T0210976

Lecture Notes in Computer Science 13295

More information about this series at https://link.springer.com/bookseries/558

Xavier Franch · Geert Poels ·
Frederik Gailly · Monique Snoeck (Eds.)

Advanced Information Systems Engineering

34th International Conference, CAiSE 2022
Leuven, Belgium, June 6–10, 2022
Proceedings

 Springer

Editors
Xavier Franch 🆔
Department of Service and Information
System Engineering (ESSI)
Universitat Politècnica de Catalunya
Barcelona, Spain

Frederik Gailly 🆔
Ghent University
Gent, Belgium

Geert Poels 🆔
Ghent University
Gent, Belgium

Monique Snoeck 🆔
KU Leuven
Leuven, Belgium

ISSN 0302-9743   ISSN 1611-3349   (electronic)
Lecture Notes in Computer Science
ISBN 978-3-031-07471-4   ISBN 978-3-031-07472-1   (eBook)
https://doi.org/10.1007/978-3-031-07472-1

This Springer imprint is published by the registered company Springer Nature Switzerland AG
The registered company address is: Gewerbestrasse 11, 6330 Cham, Switzerland

Preface

The 34th edition of the International Conference on Advanced Information Systems Engineering (CAiSE'22) was held in Leuven, Belgium, during June 6–10, 2022. CAiSE'22 was jointly organized by members of the Faculty of Economics and Business of KU Leuven and the Faculty of Economics and Business Administration of Ghent University.

The CAiSE conference continues its tradition as the premiere venue for innovative and rigorous research across the whole spectrum of information systems (IS) engineering with a special emphasis on the theme of "Information systems in the post-COVID era: reconciling the best of both worlds". During the pandemic we all experienced positive and negative aspects of increased digitization and digitalization in many different areas of our life. In the post-COVID era we should reflect on balancing "going back to normal" with reaping the benefits of what we have learned from our digital experiences. An important challenge is finding the right balance between, for instance, meeting online or face-to-face, or working in the office or remotely. Also, we became increasingly aware of the importance of finding ways to optimize, scale, and ensure a high-quality experience of the many digitized services we use at work and in our daily lives.

The call for papers solicited research papers in the categories of Technical, Empirical, and Exploratory papers, in all areas of IS engineering, including novel approaches to IS engineering; models, methods, and techniques in IS engineering; architectures and platforms for IS engineering; and domain-specific and multi-aspect IS engineering. We received a total of 203 full paper submissions. We followed a five-phase selection process. First, we desk-rejected 29 papers that were clearly out of scope or deviated substantially from the required paper layout and length limitations. Second, we assigned two Program Committee (PC) members to each of the remaining 174 papers. As an outcome of this phase, we rejected 84 papers which ended up with two negative reviews. Third, we assigned a member of the Program Board (PB) as a third reviewer for the remaining 90 papers. Fourth, we conducted an online discussion on these 90 papers and, as a result, we preliminary accepted 11 papers and rejected 14 papers, retaining 65 papers for further discussion. Fifth, we conducted an online Program Board meeting which confirmed the preliminary decisions made in the previous phase, and resulted in the PB accepting 20 more papers (14 of which were conditionally, all of which were finally accepted after checking that they satisfied the acceptance conditions stated in a meta-review), rejecting 25 other papers, and recommending the remaining 20 papers for presentation at the CAiSE Forum. Summing up, the overall evaluation process of the papers resulted in the selection of 31 papers, which amounted to an acceptance rate of 15%. In addition, we invited for presentation in the program four other papers, selected by the Journal-first Track Program Committee, published in Business & Information Systems Engineering (BISE), Data &

Knowledge Engineering (DKE) and Information System (IS), which are three academic journals with strong ties to the CAiSE conference.

Besides the 12 paper sessions presenting the 31 selected and four invited Journal First papers, the final program included the CAiSE Forum, workshops, the co-located working conferences EMMSAD and BPMDS, tutorials, a PhD consortium, and three keynote talks. Matthew Dennis (TU Eindhoven, the Netherlands) addressed "Digital well-being in the post-pandemic world", Jef Hooyberghs (VITO, Belgium) discussed "A citizen-driven ecosystem for personal health data", and Barbara Weber (University of St. Gallen, Switzerland) gave a talk on "The power of events: An IS Engineering perspective".

We are grateful to the entire team that supported the organization of the conference. We thank in the first place the General Chairs, Monique Snoeck and Frederik Gailly, and the Local Organization Chair, Liesbeth Michiels, for facilitating our work as Program Chairs, and our webmaster, Abdel-Jaouad Aberkane, for the quick updates of the website. We further wish to thank for the fruitful collaboration: the Forum Chairs, Jochen De Weerdt and Artem Polyvyanyy; the Workshop Chairs, Estefanía Serral, Jelena Zdravkovic, and Jennifer Horkoff; the Tutorial/Panel Chairs, Yves Wautelet and Saïd Assar; the Doctoral Consortium Chairs, Amy Van Looy, Michael Rosemann and Barbara Weber; the Journal-first Track Chair, Anna Perini; and the Publicity Chairs, Adela Del Rio, Marco Comuzzi, and Arik Senderovich. We believe that together we shaped a strong and varied program for this year's CAiSE conference. Of course, we thank all Program Committee and Program Board members, who played a fundamental role in the review and selection process. Finally, we would like to extend our sincerest gratitude to all those who served at the event itself as organizers, session chairs, hosts, helping students, technical staff, caterers, and the many others who went above and beyond to ensure that CAiSE continues to provide an engaging and high value forum for scientific exchange and networking within the information systems engineering community, in spite of the challenges posed by the pandemic situation.

CAiSE'22 was organized with the support of KU Leuven, Ghent University, and Springer.

June 2022   Xavier Franch
                                                         Geert Poels

In Memory of Janis A. Bubenko jr.

Janis A. Bubenko jr., Professor Emeritus at the Department of Computer and Systems Sciences, Stockholm University, passed away on January 15, 2022. He was one of the founders of the CAiSE conference series, a leader of our research community, and a beloved colleague and friend.

Janis was born 1935 in Riga, Latvia. The family immigrated to Sweden in 1945. During his education at Chalmers University of Technology, Gothenburg, Sweden, in the 1950s, he came into early contact with computers and data processing. In 1973, he received a PhD in Information Systems from the Royal Institute of Technology, Stockholm, Sweden. He was appointed Professor of Computer and Systems Sciences at the University of Gothenburg and Chalmers University of Technology in 1977 and remained there until 1981. In 1981 he was appointed Professor at the Royal Institute of Technology and Stockholm University. In 1984 Janis founded and then led the Swedish Institute for System Development (SISU) with support from the Swedish government and more than 20 businesses and public organizations in Sweden. Several research projects funded by the European Commission were conducted with SISU as a Swedish partner, such as KIWIS, TEMPORA, MILORD, NATURE, and F3.

Janis was the author, co-author, or editor of eight influential textbooks and around 150 research reports and articles covering the areas of information systems development methods, performance analysis of data processing systems, operating systems, databases, conceptual modeling methods, and enterprise modeling. In later years his research focus was on requirements engineering and enterprise modeling methods and tools, which he realized from leading positions in projects funded by the European Commission, such as ELKD, ELEKTRA, RENOIR, and HyperKnowledge.

Janis was actively involved in numerous conferences – as general chair and program chair as well as a member of their Programme Committees. His other international engagements included acting as an expert reviewer by the NSF (National Science

Foundation), the European Commission, and national research foundations (or similar) in the UK, Canada, Australia, Switzerland, Ireland, Latvia, and Austria. He was also the vice president of the VLDB Endowment during 1985–1989 and was its president during 1990–1993. He was a member of ACM, the IEEE Computer Society, and IFIP Working Group 8.1. In 2004 he was appointed ACM Fellow.

In the late 1980s Janis, together with Professor Arne Sølvberg, founded the CAiSE conference which was arranged for the first time in Sweden, in May 1989. The conference turned out to be a great success and the conference is now seen as the key event in the research community of information systems engineering.

After the collapse of the Soviet Union, Janis was among the first academics in the Nordic countries to collaborate with computer scientists in the Baltic states, by inviting researchers to Stockholm and organizing joint projects as well as helping to establish the Baltic Conference on Digital Business and Intelligent Systems. For these contributions he was awarded honorary doctorates from both Riga Technical University (2004) and the University of Latvia (2010).

Janis Bubenko can be regarded as being among the most influential researchers in the field of information systems engineering during the 80s and 90s, both in Sweden and internationally, especially in the Nordic countries. As a teacher and researcher, he was inspiring and supportive. Those who had the privilege of working with Janis remember him as a great role model, colleague, and friend. He was always ready to discuss new ideas and projects and, in these situations, often said "why not?" as a call for joint action. Janis was a warm and generous person who never put himself first. He knew how to enjoy life and had a great sense of humor. An example of his humorous side was the famous singing performance together with Arne Sølvberg at CAiSE conference dinners.

It was with deep sorrow that we received the news of Janis' passing. He was an important part of our lives, as a colleague, supervisor, role model, project partner, and friend. When the CAiSE and IFIP WG8.1 communities were informed about Janis' death, many responded with messages full of warm memories and condolences addressed to his wife Karin, daughter Anna, son Mikael, and grandchildren. This shows that Janis touched the lives of many in our community and that he will be truly missed.

June 2022   Colleagues and friends of Janis A. Bubenko jr.

Organization

General Chairs

Frederik Gailly   Ghent University, Belgium
Monique Snoeck   KU Leuven, Belgium

Program Chairs

Xavier Franch   Universitat Politecnica de Catalunya, Spain
Geert Poels   Ghent University, Belgium

Workshops Chairs

Jennifer Horkoff   Chalmers University and University of Gothenburg, Sweden
Estefania Serral   KU Leuven, Belgium
Jelena Zdravkovic   Stockholm University, Sweden

Forum Chairs

Jochen De Weerdt   KU Leuven, Belgium
Artem Polyvyanyy   Melbourne School of Engineering, Australia

Tutorial/Panel Chairs

Saïd Assar   Institut Mines-Télécom, France
Yves Wautelet   KU Leuven, Belgium

Doctoral Consortium Chairs

Michael Rosemann   Queensland University of Technology, Australia
Amy Van Looy   Ghent University, Belgium
Barbara Weber   University of St. Gallen, Switzerland

Journal-first Track Chair

Anna Perini   Fondazione Bruno Kessler, Italy

Publicity Chairs

Abdel-Jaouad Aberkane	Ghent University, Belgium
Marco Comuzzi	Ulsan National Institute of Science and Technology, South Korea
Adela del Rio Ortega	University of Seville, Spain
Arik Senderovich	University of Toronto, Canada
Seppe vanden Broucke	Ghent University, Belgium

Program Board

Sjaak Brinkkemper	Utrecht University, The Netherlands
Eric Dubois	Luxembourg Institute of Science and Technology, Luxembourg
Johann Eder	Alpen Adria Universität Klagenfurt, Germany
Giancarlo Guizzardi	University of Twente, The Netherlands
Marta Indulska	University of Queensland, Australia
John Krogstie	Norwegian University of Science and Technology, Norway
Jan Mendling	Humboldt-Universität zu Berlin, Germany
Jeffrey Parsons	Memorial University of Newfoundland, Canada
Oscar Pastor Lopez	Universidad Politécnica de Valencia, Spain
Anna Perini	Fondazione Bruno Kessler Trento, Italy
Barbara Pernici	Politecnico di Milano, Italy
Klaus Pohl	University of Duisburg-Essen, Germany
Hendrik A. Proper	Luxembourg Institute of Science and Technology, Luxembourg
Jolita Ralyté	University of Geneva, Switzerland
Hajo A. Reijers	Utrecht University, The Netherlands
Iris Reinhartz-Berger	University of Haifa, Israel
Antonio Ruiz-Cortés	University of Seville, Spain
Shazia Sadiq	University of Queensland, Australia
Ernest Teniente	Universitat Politècnica de Catalunya, Spain
Barbara Weber	University of St. Gallen, Switzerland
Jelena Zdravkovic	Stockholm University, Sweden

Program Committee

Alberto Abello	Universitat Politècnica de Catalunya, Spain
Raian Ali	Hamad Bin Khalifa University, Qatar
Hernan Astudillo	Universidad Tecnica Federico Santa María, Chile
Marco Bajec	University of Ljubljana, Slovenia
Boualem Benatallah	University of New South Wales, Wales
Palash Bera	Saint Louis University, USA
Devis Bianchini	University of Brescia, Italy
Alex Borgida	Rutgers University, USA

Cristina Cabanillas	University of Seville, Spain
Ingo Weber	TU Berlin, Germany
Joao Paolo Almeida	Federal University of Espirito Santo, Brazil
Josep Carmona	Universitat Politècnica de Catalunya, Spain
Marcela Ruiz	Zurich University of Applied Sciences, Switzerland
Raimundas Matulevicius	University of Tartu, Estonia
Eric Yu	University of Toronto, Canada

Program Committee for Journal-first Track

Sjaak Brinkkemper	Utrecht University, The Netherlands
Chiara Ghidini	Fondazione Bruno Kessler, Italy
Monique Snoeck	KU Leuven, Belgium
Pnina Soffer	University of Haifa, Israel
Anna Perini	Fondazione Bruno Kessler, Italy

Additional Reviewers

Affia, Abasi-Amefon
Akter, Yeasmin Ara
Ali, Syed Juned
Aljubairy, Abdulwahab
Alkhammash, Hanan
Atigui, Faten
Azevedo, Carlos
Bakhtina, Mariia
Batot, Edouard
Bilalli, Besim
Casamayor, Victor
Colucci, Simona
Cruz, Pablo
Dasht Bozorgi, Zahra
Dietz, Marietheres
Ehrendorfer, Matthias
Empl, Philip
Estrada Torres, Irene Bedilia
Farshidi, Siamak
Faye, Sébastien
Franceschetti, Marco
Friedl, Sabrina
Gonçalves, João Carlos De A. R.
Habibullah, Khan Mohammad
Hadad, Moshe

Heindel, Tobias
Henkel, Martin
Hobeck, Richard
Iqbal, Mubashar
Kaczmarek-Heß, Monika
Kermany, Naime
Koutsopoulos, Georgios
Lama Penin, Manuel
Léger, Bertrand
Mahmood, Adnan
Maier, Pierre
Mangat, Amolkirat Singh
Morais, Gabriel
Morichatta, Andrea
Murturi, Ilir
Müller, Kilian
Njoku, Uchechukwu
Nolte, Mario
Overeem, Michiel
Padró, Lluí
Proper, Henderik A.
Pufahl, Luise
Pusztai, Thomas
Putz, Benedikt
Sai, Catherine

Sanfilippo, Emilio M.
Scheibel, Beate
Schlette, Daniel
Schmolke, Florian
Seeba, Mari
Stertz, Florian
Su, Zihang

Suhail, Sabah
Tour, Andrei
van Dijk, Friso
Vielberth, Manfred
Wang, Kai
Winter, Karolin
Zisgen, Yorck

Contents

Graph and Network Models

Model Analysis and Comprehension

Recommender Systems

Conceptual Models, Metamodels and Taxonomies

Services Engineering and Digitalization

Tutorials

Process Mining

Decision Mining with Time Series Data Based on Automatic Feature Generation

Beate Scheibel[1](✉)[ID] and Stefanie Rinderle-Ma[2][ID]

[1] Research Group Workflow Systems and Technology, Faculty of Computer Science,
University of Vienna, Vienna, Austria
beate.scheibel@univie.ac.at
[2] Chair of Information Systems and Business Process Management,
Department of Informatics, Technical University of Munich, Munich, Germany
stefanie.rinderle-ma@tum.de

Abstract. Decision rules play a crucial role in business process execution. Knowing and understanding decision rules is of utmost importance for business process analysis and optimization. So far, decision discovery has been merely based on data elements that are measured at a single point in time. However, as cases from different application areas show, process behavior and process outcomes might be heavily influenced by additional data such as sensor streams, that consist of time series data. This holds also true for decision rules based on time series data such as 'if temperature > 25 for more than 3 times, discard goods'. Hence, this paper analyzes how time series data can be automatically exploited for decision mining, i.e., for discovering decision rules based on time series data. The paper identifies global features as well as patterns and intervals in time series as relevant for decision mining. In addition to global features, the paper proposes two algorithms for discovering interval-based and pattern-based features. The approach is implemented and evaluated based on an artificial data set as well as on a real-world data set from manufacturing. The results are promising: the approach discovers decision rules with time series features with high accuracy and precision.

Keywords: Decision mining · Time series data · Process-aware information systems · Process mining · Process analysis

1 Introduction

Process mining encompasses process discovery, conformance checking, and process enhancement [1]. An important aspect of process discovery is decision mining, which focuses on discovering decision points in processes and the underlying decision rules based on event logs [15]. Existing decision mining algorithms detect decision rules including data elements [13], overlapping rules [16] as well as incorporating linear relationships between variables [14].

© Springer Nature Switzerland AG 2022
X. Franch et al. (Eds.): CAiSE 2022, LNCS 13295, pp. 3–18, 2022.
https://doi.org/10.1007/978-3-031-07472-1_1

However, these approaches do not take into account time series data[1]. Time series data is especially relevant as many application domains collect context data outside the process as well as inside the process in the form of time series data, i.e. sensors, such as in [7], that might influence the process behavior to a great extent [5], e.g., causing concept drifts [23] and driving decisions [6].

Use cases for discovering decision rules based on time series data exist in different domains. In healthcare, for example, blood values may be decisive for the further treatment of the patient. However, not the last blood value alone might be important, but the overall trend of the blood samples, i.e., was the value decreasing or increasing over time. Another example which will be used as running example throughout the paper stems from the logistics domain and is loosely based on the use case mentioned in [6]. The corresponding process model can be seen in Fig. 1. Temperature sensitive cargo is loaded onto a transporter and moved to a destination, where the cargo is unloaded and transferred to the customer. During the transportation, the temperature is measured 15 times[2]. As the transporter reaches the destination, it is checked if the temperature exceeded 25° for more than three times. If that was the case, the goods are 'NOK' and have to be discarded, otherwise they will be transferred to the customer.

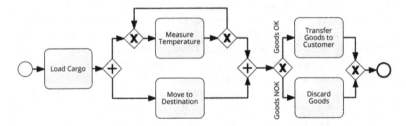

Fig. 1. BPMN model of logistics use case (modeled using Signavio©).

The corresponding decision rule looks like follows:

Rule Running Example:
IF temperature > 25 FOR number_measurements > 3 THEN discard goods.

Despite the high relevance of contextual data for process behavior [4,5,7, 22,23], only [6] has addressed decision rule discovery based on time series data so far, but in an interactive, non-automated way. Hence, this work tackles the following research question:

---

[1] Time series are defined as a sequence of time-stamped, or at least ordered, data with real-valued attribute values. Note that in this paper, we do not assume equidistant observation times.

[2] Note, that the 'Measure Temperature' task is modelled explicitly here for illustration purposes. However, it could also stem from an external source.

RQ: *How to discover decision rules based on time series data with high accuracy and high precision in an automated way?*

When exploiting time series data in decision mining approaches, it is important to achieve high accuracy and precision for the extracted rules, i.e., the goal is to discover rules that represent the underlying ground truth as closely as possible. This is important to achieve validity and robustness of the discovered rules as well as to provide interpretable, expressive rules, and transparency [20].

To answer **RQ**, we first derive three decision rule patterns based on an analysis of time series patterns and existing classification techniques from literature and use cases. In addition to the provision of necessary preprocessing steps, this paper contributes algorithms for the discovery of the derived decision rule patterns based on global and interval-based features as well as pattern-based features. The output are textual decision rules that take time series data into account. The overall approach is prototypically implemented and evaluated on synthetic data of the running example and real-world data from the manufacturing domain, i.e., production of a workpiece with accompanying sensor data. On both data sets, the approach yields decision rules with time series data at high accuracy and precision.

Sect. 2 features three decision rule patterns with time series data based on a literature analysis and use cases. Section 3 exploits the results of this analysis to provide an approach for discovering time series based decision rules, which is evaluated in Sect. 4 and discussed in Sect. 5. An overview of related work is given in Sect. 6 and a conclusion is provided in Sect. 7

2   Time Series Based Decision Rules - Analysis

For building the basis for discovering decision rules with time series data, this section analyzes literature on time series patterns and classification of time series data, with focus on expressive, interpretable decision rules. Interpretability is an important aspect in decision mining to provide transparent and explainable results [12]. The results of this analysis allow for the definition of three time series dependent decision rule patterns.

Time Series Patterns: Time series are classified into different categories, e.g., discrete or continuous time series, univariate or multivariate time series [11,17]. For this paper we focus on discrete, univariate time series where separate measurements are recorded on specific points in time. Multivariate time series, i.e., multiple time series, potentially influencing each other, will be part of future work. Especially interesting are time series patterns, as these might be insightful for underlying decision rules. In literature, different time series patterns are defined: stationary, random fluctuations, trends, level shifts, periods/cycles/seasonal variations or combinations of patterns [17]. Looking at process mining use cases, as well as the running example in Sect. 1, we add 'thresholds' as a time series pattern. Thresholds can occur once, which is a straightforward condition, or have to be met a certain amount of times to be decision relevant.

This leads to the following comprehensive, but not complete, list of decision relevant patterns: *Stationarity, Trends, Periods/Cycles/Seasonal Variations,
Shifts, Thresholds, and Pattern Combinations.*, cf. Fig. 2.

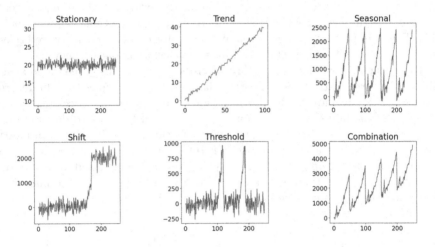

Fig. 2. Time series patterns.

Stationarity refers to a time series, where the mean stays constant over time.
A *Trend* is defined by an increasing or decreasing mean value. Both of these
patterns follow a linear trend. *Periods/Cycles/Seasonal Variations* are similar
in that the values repeatedly fluctuate over a specific time span. There are differences, for example, cycles usually refer to longer time spans than seasonal
variations. However, for this paper, it is seen as one category, i.e., *Seasonal*,
as they can be analyzed similarly. If a sudden, but lasting increase or decrease
occurs in the recorded values or the mean changes abruptly, a *Shift* was detected.
In contrast, *Thresholds* refer to sudden, non-lasting increases or decreases. Different *Combinations* of these patterns and combinations of time series dependent
rules and other decision rules can occur as well.

Existing Approaches for Time Series Data Classification: Decision mining can be understood as a classification problem, as the path that a particular
process instance takes can be seen as a category and the decision rule as classifier
[15]. Hence, we regard approaches for classification of time series data as suitable input for our further considerations. The simplest time series classification
approach is to treat each value of time series as a separate feature. However,
valuable information might be lost. A common approach is distance-based classification, i.e. calculating the distance between several time series and clustering
them based on the calculated distance [2]. However, for decision mining, we do
not want to classify instances into the right category, but extract the distinguish-
ing features to formulate textual decision rules.

Other approaches focus on extracting characteristic features from time series data to classify the instances. Which kind of features are used varies and can be calculated either on the whole time series or only on specific parts [9]. The generation of these features leads to a reduction in dimensionality which enables the application of already existing classification algorithms. As additional features enable interpretability as well as the application of existing decision mining algorithms, these approaches seem more applicable. [3] gives a comprehensive overview of existing classification algorithms for time series data. These algorithms are classified into six categories: time domain distance-based classifiers, differential distance-based classifiers, dictionary-based classifiers, shapelet-based classifiers, interval-based classifiers and ensemble classifiers. The first two classifiers fall into the distance-based category and are therefore not relevant for our purpose. Shapelet-based classifiers try to identify subsequences in a time series, that are decisive for the classification. Dictionary-based classifiers, transform time series into representative words and subsequently compare the distribution of words. Both of the latter approaches therefore explicitly take the distribution of values into account. Interval-based classifiers, split the time series into intervals and calculate different features on top of these intervals. Ensemble classifiers combine the previously described approaches. In addition, several deep learning methods [8] have been proposed. However, as we want to generate human readable, interpretable rules [20], we need interpretable approaches, i.e., standard deep learning methods are not applicable. This also applies to ensemble classifiers, as they do not provide the decisive features. Shapelet-based approaches allow to visualize the important subsequences of time series. However, they also do not allow for the extraction of expressive, textual decision rules.

Therefore, feature-based approaches, e.g., dictionary or interval-based classifiers, are suitable for decision mining, as they enable the generation of interpretable decision rules. Following the described techniques, the features can be generated on the entire time series or on specific intervals, also including the specific distribution of values.

Decision Rule Patterns: The description of patterns in combination with the described techniques allows to define some discriminating features that can be used to search for decision relevant patterns. For example, both a trend as well as stationary data can be defined by the overall slope or the overall percentage change. However, this is not applicable for the other patterns, as for example in a seasonal pattern, the overall slope is not informative, but rather the slope of parts, i.e., intervals of the time series. In a threshold pattern, we might rather look at the distribution of individual values, compare the running example, where specific values and their number of occurrence are the decisive characteristic. To discover combinations of patterns, combinations of these features might be necessary. These observations lead to the definition of decision rule patterns 2–4 in comparison to the baseline decision rule pattern 1, that can be typically seen in decision rules.

Decision Rule Pattern 1 (Baseline Decision Rule)

$$IF\ v(ariable)\ op(erator)\ c(onstant)\ THEN\ class\_x$$

with op $\in \{<, >, \leq, \geq, \neq, =\}$ *and* $c \in \mathbb{R}$

An example for a baseline decision rule is 'IF measurement_x > 2.5 THEN NOK'.

Decision Rule Pattern 2 (Global feature-based decision rule)

$$IF\ global\_feature(v)\ op\ c\ THEN\ class\_y$$

Global features are summary features, that can be calculated over the entire time series. This rule pattern will be especially useful if the underlying time series is either stationary or includes a trend.

Decision Rule Pattern 3 (Interval-based decision rule)

$$IF\ (feature(v)\ in\ interval\_n)\ op\ c\ THEN\ class\_x$$

Interval-based features, refer to the same features as the global feature, but these calculations are applied on individual intervals instead of the entire time series.

Decision Rule Pattern 4 (Pattern-based decision rule)

$$IF\ v\ op\ c\ FOR\ \{n\_times, timerange\}\ THEN\ class\_x$$

Pattern-based features take into account the distribution of values in a time series. This can be applied globally or on each interval of a time series.

Decision Rule Patterns 3 and 4 are mostly used for more complex time series, i.e., ones with seasonal variations, shifts, thresholds, or combinations of patterns. In general, decision rules can be based upon the presence or absence of a particular time series pattern.

3 Approach - EDT-TS

Based on Decision Rule Patterns 2–4 (cf. Sect. 2), we propose the *Extended Decision Tree - Time Series (EDT-TS)* approach. We base the EDT-TS approach on a decision tree as this enables the generation of interpretable rules. To allow the integration of time series data, additional features are generated, according to the analysis of decisive features in Sect. 2.

The approach involves a preprocessing stage, a feature generation stage, where additional features are created using three techniques as well as a rule extraction stage, where the actual discovery of decision rules takes place. These stages are described in more detail in the following subsections.

3.1   Preprocessing

In this paper, we assume that the time series data is part of an event log, either in form of separate, repeated tasks with one value each (cf. Table 1) or one task with a list of measurement data (cf. Table 2). Other ways of integrating sensor data into event logs are conceivable, such as aggregating sensor data based on task annotations [7], but outside the scope of this paper. For preprocessing the event logs are read and converted into a tabular form, specifically a Dataframe[3], where each row refers to one instance. To specify the candidate variables for time series analysis, all reoccurring, numeric variables are identified, these are then used as input for the feature generation. The preprocessing step has to be adapted for different use cases, as different actions have to be performed to convert an event log into a suitable dataframe. However, from this point on, the process remains the same for multiple use cases.

Table 1. Event log including measurements in one task.

UUID	Task	Data
0001	Measure	10,15,14,16,10,10,14,12,14
0001	Measure	12,13,14,12,10,11,13,15,12

Table 2. Measurements as separate tasks.

UUID	Task	Timestamp	Data
0001	Measure	2019-11-15 14:35	10
0002	Measure	2019-11-15 16:40	12
0001	Measure	2019-11-15 14:45	15
0001	Measure	2019-11-15 14:52	14
0002	Measure	2019-11-15 16:55	13
0002	Measure	2019-11-15 17:10	14

3.2   Feature Generation

After the preprocessing step, additional features are generated.

Global features are calculated for the whole time series. They can consist of simple values, for example the mean, variance, slope, percentage change or the number of peaks/lows in the time series. In addition, more complex values can be computed, e.g., a Fourier transform or auto-regressive coefficients. These global features are calculated for the time series data of each instance and added as additional features.

For **interval-based features**, the time series is split into intervals and global features are calculated for each interval. Figure 3 depicts the first interval and the n-th interval of a time series where features like the mean or percentage change vary greatly.

---

[3] https://pandas.pydata.org/pandas-docs/stable/reference/api/pandas.DataFrame.html.

The split of the time series can be done according to measurement points (as in this paper) or time spans. It is important to set the interval size appropriately, as this can have an effect on the resulting decision rules as well as the time complexity of the algorithm. For this implementation we chose to split the time series into 2, 5, and 10 intervals. However, the interval size can also be chosen manually for use cases where other interval sizes may be optimal. The generation of global features is done using an existing library, the generation of interval-based features can be seen in Algorithm 1.

Algorithm 1. EDT-TS, interval-based features

Input: event log as dataframe, candidates, number of intervals n
Output: dataframe with added generated features

1: **for** instance in event log **do**
2:     split candidates into n intervals
3: **end for**
4: **for** interval in intervals **do**
5:     **for** feature in features(mean, minimum, maximum, slope,...) **do**
6:         calculate feature
7:         add result as additional feature
8:     **end for**
9: **end for**
10: return dataframe with added columns, i.e. the generated features

---

Pattern-based features consider the distribution of values in a time series. For these features, the actual values and their number of occurrence is important. This enables for example the discovery of threshold patterns as we can identify values that occur significantly more often in one class than in the other.

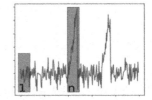

Different algorithms and approaches can be subsumed under pattern-based approaches and

Fig. 3. Time series intervals.

there exists a variety of already implemented algorithms, e.g., dictionary-based approaches. However, dictionary-based approaches combine multiple values into one letter or word and therefore loose some informative value in favor of computational complexity. In addition, existing algorithms often do not enable the extraction of the original feature-value distribution, before it was converted to a word which makes it harder to extract textual rules. Therefore, Algorithm 2 is proposed to identify possible thresholds of values based on the distribution of values in series. Note that Algorithm 2 currently works on the whole time series. However, it can also be easily adapted to work on intervals which allows to discover even more fine-grained patterns.

Algorithm 2. EDT-TS, pattern-based features

Input: dataframe, candidates, output from Alg. 1
Output: dataframe with added generated features

1: split instances by the result category, i.e. in 'OK' and 'NOK'
2: **for** category in categories **do**
3:     calculate all values and number of occurrence in candidate variables
4:     store in array
5: **end for**
6: compare value distributions of categories
7: store all values distributions (measurement, amount) that only occur in one category in array *candidate_threshold*
8: **for** c in candidate_threshold **do**
9:     add c as new column in dataframe
10:     **for** i in instance **do**
11:         **if** c.measurement occurs in i more or equal times than c.amount **then**
12:             set value for c of i "True"
13:         **else**
14:             set value for c of i "False"
15:         **end if**
16:     **end for**
17: **end for**
18: return dataframe with added columns, i.e. the generated features

---

3.3 Rule Extraction

After the additional features are created, a decision tree is applied to build the decision rules. The decision tree parameters are optimized to provide the best precision values, i.e., splits in different classes. Feature selection is used to obtain a maintainable amount of features. The last step is to output the decision tree results in human readable, textual form. This is done by following the nodes of the decision tree down for each individual class and concatenating the conditions to formulate a rule. Therefore multiple decision rules can be obtained, if different condition combinations can lead to the same class.

4 Evaluation

The approach has been implemented as a proof-of-concept prototype using Python. To generate the global features the 'tsfresh' module[4] is used, that allows to automatically create global features of a time series. To generate the decision rules, a decision tree from the 'scikit-learn' module [18] is used. In addition to the implementation of Algorithms 1 and 2, a script was written to obtain textual rules from the resulting decision tree. The implemented approach was tested on two datasets, a synthetic dataset and a real-life dataset from the manufacturing domain. The decision tree implementation is set to aim for optimal precision values. To enable comparison of the results, baseline values are created as well as

---

[4] https://tsfresh.readthedocs.io/.

individual results for each of the feature generation approaches. The source code, the datasets as well as the full results are available online: https://github.com/bscheibel/edt-ts. For the *baseline accuracy*, decision rules are calculated using a standard decision mining approach, without a component that is able to handle time series data. Therefore, only the individual values are used as input for this approach. The baseline accuracy is calculated to compare the results of 'standard' approaches, to EDT-TS. For the calculation, a 'CART' implementation from the 'scikit-learn' module was used, as this is a standard tool for decision mining [15]. The baseline results can be seen under 'Decision Rule, Baseline'.

The generated decision rule for each of the feature generation approaches (global features, interval-based and pattern-based) can be seen in the full result report online, here only the resulting, combined decision rule is shown. To test the accuracy, the data was split into a test and training set (80% training, 20% test). To calculate the accuracy, the following definition is used:

$$Accuracy := \frac{Number\ of\ correctly\ classified\ instances}{Total\ number\ of\ instances}$$

In addition to the accuracy, the precision of the result is calculated as well, using the following definition:

$$Precision := \frac{Total\ number\ of\ instances\ correctly\ classified\ in\ category}{Total\ number\ of\ instances\ classified\ as\ that\ category}$$

This definition leads to a precision value for each category, i.e., for 'OK' and 'NOK'. The depicted rules for both datasets, only contain the rules for the class 'NOK', as we assume that all instances that do not belong to 'NOK' are automatically classified as 'OK'. Accuracy and precision are choosen as evaluation metrics, as accuracy enables an intuitive assessment of the ability to identify correctly classified instances and precision, especially precision per class, provides information if the classification is imbalanced towards one class. This is especially relevant for the 'Manufacturing Dataset', as it is preferable that all 'NOK' pieces are detected early on. However it is more important that no 'OK' pieces should be wrongly disposed.

Running Example. For the running example, synthetic data was generated. In total 5000 instances for the process model shown in Fig. 1 were created, where about 50% of these instances are 'OK' (2589 instances), i.e. the cargo can be transferred to the customer, and 50% are 'NOK' (2411 instances). The temperature was randomly generated (values between 10 and 30) for 15 measurement points for each instance. Figure 4 shows the measurement time series data for two instances. It is noticeable that the 'NOK' instance reaches higher temperatures more often. However no explicit decision rule could be derived from this figure alone. The result for the baseline approach can be seen below. The feature 'temperaturelast' refers to the last temperature measurement.

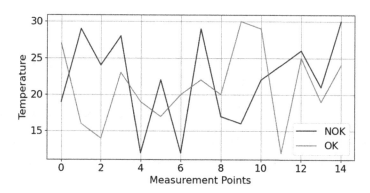

Fig. 4. Running example: visualisation of two instances. Red: 'Discard Goods'/'NOK', Green: 'Transfer Goods'/'OK'. (Color figure online)

The resulting decision tree contains 41 nodes in total, however most conditions are redundant, therefore the depicted decision rule was simplified. The precision of 59% for the class 'NOK' can be interpreted as 59% of all instances classified as 'NOK' are actually 'NOK'. The same applies for the 'OK' precision with a ratio of 56%.

Rule Running Example, Baseline:
If temperaturelast > 25.50 THEN class: NOK/Discard Goods
Accuracy: 59%
Precision: NOK - 68%, OK - 56%

Rule Running Example, EDT-TS
If temperaturelist.count(26.0)>= 4.0 == *True* THEN class: NOK/Discard Goods
Accuracy: 100%
Precision: NOK - 100%, OK- 100%

The resulting rule contains a pattern-based feature, i.e., the temperature value of 26 has to occur equal or more than 4 times, which accurately represents the underlying rule. This reflects in the high accuracy and precision values.

Manufacturing Dataset. To evaluate the applicability of the presented approach on a real world dataset, a manufacturing dataset from the production of valve lifters for gas turbines, see Fig. 5, is used. This dataset is an extension of the data used in [23] and was also used in [7].

Fig. 5. Valve lifter.

Figure 6 shows the process model. Workpieces, i.e., the valve lifters are produced using a turning machine. Subsequently, the diameter of the workpieces

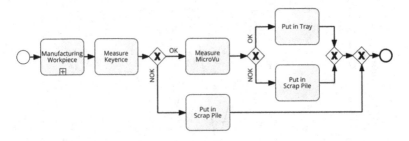

Fig. 6. Manufacturing processes (modeled using Signavio©).

is measured using the silhouette of the workpiece, the 'Keyence' measurement. This takes only a couple of seconds, but the results are not always accurate. Therefore, the workpieces are transferred to a second measuring machine, called 'MicroVu', that can measure more quality-relevant features, e,g., surface quality and flatness, resulting in more precise results. However, this step takes a couple of minutes for each workpiece. Therefore, a goal is to focus on the first decision point and filter most 'NOK' workpieces using the first measuring step. The first measuring data for two instances can be seen in Fig. 7. The diameter value is shown as a time series of values. The first part where the diameter is between 15–20 mm is the thicker part of the valve lifter, whereas the second part where the measurements are around 5–10 mm is the thinner end. The highest values at the end, technically do not belong to the workpiece, but the robot gripper that holds the workpiece through the measurement process. The dataset consists of 88 workpieces (36 - 'NOK', 52 - 'OK'). The baseline approach yields the following decision rule:

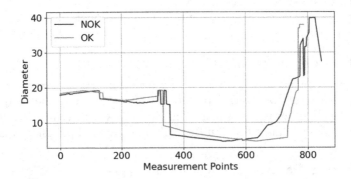

Fig. 7. Manufacturing dataset: visualisation of two instances.

Manufacturing, Baseline:
IF casename $<=$ 2242.5 AND casename $<=$ 2179 AND casename $<=$ 1932.5
AND data_diameterlast $<=$ 27.25 THEN class NOK
Accuracy: 45%
Precision: NOK - 16%, OK - 80%

The resulting decision tree contains 17 nodes, only one applicable rule is shown here, however it is representative of the other rules. We can see that in addition to the last measurement value, the 'casename', which just refers to the instance identifier was used. However, this should not have any impact on the actual quality of the workpiece, which also reflects in relatively low accuracy and precision values.

Manufacturing, EDT-TS - Combined
IF data_diameterlist2_percentchange $>$ 0.16 THEN class NOK
Accuracy: 91%
Precision: NOK - 100%, OK - 90%

The EDT-TS generated rule only has one interval-based condition that refers to the percentage change in the second interval and achieves an accuracy of 91%, as well as precision values of 100% in the 'NOK' class and 91% in the 'OK' class. A high precision value for the 'NOK' class is especially important for this use case, as we want to filter out all 'NOK' pieces beforehand, without unintentionally discarding 'OK' workpieces. The 100% precision value here means that only 'NOK' workpieces are actually classified as 'NOK'.

5   Discussion

Prerequisites for our approach are the existence of a decision point and the availability of process data up to this decision point. Therefore we do not need a complete process model to extract decision rules. The evaluation shows that EDT-TS is feasible and achieves high quality results in terms of accuracy and precision for the used datasets. The approach extracts time series based decision rules and provides them in textual form to the user. For the running example, where the actual decision rule is known, EDT-TS discovers the rule. For the manufacturing dataset the underlying rule is not known, but there are indications that the decision might depend on chips on the workpieces, influencing the quality of the produced parts. Especially the high precision for the 'NOK' is important, as the goal is to discover as many 'NOK' workpieces as possible, without discarding parts that are actually 'OK'. EDT-TS is able to include multiple independent time series and additional numeric data attributes. In terms of generalisability and comprehensiveness, the approach should be able to handle different decision rules that contain a variety of the mentioned decision patterns.

Patterns and use cases for the mentioned patterns might exist that are not covered by the proposed approach yet. Additional feature generation techniques, e.g., additional pattern-based techniques, can be added accordingly.

Limitations and Threats to Validity: We assume that the measurements are part of an explicit task and can therefore be extracted from the event logs and assigned to the correct process instance. Currently time series with separable effects are taken into account, working with intermingled effects adds another level of complexity as there is no explicit decision point and time series length may vary. So far, the robustness of the approach against noise in the data as well as the computational complexity was not taken into account. Future work will address these limitations. Additionally, future work will focus on including relational rules, e.g. the threshold of a time series is not a fixed value but a variable. Another general limitation is the availability of data. However, as described in Sect. 1 multiple use cases exist, where time series data is logged, but not explicitly part of the event log or not used as time series data.

6   Related Work

Decision mining was coined by [19], describing how to discover decision points in processes. [15] gives an overview of the state-of-the-art, e.g., [13] for the basic approach, [16] for detecting overlapping rules, and [14] for discovering the relationship between variables. These approaches have not considered time series data for decision mining yet. In general, for process mining [22] differentiates between top-down approaches where process mining is applied on process log data augmented with event data, and bottom-up approaches that apply process mining to event data in combination with complex event processing techniques. We can classify our previous work [6,7,23] into the top-down category. [6] focuses on how to merge time series data with event logs. The approach relies on manually adding features that seem relevant based on visualisations of the time series. By contrast, EDT-TS specifies textual decision rules instead of clustering instances or calculating the impact of a specific value on the end result. [23] uses time series data, in form of sensor data, to detect concept drifts during runtime, using Dynamic Time Warping and clustering. [7] uses time series data in form of sensor data to predict the process outcome, using manually added, global features as input for the proposed algorithms. Also other recent approaches consider "exogenous data" in combination with process mining. [4] propose an approach to slice time series data and adding the resulting values to specific events as data elements, as well as transformations of this data using global features which is done manually. Bottom-up approaches are proposed by, e.g., [10,21]. The goal here is to discover or enhance process models based on sensor data. Such approaches can be seen as complementary to EDT-TS.

7   Conclusion

EDT-TS is an approach to discover time series dependent decision rules. Common time series patterns as well as classification algorithms for time series data are analyzed. The analysis results in the definition of three time series dependent decision rule patterns: global feature-based decision rules, interval-based decision rules and pattern-based decision rules. EDT-TS includes three stages. Firstly, the dataset has to be preprocessed, potential time series data elements are found and added as candidate elements. The second phase, generates additional features from these candidate elements, including global features that summarize the entire time series, interval-based features that calculate features for subsequences of the time series and pattern-based features that include the distribution of values in a time series. Decision rules are then built using the generated features and a decision tree. Lastly, the rules are transformed to textual form. The evaluation on two datasets shows high accuracy (91% and 100%) and high precision (between 90% and 100%) values. In future work, we want to address the limitations discussed in Sect. 5, with a special focus on including intermingled effects and multivariate time series as well as making the approach more robust against noise. In addition, runtime detection of decision rules including decision rules based on time series, with changing rules and exceptions, will be part of future work.

Acknowledgements. This work has been partially supported and funded by the Austrian Research Promotion Agency (FFG) via the Austrian Competence Center for Digital Production (CDP) under the contract number 881843.

References

1. van der Aalst, W.M.P.: Process Mining: Data Science in Action. Springer, Heidelberg (2016). https://doi.org/10.1007/978-3-662-49851-4
2. Abanda, A., Mori, U., Lozano, J.A.: A review on distance based time series classification. Data Min. Knowl. Disc. **33**(2), 378–412 (2018). https://doi.org/10.1007/s10618-018-0596-4
3. Bagnall, A., Lines, J., Bostrom, A., Large, J., Keogh, E.: The great time series classification bake off: a review and experimental evaluation of recent algorithmic advances. Data Min. Knowl. Disc. **31**(3), 606–660 (2016). https://doi.org/10.1007/s10618-016-0483-9
4. Banham, A., Wynn, M.T.: xPM: a framework for process mining with exogenous data. In: ICPM Workshops (2021)
5. Dees, M., Hompes, B., van der Aalst, W.M.P.: Events put into context (EPiC). In: International Conference on Process Mining, pp. 65–72 (2020)
6. Dunkl, R., Rinderle-Ma, S., Grossmann, W., Anton Fröschl, K.: A method for analyzing time series data in process mining: application and extension of decision point analysis. In: Nurcan, S., Pimenidis, E. (eds.) CAiSE Forum 2014. LNBIP, vol. 204, pp. 68–84. Springer, Cham (2015). https://doi.org/10.1007/978-3-319-19270-3_5
7. Ehrendorfer, M., Mangler, J., Rinderle-Ma, S.: Assessing the impact of context data on process outcomes during runtime. In: Hacid, H., Kao, O., Mecella, M., Moha, N., Paik, H. (eds.) ICSOC 2021. LNCS, vol. 13121, pp. 3–18. Springer, Cham (2021). https://doi.org/10.1007/978-3-030-91431-8_1

8. Ismail Fawaz, H., Forestier, G., Weber, J., Idoumghar, L., Muller, P.-A.: Deep learning for time series classification: a review. Data Min. Knowl. Disc. **33**(4), 917–963 (2019). https://doi.org/10.1007/s10618-019-00619-1
9. Fulcher, B.D.: Feature-based time-series analysis. arXiv:1709.08055 [cs], October 2017
10. Kammerer, K., Pryss, R., Hoppenstedt, B., Sommer, K., Reichert, M.: Process-driven and flow-based processing of industrial sensor data. Sensors **20**(18), 5245 (2020)
11. Kitagawa, G.: Introduction to Time Series Modeling. CRC Press, Boca Raton (2010)
12. Leewis, S., Berkhout, M., Smit, K.: Future challenges in decision mining at governmental institutions. In: AMCIS 2020 Proceedings, p. 12 (2020)
13. de Leoni, M., van der Aalst, W.M.P.: Data-aware process mining: discovering decisions in processes using alignments. In: ACM Symposium on Applied Computing, p. 1454 (2013)
14. de Leoni, M., Dumas, M., García-Bañuelos, L.: Discovering branching conditions from business process execution logs. In: Fundamental Approaches to Software Engineering, pp. 114–129 (2013)
15. de Leoni, M., Mannhardt, F.: Decision discovery in business processes. In: Encyclopedia of Big Data Technologies, pp. 1–12 (2018)
16. Mannhardt, F., de Leoni, M., Reijers, H.A., van der Aalst, W.M.P.: Decision mining revisited - discovering overlapping rules. In: Nurcan, S., Soffer, P., Bajec, M., Eder, J. (eds.) CAiSE 2016. LNCS, vol. 9694, pp. 377–392. Springer, Cham (2016). https://doi.org/10.1007/978-3-319-39696-5_23
17. Montgomery, D.C., Jennings, C.L., Kulahci, M.: Introduction to Time Series Analysis and Forecasting. Wiley, New York (2015). Google-Books-ID: Xeh8CAAAQBAJ
18. Pedregosa, F., et al.: Scikit-learn: machine learning in Python. J. Mach. Learn. Res. **12**(85), 2825–2830 (2011)
19. Rozinat, A., van der Aalst, W.M.P.: decision mining in prom. In: Dustdar, S., Fiadeiro, J.L., Sheth, A.P. (eds.) BPM 2006. LNCS, vol. 4102, pp. 420–425. Springer, Heidelberg (2006). https://doi.org/10.1007/11841760_33
20. Scheibel, B., Rinderle-Ma, S.: Comparing decision mining approaches with regard to the meaningfulness of their results. arXiv:2109.07335 [cs], September 2021
21. Seiger, R., Zerbato, F., Burattin, A., García-Bañuelos, L., Weber, B.: Towards IoT-driven process event log generation for conformance checking in smart factories. In: EDOC Workshops, pp. 20–26. IEEE (2020)
22. Soffer, P., et al.: From event streams to process models and back: challenges and opportunities. Inf. Syst. **81**, 181–200 (2019)
23. Stertz, F., Rinderle-Ma, S., Mangler, J.: Analyzing process concept drifts based on sensor event streams during runtime. In: Fahland, D., Ghidini, C., Becker, J., Dumas, M. (eds.) BPM 2020. LNCS, vol. 12168, pp. 202–219. Springer, Cham (2020). https://doi.org/10.1007/978-3-030-58666-9_12

Inferring a Multi-perspective Likelihood Graph from Black-Box Next Event Predictors

Yannik Gerlach, Alexander Seeliger[✉] [ID], Timo Nolle[ID],
and Max Mühlhäuser[ID]

Telecooperation Lab, Technical University of Darmstadt, Darmstadt, Germany
{gerlach,seeliger,nolle,max}@tk.tu-darmstadt.de

Abstract. Deep learning models for next event prediction in predictive process monitoring have shown significant performance improvements over conventional methods. However, they are often criticized for being black-box models. Without allowing analysts to understand what such models have learned, it is difficult to establish trust in their abilities.

In this work, we propose a technique to infer a likelihood graph from a next event predictor (NEP) to capture and visualize its behavior. Our approach first generates complete cases, including event attributes, using the NEP. From this set of cases, a multi-perspective likelihood graph is inferred. Including event attributes in the graph allows analysts to better understand the learned decision and branching points of the process.

The results of the evaluation show that inferred graphs generalize beyond the event log, achieve high F-scores, and small likelihood deviations. We conclude black-box NEP can be used to generate conforming cases even for noisy event logs. As a result, our visualization technique, which represents exactly this set of cases, shows what the NEP has learned, thus mitigating one of their biggest criticisms.

Keywords: Process mining · Next event predictors ·
Multi-perspective likelihood graph

1 Introduction

In process mining, more and more approaches make use of *machine learning* (ML) techniques, especially deep neural networks, to better capture the behavior of a process. ML algorithms are capable of incorporating more contextual factors of a case than conventional and hand-crafted models, making them a nice fit for the application in this field. For instance, predictive process monitoring has shown significant performance improvements with respect to predictive accuracy using recurrent neural networks [3,6,17,22].

The primary goal of process mining is to obtain valuable insights for analysts to improve process performance. On the one hand, many process mining

© Springer Nature Switzerland AG 2022
X. Franch et al. (Eds.): CAiSE 2022, LNCS 13295, pp. 19–35, 2022.
https://doi.org/10.1007/978-3-031-07472-1_2

tasks are human-centric, like process discovery or conformance checking, presenting results such that humans can actually see and understand them (e.g., process models). On the other hand, ML approaches to process mining are a popular choice as their predictive power can be much better [3,17,22], despite inhibiting direct inspection of trained models by analysts. Therefore, ML models are often rightfully criticized for being black-boxes [12,14,18,19,21,23]. Recent discussions in the community voiced the need for process mining methods that can be explained and interpreted [5] by analysts to build trust [11,12,15,23] and to reduce the vulnerability of prediction errors [19]. Explainability should encompass the visualization of processes as graphs or enriched process models with decision and constraint annotations [4]. While techniques for explaining predictions made by ML models exist, they often focus on relevant parts in the input, i.e., which part in the input case is important for the prediction, on a single prediction at a time, or are not directly tailored to process mining. Therefore, extracting knowledge about what the ML model has actually learned, to build trust in its capabilities and inspect what the model "thinks" the process is, remains challenging.

In this paper, we propose a technique for inferring a multi-perspective likelihood graph of events, transitions, and event attributes given an algorithm predicting the next event of a case. Such a *next event predictor* (NEP) can be a trained ML model but can also be any other algorithm performing this task (e.g., an ensemble of NEPs). The inferred graph can be visualized and explored by analysts to outline what the NEP has learned, similar to process models. The proposed approach is a post-hoc explanation technique because it is applied after training or creation of the NEP and aims at explaining the NEP's behavior. The visual explanation through a graph further contributes to the main goal of better understanding the behavior of the predictive model [1].

Our proposed approach consists of two main steps: First, using the NEP we generate all possible cases reflecting the process behavior. Second, we convert these cases to a graph by merging nodes which share the same behavior to remove redundancies and to compact the graph. The case generation is agnostic to the architecture of the NEP and, thus, can be adapted to work with any NEP.

In summary, our contributions are:

1. A novel method for revealing the process an NEP has learned from training on an event log.
2. A visual representation of the learned behavior in form of a likelihood graph that also includes event attributes.
3. A comprehensive evaluation showing our approach is capable of accurately representing the behavior of an NEP and its decision points in the process.

The rest of the paper is organized as follows. In Sect. 2 we provide an overview of the related work, followed in Sect. 3 by some preliminaries used throughout the paper. In Sect. 4 we describe the details of our approach. Then, in Sect. 5 we present the results of the evaluation of our approach. Finally, in Sect. 7 we conclude the paper with a discussion and future work.

2   Related Work

Next Event Predictors (NEP). ML-based NEPs have previously been used for generating cases from scratch. Tax et al. [17] iteratively predict the next activity and time, choosing the most likely continuation until a case is completed. Similarly, Camargo et al. [2] use *Long Short-Term Memory* (LSTM) networks to predict sequences of next events, their timestamps, and event attributes. Both of these approaches either focus on the most likely choice for the next activity or a random selection following the predicted probability distribution. As a result, depending on the complexity of the model, it is required to generate a large number of cases to capture the entire behavior of the NEP. In contrast, we aim to explore all non-noisy cases using a threshold heuristic.

Model Discovery. An approach more focused on explainability is introduced by Shunin et al. [13], who generate a finite state machine from a neural network NEP. Similar to our approach, the neural network is trained on an event log, and is then used to generate a set of cases from scratch. Then, a process model is generated from the finite state machine. Another process model-based approach is to learn a generic mapping between event log structures and process models [16]. The idea is that a graph neural network learns the generic dependencies between relationships of events to generate the structures of the process model. The learned mapping can then be applied to new, unseen event logs.

Different from our approach, both related works do not consider noisy event logs. Furthermore, only the control-flow of a process is discovered, making it difficult to analyze decision points.

Evaluation Frameworks and Metrics. As an alternative to explanatory approaches, related work also presents evaluation frameworks and metrics. Camargo et al. [2] compare the generated cases of an NEP to the event log to evaluate their quality. However, the metric does not consider noisy cases that are typically present in real-life event logs, leading to an increase of both precision and fitness. Despite this property being undesirable, the evaluation measures do not reflect it. A framework investigating the generalization ability of neural networks is introduced by Peeperkorn et al. [9]. Their metrics are based on removing variants from an event log, training the neural network and then checking how many of the removed variants the network can reconstruct. The authors conclude that overfitting avoidance methods are important to allow the neural network to generalize beyond the training data. The approach is restricted to control-flow only and does not consider noise. Different from our approach, the approach samples from the probability distribution instead of an exhaustive search. Additionally, both presented approaches do also not visualize the generated cases, preventing efficient exploration and inspection.

3   Background

Throughout the paper, we refer to the event log, event, case, and attribute definitions from [20]:

Definition 1 (Case, Event, and Event Log). *Let $\mathcal{A} = \{a_1, \ldots, a_A\}$ be a set of ordered attributes and $\mathcal{V}$ be a set of attribute values, where $\mathcal{V}_{a_i}$ is the set of possible values for attribute $a_i \in \mathcal{A}$. Furthermore, let a_1 be the activity and a_j with $j = 2, \ldots, A$ the event attributes.*

Let $\mathcal{C}$ be the set of all cases and $\mathcal{E}$ be the set of all events. A case $c \in \mathcal{C}$ is an event sequence $c \in \mathcal{E}^*$, where $\mathcal{E}^*$ is the set of all sequences over $\mathcal{E}$. An event log is a set of cases $\mathcal{L} \subseteq \mathcal{C}$. A prefix is an ongoing, incomplete case, where the prefix length is the number of completed events.

Furthermore, let $|c|$ be the number of events in case c, $C = |\mathcal{L}|$ be the number of cases in $\mathcal{L}$, $A = |\mathcal{A}|$ be the number of attributes and $E = \max_{c \in \mathcal{L}} |c|$ be the case with the most events in $\mathcal{L}$. We denote start and end symbol by $\blacktriangleright$ and $\blacksquare$, respectively.

In process mining, next event prediction is a set of A multi-class classification problems. For the classification problem of a_i with $i = 1, \ldots, A$, the classes to be predicted are its values $\mathcal{V}_{a_i}$. The features, based on which the event at position i is determined, are the previous events, the prefix $1, \ldots, i - 1$ of the input case.

Definition 2 (Next Event Predictor). *A next event predictor is any algorithm $\mathcal{N}$ receiving a prefix as input and producing a set of next events, annotated with likelihoods for each attribute value.*

From the likelihoods for each attribute value, the likelihood of the event can be calculated and the most likely one returned, for example. The above definition of an NEP allows our approach to be applicable independently of the NEP's specific architecture.

4   Inferring Graphs from Next Event Predictors

Our approach is a post-hoc explanation technique that infers a directed and acyclic likelihood graph from an NEP to reveal the process it has learned from an event log. The resulting graph compactly represents the predictions made by the NEP and serves as a visual explanation of the NEP's behavior. The semantics of the likelihood graph is similar to that of a stochastic process model [10]. However, it may contain nodes with the same labels multiple times to model loop behavior more accurately. This allows us to model different probabilities of the same activity for different paths through the process. Additionally, the graph includes event attributes to better capture the behavior of the NEP at decision points. These can reveal dependencies between activities and event attributes that remain hidden when only constructing a process map.

The proposed approach follows two main steps to generate a likelihood graph of the determined process by the NEP:

1. **Exhaustive Case Generation.** Our approach explores the NEP to generate an exhaustive set of cases by repeatedly extending prefixes with predicted events. A heuristic strategy is applied to distinguish between normal and noisy behavior.

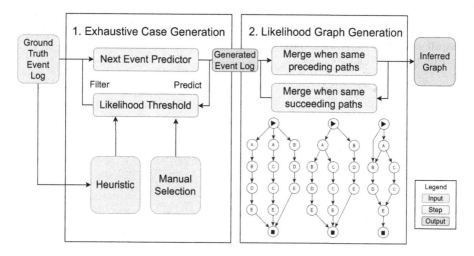

Fig. 1. Overview of the components of the proposed approach.

2. **Likelihood Graph Generation.** We use the generated set of cases to build a likelihood graph that captures the predictions made by the NEP. A merging strategy is used to compact the graph such that similar behavior is grouped.

Next, we provide a detailed description of each step. An overview of the approach is depicted in Fig. 1.

4.1 Exhaustive Case Generation

In this step, our approach extracts the knowledge about the process the NEP has learned. We perform an exhaustive search to explore all possible cases that the NEP generates and to capture its behavior in form of an event log, representing its predictions given certain prefixes. In order to avoid pursuing all possible and very unlikely cases, which may lead to a huge search space, we use a threshold heuristic to only consider case continuations with at least a certain likelihood. As a result, activities and attribute values below this threshold are not considered in the case generation; they are considered to be noise.

Algorithm 1 shows our case generation algorithm, which is a worklist algorithm that starts with an empty prefix of a case, only containing the artificial start symbol ($\blacktriangleright$) of the NEP. For each remaining prefix (line 5), the algorithm obtains all possible combinations of next events with their likelihoods in the sequence from the NEP, denoted by $\langle \ldots \rangle$ (line 8). The prefix is then extended by the continuation to generate a new prefix c_{new} (line 11). If the activity of the next event is the end symbol ($\blacksquare$, line 12), the entire case is added to the list of completed cases ($c_{complete}$). Otherwise, the new prefix is added to the worklist.

In most scenarios, our algorithm terminates when all possible cases are generated. However, in certain cases it may be that the NEP predicts looping behavior (e.g., activities a and b are predicted alternatingly). To allow the algorithm to

---

Algorithm 1. Extract all cases with normal behavior from an NEP.

Require: NEP $\mathcal{N}$, likelihood thresholds $t_1, ..., t_A$
 1: **function** GENERATECASES
 2:     $c_{complete} = \varnothing$
 3:     $c_{initial} = \langle \blacktriangleright^A \rangle \in \mathbb{R}^{1 \times A}$
 4:     $q = [c_{initial}]$
 5:     **while** $|q| > 0$ **do**
 6:         $c = q[0]$
 7:         remove c from q
 8:         $e_{next} = \mathcal{N}(c)$
 9:         **for each** $(e \in \mathbb{R}^A, l \in \mathbb{R}^A)$ in e_{next} **do**
10:             **if** $\forall i \in \{1, ..., A\} : l_i \geq t_i$ **then**
11:                 $c_{new} = \langle c, e \rangle \in \mathbb{R}^{(|c|+1) \times A}$
12:                 **if** $e_0 = \blacksquare$ **then**
13:                     $c_{complete} = c_{complete} \cup c_{new}$
14:                 **else**
15:                     $q = [c_{new}, q]$
16:     **return** $c_{complete}$

---

terminate in all scenarios, cases are discarded if an activity occurs more than ϵ-times. If a too high percentage of cases is discarded, the algorithm is terminated, indicating either a too low likelihood threshold or an inaccurate NEP. For filtering out noisy behavior, we choose to set *likelihood thresholds* $t_1, ..., t_A$ for each attribute (line 10). Therefore, for a prediction for attribute a_i to be further considered in the case generation, its probability needs to be at least t_i. We use a separate threshold for each attribute to allow a more precise filtering of noise. Related work [7] has shown that the likelihoods vary significantly between different attributes, thus, specifying individual thresholds allows fine grained control (see Sect. 4.3).

4.2 Likelihood Graph Generation

In this step, our approach constructs the likelihood graph from the set of cases, generated by the NEP. We opted for a graph because analysts are familiar with this structure (e.g., process models in process discovery), which are also used for visual exploration. As a result, we obtain a compact representation of the generated cases that serves as a visual explanation of the NEP. For obtaining such a likelihood graph, we use a merge strategy to eliminate redundant sequences of events if they behave similarly. Different from process discovery techniques, we explicitly include event attributes in the graph to better reflect branching decisions depending on the attribute probabilities.

Basic Graph Structure. We start by converting the set of cases to nodes and edges in a graph. The initial graph consists of an independent path for each case, only afterwards we merge. For each event, we convert it into a list of nodes, one for each attribute value in the event. Each node is assigned a label (activity or event attribute value name) and an unique identifier. The nodes representing attribute values are ordered and connected following the order of the attributes. Events are then linked in the order they appear in the case. To be more precise, when linking two events, the last attribute value node of the previous event is connected to the activity value node of the current event. All cases share the same start and end symbol. The conversion approach is illustrated in Fig. 1.

Merging Nodes Strategy. We merge nodes based on their context to remove redundancies and improve comprehensiveness of the resulting likelihood graph. Given any two nodes n_1 and n_2 in the graph with the same label (e.g., same activity) but different identifiers. If the two nodes share the same preceding sequences of labels (even though the nodes in the sequences might have different identifiers), one of the nodes is redundant, i.e., their behavior cannot be distinguished, up until that point in the sequence. Therefore, we merge these nodes into a single node n with possibly two outgoing edges. As a result, nodes with the same label are not merged if their behavior is different. With the same motivation, we also apply the merge strategy if two nodes share the same succeeding sequences of labels. The presented merging strategy does not change the set of cases the graph represents but only the structure of the nodes. As a result, no information (e.g., decision points or attribute values) gets lost due to merging.

To remove both types of redundancies, our approach merges once based on preceding and succeeding sequences, respectively. For generating the preceding paths of a node n, all paths between the start node and n are determined by following the ingoing edges of n backwards. For the succeeding paths of a node n, all paths between n and the end node are determined by following the outgoing edges of n forwards. Afterwards, only behavior impacting the control-flow remains. The order of merging does not affect the final result because the set of preceding or succeeding label sequences is not changed but only the structure of the graph. Note that the event attribute nodes are not entirely separated from their activity node. While activity nodes are always checked to see if they can be merged, the user may specify which event attribute nodes to attempt to merge. The proposed merging procedure contrasts process discovery algorithms, which typically merge activities with the same name, regardless of their context. Merging event attributes can further reduce the size of the graph at the expense of run time.

Example. Let us consider the following three cases: $\langle \blacktriangleright, a, b, d, e, \blacksquare \rangle$, $\langle \blacktriangleright, a, c, c, e, \blacksquare \rangle$ and $\langle \blacktriangleright, b, d, e, \blacksquare \rangle$. In the first step, the initial graph is created where every case is a single, isolated and independent path (Fig. 1, left). In the second step, nodes are merged based on their predecessor paths. Both nodes with activity a have the same preceding paths and are, thus, merged together, resulting in the middle graph in Fig. 1. After merging nodes based on predecessor paths, nodes are merged based on successor paths. Note that only nodes with the same activities are compared. The first and third case are merged because the third one is a suffix of the first one. Furthermore, activity e is always followed by the end symbol, resulting in the right graph in Fig. 1. No other nodes can be merged without changing the behavior of the graph.

4.3   Likelihood Thresholds

A main component of our approach is the threshold heuristic strategy for identifying noisy behavior predicted by the NEP. Here, the set of likelihood thresholds $t_1, \ldots, t_A$ control the predictions being considered in the extension of a prefix. While low thresholds might lead to noise being included in cases, high thresholds lead to a likelihood graph only focused on common variants. As such, the thresholds control the granularity of the inferred likelihood graph and the extent to which filter out noisy behavior.

As a strategy to determine a likelihood threshold for each attribute, we use the *(mean-centered) lowest plateau heuristic*, earlier introduced for anomaly detection in [8]. The heuristic provides an out-of-the-box threshold, which serves as a starting point for further adjustments, e.g., decreasing in steps if only few cases are generated, based solely on the prediction probabilities.

An alternative approach is to find candidate thresholds by optimizing the F-score of the likelihood graph, given the event log that was used to train the NEP. Particularly, we systematically explore different thresholds to maximize the F-score for the resulting likelihood graph. If the training event log contains much of the ground truth process behavior, this behavior will then also be reflected in the resulting likelihood graph. However, the noise that is present in the training event log, can, if incorporated in the inferred likelihood graph, have a negative impact because including the noise improves the graph's F-score, therefore resulting in an undesired optimization.

5   Evaluation

In this section, we evaluate our approach using synthetic and real-life event logs. The primary objective of our experiments is to find out how well our approach is able to capture the behavior of the ground truth event log. To ensure transparency and reproducibility of the results, we publish our source code[1] and rely on publicly available datasets. The repository also contains additional example graphs for real-life event logs.

5.1   Datasets

We use process models introduced by Nolle et al. [7] to generate likelihood graphs of activities and event attributes that serve as the ground truth in our evaluation. These graphs allow us to compare the inferred graphs to the desired outcome and, thus, are referred to as the *ground truth likelihood graphs*. These graphs vary in complexity w.r.t. the number of activities, depth, and width. We playout these graphs to obtain a *ground truth event log* that represents the entire process designed in the ground truth likelihood graph. To generate a *sampled event log*, random walks through the ground truth likelihood graph are performed in compliance with the transition probabilities. In addition, we introduce noise to

---

[1] https://github.com/yannikgerlach/likelihood-graphs-from-neps.

Table 1. Statistics of the synthetic event logs used in the evaluation

Name	# Cases	# Events	# Variants	# Activities	Avg. case length
Small	2 148	43 498	670	39	8.7
Wide	6 414	31 810	563	56	6.4
Medium	16 672	31 928	684	63	6.4
p2p	21 608	43 265	610	25	8.7
Paper	52 020	50 413	777	27	10.1
huge	102 475	43 249	890	107	8.7

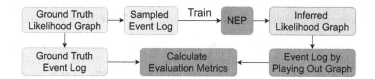

Fig. 2. Relation between ground truth graph, event log, NEP and inferred graph.

the sampled event log by randomly applying noise (skip, insert, rework, early, and late activities as well as attribute anomalies) [7] to 30% of the cases.

If the sampled event log does not contain all cases of the ground truth event log, we can be sure the NEP has not seen all ground truth cases during training. We can therefore effectively measure its generalization ability. For the used event logs, for which an overview is given in Table 1, sampled event logs with 5 000 cases each allows us to do this.

5.2 Experimental Setup

We compare the cases obtained by playing out the inferred likelihood graph to the ground truth event log, which does not contain noisy behavior. This improves upon related work, which evaluates the generated cases on the sampled event log, as described in Sect. 2. It allows to better estimate how well an NEP extracts relevant behavior from a sampled event log and metrics such as precision and fitness are more meaningful. Figure 2 shows the evaluation setup for our approach.

Training of the NEPs. For our experiments, we use the NEP by Nolle et al. [7] which is a multi-perspective NEP, predicting the next activity and event attributes. When predicting the event attributes, the predicted activity is considered, enabling the NEP to better learn dependencies.

Algorithm 2. Calculate fitness and precision between two event logs.

1: **function** WEIGHTEDLEVENSHTEINDISTANCE($\mathcal{L}_1, \mathcal{L}_2$)
2:     $\hat{\mathcal{L}}_1 = \mathcal{L}_1 \setminus \mathcal{L}_2$, $\hat{\mathcal{L}}_2 = \mathcal{L}_2 \setminus \mathcal{L}_1$
3:     $d = \sum_{c_2 \in \hat{\mathcal{L}}_2} \min_{c_1 \in \hat{\mathcal{L}}_1} LV(c_2, c_1)$
4:     $d_{weighted} = d / \sum_{c \in \mathcal{L}_2} |c|$
5:     **return** $1 - d_{weighted}$

We train an ensemble of 10 NEPs (with different seeds) on and for each sampled event log. To compare the prediction quality to a single NEP, we also use each NEP individually and average the resulting evaluation measures. For training, we use 90% of the data; the remaining 10% are used for validation.

Optimizing Likelihood Threshold. In Sect. 4.3 we propose optimizing the threshold for F-score on the sampled event log as a heuristic. To evaluate this approach, we also determine the threshold achieving the best F-score on the ground truth event log, i.e., an optimal threshold. However, this optimal threshold cannot be determined without a ground truth likelihood graph. The optimization on the sampled event log can always be performed. For optimizing, we use Bayesian optimization with 10 initial steps and 10 optimization steps. We investigate thresholds in the range of 0.02 to 0.4.

5.3 Evaluation Measures

We evaluate our approach with respect to the following aspects:

(1) We measure fitness, precision, and generalization ability to evaluate the quality of the resulting likelihood graph. For a better comparison, we also show the F_1-*measure*. To measure generalization ability, we take the set of generated cases, remove the cases present in the event log, and only take from the remaining cases those that are also present in the ground truth event log. We then divide the size of this set by the number of generated cases.

(2) We measure both the difference in likelihood prediction in single events and in the likelihood of a case to compare how well the inferred event and case likelihoods approximate the likelihoods defined in the ground truth graph.

We calculate fitness and precision between two event logs, the set of *generated cases* (GCs) and the set of *ground truth cases* (GTCs) in ground truth event log. Similar to Camargo et al. [2], who use a related measure in their evaluation, we use the normalized Levenshtein (LV) edit distance (see Algorithm 2) to compute the distance between two cases, excluding the start and end symbol. Note that for cases that are contained in both event logs, the distance is 0. Let $\mathcal{L}_1$ be the GTCs and $\mathcal{L}_2$ be the GCs. Then Algorithm 2 calculates the precision of the inferred likelihood graph. When switching the sets of cases, i.e. $\mathcal{L}_1$ are the GCs and $\mathcal{L}_2$ are the GTCs, Algorithm 2 calculates the fitness.

We define the *(average) absolute likelihood difference per event and attribute* (ALDE), as well as the *mean squared error per event and attribute* (MSEE). In comparison to ALDE, MSEE penalizes greater differences in the likelihoods more. Regarding case likelihoods, their magnitudes can be vastly different depending on the length of a case and the values are usually quite small. These two observations make the evaluation of absolute case likelihoods difficult and unintuitive. We mitigate this problem by dividing the difference in case likelihoods by the ground truth case likelihood. As a result, we obtain the relative likelihood difference, in the following called *normalized (average) likelihood difference per case* (NLDC).

As a baseline, we compare the sampled event log with the ground truth event log. Depending on the predictive performance of the NEP, it should be able to outperform the baseline. First, the NEP should filter out noise and, thus, have higher precision than the sampled event log. Second, the NEP should generalize the seen behavior and, thus, have higher fitness. Nevertheless, the reconstructed likelihood graph does not contain all attribute values and transitions because unlikely ones are filtered out using the likelihood thresholds. In contrast, the event log contains all attribute values and transitions, even those below the likelihood thresholds.

5.4   Results: Synthetic Event Logs

Table 2 lists the results for each synthetic event log. The baseline is outperformed by our approach for all event logs regarding the control-flow considerably, except for the P2P event log. Due to the structure of the P2P event log it appears to be difficult to find automatic thresholds. In general, however, optimization based on the ground truth event log yields good F-scores, with the optimization on the sampled event log being a reasonable choice as well. Interestingly, across all settings, the achieved precision is often close to 1.0, implying that mostly correct cases are generated. However, usually not all of the correct cases are generated, as indicated by the fitness values. Disregarding P2P, fitness appears to decrease with increasing size of the ground truth event log as the sampled event log size stays constant. As a result, more behavior is missing in the sampled event log. We also observe good generalization ability in the tested NEP, implying the NEP generates a good amount of correct cases that it has not seen in training.

When presented with a real-life event log, the choice is to use the lowest-plateau heuristic or optimization on the sampled event log. In the results we observe no clear tendency for one or the other, although the optimization on the event log appears to be slightly better, but also more time-intensive. Regarding the found thresholds, the threshold for the event attribute appears to be especially important for achieving good F-scores. As an activity often has multiple valid event attribute values, getting them right appears to have more impact on the F-score than getting the activity right.

When comparing the performance of single NEPs to ensembles, we observe improved prediction performance (especially when optimizing for an optimal threshold), indicating its effectiveness.

Table 2. The found thresholds (t_1 for the activity and t_2 for the event attribute), F_1-score, precision, fitness, generalization ability and quality of likelihoods for the synthetic event logs and NEP. Optimized on Event Log (EL), mean lowest-plateau threshold Heuristic (HR) or Optimal (OPT) threshold. Using a Single Model (SM) or Ensemble (EM). Note that averaging the thresholds for single models is not meaningful.

Log	Model	t_1	t_2	F_1	Prec.	Fit.	Gen.	NLDC	ALDE	MSEE
SMALL	Baseline	–	–	0.905	0.840	0.981	–	–	–	–
	EL SM	–	–	0.988	1.000	0.977	0.183	0.486	0.005	0.001
	EL EM	0.213	0.020	**0.994**	1.000	0.989	0.247	0.579	**0.004**	0.001
	HR EM	0.364	0.090	0.983	1.000	0.967	0.150	**0.367**	0.005	0.001
	OPT SM	–	–	0.991	0.999	0.982	0.205	0.533	0.005	0.001
	OPT EM	0.368	0.021	**0.994**	1.000	0.989	0.247	0.579	**0.004**	0.001
WIDE	Baseline	–	–	0.847	0.828	0.866	–	–	–	–
	EL SM	–	–	0.895	0.975	0.830	0.583	1.353	0.071	0.028
	EL EM	0.143	0.051	0.892	0.946	0.845	0.591	1.014	0.066	0.026
	HR EM	0.210	0.090	0.844	1.000	0.730	0.485	2.009	0.081	0.033
	OPT SM	–	–	0.914	0.946	0.886	0.594	0.760	0.053	0.018
	OPT EM	0.219	0.020	**0.953**	0.989	0.918	0.755	**0.416**	**0.045**	0.017
MEDIUM	Baseline	–	–	0.878	0.873	0.883	–	–	–	–
	EL SM	–	–	0.941	0.994	0.894	0.700	0.991	0.026	0.005
	EL EM	0.136	0.083	0.926	0.990	0.863	0.680	0.998	0.025	0.005
	HR EM	0.420	0.070	0.932	1.000	0.872	0.695	0.931	**0.020**	0.003
	OPT SM	–	–	0.961	0.972	0.950	0.632	0.671	0.023	0.004
	OPT EM	0.214	0.020	**0.974**	0.989	0.918	0.727	**0.519**	**0.020**	0.003
P2P	Baseline	–	–	**0.854**	0.858	0.849	–	–	–	–
	EL SM	–	–	0.782	0.982	0.652	0.469	2.270	0.030	0.005
	EL EM	0.073	0.095	0.794	0.993	0.662	0.633	1.476	0.023	0.003
	HR EM	0.140	0.080	0.802	1.000	0.670	0.713	**0.999**	**0.021**	0.003
	OPT SM	–	–	0.786	0.965	0.668	0.494	2.401	0.028	0.004
	OPT EM	0.073	0.095	0.794	0.993	0.662	0.633	1.476	0.023	0.003
PAPER	Baseline	–	–	0.883	0.899	0.868	–	–	–	–
	EL SM	–	–	0.911	0.999	0.836	0.683	5.084	0.042	0.013
	EL EM	0.102	0.112	0.908	1.000	0.831	0.660	4.626	0.039	0.013
	HR EM	0.351	0.030	**0.943**	0.990	0.900	0.837	**2.863**	**0.034**	0.011
	OPT SM	–	–	0.928	0.988	0.875	0.746	3.667	0.040	0.013
	OPT EM	0.295	0.070	0.927	0.999	0.865	0.813	3.195	0.035	0.012
HUGE	Baseline	–	–	0.843	0.890	0.801	–	–	–	–
	EL SM	–	–	0.881	0.985	0.799	0.522	3.509	**0.023**	0.006
	EL EM	0.400	0.057	**0.912**	0.987	0.848	0.620	1.781	**0.023**	0.004
	HR EM	0.130	0.050	0.842	0.827	0.857	0.274	1.452	0.028	0.007
	OPT SM	–	–	0.892	0.933	0.856	0.366	1.993	0.030	0.007
	OPT EM	0.329	0.021	**0.912**	0.917	0.907	0.124	**1.034**	0.030	0.007

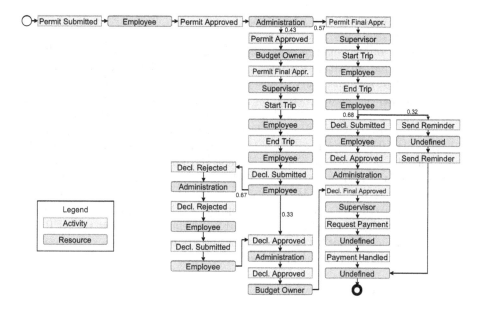

Fig. 3. Inferred graph on the travel permits log (BPIC 2020) with a single event attribute. *Undefined* user implies activity performed by the system.

The inferred transition likelihoods are typically quite close to the true likelihood (ALDE ≤ 0.04). The likelihoods of cases is also often not too far away from the true case likelihood, although it remains somewhat difficult to interpret. The best likelihood approximations correlate with the best F-scores, possibly due to the averaging of the outgoing edges.

5.5   Results: Real-Life Event Log

We apply our approach to publicly available real-life event logs from the BPI Challenge (2012, 2013, 2015, 2017, and 2020). Due to the space limitation of the paper, the details and the resulting likelihood graphs can be accessed from our repository. Here, we discuss the results of the Travel Permits event log from 2020[2], which consists of 7,065 cases and 86,581 events. The resulting likelihood graph is depicted in Fig. 3. Likelihoods of 1.0 are omitted for better readability. The NEP is trained with the activity and the resource event attribute; likelihood thresholds are set according to our threshold strategy. The likelihood graph shows three branching paths (permit approved vs. permit final approved, declaration approved vs. declaration rejected, and declaration submitted vs. send reminder) with different probabilities depending on the activity performed. Also, the additional activities executed for the permit approved-path are shown.

---

[2] van Dongen, Boudewijn (2020): BPI Challenge 2020. 4TU.ResearchData. Collection. https://doi.org/10.4121/uuid:52fb97d4-4588-43c9-9d04-3604d4613b51.

6   Discussion

The results of our evaluation show that the inferred likelihood graph reflects the behavior that an ML-based NEP has learned. Similar to a stochastic process model in process discovery, it visualizes the process of the NEP for further exploration, inspection, and debugging of the NEP. However, it should be noted that our approach is not designed as a discovery algorithm, although it similarly infers a graph with directly-follows relations. Contrary to many process discovery algorithm, which usually solely focus on the activity, our approach is able to handle an arbitrary number of event attributes (within machine memory limits) in addition to the activity if the NEP predicts those. Our approach allows analysts to better understand the decision points due to the explicit inclusion of event attributes. Therefore, we support explaining the black-box NEP and the process, besides offering a graphical representation of what the NEP has learned [4]. Dependencies between activities and event attributes are represented as separate paths through the graph, each with their respective probabilities.

6.1   Limitations

We consider that our approach exhibits mainly two limitations. One is the potential exponential explosion in the number of generated cases due to the exhaustive search that explores all combinations of activities and attributes. Thus, generating the cases can be time-intensive for processes with very long cases and a large set of attribute value combinations. The second limitation is that our approach only supports the interleaving of concurrent activities, which is susceptible to different orderings of activities. This could be addressed using the same heuristics as process discovery algorithms. Also, our approach does not create loops but unrolls them to better model probabilities for different case prefixes and attribute values. However, this can lead to large graphs containing repeating sequences of nodes. We address this issue by limiting the number of activity occurrences within a case. If this limit is exceeded, the case is discarded and, thus, excluded from the case generation. As a result, it is not included in the inferred graph and also not considered in the evaluation.

6.2   Threats to Validity

While our evaluation on a deep learning model provided relevant observations, we did not explicitly include the evaluation of the NEP itself which directly influences the quality and the interpretability of the likelihood graph. Take, for instance, a NEP randomly predicting activities which is entirely disconnected from the original input data it was "trained" on. Since the likelihood graph is inferred from the generated cases, the likelihood graph will not contain any behavior of the original input but the behavior that the NEP predicts with the noise cut off. This is the expected behavior because we want to know what the NEP has learned, and in this example we can see that it did not learn the original process. Consequently, incorporating an extensive evaluation of the NEP itself may be needed to fully understand the likelihood graph.

7   Conclusion

In this paper, we introduced a novel approach for inferring a multi-perspective likelihood graph from any NEP trained on an event log. Our proposed approach first explores the predictions of the NEP and then creates a compact visual representation of its revealed internals, combining the sequence of activities as well as the event attributes into a single likelihood graph. Therefore, the graph uncovers what black-box NEPs (e.g., ML models) have learned, thus visually explaining them, allowing analysts to better understand branching decisions and mitigating one of their biggest criticisms. Particularly, the visual explanation allows analysts to estimate if the NEP is sufficiently trained and good to deploy. By exploring the graph, the analyst can check assumptions about the process and if the learned process appears reasonable (e.g. the graph might be bigger in regions of uncertainty). As the inferred likelihood graph includes the event attributes, the analyst can identify decision points that lead to different paths and process outcomes (i.e. dependencies between activities and event attributes). For example might a process take a different path depending on the users executing a certain activity. Such decision points can provide valuable insight into how real processes are executed. In this regard, our likelihood graph also provides the probability distribution over the directly-followed activity and event attribute values, additionally allowing us to calculate likelihoods of cases and outcomes. The results of our experiments show that the inferred likelihood graphs accurately describe the original likelihood graphs from which the event logs were sampled and the NEPs were trained on.

As for future work, it is needed to systematically prune case continuations that lead to no additional knowledge about the NEP, i.e., paths or loops through the graph that are already covered by other paths. Also, our approach does not consider the concurrent execution of activities, which could reduce the complexity and increase expressiveness of the likelihood graph. Regarding the evaluation, a study with real users might give valuable insights into how business analysts can use the presented approach to generate value.

References

1. Barredo Arrieta, A., et al.: Explainable artificial intelligence (XAI): concepts, taxonomies, opportunities and challenges toward responsible AI. Inf. Fusion **58**, 82–115 (2020)
2. Camargo, M., Dumas, M., González-Rojas, O.: Learning accurate LSTM models of business processes. In: Hildebrandt, T., van Dongen, B.F., Röglinger, M., Mendling, J. (eds.) BPM 2019. LNCS, vol. 11675, pp. 286–302. Springer, Cham (2019). https://doi.org/10.1007/978-3-030-26619-6_19
3. Evermann, J., Rehse, J.R., Fettke, P.: Predicting process behaviour using deep learning. Decis. Support Syst. **100**, 129–140 (2017)
4. Gal, A., Senderovich, A.: Process minding: closing the big data gap. In: Fahland, D., Ghidini, C., Becker, J., Dumas, M. (eds.) BPM 2020. LNCS, vol. 12168, pp. 3–16. Springer, Cham (2020). https://doi.org/10.1007/978-3-030-58666-9_1

5. Galanti, R., Coma-Puig, B., de Leoni, M., Carmona, J., Navarin, N.: Explainable predictive process monitoring. In: International Conference on Process Mining (2020)

6. Mehdiyev, N., Evermann, J., Fettke, P.: A novel business process prediction model using a deep learning method. Bus. Inf. Syst. Eng. **62**(2), 143–157 (2018). https://doi.org/10.1007/s12599-018-0551-3

7. Nolle, T., Luettgen, S., Seeliger, A., Mühlhäuser, M.: BINet: multi-perspective business process anomaly classification. In: Information Systems (2019)

8. Nolle, T., Seeliger, A., Mühlhäuser, M.: BINet: multivariate business process anomaly detection using deep learning. In: Weske, M., Montali, M., Weber, I., vom Brocke, J. (eds.) BPM 2018. LNCS, vol. 11080, pp. 271–287. Springer, Cham (2018). https://doi.org/10.1007/978-3-319-98648-7_16

9. Peeperkorn, J., Vanden Broucke, S.K.L.M., De Weerdt, J.: Can deep neural networks learn process model structure ? An assessment framework and analysis. In: International Workshop on Leveraging Machine Learning in Process Mining (2021)

10. Polyvyanyy, A., Moffat, A., García-Bañuelos, L.: An entropic relevance measure for stochastic conformance checking in process mining. In: International Conference on Process Mining, pp. 97–104 (2020)

11. Rehse, J.-R., Mehdiyev, N., Fettke, P.: Towards explainable process predictions for industry 4.0 in the DFKI-Smart-Lego-Factory. KI - Künstliche Intelligenz **33**(2), 181–187 (2019). https://doi.org/10.1007/s13218-019-00586-1

12. Rizzi, W., Di Francescomarino, C., Maggi, F.M.: Explainability in predictive process monitoring: when understanding helps improving. In: Fahland, D., Ghidini, C., Becker, J., Dumas, M. (eds.) BPM 2020. LNBIP, vol. 392, pp. 141–158. Springer, Cham (2020). https://doi.org/10.1007/978-3-030-58638-6_9

13. Shunin, T., Zubkova, N., Shershakov, S.: Neural approach to the discovery problem in process mining. In: Analysis of Images, Social Networks and Texts, pp. 261–273 (2018)

14. Sindhgatta, R., Moreira, C., Ouyang, C., Barros, A.: Exploring interpretable predictive models for business processes. In: Fahland, D., Ghidini, C., Becker, J., Dumas, M. (eds.) BPM 2020. LNCS, vol. 12168, pp. 257–272. Springer, Cham (2020). https://doi.org/10.1007/978-3-030-58666-9_15

15. Sindhgatta, R., Ouyang, C., Moreira, C., Liao, Y.: Interpreting predictive process monitoring benchmarks. arXiv (2019)

16. Sommers, D., Menkovski, V., Fahland, D.: Process discovery using graph neural networks. In: International Conference on Process Mining, pp. 40–47 (2021)

17. Tax, N., Verenich, I., La Rosa, M., Dumas, M.: Predictive business process monitoring with LSTM neural networks. In: Dubois, E., Pohl, K. (eds.) CAiSE 2017. LNCS, vol. 10253, pp. 477–492. Springer, Cham (2017). https://doi.org/10.1007/978-3-319-59536-8_30

18. Tax, N., van Zelst, S.J., Teinemaa, I.: An experimental evaluation of the generalizing capabilities of process discovery techniques and black-box sequence models. In: Gulden, J., Reinhartz-Berger, I., Schmidt, R., Guerreiro, S., Guédria, W., Bera, P. (eds.) BPMDS/EMMSAD -2018. LNBIP, vol. 318, pp. 165–180. Springer, Cham (2018). https://doi.org/10.1007/978-3-319-91704-7_11

19. Theis, J., Darabi, H.: Decay replay mining to predict next process events. IEEE Access **7**, 119787–119803 (2019)

20. van der Aalst, W.M.P.: Process Mining: Data Science in Action. Springer, Heidelberg (2016). https://doi.org/10.1007/978-3-662-49851-4

21. Verenich, I., Dumas, M., La Rosa, M., Nguyen, H.: Predicting process performance: a white-box approach based on process models. J. Softw. Evol. Process (2019)

22. Weinzierl, S., et al.: An empirical comparison of deep-neural-network architectures for next activity prediction using context-enriched process event logs. arXiv (2020)
23. Weinzierl, S., Zilker, S., Brunk, J., Revoredo, K., Matzner, M., Becker, J.: XNAP: making LSTM-based next activity predictions explainable by using LRP. In: Del Río Ortega, A., Leopold, H., Santoro, F.M. (eds.) BPM 2020. LNBIP, vol. 397, pp. 129–141. Springer, Cham (2020). https://doi.org/10.1007/978-3-030-66498-5_10

Bootstrapping Generalization of Process Models Discovered from Event Data

Artem Polyvyanyy[1]([✉]) [iD], Alistair Moffat[1] [iD], and Luciano García-Bañuelos[2] [iD]

[1] The University of Melbourne, Melbourne, VIC 3010, Australia
{artem.polyvyanyy,ammoffat}@unimelb.edu.au
[2] Tecnológico de Monterrey, 64849 Monterrey, N.L., Mexico
luciano.garcia@tec.mx

Abstract. Process mining extracts value from the traces recorded in the event logs of IT-systems, with *process discovery* the task of inferring a process model for a log emitted by some unknown system. *Generalization* is one of the quality criteria applied to process models to quantify how well the model describes future executions of the system. Generalization is also perhaps the least understood of those criteria, with that lack primarily a consequence of it measuring properties over the entire future behavior of the system when the only available sample of behavior is that provided by the log. In this paper, we apply a bootstrap approach from computational statistics, allowing us to define an estimator of the model's generalization based on the log it was discovered from. We show that standard process mining assumptions lead to a *consistent estimator* that makes fewer errors as the quality of the log increases. Experiments confirm the ability of the approach to support industry-scale data-driven systems engineering.

Keywords: Process mining · Generalization · Bootstrapping · Consistent estimator

1 Introduction

Given an event log that records traces of some real-world system, the challenge of *process discovery* is to develop a plausible *model* of that system, so that the behavior of the system can be analyzed independently of the specific transactions included in that particular log. Many different models might be constructed from the same log. Thus, it is important to have tools that allow the quality of a given model to be *quantified* relative to the initial log. For example, *precision* is the fraction of the traces permitted by the model that appear in the log, and *recall* is the fraction of the log's traces that are valid according to the model. Composite measures have also been defined [1,8].

A log is only a sample of observations in regard to the underlying system, and not a specification of its actions. It is thus interesting to consider *generalization* – the extent to which the inferred model accounts for future observations of the

© Springer Nature Switzerland AG 2022
X. Franch et al. (Eds.): CAiSE 2022, LNCS 13295, pp. 36–54, 2022.
https://doi.org/10.1007/978-3-031-07472-1_3

system. Generalization poses substantial challenges, since, by its very definition, it asks about behaviors that have *not* been observed from a system that is *not* known. High generalization (and high recall) can be obtained by allowing all possible traces. But overly-permissive models of necessity compromise precision. What is desired is a model that attains high precision and recall with respect to the supplied log, and continues to score well on the universe of possible logs that might arise via continued observation. Note that process mining generalization as studied in this work differs from generalization as it applies to process model abstraction [21]. Process model abstraction considers techniques for combining several processes, activities, and events into corresponding generalized concepts, for example, identifying a semantically coherent sub-process in a process model.

In particular, we study the problem of measuring the generalization of a discovered process model, making use of the *bootstrapping* technique from computational statistics [12]. In the simplest form, the idea is to construct multiple sampled replicates of the initial log, each representing a log that might have emerged from the system. Any aggregate properties established by considering the set of replicates can then be assumed to be valid for the universe of possible traces. That is, by constructing a process model from one replicate, and then testing on another, generalization can be explored. In terms of high-level contributions, our work here:

- Presents, for the first time, an estimator of the generalization of a process model discovered from an event log, grounded in the bootstrap method;
- Shows that the estimator is consistent for the class of systems captured as directly-follows graphs (DFGs), making fewer errors on larger log replicates; and
- Confirms via experiments the feasibility of the new approach in industrial settings.

The next section introduces several key ideas, and a running example. Section 3 presents our new approach, and demonstrates its consistency. Section 4 provides an evaluation that confirms the consistency and feasibility of our approach. Related work is discussed in Sect. 5. Finally, Sect. 6 concludes our presentation.

2 Background

2.1 Systems, Models, Logs, and Their Languages

For the purpose of formalizing the problem of measuring generalization of a *process model* discovered from an *event log* of a *system*, consistent with the standard formalization in process mining [1,7], we interpret the system, model, and log as collections of traces, where a *trace* is a sequence of actions that attains, or might attain, some goal.

Let A be a set of possible *actions*; $A = \{a, b, c, d, e, f\}$ will be used throughout this section. Define A^* to be the set of all possible *traces* over A, each a finite sequence of actions. Both abbcf and addef are traces over A, as is the empty trace, denoted by ϵ.

Systems. A *system* S is a group of active elements, such as software components and agents, that perform actions and thereby consume, produce, or manipulate objects and information. A system can be an information system or a business process with its organization context, business rules, and resources [7]. Any sequence of actions that leads to the system's goal constitutes a trace. In general, a system might generate an infinite collection of traces, possibly containing infinitely many distinct traces, and hence also possibly containing traces of arbitrary length.

Models. A *process model*, or just a *model*, M is a finite description of a set of traces. Figure 1a describes a process model, represented as a *directly-follows graph* (DFG), with start node i, final node o, and all walks from i to o as valid traces. That example model, for instance, describes traces abcf and adeef; but does not describe abbcf.

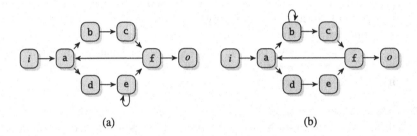

(a)   (b)

Fig. 1. (a) An example process model, and (b) an example system.

Logs. An *event log*, or just a *log*, L is a finite multiset of traces.

Languages. A *language* is a subset of the traces in Λ^*. The language of system S is the set of all traces S can generate; the language of model M is the set of traces described by M; and the language of log L is its support set, $Supp\,(L)$. Further, define $\mathcal{L} \subset \mathcal{P}(\Lambda^*)$, $\mathcal{M} \subseteq \mathcal{P}(\Lambda^*)$, and $\mathcal{S} \subseteq \mathcal{P}(\Lambda^*)$ to be sets containing all possible languages of logs, models, and systems, respectively, with $\mathcal{L}$ restricted to finite languages. When the context is clear, we will interpret logs, models, and systems as their languages – if we say that model M was discovered from log L out of system S, we may be referring to the concrete system, model, and log, or may be referring to the languages they describe.

2.2 Process Discovery

Given a log, the *process discovery problem* consists of constructing a model that represents the behavior recorded in the log [1]. For example, using superscripts to indicate multiplicity, let L = [abbbcf^5, abcf^{20}, addef, adeef^{10}, adefabcfadef^{10}, adef^{20}] be an event log that contains six distinct traces and 66 traces in total. Many comprehensive process discovery techniques have been devised over the last two decades [1]. However, model M, shown in Fig. 1a, can be constructed from L via a simple four-stage discovery algorithm: (1) filter out infrequent traces by, for example, removing the least frequent third of the distinct traces; (2) for every action in each remaining trace, construct a node representing that action; (3) for every pair of adjacent actions x and y, introduce a directed edge from the node for x to the node for y; and (4) introduce start node i and end node o, together with edges from i to every initial action in a frequent trace, and from every last action in a frequent trace to the sink node o.

Despite the simplicity of that supposed construction process, M *fits* 60 of the traces in L, failing on only six. On the other hand, the cycles in M mean that it represents infinitely many traces *not* present in L. To quantify the extent of the mismatch between L and M, the measures *recall* and *precision* can be used [7, 8, 22]. Given a suite of possible models, precision and recall allow alternative models to be numerically compared.

2.3   Generalization

An event log of a system contains traces that the system generated over some finite period *and* were recorded using some logging mechanism. That is, a log is a *sample* of all possible traces the system could have generated [26]. Hence, an alternative (and arguably more useful) definition of the process discovery problem is that a model be constructed to represent *all* of the traces the system *could* have generated, derived from the finite sample provided in the log. Such a model, if constructed, would explain the *system*, and not just the traces that happened to be recorded in that particular log. For example, the DFG S in Fig. 1b could be a

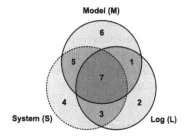

Fig. 2. Venn diagram showing languages of model M, log L, and system S, adapted from Buijs et al. [7]; the language of the system is unknown (the dotted border).

complete representation of the system that generated the 66 traces contained in L, allowing, for example, the five occurrences of abbbcf to now be understood.

If the alternative definition of the process discovery problem is accepted, then the candidate model M in Fig. 1a must be somehow benchmarked against the system S of Fig. 1b, rather than against L. Unfortunately, the actual behavior of the system is often unknown; indeed, that absence is, of course, a primary motivation for process discovery. That is, the log may be the only available information in respect of the system whose behavior it is a sample of. Given this context, Fig. 2 shows the relationship between the languages of log, model, and system. The numbered regions then have the following interpretations (again, making use of example log L, model M, and system S): (1) Traces that S does not generate, yet appear in L (perhaps by error) and are included in M; e.g., adeef. (2) Traces that S does not generate, yet appear in L without triggering inclusion in M; e.g., addef. (3) Traces permitted by S, and recorded in L, but not included in M; e.g., abbbcf. (4) Traces permitted by S, but neither observed in L nor permitted by M; e.g., abbcf. (5) Traces permitted by both S and M, but not appearing in L; e.g., adefadef. (6) Traces neither permitted by S nor observed in L, but nevertheless allowed by M; e.g., adeeef. (7) Traces permitted by S, observed in L, and included in M; e.g., adefabcfadef. Note that categories (4), (5), and (6) might be infinite, but that (1), (2), (3), and (7) must be finite, as L itself is finite.

To assess a process model against a system, a *generalization* measure is employed [1]. The objective of a generalization measure is described by van der Aalst [2] as:

> *a generalization measure [...] aims to quantify the likelihood that new unseen [traces generated by the system] will fit the model.*

On the assumption that $M \subseteq S$, Buijs et al. [7] suggest measuring the generalization of M with respect to S as the model-system recall, that is, the fraction of the system covered by the model, $(S \cap M)/M$ (when the context is clear, we use X to denote $|X|$). But this proposal requires knowledge of, or a way to approximate, the system's traces.

More broadly, generalization is probably the least understood quality criterion for discovered models in process mining. Only a few approaches have been described, and all of them diverge, in one way or another, from the intended phenomenon [23]. We elaborate on that observation in Sect. 5, which discusses related work.

3   Estimating Generalization

We now present our proposal. Section 3.1 summarizes the bootstrap method from statistics, a key component; and Sect. 3.2 presents a framework for measuring generalization using it. Then, Sect. 3.3 develops the required log sampling mechanism; Sect. 3.4 presents concrete instantiations of the framework; and Sect. 3.5 establishes the consistency of the presented estimator. Finally, Sect. 3.6 demonstrates the application of our approach to the running example of Sect. 2.2.

3.1   Bootstrapping

Bootstrapping is a computational method in statistics that estimates the sampling distribution over unknown data using the sampling distribution over an approximate sufficient statistic of the data [12]. The true sampling distribution of some quantity for a population is constructed by drawing multiple samples from the true population, computing the quantity for each sample, and then aggregating the quantities. But if the true population is unknown, drawing samples may be expensive, or even infeasible. Instead, the bootstrap method can be used, shown in Fig. 3, with dashed and solid lines denoting unknown and observed quantities, respectively. The bootstrap proceeds in four steps:

1. *Take a single sample* of the true population.
2. *Estimate the population* based on that single sample.

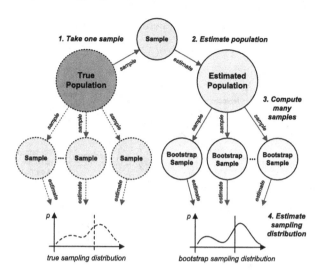

Fig. 3. The bootstrap method, adapted from lecture notes at the Pennsylvania State University, see https://online.stat.psu.edu/stat555/node/119/, accessed 26 November 2021

3. *Compute many samples* from that estimated population.
4. *Estimate the sampling distribution* based on those samples.

Estimated sampling distributions can be used to approximate properties of the sampled distribution, including the mean and its confidence interval, and variance [5, 11].

3.2   Bootstrap Framework for Measuring Generalization

We now apply the bootstrap method to estimate generalization of candidate models for representing some system, supposing that for every model the corresponding system is known, and seeking measures of the form $gen : \mathcal{M} \times \mathcal{S} \rightarrow [0, 1]$. The better M represents S, the higher is $gen(M, S)$; with $gen(M, S) = 1$ arising if every new trace from S is described by M. Conversely, $gen(M, S) = 0$ is the worst possible generalization, arising when none of the new distinct traces observed from S are captured by M.

As the system is not known, it cannot be measured directly. We thus propose assessing log-based generalization via an estimator function:

$$gen^* : \mathcal{M} \times \mathcal{L} \times \mathbb{LSM} \times \mathbb{N} \times \mathbb{N} \rightarrow [0, 1], \tag{1}$$

where $\mathbb{LSM}$ is a collection of log sampling methods, with each $lsm \in \mathbb{LSM}$ a *randomizing* function that, given an event log L and an integer n, produces a sample log $L^* = lsm(L, n)$ from L of size n. Given a model M, a log L, a log sampling method lsm, a log sample size n, and a log sample count m, Algorithm 1 implements the estimator:

$$gen^*(M, L, lsm, n, m) = \text{BootstrapGeneralization}(M, L, gen, lsm, n, m). \quad (2)$$

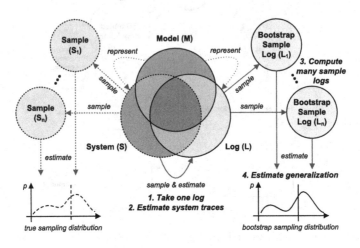

Fig. 4. Bootstrapping generalization

Figure 4 adapts Fig. 3, summarizing the input, output, and computation of Algorithm 1. The four generic stages introduced above are handled in Algorithm 1 as follows:

1. *Take one log* of the system, as a sample of all the traces the system can generate.
2. *Estimate system traces* based on that single log.
3. *Compute many samples* from the estimated system traces.
4. *Estimate generalization* based on all those sample logs.

Algorithm 1: BootstrapGeneralization(M, L, gen, lsm, n, m)

Input: Model $M \in \mathcal{M}$, log $L \in \mathcal{L}$, generalization measure $gen : \mathcal{M} \times \mathcal{S} \to [0, 1]$, log sampling method $lsm \in \mathbb{LSM}$, sample size $n \in \mathbb{N}$, and number of samples $m \in \mathbb{N}$

Output: Estimated generalization of M with respect to the system that generated L

1 $data = []$
2 **for** $i \in [1 .. m]$ **do**
3 $\quad$ sample L_i^* of size n from L using lsm, i.e., $L_i^* = lsm(L, n)$
4 $\quad$ $data = data \uplus [gen(M, L_i^*)]$
5 **return** $average(data)$

That is, given a log L (Step 1), we use L itself to define the estimated system traces (Step 2). This decision is defensible: L is a record of the system over an extended period, and, more to the point, nothing else is known in the scenario considered. Step 3 appears as line 3 of Algorithm 1, with replicate logs computed using the sampling method *lsm*. Next, lines 4 and 5 of Algorithm 1 implement Step 4 of the generic pattern, with an estimate of the generalization measurement computed for each sample log. Once the individual measurements are collected, aggregation (*bagging*) takes place at line 5. As shown, the arithmetic mean is returned, but other statistics can also be computed, including confidence intervals, variance, and skewness.

3.3 Log Sampling

We next present two log sampling methods, that is, *lsm* candidates, suitable for use in Step 2 of the generic bootstrap scheme described in Sect. 3.1.

There are two main forms of bootstrapping [11]. *Nonparametric* bootstrapping draws samples from the data using a "with replacement" methodology. The alternative, the *parametric* bootstrap, generates samples using a known distribution based on parameters estimated from the data. Nonparametric methods reuse elements from the original sample, and hence are only effective if the original sample is a good estimate of the true population. Moreover, the very essence of generalization is to measure the model's ability to handle hitherto-unseen traces. But nor is it clear what distribution of traces might be employed in a parametric bootstrap for process discovery. The first of the two log sampling techniques we explore is nonparametric. Let L be a log, a multiset of traces, and *randTrace*(L), a function that returns a randomly selected trace from L, each chosen with probability $1/|L|$. Algorithm 2 describes log sampling with replacement.

Algorithm 2: LogSamplingWithReplacement(L, n)

Input: Log L, as a multiset of traces, and sample log size $n \in \mathbb{N}$
Output: Sample log L'
1 $L' = []$
2 **for** $i = 1$ **to** n **do** $L' = L' \uplus [randTrace(L)]$
3 **return** L'

The second method we make use of is a *semiparametric* bootstrap, extending ideas from Theis and Darabi [24] (see Sect. 5). The semiparametric bootstrap assumes that the true population consists of elements similar but not necessarily identical to those in the sample; another interpretation is that a semiparametric sample is a nonparametric sample containing a certain amount of "noise." In our context, the noise is in the form of new traces; to create them, we employ a genetic *crossover* operator, also used in evolutionary computation. Two compatible *parent* traces generate two *offspring* if they contain a common subtrace of some minimum length that can become a crossover point.

Let $subseq(t, p, n)$ denote the subtrace of trace $t \in \Lambda^*$ of length $n \in \mathbb{N}$ that starts at position $p \in \mathbb{N}$ in t, with $p + n - 1 \leq |t|$; and let (t, p, n) *identify* that subtrace of t. For example, $(\text{abbbcf} 2 2)$ identifies subtrace bb. We also sometimes use underlining as a shorthand, so that $\text{ab\underline{bb}cf} = (\text{abbbcf}, 2, 2)$. In addition, $prefix(t, x)$ is the prefix of t up to and including the xth action, and $suffix(t, x)$ is the suffix of t from and including that xth action. For example, $prefix(\text{trace}, 3) = \text{tra}$ and $suffix(\text{trace}, 3) = \text{ace}$.

Algorithm 3: BreedingSites(t_1, t_2, k)

Input: Traces $t_1, t_2 \in \Lambda^*$ and length of common subtrace $k \in \mathbb{N}$
Output: Set of all breeding sites for t_1 and t_2 for common subtraces of length k
1 $sites = \{\}$
2 **for** $p_1 = 1$ **to** $|t_1| - k + 1$ **do**
3   **for** $p_2 = 1$ **to** $|t_2| - k + 1$ **do**
4   **if** $subseq(t_1, p_1, k) = subseq(t_2, p_2, k)$ **then**
5              $sites = sites \cup \{(p_1, p_2)\}$

6 **return** $sites$

Suppose that traces t_1 and t_2 share k actions, $(t_1, p_1, k) = (t_2, p_2, k)$, and that $\circ$ is a concatenation operator. Then, the *crossover* operator $\otimes$ creates a new trace by joining t_1 and t_2 across that common subtrace: $(t_1, p_1, k) \otimes (t_2, p_2, k) = prefix(t_1, p_1 + k - 1) \circ suffix(t_2, p_2 + k)$. For example, traces abbcf and abbbbcf are obtained from abbbcf via self-crossover, with bb appearing at the *breeding sites* $p_1 = 2$ and $p_2 = 3$, yielding $\text{ab\underline{bb}cf} \otimes \text{ab\underline{bb}cf} = \text{abbcf}$, and $\text{ab\underline{bb}cf} \otimes \text{ab\underline{bb}cf} = \text{abbbbcf}$. Two traces might have multiple breeding sites,

---

Algorithm 4: LogBreeding(L_1, L_2, k, p)

Input: Logs L_1 and L_2, as multisets of traces, length of common subtrace
      $k \in \mathbb{N}$, and breeding probability $p \in [0, 1]$
Output: Log L' of traces that result from breeding L_1 and L_2
1 $L' = []$
2 **for** $i = 1$ **to** $\lceil |L_1|/2 \rceil$ **do**
3      $t_1 = randTrace(L_1)$
4      $t_2 = randTrace(L_2)$
5      $sites = $ BreedingSites(t_1, t_2, k)
6   **if** $rand() < p$ **and** $sites \neq []$ **then**
7   select a random pair (p_1, p_2) from $sites$
8          $L' = L' \uplus [(t_1, p_1, k) \otimes (t_2, p_2, k), (t_2, p_2, k) \otimes (t_1, p_1, k)]$
9   **else**
10         $L' = L' \uplus [t_1, t_2]$

11 **return** L'

---

with the count determined by the traces and the value of k. Algorithm 3 identifies all breeding sites for two input traces. For example, `adeef` and `adefabcfadef` have six $k = 2$ breeding sites: $\{(1, 1), (1, 9), (2, 2), (2, 10), (4, 3), (4, 11)\}$.

In terms of a system or model, each possible candidate crossover site represents a "hyper jump" between pairs of states that share a common k-action context. We do not claim that all systems actually behave in this way; but Lemma 3.2, below, shows that some interesting classes of systems do. A noteworthy property of the crossover operator is that it allows loops to be inferred if traces that include the loop appear in the log. For example, in Fig. 1b, the state labeled `b` is the location of a loop of length one, with both of `ab` and `bb` as $k = 2$ contexts; and, as already noted, the crossover operator can spawn both `abbcf` and `abbbbcf` if `abbbcf` is available in the log.

Algorithm 5: LogSamplingWithBreeding(L, n)

Input: Log L, a multiset of traces, and sample log size $n \in \mathbb{N}$. The number of log generations $g \in \mathbb{N}$, the common subtrace length $k \in \mathbb{N}$, and the breeding probability $p \in [0, 1]$ are assumed to be constants

Output: Sample log L'

1   $G[0] = L$
2   **for** $i = 1$ **to** g **do** $G[i] = \text{LogBreeding}(L, G[i - 1], k, p)$
3   $L' = \text{LogSamplingWithReplacement}(\cup_{i=0}^{g} G[i], n)$
4   **return** L'

Algorithms 4 and 5 crystallize these ideas, assuming that $rand()$ returns a uniformly distributed value in $[0, 1]$. In Algorithm 4, traces are chosen from each of L_1 and L_2, and then, with some probability p, checked for k-overlaps, and permitted to breed. If they do breed, their offspring are added to the output set; if they do not, the strings themselves are added. That process iterates until L' contains $\approx |L_1|$ traces. Algorithm 5 then adds the notion of *generations*, with the output log L' of size n a random selection across traces formed during g generations of breeding, where the ith generation arises when the original log L is bred with the $i - 1$th generation. Algorithm 5 thus provides a semiparametric *lms* sampler that can, like Algorithm 2, be used for bootstrapping.

3.4   Generalization Measures

We now present two measures that quantify the ability of a model to represent a system.

As noted in Sect. 2.3, Buijs et al. [7] suggest that model-system recall be used to measure generalization. However, that proposal has two limitations. First, the measure is of only limited utility when models can describe infinite collections of traces, as cardinality measures over sets become problematic. Second, given a model M and system S, but where $M \nsubseteq S$, the suggested calculation is indeterminate. The first limitation can be resolved by replacing the cardinality measure over sets with $ent(\cdot)$, a measure inspired by the topological entropy of a potentially infinite language [22]. The result is a measure referred to as the *coverage of M with S*, and, in essence, is the model-system recall instantiated with the entropy as an estimation of cardinality:

$$ModelSystemRecall(M, S) = \frac{ent(M \cap S)}{ent(M)}. \tag{3}$$

By analogy, we now suggest addressing the second limitation by considering model-system precision as a second aspect that characterizes the generalization of the model[1]:

$$ModelSystemPrecision(M, S) = \frac{ent(M \cap S)}{ent(S)}. \tag{4}$$

Model-system precision and recall can both be reported, or a single blended value – their harmonic mean, for example – can be computed. We postpone discussion of which approach is preferable to future work. The entropy-based model-log measures of precision and recall satisfy all the desired properties for the corresponding class of measures [23], making it interesting to study how these measures perform, in terms of generalization properties [2], when comparing the traces of the model and system.

3.5   Consistency

Next, we show that our estimator of generalization is consistent for systems captured as DFGs, which are graphs of actions commonly used by industry to describe process models [1], making it reasonable to assume that the unknown systems they correspond to are also captured as DFGs. Figure 1 shows two DFGs.

Definition 3.1 (DFG). A *directly-follows graph* (DFG) is a tuple $(\Phi, \Psi, \phi, \psi, i, o)$; with $\Phi \subseteq \Lambda$ a set of *actions*; $\Psi \subseteq ((\Phi \times \Phi) \cup (\{i\} \times \Phi) \cup (\Phi \times \{o\}))$ a *directly-follows relation*; $\phi : \Phi \cup \{i, o\} \to \mathbb{N}_0$ an *action frequency function*; $\psi : \Psi \to \mathbb{N}_0$ an *arc frequency function*; and $i \notin \Lambda$ and $o \notin \Lambda$ the *input* and the *output* of the graph. ⌋

We define the semantics of a DFG via a mapping to a finite automaton [20].

Definition 3.2 (DFA). A *deterministic finite automaton* (DFA) is a tuple $(Q, \Lambda, \delta, q_0, A)$, with Q a finite set of *states*; Λ a finite set of *actions*; $\delta : Q \times \Lambda \to Q$ the *transition function*; $q_0 \in Q$ the *start state*; and $A \subseteq Q$ is the set of *accepting states*. ⌋

---

[1] Both can be computed using *Entropia* [19]. Recall is specified by the `-emr` option, and precision by `-emp`. Languages are compared based on exact matching of constituent traces, based on models and systems provided as Petri nets.

A sequence of actions is a trace of a DFA if the DFA accepts that sequence of actions. A DFA is *stable* if $\forall(q_1, \lambda, q_2) \in \delta \wedge \forall(q_1', \lambda', q_2') \in \delta : ((\lambda = \lambda') \Rightarrow (q_2 = q_2'))$. A DFG $(\Phi, \Psi, \phi, \psi, i, o)$ gives rise to a DFA $(\Phi \cup \{i, o\}, \Phi \cup \{o\}, \delta, i, o)$, with $\delta = \{(s, t, t) \in (\{i\} \cup \Phi) \times (\Phi \cup \{o\}) \times (\Phi \cup \{o\}) \mid (s, t) \in \Psi\}$ that is guaranteed to be stable.

Lemma 3.1 (Stable DFAs). *A DFA of a DFG is stable.*   ⌟

Indeed, an occurrence of an action is always followed by the same opportunities for future actions; and hence, any offspring that result from the crossover of two traces of a stable DFA are also traces of the DFA.

Lemma 3.2 (Trace crossover). *If $t_1, t_2 \in \Lambda^*$ are traces of a stable DFA and if $t = (t_1, p_1, 1) \otimes (t_2, p_2, 1)$, for $p_1, p_2 \in \mathbb{N}$, then t is accepted by the DFA.*   ⌟

Proof Sketch. By definition, $t = prefix(t_1, p_1) \circ suffix(t_2, p_2 + 1)$, and hence the elements in t_1 and t_2 at positions p_1 and p_2 are instances of the same action. As the DFA is stable, $prefix(t_1, p_1)$ and $prefix(t_2, p_2)$ lead to the same state q in the DFA; and because $suffix(t_2, p_2 + 1)$ leads from q to an accept state, t must also be accepted by the DFA.   ∎

If two traces share a crossover of any length, there must also be a crossover of length one that results in the same offspring pair. Consequently, a log sample that results from Algorithm 5 for an input log composed of traces from a system that is a DFG will also contain valid traces. Such a log sample estimates the system at least as well as the original log. One further condition is then sufficient to allow our main result.

Theorem 3.1 (Bootstrapping DFAs)
Let L be a set of traces from a stable DFA describing a language L^*, $L \subseteq L^*$, such that each subtrace of length two of any trace in L^* is also a subtrace of some trace in L. Then L' is a log of the DFA with $L \subseteq L'$ and $L' \subseteq L^*$ iff L' can result from log sampling with breeding (Algorithm 5) for input log L and common subtrace length $k = 1$.   ⌟

Proof Sketch. ($\Rightarrow$) If $t \in L'$ is not a crossover of two sequences in L' then t is a trace of the DFA (base case). Otherwise, let $t = (t_1, p_1, 1) \otimes (t_2, p_2, 1)$, where t_1 and t_2 are traces of the DFA. As the DFA is stable, t is a trace of the DFA, and the action at position $p_1 + 1$ in t is taken from the state of the DFA reached after the action at position p_1.
($\Leftarrow$) Let $t \in L'$, and consider two cases. (i) If $t \in L$, then t is a trace of the DFA. (ii) Suppose $t \notin L$. But $prefix(t, 0)$ is a computation of the DFA, and if $prefix(t, k)$, $k < |t|$ is a computation of the DFA, then $prefix(t, k + 1)$ is also computation of the DFA, via two subcases. (ii.a) If $t = (t_1, k, 1) \otimes (t_2, m, 1)$, $m \in \mathbb{N}$, $t_1, t_2 \in L'$ it follows (the DFA is stable) that $prefix(t, k + 1)$ is a computation of the DFA. Indeed, t_1 and t_2 are traces of the DFA, shown by structural induction on the hierarchy of crossovers over the sequences in L', and the last action in the prefix is taken from the same state of the DFA. (ii.b) Otherwise, $prefix(t, k + 1)$ is a prefix of some trace of the DFA and, thus, is its computation,

implying that t leads to an accept state, as its last action is the last action of some trace in L. ∎

Hence, the larger the bootstrapped samples of a DFG log that are generated, the better the estimate of the system – meaning that bootstrap generalization (Algorithm 1) instantiated with the entropy-based model-system measures (Eqs. 3 and 4) is consistent, a consequence of the monotonicity property of the two model-system measures [22].

3.6 Example

Consider again the running example of Sect. 2.2. For the languages M and S described by the DFGs of Fig. 1a and Fig 1b, $ModelSystemRecall(M, S) = 0.867$ and $ModelSystemPrecision(M, S) = 0.867$, noting that precision and recall are the same if the complexity of the system and model languages is the same [22].

Assuming now that S is unknown, we apply Algorithm 1 (BootstrapGeneralization) to estimate the corresponding measurements, with parameters: input model M; the log L of 66 traces presented in Sect. 2.2; the generalization measures of Eqs. (3) and (4) (gen); log sampling with breeding as described by Algorithm 5 (lsm); sample log sizes of $n = 100,000$ and $1,000,000$ traces; $m = 100$ log replicates; $g = 10,000$ log generations; breeding sites of length $k = 2$; and a breeding probability of $p = 1.0$. The estimation process yielded model-system precision and recall measurements of 0.892 and 0.912 (for $n = 100,000$), and of 0.897 and 0.908 ($n = 1,000,000$). In contrast, the original log L of 66 traces does not provide a good representation of the system, with model-log precision and recall of 0.791 and 0.935, respectively. The two computations took 457 and 575 s, respectively, on a commodity laptop running Windows 10, Intel(R) Core(TM) i7-7500U CPU @ 2.70 GhZ and 16 GB of RAM.

Table 1. Precision and recall estimates via bootstrapping, plus the number of distinct traces per replica, together with 95% confidence intervals, using $m = 100$ replicates throughout: (a) varying n, the number of traces per replicate, with $g = 10,000$ generations held constant; and (b) varying g, with $n = 10,000$ held constant. The confidence intervals for precision and recall are for the estimated values considering the input parameters and, thus, might *not* include the true values.

(a)				(b)			
n	Precision	Recall	Traces	g	Precision	Recall	Traces
100	0.83 ± 0.00	0.95 ± 0.00	12 ± 0.3	100	0.87 ± 0.00	0.92 ± 0.00	42 ± 0.8
1000	0.86 ± 0.00	0.93 ± 0.00	28 ± 0.6	1000	0.88 ± 0.00	0.92 ± 0.00	54 ± 0.8
10,000	0.88 ± 0.00	0.92 ± 0.00	57 ± 0.7	10,000	0.88 ± 0.00	0.92 ± 0.00	57 ± 0.7
100,000	0.89 ± 0.00	0.91 ± 0.00	107 ± 1.0	100,000	0.88 ± 0.00	0.92 ± 0.00	57 ± 0.7
1,000,000	0.90 ± 0.00	0.91 ± 0.00	166 ± 1.4	1,000,000	0.88 ± 0.00	0.92 ± 0.00	56 ± 0.7

Table 1 shows other values generated by bootstrapping. The simplicity of the example configuration – with just a handful of distinct traces in L, and hence a very limited range of $k = 2$ breeding sites – means that the number of distinct traces per replicate log grows relatively slowly. However, as the traces of the log contain all the subtraces of length two that can be found in traces in the language of the system it is guaranteed (Theorem 3.1) that the larger the bootstrapped logs become, the more complete the coverage of the system and, consequently, the more accurate the estimated generalization.

4   Evaluation

4.1   Data and Experimentation

Algorithms 1 to 5 were implemented[2] and used to demonstrate the feasibility of our approach when used in (close to) industrial settings. A set of 60 DFGs shared with us by Celonis SE (https://www.celonis.com) was then used as a library of ground truth systems [4,20]. Those reference DFGs were generated from three source logs (Road Traffic Fine Management Process, RTFMP [9], Sepsis Cases [17], and BPI Challenge 2012 [25]); two different discovery techniques (denoted "PE" and "VE"); and ten combinations of parameter settings (denoted "01" to "10").

For each of the 60 DFGs, we constructed a log of 100 traces by taking "random walks" through its states. Commencing at the start vertex, the first *context*, one action was chosen uniformly randomly from the edges available, and the context switched to the destination of that edge. That process was iterated until the final state of the system was reached as the context (every non-final state in these models has at least one outward edge), thereby generating one trace in the corresponding log.

Next, from each of the 60 generated logs, we discovered a process model using the Inductive Mining algorithm with a noise threshold of 0.8 [15]. In this controlled experimental setting, in which all of system (S), log (L), and discovered model (M) are known, we have the ability to compute true model-system precision and recall (Eqs. 4 and 3), that is, the ground truth generalization of the derived model.

Then we "forget" about the ground truth system, and estimate the same measurements using Algorithm 1, invoked on each combination of derived model M and log L, in conjunction with: model-system precision and recall measures (*gen*); log sampling with trace breeding (Algorithm 4 as *lsm*); a sample log size of $n = 100,000$; $m = 50$ log replicates; $g = 10,000$ log generations; a common subtrace length of $k = 2$; and a breeding probability of $p = 1.0$. All computation was on a Linux server with Intel(R) Xeon(R) Processor (Cascadelake), 32 cores @ 2.0 GHz each, and 288 GB of memory.

4.2   Results

A subset of results is shown in Table 2, covering twelve systems (three original processes, the "PE" and "VE" discovery mechanisms, and the "04" and "07"

---

[2] See https://github.com/lgbanuelos/bsgen for public software.

parameter settings), with each row showing data for a single ground truth system. The columns "*model-system*" and "*model-log*" report true model-system precision and recall and the corresponding model-log values; and the columns "*bootstrapped generalization*" give estimated model-system precision and recall computed via the new bootstrapping process, together with 95% confidence intervals. All of the bootstrapped values are closer to the true generalization values than the corresponding model-log values, confirming the applicability of the new approach. For example, in the first row in Table 2 the true value of model-system precision, which as discussed in Sect. 3.4 is used as a measure of generalization, is 0.60. The precision between that model and the log is 0.48, while the bootstrapped precision is equal to 0.55 ± 0.00, better approximating 0.60.

Table 2. True model-system precision and recall, model-log precision and recall, and estimated precision and recall via bootstrapping, plus the number of distinct traces per replica, together with 95% confidence intervals, see the text for configuration details.

System				Model-system		Model-log		Bootstrapped generalization		
	Name	Nodes	Edges	Prec.	Recall	Prec.	Recall	Precision	Recall	Traces
1	PE BPI Chall. 04	16	26	0.60	1.00	0.48	1.00	0.55 ± 0.00	1.00 ± 0.00	3541 ± 13
2	PE BPI Chall. 07	25	48	0.25	1.00	0.17	1.00	0.19 ± 0.00	1.00 ± 0.00	2489 ± 10
3	VE BPI Chall. 04	16	34	0.57	1.00	0.38	1.00	0.46 ± 0.00	1.00 ± 0.00	2384 ± 10
4	VE BPI Chall. 07	20	57	0.45	1.00	0.23	1.00	0.28 ± 0.00	1.00 ± 0.00	3089 ± 10
5	PE RTFMP 04	12	24	0.44	1.00	0.38	1.00	0.43 ± 0.00	1.00 ± 0.00	922 ± 4
6	PE RTFMP 07	13	54	0.46	1.00	0.26	1.00	0.33 ± 0.00	1.00 ± 0.00	2521 ± 9
7	VE RTFMP 04	10	29	0.60	1.00	0.40	1.00	0.49 ± 0.00	1.00 ± 0.00	2164 ± 10
8	VE RTFMP 07	13	58	0.48	1.00	0.25	1.00	0.33 ± 0.00	1.00 ± 0.00	3860 ± 13
9	PE Sepsis Cas. 04	15	35	0.47	1.00	0.23	1.00	0.29 ± 0.00	1.00 ± 0.00	5196 ± 13
10	PE Sepsis Cas. 07	17	64	0.71	1.00	0.24	1.00	0.32 ± 0.00	1.00 ± 0.00	5406 ± 18
11	VE Sepsis Cas. 04	12	23	0.70	1.00	0.54	1.00	0.58 ± 0.00	1.00 ± 0.00	202 ± 2
12	VE Sepsis Cas. 07	13	53	0.66	1.00	0.28	1.00	0.36 ± 0.00	1.00 ± 0.00	4777 ± 14

The complete version of the table is available at http://go.unimelb.edu.au/52gi.

The small systems perform consistently better. This suggests the need for further trace breeding mechanisms that target large systems. For example, the bootstrapped precision for the Sepsis Cases log (discovery technique "VE" and parameter "07", in row 12) is 0.36 ± 0.00, which is closer to the true model-system precision than is 0.28, the model-log precision, but still notably different from 0.66. Note that in this case the DFG has 53 edges, twice as many as the example in the first row of the table. Avenues for further work thus include assessing different log sampling mechanisms in terms of their accuracy (sampling traces supported by the system); their velocity (sampling accurate traces quickly); and their stability (sampling traces that lead to consistent measurements). For example, the method used in Table 2 is stable, as evidenced by the small confidence intervals of the estimates, but is slow, in that it requires many generations to breed relatively small numbers of new traces.

4.3   Threats to Validity

Several threats to validity are worth mentioning. Firstly, the discovered models were accepted as ground truth systems. These models were discovered by process mining experts independently, without the involvement of the authors of this paper. Nevertheless, they may not represent actual systems accurately. An obvious next step is thus to extend the experiments to datasets that include both the true system models and also logs induced from them. At the moment, such datasets are not available to the process mining research community. Secondly, the collection of 60 system models used in the evaluation is not representative of the full spectrum of possible systems; indeed, all of the recall measurements ended up being 1.0. They also come from a limited set of domains, namely, healthcare, loan application, and road traffic management. Hence, while the results confirm the consistency of the estimation approach shown in Sect. 3.5, they also demonstrate different behaviors – notably, convergence rates – for different (classes of) systems. Further experiments with real-world and synthetic systems and logs will help to understand such properties better.

5   Related Work

Generalization is perhaps the least-studied quality criterion of discovered process models, with just a small number of measures proposed; we now briefly survey those.

Given a function that maps log events onto states in which they occur, *alignment generalization* [3] counts the number of visits to each state, and the number of different events that occur in each state. If states are visited often and the number of events observed from them is low, it is unlikely that further events will arise, and generalization is good. van der Aalst et al. [3] also propose different forms of cross-validation methodology, including a "leave one out" approach. The bootstrap method provides more general sample reuse [11], and, as discussed in Sect. 3.1, estimates the population using the sample, and computes fresh samples from the estimated population, rather than using the single sample to both train the prediction model and to assess the prediction error.

Weighted behavioral generalization [6] measures the ratio of allowed generalizations to the allowed plus disallowed generalizations. Allowed and disallowed generalizations are determined based on "weighted negative events," which capture the fact that the event cannot occur at some position in a trace. The event weight reflects the likelihood of the event being observed in future traces of the system. The more disallowed generalizations that are identified, the lower the generalization.

Anti-alignment based generalization [10] promotes models that describe traces not in the log, without introducing new states. The underlying intuition is that the log describes a significant share of the state space of the system, and that future system traces may trigger fresh actions from known states, but not fresh states. It is implemented using a leave one out cross-validation strategy and "anti-alignments," traces from the model that are as different as possible to those in the log.

The *adversarial system variant approximation* [24] uses the log's traces to train a sequence generative adversarial network (SGAN) that approximates the distribution of system traces, and then employs a sample of traces induced by the SGAN to represent the system's behavior. Generalization is then measured using standard approaches. Trained SGANs can also be incorporated into our bootstrap-based method to obtain a parametric bootstrap strategy, an option we will explore in future work.

Other approaches to measuring generalization have also been proposed [2,7]. However, they are only partially able to analyze models with loops. van der Aalst [2] lists ten properties (including three that are subject to debate) that a generalization measure should satisfy; and it has been shown [2,23] that existing measures don't satisfy the seven properties that are agreed [2,3,6,10]. Moreover, Janssenswillen et al. [14] show that existing generalization measures assess different phenomena [3,6,7]. As the instantiations of the generalization estimator discussed and evaluated in this work rely on the entropy-based precision and recall measures [22], which were shown to satisfy all the desired properties for the corresponding classes of measures [23], it is interesting to study the properties of our generalization estimators. However, properties of the estimators must be studied in the limit (as the input grows and the estimators converge), which requires adjustments of the original properties. We will do that as future work.

An experiment with synthetic models and simulated logs analyzed whether existing model-log precision and recall, and generalization measures can be used as estimators of model-system precision and recall [13]. The experiment measured model-system and model-log properties, and performed statistical analysis to establish relationships between them. The reported results indicate that using currently available methods, it is "nearly impossible to objectively measure the ability of a model to represent the system." In our work, instead of relating model-system and model-log measurements, we use the bootstrap method to estimate the entire behavior of the system from its log, and then measure model-system properties using the model and the estimated behavior of the system. Under reasonable assumption, our estimator of generalization is consistent.

Also related to the problem of measuring generalization of a discovered model is establishing the *rediscoverability* of a process discovery algorithm, that is, identifying conditions under which it constructs a model that is behaviorally equivalent to the system and describes the same set of traces [1]. Such conditions usually address both the class of systems and the class of logs for which rediscoverability can be assured. For example, the Inductive Mining algorithm guarantees rediscoverability for the class of systems that are captured as block-structured process models [18] without duplicate actions and in which it is not possible to start a loop with an activity the same loop can also end with [16]. In contrast to rediscoverability guarantees, we study the problem of measuring how well a discovered model describes an unknown original system.

6 Conclusion

We presented a bootstrap-based approach for estimating the generalization of models discovered from logs, parameterized by a generalization measure defined over known systems, and a log sampling method. An instantiation using entropy-based generalization and log sampling based on k-overlap breeding of traces is shown to be consistent for the class of systems captured as DFGs. Thus, the larger the constructed samples and the more samples get bootstrapped, the more accurate the estimation of the generalization is. Our evaluation confirmed the approach's feasibility in industrial settings.

This work marks a first step in a study of the applicability of bootstrap methods for estimating generalization, and can be extended in several ways. In future work we will seek to develop an unbiased estimator, that is, an estimator with no difference between the expected value of the estimation and the true value of the generalization; to study the consistency of generalization estimators for different classes of systems and identify other useful components for instantiating the bootstrap-based approach for estimating the generalization, including log sampling methods and generalization measures over known systems; and to explore the quality of different bootstrap-based estimators of the generalization to overcome problems associated with noisy logs.

Acknowledgment. Artem Polyvyanyy was in part supported by the Australian Research Council project DP180102839. A presentation of this work from an earlier stage of the research project is available at https://youtu.be/8I-87iGCzNI.

References

1. van der Aalst, W.M.P.: Process Mining-Data Science in Action, 2nd edn. Springer, Heidelberg (2016). https://doi.org/10.1007/978-3-662-49851-4
2. van der Aalst, W.M.P.: Relating process models and event logs–21 conformance propositions. In: ATAED. CEUR Workshop Proceedings, vol. 2115. CEUR-WS.org (2018)
3. van der Aalst, W.M.P., Adriansyah, A., van Dongen, B.F.: Replaying history on process models for conformance checking and performance analysis. Wiley Interdiscip. Rev. Data Min. Knowl. Discov. **2**(2), 182–192 (2012)
4. Alkhammash, H., Polyvyanyy, A., Moffat, A., García-Bañuelos: Discovered Process Models 2020–08 (2020). https://doi.org/10.26188/12814535
5. Breiman, L.: Bagging predictors. Mach. Learn. **24**(2), 123–140 (1996)
6. vanden Broucke, S.K.L.M., Weerdt, J.D., Vanthienen, J., Baesens, B.: Determining process model precision and generalization with weighted artificial negative events. IEEE Trans. Knowl. Data Eng. **26**(8), 1877–1889 (2014)
7. Buijs, J.C.A.M., van Dongen, B.F., van der Aalst, W.M.P.: Quality dimensions in process discovery: the importance of fitness, precision, generalization and simplicity. Int. J. Coop. Inf. Syst. **23**(1), 1440001 (2014)
8. Carmona, J., van Dongen, B.F., Solti, A., Weidlich, M.: Conformance Checking-Relating Processes and Models. Springer, Cham (2018). https://doi.org/10.1007/978-3-319-99414-7

9. De Leoni, M., Mannhardt, F.: Road traffic fine management process (2015). https://doi.org/10.4121/UUID:270FD440-1057-4FB9-89A9-B699B47990F5

10. van Dongen, B.F., Carmona, J., Chatain, T.: A unified approach for measuring precision and generalization based on anti-alignments. In: La Rosa, M., Loos, P., Pastor, O. (eds.) BPM 2016. LNCS, vol. 9850, pp. 39–56. Springer, Cham (2016). https://doi.org/10.1007/978-3-319-45348-4_3

11. Efron, B.: The Jackknife, the Bootstrap and Other Resampling Plans. Society for Industrial and Applied Mathematics (1982)

12. Efron, B., Tibshirani, R.J.: An Introduction to the Bootstrap. Springer, New York (1993)

13. Janssenswillen, G., Depaire, B.: Towards confirmatory process discovery: making assertions about the underlying system. Bus. Inf. Syst. Eng. **61**(6), 713–728 (2019)

14. Janssenswillen, G., Donders, N., Jouck, T., Depaire, B.: A comparative study of existing quality measures for process discovery. Inf. Syst. **71**, 1–15 (2017)

15. Leemans, S.J.J., Fahland, D., van der Aalst, W.M.P.: Discovering block-structured process models from event logs - a constructive approach. In: Colom, J.-M., Desel, J. (eds.) PETRI NETS 2013. LNCS, vol. 7927, pp. 311–329. Springer, Heidelberg (2013). https://doi.org/10.1007/978-3-642-38697-8_17

16. Leemans, S.J.J., Fahland, D., van der Aalst, W.M.P.: Scalable process discovery and conformance checking. Softw. Syst. Model. **17**(2), 599–631 (2016). https://doi.org/10.1007/s10270-016-0545-x

17. Mannhardt, F.: Sepsis cases - event log (2016). https://doi.org/10.4121/UUID:915D2BFB-7E84-49AD-A286-DC35F063A460

18. Polyvyanyy, A.: Structuring process models. Ph.D. thesis, University of Potsdam (2012)

19. Polyvyanyy, A., et al.: Entropia: a family of entropy-based conformance checking measures for process mining. In: ICPM Tool Demonstration Track. CEUR Workshop Proceedings, vol. 2703. CEUR-WS.org (2020)

20. Polyvyanyy, A., Moffat, A., García-Bañuelos, L.: An entropic relevance measure for stochastic conformance checking in process mining. In: ICPM. IEEE (2020)

21. Polyvyanyy, A., Smirnov, S., Weske, M.: Process model abstraction: a slider approach. In: EDOC, pp. 325–331. IEEE Computer Society (2008)

22. Polyvyanyy, A., Solti, A., Weidlich, M., Ciccio, C.D., Mendling, J.: Monotone precision and recall measures for comparing executions and specifications of dynamic systems. ACM Trans. Softw. Eng. Methodol. **29**(3), 1–41 (2020)

23. Syring, A.F., Tax, N., van der Aalst, W.M.P.: Evaluating conformance measures in process mining using conformance propositions. ToPNoC XIV (2019)

24. Theis, J., Darabi, H.: Adversarial system variant approximation to quantify process model generalization. IEEE Access **8**, 194410–194427 (2020)

25. Van Dongen, B.B.F.: BPI challenge 2012 (2012). https://doi.org/10.4121/UUID:3926DB30-F712-4394-AEBC-75976070E91F

26. van der Werf, J.M.E.M., Polyvyanyy, A., van Wensveen, B.R., Brinkhuis, M., Reijers, H.A.: All that glitters is not gold—towards process discovery techniques with guarantees. In: La Rosa, M., Sadiq, S., Teniente, E. (eds.) CAiSE 2021. LNCS, vol. 12751, pp. 141–157. Springer, Cham (2021). https://doi.org/10.1007/978-3-030-79382-1_9

Learning Accurate Business Process Simulation Models from Event Logs via Automated Process Discovery and Deep Learning

Manuel Camargo[1,2,3], Marlon Dumas[1(✉)], and Oscar González-Rojas[2]

[1] University of Tartu, Tartu, Estonia
marlon.dumas@ut.ee
[2] Universidad de los Andes, Bogotá, Colombia
o-gonza1@uniandes.edu.co
[3] Apromore, Tartu, Estonia
manuel.camargo@apromore.com

Abstract. Business process simulation is a well-known approach to estimate the impact of changes to a process with respect to time and cost measures – a practice known as what-if process analysis. The usefulness of such estimations hinges on the accuracy of the underlying simulation model. Data-Driven Simulation (DDS) methods leverage process mining techniques to learn process simulation models from event logs. Empirical studies have shown that, while DDS models adequately capture the observed sequences of activities and their frequencies, they fail to accurately capture the temporal dynamics of real-life processes. In contrast, generative Deep Learning (DL) models are better able to capture such temporal dynamics. The drawback of DL models is that users cannot alter them for what-if analysis due to their black-box nature. This paper presents a hybrid approach to learn process simulation models from event logs wherein a (stochastic) process model is extracted via DDS techniques, and then combined with a DL model to generate timestamped event sequences. An experimental evaluation shows that the resulting hybrid simulation models match the temporal accuracy of pure DL models, while partially retaining the what-if analysis capability of DDS approaches.

Keywords: Process mining · Simulation · Deep learning

1 Introduction

Business Process Simulation (BPS) models allow analysts to estimate the impact of changes to a process with respect to temporal and cost measures – a practice known as "what-if" process analysis [1]. However, the construction and tuning

Work funded by European Research Council (PIX Project).

X. Franch et al. (Eds.): CAiSE 2022, LNCS 13295, pp. 55–71, 2022.
https://doi.org/10.1007/978-3-031-07472-1_4

of BPS models is error-prone, as it requires careful attention to numerous pit-falls [2]. Moreover, the accuracy of manually tuned BPS models is limited by the completeness of the process model used as a starting point, yet manually designed models often do not capture exceptional paths. Previous studies have proposed to extract BPS models from execution data (event logs) via process mining techniques [3]. While Data-Driven Simulation (DDS) models extracted in this way can be tuned to accurately capture the control-flow and temporal behavior of a process [4], they suffer from fundamental limitations stemming from the expressiveness of the modeling notation (e.g. BPMN, Petri nets) and from assumptions about the resources' behavior. One such assumption is that all waiting times are due to resource contention (i.e. a resource not starting a task because it is busy with another task). Another assumption is that resources exhibit robotic behavior: if a resource is available, and it may perform an enabled activity instance, the resource will immediately start it. In other words, these approaches do not take into account behaviors such as multitasking, batching, fatigue effects, and inter-process resource sharing, among others [5].

Other studies have shown that Deep Learning (DL) generative models trained from logs can accurately predict the next event in a case and its timestamp or the suffix of a case starting from a given prefix [6,7]. Suitably trained DL gener-ative models can also be used to generate entire traces and even entire logs [8], which effectively allows us to use a DL generative model as a simulation model. Camargo et al. [9] empirically show that DL models are more accurate than DDS models when it comes to generating logs consisting of activity sequences with start and end timestamps. In particular, generative DL models can emulate delays between activities that DDS models do not capture. However, unlike DDS models, DL models are not suitable for what-if analysis due to their black-box nature – they do not allow to specify a change to the process and to simulate the effect of this change.

This paper presents a method, namely DeepSimulator, that combines DDS and DL methods to discover a BPS model from a log. The idea is to use an auto-mated process discovery technique to extract a process model with branching probabilities (a.k.a. stochastic process model [10]) and to delegate the generation of activity start and end times to a DL model.

The paper is structured as follows. Section 2 discusses methods to learn gen-erative models from logs using DDS and DL techniques. Section 3 presents the proposed method while Sect. 4 presents an empirical evaluation thereof. Finally, Sect. 5 draws conclusions and sketches future work.

2   Related Work

2.1   Data-Driven Simulation of Business Processes

Previous studies on DDS methods can be classified in two categories. A subset of previous studies have proposed conceptual frameworks and guidelines to man-ually derive, validate, and tune BPS parameters from event logs [3,11], without seeking to automate the extraction process. Other studies have proposed methods that automate the extraction and/or tuning of simulation parameters from logs. In this paper, we focus on automated methods. One of the earliest such methods is that of Rozinat et al. [12], who propose a semi-automated approach to extract BPS models based on Colored Petri Nets. Later, Khodyrev et al. [13] proposed an approach to extract BPS models from data, although they leave aside the resource perspective (i.e. the discovery of resource pools). More recently, Pourbafrani et al. [14] present an approach for generating DDS models based on time-aware process trees. In all of the above studies, the responsibility for tuning these parameters is left to the user. This limitation is addressed in the Simod method [4], which automates the extraction of BPS models by employing Bayesian optimization to tune the hyperparameters used to discover the process model and resource pools as well as the statistical parameters of the BPS model (branching probabilities, activity processing times, and inter-case arrival times). This tuning phase seeks to optimize the similarity between the logs produced by the extracted BPS model and (a testing fold of) the original log.

2.2   Generative DL Models of Business Processes

A Deep Learning (DL) model is a network of interconnected layers of neurons (perceptrons) that collectively perform non-linear data transformations [15]. The objective of these transformations is to train the network to learn the patterns observed in the data. In theory, the more layers of neurons in the system, the more it will detect higher-level patterns via composition of complex functions [15]. A wide range of neural network architectures have been proposed, e.g. feed-forward networks, Convolutional Neural Networks, Variational Auto-Encoders, Generative Adversarial Networks (GAN) (often in a combination with other architectures), and Recurrent Neural Networks (RNN). The latter type of architecture is specifically designed to handle sequential data.

DL models have been widely applied in the field of predictive process monitoring. Evermann et al. [7] proposed an RNN architecture to generate the most likely remaining sequence of events (suffix) of an ongoing case. This architecture cannot handle numeric features and thus cannot generate timestamped events (timestamps are numeric). This limitation is shared by the approach in [16] and others reviewed in [17]. Tax et al. [6] use an RNN architecture known as Long-Short-Term Memory (LSTM) to predict the next event in an ongoing case and its timestamp, and to generate the remaining sequence of timestamped events from a given prefix of a case. However, this approach cannot handle high-dimensional inputs due to its reliance on one-hot encoding of categorical features. Its precision deteriorates as the number of categorical features increases. This limitation is lifted by DeepGenerator [8], which extends the approach in [6] with two mechanisms to handle high-dimensional input: n-grams and embeddings. This approach also addresses the problem of generating long suffixes (not well handled in [6]) and entire traces, by using a random next-event selection approach. It is also able to associate a resource to each event in a trace. More recently, Taymouri et al. [18] proposed a GAN-LSTM architecture to train generative models that produce timestamped activity sequences (without associated resources).

Camargo et al. [9] compare the relative accuracy of DL models against DDS models for generating sequences of the form (activity, start timestamp, end timestamp). This comparison suggests that DL models may outperform DDS models when trained with large logs, while the opposite holds for smaller logs. Camargo et al. [9] additionally show that DL models generally outperform DDS methods when it comes to predicting activity start and end timestamps.

3   Hybrid Learning of BPS Models

Figure 1 depicts the architecture of the DeepSimulator approach. The architecture is a pipeline with three phases. The first phase uses PM techniques to learn a model to generate sequences of (non-timestampted) events. The second and third phases enrich these sequences with case start times and activity start and end times. Below, we discuss each phase in turn.

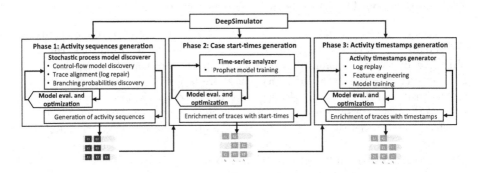

Fig. 1. Overview of the proposed BPS model discovery method

Phase 1: Activity Sequences Generation. The aim of this phase is to extract a stochastic process model [10] from the log and to use it to generate sequences of activities that resemble those in the log. A stochastic process model is a process model with branching probabilities assigned to each branch of a decision point. In this paper, we represent process models using the standard BPMN notation. Phase 1 starts with a *control-flow discovery* step, where we first discover a plain (non-stochastic) process model using the Split Miner algorithm [19]. This algorithm relies on two parameters: the sensitivity of the parallelism oracle (η) and the level of filtering of directly-follow relations (ϵ). The former parameter determines how likely the algorithm will discover parallel structures, while the latter determines the percentage of directly-follows relations between activity types are captured in the resulting model. Like other automated process discovery algorithms, the Split Miner discovers a process model that does not perfectly fit the log. The discovered process model cannot parse some traces in the log. This hinders the calculation of the branching probabilities. Accordingly, we apply the *trace alignment* algorithm in [20] to compute an alignment for each trace in the log that the model cannot parse. An alignment describes how a trace can be modified to be turned into a trace that can be parsed by the model (via "skip" operations). Based on the alignments, we either *repair* each non-conformant trace, or we *replace* it with a copy of the most similar conformant trace (w.r.t. string-edit distance). The choice between the repair and the replacement approaches is a parameter of the method.

Next, DeepSimulator uses the (conformant) event log to discover the *branching probabilities* for each branching point in the model. Here, DeepSimulator offers two options: (i) assign equal values to each conditional branch; or (ii) compute the branching probabilities by replaying the aligned event against the process model. The first approach may perform better for smaller logs, where the probabilities computed via replay are not always reliable, while the latter may be preferable for larger logs.

The DeepSimulator combines the process model and the branching probabilities to assemble a stochastic process model. In this step, the DeepSimulator uses a Bayesian optimization technique to discover the hyperparameter settings (i.e., values of ϵ, η, replace-vs-repair, and equal-vs-computed probabilities) that maximize the similarity between the generated and the ground truth sequences in terms of activity sequences. The optimizer uses a holdout method, and as a loss function, it uses the Control-Flow Log Similarity (CFLS) metric described in [4]. The CFLS metric is the mean string-edit distance between the activity sequences generated by the stochastic process model and the traces in the ground-truth log after their optimal alignment.[1] Finally, in the *sequences' generation* step, DeepSimulator uses the resulting stochastic process model to generate a bag of activity sequences without timestamps. This bag is used as the log's base structure in Phase 3.

Phase 2: Case Start-Times Generation. In this phase, we generate each process instance's start time in the output log. Traditionally, DDS models generate the start-time of cases by randomly drawing from an unimodal distribution of the interarrival times between consecutive cases. A typical BPS model captures the interarrival times using a negative exponential distribution (i.e., it models the creation of cases as a Poisson process). However, a single distribution is not realistic enough to capture real scenarios. For example, cases might be created more frequently on Mondays than on Thursdays in a claims handling process.

Instead of fitting an interarrival distribution, the DeepSimulator models the case generation as a time series prediction problem as the number of cases generated per hour of the day. This type of modeling allows us to use robust techniques such as ARIMA or ETS tested successfully in several contexts such as Stock Market Analysis or Workload Projections. DeepSimulator uses the Prophet [22]

---

[1] We did not use the stochastic conformance checking metrics over Petri nets of [10] since our method handles BPMN models with inclusive join gateways, which cannot be directly transformed to Petri Nets (without exponential blowout) as shown in [21].

model proposed by Facebook because it is one of the simplest but, at the same time, more accurate predictive models for this type of task. Prophet starts from the time series decomposition into four main components (i.e., trend, seasonality, holidays, and error) and applies specialized techniques to model each component.

The trend component decomposes those non-periodic changes in the time series values, which are modeled using logistic growth models or Piecewise linear models. The seasonality component decomposes the periodic changes repeated at fixed intervals (hours, weeks, months, or years), which are modeled by using the Fourier series. The holidays component represents the effects of holidays that occur on potentially irregular schedules over one or more days. This component is optionally modeled and is defined manually by a domain expert, since it is specific to each time series. The model automatically calculates the error, corresponding to all those unforeseen changes that the model cannot fit.

In the *time-series analysis* step, we use a saturated logistic growth model to fit the case generation trend. We chose this model, considering that the time series is limited by a lower and upper bound. The lower bound corresponds to 0, which is the minimum number of cases attended in the process, and the upper bound is theoretically limited by the capacity of the process. The parameter that most significantly affects data trend capture is changepoint-prior-scale, which determines how much the trend changes at the trend change points. This parameter needs tuning, since a too low value may cause under-fitting while a too high value may cause over-fitting. Accordingly, for this parameter, DeepSimulator explores values in the interval [0.001, 0.5]. Analogously, the parameter that most directly affects the seasonality capture is the seasonality-prior-scale. This parameter affects the flexibility of seasonality learning. If the value is too small, the model tends to focus on small fluctuations, while a large value may cause the model to focus only on large fluctuations. For this parameter, DeepSimulator explores values in [0.01, 10]. We do not define the Holidays component in the Prophet model. The holidays component could be discovered by a calendar discovery technique such as the one proposed in [5], but discovering such calendars is orthogonal to the focus of the present paper.

We use grid search for selecting the best hyperparameters of the Prophet model, as the search space consists of only sixteen configurations (cf. Sect. 4.3). We rely on the internal mechanisms embedded in Prophet for cross-validation and selection of cutoff points. During the simulation, we use the trained Prophet model to determine the number of cases to be created at each hour of the simulation. We then generate the start-times, for each simulation hour, by modeling the intercase arrival times via a normal distribution (within the hour).

Phase 3: Activity Timestamps Generation. We enhance the activity sequences generated in Phase 1 to capture waiting times and processing times in this phase.

The DeepSimulator trains two LSTM[2] models to perform two predictive tasks: the processing time of a given activity (herein called the *current activity*) and the waiting time until the start of the next activity. This task differs in two ways from approaches used to predict the next event and its timestamp [8,18]. First, we do not seek to predict the next event, since the sequences of activities are generated by the stochastic process model (cf. Phase 1). Second, we need to support changes in the process model (e.g., adding or removing tasks) for enabling what-if analysis.

Therefore, we train one model specialized in predicting the processing time of the current activity and another specialized in predicting the waiting time until the next activity. Both models differ in the set of features since

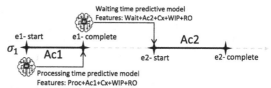

Fig. 2. Predictive models timeline and features

they act at different moments in the predictive phase, as shown in Fig. 2. The processing time predictive model uses the following features as inputs: the label and processing time of the current activity, the time of day of the current activity's start timestamp, the day of the week, and inter-case features such as the Work-in-progress (WIP) of the process and the activity and Resources' Occupation (RO) at the start of the activity. The waiting time predictive model uses the following features as inputs: the next activity's label, the time of day of the current activity's end timestamp, the day of the week, and inter-case features such as the WIP of the process and the RO at the end of the current activity.

In the *log replay* step, we calculate the waiting and processing times of each activity by replaying each trace in the input log (or in a training subset thereof) against the process model discovered in Phase 1. An activity's processing time is the difference between its end and start timestamps. An activity's waiting time is the difference between its start time and enablement time, i.e., when it was ready to be executed according to the process model. All waiting and processing times are scaled to the range [0...1] by dividing them by the largest values.

In the *feature engineering* step, we compute and encode all the remaining features used by the models. We calculate the time of the day as the elapsed seconds from the closest midnight until the event timestamp; this feature is scale over 86400 s. The day of the week is modeled as a categorical attribute and encoded using one-hot encoding. We include these latter features since they provide contextual information, allowing the model to find seasonal patterns in the data that may affect waiting and processing times. In the same way,

---

[2] We used LSTM networks as the core of our predictive models since they are a well-known and proven technology to handle sequences, as the nature of a business process event log [23]. The proposed models were based on previous works [6–8] that have extensively explored several architectural options of LSTMs, such as the use of stacked vs. unstacked models or the use of shared layers vs. specialized ones.

considering that the overall process performance is affected by the process' WIP and the RO [24], we use two inter-case features that measure these variations.

The WIP of the process measures the number of active tasks at each moment in the log transversally. The RO measures each resource pool's percentage occupancy in the log, implying that a new feature is created for each pool to record the occupation-specific variations. Since the information about the size and composition of the resource pools is not always included in the logs, we grouped resources into roles by using the algorithm described in [25]. This algorithm discovers resource pools based on the definition of activity execution profiles for each resource and the creation of a correlation matrix of similarity of those profiles. WIP and RO are calculated by replaying over time the log events, recording the variations in both features at every time point.

Finally, we encode the current activity's label using pre-trained embedded dimensions. We use embeddings for two reasons. First, embeddings help prevent exponential feature growth associated with one-hot encoding [8]. Second, embedded dimensions allow adding new categories (i.e., activity labels) without altering the predictive model's structure. These embedded dimensions are an n-dimensional space, where each category (each activity level) is encoded as a point in that space. An independent network fed with positive and negative examples of associations between activities is used to map the activity labels to points. The network maps activities that co-occur or occur close to each other to nearby points. This mechanism also allows adding a new point in that space by updating the encoding model without altering the predictive model's input size. Each time a new activity is added to the process model for what-if analysis, we generate examples of traces involving this new activity and use these examples to determine the coordinates of the new activity label to be encoded in the embedded space. Then, we update the predictive model's embedded layers with the new definition, and the predictive model can handle the new activity label from that point on.

Once encoded the features, we extract n-grams of fixed sizes from each trace to create the input sequences to train the model. As shown in Fig. 3, both models are composed of two stacked LSTM layers and a dense output. A model receives the sequences as inputs and the expected processing and waiting times as a target. The user can vary the number of units in the LSTM layers, the activation function, the size of the n-gram, and the use of all the RO inter-cases or just the one of the resource pool associated to the execution of the activity.

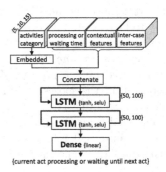

Fig. 3. DL models architectures

Assembling the Output Log. The output log is generated by assembling each generated sequence (see Phase 1), with the generated case start time (see Phase 2) and the processing and waiting times predicted iteratively (see Phase 3). In each iteration, the trained model predicts times relative to the current activity in seconds, which are transformed into absolute times by adding them to the start time of the case. Then, the DeepSimulator generates a simulated log composed of a bag of traces, each trace consisting of a sequence of triplets (activity label, start-timestamp, end timestamp).

4   Evaluation

We empirically compare the DeepSimulator method vs. DDS and DL approaches in terms of the similarity of the simulated logs they generate relative to a fold of the original log. We also evaluate the accuracy of DeepSimulator for "what-if" analysis tasks of modifying the case creation intesity and adding new activities to a process.

4.1   Datasets

We evaluated the approaches using 9 logs that contain both start and end times-tamps. We use real-life logs (R) from public and private sources and synthetic logs (S) generated from simulation models of real processes. Table 1 provides descriptive statistics of the logs. The BPI17W log have the largest number of traces and events, while CFS and P2P have fewer traces but more events/trace.

Table 1. Event logs description. (*) Private logs, (**) Generated from simulation models of real processes

Size	Source	Log	#Traces	#Events	#Act.	Avg. activities per trace	Avg. duration	Max. duration	Description
LARGE	R	BPI17W	30276	240854	8	7.96	12.66 days	286.07 days	Dutch financial institution updated
	R	BPI12W	8616	59302	6	6.88	8.91 days	85.87 days	Dutch financial institution
	S	CVS	10000	103906	15	10.39	7.58 days	21.0 days	CVS retail pharmacy**
	S	CFM	1670	44373	29	26.57	0.76 days	5.83 days	Anonymized onfidential process**
SMALL	R	INS	1182	23141	9	19.58	70.93 days	599.9 days	Insurance claims process*
	R	ACR	954	4962	16	5.2	14.89 days	135.84 days	Academic Credential Recognition
	R	MP	225	4503	24	20.01	20.63 days	87.5 days	Manufacturing Production
	S	CFS	800	21221	29	26.53	0.83 days	4.09 days	Anonymized confidential process**
	S	P2P	608	9119	21	15	21.46 days	108.31 days	Purchase-to-Pay process

4.2   Evaluation Measures

To evaluate the accuracy of a model M produced by one of the methods under evaluation, we compute a distance measure between a log generated by model M and a ground-truth log (a testing subset of the original log). In all of our experiments, we use two distance measures: the Mean Absolute Error (MAE) of cycle times and the Earth-Mover's Distance (EMD) of the normalized histograms of activity timestamps grouped by day/hour.

The *cycle time MAE* measures the temporal similarity between two logs at the *trace level.* The absolute error of a pair of traces T1 and T2 is the absolute value of the difference between their cycle times. The cycle time MAE is the mean of the absolute errors over a collection of paired traces. Given this trace distance notion, we pair each trace in the generated log with a trace in the original log using the Hungarian algorithm [26] so that the sum of the trace errors between the paired traces is minimal.

The cycle time MAE is a rough measure of the temporal similarity between the ground-truth and the simulated traces. But it does not consider the start time of each case, nor the start and end timestamps of each activity. To complement MAE, we use the *Earth Mover's Distance (EMD)* between the normalized histograms of the timestamps grouped by day/hour in the ground-truth and the generated logs. The EMD between two histograms, H1 and H2, is the minimum number of units that need to be added, removed, or transferred across columns in H1 to transform it into H2. The EMD is zero if the observed distributions in the two logs are identical, and it tends to one the more they differ.

4.3   Experiment 1: AS-IS Accuracy of Generated Models

Setup. This experiment aims to compare the accuracy of DeepSimulator models (herein called DSIM models) vs. DDS and DL models. We use SIMOD [4] as a baseline DDS approach since it is fully automated both w.r.t. parameter discovery and tuning. As DL baselines, we use an adaptation of the LSTM approach proposed by Camargo et al. [8] (herein labeled the LSTM method) as well as the GAN-LSTM approach by Taymouri et al. [18] (herein labeled GAN). Both of these DL approaches have been shown to achieve high accuracy w.r.t. the task of generating timestamped trace suffixes [23]. Figure 4 summarizes the experimental setup. We use the hold-out method with a temporal split criterion to divide the logs into two main folds: 80% for training-validation and 20% for testing. From the first fold, we took the first 80% for training and 20% for validation. We use temporal splits to prevent information leakage [8,18].

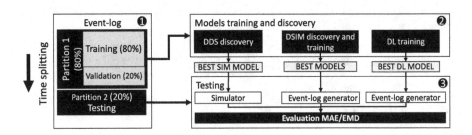

Fig. 4. Setup of experiment 1

The DDS technique (SIMOD) is set to explore 15 parameter configurations to tune the stochastic process model. For each configuration, we execute five simulation runs and compute the CFLS measure (cf. Sect. 3) between each simulated log and the validation fold. We select the stochastic model that gives the lowest average CFLS w.r.t. the validation fold. The optimizer is set to explore 20 simulation parameter configurations (i.e. the parameters that Simod uses to model resources and processing times), again using five simulation runs per configuration. We select the configuration with the lowest average EMD (cf. Sect. 4.2) between the simulated log and the validation fold. We used the parameter ranges given in Table 2 for tuning.

The LSTM technique is hyperparameter-optimized using grid search over a space of 48 possible configurations (see Table 2) For LSTM model training, we use 200 epochs, the cycle time MAE as the model's loss function, Nadam as the optimizer, and early stopping and dropout to avoid model over-training. The GAN technique is configured to dynamically adjust the size of the hidden units in each layer so that their size is twice the input's size, as proposed by the authors [18]. We use 25 training epochs, a batch of size five, and a prefix size of five. DSIM is tuned by randomly exploring 15 parameter configurations with

Table 2. Hyperparameters used by optimization techniques

Model	Stage	Parameter	Distribution	Values
SIMOD	Structure discovery	Parallelism threshold (ϵ)	Uniform	[0...1]
		Percentile for frequency threshold (η)	Uniform	[0...1]
		Conditional branching probabilities	Categorical	{Equiprobable, Discovered}
	Time-related parameters discovery	Log repair technique	Categorical	{Repair, Removal, Replace}
		Resource pools similarity threshold	Uniform	[0...1]
		Resource availability calendar support	Uniform	[0...1]
		Resource availability calendar confidence	Uniform	[0...1]
		Instances creation calendar support	Uniform	[0...1]
		Instances creation calendars confidence	Uniform	[0...1]
LSTM	Training	N-gram size	Categorical	[5, 10, 15]
		Input scaling method	Categorical	{Max, Lognormal}
		# units in hidden layer	Categorical	{50, 100}
		Activation function for hidden layers	Categorical	{selu, tanh}
		Model type	Categorical	{shared_cat, concatenated}
DSIM	Structure generation	Parallelism threshold (ϵ)	Uniform	[0...1]
		Percentile for frequency threshold (η)	Uniform	[0...1]
		Conditional branching probabilities	Categorical	{Equiprobable, Discovered}
	Cases start-times generation	Changepoint-prior-scale	Categorical	{0.001, 0.01, 0.1, 0.5}
		Seasonality-prior-scale	Categorical	{0.01, 0.1, 1.0, 10.0}
	Timestamps generation	N-gram size	Categorical	{5, 10, 15}
		# units in hidden layer	Categorical	{50, 100}
		Activation function for hidden layers	Categorical	{selu, tanh}
		Single resource-pool intercase feature	Boolean	{True, False}

five simulation runs per configuration in the stochastic model discovery phase (cf. Sect. 3, Phase 1). In Phases 2 and 3, we use grid search to explore the space of hyperparameter configurations specified in Table 2

We generate four models per log: one SIMOD, one LSTM, one GAN, and one DSIM. We then generate five logs per retained model, each with the same number of traces as the original log's testing fold to ensure the comparability. Each generated log is compared with the testing fold using the MAE and EMD measures. We report the mean of each of these measures across 5 runs.

Results. Table 3 show the results grouped by metrics, log size and source type. Note that MAE and EMD are error/distance measures (lower is better). In 3 out of 4 large logs, DSIM outperforms LSTM and SIMOD w.r.t the MAE measure. In the small logs, DSIM attains lower MAE in 3 out of 5 logs

Table 3. Evaluation results (lower values are better)

Size	Type	Log	MAE				EMD	
			GAN	LSTM	SIMOD	DSIM	SIMOD	DSIM
LARGE	R	BPI17W	828165	603688	961727	*418422*	*0.016873*	0.034584
		BPI12W	653656	*327350*	662333	548813	0.056789	*0.020098*
	S	CVS	952004	667715	1067258	*158902*	0.018955	*0.000004*
		CFM	956289	15078	252458	*8441*	0.240567	*0.239087*
SMALL	R	INS	1302337	1516368	*1090179*	1190019	0.143675	*0.142097*
		ACR	296094	341694	230363	*165411*	0.207050	*0.205106*
		MP	210714	321147	298641	*157453*	0.062227	*0.050479*
	S	CFS	717266	33016	*15297*	24326	*0.222515*	0.266749
		P2P	2347070	2495593	1892415	*1836863*	*0.130655*	0.132898

and has similar MAE w.r.t. SIMOD in one other log. Similarly, DSIM outperforms SIMOD in 6 of 9 logs w.r.t. EMD, and achieves results similar to SIMOD in two others.[3]

The results suggest that DSIM is often able to outperform the baselines when it comes to replicating the as-is behavior recorded in an event log. This conclusion should be tempered in light of two threats to validity: (i) an external threat to validity stemming from the limited number of events logs in the experiment; and (ii) a threat to construct validity created by the fact that the accuracy measures do not necessarily capture all the nuances in the control-flow and temporal behavior captured in the original and simulated event logs.

4.4 Experiment 2: What-if Analysis

In this experiment, we compare DSIM's ability to simulate a process after a change (what-if analysis). We consider two scenarios. In the first one, we assess DSIM's ability to capture variations in the inter-arrival time between cases (a.k.a. *arrival intensity*), specifically alternations between periods of lower arrival

---

[3] We cannot measure EMD for the LSTM and GAN models because EMD requires that the timestamps in the log are absolute timestamps, while the LSTM and GAN approaches produce relative timestamps (w.r.t. an unknown case start-time). It would be possible to extend the LSTM/GAN approaches to generate logs with absolute timestamps by coupling them with a model to generate start-times (e.g. based on Prophet) but this extension is outside the scope of this paper.

intensity and periods of higher intensity. In the second experiment, we evaluate the ability of DSIM (vs baselines) to estimate the impact of adding a never-before-observed activity to a process. This scenario is challenging for the DSIM and the DL models because these models need to infer the temporal behavior of the new activity using their embedding layers.

Setup Scenario 1. We create two modified versions of the three largest records (BPI12W, BPI17W, and CVS). First, to capture a periodic reduction in the arrival intensity of cases, we divide each log into six batches of the same number of cases, and then we create two alternating groups of three batches each.

The first group consists of batches 1, 3, and 5. The batches in this group are left unaltered. These groups represent periods of high arrival intensity. The second group comprises batches 2, 4, and 6. This group is used to emulate periods of low arrival intensity. To do so, we reduce the case arrival rate in these batches by 1/3, by

Fig. 5. Original vs modified case creations

randomly eliminating two out of three cases. The above altered version of the log capture a situation where the arrival intensity varies, but the waiting times within the cases remain the same. In general, when the arrival intensity goes down, the waiting times should go down. To capture this latter scenario, we create a second altered version of the log to capture decreases in waiting times associated with decreases in arrival rates. Accordingly, we take the first altered log, and we reduce the waiting times in group 2 (batches 2, 4, and 6) by 30%. For illustration, Fig. 5 sketches the modifications made to the BPI17W log.

After altering the logs as above, we train and evaluate the DSIM and SIMOD models as in Experiment 1 (see Fig. 4). Since we are particularly interested here in assessing the ability of the evaluated techniques to model the temporal dynamics of case arrivals, we also report the Dynamic Time Warping (DTW) distance between the time series of the number of cases generated per hour of the day, between the testing partition and the logs generated.

Setup Scenario 2. For each of the synthetic logs (CVS and CFM), we select a random activity A and eliminate all its occurrences from the log. We then train a DSIM simulation model using this modified log (cf. left-hand side of Fig. 6b). Next, we generate synthetic data consisting of positive and negative samples of pairs composed by the

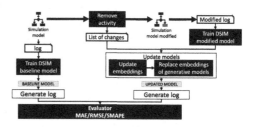

Fig. 6. Pipeline of scenario 2

activity label and associated resource (cf. Sect. 3). Using these synthetic samples, we update the embedded dimensions to include activity A (without modifying the embedding of the remaining activities). We then plug the updated embedding into the previously trained DSIM model (cf. right-hand side of Fig. 6). We calculate the errors of the DSIM model of the "as-is" process (before a change) and the DSIM model of the "what-if" process (after adding an activity). We measure the error using MAE. Additionally, we report the RMSE and SMAPE metrics to confirm that the results do not depend on the chosen metric.

Results Scenario 1. Table 4 presents the MAE, EMD and DTW results. DSIM has a lower error in cycle times in all cases. In version 2 the MAE logs are considerably reduced compared to those of the version 1. We can explain this result because the DL models in charge of predicting waiting and processing times consider inter-case attributes that capture the workload of the process, allowing their adjustment to workload variations. Regarding the results of EMD and DTW, both metrics follow the same trends. In most cases, DSIM obtains the best results. This trend is more evident in version 2, in which DSIM gets better results in all cases. These results indicate that Prophet and DL models are more effective than the baselines at capturing the temporal variations in waiting times due to a decrease in the arrival intensity. This observation should again be tempered by the threats to validity acknowledged above.

Results Scenario 2. Table 4 presents the MAE, RSME, and SMAPE grouped for each log, both for the simulation model of the as-is process vs. the model derived after the addition of the activity (what-if model). The what-if model has higher MAE than the baseline models in both event logs. The higher error values are evident in the CVS log, where the SMAPE of the updated model is 184% compared to 31.97% for the baseline model. These results suggest that embedded dimensions incorporated in DSIM can predict the presence of activities that

Table 4. Results of scenarios 1 and 2

	Log	MAE		EMD		DTW	
		SIMOD	DSIM	SIMOD	DSIM	SIMOD	DSIM
Scenario 1	*Version 1*						
	BPI17W	971151	*417572*	*0.02222*	0.03593	*3185*	3647
	BPI12W	660211	*534341*	0.11295	*0.04853*	515	*458*
	CVS	1489252	*467572*	0.03213	*0.00001*	3380	*849*
	Version 2						
	BPI17W	895524	*290980*	0.06438	*0.03218*	4528	*3431*
	BPI12W	550266	*524995*	0.25888	*0.22003*	726	*507*
	CVS	540112	*246159*	0.15674	*0.05708*	2453	*1967*
	Log	MAE		RMSE		SMAPE	
		AS-IS	WHAT-IF	AS-IS	WHAT-IF	AS-IS	WHAT-IF
Scenario 2	CFM	*7155*	17546	*22006*	33137	*0.15629*	0.28762
	CVS	*283061*	1040344	*357717*	1052255	*0.31972*	1.84601

were not present in the training set, but it is unable to adequately estimate their temporal behavior. This observation suggests that DSIM could be extended with more sophisticated embedding techniques (e.g. word2vec or transformer models) to better capture the temporal dynamics of previously unobserved activities (by analogy to activities that have been observed in similar contexts).

5 Conclusion

This paper presented a method, namely DeepSimulator, to learn BPS models from event logs based on process mining and DL techniques. The design of DeepSimulator draws upon the observation that DDS methods (based on process mining) do not capture delays between activities caused by factors other than resource contention (e.g. fatigue, batching, inter-process dependencies). In contrast, DL techniques can learn temporal patterns without assuming these patterns stem only from resource contention. Accordingly, DeepSimulator discovers a stochastic process model from a log using process mining, and then uses a DL model to add timestamps to the events produced by the stochastic model. The stochastic model can be modified (activities may be added/removed, branching probabilities may be altered), thus enabling some forms of what-if analysis.

The paper reported on an empirical comparison of the proposed technique with respect to: (i) its ability to replicate the observed as-is behavior; and (ii) its ability to estimate the impact of changes (what-if settings). The evaluation in the "as-is" setting shows that the DeepSimulator method outperforms the baselines (one DDS and two DL methods). The evaluation in the what-if analysis setting shows that DeepSimulator can better estimate the impact of changes in the arrival rate of new cases (the demand) in settings where such changes have been previously observed in the data. However, the accuracy of DeepSimulator degraded when evaluated in a previously unobserved scenario, specifically a scenario where a completely new task is added to the process. We foresee that this drawback could be at least partially addressed by adapting more sophisticated embedding techniques, such as word2vec or transformer models.

Another avenue for future work is to extend the approach to generate events with a "resource" attribute. A related avenue is to extend the approach to support a broader range of changes, such as adding or removing resources. Yet another avenue is to validate the proposed method via case studies, to complement the post-mortem evaluation reported in this paper.

Reproducibility. The source code is available at https://github.com/AdaptiveBProcess/DeepSimulator.git. The datasets, models, and evaluation results can be found at https://doi.org/10.5281/zenodo.5734443.

References

1. Dumas, M., La Rosa, M., Mendling, J., Reijers, H.A.: Fundamentals of Business Process Management. Springer, Heidelberg (2018). https://doi.org/10.1007/978-3-662-56509-4_10
2. Aalst, W.M.P.: Business process simulation survival guide. In: vom Brocke, J., Rosemann, M. (eds.) Handbook on Business Process Management 1. IHIS, pp. 337–370. Springer, Heidelberg (2015). https://doi.org/10.1007/978-3-642-45100-3_15
3. Martin, N., Depaire, B., Caris, A.: The use of process mining in business process simulation model construction. Bus. Inf. Syst. Eng. **58**(1), 73–87 (2015). https://doi.org/10.1007/s12599-015-0410-4
4. Camargo, M., Dumas, M., González-Rojas, O.: Automated discovery of business process simulation models from event logs. Decis. Support Syst. **134**, 113284 (2020)
5. Estrada-Torres, B., Camargo, M., Dumas, M., García-Bañuelos, L., Mahdy, I., Yerokhin, M.: Discovering business process simulation models in the presence of multitasking and availability constraints. Data Knowl. Eng. **134**, 101897 (2021)
6. Tax, N., Verenich, I., La Rosa, M., Dumas, M.: Predictive business process monitoring with LSTM neural networks. In: Dubois, E., Pohl, K. (eds.) CAiSE 2017. LNCS, vol. 10253, pp. 477–492. Springer, Cham (2017). https://doi.org/10.1007/978-3-319-59536-8_30
7. Evermann, J., Rehse, J.R., Fettke, P.: Predicting process behaviour using deep learning. Decis. Support Syst. **100**, 129–140 (2017)
8. Camargo, M., Dumas, M., González-Rojas, O.: Learning accurate LSTM models of business processes. In: Hildebrandt, T., van Dongen, B.F., Röglinger, M., Mendling, J. (eds.) BPM 2019. LNCS, vol. 11675, pp. 286–302. Springer, Cham (2019). https://doi.org/10.1007/978-3-030-26619-6_19
9. Camargo, M., Dumas, M., González-Rojas, O.: Discovering generative models from event logs: data-driven simulation vs deep learning. PeerJ. Comput. Sci. **7**, e577 (2021)
10. Leemans, S.J.J., van der Aalst, W.M.P., Brockhoffb, T., Polyvyanyy, A.: Stochastic process mining: earth movers' stochastic conformance. Inform. Syst. **102**, 101724 (2021)
11. Wynn, M.T., Dumas, M., Fidge, C.J., ter Hofstede, A.H.M., van der Aalst, W.M.P.: Business process simulation for operational decision support. In: ter Hofstede, A., Benatallah, B., Paik, H.-Y. (eds.) BPM 2007. LNCS, vol. 4928, pp. 66–77. Springer, Heidelberg (2008). https://doi.org/10.1007/978-3-540-78238-4_8
12. Rozinat, A., Mans, R.S., van der Aalst, W.M.P.: Discovering simulation models. Inform. Syst. **34**(3), 305–327 (2009)
13. Khodyrev, I., Popova, S.: Discrete modeling and simulation of business processes using event logs. Procedia Comput. Sci. **29**, 322–331 (2014)
14. Pourbafrani, M., van Zelst, S.J., van der Aalst, W.M.P.: Supporting automatic system dynamics model generation for simulation in the context of process mining. In: Abramowicz, W., Klein, G. (eds.) BIS 2020. LNBIP, vol. 389, pp. 249–263. Springer, Cham (2020). https://doi.org/10.1007/978-3-030-53337-3_19
15. LeCun, Y., Bengio, Y., Hinton, G.: Deep learning. Nature **521**(7553), 436–444 (2015)
16. Lin, L., Wen, L., Wang, J.: MM-Pred: a deep predictive model for multi-attribute event sequence. In: Proceedings of SIAM 2019. Society for Industrial and Applied Mathematics, pp. 118–126 (2019)

17. Tax, N., Teinemaa, I., van Zelst, S.J.: An interdisciplinary comparison of sequence modeling methods for next-element prediction. Softw. Syst. Model. **19**(6), 1345–1365 (2020). https://doi.org/10.1007/s10270-020-00789-3

18. Taymouri, F., Rosa, M.L., Erfani, S., Bozorgi, Z.D., Verenich, I.: Predictive business process monitoring via generative adversarial nets: the case of next event prediction. In: Fahland, D., Ghidini, C., Becker, J., Dumas, M. (eds.) BPM 2020. LNCS, vol. 12168, pp. 237–256. Springer, Cham (2020). https://doi.org/10.1007/978-3-030-58666-9_14

19. Augusto, A., Conforti, R., Dumas, M., La Rosa, M., Polyvyanyy, A.: Split miner: automated discovery of accurate and simple business process models from event logs. Knowl. Inf. Syst. **59**(2), 251–284 (2018). https://doi.org/10.1007/s10115-018-1214-x

20. Reißner, D., Armas-Cervantes, A., Conforti, R., Dumas, M., Fahland, D., La Rosa, M.: Scalable alignment of process models and event logs: an approach based on automata and S-components. Inform Syst **94**, 101561 (2020)

21. Favre, C., Völzer, H.: The difficulty of replacing an inclusive OR-join. In: Barros, A., Gal, A., Kindler, E. (eds.) BPM 2012. LNCS, vol. 7481, pp. 156–171. Springer, Heidelberg (2012). https://doi.org/10.1007/978-3-642-32885-5_12

22. Taylor, S.J., Letham, B.: Forecasting at scale. Am. Stat. **72**(1), 37–45 (2018)

23. Rama-Maneiro, E., Vidal, J.C., Lama, M.: Deep learning for predictive business process monitoring: review and benchmark (2021). https://arxiv.org/abs/2009.13251

24. Laguna, M., Marklund, J.: Business Process Modeling, Simulation and Design. CRC Press, New York (2018)

25. Song, M., van der Aalst, W.M.P.: Towards comprehensive support for organizational mining. Decis. Support Syst. **46**(1), 300–317 (2008)

26. Kuhn, H.W.: The Hungarian Method for the assignment problem. Nav. Res. Logist. Q. **2**, 83–97 (1955)

Multi-perspective Process Analysis: Mining the Association Between Control Flow and Data Objects

Dina Bayomie[1]([✉])[iD], Kate Revoredo[1][iD], and Jan Mendling[2][iD]

[1] Vienna University of Economics and Business (WU), Vienna, Austria
{dina.sayed.bayomie.sobh,kate.revoredo}@wu.ac.at
[2] Humboldt University, Berlin, Germany
jan.mendling@hu-berlin.de

Abstract. Process mining techniques provide process analysts with insights into interesting patterns of a business process. Current techniques have focused by and large on the explanation of behavior, partially by help of features that relate to multiple perspectives beyond just pure control flow. However, techniques to provide insights into the connection between data elements of related events have been missing so far. Such connections are relevant for several analysis tasks such as event correlation, resource allocation, or log partitioning. In this paper, we propose a multi-perspective mining technique for discovering data connections. More specifically, we adapt concepts from association rule mining to extract connections between a sequence of events and behavioral attributes of related data objects and contextual features. Our technique was evaluated using real-world events supporting the usefulness of the mined association rules.

Keywords: Association rules · Process analytic · Multi-perspective process analysis

1 Introduction

Process mining techniques provide process analysts with insights into interesting patterns of a business process [1,2]. Classical techniques in this area such as automatic process discovery or conformance checking focus on the control-flow perspective to generate process insights based on event logs. These insights are helpful for analysts to understand the performance of a process and root causes of anomalies.

A key challenge of root cause analysis is to identify as many potential explanations for a process issue as possible. Such explanations are not necessarily restricted to the control flow perspective. Indeed, the potential of multi-perspective process mining has been emphasized by several contributions [3–6]. These techniques have focused largely on the explanation of behavior, partially by help of features that relate to multiple perspectives. However, techniques to

© Springer Nature Switzerland AG 2022
X. Franch et al. (Eds.): CAiSE 2022, LNCS 13295, pp. 72–89, 2022.
https://doi.org/10.1007/978-3-031-07472-1_5

provide insights into the connection between data elements of related events have been missing so far. Such connections are particularly relevant for analysis tasks such as event correlation, resource allocation, or log partitioning.

In this paper, we address this research gap by developing a multi-perspective mining technique for the discovery of data connections. More specifically, we adapt concepts from association rule mining with pre- and post-processing [7,8] to extract connections between a sequence of events and behavioral attributes of related data objects and contextual features. During pre-processing, techniques such as filtering or partitioning can be applied. During post-processing, techniques such as rule comparison or visualization can be used. Our technique was evaluated using real-world event logs. The results show that our method is able to extract association rules that provide useful insights on the event log to support process analysts.

The rest of this paper is organized as follows. In Sect. 2 we review important concepts such as event log and association rule miner and we discuss prior research. In Sect. 3, we describe our method. In Sect. 4 we evaluate our method and discuss the findings. In Sect. 5 we conclude and provide directions for future research.

2   Background

In this section, we discuss the fundamental concepts that are used by our approach and describe some prior work. Section 2.1 introduces the basic notions of event, case and event log. Section 2.2 describes essential concepts of association rule mining. Finally, Sect. 2.3 summarizes related work.

2.1   Preliminaries

We start by introducing the basic notion of event (i.e., the atomic unit of execution) and then discuss the notions of event log and case in turn.

Definition 1 (Event, attribute). *An event e represents the execution of a process activity. An event has a set of attributes* $(\mathfrak{A})$*, that provides information about context data objects, e.g. activity* (Act)*, timestamp* (Ts)*, resource, cost,...,etc. An attribute* $Attr \in \mathfrak{A}$ *has a non-empty set of domain values Dom(Attr), such that each event is mapped to one of the attribute's domain values. We indicate the value mapped by Attr to an event e by using a dot notation, i.e., e.Attr.*

We assume the mapping of Ts to be coherent with $\leqslant$, i.e., if $e \leqslant e'$ then $e.\text{Ts} \leqslant e'.\text{Ts}$. Considering the total ordering as a mapping from a convex subset of integers, we can assign to every event a unique integer index (or *event id* for short), induced by $\leqslant$ on the events. We shall denote the index i of an event e as a subscript, i.e., e_i.

Definition 2 (Case). *A case $\sigma = \langle e_{\sigma_1}, \ldots, e_{\sigma_m} \rangle$ is a finite sequence of length m of events e_{σ_i} with $1 \leqslant i \leqslant m$ induced by $\leqslant$, i.e., such that $e_{\sigma_i} \leqslant e_{\sigma_k}$ for every $i \leqslant k \leqslant m$. We assume every case to be assigned a unique case identifier (case id for short), namely an integer in a convex subset.*

Definition 3 (Event log). *An event log $L = \{\sigma_1, \ldots, \sigma_n\}$ is a finite non-empty set of non-overlapping cases, i.e., if $e \in \sigma_i$, then $e \notin \sigma_j$ for all $i, j \in [1 \ldots n]$, $i \neq j$.*

Figure 1 depicts an example of an event log L in a tabular representation. L has three cases grouped over the *case id* attribute. The case σ_1 defined by the case id 1 is $\langle e_1, e_2, e_3, e_4 \rangle$. Notice that it preserves the order of the events within the case. L contains five attributes that describe the event, such that $\mathfrak{A} = \{\text{Activity, Timestamp, Resource, Type, Supervisor}\}$. For example, the event e_1 indicates that activity $e_1.\text{Act} = \text{Applicationsubmit}$ was executed by resource $e_1.\text{Resource} = \text{C1}$ and finished at time $e_1.\text{Ts} = \text{"01/06/2020"}$. $e_1.\text{Type} = \text{Car}$ and $e_1.\text{Supervisor} = \text{R1}$ represent additional data objects associated with the event.

Case Id	Activity	Timestamp	Resource	Type	Supervisor
1	Application submit	01/06/2020	C1	Car	R1
1	Review application	02/06/2020	R1	Car	R3
1	Accept application	03/06/2020	R3	Car	R3
1	Send notification	03/06/2020	R1	Car	R3
2	Application submit	03/06/2020	C2	House	R2
2	Review application	04/06/2020	R2	House	R3
2	Reject application	08/06/2020	R3	House	R3
2	Send notification	08/06/2020	R2	House	R3
3	Application submit	04/08/2020	C4	House	R2
3	Review application	04/08/2020	R2	House	R3
3	Request documents	07/08/2020	R2	House	R3
3	Review application	07/08/2020	R2	House	R3
3	Accept application	11/08/2020	R3	House	R3
3	Send notification	11/08/2020	R2	House	R3

Fig. 1. An event log sample

2.2 Association Rule Mining

Association rule mining is a rule-based machine learning method that searches in a transaction database (also called transaction table) for relevant relations, i.e., frequently occurring patterns, correlations, or associations, between pairs of attribute and its value [8,9]. An association rule R represents the influence of a set of pairs of attributes and their values, called *antecedent* of the rule, in another set of pairs of attributes and their values, called *consequent* of the rule, i.e. $R : \text{IF} antecedent \text{THEN} consequent$.

The mining algorithm computes different measures to rank the discovered rules, such as support, confidence and lift [10]. The support measures how frequently a rule R appears in the transaction database T:

$$support(R) = \frac{|(antecedent \cup consequent) \subseteq T|}{|T|} \quad (1)$$

The confidence measures how often the rule is satisfied in the transaction database:

$$confidence(R) = \frac{support(antecedent \cup consequent)}{support(antecedent)} \quad (2)$$

The lift is an objective interestingness measure that assesses the performance of a rule at classifying the transaction database. It measures the deviation of the support of the whole rule from the support expected under independence given the supports of the antecedent and the consequent:

$$lift(R) = \frac{support(antecedent \cup consequent)}{support(antecedent) * support(consequent)} \quad (3)$$

2.3   Prior Work

There have been various works on finding correlations between process events [11]. They have focused on different tasks such as identifying process instances, i.e. cases, for event log generation [12], also considering object-centric perspective [13] and middleware [14], for discovering a process model [15] or enriching an event log with sensor data [16]. However, the area has not received much attention from the perspective of analyzing the correlation of events and data objects behavior within an event log. Our work is most closely related to prior work in this direction.

In [6], association rules with respect to control flow, resources, and temporal process execution behaviour are learned to monitor the process for anomaly detection. The control rules indicate flow patterns, i.e. expected sequence of events. The temporal rules concern the duration of the activities. The resource rules constrain which resources execute the activities. They are split into two groups, i.e., rules covering all activities that must be executed by different resources, and rules covering all activities that must be executed by the same resource. In this work, we evaluate other data objects besides resource and also how their behavior correlate with the events.

In [3], data objects are used to revise the set of declare rules extracted from an event log. With the consideration of data objects it was possible to identify more precise correlations between the events, eliminate constraints that were not meaningful, and provide more understanding to the remaining constraints. This approach works in a broad way searching for general patterns considering the control-flow information and uses the data object to refine the patterns found.

In [5], the authors propose a multi-perspective trace clustering approach that uses the data objects to compute the case distance measure. Using the control-flow, resource and data objects perspectives improve the homogeneity of the cases within the same cluster. In this work, we focus on finding commonalities among cases by investigating associations between control-flow and data objects behavior.

In [4], the authors use multiple perspectives to compare different processes. They visualize the difference by help of the process model and data objects information available in the event log. The work provides three comparative views. The first view shows the difference in the process performance and resource perspectives over the process model. The second view focuses on showing the activity similarity between the processes. The last view focuses on comparing the time perspective. In this work, we evaluate other data objects besides resource, performance and time and also it focuses on identifying the association patterns between the control-flow and the data objects perspectives of one event log.

3   Method

In this section, we describe our method *Event Log Rule Miner*, henceforth called *EL-RM*, which extracts association rules between the control-flow and data objects behavior within an event log. It is inspired on the knowledge discovery in database (KDD) process [17], being composed of three main steps: preparation of the event log, the mining itself and a post processing of the association rules discovered. Figure 2 presents an overview of *EL-RM*.

EL-RM receives as input an event log and returns as output association rules and information about these rules. It is composed of four steps. The first step prepares the event log data based on the process analyst objectives. The second step encodes the pre-processed event log as a transaction table. In the third step, the association rule miner is applied on the transaction table to discover the association rules that define the association relation between the control flow and the data objects behavior. In the fourth step the association rules are post-processed based on the business analyst's objectives. The following sections detail these four steps.

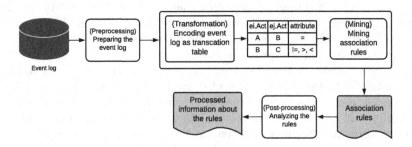

Fig. 2. EL-RM method overview

3.1   Preparing the Event Log

The main two goals of this step are to guarantee the quality of the event log and its alignment with the process analyst's analysis objectives. For addressing the former, pre-processing techniques such as data cleaning [18] are applied and for addressing the latter filtering [19] or partitioning [20] of the event log are used.

Filtering techniques select cases in the event log, i.e., $L' \subset L : L' = \{\sigma_1, \sigma_2, ..., \sigma_n\}$, based on criteria to reach the business analysts objectives. For example, selecting the non-conformed cases with the goal to investigate the reasons for this non-conformance, or selecting cases that have cycle time above a certain threshold (e.g., longest cycle time) to analyze the root cause of the delay within these cases.

Partitioning techniques split the event log into groups with common behavior allowing the process analyst to investigate behavioral differences. Various partitioning criteria can be used, for instance based on time window interval, on process variations, cycle time duration or the number of events per case. For example, partitioning the event log depicted in Fig. 1 using time window of one month as the partition criterion returns the partitioning $\{\{\sigma_1, \sigma_2\}, \{\sigma_3\}\}$, while using the cycle time duration with three days as a split criterion yields the partition $\{\{\sigma_1\}, \{\sigma_2, \sigma_3\}\}$.

3.2   Encoding the Event Log as a Transaction Table

The association rule miner runs on a transaction table. In this section, we describe the technique that we developed to encode an event log as a transaction table.

We define a transaction as the behavior of data attributes over sequences of events. We investigate the change behavior of data objects from two perspectives: *atomic* and *complex* perspectives. The former represents the behavior of a single attribute, i.e., Attr $\in \mathfrak{A}$ over the events, while the latter represents the behavior of a pair of attributes that share domain values, i.e., (Attr, Attr') $\in \mathfrak{A} \times \mathfrak{A}$: $\mathrm{Dom}(\mathrm{Attr}) \cap \mathrm{Dom}(\mathrm{Attr'}) \neq \phi$ over the events. For example, considering the event log in Fig. 1, the *atomic* perspective based on the attribute *Resource* investigates how the *Resource* changes over the events and the *complex* perspective based on the *Resource* and *Supervisor* investigate how they changed over the events. Definition 4 formally defines a transaction in *EL-RM*.

Definition 4 (Transaction). *A transaction* $t = < e_i.Act, e_j.Act, s_{Attr_1}, .., s_{Attr_m}, s_{(Attr, Attr')_0}, .., s_{(Attr, Attr')_l} >$ *is an n-tuple with the two first terms related to the control-flow perspective, i.e., activities e_i.Act and e_j.Act, the following [3,k] terms related to the status of behavior of the attributes in atomic perspective where k is bounded to the number of data attributes in the event log ($k - 3 = |\mathfrak{A}|$) and the remaining terms related to the status of behavior of the attributes in the complex perspective, if exists. The status of the attributes behavior is computed based on their values as stated in Eq. (4). Note that for the atomic perspective (Attr = Attr').*

$$status(e_i, e_j, Attr, Attr') \begin{cases} = & \text{if } e_i.Attr = e_j.Attr' \\ \neq & \text{if } e_i.Attr \neq e_j.Attr' \text{ and } Dom(Attr) \text{ is discrete} \\ > & \text{if } e_i.Attr > e_j.Attr' \text{ and } Dom(Attr) \text{ is numeric} \\ < & \text{if } e_i.Attr < e_j.Attr' \text{ and } Dom(Attr) \text{ is numeric} \end{cases}$$
$$(4)$$

Definition 5 (Transaction table). *A transaction table $T = \{t_1, t_2, ..., t_n\}$ is a set of transactions represented in a tabular structure where each item of the tuple of the transaction corresponds to a column in the table.*

Algorithm 1 presents our algorithm for encoding an event log into a transaction table.

Algorithm 1. Create transaction table from an event log

Require: Event Log $L = \{\sigma_1, ..., \sigma_n\}$, Attributes $\mathfrak{A}$, Decision attributes D,
Ensure: Transaction table T
1: $C = \{(Attr, Attrs')|Attrs, Attrs' \text{ in } \mathfrak{A} \wedge Dom(Attr) \cap Dom(Attr') \neq \phi\}$
2: $T = $ new table($e_i.Act, e_j.Act, L.\mathfrak{A}, C$)
3: **for all** $\sigma \in L$ **do**
4:      $T.append(Create\_Transactions(\sigma, \mathfrak{A}, C))$ Algorithm 2
5:      **for all** d *in* D **do**
6:          $G = $ partitions of σ based on decision attribute d values
7:          **for all** $g \in G$ **do**
8:              **if** $|g| \geqslant 2$ **then**
9:                  $T.append(Create\_Transactions(g, \mathfrak{A}, C))$ Algorithm 2
10:             **end if**
11:         **end for**
12:     **end for**
13: **end for**

It receives an event log L, the set of attributes observed in the log $\mathfrak{A}$ and an optional set of attributes D indicated by the process analyst to be considered when building the transactions. The algorithm starts by searching for the pairs of attributes that represent the complex perspective (see line 1). For example, considering the event log in Fig. 1, both "Resource" and "Supervisor" attributes share domain values, so a new complex attribute is added to represent this relation. The following steps concern with creating transactions for each case σ in L following two alternatives for event pairs selection. The first one is based on the direct successor relation between the events within a case, i.e., considering $e_i.Act$ and its direct successor event $e_{i+1}.Act$ (line 4). The second one is based on selecting the pairs of successors events i.e., considering $e_i.Act$ and its successor event $e_j.Act$ where $j > i$, based on the decision attributes chosen by the analyst (D) (lines 5-11. In this approach, the events in σ are grouped based on the values of the decision attributes D. In each group the events share the same value of $d \in D$ (lines 6). Then, for each group with at least 2 events, Algorithm 1 assesses the behavior of the atomic and complex attributes over selected subset of events g, by calling Algorithm 2 (line 9). For example, in Fig. 3 the fourth row in the transaction table is created by grouping σ_1 over "Resource" attribute as input decision attribute.

Algorithm 2. Create_Transactions(E, A, C) :Create transactions over events in a case $E \in \sigma$

Require: Set of Events E , Attributes $\mathfrak{A}$, Complex attributes C
Ensure: $set of transactions transactions$
1: $transactions =$
2: $row = 1$
3: **for** $(i = 1; i < |E| - 1; i = i + 1)$ **do**
4:     $e_i = E[i], e_j = E[i + 1]$
5:     $transactions[row][1] = e_i.\text{Act}$
6:     $T[row][2] = e_j.\text{Act}$
7:     $col = 3$
8:     **for all** a *in* $\mathfrak{A}$ **do**
9:         $transactions[row][col] = \text{status}(e_i, e_j, a, a)$
10:        $col = col + 1$
11:    **end for**
12:    **for all** (a, a') *in* C **do**
13:        **if** $\text{status}(e_i, e_j, a, a') \in \{=, >, <\}$ **then**
14:            $transactions[row][col] = "e_i." + a + \text{status}(e_i, e_j, a, a') + "e_j." + a'$
15:        **else if** $\text{status}(e_i, e_j, a', a) \in \{=, >, <\}$ **then**
16:            $transactions[row][col] = "e_i." + a' + \text{status}(e_i, e_j, a, a') + "e_j." + a$
17:        **else**
18:            $transactions[row][col] = \text{status}(e_i, e_j, a, a')$
19:        **end if**
20:        $col = col + 1$
21:    **end for**
22:    $row = row + 1$
23: **end for**

Algorithm 2 shows how we take the decision of attributes change behavior over a set of events. For each pair of events e_i and e_j in the input set of events E where e_i are followed by e_j in E, we first check the atomic attribute behavior over e_i and e_j by using $status(e_i, e_j, a, a)$ as per Eq. (4) (lines 8–11). Then, the second step checks the complex attribute (a, a') behavior over e_i and e_j by assessing if both events have the same value over a and a' by using $status(e_i, e_j, a, a')$ as per Eq. (4) (line 12-23). Figure 3 depicts the transaction table generated by Algorithm 1 when receiving a filtering of the event log showed in Fig. 1.

3.3   Mining Association Rules

The third step executes the association rule miner over the transaction table, considering only the rules that sustain the control-flow perspective.

Event log L

Case Id	Activity	Timestamp	Resource	Type	Supervisor
1	Application submit	01/06/2020	C1	Car	R1
1	Review application	02/06/2020	R1	Car	R3
1	Accept application	03/06/2020	R3	Car	R3
1	Send notification	03/06/2020	R1	Car	R3
2	Application submit	03/06/2020	C2	House	R2
2	Review application	04/06/2020	R2	House	R3
2	Reject application	08/06/2020	R3	House	R3
2	Send notification	08/06/2020	R2	House	R3

Encoding

Transaction table T

e_i.Act	e_j.Act	Resource	Type	Supervisor	(Resource,Supervisor)
Application submit	Review appllication	$\neq$	$=$	$\neq$	$\neq$
Review application	Accept application	$\neq$	$=$	$=$	e_i.Supervisor = e_j.Resource
Accept application	Send notification	$\neq$	$=$	$=$	e_i.Resource = e_j.Supervisor
Review application	Send notification	$=$	$=$	$=$	$\neq$
Application submit	Review appllication	$\neq$	$=$	$=$	$\neq$
Review application	Reject application	$\neq$	$=$	$=$	e_i.Supervisor = e_j.Resource
Reject application	Send notification	$\neq$	$=$	$=$	e_i.Resource = e_j.Supervisor
Review application	Send notification	$=$	$=$	$=$	$\neq$

Fig. 3. Encoding the event log L into the transaction table T

Definition 6 (Association rule). *EL-RM establishes the association rules with a control flow information in the antecedent, and the consequent represents the data attributes behavior as follows:*

$R : IF\ e_i.Act = a \wedge e_j.Act = b\ THEN\ e_i.Attr \lesseqgtr e_j.Attr'$

$\lesseqgtr :< | > | = | \neq$

R_1 : IF e_i. Act =" Application submit " and e_j. Act =" Review Application " THEN e_i. Resource $\neq e_j$. Resource	R_{14} : IF e_i. Act =" Review Application " and e_j. Act =" Send notification " THEN e_i. Resource = e_j. Resource
R_2 : IF e_i. Act =" Application submit " and e_j. Act =" Review Application " THEN e_i. Type = e_j. Type	R_{15} : IF e_i. Act =" Review Application " and e_j. Act =" Send notification " THEN e_i. Type = e_j. Type
R_3 : IF e_i. Act =" Application submit " and e_j. Act =" Review Application " THEN e_i. Supervisor = e_j. Supervisor	R_{16} : IF e_i. Act =" Review Application " and e_j. Act =" Send notification " THEN e_i. Supervisor = e_j. Supervisor
R_4 : IF e_i. Act =" Application submit " and e_j. Act =" Review Application " THEN e_i. Resource $\neq e_j$. Supervisor	R_{17} : IF e_i. Act =" Review Application " and e_j. Act =" Send notification " THEN e_i. Resource $\neq e_j$. Supervisor
R_5 : IF e_i. Act =" Application submit " and e_j. Act =" Review Application " THEN e_j. Resource $\neq e_i$. Supervisor	R_{18} : IF e_i. Act =" Review Application " and e_j. Act =" Send notification " THEN e_j. Resource $\neq e_i$. Supervisor
R_6 : IF e_i. Act =" Review Application " and e_j. Act =" Accept Application " THEN e_i. Resource $\neq e_j$. Resource	R_{19} : IF e_i. Act =" Review Application " and e_j. Act =" Reject Application " THEN e_i. Type = e_j. Type
R_7 : IF e_i. Act =" Review Application " and e_j. Act =" Accept Application " THEN e_i. Type = e_j. Type	R_{20} : IF e_i. Act =" Review Application " and e_j. Act =" Reject Application " THEN e_i. Resource $\neq e_j$. Resource
R_8 : IF e_i. Act =" Review Application " and e_j. Act =" Accept Application " THEN e_i. Supervisor $\neq e_j$. Supervisor	R_{21} : IF e_i. Act =" Review Application " and e_j. Act =" Reject Application " THEN e_i. Supervisor = e_j. Supervisor
R_9 : IF e_i. Act =" Review Application " and e_j. Act =" Accept Application " THEN e_i. Supervisor = e_j. Resource	R_{22} : IF e_i. Act =" Review Application " and e_j. Act =" Reject Application " THEN e_i. Supervisor = e_j. Resource
R_{10} : IF e_i. Act =" Accept Application " and e_j. Act =" Send notification " THEN e_i. Resource $\neq e_j$. Resource	R_{23} : IF e_i. Act =" Reject Application " and e_j. Act =" Send notification " THEN e_i. Resource $\neq e_j$. Resource
R_{11} : IF e_i. Act =" Accept Application " and e_j. Act =" Send notification " THEN e_i. Type = e_j. Type	R_{24} : IF e_i. Act =" Reject Application " and e_j. Act =" Send notification " THEN e_i. Type = e_j. Type
R_{12} : IF e_i. Act =" Accept Application " and e_j. Act =" Send notification " THEN e_i. Supervisor = e_j. Supervisor	R_{25} : IF e_i. Act =" Reject Application " and e_j. Act =" Send notification " THEN e_i. Supervisor = e_j. Supervisor
R_{13} : IF e_i. Act =" Accept Application " and e_j. Act =" Send notification " THEN e_i. Resource = e_j. Supervisor	R_{26} : IF e_i. Act =" Reject Application " and e_j. Act =" Send notification " THEN e_i. Resource = e_j. Supervisor

Fig. 4. The association rules extracted from transaction table T in Fig. 3

Figure 4 depicts the association rules mined from the transaction table T in Fig. 3. For example, the discovered rule R_1 states that different resources executed the activities "Application submit" and "Review Application" when they were executed in this order.

3.4   Analyzing the Rules

In the final step, EL-RM prepares the extracted association rules to align with the business analyst objectives. There are many possible post analyses to be performed to improve the usages, interpretation, and visualization of the association rules. In this paper, we discuss three post analyses options (a) combining the rules, (b) ranking the rules, and (c) Comparing the rules. These analyses can be used separately or together based on the analyst objectives.

Combine the Rules. The first option is compressing the extracted rules to improve the rules' visualization. EL-RM aggregates the rules based on common antecedent and common consequent. We propose three possible aggregations. In the first step, rules with the same antecedent are aggregated. The new consequent is the conjunction of the individual consequents. In the second step, rules with the same consequent are aggregated. The new antecedent is the disjunction of the individual antecedents. In the third step, the aggregated rules that share the same consequent or antecedent are aggregated.

For instance, antecedent aggregation applied on the association rules shown in Fig. 4 reduces the number of rules from 26 to 6 rules. R_A in Fig. 5, for example, combines rules R_1, R_2, R_3, R_4, and R_5. Consequent aggregation reduces the rules from 26 to 8 rules. R_C in Fig. 5, for example, combines rules R_1, R_6, R_10, and R_{22}. Using both aggregation reduces the rules from 26 to 4 rules. R_B in Fig. 5, for example, combines rules R_1, R_2, R_6, R_7, R_{10}, R_{11}, R_{23}, and R_{24}. By aggregating the rules, EL-RM reduces the number of the rules without losing any information. Also, it helps the analysts to focus on rules relevant to their analysis.

R_A : IF e_i. Act =" Application submit " and e_j. Act =" Review Application " THENe_i. Resource $\neq e_j$. Resource $\wedge$
e_i. Type = e_j. Type $\wedge e_i$. Supervisor = e_j. Supervisor $\wedge e_i$. Resource $\neq e_j$. Supervisor $\wedge e_j$. Resource $\neq e_i$. Supervisor

---

R_C : IF $(e_i$. Act =" Application submit " and e_j. Act =" Review Application ") $\vee$ $(e_i$. Act =" Review Application "
and e_j. Act =" Accept Application ") $\vee$ $(e_i$. Act =" Accept Application " and e_j. Act =" Send notification ") $\vee$
$(e_i$. Act =" Reject Application " and e_j. Act =" Send notification ") THENe_i. Resource $\neq e_j$. Resource

---

R_B : IF $(e_i$. Act =" Application submit " and e_j. Act =" Review Application ") $\vee$ $(e_i$. Act =" Review Application "
and e_j. Act =" Accept Application ") $\vee$ $(e_i$. Act =" Accept Application " and e_j. Act =" Send notification ") $\vee$
$(e_i$. Act =" Reject Application " and e_j. Act =" Send notification ")THENe_i. Resource $\neq e_j$. Resource $\wedge e_i$. Type = e_j. Type

---

Fig. 5. Example of combine rules from rules in Fig. 4

Ranking and Filtering. The second option is ranking and filtering the rules. The rules can be ranked based on the confidence or lift as per defined in Sect. 2.2. The lift measure is a well known objective interestingness measure, thus, the higher the lift is, the more interesting is the rule. In this step, it is also possible for the process analyst to filter the rules based on the activity represented in the antecedent or on the data objects behavior represented in the consequent to focus on specific analysis.

Comparing the Rules. If during the preparation of the event log, the process analyst decided to partitioning the event log, then in this step it is possible to compare the rules discovered in each of the partitioning. EL-RM induces various sets of rules from the extracted rules. The *All* rule set is the union of the set of rules extracted from each of the partitions (Rs) without duplicate rules:

$$All(Rs) = \bigcup_{i=1}^{|Rs|} Rs_i \tag{5}$$

The *Common* rules set is the intersection of the set of rules extracted for each of the partitions (Rs):

$$Common(Rs) = \bigcap_{i=1}^{|Rs|} Rs_i \tag{6}$$

We use the difference set operation to extract the distinct rules that distinguish each partition. We compare the rules per each partition against the common rules:

$$Difference_{com}(Rs_i, Common) = Rs_i - Common \tag{7}$$

For more distinctive rules, we compare the rules per each partition against the union set of the other partitions:

$$Difference_{partition}(Rs_i, Rs) = Rs_i - \bigcup_{\substack{j=0 \\ j \neq i}}^{|Rs|} Rs_j \tag{8}$$

Consider that time window of one month was used as the partition criterion in the event log shown in Fig. 1. The mining algorithm discovered 32 rules in total over the two partitions $(\{\{\sigma_1, \sigma_2\}, \{\sigma_3\}\})$. From these 32 rules, 16 rules are common among the partitions. The common rules spotlight the log's general rules, which exist at the intersection of all the partitions. The individual rules per each partition are found using the difference set operation with the common rules and the rest of the partitions. For example, rules in Fig. 6 distinguish the second partition as they are not satisfied by the first partition.

IF e_i. Act =" Review Application " and e_j. Act =" Request documents " THEN e_i. Type = e_j. Type
IF e_i. Act =" Review Application " and e_j. Act =" Request documents " THEN e_i. Resource = e_j. Resource
IF e_i. Act =" Request documents " and e_j. Act =" Review Application " THEN e_i. Type = e_j. Type
IF e_i. Act =" Request documents " and e_j. Act =" Review Application " THEN e_i. Resource = e_j. Resource
IF e_i. Act =" Request documents " and e_j. Act =" Review Application " THEN e_i. Supervisor = e_j. Supervisor
IF e_i. Act =" Request documents " and e_j. Act =" Review Application " THEN e_i. Resource $\neq$ e_j. Supervisor
IF e_i. Act =" Review application " and e_j. Act =" Request documents " THEN e_i. Supervisor = e_j. Supervisor
IF e_i. Act =" Review application " and e_j. Act =" Request documents " THEN e_i. Resource $\neq$ e_j. Supervisor
IF e_i. Act =" Review application " and e_j. Act =" Request documents " THEN e_j. Resource $\neq$ e_i. Supervisor
IF e_i. Act =" Request documents " and e_j. Act =" Review Application " THEN e_j. Resource $\neq$ e_i. Supervisor

Fig. 6. $Difference_{partition}(Rs_2, Rs)$

4 Evaluation

We evaluated our method using a prototypical implementation. The main steps shown in Fig. 2 were implemented as follows. For filtering and partitioning of the event log we used Disco[1] process mining tool. To encode the event log into a transaction table we implemented a script in R[2]. For the mining step we used apriori from *arules* package[3]. And for the post analysis we implemented a script in R.

We conducted three exploratory experiments to explore the usefulness of EL-RM. Section 4.1 illustrates the experiments setup over the three datasets. Then, Sect. 4.2 elaborates about the experiments finding. And finally, we discuss the usefulness of EL-RM in the lights of the experiments findings in Sect. 4.3.

4.1 Experiment Setup

We conducted three exploratory experiments with different analysis objectives to explore the usefulness of our method and the effectiveness of the association rules in understanding the relationship between the multi-perspectives observed in the event log. Table 1 summarizes the quantitative information about the three real datasets and the targeted analysis we used on each log. In all three experiment, we considered a confidence threshold of 90% and a support threshold of 2%. We used low support because of variant in the process execution behavior that leads to low number of occurrences of a sequence of events (*antecedent*) in the transaction table.

---

[1] https://www.fluxicon.com/disco/.
[2] https://github.com/DinaBayomie/EL-RM.
[3] https://www.rdocumentation.org/packages/arules/versions/1.6-8.

Table 1. Summary of the datasets and the objective of the analysis

Experiment	Dataset	#Cases	#Attributes	#Activities	Analysis objective
1	BPIC-2017	31509	16	26	Pattern analysis
2	BPIC-2020 (prepaid travel)	2099	21	21	Process drift analysis
3	Road traffic fine	150370	13	11	Variant analysis

First Experiment. We used the BPIC-2017 dataset[4], which contains the events of the loan application process of a Dutch financial institute. The events are generated from three sub-processes, i.e., application, offer and workflow. The log contains cases that started at the beginning of 2016 until the 1st of February 2017. The objective of the analysis in this experiment is exploring the association patterns within the log to understand the data object behavior over execution of the three sub-processes within the log. We follow EL-RM as in Fig. 2. For the preparation step, we did not perform any filtering or partitioning and used the entire event log to get prior insights about the whole log. For the encoding of the event log as a transaction table, we used thirteen attributes as decision attributes, i.e., all the available attributes except the attributes case id, activity and timestamp, in order to explore the different possible patterns generated by the combinations between the events. For the post analysis operations, we first ranked the rules based on the lift measure to show the most interesting rules and then we combined the rules using antecedent aggregation.

Second Experiment. We used BPIC-2020 (prepaid travel) dataset[5], which contains the events of the prepaid travel request process at Eindhoven University of Technology (TU/e). The log covers the cases from the beginning of 2017 till the 21st of February 2019. The objective of the analysis in this experiment is exploring the process evolution to understand how the process behavior change over time (from 2017 to 2018). We follow EL-RM as in Fig. 2. For the preparation step, we partitioned the log into two partitions based on the time window of 1 year. Thus, the first partition covers cases that started in 2017, and the second partition covers cases that started in 2018. For the encoding step, we used eighteen attributes as decision attributes, i.e., all the available attributes except the attributes case id, activity and timestamp, in order to explore the different possible patterns generated by the combinations between the events. For the post analysis step we compared the rules to identify the uniqueness patterns over the two partitions.

Third Experiment. We used the road traffic fine management process dataset[6], which contains the events of the road traffic fines process. The cases have a diverse cycle time duration behavior. The shortest cycle time is counted in days (less than a month), while the longest cycle time is 11.8 years. The objective

---

[4] https://doi.org/10.4121/uuid:3926db30-f712-4394-aebc-75976070e91f.

[5] https://doi.org/10.4121/uuid:5d2fe5e1-f91f-4a3b-ad9b-9e4126870165.

[6] https://doi.org/10.4121/uuid:270fd440-1057-4fb9-89a9-b699b47990f5.

of the analysis in this experiment is exploring the process variants between the shortest cycle time cases and the longest cycle time cases to understand how the process behavior change. We follow EL-RM as in Fig. 2. For the preparation step, we partition the log based on the cycle time and filter the shortest and longest cycle time partitions. Thus, the first partition covers cases with short cycle time (max 1 month cycle time), and the second partition covers cases that longest cycle time (more than 3 years cycle time). For the encoding step, we used ten attributes as decision attributes, i.e., all the available attributes except the attributes case id, activity and timestamp, in order to explore the different possible patterns generated by the combinations between the events. For the post analysis step we compared the rules to identify the common and uniqueness patterns over the two partitions.

4.2   Findings

Table 2 summarizes the quantitative findings of our experiments through different steps of EL-RM method. For each experiment, we show information about the encoded transaction table from the entire log (as in experiment one) or the partitions (as in experiments two and three). First, we show the number of encoded transactions that reflects the number of pairs of events that were used for exploring the patterns and the number of the atomic and complex attributes, which represents the number of columns within the transaction table. Second, we show information about the discovered rules. The resulting number of rules after the combination is show in table. We assumed that the analyst wanted to investigate patterns from the perspective of the control flow, and therefore the rules were combined using the antecedent perspective. Finally, the range of confidence and lift measures over the rules are shown.

First Experiment. Figure 7a shows a summary of the distribution of the rules discovered. We carried out a pattern analysis by exploring the discovered rules to understand the relationship between the events and the data objects behavior. Also, it uses the data objects to understand the execution behavior of the events with the three sub-processes and how the three sub-processes interact. For example we found the following three rules:

Table 2. Quantitative summary of the three experiments

Datasets	# Transactions		Attributes		# Discovered rules		# Combined rules		Confidence		Lift	
			Atomic	Complex					Min	Max	Min	Max
BPIC-2017	4101108		16	33	751		15		0.94	1	0.95	13.63
BPIC-2020	30004	223410	18	39	204	306	12	18	0.99	1	1	8.90
Road traffic fine	173102	306925	13	66	78	429	4	16	0.99	1	1	31.07

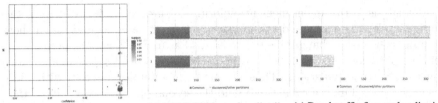

(a) BPIC 2017 - Top rules distributions

(b) BPIC 2020 - rules distributions over partitions

(c) Road traffic fine - rules distributions over partitions

Fig. 7. Summary of findings for the three experiments

R_1 : IF $e_i.Act$ = "O_Created" and $e_j.Act$ = "O_Sent(mail and online)"
THEN e_i.Offer ID = e_j.Offer ID
R_2 : IF $e_i.Act$ = "O_CreateOffer" and $e_j.Act$ = "O_Created"
THEN e_i.EventID = e_j.OfferID
R_3 : IF $e_i.Act$ = "A_Complete" and $e_j.Act$ = "W_Validateapplication"
THEN e_i.Resource = e_j.Resource

R_1 and R_2 help in explaining the correlating between the events that were executed by offer sub-process based on the data objects perspective. R_1 helps in understanding the correlation between 14% of the events within BPIC17 just that they should have the same offer ids, where there are 6872 offer ids. R_2 emphasis the correlation relation between the 'Event ID' and 'Offer ID' data objects attributes. For the interaction between application sub-process and workflow sub-process, we found R_3 that shows the resource behavior between the two sub-processes.

Second Experiment. Figure 7b shows the distribution of the association rules over the two partitions. 20% of the rules are common between the two partitions. However, 72% of the rules discovered from the second partition, i.e., cases in 2018, differ from the first partition, i.e., in 2017. For instance, the following two rules were found.

R_1 : IF $e_i.Act$ = "Permit approved by administration" and $e_j.Act$ = "Permit approved by budget owner)"
THEN e_i.Resource = e_j.Resource and e_i.org : role! = e_j.org : role
R_2 : IF $e_i.Act$ = "Permit approved by supervisor" and $e_j.Act$ = "Permit final_approved by director"
THEN e_i.(case)_organizationalEntity = e_j.(case)_permit_organizationalEntity

---

R_1 applies for 24% of the cases that occurred in 2018, while it does not apply for the cases executed in 2017, while R_2 applies in cases executed in 2017 but does not apply for cases in 2018.

Third Experiment. Figure 7(c) shows the distribution of the association rules over the two variants, 6% of the rules are common between the two partitions.

We compared the rules to understand the different behavior between the longest and shortest cycle time cases. For example, the following three rules were found.

R_1 : IF $e_i.Act$ = "Insert Fine Notification" and $e_j.Act$ = "Insert Date Appeal to Prefecture"
THEN e_i.NotificationType $\neq$ e_j.NotificationType
R_2 : IF $e_i.Act$ = "Create Fine" and $e_j.Act$ = "Payment"
THEN e_i.NotificationType = e_j.NotificationType
R_3 : IF $e_i.Act$ = "Create Fine" and $e_j.Act$ = "Send Fine"
THEN e_i.Resource $\neq$ e_j.Resource

Cases with long cycle time used different type of notification as in R_1 While, in the short cycle time cases, they tend to use the same notification type as in R_2. Also, the longest cycle time cases used different resources for creating the fine and sending it as in R_3, unlike in the cases with shortest cycle time they used the same resource.

4.3 Discussion

The three exploratory experiments showed that EL-RM is a useful method that provides insights to understand the association relations between the events and data objects behavior perspectives. EL-RM explores the correlation relation between the data object attributes through attributes complex view and highlights these attributes behavior over the control-flow perspective for the analyst. Moreover, our exploratory experiments showed that the association rules support pattern analysis, process drift analysis and variant analysis.

Our work contributes to research on process mining, as it shows how association rules can represent multi-perspective patterns over the event log. Our work also has a potential impact on industry by providing a new tool that supports the process analysts in their decision making process.

5 Conclusion

In this paper, we proposed a multi-perspective mining technique for the discovery of data connection. Our method uses association rules to represent the relation between the control-flow perspective and its impacts on the behavior of the data objects perspective. Our method has a pre-processing step that allows the analysts to prepare the data for their analysis by applying several techniques such as filtering or partitioning techniques. Moreover, our method has a post-processing step that allows the analysts to improve the usages, interpretation and visualization of the association rules such as combining, comparing and ranking the rules. The results of our evaluation showed the potential of the approach to extract relevant insights about the change behavior of the attributes over the events.

As future work, we will investigate methods to discover further correlation patterns to improve the interest of the rules and to measure their interestingness.

References

1. Dumas, M., Rosa, M.L., Mendling, J., Reijers, H.A.: Fundamentals of Business Process Management, 2nd edn. Springer, Heidelberg (2018). https://doi.org/10.1007/978-3-662-56509-4
2. van der Aalst, W.: Process Mining - Data Science in Action, 2nd edn. Springer, Heidelberg (2016). https://doi.org/10.1007/978-3-662-49851-4
3. Bose, R.P.J.C., Maggi, F.M., van der Aalst, W.M.P.: Enhancing declare maps based on event correlations. In: Daniel, F., Wang, J., Weber, B. (eds.) BPM 2013. LNCS, vol. 8094, pp. 97–112. Springer, Heidelberg (2013). https://doi.org/10.1007/978-3-642-40176-3_9
4. Pini, A., Brown, R., Wynn, M.T.: Process visualization techniques for multi-perspective process comparisons. In: Bae, J., Suriadi, S., Wen, L. (eds.) AP-BPM 2015. LNBIP, vol. 219, pp. 183–197. Springer, Cham (2015). https://doi.org/10.1007/978-3-319-19509-4_14
5. Jablonski, S., Röglinger, M., Schönig, S., Wyrtki, K.M.: Multi-perspective clustering of process execution traces. Enterp. Model. Inf. Syst. Archit. Int. J. Concept. Model. **14**, 2:1–2:22 (2019). https://doi.org/10.18417/emisa.14.2
6. Böhmer, K., Rinderle-Ma, S.: Mining association rules for anomaly detection in dynamic process runtime behavior and explaining the root cause to users. Inf. Syst. **90**, 101438 (2020)
7. Agrawal, R., Srikant, R., et al.: Fast algorithms for mining association rules. In: Proceedings of the 20th International Conference on Very Large Data Bases, VLDB, vol. 1215, pp. 487–499. Citeseer (1994)
8. Dongre, J., Prajapati, G.L., Tokekar, S.V.: The role of apriori algorithm for finding the association rules in data mining. In: International Conference on Issues and Challenges in Intelligent Computing Techniques (ICICT) 2014, pp. 657–660 (2014)
9. Agrawal, R., Imielinski, T., Swami, A.N.: Mining association rules between sets of items in large databases. In: SIGMOD Conference, pp. 207–216. ACM Press (1993)
10. Hornik, K., Grün, B., Hahsler, M.: arules-a computational environment for mining association rules and frequent item sets. J. Stat. Softw. **14**(15), 1–25 (2005)
11. Diba, K., Batoulis, K., Weidlich, M., Weske, M.: Extraction, correlation, and abstraction of event data for process mining. Wiley Interdiscip. Rev. Data Min. Knowl. Discov. **10**(3), e1346 (2020)
12. Bayomie, D., Di Ciccio, C., La Rosa, M., Mendling, J.: A probabilistic approach to event-case correlation for process mining. In: Laender, A.H.F., Pernici, B., Lim, E.-P., de Oliveira, J.P.M. (eds.) ER 2019. LNCS, vol. 11788, pp. 136–152. Springer, Cham (2019). https://doi.org/10.1007/978-3-030-33223-5_12
13. Li, G., de Carvalho, R.M., van der Aalst, W.M.P.: Configurable event correlation for process discovery from object-centric event data. In: ICWS, pp. 203–210. IEEE (2018)
14. Bala, S., Mendling, J., Schimak, M., Queteschiner, P.: Case and activity identification for mining process models from middleware. In: Buchmann, R.A., Karagiannis, D., Kirikova, M. (eds.) PoEM 2018. LNBIP, vol. 335, pp. 86–102. Springer, Cham (2018). https://doi.org/10.1007/978-3-030-02302-7_6

15. Pourmirza, S., Dijkman, R.M., Grefen, P.: Correlation miner: mining business process models and event correlations without case identifiers. Int. J. Cooperative Inf. Syst. 26(2), 1742002:1–1742002:32 (2017)
16. Senderovich, A., Rogge-Solti, A., Gal, A., Mendling, J., Mandelbaum, A.: The ROAD from sensor data to process instances via interaction mining. In: Nurcan, S., Soffer, P., Bajec, M., Eder, J. (eds.) CAiSE 2016. LNCS, vol. 9694, pp. 257–273. Springer, Cham (2016). https://doi.org/10.1007/978-3-319-39696-5_16
17. Han, J., Kamber, M., Pei, J.: Data Mining: Concepts and Techniques, 3rd edn. Morgan Kaufmann, Burlington (2011)
18. Wynn, M.T., Sadiq, S.: Responsible process mining - a data quality perspective. In: Hildebrandt, T., van Dongen, B.F., Röglinger, M., Mendling, J. (eds.) BPM 2019. LNCS, vol. 11675, pp. 10–15. Springer, Cham (2019). https://doi.org/10.1007/978-3-030-26619-6_2
19. Vidgof, M., Djurica, D., Bala, S., Mendling, J.: Interactive log-delta analysis using multi-range filtering. Softw. Syst. Model. 1–22 (2021). https://doi.org/10.1007/s10270-021-00902-0
20. de Leoni, M., van der Aalst, W.M.P., Dees, M.: A general process mining framework for correlating, predicting and clustering dynamic behavior based on event logs. Inf. Syst. 56, 235–257 (2016)

Sustainable and Explainable
Applications

Towards Greener Applications: Enabling Sustainable-aware Cloud Native Applications Design

Monica Vitali[✉]

Department of Electronics, Information and Bioengineering,
Politecnico di Milano, Milan, Italy
`monica.vitali@polimi.it`

Abstract. Data centers energy demand is increasing. While a great deal of effort has been made to reduce the amount of CO_2 generated by large cloud providers, too little has been done from the application perspective. We claim that application developers can impact the environmental footprint by enhancing the application design with additional features. Following the proposed Sustainable Application Design Process (SADP), the application design is enriched with information that can be leveraged by cloud providers to manage application execution in an energy-aware manner. This exploratory work aims to emphasize the awareness on the sustainability of applications by proposing a methodology for its evaluation. To this end, we first suggest possible actions to enrich the application design towards sustainability, and finally describe how this additional information can be leveraged in the application workflow. We discuss the feasibility of our methodology by referring to existing tools and technologies capable of supporting the design features proposed in a production environment.

Keywords: Sustainable applications · Cloud-native · Workflow design · Sustainability-awareness · Energy-efficiency

1 Introduction

The last 10 years have seen an exponential growth in data centers energy demand. Recent studies have demonstrated that data centers are responsible for 3% of the global electricity supply and 2% of total greenhouse gas emissions[1]. Efforts have been made, and are still ongoing, by leading cloud providers and IT companies, such as Facebook, Google, and Apple, towards environmental sustainability[2]. To improve the efficiency and effectiveness of data centers, two complementary approaches can be adopted: (i) design efficient facilities [31] and (ii) improve

---

[1] http://www.independent.co.uk/environment/global-warming-data-centres-to-consume-three-times-as-much-energy-in-next-decade-experts-warn-a6830086.html.
[2] https://cloudscene.com/news/2016/12/going-green/.

© Springer Nature Switzerland AG 2022
X. Franch et al. (Eds.): CAiSE 2022, LNCS 13295, pp. 93–108, 2022.
https://doi.org/10.1007/978-3-031-07472-1_6

server utilization [30]. The first can be pursued by building data center facilities in cold locations and taking advantage of local renewable resources to power up the data center. The second strategy adopts server consolidation exploiting virtualization techniques. To date, most of the efforts have been addressed to the optimization of the Power Usage Effectiveness (PUE), a metric comparing the amount of energy consumed in a data center by the IT facilities and the overall energy consumed to power the whole data center (including cooling and uninterruptible power supply units). PUE gives hints about the energy efficiency of a data center but fails in expressing how efficiently IT resources are employed for running the applications [41]. Even if big companies have adopted both strategies, the overall carbon footprint of data centers has not changed significantly. While data centers are more efficient, the demand for data center services is increasing[3] [25]. Computationally demanding applications, including AI, machine learning, and Big Data analytics, consume a significant amount of energy, increased 300'000 times over the past 10 years [19,24]. Therefore, the improvement in the efficiency of the infrastructure is followed by an increase in demand, making current efforts towards energy efficiency less relevant. At the same time, the architectural style of the applications is shifting from monolith to cloud native applications, designed to take advantage of the characteristics of cloud computing [11,20]. Cloud native applications are implemented through microservices: a large set of simple, single-function, and loosely coupled components interacting to provide the overall service. From the cloud provider perspective, these components are black boxes whose internal logic is neither declared nor modifiable, and whose interaction is mainly hidden. Even though recent, this kind or architecture is getting more popular every day and is becoming the de facto standard in industry [9].

The main goal of the methodology proposed in this exploratory paper is to engage application designers in the path towards IT and Information Systems (IS) sustainability. This paper focus the attention on the active role of applications in the energy footprint of IT and aims at increasing the awareness of application providers on the environmental footprint of their applications. The main contributions are:

- a Sustainable Application Design Process (SADP), defining steps the designers need to perform to increase the sustainability of applications;
- a set of best-practices, guiding the application designers in improving the sustainability level of applications;
- insights on how SADP can be exploited in the application workflow.

The paper is organised as follows. Section 2 describes existing work. Section 3 motivates the proposed approach with a running example. Section 4 introduces SADP in more details. Section 5 describes the employment of SADP at runtime. Section 6 validates the methodology mapping its steps to existing tools and technologies, while Sect. 7 summarizes the approach and outlines future developments.

---

[3] http://fortune.com/2016/06/27/data-center-energy-report/.

2   State of the Art

The energy consumption in data centers has been taken into consideration for several years. Research has focused on the energy efficiency of data centers, with approaches related to the employment of renewable energy [14] and the improvement of cooling efficiency [21]. The focus on cooling has been driven by adopting the Power Usage Efficiency (PUE) metric to measure data centers' energy efficiency, computed as the ratio of the amount of energy consumed for IT operations and the overall amount of energy. PUE has several limitations as it does not account for the type of energy used (brown or renewable) and the efficiency of IT operations [12]. Some approaches have focused on IT resource management in data centers. In [38], approaches to green IT have been classified into three main categories: assessment, measurement, and improvement. Most of the approaches in improving energy efficiency are related to the infrastructure, exploiting the intermittent availability of renewable energy [18,35]. These involve operations such as server consolidation [13,30]. When enacting consolidation, shut down policies must be taken into account to ensure a trade-off between energy efficiency and performance [4]. To express non-functional requirements of applications, a Goal-Oriented Requirement Engineering approach can be used [17]. Other approaches have considered several improvement actions, including consolidation, migration, CPU frequency and voltage scaling, and virtual machine resources vertical scaling [34,39,40]. Some best practices have been suggested over the years to promote data center efficiency improvement, as the EU Code of Conduct [1] and the Data Center Maturity Model [33]. From an IT perspective, plenty of works have been investigating how to make data centers greener, while some limited attempts have been made to include sustainability in the application design of Green Information Systems [5,8,22,27]. These approaches propose general principles and lacks practical solutions. Some proposal aimed to estimate energy efficiency of specific applications in embedded systems [10], but cannot be applied in complex cloud infrastructures. From a design perspective, in [32] more specific guidelines are provided focusing only on data mining. Current research mainly focuses on dynamic resource allocation and scheduling according to energy efficiency optimization [2,37]. All these techniques are not exploiting the differences between microservices and their interaction. Some efforts have been made to estimate the environmental footprint of applications. The CodeCarbon initiative [23] provides a tool for estimating CO_2 emissions the geographical location and the energy mix of the country in which the application is deployed. Power is also one of the metrics considered in [7], providing black-box monitoring for multi-component applications. This is a first step for enabling energy-awareness in microservice-oriented applications but the workflow enhancement perspective is still missing.

Cloud native applications empower organizations to design and execute scalable, loosely coupled, resilient, manageable, and observable applications [11]. Cloud native adoption is increasing, thus we need to refer to this kind of model for future developments in cloud computing application management. These applications generate complex workflows due to the adoption of the microservice architectural style. A standard way to model the interaction between microservices is missing, even though this information is crucial to enhance their management. In [36], microservice choreography is represented through BPMN fragments, thus exploiting a well-known process modeling notation for representing microservice interactions. However, the dynamicity of this interaction cannot be mapped in such an approach. To introduce dynamicity in microservice coordination, it is possible to enrich the model using the DMN specification [29], expressing business rules to define under which condition a task should be executed. An integration between BPMN and DMN is proposed in [16,26], implementing the separation of concern between the process and decision model.

This work focuses on enriching the design of cloud native applications and of their workflow in order to enable the sustainability of applications.

3   Motivating Scenario

In this section, we describe the main motivations driving this work and how the proposed approach is mapped on the current cloud scenario.

Our main goal is to raise attention towards sustainability of applications, and not only of the infrastructure in which they are deployed. In order to do so, we need to know the current state of the art in terms of cloud applications. For this reason, in this work we refer to cloud native applications, which are the current best practice for cloud applications. In fact, more and more developers are shifting towards the cloud native paradigm which requires to implement applications as a set of composite microservices, uncoupled and independent, interacting with each others through synchronous and asynchronous messages. A typical application is composed of dozens to hundreds of independent microservices, all implicitly cooperating to reach the overall goal of the organization implementing the application. However, **not all the components have the same relevance**, being some of them necessary for reaching the goal, while other just enriching the application with additional accessory functionalities that might increase the overall Quality of Experience (QoE) of the customer or the income of the service provider. Moreover, **each microservice has different requirements** in terms of computational resources and different constraints in terms of Quality of Service (QoS). From this perspective, microservice based architectures are really effective since they allow the scale-out of the single components that are experiencing performance issues. Microservices can be sensitive to the context in which they are executed. Each microservice provides a specific functionality, however, the way in which this functionality is carried out might depend on the context of execution, and slightly different **alternative implementations of the same functionality can be provided**, i.e., with fail-over mechanisms.

To make the discussion more practical, an example of application presenting the features we have just introduced is described. We consider a Flight Booking service allowing customers to check for specific itineraries and compare prices of several airlines. This service consists of several microservices (Fig. 1):

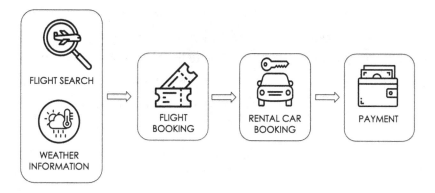

Fig. 1. Microservices of a flight booking application

- *Flight Search*: it collects the itinerary request of the customers and returns a list of solutions obtained by querying the information systems of all the airlines. The solutions are ranked according to specific policies (e.g., price, duration, number of stops). This service can be provided with some variations according to the specific context of execution:
  - **variation 1:** the information collected profiling the customer can be used to suggest routes or rank the results. This variation requires a recommendation engine to run in the background increasing the computational cost of the service while providing a better QoE to the customers;
  - **variation 2:** results of recent searches by the same or other users can be reused. The actual query is executed only if the solution is selected. This might generate out of date results (e.g., not updated the cost of tickets for an airline) while reducing the computation time and cost.
- *Weather Information:* the search service can be complemented with information useful to the customers in selecting their itinerary. A weather service shows forecasts and statistics of temperatures and precipitations for the selected destination and dates that can be valuable for the customer.
- *Flight Booking:* it is executed when a customer selects a solution after the search microservice. It includes all the activities related to the booking, including configurations (e.g., seat selection, baggage options) and the interaction with the airline's information system.
- *Rental Car Booking:* additional services are proposed to the customer as the rental car booking. This service is provided by a partner but generates an income for the organization in case the customer books a vehicle.
- *Payment:* the payment service manages all the activities related to the payment of the selected flight solution.

Even in this very simple example, it is possible to see how some components of the application are mandatory (i.e., necessary to reach the goal of the application) while others are optional (i.e., contributing to the QoE but not affecting the overall goal). Examples of optional microservices are the *Weather Information* and the *Rental Car Booking* microservices. Moreover, the same functionality

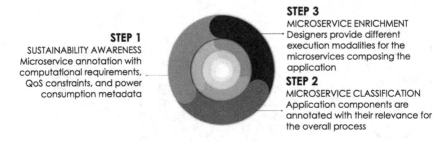

STEP 1
SUSTAINABILITY AWARENESS
Microservice annotation with
computational requirements,
QoS constraints, and power
consumption metadata

STEP 3
MICROSERVICE ENRICHMENT
Designers provide different
execution modalities for the
microservices composing the
application

STEP 2
MICROSERVICE CLASSIFICATION
Application components are
annotated with their relevance for
the overall process

Fig. 2. Steps of the SADP

can be provided with some variations that might affect the QoS, the QoE, or
the resource demand of the application, as demonstrated for the *Flight Search*
microservice. Finally, each microservice has different resources and QoS requirements. For instance, the *Flight Search* might require some time to be executed
(especially when querying all the airlines' systems) but results should be provided
to the customers in a limited time to avoid that they turn to a competitor. On
the contrary, a delay in showing the weather forecasts provided by the *Weather
Information* microservice is not problematic, although it is not desirable.

Most of these features, enclosing the complexity and dynamicity of cloud
native applications, are hidden in configurations set by the application developer. These configurations are usually decided a priori and rarely adapt with
the context of execution. The cloud provider, who is the one in charge of managing most of the deployment aspects of the application, has no access to this
information. Giving the provider the faculty of managing these configurations
might severely improve the QoS of the application as well as its sustainability.
Thus, it is important that the two stakeholders share relevant information for
the effective management of the application. The goal of this paper is to define
which are the key features in the application design that can be exploited to
improve the sustainability of the application. Secondly, it suggests how these
features can be made explicit in the design of an application, and finally it discusses how to exploit them for improving the sustainability of the application
workflow.

4   Sustainable Application Design Process

The proposed Sustainable Application Design Process (SADP) aims at supporting designers in the achievement of sustainable microservice based applications.
SADP focuses on an application perspective by providing goals and directions
for designing sustainable applications. The steps in Fig. 2 have been identified.

The initial point is the current state of the art, where the application designer
is not putting effort in designing sustainable applications. An application can be
described as a graph $A = \{M, E\}$ where M is the set of microservices composing
the application and E is the set of edges connecting the microservices.

Step 1 is a first step towards sustainable applications. It consists in adding basic sustainability-aware information to the application design. The goal is to enrich the application model with additional information that can drive the deployment decisions of the cloud provider when the single components are deployed. This information is not only related to the energy aspect, but also to functional and QoS requirements. The set R contains the specification of all the requirements that can be expressed for an application as $R = \{F, Q, S\}$ where: F is the set of functional requirements regarding the amount of required resources (e.g., the size of the VM required for deploying that component); Q is the set of quality related non-functional requirements (e.g., response time or throughput constraints), and S is the set of sustainability related non-functional requirements (e.g., the estimated power consumption for executing the microservice). Estimating power consumption of a microservice is not trivial, since providing such information is not straightforward. However, from a simple profiling activity it is possible to estimate the computational power required by a specific VM or container configuration. Models available in the state of the art, transforming computational power in energy consumption, can then be exploited [6]. For each microservice $m_i \in M$, a set of requirements $R_i \subseteq R$ can be expressed. A score can be assigned to the application measuring the extent to which the application design implements SADP's Step 1 best practices. Given the set R of expressible requirements, the score is assigned according to the coverage of the annotation:

$$A.score_1 = \Sigma_i |R_i|/|R||M| \quad A.score_1 \in [0, 1] \tag{1}$$

where $|R_i|$ is the number of requirements expressed for a microservice $m_i \in M$, and $|R||M|$ is the total amount of requirements that can be expressed for A.

Step 2. The application designer provides information on which components of the application are mandatory and which are optional: $M_M \cup M_O \subseteq M$ where M_M is the set of mandatory microservices and M_O is the set of optional microservices. Considering the flight reservation application example in Fig. 1, the rental car service can provide additional value for the customer and additional revenue for the application owner, but it is not a key component of the main application. If information about the relevance of each component is provided at design time, this information can be exploited to decide when to execute or when to skip a component according to the execution context. This information is relevant not only for the sustainability of the application (e.g., skip an optional component when renewable power source is not available), but also for QoS (e.g., avoid optional components when the application is experiencing response time or latency issues). Two possible approaches can be used to implement Step 2: i) all components require annotations stating if they are necessary or not for the overall workflow, ii) only optional components are annotated, while mandatory components are not explicitly identified. In the first case, a score can be assigned according to the amount of components explicitly annotated in the workflow:

$$A.score_2 = (|M_O|+|M_M|)/|M| \quad A.score_2 \in [0, 1] \tag{2}$$

However, this approach is more time consuming. In the second approach, instead, a refined score cannot be associated, since it is not possible to differentiate between not annotated and implicitly annotated components. Thus, for the second approach, the score can only be 0 if no annotation is provided, and 1 if at least one component has been annotated as optional:

$$A.score_2 = \begin{cases} 0 & if \ M_O \cup M_M = \emptyset \\ 1 & otherwise \end{cases} \tag{3}$$

Step 3. It consists in the enrichment of the microservices composing the application through the definition of different modalities of execution for each component. Alternative execution modalities can be defined for a single microservice and the one to enact might depend on the current context. Here, three different execution modalities (or versions) are proposed: $V = \{N, HP, LP\}$.

- Normal (N): this is the basic execution modality of the microservice;
- High-Performance (HP): the performance of the microservice is stressed so that the QoS and/or QoE of the customer is maximized at the cost of a higher computational resource demand and power consumption. As an example, in the flight reservation application, the "Search flight" component might take into account the previous activities of the customer in ranking the results to provide a better QoE. This additional functionality has a relevant cost in terms of resources needed for the computation.
- Low-Power (LP): it is a simplified version of the microservice aiming at reducing the amount of energy consumed. To guarantee the performance level, some sub-activities are skipped or executed differently. As an example, in the flight reservation application, the "Search flight" component might ignore specific user information when proposing flight solutions, thus saving computational resources.

For each microservice, both optional and mandatory, it is possible to define several versions: $m_i.V = \{m_i.v\} \mid m_i \in M \ , \ v \in V \ , \ |m_i.V| \leq |V|$; where m_i is a microservice of the application, $m_i.V$ is the set or modalities defined for m_i, and $m_i.v$ is a specific modality of the microservice (Normal, Low-Power, or High-Performance). A score can be assigned according to the number of alternative versions provided compared to the overall amount of required versions:

$$A.score_3 = \Sigma_i |m_i.V|/|M||V| \quad A.score_3 \in [0,1] \tag{4}$$

Different modalities correspond to different power consumption, QoS, and QoE, thus a trade-off is to be considered when selecting the proper modality. The overall SADP approach and the suggested best practices are summarized in Fig. 2. The three steps are incremental refinements. At each step, additional information is provided by the application designer and, at the same time, the complexity in the management of the application increases together with the degree of freedom of how to execute the application. The process is incremental: at each loop, the designer can focus on a single component or on a subset of components, enriching the model step by step.

5   Sustainable Workflow Design with SADP

SADP provides a methodology for improving and evaluating the sustainability in the design of a cloud-native application, enriching each component with additional details and metadata. This section describes how it is possible to exploit these features designing sustainable workflows.

Designing a sustainable workflow requires to select the best configuration for all the components of the application according to the context, aiming at improving energy efficiency, cost, and QoS. The composition of the application will dynamically change selecting a different pool of microservices according to the context of execution. Exploiting all the features added in the process design described in Sect. 4, the workflow can be executed in different modalities:

- **Normal execution** is the typical behaviour of an application; all the microservices composing the application are executed when a request arrives.
- **Basic execution** only a subset of the tasks composing the application are executed. Not mandatory tasks are skipped to reduce the energy consumption or to improve the QoS. It is supported by the Step 2 of the SADP.
- **Low-power execution** tasks composing the application are executed using a low power modality if available (e.g., using editorial content instead of computing personalized content);
- **High-performance execution** tasks composing the application are executed using a performance enhanced modality if available (e.g., providing additional personalizations and functionalities to improve the QoE).

In order to enable the **Low-power execution** and the **High-performance execution**, all the microservices, or part of them, have to be designed according to the Step 3 of the SADP: different interfaces to execute the microservice are provided for each supported modality. These workflow execution modalities are not exclusive, in fact they can be combined together. As an example, if a Low-power execution is activated together with a Basic execution, all the optional tasks are skipped, while regular tasks are executed using their low-power version if available. Two different approaches can be applied for the enactment of the workflow modalities just described:

- **All in:** the execution modality is globally selected for all the components of the application. With the Low-power execution, all the microservices providing this behaviour are executed in this modality without any distinction. Similarly, with the Basic execution, all the optional tasks are skipped.
- **Optimized selection:** the decision about which modality to activate is performed at the microservice level. The execution is optimized by selecting the best combination for reaching the overall desired performance.

While the second approach enables a fine grained optimisation, it increases the complexity of the workflow design and management, which makes necessary the introduction off a complex decision process at run-time. Thus, the workflow design has to be enriched with decision points that are able to provide the logic for deciding the execution modality according to the actual context of execution.

6   Validation

This section demonstrates the feasibility of the proposed methodology given the current technological stack and the cloud native landscape.

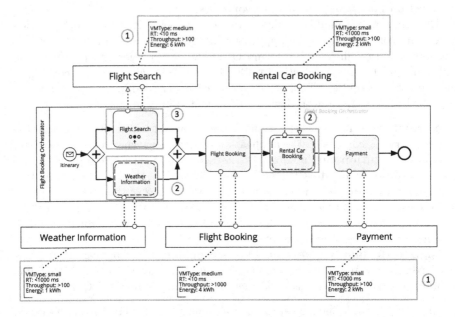

Fig. 3. BPMN representation of the Flight Booking application redesigned with SADP

6.1   Designing Sustainable Applications

In Sect. 4 we introduced SADP, identifying the features to obtain sustainability-aware applications. This section proposes some solutions for designing sustainable applications based on microservices. Here we propose to represent the application and its components using the BPMN notation [28], a standard used to represent both internal processes of an organization as well as collaborations and orchestrations between different organizations. In this work, applications are a workflow of operations performed by different microservices, that might belong to different organizations. Following the representation adopted in [36], the application can be represented as a set of microservices orchestrated by a general process defining their order of execution. In this way, we can model the interaction between different microservices through message events generated during the execution of a microservice or at its end, triggering the execution of another microservice or influencing its activities. As an example, the BPMN model of the Flight Booking application is represented in Fig. 3. The details of the logic of the single microservices are hidden since they are not relevant for the discussion. The interaction is made explicit through the orchestrator process.

Following the steps presented in Sect. 4, the process model can be enriched with metadata regarding the functional and non functional requirements of each microservice. In order to do so, it is possible to use annotations. Annotations are already defined in BPMN and they are used to add additional information on the task execution. Here, annotations are used to add details on the microservice functional and non functional requirements (e.g., required computational resources, QoS constraints), execution cost, power consumption, and eventual reward associated to the microservice execution. These meta-data are useful to predict which will be the outcome of executing a specific microservice in the process workflow. The outcome of Step 1 applied to the flight booking application is shown in Fig. 3. Metadata are modeled with the annotation artifact of BPMN using a semi-structured notation. In order to obtain a consistent annotation, each aspect is represented as an attribute-value pair and the set of allowed attributes and values is predefined. The score is assigned according to the coverage of the current annotation. As an example, assuming that only 4 attributes can be expressed, the process in Fig. 3 has a Step 1 score of 100% since all the attributes are defined for all the components. The Step 2 process representation is enriched with the information about the optional tasks. This can be implemented enriching the BPMN notation with an additional type of task represented with an internal dashed border, indicating that the execution of a component is optional. For instance, in the flight booking application, the *Weather Information* and the *Rental Car Booking* microservices are indicated as optional, as shown in Fig. 3. This is because they don't affect the reach of the final goal of the process (booking a flight) even if their execution improves the QoE providing the customer with additional information and functionalities. In case these functionalities are provided by third parties, skipping their execution might reduce the income for the organization. As an example, the flight booking service might have an agreement with the rental car company consisting in a percentage gain of the overall rental contracts stipulated through the booking service. Skipping this task results in the lost of the possible revenue originated by a car rental. This step is not associated with a refined score, since it is not possible for anyone to know which are the necessary steps of the process but for the owner of the process. At Step 3, the process is enriched with alternative execution modalities. It is represented enriching the BPMN notation with a type identifier for the task representing the call to the component in the orchestrator. As an example, in Fig. 3 the *Flight Search* microservice is identified as a component with alternative execution modes. In the example, five microservices are involved but only one has been refined with the alternative versions (both low power and performance enhanced). Thus, the score will be 20%.

6.2   Designing Sustainable Workflows

In order to exploit the features provided by SADP and enable the different execution modalities introduced in Sect. 5, the process model is enriched with

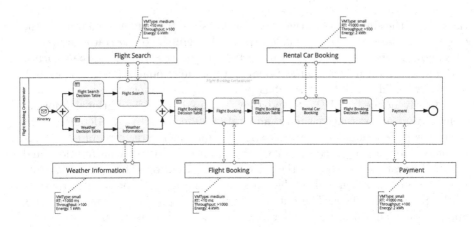

Fig. 4. Flight Booking workflow orchestrator model

business rules. Business rules enable to express conditions on the execution of an activity in a business process. They hide the complexity of the logic preventing the model to become too complex. In this case, business rules are included to define the execution modality of each task according to the values of a set of contextual variables collected by the monitoring system of the application and each of its microservices. Each business rule is linked to a DMN model [29], which makes explicit the involved variables and the decision tables containing the business rules used in the process. A decision table contains rules in the form if-then, where the condition is based on the value of the contextual variables. An example for the Flight Booking application is shown in Fig. 4. Each component is preceded by a business rule, linked to a DMN model, defining the modality of execution for the following microservice. Examples of business rules are:

– *Rental Car Booking*: if `response_time > 1000 ms then skip`;
– *Flight Search*: if `power > 5 kW then low-power execution`.

These are very simple rules, but a general rule can combine different variables and more complex reasoning. As an example, rules can be derived from a goal-oriented decision model where the different non-functional requirements of the service provider (goals) are mapped and linked to effective design actions. An attempt in integrating goal-oriented models and DMNs has been discussed in [15]. Using a more complex way to express requirements enable complex reasoning and the management of trade-off situations. However, this paper demonstrated that the logic behind the execution modality can be included in the application design.

Business rules will depend on the workflow modality enactment approach. In the case of the **All in** approach, an execution modality is selected at the process level, thus a single DMN model is referred by the business rules for establishing if the normal, basic, low-power, or high-performance execution should be enacted. For instance, in case of poor energy efficiency, the low power execution and the basic execution modalities can be selected, resulting in the execution of the *Flight Search* microservice in low power mode and in the skipping of both the *Weather Information* and the *Rental Car Booking* microservices. On the contrary, in the case of **Optimized execution** a custom modality will be selected for each microservice, thus requiring more complex DMN models.

6.3   Feasibility and Open Challenges

In the previous sections, the proposed approach has been validated by demonstrating that modeling tools are available to capture all the features introduced in the proposed methodology. We will now look at how these features can be supported in the cloud native ecosystem. The outcome of the design step will be an annotated and enriched BPMN model containing all the relevant information for the management of sustainability-aware applications. BPMN models can be translated in machine-readable formats like XML or JSON, including annotations and task types that will enrich the description of each task. It is thus possible to translate the model into a set of features that can be exploited by an orchestrator. As an example, a BPMN-driven microservice coordination approach is provided by some existing tools in the state of the art. For instance, Camunda[4] and Zeebee[5] are workflow engines supporting BPMN and DMN for designing workflow orchestrations. The other aspect is related to the management of dynamic execution modalities for microservices. The concept of alternative execution paths for microservices, activated according to the current context is supported by the state of the art technological stack. When a microservice of the pipeline experiences performance issues it can be replaced by a different one until the problem is not solved (fail-over management). Even if these approaches are traditionally related to the QoS management [3], their mechanism can be easily adapted to other goals such as sustainability.

SADP is based on the assumption that monitoring the energy consumption (and even better the CO_2 emissions) of each single component of an application is possible. At the moment this information is not provided by any cloud provider natively. However, several initiatives are proposing solutions for estimating both energy and emissions at the application level[6]. This shows a growing interest in the topic that is expected to result in additional improvement of existing third party tools and in the involvement of cloud providers in the process. Another critical aspect is the increased complexity in the application design, requiring to define several versions for each microservice. From a design perspective, the proposed approach is incremental, leaving the application owner the right to decide to what extent to refine the existing application model. The initial effort can be limited on the most affecting components and extended only in future

---

[4] Camunda: Microservices and BPMN: https://bit.ly/3pxYPbS.

[5] Zebee: A Workflow Engine for Microservices Orchestration: https://zeebe.io.

[6] Cloud Jewels: https://codeascraft.com/2020/04/23/cloud-jewels-estimating-kwh-in-the-cloud/ Cloud Carbon Footprint: https://www.cloudcarbonfootprint.org/ CodeCarbon: https://mlco2.github.io/codecarbon/visualize.html.

steps to other components. From a management perspective, costs will probably increase. Thus, the problem is how to motivate application providers to invest in sustainable applications. Existing studies have demonstrated how sustainability can become a strategic value for both organizations and their customers thanks to a proper awareness of the impact on the environment [32].

7 Conclusion

This paper introduced the SADP methodology to support the design of sustainable applications. SADP proposes an incremental process, defining levels of sustainability for application design and numerous enrichments that can be exploited to improve the application energy-efficiency while maintaining the QoS. The paper demonstrates how the proposed solution can be supported by existing tools and technologies. The SADP methodology is a first step towards energy-aware application management and aims at engaging application owners in the path towards sustainable IT. However, there are still several challenges to motivate application developers' effort to make their applications more sustainable, but we believe these benefits can compensate the additional costs and efforts in the long term. In future work we will provide a framework supporting SADP and implement a prototype exploiting all the introduced features for sustainable applications design and execution. We will also consider an additional step: how to optimize the deployment of microservices in a heterogeneous fog environment to minimize the energy footprint of applications at run-time.

References

1. Acton, M., et al.: 2018 best practice guidelines for the EU code of conduct on data centre energy efficiency. Technical report. EUR 29103 EN, 2018, Publications Office of the European Union, Luxembourg (2017)
2. Ajibola, O.O., El-Gorashi, T.E., Elmirghani, J.M.: Energy efficient placement of workloads in composable data center networks. J. Lightwave Technol. **39**(10), 3037–3063 (2021)
3. Aldwyan, Y., Sinnott, R.O.: Latency-aware failover strategies for containerized web applications in distributed clouds. FGCS **101**, 1081–1095 (2019)
4. Benoit, A., Lefevre, L.E.A.: Reducing the energy consumption of large-scale computing systems through combined shutdown policies with multiple constraints. Int. J. High Perform. Comput. Appl. **32**(1), 176–188 (2018)
5. vom Brocke, J., et al.: Green information systems: directives for the IS discipline. Commun. Assoc. Inf. Syst. **33**(1), 30 (2013)
6. Brondolin, R., et al.: DEEP-Mon: dynamic and energy efficient power monitoring for container-based infrastructures. In: IEEE International Parallel and Distributed Processing Symposium Workshops (IPDPSW), pp. 676–684, May 2018
7. Brondolin, R., Santambrogio, M.D.: A black-box monitoring approach to measure microservices runtime performance. ACM Trans. Arch. Code Optim. (TACO) **17**(4), 1–26 (2020)
8. Cappiello, C., Fugini, M., Ferreira, A.M., Plebani, P., Vitali, M.: Business process co-design for energy-aware adaptation. In: ICCP, pp. 463–470. IEEE (2011)

9. CNCF: Cloud Native Computing Foundation Annual Survey 2021. Technical report, CNCF, February 2022. https://www.cncf.io/wp-content/uploads/2022/02/CNCF-AR_FINAL-edits-15.2.21.pdf

10. Béziers la Fosse, T., Tisi, M., Mottu, J.M., Sunyé, G.: Annotating executable DSLs with energy estimation formulas. In: Proceedings of the 13th ACM SIGPLAN International Conference on Software Language Engineering, pp. 22–38 (2020)

11. Gannon, D., Barga, R., Sundaresan, N.: Cloud-native applications. IEEE Cloud Comput. **4**(5), 16–21 (2017)

12. Garrett-Peltier, H.: Green versus brown: comparing the employment impacts of energy efficiency, renewable energy, and fossil fuels using an input-output model. Econ. Model. **61**, 439–447 (2017)

13. Gholipour, N., et al.: A novel energy-aware resource management technique using joint VM and container consolidation approach for green computing in cloud data centers. Simul. Model. Pract. Theory **104**, 102127 (2020)

14. Goiri, Í., et al.: Parasol and greenswitch: managing datacenters powered by renewable energy. ACM SIGPLAN Not. **48**(4), 51–64 (2013)

15. Guizzardi, R.S., Perini, A.: Goal-oriented decision modeling: a position paper. In: iSTAR@ CAiSE (2018)

16. Hasić, F., De Smedt, J., et al.: Augmenting processes with decision intelligence: principles for integrated modelling. Decis. Support Syst. **107**, 1–12 (2018)

17. Horkoff, J., et al.: Goal-oriented requirements engineering: an extended systematic mapping study. Requirements Eng. **24**(2), 133–160 (2017). https://doi.org/10.1007/s00766-017-0280-z

18. Hu, X., Li, P., Sun, Y.: Minimizing energy cost for green data center by exploring heterogeneous energy resource. J. Mod. Power Syst. Clean Energy **9**(1), 148–159 (2021)

19. Knight, W.: AI can do great things - if it doesn't burn the planet. https://www.wired.com/story/ai-great-things-burn-planet (2020)

20. Kratzke, N., Quint, P.C.: Understanding cloud-native applications after 10 years of cloud computing-a systematic mapping study. J. Syst. Softw. **126**, 1–16 (2017)

21. Liu, Z., et al.: Renewable and cooling aware workload management for sustainable data centers. In: Proceedings of the 12th International Conference on Measurement and Modeling of Computer Systems, pp. 175–186 (2012)

22. Loos, P., Nebel, W., et al.: Green it: a matter of business and information systems engineering? Bus. Inf. Syst. Eng. **3**(4), 245–252 (2011)

23. Lottick, K., Susai, S., Friedler, S.A., Wilson, J.P.: Energy usage reports: environmental awareness as part of algorithmic accountability. arXiv:1911.08354 (2019)

24. Lucivero, F.: Big data, big waste? A reflection on the environmental sustainability of big data initiatives. Sci. Eng. Ethics **26**(2), 1009–1030 (2020)

25. Masanet, E., Shehabi, A., Lei, N., Smith, S., Koomey, J.: Recalibrating global data center energy-use estimates. Science **367**(6481), 984–986 (2020)

26. Neumann, J., Franke, S., Rockstroh, M., Kasparick, M., Neumuth, T.: Extending BPMN 2.0 for intraoperative workflow modeling with IEEE 11073 SDC for description and orchestration of interoperable, networked medical devices. Int. J. Comput. Assist. Radiol. Surg. **14**(8), 1403–1413 (2019). https://doi.org/10.1007/s11548-019-01982-6

27. Nowak, A., Binz, T., et al.: Pattern-driven green adaptation of process-based applications and their runtime infrastructure. Computing **94**(6), 463–487 (2012)

28. OMG: Business Process Model and Notation (BPMN), Version 2.0. Technical report, Object Management Group, January 2011. http://www.omg.org/spec/BPMN/2.0

29. OMG: Decision model and notation version 1.3. Technical report, OMG (2019)
30. Pedram, M.: Energy-efficient datacenters. IEEE Trans. Comput. Aided Des. Integr. Circuits Syst. **31**(10), 1465–1484 (2012)
31. Pierson, J.M., Baudic, G., et al.: Datazero: datacenter with zero emission and robust management using renewable energy. IEEE Access **7**, 103209–103230 (2019)
32. Schneider, J., Basalla, M., Seidel, S.: Principles of green data mining. In: Proceedings of the 52nd Hawaii International Conference on System Sciences (2019)
33. Singh, H., et al.: Data center maturity model. Techn. Ber, The Green Grid (2011)
34. Stavrinides, G.L., Karatza, H.D.: An energy-efficient, QoS-aware and cost-effective scheduling approach for real-time workflow applications in cloud computing systems utilizing DVFS and approximate computations. FGCS **96**, 216–226 (2019)
35. Thi, M.T., Pierson, J.M., Da Costa, G.: Game-based negotiation between power demand and supply in green datacenters. In: 18th International Symposium on Parallel and Distributed Processing with Applications (ISPA 2020) (2020)
36. Valderas, P.e.a.: A microservice composition approach based on the choreography of BPMN fragments. Inf. Softw. Technol. **127**, 106370 (2020)
37. Valera, H., Dalmau, M., et al.: DRACeo: a smart simulator to deploy energy saving methods in microservices based networks. In: IEEE International Conference on Enabling Technologies: Infrastructure for Collaborative Enterprises, pp. 94–99 (2020)
38. Vitali, M., Pernici, B.: A survey on energy efficiency in information systems. Int. J. Cooper. Inf. Syst. (IJCIS) **23**(03) (2014)
39. Vitali, M., et al.: Learning a goal-oriented model for energy efficient adaptive applications in data centers. Inf. Sci. **319**, 152–170 (2015)
40. Wajid, U., et al.: On achieving energy efficiency and reducing CO_2 footprint in cloud computing. IEEE Trans. Cloud Comput. **4**(2), 138–151 (2015)
41. Yuventi, J., Mehdizadeh, R.: A critical analysis of power usage effectiveness and its use in communicating data center energy consumption. Energy Build. **64**, 90–94 (2013)

Towards Explainable Artificial Intelligence in Financial Fraud Detection: Using Shapley Additive Explanations to Explore Feature Importance

Philipp Fukas[1,2,3](✉) [ID], Jonas Rebstadt[2,3] [ID], Lukas Menzel[1], and Oliver Thomas[1,2]

[1] Osnabrück University, Osnabrück, Lower Saxony, Germany
{philipp.fukas,lumenzel,oliver.thomas}@uni-osnabrueck.de
[2] German Research Center for Artificial Intelligence, Osnabrück, Lower Saxony, Germany
{philipp.fukas,jonas.rebstadt,oliver.thomas}@dfki.de
[3] Strategion GmbH, Osnabrück, Lower Saxony, Germany
{philipp.fukas,jonas.rebstadt}@strategion.de

Abstract. As the number of organizations and their complexity have increased, a tremendous amount of manual effort has to be invested to detect financial fraud. Therefore, powerful machine learning methods have become a critical factor to reduce the workload of financial auditors. However, as most machine learning models have become increasingly complex over the years, a significant need for transparency of artificial intelligence systems in the accounting domain has emerged. In this paper, we propose a novel approach using Shapley additive explanations to improve the transparency of models in the field of financial fraud detection. Our information systems engineering procedure follows the cross industry standard process for data mining including a systematic literature review of machine learning methods in fraud detection, a systematic development process and an explainable artificial intelligence analysis. By training a downstream Logistic Regression, Support Vector Machine and eXtreme Gradient Boosting classifier on a dataset of publicly traded companies convicted of financial statement fraud by the United States Securities and Exchange Commission, we show how the key items for financial statement fraud detection and their directionality can be identified using Shapley additive explanations. Finally, we contribute to the current state of research with this work by increasing model transparency and by generating insights on important financial statement fraud detection variables.

Keywords: Machine learning · Fraud detection · Financial auditing · Explainable artificial intelligence · Shapley additive explanations

1 Introduction

Fraud detection has been extensively studied in academia and practice in the past, but successfully identifying fraudulent firms remains a complex task. Since financial fraud techniques are evolving and becoming more international, detecting fraud has become a

© Springer Nature Switzerland AG 2022
X. Franch et al. (Eds.): CAiSE 2022, LNCS 13295, pp. 109–126, 2022.
https://doi.org/10.1007/978-3-031-07472-1_7

difficult task making the battle against it more crucial than ever [1]. Traditionally, external auditors have been in charge of detecting financial statement fraud. As the number of organizations as well as their complexity has grown and powerful machine learning (ML) methods became available, ML became paramount in trying to reduce the auditors' workload and to increase the audit quality [2–4]. But despite these potentials, auditing still lags behind other industries regarding the application of artificial intelligence (AI) [4, 5]. One reason for this are the uncertainties of the strict regulations and laws, which limit the use of AI without explicitly regulating the adoption of it [5]. In this context, the need for transparency and documentation of the decision-making process is a major aspect [6, 7]. To address this aspect, the development of transparent models and the integration of post-hoc explanatory methods is crucial for the adoption and diffusion of AI and ML in auditing. Due to this, ML-based fraud detection and its explanatory approaches are a broad area of research both regarding the fraud types and the methods for its detection. Recently, new approaches like Shapley Additive Explanations (SHAP) have already led to promising results for various types of fraud such as electrical energy consumption fraud [8], property insurance fraud [9] and credit card fraud [10]. However, there is a research gap regarding explainable ML models and the use of new approaches like SHAP in the specific area of financial statement fraud detection. With this paper, we fill this gap by presenting one of the first publicly available, technical studies on explainable AI (XAI) in financial fraud detection as well as by applying SHAP values for financial statement fraud detection for the first time. Therefore, this paper addresses the following two research questions (RQ):

RQ1: How is machine learning used in the current scientific literature to detect financial fraud?

RQ2: How can Shapley additive explanations foster the understanding of machine learning-based financial fraud detection?

To address RQ1, a systematic literature review (SLR) to portray the current state of research regarding the financial fraud types covered and the methods used for its detection is conducted. This results in a 3-dimension (author(s), fraud type, ML-method) Webster-Watson matrix [11] to summarize the current state of research (cf. Sect. 4.1). Based on the results to RQ1 and in preparation to answer RQ2, three major ML models inspired by Cecchini et al. [12], Dechow et al. [13] and Bao et al. [14] were implemented, benchmarked and ranked using the same dataset (cf. Sect. 4.1). Finally, we applied SHAP to the best performing model to answer RQ2 (cf. Sect. 4.2).

2 Artificial Intelligence in Fraud Detection and Its Need for Transparency

2.1 Financial Fraud Detection

Fraud is a complex and ambiguous topic both in behavioral and legal sciences without broad consensus upon a single definition [15, 16]. While there are many types and contexts for fraud such as customs-, subscription- or auction fraud [17], financial fraud is best described as deliberate falsification or manipulation of financial data [18]. This information is critical for financial market transactions, where the present and future value of the traded intangible rights is determined by the performance of the issuer in the future [19]. In order to assess the future performance of a firm or the credit risk in case of mortgages, accurate information is fundamental. To facilitate information disclosure between both parties and to establish information integrity, state authorities issue rules in the realm of regulatory rules, statutory, civil as well as criminal laws and their accompanying sanctions [15]. One of the foundations of such regulation are disclosure requirements [20, 21]. These requirements enforce the disclosure of all relevant information for assessment to the public in a timely manner and with equal access to all market participants. To achieve a high level of reliability and to strengthen the confidence of the addressees in the published financial information, external auditors have the responsibility to ensure that the information on which a company's financial statements are based has been provided correctly in accordance with the relevant legal regulations [22]. In total, there are numerous types of financial fraud ranging from credit card fraud to insurance fraud. To understand the variability of financial fraud, we selected the following fraud types according to the list provided by the Federal Bureau of Investigation (FBI) and previous literature applying similar classification frameworks [23–26]. The classification framework consists of two layers, category and type. Category groups of similar fraud types are based on the context or setting they generally occur in such as banking, corporate or insurance. The type layer provides a more granular description of the fraud types (cf. Fig. 1).

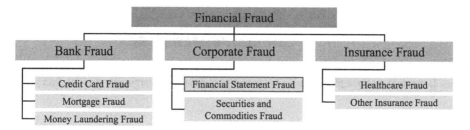

Fig. 1. Classification of financial fraud types [24].

As the literature on XAI in financial fraud detection is still immature, the SLR to answer RQ1 considers all of the previous types of financial fraud whereas the further focus to answer RQ2 lies only on financial statement fraud.

2.2 Explainable Artificial Intelligence with Shapley Additive Explanations

Transparency is an important issue for the implementation of AI-based information systems (IS) in the auditing domain and thus also for the automatic detection of fraud cases [6, 7]. Similar to the term AI, the definition and use of the terms transparency, interpretability or explainability is highly inconsistent [27–30]. In this publication, we follow the definition of transparency as a superordinate term as characterized by the European

Union (EU) [31], the specification of interpretability as inherently understandable models and explainability as post-hoc explanation of black box models as proposed by Rudin [29]. One approach in this field that has become increasingly prominent in recent years as theoretically well-founded model agnostic explanation method are Shapley Additive Explanations (SHAP). SHAP was first introduced in 2017 by Lundberg and Lee [32] as a form of model explanation and is based on Shapley values which were invented by Lloyd S. Shapley [33] in 1953 to find an optimal and fair distribution of rewards in a collaborative game. The SHAP method explains the prediction of an instance by calculating the marginal contribution of each feature to the prediction. Accordingly, Shapley values represent estimates of a feature's importance (magnitude of contribution) as well as the direction (e.g. positive or negative impact on the predicted label). For a detailed description of the computation of SHAP values please refer to Lundberg and Lee [32] as well as to Shapley [33]. In the context of fraud detection, a positive SHAP value increases the probability for a firm to be predicted fraudulent while a negative SHAP value decreases it. If a feature has a SHAP value of 0 it means that it did not influence the model at all. The absolute value describes the overall contribution of a feature. By taking the absolute value, the model's prediction can be explained by calculating the impact of each feature's value on the output. SHAP values and other game theoretic approaches can be used for AI algorithms as post-hoc method or as optimization criteria in human-in-the-loop approaches [34]. There are several possibilities to visualize these interrelations, but one of the most prominent is the force plot as motivated by Lundberg, Erion and Lee [35]. As shown in Fig. 2, these plots can show how each variable decreases or increases the predicted fraud probability.

Fig. 2. Exemplary force plot of single prediction of our machine learning models (cf. Sect. 4).

3   Information Systems Engineering Approach

IS engineering deals with the design, development, testing and maintenance of IS [36]. To develop AI-based IS, the cross-industry standard process for data mining (CRISP-DM) is often used [37]. Since in addition to software development, the deployment and maintenance are of particular importance in IS engineering, new challenges for AI-based IS arise. Especially the explainability of ML models in domains like financial auditing requires novel approaches [6, 7]. Only when the developed AI application meets the requirements for explainability the *line of governance*, which symbolizes the transition to operational use, can be overcome [38]. Thus, we extend the known CRISP-DM with a novel XAI analysis in our overall research approach: *(1) Business Understanding* with a SLR, *(2) Data Understanding* to calculate the descriptive statistics about the dataset such as fraud percentage each year, the description and box plots for each variable showing mean, minimum and maximum values as well as the inter variable correlation, the *(3) Data Preparation*, the *(4) Modeling* describing which models will be constructed and which hyperparameters will be tuned and the final *(5) Evaluation* of the results together with a SHAP analysis (cf. Fig. 3).

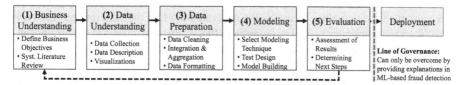

Fig. 3. Research approach based on CRISP-DM [37] and Thomas et al. [38].

First, the *(1) Business Understanding* phase is conducted. This phase consists of determining the business objectives, assessing the situation and defining the data mining goals. For a research project, the business objectives can be additionally seen as the (scientific) motivation for the underlying topic. Therefore, we extend the business understanding by an extensive SLR since the focus of this work lies on scientific goals in addition to the business objectives. The general approach to the SLR follows the guidelines by vom Brocke et al. [39], Kitchenham and Charters [40] as well as Webster and Watson [11]. First, the search terms must be constructed. According to RQ1, the focus lies on the use of AI or ML for fraud detection. Therefore, two general search brackets were connected. The first part focuses on the technology and includes words such as "Artificial Intelligence" or "Machine Learning" while the second part focuses on the application domain with words such as "Financial Fraud Detection", "Audit" or "Financial Statement Fraud". A total of seven search terms were constructed to identify relevant studies. The databases Wiley, AISeL, SpringerLink, Emerald, Web of Knowledge and Ebscohost were used to gather the relevant literature with the seven search phrases. Furthermore, a search on Google Scholar was also conducted to perform a basic search on all the missing scientific databases. These databases were chosen because they cover most of the important journals and conferences. Due to their search algorithms, Google Scholar and SpringerLink led to a lot of search hits of descending quality. For these searches, the scanning was limited to the first 20 results pages. The search results are screened based on their language, title, keywords and abstract. Then, the remaining inclusion and exclusion criteria were applied to the results especially focusing on a practical contribution to the field. The initial overall hits of 96545 were reduced to 65 after the initial screening based on the title. After the application of the other criteria, a total of 53 studies were included into the analysis and the literature matrix. As the second step of our overall software engineering approach in the *(2) Data Understanding* phase, all data is collected and briefly described including its format, quantity like number of records and fields as well as the column identifiers. Querying, visualization and reporting techniques are applied to answer data mining questions. These include the distribution of key attributes, results of simple aggregations and simple statistical analyses. During the *(3) Data Preparation* the data is selected, cleaned, constructed, integrated and formatted. The data is first selected upon criteria like relevance to the data mining goals, quality and technical constraints. Data cleaning methods aim to raise the data quality upon matching data analysis requirements. The *(4) Modeling* phase includes selecting a modeling technique, generating a test design, building the model and assessing its performance. First, a specific modeling technique appropriate for the data is selected and all modeling assumptions about the data are recorded. Before the actual model training, a test design is selected, which includes the exact separation of test and training set(s) and the error rates to measure the model quality. To assess the generated models, they are ranked based on the accuracy measurement as well as regarding other evaluation criteria that were chosen beforehand. The last phase in our prototyping approach is the *(5) Evaluation*, review and determination of the next steps. The evaluation assesses the results against business and academic success criteria and determines whether the project meets the initial business and academic objectives.

4   Results: An Explainable Financial Fraud Detection Pipeline

4.1   Developing Machine Learning Models for Financial Fraud Detection

(1) Business Understanding. The literature overview in Table 1 is grouped by the specific fraud types described in Sect. 2.1 that the papers address. Afterward, the central results of the SLR are briefly described and concluded with the (business) goals of our IS engineering approach.

Table 1. Condensed concept matrix of the systematic literature review.

Fraud type	Machine learning methods (hits)	Total hits	Reference publications
Credit card fraud	Artificial immune systems (3), Bayesian belief network (2), Decision forests (4), Genetic algorithms and programming (1), Logistic regression model (2), Neural network (6), Support vector machine (4), Self-organizing map (3), Hybrid methods (3)	21	[41–43]
Financial statement fraud	Bayesian belief network (3), Decision forests (10), Genetic Algorithms and programming (2), Logistic regression model (7), Neural network (9), Support vector machine (9), Text mining/Natural language processing (2), Hybrid methods (8)	25	[12–14]
Insurance fraud	Logistic Regression Model (3), Process Mining (1), Hybrid Methods (1)	5	[44–47]
Money laundering	Bayesian belief network (1), Decision forests (3), Logistic regression model (1), Neural network (3), Support vector machine (1), Text mining/Natural language processing (1)	6	[48–50]

(continued)

Table 1. (*continued*)

Fraud type	Machine learning methods (hits)	Total hits	Reference publications
Mortgage fraud	Decision forest (1), Support vector machine (1), Hybrid methods (1)	2	[51, 52]
Securities & commodities fraud	Text mining/Natural Language processing (1), Hybrid methods (2)	3	[53–55]

According to our results, credit card fraud and financial statement fraud are the most researched fraud types in combination with ML methods in recent years. Moreover, the variety of applied ML methods to different types of fraud is huge and does not follow a clear pattern. Methods, that are interpretable by design like Logistic Regression (logit) models are used as well as black box methods like decision forests and neural networks. But in recent years, the latter seems to gain higher interest in research as there are more and more publications examining black box models in the financial fraud detection domain. Although there is a clear need for transparency in financial fraud detection, only a few approaches already laid their research focus on this topic. For instance, SHAP values were already successfully applied in credit card fraud detection [10]. But regarding financial statement fraud, no research addressed the use of SHAP to explain automatic fraud detection algorithms yet. Therefore, this research is based on previous results in the field of ML-based financial statement fraud detection by applying similar models like Bao et al. [14], Cecchini et al. [12] and Dechow et al. [13] and extending their analysis by an XAI approach with SHAP. Finally, we define our (business) objectives as follows: First, an equal or a higher AUC than previously developed models by Bao et al. [14] and the earlier benchmarks by Dechow et al. [13] and Cecchini et al. [12] should be achieved. Second, the model should be transparent to some degree yielding insights into which variables are important for the classification.

(2) Data Understanding. The dataset for our financial statement fraud detection pipeline is provided by Bao et al. [14]. It covers all publicly listed companies in the United States (U.S.) during the period 1990–2014 and was downloaded from GitHub on 01.03.2021[1]. The full sample by Bao et al. [14] includes data from 1979–2014. The data before 1990, even though it is available, is omitted because of a significant shift in U.S. firms' fraudulent behavior as well as the type of Securities and Exchange Commission (SEC) enforcement starting in that timeframe. The sample period from 2009–2014 will be also omitted because on the one hand, this replicates the approach by Bao et al. [14] and ensures that the findings of this work can be benchmarked against their results and on the other hand, there is a noticeable change in the enforcement of accounting fraud

---

[1] https://github.com/JarFraud/FraudDetection.

by the regulators that roughly coincided with the 2008 financial crisis. The fraud sample features data from the SEC's Accounting and Auditing Enforcement Releases (AAER), was initially provided by the University of California-Berkeley Centre for Financial Reporting and Management (CFRM) and was finally assembled by Bao et al. [14]. The CFRM database offers an accurate identification of all fraud cases [56]. While there are several more similar databases about financial statement fraud such as the Audit Analytics (AA) or Government Accountability Office's (GAO) database, the CFRM offers the most comprehensive list, albeit not being the fastest database to include a fraud case after the start of an initial investigation [56]. Furthermore, the use of the AAER database enables the interpretation of the results against two more comprehensive studies by Cecchini et al. [12] and Dechow et al. [13]. Both studies utilize the CFRM database. In total, 28 raw data variables of the dataset are used, which were also used in previous fraud detection studies. The variables range from balance sheet items such as receivables or long-term debt to market value items like common shares outstanding (cf. Table 4). Moreover, we followed Bao et al. [14] and Dechow et al. [13] by including constructed financial ratios based on the raw data variables. With three more financial ratios based on other literature in addition to the dataset by Bao et al. [14] we finally obtained 14 additional financial ratios [57, 58]. For a detailed description of the computation of the ratios please refer to Dechow et al. [13].

(3) Data Preparation. During the data preparation phase, the final dataset is constructed by selecting, cleaning, constructing, integrating and formatting the available data. All the necessary steps of the data preparation were conducted by Bao et al. [14]. They selected the 1990–2014 timeframe for their dataset and chose the variables based on previous works. After constructing the previously described 14 financial ratios in addition to the 28 raw variables, items that had more than 25% of their values missing were omitted from the dataset. For a detailed description of the data preparation steps please refer to Bao et al. [14] and their corresponding GitHub repository.

(4) Modeling. The model construction is based on the programming language Python and is utilizing several standardized packages for fast and reproducible results. To compare the results to the benchmarks set by Bao et al. [14], Cecchini et al. [12] and Dechow et al. [13], several models are constructed to mimic their approaches on the available dataset. The Dechow et al. [13] model is replicated by using a logistic regression algorithm on multiple subsets of the data. The model is trained on 14 financial ratios, 28 raw variables and the full set of 42 variables. Not only can the model then be compared to other algorithms, but it can also be determined if adding additional variables improves the performance of the classifier. Cecchini et al. [12] developed a novel SVM method with a financial kernel, in short to be referred to as SVM-FK. Compared to a traditional SVM, the SVM-FK is based on a financial kernel that maps raw financial data to a set of predefined ratios. Instead of the specific SVM-FK, we used a standard *scikit-learn* SVM implementation. Therefore, the results are not completely comparable to the work by Cecchini et al. [12]. Cecchini et al. [12] only used a set of raw variables, so this method is only trained on a dataset of 28 raw variables. Bao et al. [14] evolved the field by applying the RUSBoost algorithm to the problem space and advancing on the previous approaches by Dechow et al. [13] and Cecchini et al. [12]. The RUSBoost algorithm is a variant of AdaBoost and uses random undersampling (RUS) to address the problem of class imbalance [59]. This approach is replicated by using the XGBoost algorithm, a newer and more powerful ensemble learning method that might outperform the RUS-Boost algorithm. XGBoost, developed in 2015, is one of the best performing algorithms for structured data and is widely used in academia and industry [60]. Furthermore, it has the advantage of being relatively computationally efficient as well as accurate and it can handle missing values efficiently [60]. The RUSBoost model by Bao et al. [14] will act as the primary benchmark model. The Support Vector Machine (SVM) and the logit models were implemented by using the corresponding classes of the *scikit-learn* package whereas the eXtreme Gradient Boosting (XGBoost) model was implemented by using the *XGBoost* package. Please refer to the official *scikit-learn* [61] and *XGBoost* [60] documentation as a guide for reproducibility. The training period is 1991–2001, while the testing period is 2003–2008. Hyperparameters are tuned using GridSearchCV of the *scikit-learn* package with 3-fold cross-validation on a holdout validation set from 2001–2002 (cf. Table 2).

Table 2. XGboost hyperparameter grid.

Hyperparameter	Values	Best value
Learning rate	0.001; 0.01; 0.1; 0.2; 0.8	0.1
Minimum child weight	1; 5; 10	1
Subsample	0.6; 0.8; 1.0	0.8
Colsample bytree	0.6; 0.8; 1.0	0.6
Max depth	3; 4; 5	4
Number of estimators	50; 100; 150; 200	150

(5) Evaluation. After constructing, optimizing and testing all models, the models' out-of-sample classification performance is compared (cf. Table 3). The reported results refer to the previously described dataset averaged on the test years 2003–2008. The evaluation metrics area under the receiver operator curve (AUC) [62], normalized discounter cumulative gain at position k (NDCG@k) [63], recall and precision are reported. All evaluation metrics were also implemented for better reproducibility with the *scikit-learn* package [61]. For a detailed description of the computation of the metrics please refer to Metz [62] as well as Järvelin and Kekäläinen [63].

Table 3. Out-of-sample performance metrics of the baseline models on the 2003–2008 test set.

Input variables	Method	Performance metrics on the test set 2003–2008			
		AUC	NDCG@k	Recall	Precision
14 financial ratios	Logit	0.685	0.036	3.83%	2.84%
28 raw variables	Logit	0.689	0.025	2.68%	1.99%
	SVM	0.443	0.046	4.98%	3.69%
	XGBoost	0.761	0.050	5.36%	3.98%
28 raw variables and 14 financial ratios	Logit	0.695	0.025	2.68%	1.99%
	XGBoost	0.735	0.043	4.60%	3.41%

With exception of the SVM model trained on the 28 raw variables all models have an AUC higher than 0.50, which can be achieved by random guessing. The AUC for random guesses is represented by the straight dashed line in Fig. 4. Please note that the individual models are denoted as logit-14 for the replication Dechow et al [13] trained on a subset of 14 financial ratios, SVM-28 for the replication of the Cecchini et al. [12] SVM-FK model trained on the 28 raw variables and XGB-28/XGB-42 as a replication of the Bao et al. [14] RUSBoost model. The models logit-28 and logit-42 are constructed for supplemental analysis, where the 42 is referring to the use of the full variable set of 14 ratios and 28 raw variables. The following XGBoost hyperparameters yielded the best performance on the testing set with 28 raw variables: *learning rate* $= 0.1$, *minimum child weight* $= 1$, *subsample* $= 0.8$, *colsample bytree* $= 0.6$, *max depth* $= 4$ and *number of estimators* $= 150$ (cf. Table 2 and Table 3).

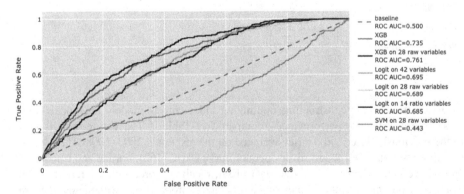

Fig. 4. Receiver operating characteristic curves of the different machine learning models.

4.2 Explaining Machine Learning Models by Shapley Additive Explanations

The best performing classifier XGBoost suffers like many ML algorithms from a lack of transparency regarding the inner workings of its model. Some classifiers such as decision trees can be interpreted by visualizing the tree structure. This makes it easier to understand why a decision tree model made a particular decision by simply following the tree structure. Ensemble learning models like XGBoost though consist of hundreds of individual trees and thus cannot be understood by simply looking at the tree structure.

Table 4. Average impact of the 28 raw data items in the XGBoost-28 model.

#	Item	SHAP value	Item category	References
1	Property, plant and equipment, total	0.515	Balance sheet	[12–14, 57]
2	Price close, annual, fiscal	0.374	Market value	[12–14]
3	Sales of common preferred stock	0.360	Cash flow statement	[13, 14]
4	Receivables, total	0.221	Balance sheet	[12–14, 57]
5	Debt in current liabilities, total	0.195	Balance sheet	[12–14, 57]
6	Depreciation and amortization	0.182	Income statement	[12–14, 57]
7	Long-term debt issuance	0.181	Cash flow statement	[13, 14]
8	Inventories, total	0.171	Balance sheet	[12–14]
9	Current assets, total	0.168	Balance sheet	[12–14, 58]
10	Retained earnings	0.160	Balance sheet	[12, 14]
11	Common shares outstanding	0.145	Market value	[12–14]
12	Common/ordinary equity	0.139	Balance sheet	[12–14]
13	Accounts payable, trade	0.124	Balance sheet	[13, 14]
14	Short-term investments, total	0.105	Balance sheet	[12–14]
15	Cash and short-term investments	0.104	Balance sheet	[12–14, 57]
16	Costs of goods sold	0.099	Income statement	[12–14, 57]
17	Current liabilities, total	0.090	Balance sheet	[12–14, 57]
18	Liabilities, total	0.090	Balance sheet	[12–14, 58]
19	Assets, total	0.089	Balance sheet	[12–14, 58]
20	Sales/turnover, net	0.087	Income statement	[12–14, 58]
21	Income before extraordinary items	0.084	Income statement	[12–14]
22	Investments and advances, total	0.068	Balance sheet	[12–14]
23	Income taxes payable	0.063	Balance sheet	[12–14, 58]
24	Preferred/preference stock (capital)	0.061	Balance sheet	[12–14]

(*continued*)

Table 4. (*continued*)

#	Item	SHAP value	Item category	References
25	Interest and related expense, total	0.057	Income statement	[12, 14, 58]
26	Income taxes, total	0.050	Income statement	[12, 14, 58]
27	Long-term debt, total	0.049	Balance sheet	[12–14, 57]
28	Net income (loss)	0.045	Income statement	[12, 14]

As explained in Sect. 2.2 the concept of SHAP can be used to explain any machine learning model's output. The SHAP values in Table 4 are calculated for the best performing model, namely the XGBoost model trained on 28 raw financial variables. The calculation of the SHAP values was implemented with the *shap* package for the programming language Python. Please refer to the official *shap* documentation as a guide for reproducibility [32]. Table 4 lists the 28 items, their item category and other references that have used the variable in previous fraud detection studies sorted from high to low based on the mean of the absolute SHAP value. The related variable categories do not show a distinct pattern in whether a particular category is more important for the model's prediction. All categories are represented in the top 10 variables with the highest average impact on the model's prediction. Nonetheless, both cash flow statement items and one out of two (with *common shares outstanding* also ranking 11th) market value items are found in the top 10. This indicates that items with special importance to the public such as the *common shares outstanding* or *sales of common preferred stock* may be of high importance for the prediction of accounting fraud.

Given that Bao et al. [14] performed a similar feature importance analysis with a similar machine learning algorithm on the same dataset it is important to check whether our results significantly differ from theirs. Albeit using a different method for calculating the feature importance, six variables in the top ten of most important features are also found in the top ten variables by Bao et al. [14]. The six common variables in the top ten are: *(1) Property, plant and equipment, total, (2) Price close, annual, fiscal, (3) Sales of common preferred stock, (4) Inventories, total, (5) Current assets, total* and *(6) Retained earnings.* This demonstrates a high validity of the trained machine learning model and with the similarity of the training approach, our SHAP analysis is comparable to the performance evaluation metrics of Bao et al. [14] with a percentage of 60% within the top ten variables. While the mean absolute SHAP value gives a good overview of the ranking and the overall impact of each variable it does not cover an important aspect: The impact of a variable in dependence of its value. With other, previously applied methods for feature importance, one would not know, if for instance a high *sales of common preferred stock* leads to an increase or decrease in predicted fraud probability. To highlight the direction of these influences, the SHAP summary plot in Fig. 5 shows the impact of each variable depending on its feature values. The SHAP summary plot was also implemented with the *shap* package for better reproducibility [32]. The summary plot combines the feature importance with their corresponding effects. Each point in the summary plot is a SHAP value for the feature listed on the left side. The position on the

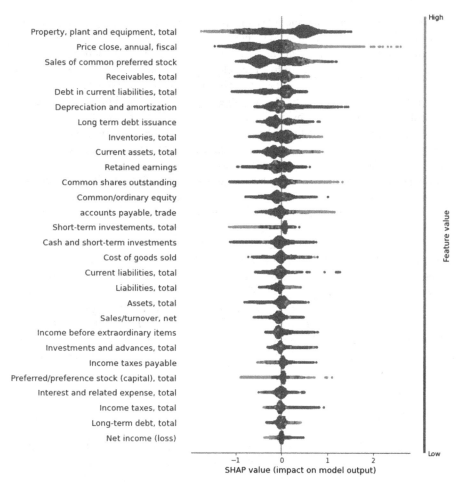

Fig. 5. SHAP summary plot of the 28 raw data items in the XGBoost-28 model.

x-axis is determined by the SHAP value as negative or positive impact on the feature. The color represents the value of the feature from low (blue) to high (red). Overlapping points are shifted slightly up or down, giving an impression of the distribution of SHAP values per feature. Again, the variables are ordered from high to low based on the mean SHAP impact value. Most variables show a significant difference between the impact of high and low feature values indicating that there is indeed a significant difference in feature values between misstating and non-misstating firms. For the most important variable *property, plant and equipment, total* a high feature value significantly lowers the predicted fraud probability whereas a low feature value raises the probability. This is in line with preceding works regarding the influence of investments and earnings management on accounting fraud. Kedia and Philippon [64] have shown that in the years leading up to the restatement period a fraudulent firm has a higher investment growth rate than usual. Although the variable *property, plant and equipment* measures the total and not the growth, it makes economic sense that prior to the growth in property investment the total property is smaller compared to those of non-misstating firms. The second most important variable *price close, annual, fiscal* also has a clear distinction in its feature value between firms with a high or low predicted fraud probability: High closing prices significantly increase the probability for a firm to be predicted fraudulent while low closing prices cause the opposite. This variable presumably has a significant impact on the model's output because of insider trading before and during the misstatement period hoping to profit from inflated stock prices by company employees or other stakeholders [64–66]. The same reasoning also explains the influence of the variable *sales of common preferred stock* on the predicted fraud likelihood. Due to insider trading, the sales of common preferred stock are likely to be high in order to profit from inflated prices – a behavior also seen in the SHAP values, where high feature values increase the predicted probability for accounting fraud. High feature values of the variable *receivables* also raise the predicted likelihood for fraud, while low values decrease it. Interestingly, either very high or low feature values of the variable *debt in current liabilities* increase or decrease the fraud probability while values towards the center are more prevalent with firms predicted fraudulent. A similar behavior can also be found in the variable *depreciation and amortization*, even though it is rather skewed towards an increase in the predicted fraud likelihood whereas *debt in current liabilities* is skewed towards predicting non-fraudulent. High feature values for the variables *inventories, total* and *current assets, total* increase the predicted likelihood for fraud. As inventories typically are a part of current assets, it appears rational that both variables influence the XGBoost algorithm in the same way.

5   Conclusion

In this work, we addressed the topic of XAI in financial statement fraud detection. Our IS engineering approach has been split up into two parts starting with the identification and evaluation of approaches for machine learning in financial fraud detection based on the current state of the art in the literature to answer RQ1. We tested different variable and algorithm configurations and found that an XGBoost classifier trained on 28 raw financial variables yielded the best results. Due to the explicit need for a transparent design of algorithms used in auditing, SHAP values have been considered as model agnostic explanation approach for XGBoost to answer RQ2. With our work, we contribute to the current state of research by increasing model transparency as well as by generating insights on important financial statement fraud detection variables and their direction-ality. To this date, this study is one of the first with an XAI approach using SHAP to build an explainable machine learning model for financial fraud detection with feature importance. This method advances on a similar feature importance analysis done by Bao et al. [14] by not only yielding an overall feature importance but also the directionality of each variable. Furthermore, the top three variables are also found to be consistent with current fraud detection literature adding a better explainability by stating whether a particular low or high feature value increases or decreases the predicted fraud probability. As central interface between users and AI algorithms, the increased transparency plays a crucial role to overcome the *line of governance* in the development of AI applications and according to this, deploy the algorithms as part of complex IS. Using our insights, the gap between the development of prototypical AI algorithms and AI-based IS engineering can be tightened. In the next step, further research regarding the integration of SHAP values in audit-related ML systems may be promising.

References

1. Bouazza, I., Ameur, E.B., Ameur, F.: Datamining for fraud detecting, state of the art. In: Ezziyyani, M. (ed.) Advanced Intelligent Systems for Sustainable Development (AI2SD'2018), pp. 205–219. Springer, Cham (2018)
2. Kokina, J., Davenport, T.H.: The emergence of artificial intelligence: how automation is changing auditing. J. Emerg. Technol. Account. **14**, 115–122 (2017)
3. Downar, B., Fischer, D.: Wirtschaftsprüfung im Zeitalter der Digitalisierung. In: Obermaier, R. (ed.) Handbuch Industrie 4.0 und Digitale Transformation, pp. 753–779. Springer, Wiesbaden (2019). https://doi.org/10.1007/978-3-658-24576-4_32
4. Issa, H., Sun, T., Vasarhelyi, M.A.: Research ideas for artificial intelligence in auditing: the formalization of audit and workforce supplementation. J. Emerg. Technol. Account. **13**(2), 1–20 (2016)
5. Munoko, I., Brown-Liburd, H.L., Vasarhelyi, M.: The ethical implications of using artificial intelligence in auditing. J. Bus. Ethics **167**(2), 209–234 (2020). https://doi.org/10.1007/s10551-019-04407-1
6. Fukas, P., Rebstadt, J., Remark, F., Thomas, O.: Developing an artificial intelligence maturity model for auditing. In: ECIS 2021 Research Papers, 133 (2021)
7. Rebstadt, J., Remark, F., Fukas, P., Meier, P., Thomas, O.: Towards personalized explanations for AI systems: designing a role model for explainable AI in auditing. In: Wirtschaftsinformatik 2022 Proceedings, 2 (2022)
8. Santos, R.N., et al.: Gradient boosting and Shapley additive explanations for fraud detection in electricity distribution grids. Int. Trans. Electr. Energy Syst. **31**, e13046 (2021)
9. Severino, M.K., Peng, Y.: Machine learning algorithms for fraud prediction in property insurance: empirical evidence using real-world microdata. Mach. Learn. with Appl. **5**, 100074 (2021)
10. Psychoula, I., Gutmann, A., Mainali, P., Lee, S.H., Dunphy, P., Petitcolas, F.: Explainable machine learning for fraud detection. Computer **54**(10), 49–59 (2021)
11. Webster, J., Watson, R.T.: Analyzing the past to prepare for the future: writing a literature review. Manag. Inf. Syst. Q. **26**, xiii–xxiii (2002)
12. Cecchini, M., Aytug, H., Koehler, G.J., Pathak, P.: Detecting management fraud in public companies. Manag. Sci. **56**(7), 1146–1160 (2010)
13. Dechow, P.M., Ge, W., Larson, C.R., Sloan, R.G.: Predicting material accounting misstatements. Contemp. Account. Res. **28**(1), 17–82 (2011)
14. Bao, Y., Ke, B., Li, B., Yu, Y.J., Zhang, J.: Detecting accounting fraud in publicly traded U.S. firms using a machine learning approach. J. Account. Res. **58**(1), 199–235 (2020)
15. Reurink, A.: Financial fraud: a literature review. J. Econ. Surv. **32**(5), 1292–1325 (2018)
16. Green, S.P.: Lying, Cheating, and Stealing: A Moral Theory of White-Collar Crime. Oxford University Press, Oxford (2006)
17. Laleh, N., Azgomi, M.A.: A taxonomy of frauds and fraud detection techniques. In: Prasad, S.K., Routray, S., Khurana, R., Sahni, S. (eds.) Information Systems, Technology and Management, pp. 256–267. Springer, Berlin, Heidelberg (2009)
18. Fligstein, N., Roehrkasse, A.: All of the incentives were wrong: opportunism and the financial crisis. In: American Sociology Annual Meeting, New York (2013)

19. Lomnicka, E.: Investor protection in securities markets. In: Cane, P., Conaghan, J. (eds.) The New Oxford Companion to Law, pp. 40–65. Oxford University Press, Oxford (2008)

20. Selden, S.R.: (Self-)policing the market: congress's Flawed approach to securities law reform. J. Legis. **33**(1), 3 (2007)

21. Guttentag, M.: An argument for imposing disclosure requirements on public companies. Florida State Univ. Law Rev. **32**(1), 3 (2004)

22. ISA 200: ISA 200: Overall Objectives of the independent auditor and the conduct of an audit in accordance with international standards on auditing. In: International Federation of Accountants (IFAC) (ed.) International Standards on Auditing (ISAs). Institut der Wirtschaftsprüfer (IDW) Verlag GmbH, Düsseldorf (2009)

23. FBI: Financial Crimes Report to the Public (2012)

24. Barman, S., Mandal, P., Mahata, A., Biswas, B., Pal, U., Sarfaraj, M.A.: A complete literature review on financial fraud detection applying data mining techniques. Int. J. Trust Manag. Comput. Commun. **3**(4), 336–359 (2016)

25. Ngai, E.W.T., Hu, Y., Wong, Y.H., Chen, Y., Sun, X.: The application of data mining techniques in financial fraud detection: a classification framework and an academic review of literature. Decis. Support Syst. **50**(3), 559–569 (2011)

26. West, J., Bhattacharya, M.: Intelligent financial fraud detection: a comprehensive review. Comput. Secur. **57**, 47–66 (2016)

27. Lipton, Z.C.: The mythos of model interpretability. Commun. ACM. **61**(10), 36–43 (2018)

28. Tomsett, R., Braines, D., Harborne, D., Preece, A., Chakraborty, S.: Interpretable to whom? A role-based model for analyzing interpretable machine learning systems. arXiv (2018)

29. Rudin, C.: Stop explaining black box machine learning models for high stakes decisions and use interpretable models instead. Nat. Mach. Intell. **1**(5), 206–215 (2019)

30. Dhurandhar, A., Iyengar, V., Luss, R., Shanmugam, K.: TIP: typifying the interpretability of procedures. arXiv (2017)

31. European Commission: High-Level Expert Group on Artificial Intelligence: Ethics Guidelines for Trustworthy AI, Brüssel (2018)

32. Lundberg, S.M., Lee, S.-I.: A unified approach to interpreting model predictions. In: von Luxburg, U., Guyon, I., Bengio, S., Wallach, H., Fergus, R. (eds.) Proceedings of the 31st International Conference on Neural Information Processing Systems (NIPS 2017), pp. 4768–4777. Curran Associates Inc., Red Hook (2017)

33. Shapley, L.S.: A Value for N-Person Games. RAND Corporation, Santa Monica (1952)

34. Gianini, G., GhemmogneFossi, L., Mio, C., Caelen, O., Brunie, L., Damiani, E.: Managing a pool of rules for credit card fraud detection by a Game Theory based approach. Futur. Gener. Comput. Syst. **102**, 549–561 (2020)

35. Lundberg, S.M., Erion, G.G., Lee, S.-I.: Consistent individualized feature attribution for tree ensembles. arXiv (2018)

36. Wangler, B., Backlund, A.: Information systems engineering: what is it? In: Castro, J., Teniente, E. (eds.) CAiSE 2005 Workshops, pp. 427–437. FEUP Edições, Porto (2005)

37. Chapman, P., et al.: CRISP-DM 1.0 (2000)

38. Thomas, O., Bruckner, A., Leimkühler, M., Remark, F., Thomas, K.: Konzeption, Implementierung und Einführung von KI-Systemen in der Wirtschaftsprüfung. Die Wirtschaftsprüfung. **74**, 551–562 (2021)

39. vom Brocke, J., Niehaves, B., Simons, A., Riemer, K.: Reconstructing the giant : on the importance of rigour in documenting the literature search process. In: ECIS 2009 Proceedings, vol. 161 (2009)

40. Kitchenham, B.A., Charters, S.M.: Guidelines for performing systematic literature reviews in software engineering (2007)

41. Wong, N., Ray, P., Stephens, G., Lewis, L.: Artificial immune systems for the detection of credit card fraud: an architecture, prototype and preliminary results. Inf. Syst. J. **22**(1), 53–76 (2012)
42. Sahin, Y., Bulkan, S., Duman, E.: A cost-sensitive decision tree approach for fraud detection. Expert Syst. Appl. **40**(15), 5916–5923 (2013)
43. Fiore, U., De Santis, A., Perla, F., Zanetti, P., Palmieri, F.: Using generative adversarial networks for improving classification effectiveness in credit card fraud detection. Inf. Sci. **479**, 448–455 (2019)
44. Yang, W.S., Hwang, S.Y.: A process-mining framework for the detection of healthcare fraud and abuse. Expert Syst. Appl. **31**(1), 56–68 (2006)
45. Pinquet, J., Ayuso, M., Guillén, M.: Selection bias and auditing policies for insurance claims. J. Risk Insur. **74**(2), 425–440 (2007)
46. Bermúdez, L., Pérez, J.M., Ayuso, M., Gómez, E., Vázquez, F.J.: A Bayesian dichotomous model with asymmetric link for fraud in insurance. Insur. Math. Econ. **42**, 779–786 (2008)
47. Caudill, S.B., Ayuso, M., Guillen, M.: Fraud detection using a multinomal logit model with missing information. J. Risk Insur. **72**(4), 539–550 (2005)
48. Wang, S., Yang, J.: A money laundering risk evaluation method based on decision tree. In: International Conference on Machine Learning and Cybernetics, pp. 283–286 (2007)
49. Le Khac, N.A., Markos, S., Kechadi, M.T.: A data mining-based solution for detecting suspicious money laundering cases in an investment bank. In: 2010 Second International Conference on Advances in Databases, Knowledge, and Data Applications, pp. 235–240 (2010)
50. Larik, A.S., Haider, S.: Clustering based anomalous transaction reporting. Procedia Comput. Sci. **3**, 606–610 (2011)
51. Zhan, Q., Yin, H.: A loan application fraud detection method based on knowledge graph and neural network. In: Guan, S.-U., Jiannong, C., Du, H., Huang, N.-F. (eds.) ICIAI 2018: Proceedings of the 2nd International Conference on Innovation in Artificial Intelligence, pp. 111–115. Association for Computing Machinery, New York (2018)
52. Błaszczyński, J., de Almeida Filho, A.T., Matuszyk, A., Szeląg, M., Słowiński, R.: Auto loan fraud detection using dominance-based rough set approach versus machine learning methods. Expert Syst. Appl. **163** (2021)
53. Holton, C.: Identifying disgruntled employee systems fraud risk through text mining: a simple solution for a multi-billion dollar problem. Decis. Support Syst. **46**, 853–864 (2009)
54. Jans, M., Van Der Werf, J., Lybaert, N., Vanhoof, K.: A business process mining application for internal transaction fraud mitigation. Expert Syst. Appl. **38**(10), 13351–13359 (2011)
55. Sarno, R., Dewandono, R., Tohari, A., Naufal, M., Sinaga, F.: Hybrid association rule learning and process mining for fraud detection. Int. J. Comput. Sci. **42**(2), 59–72 (2015)
56. Karpoff, J.M., Koester, A., Lee, D.S., Martin, G.S.: Proxies and databases in financial misconduct research. Account. Rev. **92**(6), 129–163 (2017)
57. Beneish, M.D.: The detection of earnings manipulation. Financ. Anal. J. **55**, 24–36 (1999)
58. Summers, S.L., Sweeney, J.T.: Fraudulently misstated financial statements and insider trading: an empirical analysis. Account. Rev. **73**(1), 131–146 (1998)
59. Seiffert, C., Khoshgoftaar, T., Van Hulse, J., Napolitano, A.: RUSBoost: a hybrid approach to alleviating class imbalance. Syst. Man Cy. Part A Syst. Hum. **40**, 185–197 (2010)
60. Chen, T., Guestrin, C.: XGBoost: a scalable tree boosting system. In: KDD 2016: Proceedings of the 22nd ACM SIGKDD International Conference on Knowledge Discovery and Data Mining, pp. 785–794. Association for Computing Machinery, New York (2016)
61. Pedregosa, F., et al.: Scikit-learn: machine learning in Python. J. Mach. Learn. Res. **12**, 2825–2830 (2011)
62. Metz, C.E.: Basic principles of ROC analysis. Semin. Nucl. Med. **8**(4), 283–298 (1978)

63. Järvelin, K., Kekäläinen, J.: Cumulated gain-based evaluation of IR techniques. ACM Trans. Inf. Syst. **20**(4), 422–446 (2002)
64. Kedia, S., Philippon, T.: The economics of fraudulent accounting. Rev. Financ. Stud. **22**(6), 2169–2199 (2009)
65. Agrawal, A., Cooper, T.: Insider trading before accounting scandals. J. Corp. Financ. **34**, 169–190 (2015)
66. Bartov, E., Mohanram, P.: Private information, earnings manipulations, and executive stock-option exercises. Account. Rev. **79**(4), 889–920 (2004)

Tools and Methods to Support Research and Design

Systematic Literature Review Search Query Refinement Pipeline: Incremental Enrichment and Adaptation

Maisie Badami[1(✉)], Boualem Benatallah[1], and Marcos Baez[2]

[1] University of New South Wales (UNSW), Sydney, Australia
{m.badami,b.benatallah}@unsw.edu.au
[2] LIRIS - University of Claude Bernard Lyon 1, Villeurbanne, France
marcos.baez@liris.cnrs.fr

Abstract. Systematic literature reviews (SLRs) are at the heart of evidence-based research, collecting and integrating empirical evidence regarding specific research questions. A leading step in the search for relevant evidence is composing Boolean search queries, which are still at the core of how information retrieval systems work to perform an advanced literature search. Building these queries thus requires going from the general aims of the research questions into actionable search terms that are combined into potentially complex Boolean expressions. Researchers are thus tasked with the daunting and challenging task of building and refining search queries in their quest for sufficient coverage and proper representation of the literature. In this paper, we propose an adaptive Boolean query generation and refinement pipeline for SLR search. Our approach utilizes a reinforcement learning technique to learn the optimal modifications for a query based on the feedback collecting from the researchers about the query retrieval performance. Empirical evaluations with 10 SLR datasets showed our approach to achieve comparable performance to that of queries manually composed by SLR authors.

Keywords: Systematic reviews · Query enrichment · Query adaptation · Reinforcement learning · Word embedding

1 Introduction

Systematic literature reviews (SLRs) offer robust and transferable evidence for evaluating and interpreting relevant research on a topic of interest [13]. SLRs are used to set the foundation for future research, allowing researchers to formally plan and systematically collect and integrate available evidence in order to answer research questions [2]. Given their demonstrated value, SLRs are becoming a popular type of publication in empirical research domains such as evidence-based software engineering [13]. The identification of relevant studies is a fundamental step in the SLR process, as it can impact the overall *quality* and *workload* of the SLRs. This step is guided by the definition of research questions

© Springer Nature Switzerland AG 2022
X. Franch et al. (Eds.): CAiSE 2022, LNCS 13295, pp. 129–146, 2022.
https://doi.org/10.1007/978-3-031-07472-1_8

that set the tone and scope for the entire SLR [2,13]. Researchers are then tasked with capturing this scope in a search strategy that typically involves composing Boolean search queries for scientific digital libraries [13].

The ability of the search query to capture relevant works will determine whether the review has a proper representation of the literature for accurate synthesis of the literature downstream of the process [31]. It also greatly impact the workload as researchers need to screen the volume of returned results to filter out irrelevant work. It is not thus surprising that a large part of the SLR effort goes to the identification of relevant studies [37]. To make things more complicated for such a critical task, SLR authors might have limited knowledge of the review topic and the search terms at the beginning of the process, and the primary studies themselves may adopt different terminology to refer to similar concepts [17]. All these circumstances make building proper SLR search queries challenging task and a potential point of failure.

The challenges in SLR search have motivated research on how to automate query generation for SLR search. The existing solutions for building the SLR search query task mainly focused on automatically building search queries (e.g., [19,20]) or automatically refining existing search queries (e.g., [11,31]). These proposed methods, while valuable, are limited to specific research domains (e.g., medical domain). This limitation imposes challenges for generalizing and adopting these methods in different SLRs and research domains. In addition, these methods rely on machine learning algorithms (e.g., classifiers) that require domain-specific training data to predict the performance and rank the generated queries. Moreover, these methods require authors to compose and provide an initial query, which poses challenges to researchers who have less knowledge about building search queries and especially who are new to a research topic [17].

This calls for solutions that can better adapt to different domains and SLRs while supporting SLR authors in the early the stage of review process where knowledge is still limited. We addressed these gaps by devising an adaptive query *building* and *refining* pipeline that relies on a reinforcement learning approach for incrementally refining a generated search query based on authors feedback. More precisely, given a seed expressing the scope of the literature review (e.g., research questions or a set of relevant abstracts), the pipeline automatically generates a search query from the initial seed. Through an interactive process, the pipeline then leverages author feedback on the query search results to incrementally improve the generated query. The aim is to maximize recall while minimizing the workload that would impose on later screening steps. The rationale behind our approach is to leverage SLR authors' knowledge about the scope of the review and what is relevant, for automatically building and incrementally learning to refine the search queries. In sum, the contributions of this paper are as follows:

– We propose a method that exploits a high-level expression of the SLR scope to build initial search queries and semantically enrich them to deliver an applicable search query;

- We devise an incremental and adaptive process to refine search queries for SLRs. The proposed reinforcement learning approach learns to modify and adjust the search queries by observing the relevance feedback provided by researchers on query search results;
- We empirically show, in an evaluation with 10 SLR datasets, that the proposed pipeline can generate effective search queries (in terms of recall and workload), that have a performance comparable to the queries that domain experts manually compose.

The rest of this paper proceeds as follows. Related work is given in Sect. 2. Section 3 presents our proposed approach. The experiments and evaluations are presented in Sect. 4. And finally, Sect. 5 concludes the paper.

2   Related Work

While most of the literature on SLR automation focuses on study selection (see [6] for a review), interest in SLR search support has recently sparked. These efforts can be categorised into two main groups: i) automatic techniques for *generating* search queries, and ii) automatic *refining* of SLR search queries.

In the **search query generation task**, studies have leveraged information from the review protocol (e.g., review questions, inclusion and exclusion criteria) or a set of relevant abstracts to extract relevant keywords to build search queries [19,20]. These studies generally rely on text mining techniques (e.g., terms frequency-inverse document frequency (TF-IDF) [27]) to find the most relevant terms from a given corpus [19,20]. However, these approaches only focus on suggesting terms to help researchers building queries and do not provide an end-to-end solution for query adaptation and refinement. Yet, the techniques serve as an inspiration for building the query generation component.

In the context of systematic reviews, **query refinement** is depicted as modifying a query to improve its recall or to reduce the number of studies retrieved [31]. Several studies explored techniques to achieve these goals [11,31]. By leveraging techniques in the form of query expansion (e.g., adding synonyms of the search terms), query reduction (e.g., removing unnecessary terms), or query transformation (e.g., rewriting query by replacing the Boolean operators).

Notably, Scells et al. in a series of studies [30,31] proposed a query refinement technique for medical SLR search queries comprised of query expansion (e.g., logical operator replacement (A AND B)→(A OR B)) and semantic transformations (e.g., using medical embeddings)) and query reduction (e.g., removing unnecessary terms) and then automatically selecting the best query candidate.

While valuable, current query refinement techniques in SLRs have some limitations. These solutions require authors to compose an initial query which poses challenges to researchers who have less knowledge about building search queries and especially who are new to a research topic [17]. They also rely on machine learning techniques that require domain-specific training data, making them less reusable across domains. We note that the need for domain-specific data and training is a significant obstacle for the adoption of automation for SLRs [37].

The use of **human-machine approaches** has the potential to adapt to specific domains and incrementally improve outcomes by learning from human feedback. In SLRs, the active learning approach has shown significant success in reducing citation screening workload and cost [23,37]. Due to this success, some tools (e.g., Rayyan) have adopted this approach to support researchers in citation screening. However, the use of human-machine approaches for SLR query refinement remains unexplored.

In this paper we aim at filling the above gaps by designing an end-to-end pipeline that takes a seed expressing the scope of the review, to generate a Boolean search query and refine it following a human-machine approach. We take inspiration from previous research in automatic query expansion to generate a SLR search query from a seed (research questions or abstracts). We then propose a novel reinforcement learning method for refining SLR search queries, adopting reinforcement learning models to solve the query refinement as multi-armed bandit problem [34,38]. We contribute with empirical evidence characterising the performance of the query building and refinement components under various meaningful dimensions.

3   Incremental Query Building and Refining Pipeline

In our proposed query generation and refinement approach, the aim is to leverage minimum information available to the researchers on the scope of a review to build initial search queries. Then, through a refinement process, based on researcher feedback, incrementally refine and improve those initially generated queries. In the context of this work, the query quality associates with the performance of a query to i) retrieve relevant literature as defined by the scope of the review (recall), and ii) minimise the (unnecessary) screening effort that the number of studies in retrieved results imposes on the eligibility screening efforts. It is worth noting that this balance is important as very "open" search queries may be effective in retrieving the majority of relevant works but return a massive number of search results. Conversely, narrow search queries may be easily manageable but miss important relevant works.

To realise this goal, we devised the query building and refinement pipeline illustrated in Fig. 1. In summary, the pipeline receives a seed representing the scope of the SLR (e.g. research questions). Then, it uses the seed to extract candidate terms to build an initial query. The pipeline expands the initial query by enriching the terms in the initial query. The generated query is then automatically executed on a digital library (DL) search engine to retrieve the search results. The pipeline uses relevance feedback from researchers on the search results to measure the performance of the executed query. Finally, the pipeline uses these observations to refine the query using a reinforcement learning approach. In what follows, we elaborate on each component of our proposed pipeline.

3.1   Initial Query Builder

The first component of the pipeline is *Initial Query Builder* which leverages a high-level expression of the scope of an SLR to build an initial query. The input to this component is a *seed*, which can be partially defined research questions or multiple relevant abstracts. This component first, removes non-contributing terms (e.g., stop words and special characters). Next, it extracts all the terms (nouns, verbs) from the given seed using Stanford's CoreNLP library [18]. This component relies on the terms TF-IDF as a criterion to select terms to construct an initial query when the seed contains more than one document. When the input seed contains only one document (e.g., one relevant abstract), the terms frequency (TF) is used to select top-n relevant terms. The selected terms at this stage represent concepts that should be present in relevant literature (i.e., matching results). We refer to these terms as *main terms* of the query. Therefore, *Initial Query Builder* constructs the initial query by joining the main terms using *'AND'* operator. For instance, for given research question *RQ: "Which techniques perform best when used to predict software fault?"* as the seed, *Initial Query Builder* extracts the main terms and generates an initial query denoting: $q =$ (software AND fault AND predict).

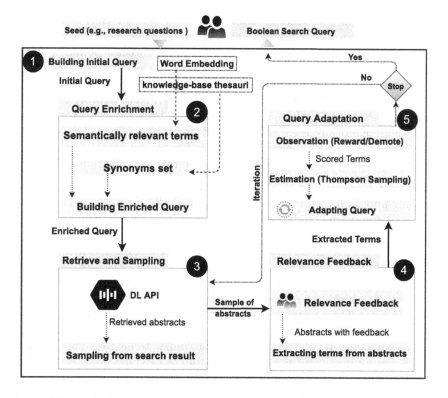

Fig. 1. Architecture of the query building and refinement pipeline

The generated initial query search results will be narrow and not suitable for recall-oriented SLR search. The reason is that authors of scientific literature use different terminologies to express same concept [8]. To address this, we devise the pipeline with a query enrichment component which we explain next.

3.2   Query Enrichment

We devised the pipeline with two query enrichment techniques: i) a knowledge-base approach for finding the synonyms of main query terms [5], and ii) an embedding approach to find alternative terms that are relevant to the query terms but may not be synonyms to the main terms [5].

Knowledge-Base Enrichment. This component finds all the synonyms of a given query term using WordNet [22]. It builds a *synonym set* for each query term, containing the term and its synonyms. WordNet collects English words into groups of synonyms, called *synsets* [22]. One word in WordNet may have more than one synset. WordNet records the semantic relations between the synsets that describes the specific concept (hyponym) or generalized concept (hypernym) of a synset [22].

To enrich a given search term, this component selects a synset from WordNet that has a hyponym similar to other terms in the query. For instance, in the initial query q (from our ongoing example), the term "fault" has a synset that denotes the concept of "geography" and a synset that denotes "programming". The synset that denotes "programming" is selected because it has a similar hyponym to the term "software" in the query. As a result, for each term in query q, the following synset is selected for fault:{fault, defect, error,...}.

The described enrichment approach has the potential to improve the query's retrieval performance [5]. However, the knowledge-based thesauri often do not hold all the semantically relevant terms that are not synonyms [21]. Therefore, we introduced another enrichment technique to further improve the query performance in retrieving papers that use alternative terms to express similar concept.

Embedding Enrichment. This enrichment component builds upon a word embedding approach [21]. In word embeddings, similar words have similar vectors in a vector space [21]. This component uses a word embeddings model to find the most relevant terms to each *synonym set* and collects these terms into an *enriched set*. First, it calculates the mean vector of each synonym set using the vectors of all the terms within the synonym set $(\vec{set}_s = 1/|set_s| \sum_{s \in set_s} \vec{s})$. Herein, set_s denotes a synonym set. Next, the component uses the cosine similarity score of embedding terms and the mean vector of each synonym set $(\vec{set}_s)$ to find top-n candidate terms in the embedding that have similarity to the synonym set. These top-n selected candidate terms form a candidate set (W) for each synonym set. Finally, to select the most similar terms from the candidate set, *Embedding Enrichment* ranks the terms in the candidate set (W) based on their cosine similarity to the mean vector of the *initial query*. We chose to rank the terms in the candidate sets (W) based on their similarities to the query instead of their synonym sets (set_s). This way, we ensured the terms that are more relevant to the query are ranked higher and selected for enrichment [15]. A query's mean vector is calculated by averaging the vectors of all the terms in the query ($\vec{q} = 1/|q| \sum_{t \in q} \vec{q}$). Herein, q denotes a query. Therefore, the score of term w from the candidate sets (W) is calculated as: $score(w, q) = cos(\vec{q}, \vec{w})$. Herein, $\vec{w}$ denotes vector of a term w in a candidate set (W). In our experiment, a minimum similarity threshold (α) is used to select top-n terms. These top-n terms form an *enriched set* for each corresponding synonym set.

Query Composer. Once all the *enriched sets* are generated, *Query Composer* component builds an enriched query by applying Boolean logic. It is assumed that the terms in the enriched sets are alternative to the *main terms* in the initial query. Therefore, *Query Composer* assembles the alternative terms in the enriched set using *OR* operator and forms a *query cluster* for each *enriched set*. For instance, the main term *predict* and its enriched set {predict, estimate, model} results in a cluster as: (predict OR detect OR model). The final query is then formed by concatenating all the query clusters, using an *'AND'* operator. Therefore, for initial query q, enriched query q^* will be generated: $q^* =$ (software OR program...) AND (fault OR defect OR...) AND (predict OR detect...). At this stage the queries are built using only OR and AND operation. Using other operations are left to the future work.

3.3 Query Adaptation

Query adaptation is a common practice in SLR search. Researchers modify search queries based on the knowledge gained by screening more candidate papers over time. In practice, this process can take many iterations and is prone to error. Furthermore, due to the large and expanding number of publications, researchers can spend significant time evaluating and appraising search results and accordingly adapting the queries [32]. To help researchers with this time-consuming task, we formulated the query adaptation problem in the form of a reinforcement learning model which learns to adapt queries by observing changes in the retrieved papers. We built our approach on a multi-armed bandit problems [14]. In multi-armed bandit problems, the algorithm continually allows a choice of which action to take and each action results in a reward based on an underlying probability distribution [33]. The algorithm learns to take the actions that maximise the accumulative rewards, by repeating the action and observing the results [33]. In what follows, we elaborate on the components of our proposed query adaptation approach.

Observation. The first step in the query adaptation is *observation*. It consists of three components: i) search and retrieve; ii) sampling; and iii) relevance feedback.

Search and Retrieve. This component facilitates the search on various digital libraries. It contains adapters for executing search queries by calling digital libraries API. It executes the queries and retrieves the results for processing.

Sampling. In practice, researchers examine the query performance by screening a subset of retrieved papers [16]. Building on this practice, we aim at improving the retrieval performance of the search query by learning about the relevance of a sample set from the query search results. For this, we introduced a *sampling* mechanism to the pipeline. The sampling component has the task of selecting S items from the search result based on a learning strategy introduced next. This component first extracts all the terms (nouns, verbs) from the retrieved abstracts using Stanford's CoreNLP library [18]. Next, it extracts the corresponding word vectors for these terms using an embedding model (e.g., Glove [24]). It then averages all these terms vectors to find the mean vector of each abstract. The *sampling* component also calculates the mean vector of the query by averaging corresponding vectors of all its terms. It makes use of the cosine similarity metric to calculate the similarity between the vector of each abstract and the vector of the query: $Score(a, q*) = Sim_a = cos(\vec{q*}, \vec{a})$. Here, $\vec{a}$ represents the vector of the abstract and $\vec{q*}$ is the vector of the executed query. Then, it ranks the abstracts in descending order based on their similarity score. Finally, it selects a set of samples based on a sampling strategy. The sampling strategy is applied either by seeking feedback on *uncertain* or *certain* abstracts. To this end, a lower η and a higher ζ similarity score thresholds define the sampling strategy. In sampling based on uncertainty, abstracts are those that the pipeline is less confident about their relevance ($\eta < Sim_a < \zeta$). Instead, sampling based on certainty seeks confirmation on abstracts with the highest similarity scores ($Sim_a > \zeta$). The choice for the sampling method is a configuration parameter of the pipeline.

Relevance Feedback. This component presents the selected samples to researchers for receiving feedback. Leveraging a binary relevance feedback [29], researchers can screen the sample abstracts and label them as *relevant* or *irrelevant*, based on whether they fit the scope of the review or not. They can also screen additional abstracts from the search results. The abstracts with feedback are then used in the next component of the pipeline to modify the search query.

Estimation. The next step in query adaptation process is *estimation* which includes two components: i) reward/demote schema and ii) terms performance estimator that computes the retrieval performance of the query terms.

Reward/Demote Scheme. This component keeps records of the accumulated rewards and demotes for each query term. It also finds candidate terms in the relevant abstracts that are not yet part of the query but have shown positive performance (i.e., candidate terms). Reward/Demote Scheme complies with two main functions: i) Rewards/Demotes Calculator, and ii) Candidate Terms Finder. Each time new relevant/irrelevant abstracts are received, the Rewards/Demotes extracts all terms (nouns, verbs) from each abstract, using Stanford's CoreNLP [18]. It then updates the rewards and demotes of the query terms, based on their presence in relevant or irrelevant abstracts. Each query term has default value of 1 for reward and demote in the first iteration. Each time a query term appears in a new irrelevant abstract, it will be demoted ($d_t = +1$). In turn, every time a query term appears in a new relevant abstract, it will be rewarded ($r_t = +1$). This component updates the term rewards and demotes in each iteration. Therefore, after n iterations the accumulated rewards and demotes for query term t would be: $r_t = \sum_{i=1}^{n-1} r_{ti}$ and $d_t = \sum_{i=1}^{n-1} d_{ti}$. In addition to keeping the record of query terms' rewards and demotes, Reward/Demote Scheme has another function that finds new candidate search terms. These are the terms that frequently appear in relevant abstracts but are not part of the query, yet. When all the terms are extracted from relevant abstracts, *Candidate Terms Finder* uses the TF-IDF of those terms as a filtering mechanism and selects candidate terms when their TF-IDF score is above a minimum threshold. Terms that meet these criteria are added to a *candidate terms* set. The candidate terms are used by the *Query modifier* component when a term in a query must be replaced with a more suited term. The terms' accumulated rewards and demote are used by the *Terms Performance Estimator* to estimate the retrieval performance of each term.

Terms Performance Estimator. Having the terms with rewards and demotes, the only remaining question is: "how to choose a term for adding to or removing from a query?". Instead of choosing an uncertain heuristic, we used Thompson Sampling [28], in which this question is answered by capturing this uncertainty in a probability distribution [28].

In our query adaptation problem, Thompson Sampling holds a *policy* for deciding which term should be modified in a query. It also provides an algorithm for finding new candidate terms that could update this policy [38]. We utilized Thompson Sampling for our multi-armed bandit problem because it has provided near-optimal regret[1] found in previous research [34]. For candidate term t, Thompson sampling estimates a probability distribution $\theta = Beta(r_t, d_t)$, using the accumulated rewards (r_t) and demotes (d_t). This distribution shows the expected reward when a particular term is chosen and also how variable reward is, which affect the action that is taken (removing or replacing a term) [38]. This distribution probability value is updated based on the algorithm observation (i.e., whether the term appears on relevant or irrelevant abstracts).

Each time terms with rewards and demotes are received, the algorithm updates their θ value based on their rewards and demotes. More specifically, when the algorithm obtains a set of candidate terms $C = \{t_1, t_2, ..., t_n\}$ along with their accumulated rewards and demotes, it updates the terms probability distributions, $\theta = \{\theta_1, \theta_2, ..., \theta_n\}$, where $0 < \theta < 1$ using Bayes rule as: $P(\theta|t) = \frac{P(t|\theta)P(\theta)}{P(t)}$. If $\beta(r_t, d_t)$ is the β value for term t in iteration i, then after observing a win $r = 1$, its β value would be $\beta(r_t + 1, d_t)$. Conversely, after observing a loss $d = 1$ its β value will be: $\beta(r_t, d_t + 1)$. The candidate term is then selected according to its probability (θ_t) satisfies: $argmax_t P(\theta|t) = E[reward|\theta_t]p(\theta_t|A)$ where A is the set of observed abstracts (relevant and irrelevant) and θ_t is the parameters of the Beta distribution for term t. It is worth noting that our query adaptation problem is a Bernoulli problem, meaning that the generated random variable by each term has only two possible outcomes: 0 or 1 and the value of

---

[1] The per-iteration regret is the mean of rewards of a choice with the best rewards and the action taken by the algorithm [28].

$Beta(\alpha, \beta)$ is within the interval [0, 1]. Therefore, instead of the result varying per term, the probability of term generating rewards varies [4].

Query Modifier. The last component of query adaption is *Query Modifier* that modifies the query by adding or removing terms from the query based on their observed performance. To adapt a query, it first identifies query clauses[2] which their performance values are below a minimum threshold γ. The threshold outlines the minimum accumulative rewards and demotes that a query clause should have to be considered efficient for query retrieval performance. After identifying inefficient query clauses, this component finds the term in the clause that makes the clause inefficient. It compares the performance of the term with its sibling terms' performance[3]. *Query Modifier* would replace a term in the query clause if the number of relevant abstracts that the term appears on is below the average number of relevant abstracts its sibling terms appear on. This indicates that the term is not sufficient in retrieving relevant abstracts. Moreover, *Query Modifier* replaces this term with a *candidate term* which is estimated to yield the highest probability distribution (θ) by the Bayesian algorithm.

For instance, as illustrated in Fig. 2, suppose that after i iterations *Query Modifier* identifies t_3 is to underperform. It would remove t_3 and replaces it with t_6, the candidate term that has the highest probability value θ in iteration i. When to stop the adaptation is a problem that could be addressed with different strategies. Currently we assume that the authors decide when to stop.

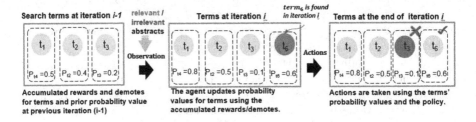

Fig. 2. Query modifier removes and adds terms in iteration i

4   Evaluation

The main goal of the evaluation was to assess the two main design decisions in our proposed pipeline: the (i) *automatic generation* of the search query from the initial user input, and (ii) *incremental refinement* of the initial search query by

---

[2] We define a *query clause* as a conjunction of a set of terms such as (t_1 AND t_3).

[3] In a query cluster such as (t_1 OR t_2) , t_1 is considered as sibling term to t_2.

leveraging user feedback. To this end, we designed two experiments that evaluated the *initial* and *refined* queries according to relevant performance metrics.[4]

4.1 Methods

Datasets. We performed the evaluation on SLR datasets that were made publicly available by their authors. To identify these datasets, we looked for SLRs in computer science that had published their search and screening data, by systematically searching datasets at Zenodo and Figshare.[5] As a result, we identified 10 SLRs that included research questions, the SLR search query, the search result dataset, and final relevance assessment. Of these SLRs, 5 also included the relevance assessment from the title and abstract screening phase. We consider the SLR authors' relevance assessment to be the gold label in our experiments.

Experiment 1- Initial Query Generation. In this experiment, we assessed our approach in generating the search query directly from an initial seed, by applying the query generation and enrichment components. To understand the impact of the amount of information in the seed on these components, we tested three conditions having:**i)** only research questions (*GEN-RQ*), **ii)** abstracts from (1 or 3) relevant papers (*GEN-ABS(1,3)*); **iii)** and a combination including the research questions and one abstract (*GEN-RQA*). Notice that we only used the abstracts of the relevant papers for building the seeds, as they capture a meaningful summary of the paper. We generated search queries for the 10 SLR datasets, taking the seed from each SLR. For comparison, we took as baseline (*BASE-OG*) the performance of the original search queries from each SLR adapted and scoped to our target digital library and the fields currently supported (title, abstract).

Experiment 2- Query Adaptation and Refinement. Here, we evaluated the performance of the query adaptation based on author relevance feedback when incrementally refining the initial search query. To do so, we took the initial queries generated with research questions (*GEN-RQ*) in Experiment 1. Then we simulated the author feedback by leveraging the relevance assessment already present in the SLR datasets, i.e., screening relevance feedback made strictly based on title and abstract. We assessed the changes in query performance within 5 iterations, where for the sampling method we tested two different approaches: i) *uncertainty sampling*, where abstracts for feedback are drafted from those where the pipeline is less confident about their relevance (low similarity score); ii) *certainty sampling*, where abstracts are drafted from those the pipeline is most certain about their relevance (high similarity score). The idea of these two methods was to test the impact of the class distribution (ratio relevant to irrelevant papers) in authors' feedback since these contribute differently to the

---

[4] For full details about the datasets, experimental details and in-depth results please refer to our supplementary material at https://tinyurl.com/496zuar3 and implementation details on https://tinyurl.com/2rp4m5cs.

[5] Popular dataset repositories, at https://zenodo.org and http://figshare.com.

query adaptation. The uncertainty sampling returns predominately irrelevant papers, while the certainty sampling returns predominantly relevant papers.

For both sampling methods, we used 0.80 as the highest and 0.30 as the lower similarity thresholds for estimating relevance. The sampling size in the experiment was five papers for each SLR and in each iteration. We compared the performance of the query adaptation conditions against the initial generated search query (*GEN-RQ*) and the original search query (*BASE-OG*).

Data Processing and Analysis. In our analysis, we relied on metrics to help us capture how effective search queries are in identifying relevant papers while lowering the workload of the screening process. To capture the **effectiveness** we relied on standard precision and recall metrics applied to this context. *Precision* measures the proportion of retrieved relevant papers to the total number of retrieved papers. *Recall* computes the proportion of relevant papers retrieved to the total relevant papers in the relevance assessment dataset.

As a proxy for **workload**, we assess the *number of retrieved papers*. This number gives us a raw indication of the effort that authors would need to put into screening the search results for identifying relevant papers. As previously mentioned, a large number of retrieved papers will significantly impact the cost and effort required by the authors and could dictate the feasibility of performing the review. Notice that we take the number of relevant papers from each SLR dataset as the gold standard. However, since most SLR datasets include results from multiple libraries, we recalculated the number of relevant papers to those that could be identified by the original query on our target digital library (IEEEXplore).

Table 1. Performance of generated queries based on different seed input, compared to manually formulated queries by SLR authors (#Ret= #Retrieved; #Rel=#Relevant).

Dataset	#Rel	BASE-OG			GEN-RQ			GEN-RQA			GEN-ABS-3		
		#Ret	Recall	Prec.	#Ret	Recall	Prec.	#Ret	Recall	Prec.	#Ret	Recall	Prec.
SLR_1 [36]	71	44,431	**0.59**	0.0009	996	0.37	0.0261	1045	0.40	0.0268	1,220	0.42	0.0246
SLR_2 [9]	208	5,852	**0.50**	0.0178	1,650	**0.50**	0.0630	1,780	0.51	0.0596	540	0.54	0.2074
SLR_3 [26]	89	3605	**0.47**	0.0117	552	0.45	0.0725	1,525	0.45	0.0262	1,049	0.37	0.0315
SLR_4 [10]	23	101	**0.95**	0.2178	260	0.83	0.0731	260	0.83	0.0731	146	0.87	0.1370
SLR_5 [12]	160	1,886	**0.28**	0.0239	13,300	0.24	0.0029	13,300	0.24	0.0029	2,019	0.28	0.0223
SLR_6 [3]	99	11,713	**0.93**	0.0079	350	0.80	0.2257	352	0.80	0.2244	220	0.59	0.2636
SLR_7 [7]	34	1,462	**0.76**	0.0178	169	0.35	0.0710	261	0.44	0.0575	1,245	0.38	0.0104
SLR_8 [1]	19	1,652	**0.95**	0.0109	800	0.74	0.0175	800	0.74	0.0175	205	0.42	0.0390
SLR_9 [25]	75	144	0.43	0.2222	730	**0.63**	0.0644	45	0.21	0.3556	79	0.16	0.1519
SLR_{10} [35]	49	82,009	0.71	0.0004	604	0.82	0.0662	27,618	**0.84**	0.0015	785	0.49	0.0306
Median		2,746	0.66	0.0531	667	0.56	0.0653	923	0.48	0.0421	663	0.42	0.0357
Relative median performance					24.3%	87.7%	121.9%	33.6%	72.8%	79.3%	24.1%	64.1%	66.3%

4.2 Results

Experiment 1. The results of query generation are presented in Table 1[6], and the full details of the generated queries are available in the online Appendix.

In comparison to the baseline (BASE-OG), queries generated with the best variant of our approach (GEN-RQ), achieve 87.7% of the median recall, and 121.57% of the accuracy of the expert queries, with only 24% of the results.

When comparing the impact of the three types of seed, we see the results to be similar across the various SLRs. However, the most consistent performance was achieved by GEN-RQ, i.e., it shows higher mean values of precision and recall with lower-to-comparable numbers of retrieved papers. These results suggest that, with our current approach, RQs are generally better for identify key concepts for the search query than having one or three relevant abstracts. An inspection of the results tells us that, in addition to the type of seed (e.g., RQs or relevant abstracts), the information presented in the seed also impact the quality of generated queries. For example, in our experimental scenario, RQs are collected from published SLRs. Thus they are more likely to be properly formed and representative of the scope of the reviews. In contrast, the randomly selected relevant abstracts in the GEN-ABS and GEN-RQA approach may contain more repeating words, possibly introducing noise and reducing the relevance of important terms. However, going from a seed with one to three abstracts does show some performance increase in mean recall albeit with a higher number of results.

A closer look at the generated queries gives us hints into the characteristics of produced queries. As illustrated in Fig. 3**A**, our approach is effective at identifying the main query components (e.g., fault, prediction, software). Yet some refinement (e.g., removing non relevant terms) could improve its performance.

Research Questions	Original Query	Ⓐ Initial generated query	Ⓑ Final search query
• How does context affect fault prediction? • Which independent variables should be included in fault predictions? • Which modelling techniques perform best when used in fault prediction?	(Fault* OR bug* OR defect* OR errors OR corrections OR corrective OR fix*) **AND** (Software)	(mistake OR error OR fault OR defect OR demerit OR faulting OR break) **AND** (predict OR anticipate OR prevision OR foretell OR forecast OR prognosticate) **AND** (software OR software_program OR computer_software OR software_system OR software_package OR package)	(fault OR defect OR quality OR error-prone) **AND** (predict OR assess OR detect) **AND** software OR software_program OR computer_software OR software_system OR software_package)

Fig. 3. Example queries generated for SLR_2 after the (A) initial query generation step (GEN-RQ) and (B) final query refinement iteration I_5 using certainty sampling

---

[6] We only included the results of three seed types in the table, the full list is available in Appendix at https://tinyurl.com/496zuar3.

The above tells us that our approach provides a good foundation for generating queries and improving upon. Having properly formulated research questions might not be the case in the early stages when planning a literature review process. Therefore, the possibility of having relevant abstracts as seeds provides a solid base for composing and refining search queries.

Experiment 2. The results of the query adaptation and refinement step, for the uncertainty and certainty sampling, are shown in Table 2. Compared to the **input query** generated by GEN-RQ (I_0), the final refined queries consistently improved on the recall when applying either of the two sampling methods, though, the improvements are more pronounced for certainty sampling. However, the improvements came at the cost of an increase in the number of retrieved results for 3 of the 5 SLRs. Precision was also improved only in 2 of the 5 SLRs (refer to the supplementary materials for precision results). Looking at performance through the iterations, we can see that uncertainty sampling improves more slowly, or stalls in terms of recall, compared to certainty sampling. The increase in the number of papers in search results is also more conservative in the uncertainty sampling approach. This can be attributed to the fact that negative samples (irrelevant abstracts) contribute more to removing irrelevant terms.

To contextualise the practical implications of the higher recall at the cost of more search results, we compare refined queries to the queries formulated by the SLR authors. When comparing the performance to the **baseline query** (BASE-OG), the difference is more noticeable. Certainty sampling was significantly improving (or matching) the recall of the expert formulated queries BASE-OG (Q). As seen in the grayed out cells, this was achieved while reducing the number of retrieved papers in two instances (SLR_1, SLR_2) and with a modest increase in other cases. The outlier with a significant increase is due to the unusual case of having only 101 search results in the baseline (SLR_4). What these results tell us is that our approach is **able to match or improve the performance of expert formulated queries** when it comes to recall, while adapting to different SLRs by learning from author feedback. All of this, reducing at times the number of results – though results in this regard are inconclusive. Notice that recall, and in particular avoiding missing out on relevant work, is paramount in SLRs, and our approach is able to build and refine queries towards this goal.

As illustrated in Fig. 3, the refinement process is indeed able to reduce the non-relevant search terms (e.g., for "fault", removing "demerit") and add relevant terms (e.g., for "fault" adding "quality") to the query, contributing to better performance. However, we should also note that the generated query is currently not the optimal expression of the query, as we can still find redundant terms (e.g., having "software" makes the term "computer software" redundant). To inspect all the generated queries, please refer to the online Appendix.

Table 2. Performance of the query refinement approach for two competing sampling methods. Values are shown for the first five iterations (I_1 - I_5). Performance is compared to the input query ($I_0^\uparrow$) generated by GEN-RQ, and the baseline query ($Q^\uparrow$) BASE-OG.

DS	Uncertainty							Certainty						
Recall	I_1	I_2	I_3	I_4	I_5	$I_0^\uparrow$	$Q^\uparrow$	I_1	I_2	I_3	I_4	I_5	$I_0^\uparrow$	$Q^\uparrow$
SLR_1	0.37	0.38	0.44	0.44	0.56	51%	−5%	0.46	0.51	0.56	0.61	0.66	78%	12%
SLR_2	0.51	0.51	0.52	0.52	0.54	8%	8%	0.93	0.95	0.97	0.99	**1.00**	100%	100%
SLR_3	0.45	0.45	0.48	0.55	0.60	33%	28%	0.83	0.88	0.92	0.96	**1.00**	122%	113%
SLR_4	0.83	0.87	0.87	0.87	0.87	5%	−8%	0.85	0.85	0.88	0.91	0.95	14%	0%
SLR_5	0.24	0.24	0.24	0.26	0.26	8%	−7%	0.35	0.35	0.35	0.44	0.53	121%	89%
#Ret	I_1	I_2	I_3	I_4	I_5	$I_0^\uparrow$	$Q^\uparrow$	I_1	I_2	I_3	I_4	I_5	$I_0^\uparrow$	$Q^\uparrow$
SLR_1	996	862	813	756	952	−4%	−98%	1320	992	855	767	705	−29%	−98%
SLR_2	2052	2038	1904	1760	2362	43%	−60%	6893	6861	5528	5477	5161	213%	−12%
SLR_3	1050	890	1473	1563	1420	157%	−61%	6904	7120	7311	7366	7542	1266%	109%
SLR_4	315	420	421	495	452	74%	348%	1955	1777	1687	1674	1561	500%	1446%
SLR_5	12754	9835	8920	8635	7432	−44%	294%	4667	3733	3237	3352	2423	−82%	28%

5   Conclusion and Future Work

In summary, our evaluation showed that our approach is able to generate effective queries from high level expressions of the scope of a review. The initial query generation and enrichment process is able to generate search queries that deliver 87.7% of the median recall of the manual approach, with only 24% of the results (number of items retrieved). While a solid approximation, we observed this process to be sensible to the amount of information provided in the seed and limited by the query enrichment methods that might introduce non semantically relevant terms to the query. On this, the proposed query adaptation is able to significantly improve on the initial generated query and archives the performance (and in some cases improve) of expert formulated queries in the course of 5 iterations with 5 relevance feedback each. Sampling methods were shown to have a significant impact, with a sampling strategy biased towards positive examples found to be the most effective. Overall, our empirical evaluation has shown the potential of the reinforcement learning approach to adapting search queries based on author feedback, without the need for domain-specific training.

While this approach and its evaluation showed some initial promise in generating search queries, there are limitations to the current pipeline and the evaluation methods. One limitation of our proposed enrichment approach is when the extracted terms from the seeds do not have many relevant terms in the embeddings. Therefore, selecting the most relevant terms becomes uncertain. Yet, replacing the general-embedding models with a domain-specific embeddings model could improve query enrichment process. The other limitation in our proposed approach is that pipeline only uses AND and OR operations for generating boolean queries, we leave exploring the impact of using NOT operator for generating and refining queries to future research. One limitation to our experiment is regarding taking the SLR datasets as gold-standard to measure the query performance. It is also required to measure the effectiveness of our proposed approach in building search queries that could retrieve relevant papers that are missing in the baseline SLR datasets (e.g., relevant papers that were excluded in published SLRs by mistake). This also requires further development in the pipeline and a scale user study. We leave this experiment for future research.

References

1. Adamo, G., Ghidini, C., Di Francescomarino, C.: What is a process model composed of ? A systematic literature review of meta-models in bpm. arXiv preprint arXiv:2011.09177 (2020)
2. Badami, M., Baez, M., Zamanirad, S., et al.: On how cognitive computing will plan your next systematic review. arXiv preprint arXiv:2012.08178 (2020)
3. Barišić, A., Goulão, M., Amaral, V.: Domain-specific language domain analysis and evaluation: a systematic literature review. Universidade Nova da Lisboa, Faculdade de Ciencias e Technologia (2015)
4. Brochu, E., Cora, V.M., et al.: A tutorial on Bayesian optimization of expensive cost functions, with application to active user modeling and hierarchical reinforcement learning. arXiv preprint arXiv:1012.2599 (2010)
5. Carpineto, C., Romano, G.: A survey of automatic query expansion in information retrieval. ACM Comput. Surveys (CSUR) **44**(1), 1–50 (2012)
6. van Dinter, R., Tekinerdogan, B., Catal, C.: Automation of systematic literature reviews: A systematic literature review. Information & Soft. Tech, p. 106589 (2021)
7. Frank, M., Hilbrich, M., Lehrig, S., Becker, S.: Parallelization, modeling, and performance prediction in the multi-/many core area: a systematic literature review. In: 2017 IEEE 7th International Symposium on Cloud and Service Computing (SC2), pp. 48–55. IEEE (2017)
8. Garousi, V., Felderer, M.: Experience-based guidelines for effective and efficient data extraction in systematic reviews in software engineering. In: Proceedings of EASE 2017, pp. 170–179 (2017)
9. Hall, T., Beecham, S., Bowes, D., Gray, D., Counsell, S.: A systematic literature review on fault prediction performance in software engineering. IEEE Trans. Softw. Eng. **38**(6), 1276–1304 (2011)
10. Jamshidi, P., Ahmad, A., Pahl, C.: Cloud migration research: a systematic review. IEEE Trans. Cloud Comput. **1**(2), 142–157 (2013)
11. Kim, Y., Seo, J., Croft, W.B.: Automatic Boolean query suggestion for professional search. In: Proceedings of SIGIR, pp. 825–834 (2011)
12. Kitchenham, B., Brereton, O.P., Budgen, D., Turner, M., Bailey, J., Linkman, S.: Systematic literature reviews in software engineering-a systematic literature review. Inf. Softw. Technol. **51**(1), 7–15 (2009)
13. Kitchenham, B., Charters, S.: Guidelines for performing systematic literature reviews in software engineering (2007)
14. Kohavi, R., Longbotham, R., Sommerfield, D., et al.: Controlled experiments on the web: survey and practical guide. DMKD **18**(1), 140–181 (2009)

15. Kuzi, S., Shtok, A., Kurland, O.: Query expansion using word embeddings. In: Proceedings of CIKM, pp. 1929–1932 (2016)
16. Lee, G.E., Sun, A.: Seed-driven document ranking for systematic reviews in evidence-based medicine. In: SIGIR, pp. 455–464 (2018)
17. Li, H., Scells, H., Zuccon, G.: Systematic review automation tools for end-to-end query formulation. In: Proceedings of the 43rd International ACM SIGIR Conference on Research and Development in Information Retrieval, pp. 2141–2144 (2020)
18. Manning, C.D., Surdeanu, M., et al.: The stanford coreNLP natural language processing toolkit. In: Proceedings of ACL, pp. 55–60 (2014)
19. Marcos-Pablos, S., García-Peñalvo, F.J.: Decision support tools for SLR search string construction. In: Proceedings of TEEM 2018, pp. 660–667 (2018)
20. Mergel, G.D., Silveira, M.S., da Silva, T.S.: A method to support search string building in systematic literature reviews through visual text mining. In: Proceedings of the 30th Annual ACM Symposium on Applied Computing, pp. 1594–1601 (2015)
21. Mikolov, T., Sutskever, I., Chen, K., et al.: Distributed representations of words and phrases and their compositionality. In: NeurIPS, pp. 3111–3119 (2013)
22. Miller, G.A.: WordNet: An Electronic Lexical Database. MIT Press, Cambridge (1998)
23. Ouzzani, M., Hammady, H., Fedorowicz, Z., Elmagarmid, A.: Rayyan-a web and mobile app for systematic reviews. Syst. Rev. **5**(1), 210 (2016)
24. Pennington, J., Socher, R., Manning, C.D.: GloVe: global vectors for word representation. In: Proceedings of EMNLP, pp. 1532–1543 (2014)
25. Qin, C., Eichelberger, H., Schmid, K.: Enactment of adaptation in data stream processing with latency implications-a systematic literature review. Inf. Softw. Technol. **111**, 1–21 (2019)
26. Radjenović, D., Heričko, M., Torkar, R., Živkovič, A.: Software fault prediction metrics: a systematic literature review. Inf. Softw. Technol. **55**(8), 1397–1418 (2013)
27. Robertson, S.: Understanding inverse document frequency: on theoretical arguments for IDF. J. Doc. **60**(5), 503–520 (2004)
28. Russo, D., Van Roy, B., Kazerouni, A., et al.: A tutorial on Thompson sampling. arXiv preprint arXiv:1707.02038 (2017)
29. Salton, G., Buckley, C.: Improving retrieval performance by relevance feedback. J. Am. Soc. Inf. Sci. **41**(4), 288–297 (1990)
30. Scells, H., Zuccon, G.: Generating better queries for systematic reviews. In: ACM SIGIR, pp. 475–484 (2018)
31. Scells, H., Zuccon, G., Koopman, B.: Automatic Boolean query refinement for systematic review literature search. In: WWW, pp. 1646–1656 (2019)
32. Scells, H., Zuccon, G., Koopman, B.: A comparison of automatic Boolean query formulation for systematic reviews. Inf. Retrieval J. **24**(1), 3–28 (2021)
33. Sutton, R.S., Barto, A.G.: Reinforcement Learning: An Introduction. MIT Press, Cambridge (2018)
34. Tabebordbar, A., Beheshti, A., Benatallah, B., et al.: Feature-based and adaptive rule adaptation in dynamic environments. DSE **5**(3), 207–223 (2020)
35. Teixeira, E.N., Aleixo, F.A., de Sousa Amâncio, F.D., OliveiraJr, E., Kulesza, U., Werner, C.: Software process line as an approach to support software process reuse: a systematic literature review. Inf. Softw. Technol. **116**, 106175 (2019)
36. Wahono, R.S.: A systematic literature review of software defect prediction. J. Softw. Eng. **1**(1), 1–16 (2015)

37. Wallace, B.C., Small, K., Brodley, C.E., et al.: Who should label what ? Instance allocation in multiple expert active learning. In: SDM, pp. 176–187. SIAM (2011)
38. Williams, J.J., Kim, J., Rafferty, A., et al.: AXIS: generating explanations at scale with learner sourcing and machine learning. In: L@Scale, pp. 379–388 (2016)

A Model-Driven Approach for Systematic Reproducibility and Replicability of Data Science Projects

Fran Melchor$^{(\boxtimes)}$, Roberto Rodriguez-Echeverria , José M. Conejero ,
Álvaro E. Prieto , and Juan D. Gutiérrez

INTIA, Universidad de Extremadura, Cáceres, Spain
{fmelchor,rre,chemacm,aeprieto,andy}@unex.es

Abstract. In the last few years, there has been an important increase
in the number of tools and approaches to define pipelines that allow the
development of data science projects. They allow not only the pipeline
definition but also the code generation needed to execute the project
providing an easy way to carry out the projects even for non-expert
users. However, there are still some challenges that these tools do not
address yet, e.g. the possibility of executing pipelines defined by using
different tools or execute them in different environments (reproducibility and replicability) or models validation and verification by identifying
inconsistent operations (intentionality). In order to alleviate these problems, this paper presents a Model-Driven framework for the definition
of data science pipelines independent of the particular execution platform and tools. The framework relies on the separation of the pipeline
definition into two different modelling layers: conceptual, where the data
scientist may specify all the data and models operations to be carried
out by the pipeline; operational, where the data engineer may describe
the execution environment details where the operations (defined in the
conceptual part) will be implemented. Based on this abstract definition
and layers separation, the approach allows: the usage of different tools
improving, thus, process replicability; the automation of the process execution, enhancing process reproducibility; and the definition of model
verification rules, providing intentionality restrictions.

Keywords: Reproducibility · Replicability · Process · Data science ·
Model-driven engineering

1 Introduction

The rapid increase of data generated in our daily lives has fostered the democ-
ratization of Big Data platforms that are used once and again for exploring

This work has been partially funded by the Spanish government (LOCOSS project -
PID2020-114615RB-I00), and (ii) European Regional Development Fund (ERDF) and
Junta de Extremadura: IB18034, and GR18112 projects.

© Springer Nature Switzerland AG 2022
X. Franch et al. (Eds.): CAiSE 2022, LNCS 13295, pp. 147–163, 2022.
https://doi.org/10.1007/978-3-031-07472-1_9

those data to extract knowledge from them. These platforms have even become *commodities* used in all kind of research or commercial studies related to many different fields such as education [26], finances [13] biology [28], or medicine [16].

However, despite of the quick emergence and mature development of these tools, there are still some challenges that the research community has identified to be faced up. One of these challenges is known as the reproducibility crisis [12] and refers to the difficulties for reproducing and replicating the experiments developed in artificial intelligence in general and data science projects in particular. According to [15], reproducibility of an experiment refers to the action of obtaining consistent results using the same input data, computational steps, methods, code, and conditions of analysis. Whereas replicability refers to the action of obtaining consistent results across studies aimed at answering the same scientific question, each of which has obtained its own data.

Although there could be found different reasons explaining why many data analysis projects are continuously struggling with reproducibility and replicability (R&R) [1,9,10,17,21] the infrastructure problem is considered one major factor [27]. In that sense, the definition of platform-agnostic pipelines would aim at alleviating this problem by improving separation of concerns since the different roles in teams involved in data projects (e.g. data scientist and engineer) could focus on their specific tasks, as MLOps approaches claim [4,11,24]. While data scientists are responsible for exploring the data and building a minimum viable product (MVP) version of a function, feature, or product; data engineers design the infrastructure to support the data scientists' pipeline definition [4].

Other important reasons that hinder R&R in data science projects are both the complexity of the underlying data science pipelines [20] and the lack of standards for defining these pipelines (these workflows are still in flux due to being a young research field [4]). These problems force data scientists and engineers to manually define these pipelines on top of a plethora of tools and technologies. These pipelines are usually error-prone and difficult to trace especially when the users defining them have limited knowledge about data science [23]. Indeed, as authors claim in [23], *prior research shows that they could be potentially making mistakes that invalidate the findings of their data science pipelines.*

In that context, although PMML and PFA have come to the scene as standards to improve platforms interoperability, they still have some limitations that must be overcome. They provide a particular Domain Specific Language (DSL) for the representation of models and pre- and post-processing transformations. However, neither they cover the definition of the whole pipeline (e.g. there are many data manipulation operations that may not be represented) nor the standard is supported by all the tools yet.

In this work, we focus on the next three challenges that hinder reproducibility and replicability (R&R) in data science projects:

- Manual ad hoc pipelines are defined on top of a variety of tools and technologies. Pipelines' stages are not always the same, so flexibility is mandatory. Each stage (or partial stage) could be implemented by a different tool increasing the complexity of its execution and monitoring. Flexibility and heterogeneity are relevant properties of this kind of projects, but we need to manage them in a systematic way in order to make the process measurable and traceable to satisfy R&R.

- Trial-and-error processes are commonly followed by exploring different alternatives along the pipeline. Versioning code and data is possible, but doing it systematically is a different challenge. Moreover, versioning decisions and tool usage also remains a challenge. The final pipeline becomes then a particular path (along particular versions of stages) inside the exploration tree organically generated in the process of its definition.

- Data consistency verification can easily become complex. Data pipelines define a sequence of transformations on input datasets. Different tools may provide different implementations of such transformations (data operations). Therefore, different executions of the same pipeline could imply divergent data derivations making data inconsistent among execution tools. As a result, R&R may be compromised.

With these challenges in mind, this paper presents a Model-Driven approach for the definition of R&R data science pipelines. The approach is based on the definition of a metamodel that allows separating the pipeline definition into two different abstraction levels: conceptual and operational. While the former provides the data scientist with a language for specifying a platform-agnostic data science pipeline, the latter allows the data engineer to define the concrete execution environment where the pipeline will be deployed. Based on this two-levels separation, the code for running the pipeline could be completely generated and executed for a particular platform gaining, thus, in R&R since the pipeline could be deployed once and again in a systematic way. The systematic definition of pipelines and the automatic execution of the supporting infrastructure would aim at tackling the complexity of the aforementioned challenges. Moreover, some of these challenges could be solved at model level by applying, for example, model verification methods and techniques. As a result, those solutions also remain technology independent, so they can be reused in different executions of the same pipeline, eventually improving R&R.

The rest of paper is organized as follows. Section 2 describes our approach, namely a new metamodel for the definition of reproducible and replicable pipelines. In order to clarify the approach, Sect. 3 introduces an illustrative example. Section 4 evaluates the approach by presenting the results obtained in the execution of the example in two different platforms. In Sect. 5 related works are presented. Section 6 discusses some open points of our approach and presents future research lines. Finally, Sects. 7 concludes the paper.

2   Model-Driven Data Science Projects R&R

Model Driven Engineering (MDE) makes use of models as a primary artifact in the development lifecycle [3]. One of the most extended applications of MDE is the creation of Domain Specific Modeling Languages (DSMLs) for describing the characteristics of a particular domain where some tasks must be automated. Based on models and transformations, software code may be automatically generated mitigating common software engineering problems, improving productivity and overall quality [18], a.k.a. Model-Driven Development (MDD). Model Driven Architecture (MDA)[1] is a particular realization of MDD on top of OMG's standards, which provides guidelines for structuring software specifications that are expressed as models. MDA separates business and application logic from underlying platform technology. An MDA specification consists mainly of a platform-independent model (PIM), plus one or more platform-specific models (PSM) and complete implementations on each platform supported. Moreover, using models raises the level of abstraction providing a better separation of concerns for the different roles of a project. Furthermore, error detection and quality control may be also raised to model level, as [19] suggests.

In this section the main points of our Model-Driven Data Science Projects R&R (MD4DSPRR) approach are presented, whose core relies in the definition of two complementary DSMLs for data science projects. From an MDA perspective, those DSMLs are conceived to specify the PIM in data science projects.

2.1 Overview

As shown in Fig. 1, the core of our MDE approach is composed of two primary models: the conceptual and the operational model. That division follows the responsibility organization into two main roles in data science projects: data scientists and data engineers. While scientists are concerned about specifying the correct pipeline to generate, for instance, prediction models from the available data, data engineers are occupied provisioning and configuring the necessary infrastructure to, firstly, support data scientists in model generation and, secondly, to operate the resulting model integrated into larger information systems.

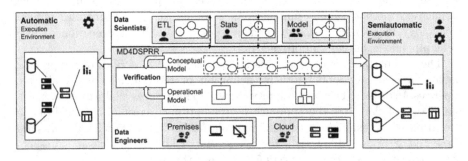

Fig. 1. MD4DSPRR approach overview.

The conceptual model allows the description of data pipelines (data + operations) in a technology agnostic manner by raising the level of abstraction. Based on this high level description and the large spectrum of model-driven engineering methods and tools, data scientists could (i) analyze the pipeline by means

---

[1] https://www.omg.org/mda/.

of model verification methods and tools to find any existing pitfall, as exemplified by [19] (ii) compare different complex pipelines easier, (iii) reuse pipelines, totally or partially, (iv) version control pipeline alternatives and the involved data, (v) better collaborate in pipeline definitions, among others. Moreover, different data scientist teams (ETL, Stats, Model) may need to use different tools or platforms to better specify their pipeline portions; therefore, our approach needs to support the integration with those tools by means of import/export operations to/from the conceptual model.

Regarding data engineers, they are responsible for providing the technological infrastructure for pipeline definition and operation. The operational model mission is to support the detailed specification of such infrastructures. Different data engineer teams with different capabilities are also common in data science projects. For instance, as a basic organization, there may be a team with cloud expertise apart from another one with local systems knowledge, as illustrated in the figure. The operational model should provide the proper concepts and tools to engineering teams to describe how the pipeline (partially or totally) must be executed.

This conceptual and operational separation, together with the unidirectional dependency from the operational to the conceptual part, may allow the definition of (conceptual) pipelines with multiple execution environments, which can also be maintained and migrated to new versions of the tooling, while ensuring the new results obtained are coherent with the previous ones. Moreover, given a pipeline specification and multiple execution environments for it, multiple properties could be verified by means of model-driven methods and tools.

Regarding workflow, although somehow final operational models are coupled with conceptual models (unidirectional dependency), actually they can be developed independently from each other until a operational model is bound to a conceptual one. Data scientists can collaborate to define new pipelines by creating conceptual models, validating and verifying them at model level, and eventually use predefined execution environments to test them. Likewise, data engineers can define infrastructures based on a concrete container technology for deployment and execution, according to technical requirements, but no concerning any particular conceptual model. Once the binding is done, all the (meta)data for code generators (M2T transformations) need to be provided, e.g. data sources.

Finally, based on these models, all the infrastructure for the automatic execution of pipelines could be generated as code. This systematic specification of the pipeline and automatic generation of the environment configuration and execution will contribute to a significant improvement of R&R in data science projects. Note, however, that given the great heterogeneity of the eligible tools the full automation of a pipeline cannot always be ensured, because some of the GUI tools might not allow headless execution (i.e., CLI execution). In those cases, our approach may need to be able to interrupt the execution, provide the next step artifacts and, once engineers perform the expected manual operation, collect the results to resume the automatic execution. Furthermore, the impact of such situations on the R&R of a pipeline may also be expressed in our models by means of uncertainty specification [2], providing more information to the R&R verification process.

2.2   Metamodels

The abstract syntax of the conceptual and operational DSMLs have been defined as metamodels by means of the Eclipse Modeling Framework (EMF)[2].

Figure 2 shows a representative excerpt of our conceptual metamodel. Its core element is the DataProcessingElement class, which may be classified into two types: (i) DataOperation, atomic operations applied on the data, and (ii) Job, a collection of related data operations or nested jobs. That way projects of different sizes and granularity can be easily specified.

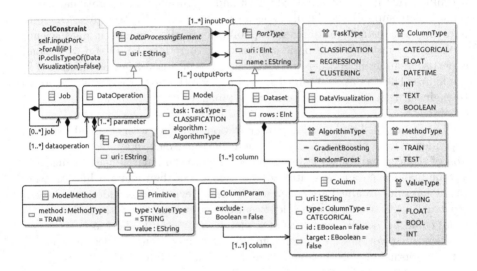

Fig. 2. Conceptual metamodel

Each DataProcessingElement contains one or more input or output ports. Output ports may be a machine learning model, a dataset or a data visualisation, whilst input ports may be just learning models or datasets. An OCL[3] expression constrains the types of input ports allowed. Datasets are described by means of its columns. Columns can be marked as target variables for machine learning models. The main properties of learning models are their task (e.g. Classification, Regression) and the algorithm involved. Each DataOperation is composed of a set of parameters, represented through the Parameter class in our metamodel.

There are three types of parameters: (1) ColumnParam references a set of columns of the dataset to include or not as parameter (exclude attribute); (2) Primitive indicates common primitive types; (3) ModelMethod sets the machine learning operation mode.

---

[2] https://www.eclipse.org/modeling/emf/.
[3] https://www.omg.org/spec/OCL/2.4.

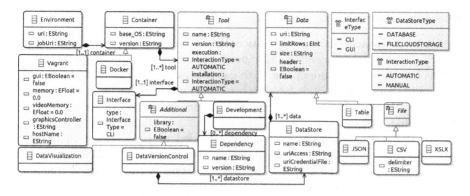

Fig. 3. Operational metamodel

Figure 3 shows an excerpt of our operational metamodel. Its main element is the Environment class, which specifies an execution environment to implement and execute the pipeline defined in the conceptual model. An environment is formed by a container, which could be either a Vagrant[4] or a Docker[5] element. Each container contains a toolkit (Tool) for pipeline development and execution. For each tool we need to know the name, version, user interface, and execution type and installation type (automatic or manual). Note that automatic installation or execution imply no need of human intervention on the whole process. Such automation is not always possible, so the type of user interface is also specified for each tool: (gui or cli). Moreover, an environment defines a relationship with a particular Job of the conceptual model (job attribute), which means that all the data operations specified inside that job will be executed in this environment.

Currently tools are organized into two different classes: Development and Additional. Development tools can implement and execute the pipeline defined, e.g. a programming language as Python. These tools can also reference a collection of Dependency elements (e.g. Python libraries), whose compatibility could verified at model level.

Additional Tools are the tools not mandatory for the execution of the pipeline, but useful to define the complete process in a systematic way, such as data version control or data visualization tools. If they are set as libraries, their installation will be automatic and mediated by the dependency installer of the related development tool. Moreover, version control tools must specify a DataStore where versions can be stored.

Finally, the Data to be imported or exported from this pipeline must be also specified. This data can be imported or exported as a table or as a file, depending on the type of data source used. In both cases, we need to know the name, the row limit (if any), the size of the data, and if header matters.

---

[4] https://www.vagrantup.com/.
[5] https://www.docker.com/.

2.3 Libraries

Both models (conceptual and operational) can be created from scratch, thus requiring a huge modeling effort. Moreover, a great number of elements in those models can become redundant, e.g. each data operation only needs to be defined once, and a similar situation is faced by tools and environments in the operational model. For this reason, we expect to collect those elements in reusable libraries.

As a first step, several known data mining tools (RapidMiner[6], KNIME[7], Orange Data Mining[8]) were thoroughly analyzed to collect their main data operations and map them[9]. A small excerpt of the results obtained is shown in Table 1. Note that the existence of each operation in the PMML[10] standard version 4.2 is also indicated.

Table 1. Data operations mapping.

RapidMiner	KNIME	Orange	PMML	MD4DSPRR
Nominal to numerical	One to many	Continuize	Yes	Get dummy variables
Remove attribute range	Column filter	Select columns	Yes	Remove columns
SMOTE upsampling	SMOTE	–	No	SMOTE
Split data	Partitioning	Data sampler	No	Split data
Gradient boosted	GB trees learner	Gradient boosting	Yes	Gradient boosting (train)
Apply model	GB trees predictor	Predictions	Yes	Gradient boosting (predict)
Performance	Scorer	Test & score	No	Performance measures

Following, we provide a brief description of those operations. GET DUMMY VARIABLES transforms categorical columns into numerical ones (i.e. one-hot encoding). REMOVE COLUMNS deletes a set of columns. The SMOTE algorithm oversamples the dataset (i.e. adds artificial rows), adding instances of the minority class. SPLIT DATA splits the input dataset into two partitions (i.e. row-wise). GRADIENT BOOSTING (TRAIN) represents the training of a machine learning model using the Gradient Boosting algorithm. GRADIENT BOOSTING (PREDICT) represents the execution of a ML model. PERFORMANCE MEASURES calculates the most relevant metrics for a classification model (e.g. confusion matrix, accuracy, recall, etc.) by comparing the prediction made with the real value.

3 Illustrative Example

Next, an illustrative example is presented to better convey how the previously defined metamodels can be used to specify data science projects. This example

---

[6] https://rapidminer.com/.
[7] https://www.knime.com/.
[8] https://orangedatamining.com/.
[9] https://bit.ly/3FXDbp5.
[10] http://dmg.org/pmml/pmml-v4-2-1.html.

was excerpted from a previous project on academic dropout prediction developed by our team [7]. The primary objective of this project was to predict whether an engineering student is going to drop out of her degree at the end of each semester, so correction actions may be triggered to reduce the existing high-rate dropout in technical careers. For this purpose, a machine learning model was trained from academic and personal data. Concretely, an ensemble model was applied integrating the results of three different machine learning algorithms: Gradient Boosting, Random Forest and Support Vector Machines.

For the sake of brevity, here we present the pipeline fragment for the creation of the Gradient Boosting learning model as an illustrative example, because its reduced size and representative operations flow. This flow contains (i) operations involved in the learning model generation (training and testing), (ii) common data processing operations, and (iii) feature engineering operations. More information and materials are available at the project repository[11].

3.1   Conceptual Model

The input dataset structure is presented in Table 2. Each row shows the data needed to define each column of the dataset with our conceptual DSML. Two

Table 2. Dataset definition

Columns	Data types	ID	Target	Description	Examples
degree_name	categorical	0	0	Name of degree	Computer science
call_year	categorical	0	0	Year of the call for access	2007–08, 2008–09
call	categorical	0	0	Call for access	June, September
access_description	categorical	0	0	Access type description	Exam, transferred
gender	categorical	0	0	Gender of student	H, M
interval_year_birth	categorical	0	0	Year of birth divided into 5-year intervals	(1990–1995], (2000–2005]
scholarship	categorical	0	0	Indicate if the student has a scholarship	N, S
cum_pass_ratio	float	0	0	Ratio of subjects passed per taken	0,5; 0,7
marks	float	0	0	Mark obtained in University Entrance Exam (0–14)	10, 11, 9
cum_absent_ratio	float	0	0	Ratio of subjects not presented to the exam per taken	0,8; 0,9
record_id	categorical	1	0	Student ID by degree	1, 5, 105
degree_id	categorical	1	0	Unique Degree Identifier	233, 1623, 1627
dropout	categorical	0	1	Indicates if the student has dropped out	0, 1

---

[11] https://github.com/i3uex/education_drop.

additional columns present a brief description and some example values for each column (feature) respectively.

Once the input dataset has been specified according to our DSML (not shown here), we proceed to define the data pipeline, presented in Fig. 4. Note that an ad-hoc concrete syntax (described in the legend) is used to better illustrate this example. Here we just explain the parameters of the most relevant operations previously described in Sect. 2.3.

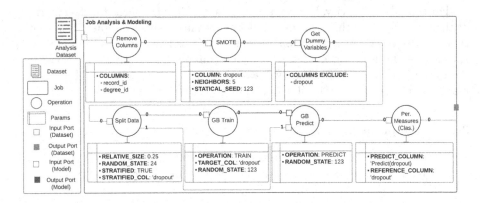

Fig. 4. Conceptual model

In SMOTE, the COLUMN parameter (ColumnParam type) refers to the categorical column to generate new cases (dropout column in our dataset), while NEIGHBORS and STATISTICAL_SEED (Primitive type) are internal parameters of the algorithm.

In SPLIT DATA, the RELATIVE_SIZE parameter indicates the percentage of rows for the first partition. In this case it is 0.25 because we want to use the 75% of the input rows for training and the remaining 25% for testing. The RANDOM_STATE parameter (Primitive type) indicates a fixed random seed for the split. The STRATIFIED parameter (Primitive type) is set to true to indicate that the distribution of the values in the STRATIFIED_COL column should be maintained in the partitions. Finally, this operation returns the first partition on port 0 (training) and the second partition on port 1 (testing).

In GRADIENT BOOSTING TRAIN, the OPERATION parameter (ModelMethod type) set the operation mode: train or predict.

The TARGET_COL parameter (ColumnParam type) indicates that dropout values will be later predicted by the ML model. This operation returns the trained ML model to use as input of the GRADIENT BOOSTING PREDICT operation, which will return a dataset with an additional column, PREDICT(DROPOUT), containing the predicted values.

3.2   Operational Model

For illustrative purposes, two different execution environments were defined in the operational model. Figure 5 presents the commonalities of both execution environments, while Fig. 6 shows their specificities. Figure 5 also illustrates the binding between both environments and the Analysis & Modeling job.

The information system used for data storage was a Cloud File System, so its URI (uriAccess) and credentials file (credentialFileUri) are specified. CSV data files were used for both input and output with the same configuration: header is True and delimiter is '|'.

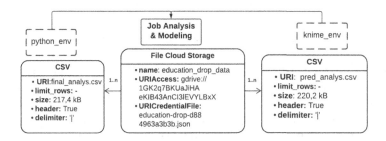

Fig. 5. Operational model

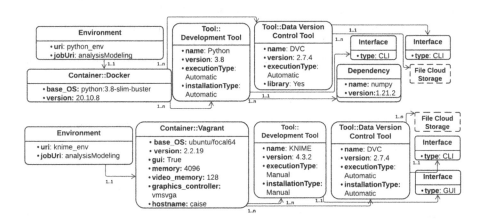

Fig. 6. Execution environment details

The Python environment uses a Docker container with a Linux OS image. Python[12] is selected as development tool with automatic installation and execution (preinstalled in the OS image) and CLI as its interface. Python dependencies are also specified in the model. DVC[13] is the data versioning control tool

---

[12] https://www.python.org/.
[13] https://dvc.org/.

selected, configured as a library of the development tool (installed and executed automatically). Its **DataStore** configuration is shown in Fig. 5. The KNIME environment uses a Vagrant container preinstalled with a particular distribution of Linux OS. Given the small size of the dataset and the simple pipeline defined, data engineers decided to allocate 4 GB of RAM. KNIME[14] is the development tool, which requires manual installation, because no package is available, and also manual execution through its GUI. In this second environment, DVC is not set as a library of the development tool, but as a external tool.

4   Evaluation

Our goal is to assess we can get equivalent results from different executions of the same conceptual pipeline (R&R). For that purpose, we have manually generated the two previous execution environments from their specifications, executed them and compared both results. Given our approach is in an exploratory stage, functional code generators are not still available.

In concrete, we have divided this evaluation into two steps: (1) verifying datasets remain equivalent along the process, and (2) checking final prediction results (testing) are consistent. Regarding the first step, our aim is to assert that no divergent data derivations have been produced when data operations are executed in any of the environments. For that purpose, for every data operation we also specify a collection of post-conditions affecting the output dataset. Their formalization and model-based representation is out of the scope of this work. Hence here we are just illustrating them in Table 3 (top half). As shown, both datasets satisfy all the conditions when **Split Data** operation finishes. Therefore, they can be considered equivalent, though they may contain different data rows.

Table 3. Conditions and results

Operation	Condition	In the example	KNIME	Python
Remove cols.	Columns not present	record_id, degree_id	true	true
SMOTE	Target variable distr.	0.5 for each class	0.5	0.5
Get Dummy Vars.	New column for each different value	# values 7 first cols.: 7, 9, 5, 2, 2, 2, 5	32	32
Split Data	# rows per split	75%/25%	1194/396	1194/396
	Target variable distr	0.5 for each class	0.5	0.5
Operation	Metric	Δ	KNIME	Python
Per. measures	accuracy	+− 0.0256	0.7679	0.7423
	Recall	+− 0.0436	0.8214	0.7778
	Precision	+− 0.0633	0.7419	0.6786
	Specificity	+− 0.0061	0.8000	0.8061

Regarding the second step, Table 3 (bottom half) present the resulting performance metrics for both executions, which are consistent (not yet identical).

---

[14] https://www.knime.com/.

Such difference may be mainly due to slightly different implementations of the same operations in different execution environments.

Although these differences may be further analysed, as a main conclusion, our approach would increase R&R by the automatic generation of the deployment and execution code for data pipelines and by raising verification and validation issues to model level.

5   Related Works

First of all, it is worth mentioning that the work in [14] reviews eleven applications focused on assisting researchers in publishing reproducible research, including executable code and data. Among them, the REANA platform [30] aims at facilitating reproducible science practices using container technologies for preserving and reinstantiating runtime environments. Basically, a cluster composed of a set of micro-services permit to instantiate, launch and monitor container-based computational workflows on remote compute clouds. On the other hand, ReproZip [22] not only provides reproducibility but also basic replicability by allowing the substitution of datasets if researchers have previously ensured compatibility. Basically, it allows encapsulating data, code, and the computational environment. In this case, researchers can choose either execute the result on a ReproZip server or locally without tracking down and installing the dependencies.

Specifically focused on replicability, MORF [8] is an open-source platform which provides a Python API for predictive modeling or production rule analysis in education. It also uses Docker for reproducibility. Moreover, DataDeps.jl [25] is a julia package that facilitates to automate the data setup step in data driven research. It allows joining code and data, so that different projects can be reproduced and replicated avoiding human errors in this part of a Data Science process. It is similar to one part of our approach, but in a simplest way.

Finally, focusing on reproducibility and reusability, ML-flow[29] allows ensuring both aspects by offering itself as an API available for Python, Java and R languages. Researchers can define a pipeline using a YAML specification that can be reproduced managing dependencies through Conda or Docker. Subsequently ml-experiment [6] integrates it into a Python Framework to create reproducible Data Science projects. This framework shares with our approach features such as the use of containers (Docker) or the use of Jobs to encapsulate code.

In general, we have some commonalities with some of the above works. However, first, our approach is technology independent, second, it makes an explicit separation between data scientist and data engineering roles and responsibilities, and third, it raises the level of abstraction for verification, comparison and reusability of data science artifacts.

6 Discussion and Future Work

Given the exploratory essence of this work, we finally discuss some open points.

R&R Verification at Model Level. In this work, we briefly illustrate how formally specifying post-conditions for every data operation would allow verifying datasets processed in a pipeline remain equivalent in different execution environments. We could obtain a model from the output dataset (T2M transformation) resulting from the execution of each job (or data operation) in the pipeline, and automatically verify those conditions by model-driven techniques and tools, as OCL, for example. As [5] states, the development of a formal model for recording data derivations at the level of the atomic elements in the dataset is a subject of current research. Furthermore, conceptual and operational models provide enough information to define specific (and reusable) R&R constraints. For instance, a concrete execution environment (e.g. a Linux PC with KNIME) may be adequate to execute its associated pipeline for a small volume of data, however it turns out unresponsive when the expected volume of data grows significantly. We intend to work on those lines in the future.

Usability and Efficiency. Although a full discussion of those properties is out of the scope of this work, they are relevant topics to address in the future. Regarding usability, our modeling framework is mainly conceived as an integration hub of pipeline definitions and operational environment configurations made by specific well-known tools and technologies. Once conceptual and operational concerns are completely defined for a DS pipeline, model-driven methods can be used for validation, and verification, but also for automatic deployment and execution. As a result, we expect the efficiency of the whole process will be improved. One of the keys to improve usability and efficiency is to create a library of modeling assets for our approach, containing reusable data operations and their constraints as well as reusable execution environments provisioning. Furthermore, we already elaborated a mapping of data operations among different well-known tools as a foundation for their integration and the automatic generation of pipelines specification on them.

Available Notations and Languages. We have defined our own metamodels as a means to explore the domain and elicitate the main concepts and their relationships. However, existing languages and notations from different domains may be used for conceptual and operational models in future work.

7 Conclusions

Although there exits a plethora of tools and platforms for data science projects development, their reproducibility and replicability remains still an open challenge. This paper presents a Model-Driven approach for the definition of reproducible and replicable data science pipelines by fostering the systematization and automation of their execution. The two main roles in these projects, data scientists and data engineers, are specifically considered to provide a particular view of the system for each of them, the conceptual and operational perspectives respectively. Moreover, a representative example, excerpted from a previous project, was presented to illustrate and evaluate our approach. Our first results in R&R for that example were promising and we expect to apply our approach in next data science projects. Finally, some open questions were briefly discussed to lead future research.

References

1. Baker, M.: 1,500 scientists lift the lid on reproducibility. Nature **533**, 452–454 (2016). https://doi.org/10.1038/533452a, https://www.nature.com/articles/533452a
2. Bertoa, M.F., Burgueño, L., Moreno, N., Vallecillo, A.: Incorporating measurement uncertainty into OCL/UML primitive datatypes. Softw. Syst. Model. **19**(5), 1163–1189 (2019). https://doi.org/10.1007/s10270-019-00741-0
3. Brambilla, M., Cabot, J., Wimmer, M.: Model-driven software engineering in practice, second edition. Synthesis Lect. Softw. Eng. **3**(1), 1–207 (2017). https://doi.org/10.2200/S00751ED2V01Y201701SWE004
4. Byrne, C.: Development Workflows for Data Scientists. O'Reilly Media, Inc., Newton (2017)
5. Chapman, A., Missier, P., Simonelli, G., Torlone, R.: Capturing and querying fine-grained provenance of preprocessing pipelines in data science. Proc. VLDB Endow. **14**, 507–520 (2020). https://doi.org/10.14778/3436905.3436911
6. Domenech, A.M., Guillén, A.: ml-experiment: A Python framework for reproducible data science. J. Phys. Conf. Ser. **1603**(1), 012025 (2020). https://doi.org/10.1088/1742-6596/1603/1/012025
7. Fernández-García, A.J., Preciado, J.C., Melchor, F., Rodriguez-Echeverria, R., Conejero, J.M., Sánchez-Figueroa, F.: A real-life machine learning experience for predicting university dropout at different stages using academic data. IEEE Access **9**, 133076–133090 (2021)
8. Gardner, J., Brooks, C., Andres, J.M., Baker, R.S.: Morf: a framework for predictive modeling and replication at scale with privacy-restricted MOOC data. In: Proceedings - 2018 IEEE International Conference on Big Data, Big Data 2018, pp. 3235–3244, January 2019. https://doi.org/10.1109/BIGDATA.2018.8621874
9. Gundersen, O.E., Kjensmo, S.: State of the art: reproducibility in artificial intelligence. In: Proceedings of the Thirty-Second AAAI Conference on Artificial Intelligence and Thirtieth Innovative Applications of Artificial Intelligence Conference and Eighth AAAI Symposium on Educational Advances in Artificial Intelligence. AAAI 2018/IAAI 2018/EAAI 2018, pp. 1644–1651. AAAI Press (2018)
10. Haibe-Kains, B., et al.: Transparency and reproducibility in artificial intelligence. Nature **586**, E14–E16 (2020). https://doi.org/10.1038/s41586-020-2766-y
11. van den Heuvel, W.-J., Tamburri, D.A.: Model-driven ML-ops for intelligent enterprise applications: vision, approaches and challenges. In: Shishkov, B. (ed.) BMSD 2020. LNBIP, vol. 391, pp. 169–181. Springer, Cham (2020). https://doi.org/10.1007/978-3-030-52306-0_11
12. Hutson, M.: Artificial intelligence faces reproducibility crisis. Science **359**(6377), 725–726 (2018). https://doi.org/10.1126/science.359.6377.725

13. Jaiswal, A., Bagale, P.: A survey on big data in financial sector. In: 2017 International Conference on Networking and Network Applications (NaNA), pp. 337–340. IEEE (2017). https://doi.org/10.1109/NaNA.2017.46

14. Konkol, M., Nüst, D., Goulier, L.: Publishing computational research - a review of infrastructures for reproducible and transparent scholarly communication. Res. Integrity Peer Rev. **5**, 1–8 (2020). https://doi.org/10.1186/S41073-020-00095-Y/TABLES/2

15. National Academies of Sciences, Engineering, and Medicine: Reproducibility and Replicability in Science. The National Academies Press, Washington, DC (2019). https://doi.org/10.17226/25303

16. Obermeyer, Z., Emanuel, E.J.: Predicting the future - big data, machine learning, and clinical medicine. N. Engl. J. Med. **375**, 1216–1219 (2016). https://doi.org/10.1056/NEJMp1606181

17. Raff, E.: A step toward quantifying independently reproducible machine learning research. In: Proceedings of the 33rd International Conference on Neural Information Processing Systems, pp. 5485–5495. Curran Associates Inc. (2019)

18. Rahad, K., Badreddin, O., Mohsin Reza, S.: The human in model-driven engineering loop: a case study on integrating handwritten code in model-driven engineering repositories. Softw. Pract. Exp. **51**(6), 1308–1321 (2021). https://doi.org/10.1002/spe.2957

19. Rajbahadur, G.K., Oliva, G.A., Hassan, A.E., Dingel, J.: Pitfalls analyzer: quality control for model-driven data science pipelines. In: 2019 ACM/IEEE 22nd International Conference on Model Driven Engineering Languages and Systems (MODELS), pp. 12–22 (2019). https://doi.org/10.1109/MODELS.2019.00-19

20. Rupprecht, L., Davis, J.C., Arnold, C., Gur, Y., Bhagwat, D.: Improving reproducibility of data science pipelines through transparent provenance capture. Proc. VLDB Endow. **13**, 3354–3368 (2020). https://doi.org/10.14778/3415478.3415556

21. Samuel, S., König-Ries, B.: Understanding experiments and research practices for reproducibility: an exploratory study. PeerJ **9**, e11140 (2021)

22. Steeves, V., Rampin, R., Chirigati, F.: Using reprozip for reproducibility and library services. IASSIST Q. **42**, 14–14 (2018). https://doi.org/10.29173/IQ18

23. Tantithamthavorn, C., Hassan, A.E.: An experience report on defect modelling in practice: pitfalls and challenges. In: Proceedings - International Conference on Software Engineering, pp. 286–295 (2018). https://doi.org/10.1145/3183519.3183547

24. Treveil, M., et al.: Introducing MLOps: How to Scale Machine Learning in the Enterprise. O'Reilly Media, Inc., Newton (2021). https://www.oreilly.com/library/view/introducing-mlops/9781492083283/

25. White, L., Togneri, R., Liu, W., Bennamoun, M.: DataDeps.jl: Repeatable data setup for reproducible data science. J. Open Res. Softw. **7**(1), 33 (2019). https://doi.org/10.5334/jors.244

26. Williamson, B.: Digital education governance: data visualization, predictive analytics, and 'real-time' policy instruments. J. Educ. Policy **31**, 123–141 (2016). https://doi.org/10.1080/02680939.2015.1035758

27. Willis, C., Stodden, V.: Trust but verify: how to leverage policies, workflows, and infrastructure to ensure computational reproducibility in publication. Harvard Data Sci. Rev. **2**(4) (2020). https://doi.org/10.1162/99608f92.25982dcf

28. Yin, Z., Lan, H., Tan, G., Lu, M., Vasilakos, A.V., Liu, W.: Computing platforms for big biological data analytics: perspectives and challenges. Comput. Struct. Biotechnol. J. **15**, 403–411 (2017). https://doi.org/10.1016/j.csbj.2017.07.004

29. Zaharia, M., et al.: Accelerating the machine learning lifecycle with MLFlow. IEEE Data Eng. Bull. **41**, 39–45 (2018). https://www-cs.stanford.edu/people/matei/papers/2018/ieee_mlflow.pdf

30. Šimko, T., Heinrich, L., Hirvonsalo, H., Kousidis, D., Rodríguez, D.: Reana: a system for reusable research data analyses. EPJ Web Conf. **214**, 06034 (2019). https://doi.org/10.1051/epjconf/201921406034

The Aircraft and Its Manufacturing System: From Early Requirements to Global Design

Anouck Chan⬤, Anthony Fernandes Pires⬤, Thomas Polacsek$^{(\boxtimes)}$⬤,
and Stéphanie Roussel⬤

ONERA, Toulouse, France
{anouck.chan,anthony.fernandes_pires,thomas.polacsek
stephanie.roussel}@onera.fr

Abstract. The design of an aircraft manufacturing system depends highly on the design of the aircraft itself. In this work, we propose an approach based on conceptual modelling and optimization methods that allows to take into account the impact of an aircraft design on its assembly line design. We start by eliciting early requirements in a real industrial use case context. Using Goal Oriented Requirements Engineering, we highlight the dependencies between the systems as well as the key elements that must be optimized to obtain an optimal global system. Then, based on a conceptual model and operational research, we present the tool that we have developed to support the development of an optimal overall system. We analyse the experiments realized on different aircraft designs, and we identify and summarize the lessons learned from this experience.

Keywords: Requirements · Optimization · Co-design · Aeronautics · Industry 4.0

1 Introduction

In industry, there are systems that are designed in an asynchronous way and that are dependent on each other. Such systems can be found, for example, in the context of software development and operations, where operational environment system is based on software design. In the embedded systems context, hardware and software designs can also sometimes be out of synchronization but depend on each other. If hardware is decided first, choices made on it strongly impact software (*e.g.* because of memory limitations).

In this paper, we focus on another example of such systems, namely an aircraft and its manufacturing system. Indeed, aircraft development is not only limited to the elaboration of an aircraft design, but also includes means to build it. For each new aircraft family, a dedicated industrial system must be developed. Even if it is built upon existing means like basic plants, new assembly

ⓒ Springer Nature Switzerland AG 2022
X. Franch et al. (Eds.): CAiSE 2022, LNCS 13295, pp. 164–179, 2022.
https://doi.org/10.1007/978-3-031-07472-1_10

lines (along with new tools, robots, *etc.*) must be developed to cope with the specificity of each new aircraft family and with production objectives (*e.g.* number of aircraft to produce, rate). An aircraft and its manufacturing system are strongly linked to each other. Every time the design of the first changes, it may be necessary to redesign the latter. In addition, it is impossible to design the manufacturing system until certain aircraft design choices are made. Lastly, the performance of the manufacturing system highly depends on the aircraft design.

For designing these two systems, it is essential to anticipate as soon as possible the impacts of aircraft design choices on its manufacturing system. For instance, it could be possible that a manufacturing requirement such as *reach a production rate of 50 aircraft per month* is not satisfied because of the aircraft specifications (*e.g.* the chosen material which requires a complex process for drilling and junctionning). In this example, the aircraft design must be modified, which is quite heavy. In fact, it requires to make new high-level changes (*e.g.* material choice), cascade them and then assess if this new design is consistent with the manufacturing requirement. Being able to assess, even partially, the impact of the aircraft design on the manufacturing goals would allow earlier trade-offs in case of conflict and thus a more satisfactory overall specification. It would also prevent high costs due to late design modifications. A good design for the two systems is more a matter of global optimum than of the separate optimization of each of them.

In this paper, we introduce an approach that combines proven modelling techniques and optimization methods to support the design of the aircraft and its manufacturing systems. The aim of this approach is to provide methods and tools for taking into account, from the early design phases, the manufacturing performance in the design of the aircraft.

This paper is organized as follows: in Sect. 2, we describe our industrial case study. Sections 3 and 4 are respectively dedicated to goals elicitation and to overall optimization and provide details about the application on the case study. Then, we discuss lessons learned in Sect. 5. Section 6 is dedicated to related work and we conclude in Sect. 7.

2   Industrial Case Study

In this section, we detail the main features of the industrial case study we have worked on. The design of the aircraft has an impact on many aspects of manufacturing: the workplace ergonomics, the space available to perform assembly operations, the need for very specific tools and machines, the means of transporting the aircraft components according to their size, *etc*. Moreover, the way the aircraft is broken down into parts can induce more or less assembly operations. For instance, installing several light parts could be easier than a large heavy one. However, it could require much more connection operations. Therefore, the objective of reaching a high industrial efficiency is also linked to the aircraft design choices.

Our industrial study framework deals with the design and manufacture of a specific component: the structure of the aircraft's fuselage, namely the *airframe*, and its assembly line. The fuselage is designed to provide spaces for the crew, passengers and cargo and to withstand the aerodynamic forces. It is also the link between the wings, the tail and the nose. The airframe is composed of a keel beam, circular frames, linear spars and skin panels which must be assembled. An assembly line is a sequence of workstations that corresponds to all the assembly stages of a product. In the aeronautics industry, assembly lines can be found at both Boeing [18] and Airbus [16,25].

In this case study, we have worked with two *aircraft architects*, who design the fuselage, and one *assembly architect*, who designs assembly lines. All three of them have been working for a major aircraft manufacturer for many years. The aircraft architects are specialised in architectural design, *i.e.* making choices and designing the elements and systems of the aircraft without going into details. For instance, they do not consider the number or the position of each bolt. The assembly architect works on the assembly line organisation and the new assembly tools definition. In this project, he was in charge of the design of a new assembly line for the airframe production. An important point is that the two aircraft architects work in a different department and on a different site from the assembly architect. This is a real silo situation. This project was an opportunity to have a more integrated vision and to take into account the impact of the product on the production. Through five half-day working sessions over a period of three months, we supported the architects to clarify the goals, the constraints and what was not in the scope of this case study. To this end, we proposed a *Goal-Oriented Requirements Engineering* (GORE) model and briefly trained architects in this approach. Then, for three months, at the frequency of a meeting every week with the architects, we worked on the problem formalisation and on the design of the tool presented in the following sections. The architects provided us with all the information regarding the assembly operations related to the different aircraft designs and the assembly methods and tools. From our side, we helped them to clarify their objectives and we provided them with a tool to evaluate the impacts of the product on the production.

In our use case, the problem was to design an aircraft fuselage as manufacturable as possible, *i.e.* as easy and as fast as possible to assemble and with a not too expensive factory. More precisely, architects want to be able to evaluate aircraft design solutions at early stages of the design process and, to do this, assess them with respect to the industrial performance of their corresponding assembly lines. Note that the concept of industrial performance was not clearly defined at the beginning of our study.

In the two following sections, we describe how we tackled this problem. Starting from requirements elicitation, we explain the relevant metrics we have identified to measure the assembly line performances. Then, we present a tool that allows to perform numerical comparison of two fuselage airframe designs.

3   Identify Goals and Objectives

The first step of our work was to understand the dependencies between the aircraft and its manufacturing system and specifically how the design choices impact assembly line performance. Expressing such dependencies is not an easy task, as aircraft design and manufacturing design are two different domains. In this section, we show how GORE modelling techniques allow to elicit and understand the goals of each system and their dependencies.

3.1   Model the Goal Oriented Requirements

GORE approaches focus on finely characterizing the interactions among goals of the system and interactions among goals and some other elements. These elements can be internal or external to this system, like actors or resources [6,17]. Most of GORE frameworks identify two types of goals, namely *goals* and *soft goals*. Soft goals are objectives for which *no clear-cut criteria* indicating whether they are fulfilled can be expressed [13,22]. Such a distinction is used in frameworks such as *Non-Functional Requirements* (NFR) [6,21] or i^* [7,30]. In our context, this distinction is crucial. It allows us to distinguish between what is a non-negotiable constraint and what is flexible. Therefore, we consider that a goal is a constraint, a non-negotiable mandatory objective that a system must satisfy. In reverse, a soft goal is a possible trade-off point, its satisfaction being negotiable. It represents an element of negotiation between the aircraft and the manufacturing systems.

As expressed earlier, the manufacturing system design depends on the aircraft design. Because the designs of these systems are asynchronous, this dependency is a strong one, *i.e.* the manufacturing system cannot exist without the aircraft. This corresponds to the i^* notion of vulnerability of the manufacturing system. This vulnerability is materialised through *dependency relationships*. In i^*, the dependency relation is composed of three elements. The first two elements can be goals or tasks and belong to two different actors and the third is the dependence object (the dependum). It is a unidirectional relationship that indicates a dependency of one actor on another. For instance, the choice of a robot (the depender) depends on the assembly operation to be performed (the dependum), and this operation is defined during the aircraft design (the dependee). Because the dependency relationship is at the heart of i^* framework, we chose i^* for the modelling of our use case goals.

3.2   Application

In our case study, aircraft and assembly architects were not familiar with GORE approaches. None of the goals, soft goals, tasks and dependencies were clearly identified. It took many iterations with the three architects to elicit them and to reach the exploitable goals model given in Fig. 1.

In this goals model, the task *Design the fuselage airframe* is the main activity of the Aircraft Architect. This task is the mean to satisfy the main goal *The fuselage airframe design is defined* and it is decomposed into three goals that qualify the task: *Spaces for the crew, passengers and cargo are provided*, *The aerodynamic forces are withstood* and *Mastered materials are used*.

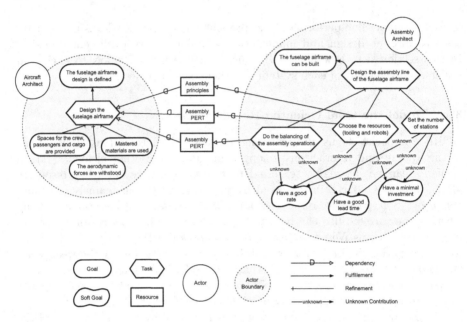

Fig. 1. i^* Strategic Rationale model for the design of the fuselage airframe and its assembly line (Model in i^* 1.0)

For the design of the assembly line, the Assembly Architect main task is to *Design the assembly line of the fuselage airframe*, answering the main goal *The fuselage airframe can be built*. This main task is decomposed into three sub-tasks: *Do the balancing of the assembly operations* which corresponds to the scheduling of the assembly operations based on the *Assembly PERT* (Program Evaluation and Review Technique); *Choose the resources* corresponds to the choice of the resources to perform the assembly depending on the *Assembly principles* and the *Assembly PERT*; and *Set the number of stations* corresponds to the choice of the number of stations composing the assembly line.

Assembly PERT and *Assembly principles* are information produced by the Aircraft Architect. The *Assembly PERT* describes the precedence relationship among assembly operations and their duration. The *Assembly principles* describe how to join the skin panels together and how to fix all the elements together (for instance with joints, fasteners or welding).

In addition, the Assembly Architect has three soft goals that altogether represent the industrial performance of the manufacturing system. *Have a good rate* indicates that the factory must produce as many aircraft as possible. This soft goal is limited by the investments that are made to build the factory, which is expressed by the second soft goal *Have a minimal investment*. The third soft goal, *Have a good lead time*, asserts that the duration to build a single aircraft must be acceptable. They are soft goals because their acceptance is subject to interpretation.

Usually in i^*, tasks impact soft goals. There are various impact types: *make, help, hurt* or *break*. For trade-offs, tasks can be refined into aircraft design alternatives and assembly line design alternatives. Each alternative impacts goals positively or negatively. From there, many works use these links and propose propagation rules to evaluate the alternatives [3,11]. In our case, and this is a key consideration, assessing these impacts within the model is impossible: relationships among tasks and soft goals are not monotonic. For example, let us consider the task *Choose the resources*. On the one hand, choosing cutting edge technology resources can help the goal *Have a good lead time*, but might hurt *Have a minimal investment*. On the other hand, choosing cheaper resources that are less efficient can help to *Have a minimal investment* but may hurt the goal *Have a good lead time*. Moreover, refining the different alternatives does not give us more information. It is not obvious that having 6 stations allows to have a better rate than with 5. Even regarding the investment, stations number is not the only cost factor, there are also the tools and machines.

Therefore, due to the combinatory explosion, we are faced with the impossibility of expressing all the alternatives and to manually assess their impacts on goals. So, we choose to model the contribution links to the soft goals as *unknown* and, unlike other works, to perform trade-offs assessment not in i^*, but by using automatic calculus outside of the model. We even go further: besides assessment, we automatically find the best assembly line alternatives for a given aircraft design. To do this, we need to elicit all elements and their relationships that are involved in the satisfaction of the soft goals.

Note that the obtained model looks rather simple. In fact, our problem is to take into account the manufacturing performance for an airframe design. So we do not need to consider all goals involved in the airframe design or in the industrial system design but only the relevant ones. Moreover, we focus on early design phases. Therefore, a refined version of goals is pointless as they would result in the alternatives described previously. Finally, it took several collaborative working sessions to converge towards the goal model presented here. This highlights that all the elements (goals and soft goals, associated tasks and dependencies) were not clear at the beginning of the study.

4   Support the Optimal Overall System Design

In this section, we first present several considerations that we had to take into account in our approach. Then, we describe the methods and tools developed to support the development of an optimal overall system. They are based on a conceptual model and operational research optimization methods.

4.1   Support the Design of an Optimal Solution

Our aim is to support the design of the global system composed by the aircraft fuselage and the assembly line. To do this, it is necessary to have an impact assessment of the fuselage airframe design choices on the assembly line. In order to be useful, this assessment should satisfy four properties. Firstly, the method used to perform the assessment should be clear and accepted by the teams involved in the project development. Secondly, the time required to perform the assessment should be short, in order to allow the teams to quickly have feedback on the current project development when they need one. Thirdly, it should not be subjective, *i.e.* its value should be the same regardless of who performs it. In order to be objective, metrics can be used along with documentation on how the metrics are computed. That way, anyone can reproduce the assessment and should obtain the same value. Finally, this assessment should not require additional work. An intuitive way to meet these four properties is to automatize the assessment.

Of course, assessing the impact of the airframe design on the assembly line is not new. Today, this activity is carried out by experts judgment. However, this expert judgment is quite arbitrary, slightly unclear and difficult to reproduce. It does not fit regarding our expectations. In addition, in our context, assessment comes to solve a highly combinatorial problem whose optimal solution is hardly findable by humans. To overcome these limitations, we propose an assessment based on automated calculus that can support experts in their design decision-making. The criteria and metrics used for this assessment correspond to the soft goals that have been described in the previous section. As these soft goals have been validated by the architects, this eases the assessment acceptation by the teams.

To formally define and to automatize the assessment, it is necessary to model the elements targeted by these criteria and also the elements that interact with them. The idea here is not to fully model the two systems, but only the parts that are relevant for expressing the problem. Modelling is playing a substantial role in engineering today, as it allows to manage complexity, formalize or run automatic reasoning on it. In our case, we have chosen a conceptual modelling expressed in SysML, as it allows the representation of elements, their properties or attributes, and their relationships.

4.2   Application: Conceptual Model

Applied to our case study, the conceptual model in Fig. 2 uses the SysML formalism to describe the main elements composing an aircraft section for the product side and the main elements composing an assembly line for the manufacturing side.

On the product side, the main element is the *Aircraft Section* (the fuselage in our application). It is composed of several *Airframe Components*. An *Airframe Component* can be an *Airframe part, i.e.* a unitary element made in a unique material, or an *Airframe Assembly, i.e.* a composition of *Airframe Components* in a tree structure.

On the manufacturing side, the main element is an *Assembly Line*. An *Assembly Line* is composed of *Resources*, which represent infrastructures, machines or tooling. *Resources* are associated to a *Resource Type* that represents the

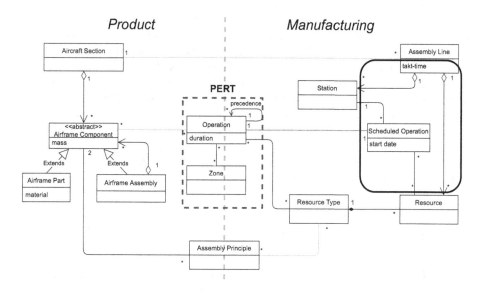

Fig. 2. SysML model for the design of an aircraft section and its assembly line

type of resource used (*e.g.* drilling robots). An *Assembly Line* is also composed of *Stations*. A *Station* represents a physical space in the factory used to perform several *Scheduled Operations*. Each *Scheduled Operation* has a *start date* and uses a set of *Resources*. The duration spent on each station of an assembly line is called the *takt-time* and is the same for all the stations. So, a shorter *takt-time* means a higher rate. Note that the *takt-time*, the *lead time* and the number of stations are mathematically related by the following formula: *lead time = number stations ∗ takt-time*.

In the middle of Fig. 2, there are elements associated with dependencies between the product side and the manufacturing side identified in the i^* model. The Assembly PERT is represented by two elements. The first element is the *Operation*. It has a *duration* and a link on itself to represent the precedence relation. The Assembly PERT is also linked to the *Zone*. *Zone* corresponds to a physical zone of the aircraft section where the *Operation* is performed. Each *Zone* has specific constraints with regards to working conditions that are not detailed here for readability. Each *Operation* can require *Resource Type* to be performed. It is linked to a *Scheduled Operation*. Finally, on the product side, each *Operation* is also linked to an *Airframe Component*, which is the element addressed by the *Operation*.

The *Assembly Principles* identified in Fig. 1 is also present in Fig. 2. Each couple of *Airframe Components* can have one or many *Assembly Principles* if they are meant to be assembled together. An *Assembly Principle* is the mean by which *Airframe Components* are connected together. For example, it can be by drilling and using bolts or by welding, *etc.* In addition, each *Assembly Principle* requires specific *Resource Types* for the assembling.

Several elements are circled in black. We call them *calculated elements*. They correspond to the tasks outputs identified in the goal model presented in Sect. 3. The instantiation of these calculated elements is therefore the result of an assembly architect's design task. More precisely, the task *Do the balancing of the assembly operations* corresponds to the instantiation of the class *Scheduled Operation* and to the choice of a *takt-time* for the *Assembly line*. The task *Choose the resources* corresponds to the choice of the number of *Resources* of each type in the *Assembly Line* (multiplicity value of the link between *Assembly Line* and *Resource*) and to the choice of resources for performing *Scheduled Operations*. Finally, the task *Set the number of stations* corresponds to the number of stations in the *Assembly Line* (multiplicity value of the link between *Assembly Line* and *Station*).

4.3   Application: Assembly Line Design Optimization Tool

In order to evaluate the impact of the aircraft design on the manufacturing soft goals and to support assembly line design, we have developed an Assembly Line Design Optimization tool (ALDO) that computes the best assembly line associated with this design. ALDO is based on the conceptual model defined previously: its inputs are instances of all the elements of the conceptual model, except the *calculated elements* that are its outputs.

Practically speaking, the tool explores assembly line alternatives. These alternatives correspond to the tasks *Choose the resources* and *Set the number of stations* and therefore have an impact on the soft goals. Then, the objective of ALDO is to minimize the takt-time, which contributes to the goals *Have a good rate* and *Have a good lead time*. In fact, as the number of stations is fixed in the explored alternatives, minimizing the takt-time also minimizes the lead time. Based on this objective, ALDO creates a *Scheduled Operation* along with its *start date* for each *Operation* of the PERT. This corresponds to the task *Do the balancing of the assembly operations*.

The optimization problem solved by ALDO consists in scheduling operations according to several types of constraints. The first set of constraints addresses the operation precedence relation. The second deals with the fact that at most one technician can work in a zone at each time and that some zones can be blocked when performing some operations (*e.g.* for security reasons). The last set of constraints focuses on the number of available resources and the fact that some pairs of resources cannot be both installed in the same station. Concerning the objective, the tool minimizes the maximum use duration of each resource, which is an approximation of the takt-time. Following classical approaches such as [26] or [5], such a problem can be encoded in Constraint Programming. In our case, ALDO uses CP Optimizer 20.1.

We have run experiments with ALDO on benchmarks that represent two aircraft designs along with their PERT. They are composed of 150 operations on average. We consider 5 types of resources in the assembly line, mainly drilling robots and arm robots. There are approximately 20 working zones. We use two parameters to define assembly line alternatives: the number of stations and the number of resources for each resource type.

Table 1. *Takt-time* obtained for a number of stations and for some available resources.

Number of stations	1 robot of each type		One additional drilling robot	
	Design 1	Design 2	Design 1	Design 2
4	9h54	**9h51**	9h54	**9h08**
5	**8h53**	9h07	8h09	**7h30**
6	**6h50**	9h07	6h47	**6h21**
7	**5h51**	9h07	5h51	**5h30**
8	**5h30**	9h07	**5h30**	**5h30**

In Table 1, we present a representative set of results. The number of stations varies between 4 and 8 and we compare only two resource alternatives: in the first column there is exactly one robot of each type and in the second column there is one additional drilling robot. Note that the one robot of each type alternative helps more the soft goal *Have a minimal investment* than the one with the additional robot. The tool was given 2 min for each alternative, which allowed to get solutions close to optimal ones. The lead time for each alternative can be computed by multiplying the number of stations with the takt-time value.

Within the one robot of each type alternative, Design 1 has a smaller takt-time than Design 2 with a number of stations between 5 and 8 (which corresponds to a higher rate), while Design 2 is better only for 4 stations. The takt-time stops being improved after 8 stations for Design 1 and 5 stations for Design 2. It is because it is not possible to schedule in a shorter amount of time some activities that use a specific resource that must belong to a unique station. To overcome this, the assembly architect proposed a new alternative with one additional drilling robot. With this new robot, Design 2 has a strictly better takt-time for all the station numbers except for the 8 stations one in which both designs have the same value.

As a result of these experiments, we allowed architects to compare designs and to propose quickly the best possible assembly line alternatives. It should be noted that we do not obtain one best solution but a Pareto front of takt-time, lead time, number of stations and resources. Choosing among these aircraft designs and assembly line alternatives would require a trade-off among assembly line soft goals based on business knowledge. This is clearly outside the scope of this study.

5 Lessons Learned

As stated in the introduction, our aim is to *take into account the performance of the manufacturing system in the design of the aircraft*. The models and tools presented in this paper clearly provide insight on the impact of certain aircraft design choices on the manufacturing system. It is important to note that the architects did not know GORE approaches at the beginning of the study. The

i^* framework allowed us to elicit the key elements of assembly line design and to understand their interactions with airframe design. The resulting goal model, although simple, ensures that we did not miss any relevant elements and that their dependencies were correct. The architects considered this contribution very valuable and this opinion was shared by an expert from the company's digital transformation department to whom they showed this work. In addition, our automatic tool allows users to automatically compute optimized assembly line alternatives which would be extremely challenging to be created manually. It also shows that some alternatives appear more promising than others. The aircraft and assembly architects were very enthusiastic about the results found and the ability to measure the impact of aircraft design choices on the assembly line in a very short time. However, a limit of our approach is that it does not trace nor clearly identify the root decision in the aircraft design that has an impact on each soft goal on the manufacturing system side.

We can also observe that our interlocutors were not able to choose only one satisfactory scenario among the ones generated by the tool, but to identify some suitable alternatives. Indeed, at this stage, it was not possible for them to decide which costs should be reduced in priority, among the ones generated by the number of robots, by the number of stations, by the lead time or by the rate. However, our results allowed them to brainstorm and discuss these points in the early stages of the design, which they had never been able to do before.

Regarding the two different aircraft designs in our case study, we can note that they are equivalent in terms of aircraft architect's goals. Of course the two structure designs are not equivalent in terms of configuration and layouts, and even less identical, but they both satisfy the goals considered in the early aircraft design phase. There is therefore no trade-off between the goals associated with the aircraft design and the ones associated with the assembly line design. Practically speaking, this absence of a trade-off possibility is due to the absence of soft goals on the aircraft design side. Future work should introduce trade-offs between aircraft and manufacturing goals, such as reduce the aircraft weight and reduce the assembly time.

However, by giving the aircraft architects the possibility to compare different designs in terms of industrial performance and by allowing the assembly architect to measure the impact of choices such as the number of robots, we have laid the first steps of a methodology and tools for co-design. Historically, co-design, or concurrent engineering, aims at the early detection of potential problems between design and manufacturing [28]. Nowadays, co-design encompasses a much larger issue. It ensures that all stakeholders, not only design and manufacturing engineering, but also supply chain, maintenance, environmental impact or recycling, cooperate in the early design phases [19].

If we take a step back and look closer at the methodology we followed, we identify two steps. In a first step, we model the objectives of each system and their dependencies. These dependencies represent the point in the design activity where decisions can be made to find optimal solutions for both systems. Note that we are independent of the used GORE approach. As long as the dependencies among systems design can be represented, their rationale are detailed and their soft goals are elicited, we are confident that any GORE language can be used. In addition, even though we did not explore this direction, specification of links along requirements and interactions with them is not specific to GORE modelling. Similar modelling problems are studied in systems engineering approaches like, for instance, SysML.

In a second step, we focused on assessment and optimization. Using conceptual model, we provided a clear view of relationships among the drivers and a structure for the data. By drivers, we mean the constraints and the decision variables that affect the satisfaction of the objectives of interests. Once the problem is structured, we use automatic calculation to find optimal solutions with respect to criteria derived from the goal model.

Thus, we can observe that we couple here two different ways of modelling in order to support the assessment and optimization of solutions for our problem. Both models are complementary, bringing their own benefits at different steps of the approach.

6 Related Work

The approach presented in this paper is related to many research topics, going from the optimal design of a product and its production system to the use of multi-modelling approaches. In this section, we give a non-exhaustive view of related work.

6.1 Optimal Design of a Product and Its Production System

Many works exist in the aeronautical industry which aims at improving the manufacturing system performance. For example, at Airbus, [16] focuses on improving the existing production line relying on a collective exploratory approach. Another example at Boeing focuses on optimizing the production flow and processes, relying on modeling and simulation analysis [18]. However, few works focus on the optimal global design, even though *concurrent engineering* is a common practice in aeronautic corporations such as Airbus [1]. In recent works, Donelli *et al.* describes a value-driven model-based approach to assess a solution trade space for the aircraft design, manufacturing and supply chain [9]. Their main objective is to support decision makers in the early stages of aircraft development by coupling these different domains. Even though our objectives could appear similar, they consider a much more abstract design level. For instance, they model the dependency between the manufacturing and the aircraft with a single numeric impact factor. Another work studies the links between the factory and the aircraft [24]. They propose a conceptual model pattern to represent and apprehend the links between them but unlike us, they do not tackle the problem of finding an optimal factory. Note that the conceptual model we have used is compliant with this pattern.

There is a lot of work on *concurrent engineering* to answer our problematic, but they are not specific to the aeronautic field. For example, it is mainly applied in the automotive supply chain where it has been focusing for a long time on manufacturability issues [12]. In this approach, collaborative engineering considers mostly physical parts of a system and aims to design things that are assembled [31], or have the best assembly sequence [8,14]. Focusing only on ease of assembly *Design for Assembly* (DFA) [4] and Design for Manufacturing (DFM) [20] aim to solve manufacturing problems at the design stage.

Stoffels and Vielhaber study a concurrent engineering approach for a product and its production system [29]. This approach is based on correlation matrices between characteristics of both systems. They also define a method in which solutions of all product functions are evaluated by experts with regards to solutions of all production functions. This human-based evaluation is done on several dimensions that can be technological, economical, ecological, *etc.*

Hanafy *et al.* [15] try to automatically compute interdependencies between product features and capabilities of machines for production. The authors use Bayesian Network on several instances of product and production systems to capture interdependencies without explicitly expressing them. This approach relies on the hypothesis that the product features and machine capabilities are already known whereas this might not be the case when reasoning at goal level. Moreover, the approach might not scale up to the complexity of an aircraft.

6.2   Trade-off Between Design Choices in Other Fields

Out of the context of a product and its production system but still related to the trade-off design choices we are tackling, a method mixes goals, non-functional requirements, scoring with fuzzy rankings by stakeholders [32]. Based on this scoring, in a situation of conflicting goals, the authors introduce measurement of design solution alternative's influence on two goals satisfaction to help designers to make the best trade-off decision. This method focuses mainly on two goals comparisons and may not be sufficient enough to study bigger conflicts.

In another direction, Lightswitch [27] is an approach to define IT systems early requirements while taking into account the evolution of the enterprise's environment. Indeed, environment has an influence on the enterprise goals, and thus on the IT system ones, which must therefore be adapted over time. The approach stands on a process to build a model of the relationships between the enterprise and its environment, analyse and improve the way a company regulates these relationships and lastly specify the IT system goals. This approach allows to negotiate high-level goals trade-offs for the enterprise and the environment, but is very informal.

6.3   The Relation with Systems of Systems

One could see similarities between the systems we are describing and Systems of Systems (SoS). However we think our systems are much more dependent. Nevertheless, we can relate to some SoSs Requirements Engineering work. For instance, Ncube and Lim give perspective and research agenda [23], and they recommend some research topics very close to our work. The first topic is "*Tools for*

SoSs Requirements Trade-Off Decision" where the authors advocate the development of techniques and tools to permit efficient trade-off decisions among a large trade space. The second topic is *"Multi-Level Modelling techniques for SoSs requirements"*, where the authors discuss different modelling approaches, goal modelling included, and prone combination of approaches to take advantage of different perspectives.

6.4   The Use of Multi-modelling Approaches

Some works advocate the use of multi-modelling techniques for Requirements Engineering. For instance, Franch *et al.* study the joint use of i^* with other modelling techniques [10]. In this context, they reviewed existing work and identified different scenarios of use. Our work belongs to a scenario of Model Coupling, where the goal model and other modelling notations coexist without being merged, in order to gain benefits. Closer to our approach, Alencar *et al.* go from an i^* model to a conceptual model in UML [2], but we differ on the final objectives. Indeed, we are dealing with the development of design-dependent systems and their optimization while they are interested in going from a goal model to a UML representation for software development. Their work is mainly centred on the model transformation guidelines.

7   Conclusion and Future Work

In this paper, we have presented methods and tools to support the design of an aircraft and its manufacturing system in order to take into account the impacts of the former on the latter. We have provided an approach that combines goal modelling, conceptual modelling and constraint programming in order to automatically compute optimized solutions applied to the design of an aircraft fuselage airframe and its assembly line. This approach has been very well received by the architects and has allowed them to discuss design alternatives at an early stage in the design.

Among the future work, we have already identified some of them in the lessons learned. We have observed that there is no possible trade-off between the goals impacting the aircraft designs and the ones impacting the assembly line, due to the absence of soft goals on the aircraft design side in our case study. One future work could be to introduce them to the problem in order to enable and explore this kind of trade-off. New case studies will be an opportunity to test our approach and clarify how it should be used.

The improvement of the optimization tool is also a possible future work. We could explore the generation of explanations for the values obtained on the criteria and link them to particular aircraft design decisions, in order to guide the architects in a better way.

We could also strengthen the approach by investigating in detail the relationship between the two modelling techniques we have used. In this direction, we could try to establish guidelines to express how to progress from one model type to the other. In addition, in a model-based approach perspective, we could explore the possibility to return the computed solutions in the form of a complete conceptual model instantiation.

Finally, we could generalize our work to other systems which are designed in an asynchronous way and are dependent on each other. As we have seen in Sect. 1, this kind of systems can be found in other domains and may benefit from our approach. In this context, we have just started working on a case study coming from the space industry.

References

1. Airbus: Design webpage. https://www.airbus.com/en/products-services/commercial-aircraft/the-life-cycle-of-an-aircraft/design. Accessed 17 Mar 2022
2. Alencar, F., Marín, B., Giachetti, G., Pastor, O., Castro, J., Pimentel, J.H.: From $i*$ requirements models to conceptual models of a model driven development process. In: Persson, A., Stirna, J. (eds.) PoEM 2009. LNBIP, vol. 39, pp. 99–114. Springer, Heidelberg (2009). https://doi.org/10.1007/978-3-642-05352-8_9
3. Amyot, D., Ghanavati, S., Horkoff, J., Mussbacher, G., Peyton, L., Yu, E.S.K.: Evaluating goal models within the goal-oriented requirement language. Int. J. Intell. Syst. **25**(8), 841–877 (2010)
4. Boothroyd, G.: Product design for manufacture and assembly. Comput. Aided Des. **26**(7), 505–520 (1994)
5. Borreguero Sanchidrián, T.: Scheduling with limited resources along the aeronautical supply chain: from parts manufacturing plants to final assembly lines. Ph.D. thesis, E.T.S.I. Industrials (UPM) (2019)
6. Chung, L., Nixon, B.A., Yu, E., Mylopoulos, J.: Non-Functional Requirements in Software Engineering, International Series in Software Engineering, vol. 5. Springer, Heidelberg (2000). https://doi.org/10.1007/978-1-4615-5269-7
7. Dalpiaz, F., Franch, X., Horkoff, J.: istar 2.0 language guide. CoRR abs/1605.07767 (2016)
8. Demoly, F., Yan, X., Eynard, B., Rivest, L., Gomes, S.: An assembly oriented design framework for product structure engineering and assembly sequence planning. Robot. Comput. Integr. Manuf. **27**(1), 33–46 (2011)
9. Donelli, G., et al.: A model-based approach to trade-space evaluation coupling design-manufacturing-supply chain in the early stages of aircraft development. In: AIAA Aviation Forum, vol. 2021–3057 (2021)
10. Franch, X., Maté, A., Trujillo, J.C., Cares, C.: On the joint use of $i*$ with other modelling frameworks: a vision paper. In: Proceedings of RE 2011, pp. 133–142 (2011)
11. Giorgini, P., Mylopoulos, J., Sebastiani, R.: Goal-oriented requirements analysis and reasoning in the tropos methodology. Eng. Appl. Artif. Intell. **18**(2), 159–171 (2005)
12. Göpfert, I., Schulz, M.: Logistics integrated product development in the German automotive industry: current state, trends and challenges. In: Kreowski, HJ., Scholz-Reiter, B., Thoben, KD. (eds.) Dynamics in Logistics. LNL, pp. 509–519. Springer, Heidelberg (2013). https://doi.org/10.1007/978-3-642-35966-8_43
13. Guizzardi, R.S.S., Li, F., Borgida, A., Guizzardi, G., Horkoff, J., Mylopoulos, J.: An ontological interpretation of non-functional requirements. In: Proceedings of FOIS. Frontiers in Artificial Intelligence and Applications, vol. 267, pp. 344–357. IOS Press (2014)

14. Hadj, R.B., Belhadj, I., Trigui, M., Aifaoui, N.: Assembly sequences plan generation using features simplification. Adv. Eng. Softw. **119**, 1–11 (2018)
15. Hanafy, M., ElMaraghy, H.: Co-design of products and systems using a Bayesian network. Procedia CIRP **17**, 284–289 (2014)
16. Harlé, H., et al.: Innovative design on the shop floor of the Saint-Nazaire Airbus factory. Res. Eng. Des. **33**(1), 69–86 (2022)
17. van Lamsweerde, A.: Goal-oriented requirements engineering: a guided tour. In: Proceedings of RE 2001, pp. 249–262. IEEE Computer Society (2001)
18. Lu, R., Sundaram, S.: Manufacturing process modeling of Boeing 747 moving line concepts. In: Proceedings of the Winter Simulation Conference, vol. 1, pp. 1041–1045 (2002)
19. Ma, Y.S., Chen, G., Thimm, G.: Paradigm shift: unified and associative feature-based concurrent and collaborative engineering. J. Intell. Manuf. **19**(6), 625–641 (2008)
20. Molloy, E., Yang, H., Browne, J., Davies, B.: Design for assembly within concurrent engineering. CIRP Ann. **40**(1), 107–110 (1991)
21. Mylopoulos, J., Chung, L., Nixon, B.A.: Representing and using nonfunctional requirements: a process-oriented approach. IEEE Trans. Softw. Eng. **18**(6), 483–497 (1992)
22. Mylopoulos, J., Chung, L., Yu, E.S.K.: From object-oriented to goal-oriented requirements analysis. Commun. ACM **42**(1), 31–37 (1999)
23. Ncube, C., Lim, S.L.: On systems of systems engineering: a requirements engineering perspective and research agenda. In: Proceedings of RE 2018, pp. 112–123. IEEE Computer Society (2018)
24. Polacsek, T., Roussel, S., Bouissiere, F., Cuiller, C., Dereux, P.-E., Kersuzan, S.: Towards thinking manufacturing and design together: an aeronautical case study. In: Mayr, H.C., Guizzardi, G., Ma, H., Pastor, O. (eds.) ER 2017. LNCS, vol. 10650, pp. 340–353. Springer, Cham (2017). https://doi.org/10.1007/978-3-319-69904-2_27
25. Polacsek, T., Roussel, S., Pralet, C., Cuiller, C.: Design for efficient production, a model-based approach. In: Proceedings of RCIS 2019, pp. 1–6. IEEE (2019)
26. Pralet, C., et al.:: A scheduling tool for bridging the gap between aircraft design and aircraft manufacturing. In: Proceedings of ICAPS 2018, pp. 347–355. AAAI Press (2018)
27. Regev, G., Wegmann, A.: Defining early IT system requirements with regulation principles: the Lightswitch approach. In: Proceedings of RE 2004, pp. 144–153. IEEE Computer Society (2004)
28. Shenas, D.G., Derakhshan, S.: Organizational approaches to the implementation of simultaneous engineering. Int. J. Oper. Prod. Manag. **14**(10), 30–43 (1994)
29. Stoffels, P., Vielhaber, M.: Methodical support for concurrent engineering across product and production (system) development. In: Proceedings of ICED 2015, vol. 4, pp. 155–162 (2015)
30. Yu, E.S.: Towards modelling and reasoning support for early-phase requirements engineering. In: Proceedings of ISRE 1997, pp. 226–235. IEEE (1997)
31. Zha, X.F., Du, H.J., Qiu, J.H.: Knowledge-based approach and system for assembly oriented design, part i: the approach. Eng. Appl. Artif. Intell. **14**(1), 61–75 (2001)
32. Zhang, X., Wang, X.: Tradeoff analysis for conflicting software non-functional requirements. IEEE Access **7**, 156463–156475 (2019)

Process Modeling

Causal Reasoning over Control-Flow Decisions in Process Models

Sander J. J. Leemans[1]([✉]) and Niek Tax[2]

[1] Queensland University of Technology, Brisbane, Australia
s.leemans@qut.edu.au
[2] Meta, London, UK
niek@fb.com

Abstract. Process mining aims to provide analysts with insights, such that business processes supported by information systems can be improved. Traditionally, insights from process mining projects and techniques have been associational rather than causal, thus only describing the current state of the process, without predictive capabilities over effects of hypothetical process changes, which inherently limits business process optimisation efforts. In this paper, we introduce causal analysis for control-flow decisions taken during the execution of process models: using an event log and the structure of a process model, we (i) extract the set of decision points in the process, (ii) apply a causal discovery approach to obtain a collection of causal graphs that are consistent with the observations in the event log, (iii) extract ordered pairs of decision points between which a causal connection can be ruled out based on the temporal ordering that is implied by the process model specification, and use these to narrow down the set of possible causal graphs. This technique addresses the problem of mining dependencies, which has long been a challenge in the process discovery field. The technique has been implemented in the Visual Miner as part of the ProM framework. We illustrate the technique using examples and demonstrate its applicability on real-life logs.

Keywords: Process mining · Causal discovery · Intra-model dependencies · Long-distance dependencies

1 Introduction

Process mining aims to gain insights into business processes of organisations from event data recorded in information systems. Typical process mining projects aim to gain such insights such that the process can subsequently be improved, for instance to reduce cost, reduce cycle time or increase efficiency. Gaining insights into business processes can be supported by several automated process mining techniques, such as the discovery of a process model from recorded event data, the study of conformance checking and the projection of data such as costs, performance information and other data on process models. Using such enriched

© Springer Nature Switzerland AG 2022
X. Franch et al. (Eds.): CAiSE 2022, LNCS 13295, pp. 183–200, 2022.
https://doi.org/10.1007/978-3-031-07472-1_11

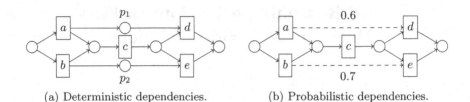

(a) Deterministic dependencies.   (b) Probabilistic dependencies.

Fig. 1. A Petri net with dependencies.

process models, process mining techniques have been developed that recommend interventions or optimal pathways through the process for ongoing cases by predicting process outcomes.

Typical process mining techniques are inherently *associational*, that is, they merely describe or visualise the data and cannot be used to reason in retrospect (i.e.. counterfactual) or to identify *causes* of identified phenomena. For instance, a negative association between identified fraud cases and the performed thorough checks earlier in a process does not suffice to conclude that the number of identified fraud cases can be lowered by performing more thorough checks earlier in the process. Similarly, a positive association between the sales of ice cream and deaths by drowning does not suffice to conclude that deaths by drowning can be prevented by lowering the sales of ice cream. Thus, such associational insights have limited value in assisting redesigns of the process.

Causal reasoning has been leveraged to, for instance, predict the influence of trace-based interventions on cycle time [4], to influence the likelihood of a given outcome [3], and to explain why a certain negative outcome was achieved in a particular trace [22]. However, none of these causal process mining techniques are tailored towards process discovery, make the connection to (long-distance) dependencies, or in any way leverage process models.

An often overlooked aspect of process models is *dependencies*: the dependence of decisions in the process on earlier decisions. For instance, the Petri net in Fig. 1a contains two long-distance dependencies: d can only be executed if a was executed earlier in the process and e can only be executed if b was executed earlier in the process. As d cannot be executed without a having been executed, this is a *deterministic* dependency, enforced by places p_1 and p_2. Rather, in this paper, we consider *probabilistic* dependencies. For instance, the Petri net in Fig. 1b is annotated with long-distance dependencies indicating that after execution of a, the probability of executing d is 60%, while after execution of b, this probability is 30%. Obviously, Petri nets can only capture deterministic dependencies. For process discovery, we argue that we might still want to visualise probabilistic dependencies to the process analyst *as long as these dependencies are causal*.

In this paper, we aim to identify causal relationships among decision points in the process. The motivation behind these causal relationships includes the following use cases:

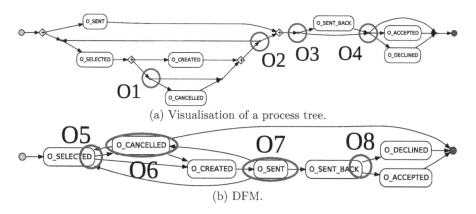

(a) Visualisation of a process tree.

(b) DFM.

Fig. 2. Two models of the BPI Challenge 2012 log - O_ activities. Red circles indicate option sets. (Color figure online)

Informing Process Interventions and Design. If activity d in Fig. 1b affects the business positively (e.g., a purchase of a certain product) while e represents a negative outcome (e.g., ending the process without a purchase), then it is useful to know whether the decision between a and b has a causal effect on the decision between d and e. If this relation is causal, then information about this causal relation could influence process participants' decisions as well as process redesign efforts, e.g. by preferring a over b.

Discovering Long-Distance Dependencies in Process Models. The control flow perspective of process models is inherently causal: the execution of a transition may enable other transitions and is thus, according to the model, causal. For instance, in Fig. 1a, executing a has a causal influence on whether d is executed later on in the process. It is thus natural to extend the model with only causal probabilistic dependencies.

We introduce a method to study causal control-flow dependencies in process models. Using this causal knowledge, control-flow decisions in processes that could be leveraged to influence the decision can be identified. To this end, given a process model and an event log, our technique derives the causal structure of decision points in the model, after which causal reasoning is applied to provide analysts with insights into the causal dependencies in a process. The method has been implemented and we evaluate it using synthetic and real-life examples, and we demonstrate its applicability on real-life logs.

This paper is organised as follows: Sect. 2 introduces a motivating example; Sect. 3 discusses related work; Sect. 4 introduces existing concepts; Sect. 5 introduces our method; Sect. 6 evaluates it and Sect. 7 concludes the paper.

2   Motivating Example

As an example, we study the choices made in a loan application process (BPI Challenge 2012 - O_ activities). To this log, we applied a discovery technique to

Table 1. Some probabilistic dependencies of the model in Fig. 2a.

(a) O1 vs. O1 (unfolding 2) $\chi^2 = 642$, $p < 0.00001$		(b) O1 vs. O2 $\chi^2 = 129$, $p < 0.00001$		(c) O1 vs. O2 (unfolding 2) $\chi^2 = 0.58$, $p = 0.45$	
	o_cancelled	skip	[loop redo]	[loop exit]	[loop redo]	[loop exit]
o_cancelled	278	462	740	1222	205	535
skip	698	0	698	2355	206	492

obtain a process tree (see Fig. 2a). This model has four decisions points (*option sets*), labelled O1-O4. Option sets O1 and O2 form a loop: the options of O2 entail either exiting the loop or doing it again, and O1 is part of that loop. For every time a trace traverses the loop, a decision must be made on O1 and O2. Thus, each trace might have multiple *choices* corresponding to the option sets O1 and O2. That is, the option sets that are part of the loop can be *unfolded* into *choices*. We formalise option sets and choices in Sect. 5.1.

To study probabilistic dependencies, Table 1 shows how often certain decisions appeared together. If in the first unfolding of O1, o_cancelled is chosen, then in O3, o_sent_back is chosen 406 times (21%), while o_sent_back is skipped 1556 times (79%). However, if o_cancelled is skipped in the first unfolding of O1, then in O3, o_sent_back is executed 2568 times (84%) and skipped 485 times (16%). With a Benjamini-Hochberg correction [2] for the 14 tests performed (assuming at most 2 unfoldings), a χ^2 test confirms that this difference is statistically significant. Yet, this is insufficient information for stakeholders to decide how to best decrease the relative number of loan applications that are sent back (O3), since this is not yet shown to be a *causal* relation. In the remainder of this paper, we study these two models as running examples.

3   Related Work

Long-Distance Dependencies. Many discovery techniques explicitly support long-distance dependencies, including the Flexible Heuristics Miner [32], Fodina [5], some variants of the α algorithm [33], the ILP algorithm [34] and Declare [19]. Most of these techniques apply a threshold to decide on the presence of a long-distance dependency and thus still produce deterministic dependencies, or only include long-distance dependencies if they do not violate fitness at all (e.g. ILP), thus all produce only deterministic dependencies. An exception is [27], which considers probabilistic dependencies through association rules in one particular Petri net structure (though not causal). Thus, while deterministic dependencies in models have been studied (e.g.. ILP, HM, Fodina), to the best of our knowledge, causal dependencies have not.

Some discovery techniques are limited by their representational bias in representing long-distance dependencies. For instance, process trees cannot represent long-distance dependencies due to their block structure [13]. As the state of directly follows-based models consists only of the last executed state, these models cannot represent long-distance dependencies either [9,16]. BPMN models can represent a limited set of long-distance dependencies, due to a lack of an explicit state and a waiting-less semantics.

Prediction. Given an enriched process model, several approaches have been proposed that aim to predict certain aspects of ongoing cases, such as the likelihood of undesirable events [6], timeliness [10,12,29], the next executed activity [30], the utilisation of resources [20] or in general event data [7]. While a recent approach [11] uses counterfactual reasoning to explain predictions, these approaches to prediction do not provide information on intervention (what-if), for which a causal approach is necessary,

Causal Analysis in Process Mining. Causal inference has been used to determine the influence of process steps on the outcomes of ongoing traces [24], and to maximise the likelihood of a desirable outcome for a running case [3]. Similar approaches have been proposed to decrease service time [21] or cycle time [4] of a case, or the root causes of performance issues [26]. Counterfactual reasoning has been applied to process mining as well, to explain why an undesirable outcome was achieved for a particular case [22]; a diversified range of potential scenarios is presented to the analyst.

Bayesian network structure learning from event logs is proposed in [28,29]. Bayesian networks can in principle be causal models if their structure coincides with the structure of the causal graph, however, the Bayesian networks in [28,29] are not causal, as they focus on optimising the structure for predictive accuracy rather than on attempting to find causal relations.

To the best of our knowledge, only two causal approaches in process mining advocate the use of a process model: [17] uses Structural Causal Models to answer what-if questions by quantifying the improvement of proposed process changes; [17] mentions a broad range of causal principles, including using the structure of process models. Both techniques however provide no guidance or detail on how to apply these, and do not consider the causal dependencies between model choices. Similarly, [23] proposes root-cause analysis and mentions the potential use of process models, but does not detail how process models can be leveraged.

More generally, while existing work in the area of causality in process mining focuses on identifying or quantifying causal effects on process outcomes or process performance, this work, in contrast, focuses on causal effects of control-flow decisions on other control-flow decisions later in the process. Thereby, this work is positioned at the intersection of causal inference and process discovery, rather than at the intersection of causal inference and business process improvement.

4   Preliminaries

In this section, we introduce existing concepts and notations.

A *multiset* is a function from a set of elements Σ to the natural numbers, indicating how often each element appears in the multiset. For instance, $[a^2, b^7]$. For a multiset M, $[.\ |\ .]$ denotes multiset composition, such that $[a\ |\ a \in M] = M$.

A *trace* is a sequence of events, representing the activities executed for a particular case in a process. An *event log* is a multiset of traces. For instance, $[\langle a, b, c \rangle^2, \langle a, d \rangle^3]$ represents a log with 5 traces, of which 2 traces have 3 activities. The empty trace is denoted with ϵ; the set of all logs is $\mathcal{L}$.

$\mathcal{M}$ is the set of all process models (regardless of formalism). A *directly follows model* (DFM) is a directed graph consisting of transitions T and edges E, such that $start \notin T$ and $end \notin T$. A DFM expresses a set of traces as each trace starts in $start$ and moves over the edges to end, executing the activities annotated on the transitions along the path. See [16] for a full formal definition. Figure 2b shows an example of a DFM, which supports the trace $\langle$o_selected, o_cancelled$\rangle$ amongst other traces.

A *process tree* is a block-structured process model, defined recursively [13]. Each node in the tree describes a language; a *leaf* $a \in \Sigma$ describes the singleton language of its activity, a *silent leaf* τ) describes the language with the empty trace $\{\epsilon\}$ and a *node* describes a combination of the behaviour of its sub-trees using an operator $\oplus$. In this paper, we consider six n-ary operators: the sequential composition $\mapsto$, exclusive choice $\times$, inclusive choice $\vee$, interleaved $\leftrightarrow$, concurrent $\wedge$, and $\circlearrowleft$; where $\circlearrowleft (T_1, T_2, T_3)$ combines three sub-trees as an always-executed body T_1, and then a choice between executing T_2 followed by T_1 and back to the same choice, or exiting the loop by executing T_3. For a formal definition, please refer to [13]. As an example, Fig. 2a shows a visualisation of the process tree $\mapsto ($ $\wedge($ o_sent, $\circlearrowleft ($ $\mapsto($ o_selected, $\wedge($ o_created, $\times (\tau$, o_cancelled $))), \tau, \tau)), \times (\tau,$ o_sent_back), $\times (\tau,$ o_accepted, o_declined)).

A *structural causal model* [18] over a set of variables V is a system of equations of the form $v_i = f_i(\mathrm{pa}(v_i), U_i)$ for all $v_i \in V$, where $\mathrm{pa}(v_i)$ denotes the set of variables that directly determine the value of v_i (i.e., the parents), and U_i represents errors that might arise as a result of either true randomness (i.e., a coin flip) or residual errors due to omitted variables. A *causal graph* [18] of a set of variables V is a directed acyclic graph consisting of nodes V and edges $E = \{(v_i, v_j) \in V \times V \mid v_i \in \mathrm{pa}(v_j)\}$, i.e., the causal graph denotes the *structural form* of the structural causal model without specifying the *functional form*. We write $v_i \rightarrow v_j$ for $(v_i, v_j) \in E$, representing that v_i has a causal effect on v_j. Furthermore, we write $v_i - v_j$ for $v_i \rightarrow v_j \vee v_i \leftarrow v_j$.

Random variables X and Y are *conditionally independent* given a set of random variables Z, denoted $X \perp\!\!\!\perp Y \mid Z$, if and only if $P(X \mid Y, Z) = P(X \mid Z)$, i.e., given that we already know Z, knowing additionally Y provides no addition information about X, and vice versa[1]. When $Z = \emptyset$, i.e., $P(X \mid Y) = P(X)$, X and Y are *marginally independent*, denoted $X \perp\!\!\!\perp Y$.

A causal graph G on variables V and a probability distribution $P(v_1, \ldots, v_{|V|})$ satisfies the *causal Markov condition* if and only if $\forall_{v_i, v_j \in V, v_i \neq v_j} \Rightarrow v_i \perp\!\!\!\perp v_j | \mathrm{pa}(v_i)$, i.e. each variable is independent of all its non-descendants given its parents G.

A *path* on a causal graph $G = (V, E)$ is a sequence of distinct vertices $\langle v_1, \ldots v_n \rangle$ such that $\forall_{1 \leq i < n} v_i - v_{i+1}$. A *directed path* is a path such that $\forall_{1 \leq i < n}$

---

[1] By symmetry, also $P(Y \mid X, Z) = P(Y \mid Z)$.

Fig. 3. Overview of our method.

$v_i \to v_{i+1}$. A vertex v_i on a path $\langle v_1, \ldots v_n \rangle$ is called (i) a *chain* if $v_{i-1} \to v_i \to v_{i+1}$ or $v_{i-1} \leftarrow v_i \leftarrow v_{i+1}$; (ii) a *collider* if $v_{i-1} \to v_i \leftarrow v_{i+1}$ (i.e.., v_i is a common effect of its neighbours); and (iii) a *confounder* if $v_{i-1} \leftarrow v_i \to v_{i+1}$ (i.e.., v_i is a common cause of its neighbours).

A path p in causal graph G is *d-separated* [8,18] by $Z \subseteq V$ if and only if either p contains a chain $v_{i-1} \to v_i \to v_{i+1}$ or confounder $v_{i-1} \leftarrow v_i \to v_{i+1}$ such that $v_i \in Z$, or p contains a collider $v_{i-1} \to v_i \leftarrow v_{i+1}$ such that $v_i \notin Z$ and no descendent of v_i is in Z. A set $Z \subseteq V$ is said to *d-separate* $X \subseteq V$ from $Y \subseteq V$ if and only if Z d-separates every path from a node in X to a node in Y.

For example, in causal graph $G_1 = v_1 \leftarrow v_2 \to v_3$, set $\{v_2\}$ d-separates $\{v_1\}$ from $\{v_3\}$, while set $Z = \emptyset$ does not. In contrast, in causal graph $G_2 = v_4 \to v_5 \leftarrow v_6$, $\emptyset$ d-separates $\{v_1\}$ from $\{v_3\}$, while set $\{v_2\}$ does not. While *d-separation* is a property of sets of nodes in a causal graph, it has a direct link with conditional independence: if $X \subseteq V$ is d-separated from $Y \subseteq V$ given $Z \subseteq V$ in causal graph G, then $X \perp\!\!\!\perp Y \mid Z$ in every probability distribution that satisfies the causal Markov condition with respect to G. For example, in example causal graph G_1, imagine that v_2 represents age, while v_1 and v_3 respectively represent the presence of arthritis and cardiovascular disease, two common age-related diseases. Now, $\{v_2\}$ d-separates $\{v_1\}$ from $\{v_3\}$, which means that in all probability distributions that satisfy the causal Markov condition w.r.t. G_1 it must be the case that the presence of arthritis and of cardiovascular disease are independent once the age is known.

Causal graphs that imply the same set of conditional independence relations, i.e., graphs that have the same set of d-separation properties, are *Markov equivalent*, and the set of all Markov equivalent causal graphs is a *Markov equivalence class* (MEC). In the case of two variables, graphs $v_1 \to v_2$ and $v_1 \leftarrow v_2$ are Markov equivalent, as the set of condition independence relations that both graphs imply is $\emptyset$. Markov equivalent causal graphs cannot be distinguished purely based on observational data. *Causal discovery* algorithms aim to reconstruct the causal graph from observational data, however these algorithms can thus merely identify the correct MEC of possible causal graphs [18].

5   Our Method

Our method consists of five steps, illustrated in Fig. 3, that combine the information available in a process model and an event log. First, we obtain an *upper bound* on the causal graph (UBCG) that consists of all causal edges that are possible according to the process model. Second, we extract the choices made in the traces of the event log to obtain a data set of made choices (Sect. 5.2). Third, we apply a causal discovery technique to obtain the MEC that is consistent with this choice data set. Fourth, in Sect. 5.3 we combine the MEC with the UBCG, i.e., we shrink the MEC to contain only causal graphs that do not contradict the process model. Often, this MEC is a single causal graph. Finally, we estimate the size of the causal effects using this causal graph and a standard application of regression with backdoor adjustment [18].

5.1 Upper-Bound Causal Graphs

Given a process model, an *upper-bound causal graph* (UBCG) is a causal graph that contains all causal edges that do not violate the model. In this section, we describe how a UBCG can be computed for any DFM or process tree. The nodes of a causal graph indicate choices in the model. As causal graphs conceptually do not support loops – every choice in a causal graph can be made at most once –, if a model-choice is encountered multiple times in a trace, it must be represented multiple times in a causal graph. Thus, while the nodes of causal graphs differ slightly between DFMs and process trees, they both contain unfolding identifiers.

Directly Follows Models
For DFMs, we use both the DFM and an event log for the construction of the UBCG. In constructing the UBCG, for each event it must be decided whether the event enters the "next" unfolding. We aim to minimise the number of unfoldings, as to minimise the number of nodes in the causal graph and to maximise the amount of information per node.

Intuitively, our starting point is the set of not-unfolded choices in the model. Our strategy is to create a total order of these choices: whenever the sequence of choices in a trace in the log goes backwards in this total order, we enter a new unfolding. Thus, our aim is to create a total order that minimises the total number of such backward steps.

We first create a *non-unfolded-choice graph* (*nucg*). To this end, each trace t of a log L is transformed using a function choicesTrace that takes a trace and a model, and returns the sequence of choices in the trace corresponding to the model. Such a function could be implemented using alignments [1]. Then, an edge is added between every pair of encountered options:

$$nucg(L, M) = [(o_i, o_j) \mid \langle \ldots o_i \ldots o_j \ldots \rangle = \text{choicesTrace}(t, M) \wedge t \in L] \quad (1)$$

For instance, Fig. 4a shows the *nucg* of the DFM of Fig. 2b.

Next, we create a total order of choices (*nucto*) by repeatedly greedily adding choices with the least incoming edges: ((2))

$$nucto(L, M) = nucto'(nucg(L, M), 1, \{o \mid o \in \text{choicesTrace}(t, M) \wedge t \in L\})$$

$$nucto'(G, r, O) = \begin{cases} \{o \to r\} & \text{if } |O| = 1 \\ nucto'(G, r + 1, O \setminus \{o\}) \cup \{o \to r\} & \text{otherwise} \end{cases}$$

$$\text{with } o = \underset{o \in O}{\arg\min} \sum_{o' \in O \wedge o \neq o'} G((o', o)) \quad (2)$$

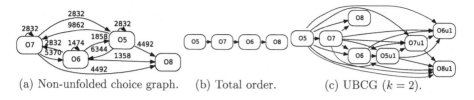

(a) Non-unfolded choice graph.   (b) Total order.   (c) UBCG ($k = 2$).

Fig. 4. Constructing a UBCG from the DFM in Fig. 2b.

For instance, Fig. 4b shows the total order for our example of Fig. 2b.

Then, the UBCG function $ubcg$ takes a log and a model and returns a set of edges between choices. Intuitively, in a UBCG there is an edge between two choices if there is a potential causal relation between the source and target of the edge. In the context of a DFM, two choices can only have influenced one another if they appeared consecutively in a trace in the log. Thus, we add all such edges. To avoid cycles, whenever an edge goes *backwards* in the total order $nucto$, we increase the unfolding identifier u (3).

$$ubcg(L, M) = \bigcup_{t \in L} ubcg'(\langle \rangle, \text{choicesTrace}(t), nucto(L, M), 1)$$

$$ubcg'(t_c, \langle \rangle, R, u) = \emptyset$$

$$ubcg'(\langle \rangle, \langle o \rangle \cdot t_o, R, u) = ubcg'(\langle (o, \langle u \rangle) \rangle, t_o, R, u)$$

$$ubcg'(t_c \cdot \langle c \rangle, \langle o \rangle \cdot t_o, R, u) = \{(c', c'') \mid c' \in t_c \cdot \langle c \rangle\} \cup ubcg'(t_c \cdot \langle c, c'' \rangle, t_o, R, u')$$

$$\text{with } c'' = (o, \langle u' \rangle)$$

$$\text{and } u' = \begin{cases} u & \text{if } R(o_c) < R(o), c = (o_c, t_x) \\ u + 1 & \text{otherwise} \end{cases} \tag{3}$$

To limit the size of the UBCG, the unfoldings can be maximised using a parameter k, which stops processing a trace if it reaches k unfoldings – processing the remainder of the trace remains future work.

In our example, the UBCG truncated to 2 unfoldings is shown in Fig. 4c.

Process Trees. For process trees, it is trivial to decide when the "next" unfolding starts – with each execution of the second child of a loop –, thus we can construct the UBCG directly.

First, we describe the choices in a process tree recursively. • The silent and activity nodes τ and $a \in \Sigma$ do not possess any choices (4). • The sequence, concurrent and interleaved operators do not add any choices (5). • The exclusive choice operator adds a choice between its children (6). • For each execution of an inclusive choice node, at least one child must be executed. Thus, there is one choice – which child to execute first – and another choice for each child – whether that child is executed as a non-first child (7). • For each execution of a loop node, a different choice is made – to proceed with the redo T_2 or to exit using T_3 (8). As loops can be arbitrarily nested, the unfolding identifier is a sequence of integers indicating the unfolding number of each encountered loop node. While a loop node thus describes a sequence of potentially infinitely many choices, every event log has finitely many finite traces. Therefore, we introduce a parameter k which indicates the times a loop node must be unfolded. In the following, I is initially $\langle\rangle$.

$$\mathrm{cs}(\tau, I) = \mathrm{cs}(a, I) = \emptyset \tag{4}$$

$$\mathrm{cs}(\oplus(T_1, \ldots T_n), I) = \bigcup_{1 \le i \le n} \mathrm{cs}(T_i, I) \text{ for } \oplus \in \{\mapsto, \wedge, \leftrightarrow\} \tag{5}$$

$$\mathrm{cs}(\times(T_1, \ldots T_n), I) = \bigcup_{1 \le i \le n} \mathrm{cs}(T_i, I) \cup \{(T_1, \ldots T_n, I)\} \tag{6}$$

$$\mathrm{cs}(\vee(T_1, \ldots T_n), I) = \{(\{T_l | 1 \le l \le n\}, I)\} \cup \{(T_i, \neg T_i, I) \mid 1 \le i \le n\} \tag{7}$$

$$\mathrm{cs}(\circlearrowleft(T_1, T_2, T_3), I) = \bigcup_{1 \le j \le k} \bigcup_{1 \le i \le 3} \mathrm{cs}(T_i, I \cdot \langle j \rangle) \cup \bigcup_{1 \le j \le k} \{(T_2, T_3, I \cdot \langle j \rangle)\} \tag{8}$$

Then, we can define the UBCG as a function $ubcg$, which produces a set of directed edges between (unfolded) choices of a process tree. • Intuitively, concurrency nodes do not induce any relation between their sub-trees: concurrent sub-trees are independent by definition, thus the choices in sub-trees cannot have causal relations with one another either (10). • For exclusive choice, the choices made in its sub-trees depend on the choice made to select a sub-tree to execute. As the sub-trees themselves are mutually exclusive, the choices in these sub-trees cannot have causal relations with one another (11). • For sequence nodes, the choices in each sub-tree may causally depend on all choices in sub-trees before the current sub-tree (12). Initially, I is $\langle\rangle$.

$$ubcg(\tau, I) = ubcg(a, I) = \emptyset \tag{9}$$

$$ubcg(\oplus(T_1, \ldots T_n), I) = \bigcup_{1 \le i \le n} ubcg(T_i, I) \text{ for } \oplus \in \{\wedge, \leftrightarrow\} \tag{10}$$

$$ubcg(\times(T_1, \ldots T_n), I) = \bigcup_{1 \le i \le n} ubcg(T_i, I) \cup (\{(T_1, \ldots T_n, I)\} \times \mathrm{cs}(T_i, I)) \tag{11}$$

$$ubcg(\mapsto(T_1, \ldots T_n), I) = \bigcup_{1 \le i \le n} ubcg(T_i, I) \cup \bigcup_{1 \le i < j \le n} (\mathrm{cs}(T_i, I) \times \mathrm{cs}(T_j, I)) \tag{12}$$

• To construct the UBCG of an inclusive choice node, we may assume that first a choice is made to execute a child, after which choices are made whether the remaining children are executed. Thus, all subsequent choices may depend on this first choice (14). Second, the choices within a child might also depend on the choice whether to execute that child (15). Figure 5 illustrates this for 3 children.

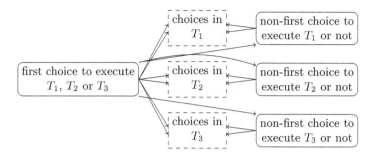

Fig. 5. An UBCG of the execution of an inclusive choice $\vee(T_1, T_2, T_3)$.

$$ubcg(\vee(T_1, \ldots T_n), I) = \bigcup_{1 \leq i \leq n} ubcg(T_i, I) \cup \qquad (13)$$

$$\{(\{T_1, \ldots T_n\}, I)\} \times \bigcup_{1 \leq i \leq n} \{(\{T_i, \neg T_i\}, I)\} \cup cs(T_i, I) \cup$$
$$\qquad (14)$$

$$\bigcup_{1 \leq i \leq n} \{(T_i, \neg T_i, I)\} \times cs(T_i, I) \qquad (15)$$

- The causal relations of a loop node consist of the relations of its sub-trees (16), relations within an unfolding of the loop (17)–(21) (see Fig. 6a) and relations between subsequent unfoldings (22) (see Fig. 6b).

$$ubcg(\circlearrowleft (T_1, T_2, T_3), I) = \bigcup_{1 \leq j \leq k} \bigcup_{1 \leq i \leq 3} ubcg(T_i, I \cdot \langle j \rangle) \cup \qquad (16)$$

$$\bigcup_{1 \leq j \leq k} (cs(T_1, I \cdot \langle j \rangle) \times \{(T_2, T_3, I \cdot \langle j \rangle)\}) \cup \qquad (17)$$

$$(cs(T_1, I \cdot \langle j \rangle) \times cs(T_2, I \cdot \langle j \rangle)) \cup \qquad (18)$$
$$(cs(T_1, I \cdot \langle j \rangle) \times cs(T_3, I \cdot \langle j \rangle)) \cup \qquad (19)$$
$$(\{(T_2, T_3, I \cdot \langle j \rangle)\} \times cs(T_2, I \cdot \langle j \rangle)) \cup \qquad (20)$$
$$(\{(T_2, T_3, I \cdot \langle j \rangle)\} \times cs(T_3, I \cdot \langle j \rangle)) \cup \qquad (21)$$

$$\bigcup_{1 \leq j < j' \leq k} \bigcup_{1 \leq i' \leq 3} (cs(T_1, I \cdot \langle j \rangle) \times cs(T_{i'}, I \cdot \langle j' \rangle)) \cup$$
$$(cs(T_2, I \cdot \langle j \rangle) \times cs(T_{i'}, I \cdot \langle j' \rangle)) \cup$$
$$(\{(T_2, T_3, I \cdot \langle j \rangle)\} \times cs(T_{i'}, I \cdot \langle j' \rangle)) \qquad (22)$$

The parameter k can be chosen per node as to cover the longest unfolding of a loop in any trace of the log minus one, as the last unfolding always exits the loop. As some causal discovery techniques are exponential in the number of variables, a smaller k can be chosen. For example, Fig. 7a shows the UBCG derived from the process tree in Fig. 2a with maximum unfolding $k = 2$ for all nodes.

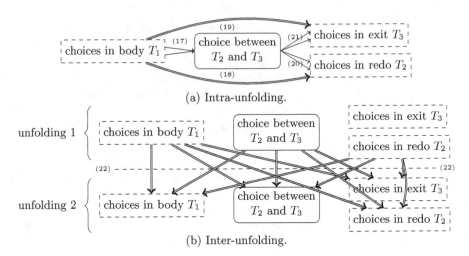

(a) Intra-unfolding.

(b) Inter-unfolding.

Fig. 6. UBCG of $\circlearrowleft (T_1, T_2, T_3)$. Double edges indicate that every choice in the source of the edge is connected to every choice in the target of the edge.

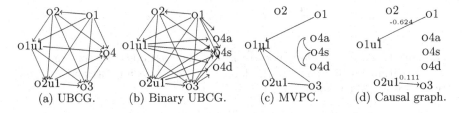

(a) UBCG.   (b) Binary UBCG.   (c) MVPC.   (d) Causal graph.

Fig. 7. Our method applied to a process tree (Fig. 2a), with $k = 2$.

Binary UBCGs. The causal discovery technique we will use in Sect. 5.3 requires binary choices. Therefore, we transform each n-ary choice into a set of binary choices using one-hot encoding in a post-processing step. That is, a choice between a, b and c is transformed into three choices: a vs. $\neg a$, b vs. $\neg b$ and c vs. $\neg c$. Figure 7b shows an example, where choice o4 has been split into o4s(kip), o4a(ccepted) and o4d(eclined). The introduced binary choices have no causal relation.

5.2   Choice Data

The next step is to create a table of the decisions made in the event log. In this table, each row represents a trace, each column represents a choice from the model, and each cell indicates which option was chosen. As decisions depend on both model and log, we use alignments [1] to extract the decisions made for the choices in each trace according to the model. That is, steps in the log that have no equivalent in the model are ignored.

Table 2. Table of choice data of Fig. 2a.

	o1	o2	o1u1	o2u1	o3	o4a	o4s	o4d
⟨o_sent, o_selected, o_created, o_accepted⟩	true	true	—	—	false	true	false	false
⟨o_selected, o_created, o_sent⟩	true	true	—	—	false	false	true	false

Certain choices are not encountered on certain paths through the process, resulting in missing data in the choice data set. For instance, the process tree model $\times(a, \mapsto(b, \times(c, d)))$ contains two decision points, however the trace $\langle a \rangle$ yields a for the first choice, but the second choice is not encountered. Another source of missing data are loop executions. For instance, for the model in Fig. 2a and the UBCG in Fig. 7a, an example choice data table is shown in Table 2

5.3 Causal Discovery

One of the oldest causal discovery algorithms is PC [25], which is able to identify the MEC under the assumption that there are no unobserved confounders. The PC algorithm starts from a fully connected undirected graph over all variables, and iteratively removes edges based on a series of statistical tests for conditional independence. The resulting graph summarises the MEC by keeping both directed and undirected edges, where the undirected edges mean that an edge between those nodes in either direction yields the same set of conditional independence relations and thus could not be distinguished.

Most causal discovery algorithms are unable to deal with missing values in the choice data. Therefore, we use the Missing Value PC (MVPC) algorithm [31], which is an extension of the PC algorithm that is able to handle missing data. If a value is missing, this is due to an earlier choice in the model, thus the cause of missing data is fully observed (*Missing At Random* (MAR)). This is a step up from Missing Not At Random, for which MVPC is less precise.

We know from the UBCG that certain causal edges contradict the process model. Therefore, we filter these edges from the MEC (considering undirected edges as two directed edges). This modification makes the MVPC algorithm process-aware, i.e., it leverages domain knowledge from the process model to reduce the MEC of observationally equivalent causal graphs. This reduction generally yields a single causal graph since the UBCG contains no undirected edges.

Finally, we take the obtained causal graph and estimate the size of the causal effect of each the edge in the causal graph. We estimate these causal effect sizes using a regression with backdoor adjustment [18]. When estimating the causal effect for an edge $v_i \to v_j$ in the causal graph, the backdoor adjustment achieves d-separation between v_i and v_j for all paths between v_i and v_j other than the direct causal path $v_i \to v_j$. After this adjustment, the regression coefficient can be given causal interpretation as the *average treatment effect* (ATE).

For example, Fig. 7c shows the output of the MVPC step for our process tree of Fig. 2a. Combining this graph with UBCG yields the causal graph in Fig. 7d.

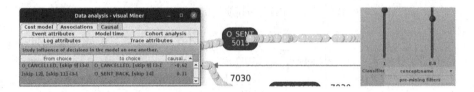

Fig. 8. Implementation of causal analysis in the Visual Miner.

6 Evaluation

Implementation. Our method has been implemented as a prototype in the Visual Miner [15,16]: it shows the results of the analyses of this table in a tabular format, as shown in Fig. 8. Intermediate steps are available to developers; future enhancements could include causal-graph editors and graph-based visualisations of identified causal dependencies.

Illustration: Synthetic Example. We apply our method to a synthetic process tree shown in Fig. 9, and generate a log of 10 000 traces, while injecting the causal dependencies of Fig. 9a. For instance, a choice for a in $\times(a, b)$ adds 0.4 to the probability of observing an h in $\times(g, h)$. This example contains several challenges: (i) *missing values* [by $\times(y, .)$]; (ii) *nested dependencies* [$\times(a, b)$ impacts $\times(g, h)$ and $\times(c, d)$ impacts $\times(e, f)$]; (iii) *indirect effects* [$\times(a, b)$ impacts $\times(g, h)$, which impacts $\times(i, j)$ without direct effect]; and (iv) *direct effect after an indirect effect* [$\times(k, l)$ is yet again impacted by $\times(a, b)$]. Choosing a synthetic example with these edge cases demonstrates that our method can handle these challenges.

Then, we apply our method, yielding a UBCG (Fig. 9b), the result of MVPC (Fig. 9c), and the causal graph obtained by combining UBCG and MVPC (Fig. 9d). Finally, ordinary least square regressions with backdoor adjustments for the true causal graph (Fig. 9d) recovers estimates of the true causal effect s, up to sampling variation. Note that our method is successful in retrieving the structure of the causal graph, despite the challenges.

Demonstration: Illustrative Example. Continuing from Sect. 2 and Fig. 2a, our method identifies two causal relationships: the first occurrence of o1 skipping o_cancelled *causes* a reduction of the second occurrence of o1 executing o_cancelled by 0.624. Furthermore, executing the loop exactly two times (o2u1 exit) *causes* o_sent_back to be executed 0.111 more. This means that if the execution of o_sent_back is of concern (e.g., wasteful), the process can be optimised by reducing the number of times the loop is executed exactly two times. Notice that some of the associations identified in Sect. 2 were in fact *not* causal.

Applicability: Real-Life Logs. To evaluate the practical applicability of our method, we applied it to several real-life event logs published by the IEEE Task Force on Process Mining, and models discovered by two miners: DFM Miner [16] (DFMM) and Inductive Miner - infrequent [14] (IMf). We measured the number

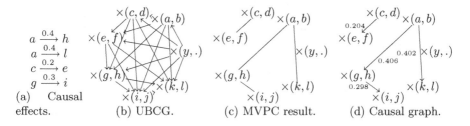

$a \xrightarrow{0.4} h$
$a \xrightarrow{0.4} l$
$c \xrightarrow{0.2} e$
$g \xrightarrow{0.3} i$

(a) Causal effects.   (b) UBCG.   (c) MVPC result.   (d) Causal graph.

Fig. 9. Synthetic example $\times(y, \mapsto(\times(a,b), \times(c,d), \times(e,f), \times(g,h), \times(i,j), \times(k,l)))$.

Table 3. Results of the applicability experiment.

Log	Miner	Choices	UBCG edges	MVPC edges → (−)	Causal graph edges	Run time (s) mean ± std.dev
BPIC12-a	DFMM	3	3	0 (6)	6	1.18 ± 0.22
BPIC12-a	IMf	4	6	0 (4)	4	0.59 ± 0.13
BPIC12-o	DFMM	42	594	7 (0)	4	1.29 ± 0.23
BPIC12-o	IMf	16	120	1 (5)	7	3.80 ± 0.29
Roadfines	DFMM	2	1	0 (0)	0	0.09 ± 0.08
Roadfines	IMf	8	27	2 (3)	5	7.80 ± 0.69
Sepsis	DFMM	288	23 776	not enough data for a particular edge		
Sepsis	IMf	148	5 485	0 (5)	5	74.52 ± 3.63
BPIC17-o	DFMM	2	1	0 (0)	0	0.04 ± 0.07
BPIC17-o	IMf	3	3	0 (4)	4	2.98 ± 0.50

of choices with log-bounded k, the edges in each of the graphs, and run time to apply MVPC (repeated 25 times on an i9-9980HK CPU with 32 GB RAM). Table 3 shows the results; for one instance, the MVPC algorithm did not produce a result as one particular edge had a constant choice. In all cases, the run time of MVPC was in the order of a minute, which makes it faster than alignment computations. We conclude that it is practically feasible to run our method on real-life logs. Furthermore, at most 7 causal relations are identified, which seems promising as to not overload analysts.

Discussion. Our method assumes that there are no unobserved confounders for model decisions, which is a rather substantial assumption. While any technique would need to make this assumption, potential bias could be reduced by using more data from event logs. Future work could explore integrating trace or event attributes in the choice graph. For trace attributes, this would require to precisely determine the moment in time when the attribute value became known, which might require domain expert knowledge. For causal analysis of choices, the moment of choice matters: the models $\mapsto(a, \times(b,c))$ and $\times(\mapsto(a,b), \mapsto(a,c))$ have the same language, but their moments of choice are different. In the first model a might have influenced the decision between b and c, but in the second model this is not possible. Event logs do not provide information about choices, so this cannot be verified using logs; our technique assumes that the given process model is correct.

7 Conclusion

Process mining aims to obtain insights from event logs, recorded from historic executions of business processes in organisations. In this paper, we introduced a causal method to study dependencies between choices within the control flow of process models. This method first derives an upper bound causal graph (UBCG) of choices in the model (for DFMs and process trees). Second, it transforms the log to a tabular data structure representing the choices made in each trace. Third, it applies an adjusted PC causal graph discovery algorithm, taking the UBCG into account. Fourth, it applies causal regression to find the causal relations. We illustrated the method and how it can be applied on an artificial and a real-life example, and applied the method in practice on several real-life event logs.

As future work, UBCGs for Petri nets could be constructed leveraging combined concepts of DFMs (markings/arbitrary loops) and process trees (concurrency). Furthermore, trace and event data can reveal additional confounding factors. Finally, the causal analysis could be summarised over unfoldings and projected on a model for easier analysis.

References

1. Adriansyah, A., Sidorova, N., van Dongen, B.F.: Cost-based fitness in conformance checking. In: ACSD, pp. 57–66. IEEE (2011)
2. Benjamini, Y., Hochberg, Y.: Controlling the false discovery rate: a practical and powerful approach to multiple testing. J. Royal Stat. Soc. **57**(1), 289–300 (1995)
3. Bozorgi, Z.D., Teinemaa, I., Dumas, M., Rosa, M.L., Polyvyanyy, A.: Process mining meets causal machine learning: discovering causal rules from event logs. In: ICPM, pp. 129–136. IEEE (2020)
4. Bozorgi, Z.D., Teinemaa, I., Dumas, M., Rosa, M.L., Polyvyanyy, A.: Prescriptive process monitoring for cost-aware cycle time reduction. In: ICPM, pp. 96–103. IEEE (2021)
5. vanden Broucke, S.K.L.M., Weerdt, J.D.: Fodina: a robust and flexible heuristic process discovery technique. Decis. Support Syst. **100**, 109–118 (2017)
6. Brunk, J., et al.: Cause vs. effect in context-sensitive prediction of business process instances. Inf. Syst. **95**, 101635 (2021)
7. Choueiri, A.C., Portela Santos, E.A.: Discovery of path-attribute dependency in manufacturing environments: a process mining approach. JMS **61**, 54–65 (2021)
8. Geiger, D., Verma, T., Pearl, J.: Identifying independence in Bayesian networks. Networks **20**(5), 507–534 (1990)
9. Günther, C.W., Rozinat, A.: Disco: discover your processes. In: BPM Demos, vol. 940, pp. 40–44. CEUR-WS.org (2012)
10. Hompes, B.F.A., Maaradji, A., La Rosa, M., Dumas, M., Buijs, J.C.A.M., van der Aalst, W.M.P.: Discovering causal factors explaining business process performance variation. In: Dubois, E., Pohl, K. (eds.) CAiSE 2017. LNCS, vol. 10253, pp. 177–192. Springer, Cham (2017). https://doi.org/10.1007/978-3-319-59536-8_12

11. Hsieh, C., Moreira, C., Ouyang, C.: Dice4el: interpreting process predictions using a milestone-aware counterfactual approach. In: ICPM, pp. 88–95. IEEE (2021)
12. Kamal, I.M., Bae, H., Utama, N.I., Yulim, C.: Data pixelization for predicting completion time of events. Neurocomputing **374**, 64–76 (2020)
13. Leemans, S.J.J., Fahland, D.: Information-preserving abstractions of event data in process mining. Knowl. Inf. Syst. **62**(3), 1143–1197 (2019). https://doi.org/10.1007/s10115-019-01376-9
14. Leemans, S.J.J., Fahland, D., van der Aalst, W.M.P.: Discovering block-structured process models from event logs containing infrequent behaviour. In: Lohmann, N., Song, M., Wohed, P. (eds.) BPM 2013. LNBIP, vol. 171, pp. 66–78. Springer, Cham (2014). https://doi.org/10.1007/978-3-319-06257-0_6
15. Leemans, S.J.J., Fahland, D., van der Aalst, W.M.P.: Exploring processes and deviations. In: Fournier, F., Mendling, J. (eds.) BPM 2014. LNBIP, vol. 202, pp. 304–316. Springer, Cham (2015). https://doi.org/10.1007/978-3-319-15895-2_26
16. Leemans, S.J.J., Poppe, E., Wynn, M.T.: Directly follows-based process mining: exploration & a case study. In: ICPM, pp. 25–32. IEEE (2019)
17. Narendra, T., Agarwal, P., Gupta, M., Dechu, S.: Counterfactual reasoning for process optimization using structural causal models. In: Hildebrandt, T., van Dongen, B.F., Röglinger, M., Mendling, J. (eds.) BPM 2019. LNBIP, vol. 360, pp. 91–106. Springer, Cham (2019). https://doi.org/10.1007/978-3-030-26643-1_6
18. Pearl, J.: Causality: Models, Reasoning, and Inference. Cambridge UP, Cambridge (2009)
19. Pesic, M., Schonenberg, H., van der Aalst, W.M.P.: DECLARE: full support for loosely-structured processes. In: EDOC, pp. 287–300. IEEE (2007)
20. Peters, S., et al.: Fast and accurate quantitative business process analysis using feature complete queueing models. Inf. Sys. **104**, 101892 (2022)
21. Qafari, M.S., van der Aalst, W.: Root cause analysis in process mining using structural equation models. In: Del Río Ortega, A., Leopold, H., Santoro, F.M. (eds.) BPM 2020. LNBIP, vol. 397, pp. 155–167. Springer, Cham (2020). https://doi.org/10.1007/978-3-030-66498-5_12
22. Qafari, M.S., van der Aalst, W.M.P.: Case level counterfactual reasoning in process mining. In: Nurcan, S., Korthaus, A. (eds.) CAiSE 2021. LNBIP, vol. 424, pp. 55–63. Springer, Cham (2021). https://doi.org/10.1007/978-3-030-79108-7_7
23. Qafari, M.S., van der Aalst, W.M.P.: Feature recommendation for structural equation model discovery in process mining. CoRR abs/2108.07795 (2021)
24. Shoush, M., Dumas, M.: Prescriptive process monitoring under resource constraints: a causal inference approach. CoRR abs/2109.02894 (2021)
25. Spirtes, P., Glymour, C., Scheines, R.: Causation, Prediction, and Search, 2nd edn. MIT Press, Cambridge (2000)
26. Stierle, M.: Exploring Cause-Effect Relationships in Process Analytics - Design, Development and Evaluation of Comprehensible, Explainable and Context-Aware Techniques. Ph.D. thesis, FAU Erlangen-Nürnberg (2021)
27. Sun, H., Liu, W., Qi, L., Ren, X., Du, Y.: An algorithm for mining indirect dependencies from loop-choice-driven loop structure via petri nets. IEEE TSMC (2021)
28. Sutrisnowati, R.A., Bae, H., Park, J., Ha, B.: Learning Bayesian network from event logs using mutual information test. In: ICSOC, pp. 356–360. IEEE (2013)
29. Sutrisnowati, R.A., Bae, H., Song, M.: Bayesian network construction from event log for lateness analysis in port logistics. Comput. Ind. Eng. **89**, 53–66 (2015)
30. Tax, N., Teinemaa, I., van Zelst, S.J.: An interdisciplinary comparison of sequence modeling methods for next-element prediction. Softw. Syst. Model. **19**(6), 1345–1365 (2020). https://doi.org/10.1007/s10270-020-00789-3

31. Tu, R., Zhang, C., Ackermann, P., Mohan, K., Kjellström, H., Zhang, K.: Causal discovery in the presence of missing data. In: AISTATS, pp. 1762–1770 (2019)
32. Weijters, A.J.M.M., Ribeiro, J.T.S.: Flexible heuristics miner (FHM). In: CIDM, pp. 310–317. IEEE (2011)
33. Wen, L., van der Aalst, W.M.P., Wang, J., Sun, J.: Mining process models with non-free-choice constructs. Data Min. Knowl. Discov. 15(2), 145–180 (2007)
34. van Zelst, S.J., van Dongen, B.F., van der Aalst, W.M.P., Verbeek, H.M.W.: Discovering workflow nets using integer linear programming. Computing 100(5), 529–556 (2017). https://doi.org/10.1007/s00607-017-0582-5

Crop Harvest Forecast via Agronomy-Informed Process Modelling and Predictive Monitoring

Jing Yang[1,2(✉)] , Chun Ouyang[1,2] , Güvenç Dik[1,2] , Paul Corry[1,2] , and Arthur H. M. ter Hofstede[1]

[1] Queensland University of Technology, Brisbane, QLD 4000, Australia
{roy.j.yang,c.ouyang,g.dik,p.corry,a.terhofstede}@qut.edu.au
[2] Food Agility Cooperative Research Centre, Sydney, NSW 2000, Australia

Abstract. Reliable and timely forecasts on crop harvest bring significant benefits to agri-food industries by providing valuable input to complex decisions on production planning. Useful predictions on crop harvest require continual effort by seasoned field agronomists. However, they are often scarce resources in the real-world. A feasible way to facilitate crop harvest forecast is through developing predictive models that can exploit data relevant to crop growth and automatically generate consistent predictions. To this end, this paper presents our design of a systematic and data-driven approach to supporting online forecasts on crop harvest. Underpinned by process modelling and predictive monitoring techniques, our approach can utilise crop-growth-related information from multiple data sources and progressively generate crop harvest predictions within the crop growing season. The approach has a flexible design informed by agronomic knowledge applicable to crop growth in general, and may be tailored to different crops and production scenarios. A case study with a local farming company using its real-life production data demonstrates the feasibility and efficacy of our approach.

Keywords: Crop forecast · Predictive process monitoring · Event logs · Process modelling · Knowledge discovery

1 Introduction

The resilience of agriculture and food production is one of the key challenges in today's world. Growers of fresh produce often have to make fast and complex decisions about production planning based on outcomes of crop harvest. Reliable and timely forecasts on crop harvest can bring significant benefits to agri-food industries, as they provide valuable input to support growers' decision-making, e.g., schedule for appropriate harvest dates to ensure the quality of yield [10]. However, forecasting crop harvest is complicated by the fact that (i) crop growth is affected by many factors, such as climate variability, geographical location, soil

© Springer Nature Switzerland AG 2022
X. Franch et al. (Eds.): CAiSE 2022, LNCS 13295, pp. 201–217, 2022.
https://doi.org/10.1007/978-3-031-07472-1_12

and water quality, and (ii) the impact of relevant factors on crop production is often dynamic, i.e., it changes along the crop growing process.

Effective forecasts on crop harvest concern various aspects and factors related to crop growth, and demand efforts by experienced agronomists working in the fields [2]. However, they are often scarce resources in the real-world. Recent advancement in digitalisation and Internet of Things (IoT) technologies enables the recording of various data relevant to crop production by information systems deployed in the agri-food sector [10] (e.g., farm management systems). It becomes an interesting yet challenging problem how to exploit such relevant and multi-sourced data to provide accurate and timely crop forecasts within the crop growing season automatically.

To this end, we propose a systematic and data-driven approach to supporting online forecasts on crop harvest. By modelling the process nature of crop growth, our approach can integrate static and dynamic crop-growth information from various data sources into one consistent data input and utilise it for reliable crop harvest predictions. Built upon process modelling and predictive monitoring [16] capabilities, the approach enables predictions to be generated automatically and progressively during the crop growing season. Furthermore, the approach has a flexible design informed by agronomic knowledge applicable to crop growth in general, and may be tailored to different crops and production scenarios. A case study with a local farming company using historical real-life crop production data demonstrates the feasibility and efficacy of the approach.

Our research contributes an effective approach to forecasting crop harvest based on process science and machine learning. The contribution is three-fold. Firstly, it presents a novel attempt to adapt a predictive process monitoring framework in the domain of agri-food production. Secondly, the proposal of using process modelling to integrate multi-sourced crop-growth data into one standardised, consistent data input in the form of event logs, is a potential contribution to the field of Information Systems Engineering. Last but not least, for the farming company engaged in the case study, our work lays the technical foundation for the company's capability building in data-driven crop forecast and contributes to improved production planning and resource deployment.

2   Background and Related Work

Forecasting crop harvest within crop growing seasons plays a vital role in crop production planning and decision-making. There are three types of approaches to crop forecasting [2]. Field survey is a traditional yet expensive way. Farm managers and farmers collect and assess information such as the number of pods and pod weight close to the harvest period and give estimation of the final yield [12]. Field surveys usually require trained operators to carry out data collection across multiple locations. A typical example concerns the Objective Yield surveys conducted by the US Department of Agriculture. Field survey data can be used to make forecasts, which often depend on agronomists' opinions about growing-season conditions (like weather events) and their expectations on the final yield. As a result, field surveys may risk uncertainty and inconsistency due to their reliance on agronomists' expertise [2].

Crop simulation modelling is an effective way to deriving crop forecasts. Simulation models consist of mathematical equations to characterise plant development and growth processes, considering factors of genotypes, environment, management, and their interactions [13]. Historical data, such as actual observed weather and averaged weather data, as well as climate model outputs, can be used to establish parameters of a simulation model. Predictions on the end-of-season harvest outcomes are then generated by running the instantiated model. Since simulation models do not predict based on real-time observed data, they are prone to risks of unknown climate situations between forecast dates and harvest dates [2]. To overcome this issue, some research (e.g., [5]) studies how to calibrate simulation models at runtime within crop growing seasons.

Another promising way to approach crop harvest forecasting is through the use of machine learning techniques, which has received growing interest in recent years. Machine learning models, e.g., linear regression or neural network, are trained to fit crop data from historical seasons, and can then be applied to new crop data and make predictions for coming seasons. Crop data may cover various types of information, including weather (e.g., temperature and solar radiation), soil (e.g., soil type and nutrients), water (e.g., rainfall and humidity), and the crop itself (e.g., crop variety and plant weight) [15]. Recent advancement in sensor technologies has enabled possibilities to use data collected by dedicated proximal sensors (e.g., Internet of Things devices deployed on fields) and remote sensing platforms (e.g., satellites and Unmanned Aerial Vehicles or UAVs) [17] as inputs to machine learning techniques. These data are usually images, from which various vegetation indices and biophysical parameters can be derived and utilised for prediction and change analysis [8]. For example, remotely-sensed images acquired by UAVs are used to calculate the Normalized Difference Vegetation Index, contributing an important feature alongside weather variables for predicting pasture biomass development [4]. Notably, a recent systematic literature review on application of machine learning to crop yield prediction [15] highlights the need and challenge for future work to utilise data from different data sources to improve predictions.

To automatically generate reliable forecasts on crop harvest within crop growing seasons, it is vital to integrate multi-sourced data relevant to crop growth—data reflecting aspects of the plant nature, growing environment, and production management—and to be able to utilise such data and synchronise with dynamic changes during growing seasons. Event logs provide a flexible view that aggregates multi-dimensional, time-series data relevant to the same process and potentially from multiple data sources [1]. Crop growing seasons adhere to the plant's phenological nature [2] and can be captured using a process notation. This makes event logs a suitable choice for integrating multi-sourced data relevant to crop growth.

Predictive process monitoring techniques can be used to exploit event log data and make predictions on running processes with regard to performance, outcomes, risks, or future states [11]. These techniques use machine learning algorithms with a process focus [16] and strengthen organisations' capabilities of making timely decisions about processes at runtime.

In this paper, we propose an approach to integrating multi-sourced, crop growth-related data into the form of event logs and using predictive process monitoring techniques for online predictions of crop harvest. In the context of research on process analytics [1] and predictive process monitoring [11], our approach represents an application of these techniques to address key problems in the agri-food domain.

3 Approach

In this section, we present our approach to supporting online predictions of crop harvest. Figure 1 depicts an overview of the approach, which takes as input multiple data sources related to crop growing and generates predictions related to crop growth and harvest (e.g., *days to harvest* and *yield*). The design of the approach is informed by the relevant agronomic knowledge and is built upon a benchmark predictive process monitoring workflow [16]. As such, it is capable of addressing the need of making timely crop predictions automatically and progressively during the crop growing season. There are two key components—data fusion guided by a crop growing process model, and an agronomy-informed process-aware (AIPA) predictive model for crop forecast.

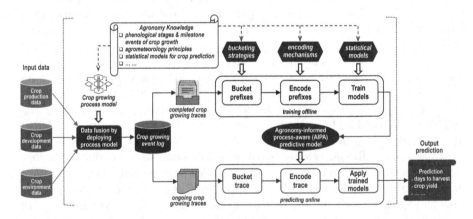

Fig. 1. An overview of the approach supporting online forecasts on crop harvest

3.1 Data Fusion

We consider three main data sources which provide useful information related to crop growing. *Crop production data* records information of crop production relevant to farm and supply chain management, such as production order, crop plant variety, growing location, sowing date, and harvest date and yield (only available in historical data). *Crop development data* contains information about crop growth, including important events like sowing and flowering; and physical characteristics of growing plants like size of the plant, tiller number, etc. *Crop environment data* records information concerning the crop growing environment like soil and water quality and, in particular, *weather information* of the crop growing locations such as temperature, radiation, and rainfall.

We use rice production as an example to explain how data fusion is carried out, as illustrated in Fig. 2. While the three data sources are inherently different from each other, the purpose of data fusion is to integrate them into one crop growing dataset as the input for prediction.

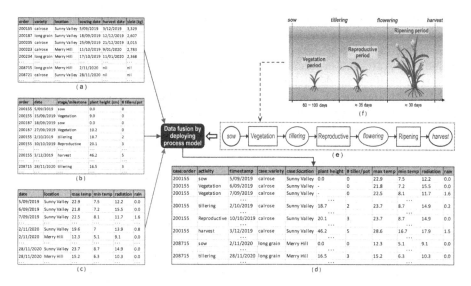

Fig. 2. Illustration of data fusion using a simple hypothetical example, where (a) rice production data, (b) rice plant development data and (c) weather data of rice growing locations are integrated into (d) rice growing event log data, by referring to (e) a rice growing process model (in a simplified view) of which the design is informed by (f) three main phenological growth stages and milestone events of rice crop (adapted from [7])

The key to enabling data fusion in our approach is the design of a crop growing process model which captures the phenological process of a given crop. Consider the example of rice crop in Fig. 2(f). The growth of a rice crop consists of three main phenological stages—Vegetation, Reproductive and Ripening, and two intermediate milestone events—*tillering* which indicates the transition from Vegetation to Reproductive growth, and *flowering* which marks the transition from Reproductive to Ripening growth [7]. Such agronomic knowledge can be used to inform the design of a rice growing process model. Figure 2(e) depicts a simplified view of such a model capturing rice growing activities in terms of three main phenological growth stages and two milestone events between *sow* (the start event of rice growth) and *harvest* (the end event of rice growth).

Once a crop growing process model is established, it can be deployed to replay or monitor the process of crop growth by incorporating the input data from available data sources. As a result, a log of events recording the occurrences of crop growing activities can be generated, where data from the various sources is systematically and consistently integrated into relevant data attributes associated with individual events. For example, Fig. 2(d) shows a fragment of a rice growing event log generated by deploying the rice growing process model in (e) with the input data of rice production in (a), rice plant development in (b) and relevant weather information in (c).

Concepts and Notations. We define several key concepts and notations for describing crop growing event log data.

A *crop growing event* (denoted e) is an instance of a crop growing activity (including a start, end or intermediate milestone event), and has *attributes* carrying crop production, development, and environment data associated with the activity. Each crop growing event e has three mandatory attributes—production order (denoted o), crop growing activity (a) and timestamp (t), and is uniquely identified by a combination of the values carried by these attributes. Hence, e can be represented as a tuple (o, a, t). For example, in Fig. 2(d) each row corresponds to a rice growing event and each column to an attribute, and the rice growing event on the first row can be written as (200155, *sow*, 5/09/2019).

A *case-level attribute* is an attribute of which values remain identical across all crop growing events that belong to the same production order. By definition, production order is always a case-level attribute of a crop growing event. Revisiting the example in Fig. 2(d), each rice growing event has three case-level attributes—crop production order, variety, and location.

A *crop growing trace* (denoted σ) is a non-empty finite sequence of crop growing events that belong to the same production order. For each crop growing trace σ, the order of crop growing events in σ is determined by event timestamps. Let σ_o represent the crop growing trace of production order o, σ_o can be written as $[(o, a_1, t_1),\ldots,(o, a_n, t_n)]$ (where $t_1<\ldots<t_n$). Revisiting the example in Fig. 2(d), the following two rice growing traces can be observed:

- σ_{200155}: [(200155, *sow*, 5/09/2019), (200155, *Vegetation*, 6/09/2019), (200155, *Vegetation*, 7/09/2019), . . . , (200155, *harvest*, 3/12/2019)]
- σ_{208715}: [(208715, *sow*, 2/11/2020), . . . , (208715, *tillering*, 28/11/2020)]

A *crop growing event log* is a set of crop growing traces. There are: *completed crop growing traces*, which begin with the start event (e.g., *sow*) of a crop growing process and finish with the end event (e.g., *harvest*) of the process; and *ongoing crop growing traces*, which begin with the start event but finish with an event other than the end event. In the above example, σ_{200155} is a completed rice growing trace, and σ_{208715} is an ongoing rice growing trace.

3.2 AIPA Predictive Model

The availability of crop growing event log data (as output of data fusion) makes it possible to develop a predictive model to forecast crop harvest by exploiting predictive process monitoring capabilities. We adopt a benchmark predictive process monitoring workflow [16]. The main idea is to train a predictive model using historical data of completed crop growing traces, and then use the trained model to make predictions for ongoing crop growing traces (see Fig. 1). In particular, we focus on applying agronomic knowledge and domain expertise and support model explainability in the design of our approach.

Bucket Prefixes. The first step is to extract *prefixes* from completed traces and group them into *buckets* (or bins) according to certain criteria. Given a completed trace σ, a prefix of σ is defined as a sequence of the first l ($1 \leq l \leq |\sigma|$) events of σ. Hence, a completed trace σ can be used to extract $|\sigma|$ prefixes. These prefixes capture the history of crop growth related to the trace progressively, and are the input for feature encoding and model training. A *bucketing strategy* is used to specify the criteria for grouping the extracted prefixes into buckets. A typical example known as prefix-length-based bucketing is to group prefixes of the same length into the same bucket. For crop prediction, we propose to apply the relevant agronomic knowledge to the design of a bucketing strategy. For example, the growth of a crop plant consists of different phenological stages. Each stage is associated with a specific set of factors affecting crop harvest outcome. According to this, prefixes of crop growing traces can be grouped into buckets depending on which phenological stage each prefix belongs to.

Encode Prefixes. In the second step, prefixes in each bucket are encoded as feature vectors using an *encoding mechanism*. Our focus is on how to encode *event-specific* attributes, which change from event to event and are considered *dynamic* attributes of an event log. Although there exist various feature encoding techniques in data mining research, they are not necessarily suitable for crop prediction. For example, weather data attributes are typical event-specific attributes of a crop growing event log. Since weather plays an important role in crop growth, it has been studied in the field of agrometeorology, where specific measures and algorithms for aggregation of weather attributes are established with an emphasis on their impact on crop production. Hence, we propose that relevant agronomic knowledge such as agrometeorology principles should be used to guide the design of encoding mechanisms for crop prediction.

Train Models. In this step, feature vectors in each bucket are used to train a predictive model. While there are various machine learning techniques that one can choose from, we propose two key rationales for making a design decision. Firstly, since complex machine learning models developed to build advanced predictive capabilities are often used as a 'black-box', the recent body of literature in machine learning has emphasised the importance to apply models that are transparent and explainable [14]. Secondly, among the models that are explainable by design, statistical models are a good choice as they have already been used to make crop predictions (see Sect. 2). A typical example is the use of statistical regressions for predicting crop yield, where the applicability of such a model is often driven by its simplicity and transparency [2]. Hence, we consider the use of statistical models for crop prediction in our approach.

At the end of this step, a predictive model that is agronomy-informed and process-aware (i.e., an AIPA predictive model) is generated. It comprises a set of buckets of prefixes, and encoded feature vectors and trained models associated with each of the buckets. The performance of an AIPA predictive model can be assessed using appropriate evaluation measures for the given predictive target.

Online Prediction. During the online phase, a trained AIPA predictive model is used to make predictions for ongoing crop growing traces. Given an ongoing trace, the correct bucket for the trace is firstly determined, then the feature encoder for the bucket is used to encode the trace data into a feature vector, and finally the trained model for the bucket is deployed to obtain a prediction.

4   Case Study

This section reports on a case study using real-life data provided by a farming company X in Australia to predict the harvest of a crop Y.[1]

4.1   Context

Crop Y is a common type of crop grown by company X. To increase market value of crop Y, the company wishes to develop a scientific solution that provides timely predictions about the crop's harvest date and yield, using historical crop production and meteorological data. While its current predictions rely heavily on the manual labour of field agronomists, company X expects the solution to automatically produce predictions on a weekly basis during the crop growing season. We applied our approach to address this need.

For this case study, company X provided us with historical crop production data recording the actual production orders (*orders* for short) of Y over the past five years. Each order in the dataset can be uniquely identified and records information on the growth period of a certain amount of crop Y. More specifically, an order record has four types of information, including (i) location and area of the production unit, (ii) variety of crop Y, (iii) key dates during the crop growth period, e.g., harvest dates, (iv) quantities of the order, i.e., the ordered quantity (corresponded to sales orders) and the delivered quantity (i.e., yield).

For crop environment data, we collected and used the public weather data released by the state government. For each local area in the state, the weather dataset records the daily maximum and minimum temperature, radiation, rainfall, evaporation, and vapour pressure.

---

[1] For confidentiality reasons, we cannot disclose the company's name and the specific crop considered in this case study.

4.2   Application of the Approach

Data Fusion and Preprocessing. We discussed with agronomists from company X and built a process model capturing the phenological growth process of crop Y. As shown in Fig. 3, the growing season of crop Y is divided into two stages marked by two milestone events, namely "PF" and "HA".

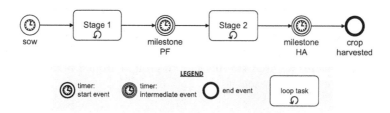

Fig. 3. Process model capturing the growth of crop Y using BPMN

We utilised the created crop growing process model to integrate the collected order data and weather data, and generated the crop growing event log for the given orders of crop Y. By matching the production unit locations in the order data against the geographical locations in the weather data, we were able to extract the daily weather observations during the crop growing season for every order. Then, the created process model was deployed to generate for each order a crop growing trace containing daily crop growing events. As a result, we obtained a crop growing event log with 348 completed traces consisting of 22, 115 events. Table 1 shows a fragment of the event log.

Table 1. A fragment of the anonymised event log used in the case study

Order	Event/ subprocess	timestamp	Days to PF	Days to harvest	case: unit_loc	case: unit_area	case: var	case: order_qty	case: deliv_qty	radn	max_t	min_t	rain	evap	vp
12763	sow	2016-08-10	74	56	M1	4.2	VG	32320	38350	17.4	24	5.4	0	2.4	11.6
12763	Stage 1	2016-08-11	73	55	M1	4.2	VG	32320	38350	8.1	22.9	7.2	0	2.9	13
12763	Stage 1	2016-08-12	72	54	M1	4.2	VG	32320	38350	16	21.9	8.5	2.9	3	12.4
...															
12763	Stage 1	2016-10-05	0	18	M1	4.2	VG	32320	38350	25.8	26	7.1	0	6	9.7
12763	Stage 2	2016-10-06	n/a	17	M1	4.2	VG	32320	38350	25.5	28.3	6.6	0	5.4	7.2
12763	Stage 2	2016-10-07	n/a	16	M1	4.2	VG	32320	38350	26.3	29.8	5.8	0	5.2	10.5
...															
13687	sow	2019-10-14	60	45	M3	2	W	3900	5700	20.1	29.6	15.4	0.8	5.3	17.8
13687	Stage 1	2019-10-15	59	44	M3	2	W	3900	5700	22	34.3	16.3	0	7.5	20.4
...															

(i) Attributes derived from the order data: "days to PF", days from the recorded event to PF; "days to harvest", days from the recorded event to the harvest date; "case:unit_loc", location of the production unit; "case:unit_area", area of the production unit (hectare); "case:var", crop variety; "case:order_qty", ordered quantity (kg); "case:deliv_qty", delivered quantity (kg). (ii) Attributes derived from the weather data: "radn", solar radiation (MJ/m^2); "max_t", maximum temperature (°C); "min_t", minimum temperature (°C); "rain", rainfall (mm); "evap", evaporation (mm); "vp", vapour pressure (hPa). Attributes that start with "case" are case-level attributes.

In a real-life scenario, historical crop growing traces are used to train an AIPA predictive model offline, which is then used for making predictions about ongoing crop growing traces. In our evaluation, we simulated such a scenario by splitting the event log dataset into two subsets. We ordered all traces by their sowing dates. The first 75% was used for training the AIPA model (as "historical" traces), while the more recent 25% was used for testing the derived model (as "ongoing" traces).

Bucketing. We applied a bucketing strategy based on the crop's phenological growth stages. As mentioned, the growing season of crop Y is divided into two stages. Therefore, we used two buckets to group encoded prefixes based on whether milestone PF was reached.

Encoding. We consulted agronomists from company X to identify and model factors impacting the growth of crop Y. It was suggested that temperature and radiation are the most important weather attributes. Specifically, temperature can be characterised by two measures in agronomy, namely, growing degree days (GDD) [9] and heat stress days [6]. These measures can be derived[2] based on the daily maximum and minimum temperature in our dataset. For radiation, we applied numerical aggregation functions including *sum, mean, max, min* and *std* to encode features [16].

Furthermore, in terms of predicting harvest date, the agronomists advised that the length of stage 1 (from sowing to milestone PF) is a good indicator for estimating final harvest dates in practice. Therefore, for prefixes in the second bucket (at stage 2), we included the duration from sowing to milestone PF as an encoded feature. We set the field "days to harvest" as the prediction target.

For predicting yield, the agronomists suggested that the number of heat stress days occurred during the first five days after milestone PF may be a useful predictor besides the foregoing features. We included this for prefixes in the second bucket. We set the delivered quantity per unit area as the prediction target to eliminate the area difference across production units. This variable can be derived from dividing "case:delivered_qty" by "case:unit_area".

Statistical Model. In this case study, we employed ordinary linear regression models with least squares. The reasons are two-fold. First, applying a linear regression model requires minimal configuration, which helps avoid hyperparameter tuning often required by other more complex regression techniques. Second, the simplicity and transparency of a linear model helps us better communicate our prediction results with company X when explaining how predictions are obtained and identifying factors that have high impact on the predictions.

---

[2] Calculation of those meteorological measures was done based on an R-package `cropgrowdays` (https://gitlab.com/petebaker/cropgrowdays).

Model Evaluation. When selecting the evaluation metrics, we refer to the goals set by company X: (i) predicted harvest dates are expected to be within 2 days on either side of the actual harvest dates, and (ii) predicted yield (as delivered quantity per unit) values are expected to deviate no more than 35% (either side) from the actual delivered yield. Given these goals, we employed Mean Absolute Error (MAE) for evaluating harvest date prediction and Mean Absolute Percentage Error (MAPE) for yield prediction, respectively.

$$\text{MAE} = \frac{1}{n} \sum_{i=1}^{n} |y_i - \hat{y}_i| \, , \text{MAPE} = \frac{1}{n} \sum_{i=1}^{n} \left| \frac{y_i - \hat{y}_i}{y_i} \right| ,$$

where n is the number of samples, y_i and $\hat{y}_i$ are the observed and predicted target values of the i-th sample [16]. Furthermore, we also included the adjusted R^2 score (i.e., coefficient of determination) considering the regression nature of the tasks.

We also considered earliness [16] in our evaluation, which refers to the earliest point of time when the prediction accuracy (in terms of a selected measure) satisfies a given goal. To enable earliness evaluation, we applied two filters on prefixes in both the training and testing data set: (i) we excluded the final event for all prefixes (i.e., event recording harvests), since predictions obtained on the day of harvest will be trivial, and (ii) we excluded prefixes with excessive length[3] to avoid unreliable results due to an unbalanced number of samples [16].

In our experiments, we conducted model evaluation in two ways. First, we performed an overall model evaluation by calculating prediction scores and errors for prefixes in the two buckets separately, i.e., stage 1 (pre-PF) and stage 2 (post-PF). In this way, we were able to obtain an overview on the efficacy of linear regression models using different features. Second, we performed a weekly-based evaluation to assess how our approach generates predictions within the crop growing season. We took all prefixes from both buckets and re-grouped them by prefix length based on weeks, e.g., prefixes with lengths ranged from 1 to 7 comprise the first group and those from 8 to 14 comprise the second group, etc. We then calculated the prediction errors for each weekly group and compared the results against the prediction goal.

4.3 Results Analysis and Discussion

Overall Model Evaluation. Table 2 show the results of the overall model evaluation by prediction errors and scores. In predicting days to harvest, the average adjusted R^2 scores show that regression models built for both buckets have decent performance. Meanwhile, the MAE values are 2.77 and 1.85. The decrease in errors signifies that including the duration from sowing to milestone PF as a feature contributes to making better predictions, which aligns with the advice given by the agronomists of company X.

---

[3] Note that this does not reduce the size of the training or the testing set, in terms of the number of traces (orders).

Table 2. Results of overall model evaluation

Prediction task	Metric	Bucket 1: pre-PF	Bucket 2: post-PF
Days to harvest	Adj.R^2	0.93	0.85
	MAE	2.77	1.85
Yield	Adj.R^2	0.62	0.60
	MAPE	0.37	0.31

In predicting yield, we obtained adjusted R^2 scores of 0.62 and 0.60, respectively. The scores are lower compared to those in the previous task, but this is expected—in predicting yield, all prefixes of the same trace have an identical target value (i.e., the final unit quantity delivered), due to the lack of data tracking crop development in terms of its final yield. This limitation of data impeded the yield predictive model in capturing how weather conditions within the growing season may have impacted the final yield.

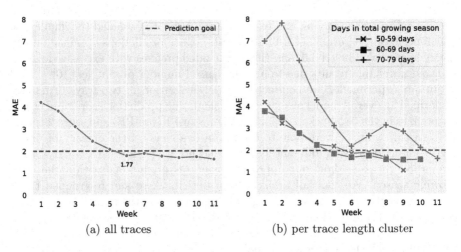

(a) all traces   (b) per trace length cluster

Fig. 4. Weekly evaluation by Mean Absolute Error on predicting days to harvest

Weekly-Based Model Evaluation. In terms of predicting days to harvest, Fig. 4a shows the results of weekly evaluation by MAE over prefixes of all traces. It is clear that the prediction error decreases weekly as the crop growing season proceeds weekly. Also, the developed models show good performance in terms of earliness, since the prediction errors satisfy the goal set by company X as early as week 6 (when MAE = 1.77 < 2).

Furthermore, we unfolded the evaluation results to investigate how our approach performed on traces related to crop growing seasons of different lengths. We did this by classifying traces into three clusters based on the number of days from crop sowing to harvest: 50–59 days, 60–69 days, and 70–79 days, respectively. Figure 4b shows the results. We can observe that the predictive models performed well on the 50-day and 60-day clusters, with a similar trend of progressively decreasing error as seen before. However, the longer traces (i.e., those in the 70-day cluster) seem to be the outliers. Even though the prediction error decreases in general, it has an unexpected increase after week 6, which is approximately the point that splits the two buckets by milestone PF. Also, the prediction error never reaches a satisfactory level until the last week (week 11), which would then have very little value in terms of earliness. A possible reason is that it is less common that the total growing season spans over 70 days. We confirmed this by examining the distribution of traces in our dataset. It was found that the longer traces comprise a small percentage of all traces, only around 15% in both the overall dataset and the subset used for model training. Therefore, the predictive models may likely have under-fitted data of the longer traces.

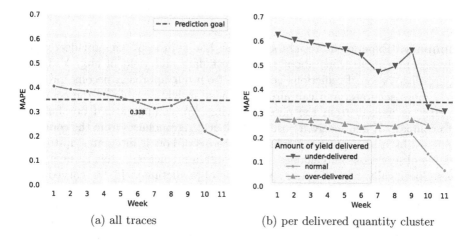

(a) all traces   (b) per delivered quantity cluster

Fig. 5. Weekly evaluation by Mean Absolute Percentage Error on predicting yield

In terms of predicting yield, Fig. 5a show the results of weekly evaluation by MAPE over prefixes of all traces. At first, the prediction error decreases in general, albeit at a small scale, and meets the prediction goal in week 6 (MAPE = 33.8% < 35%). During week 8 to week 9, there is an unexpected increase, but the prediction error stays close to the accepted level. From week 10 onwards, the prediction error becomes much lower to around 20%. These observations provide further evidence to our previous conclusion that predicting yield with the current dataset is challenging due to the limitation of the data—yield predictions become much more accurate in terms of the actual final yield only when the crop growing season enters its later stages.

We further examined the yield prediction results. Again, traces were clustered but, in this case, by calculating the ratio of delivered quantity to ordered quantity (see data attributes in Table 1), which then represents the percentage of ordered quantity delivered. We considered three clusters: (i) "normal", if the ratio is between 90% and 110%; (ii) "over-delivered", if the ratio is higher than 110%; and (iii) "under-delivered", if the ratio is lower than 90%. Figure 5b shows the unfolded results per cluster. Clearly, the predictive models performed well on the "normal" cluster, showing an expected pattern of both low and progressively decreasing error. Performance on the "over-delivered" cluster is acceptable and remains stable over time. The most interesting finding concerns the "under-delivered" cluster, where prediction error is consistently high in the early weeks and merely reaches the prediction goal from week 10 onwards. Consider that "under-delivered" traces accounted for 42% of the training set, the underperformance of the models is unlikely to be caused by insufficient data. We surmised that crop growth relevant to those "under-delivered" traces was impacted by unseen factors not captured by information in the current dataset. This speculation was later confirmed through our discussion with the agronomists reported below. The relatively high proportion of "under-delivered" traces also explains the increase of prediction error in week 7 as previously shown in Fig. 5a.

Summary. Experiment results show that our approach can provide reasonably accurate predictions about the harvest date and yield of crop Y during its growing season. Predictions generated from our approach become progressively more accurate, and can already provide insights usable by the company as early as week 6 from the date of sowing. We communicated our findings with company X and received positive feedback. Agronomists from the company expressed high interest in our solution in terms of how it integrates up-to-date weather observations and enables them to obtain prediction outcomes on a daily basis. Specifically, regarding our speculation of predicting yield, we learned from the discussion that the "delivered quantity" recorded in the dataset (which we specified as the target of yield prediction) does not fully represent the amount of fresh yield. Instead, the delivered quantity records the result from a quality control process which took place after crop harvest. Not surprisingly, data in the "under-delivered" clusters are related to more human intervention in quality control, compared to other clusters. Since the dataset we used does not cover any information about that post-processing step, it makes sense that the derived predictive models did not perform well on the "under-delivered" clusters.

5   Discussion

Our work reported in this paper paves new avenues to some interesting future work. For one, our approach has a flexible design which enables it to be generalised to potentially any field crop for which phenological events can be identified and captured by process modelling. Also, the use of a general predictive process monitoring workflow allows many machine learning techniques to be plugged in. For example: (i) when given data that embeds complex, non-linear patterns, advanced regression algorithms, e.g., Support Vector Machine (SVM), can be used to potentially improve the prediction accuracy [15]; and (ii) when encoding prefixes, feature selection methods for sequence prediction [18] can be applied to complement the use of expert knowledge from agronomists.

With this flexibility, it is worthwhile to investigate guidelines on how to configure different steps of the approach according to factors like actual crops, ecosystems (soil, growing season, etc.), and input data characteristics [8].

The use of process modelling in our approach can transcend the purpose of integrating data from multiple, various sources to feed the predictive process monitoring workflow. Process models formally capturing the phenology of crop growth enable many existing process analytics tools to be applied "off-the-shelf". For example, historical crop growth can be visually analysed by replaying crop growing event logs [3], so that agronomists can leverage the collated data to examine how crop harvests were impacted by geographical locations, date-times, weather conditions, etc. We consider the use of process modelling an enabler of future deployment and application of process analytics over data integrated from various non-standard data sources—this can potentially be extended to domains other than forecasting crop harvest, making a contribution to the field of Information Systems Engineering.

Last but not least, an interesting direction concerns how to integrate this approach into the decision workflow of production planning for growers, specifically how it can synergise with the management of other business processes in crop production, e.g., delivery after crop harvest.

A limitation of our work is that the case study is subject to one crop grown in the local area, and the collected data contains only crop production data and crop environment data recording weather conditions. Therefore, an immediate next step is to extend the case study to other crops and include more relevant data. In particular, we are interested in exploring the use of crop development data, for example, as collected by agronomists through field visits or by dedicated sensors and remote sensing platforms [17]. Such ancillary data will provide precise information on crop growth monitoring and thus the opportunity to improve the efficacy of our approach. We also seek to improve the input data quality, e.g., to use production data that captures the fresh yield rather than the processed one.

6   Conclusion

Reliable and timely forecasts on crop harvest benefits decision-making in the agri-food industries and contribute to the resilience of agriculture and food production. In this paper, we present an approach that systematically utilises crop-growth data from multiple sources and generates online predictions on crop harvest automatically and progressively. Our approach offers a flexible solution for crop harvest predictions and can be tailored according to different crops (by redesigning the crop growing process model) and relevant agronomic knowledge (by altering the strategies for bucketing, encoding, and the statistical models). Meanwhile, our research findings contribute to the field of process science by making a novel and successful attempt to use process modelling and predictive monitoring techniques to address a key problem in the agri-food domain.

Acknowledgments. This work was supported by Food Agility CRC Ltd, funded under the Commonwealth Government CRC Program. We also received highly valuable input from A/Prof Miranda Mortlock, a specialist in agronomy and statistics, and Dr David Carey, a senior horticulturist from Queensland Department of Agriculture and Fisheries.

References

1. Van der Aalst, W.M.P.: Process Mining - Data Science in Action. Springer, second edn. (2016). https://doi.org/10.1007/978-3-662-49851-4, https://doi.org/10.1007/978-3-662-49851-4_1

2. Basso, B., Liu, L.: Chapter Four - Seasonal Crop Yield Forecast: Methods, Applications, and Accuracies. Advances in Agronomy. Academic Press, vol. 154, pp. 201–255 (2019)

3. De Leoni, M., Suriadi, S., ter Hofstede, A.H.M., van der Aalst, W.M.P.: Turning event logs into process movies: animating what has really happened. Softw. Syst. Model. **15**(3), 707–732 (2014). https://doi.org/10.1007/s10270-014-0432-2

4. De Rosa, D., et al.: Predicting pasture biomass using a statistical model and machine learning algorithm implemented with remotely sensed imagery. Comput. Electron. Agric. **180**, 105880 (2021)

5. Inoue, Y., Moran, M.S., Horie, T.: Analysis of spectral measurements in paddy field for predicting rice growth and yield based on a simple crop simulation model. Plant Prod. Sci. **1**(4), 269–279 (1998)

6. Kaushal, N., Bhandari, K., Siddique, K.H.M., Nayyar, H.: Food crops face rising temperatures: an overview of responses, adaptive mechanisms, and approaches to improve heat tolerance. Cogent Food Agric. **2**(1), 1134380 (2016)

7. Krishnan, P., Ramakrishnan, B., Reddy, K.R., Reddy, V.: Chapter Three - High-Temperature Effects on Rice Growth, Yield, and Grain Quality. Advances in Agronomy. Academic Press, vol. 111, pp. 87–206 (2011)

8. Lhermitte, S., Verbesselt, J., Verstraeten, W.W., Coppin, P.: A comparison of time series similarity measures for classification and change detection of ecosystem dynamics. Remote Sens. Environ. **115**(12), 3129–3152 (2011)

9. McMaster, G.S., Wilhelm, W.: Growing degree-days: one equation, two interpretations. Agric. Forest Meteorol. **87**(4), 291–300 (1997)

10. Miranda, J., Ponce, P., Molina, A., Wright, P.K.: Sensing, smart and sustainable technologies for agri-food 4.0. Comput. Ind. **108**, 21–36 (2019)

11. Márquez-Chamorro, A.E., Resinas, M., Ruiz-Cortés, A.: Predictive monitoring of business processes: a survey. IEEE Trans. Serv. Comput. **11**(6), 962–977 (2018)

12. Nandram, B., Berg, E., Barboza, W.: A hierarchical Bayesian model for forecasting state-level corn yield. Environ. Ecol. Stat. **21**(3), 507–530 (2013). https://doi.org/10.1007/s10651-013-0266-z

13. Reynolds, M., et al.: Role of modelling in international crop research: overview and some case studies. Agronomy **8**(12), 291 (2018)

14. Rudin, C.: Stop explaining black box machine learning models for high stakes decisions and use interpretable models instead. Nat. Mach. Intell. **1**(5), 206–215 (2019)

15. Van Klompenburg, T., Kassahun, A., Catal, C.: Crop yield prediction using machine learning: a systematic literature review. Comput. Electron. Agric. **177**, 105709 (2020)

16. Verenich, I., Dumas, M., Rosa, M.L., Maggi, F.M., Teinemaa, I.: Survey and cross-benchmark comparison of remaining time prediction methods in business process monitoring. ACM Trans. Intell. Syst. Technol. **10**(4), 34:1–34:34 (2019)
17. Weiss, M., Jacob, F., Duveiller, G.: Remote sensing for agricultural applications: a meta-review. Remote Sens. Environ. **236**, 111402 (2020)
18. Xing, Z., Pei, J., Keogh, E.: A brief survey on sequence classification. ACM SIGKDD Explor. Newslett. **12**(1), 40–48 (2010)

Guiding Knowledge Workers Under Dynamic Contexts

Zeynep Ozturk Yurt[1]([✉])[iD], Rik Eshuis[1][iD], Anna Wilbik[2][iD],
and Irene Vanderfeesten[1,3][iD]

[1] Eindhoven University of Technology, Eindhoven, The Netherlands
z.ozturk.yurt@tue.nl
[2] Maastricht University, Maastricht, The Netherlands
[3] Open Universiteit, Heerlen, The Netherlands

Abstract. A knowledge-intensive process (KiP) is a flexible process
where knowledge workers have the control over the actions to be taken
towards fulfilling the process goals. Yet, the context of a business process impacts how the goals are met by the knowledge worker throughout
the process. The context of a business process can be dynamic, i.e., the
context might be subject to changes during the process execution based
on the decisions and interpretations of the knowledge worker. Moreover,
there can be multiple ways to fulfill the goals depending on the dynamic
context. In such a case, the knowledge worker faces a difficult decision
on prioritizing the available tasks in the process to execute this flexible
process and fulfill the goals as efficient as possible. This paper presents
a method that provides knowledge workers a prioritization ranking for
the available tasks, to help them efficiently collect the information they
need to evaluate the fulfillment of goals in dynamic contexts. Our method
guides the knowledge worker in executing KiPs more efficiently by giving
higher priority to tasks that provide information required for the goals of
multiple dynamic contexts. We present our approach on a real-life case
and evaluate the improvement gained by following the recommendations
of our method through simulation.

Keywords: Knowledge-intensive processes · Guidance ·
Context-awareness

1 Introduction

Knowledge-intensive processes (KiP) are goal-oriented [7]. The course of actions
in a KiP evolves through a set of intermediate goals and is determined by the
knowledge-intensive decisions made by knowledge workers based on the emergent
knowledge in the process. Consequently, a KiP requires flexible execution where
the knowledge workers have the control to determine the course of actions to be
performed to achieve the goals [7].

© Springer Nature Switzerland AG 2022
X. Franch et al. (Eds.): CAiSE 2022, LNCS 13295, pp. 218–234, 2022.
https://doi.org/10.1007/978-3-031-07472-1_13

Context of a business process is an important concept when talking about goals of a process. Context factors, e.g., weather or location, determine the context for a business process and hence determine how the process should be executed to achieve process goals. For instance, weather determines the context for the insurance claim handling process and a faster way of lodging the claims can be required in the context of stormy weather to reduce the waiting time [20]. Typically, process context is considered to be either static or dynamic. Static context is fixed, it is defined before the process starts and does not change throughout the process execution, e.g., season in an airline booking process. Yet, the dynamic context is not fixed and can change during the process execution, e.g., weather in an airline booking process.

Conventionally, context-awareness in business processes deals with adapting processes to unexpected or uncontrolled changes in the dynamic context due to a change in the environment. Accordingly, the dynamism of the context of a business process usually originates from the changes in the environment of the process. For a KiP, however, the context can also dynamically change based on the interpretations and decisions made by the knowledge workers throughout the process execution. For instance in a medical diagnosis process, the goal is to Complete the diagnosis by doing some tests (e.g., blood tests, x-ray etc.). Depending on the suspected disease, the clinician should perform different tests to confirm the diagnosis and achieve this process goal. Since the suspected disease affects how the process goal is achieved, it is a context factor defining the context of the diagnosis process. The specific suspected disease defines a dynamic context, since at the beginning, the clinician might consider multiple suspected diseases and investigate them throughout the process, but the final diagnosis is determined by looking at the results of the tests performed throughout the diagnosis process. Therefore, throughout the process execution, multiple contexts (different suspected diseases) are investigated and context is subject to changes until the final diagnose is made. In such KiPs, the change in the context is not uncontrolled or unexpected, but rather a part of the business logic, and the dynamism of the context originates from the interpretations and decisions made by the knowledge worker throughout the process rather than a change in the environment.

Since a KiP requires flexible execution, there should be no strictly-defined process that dictates the tasks to be performed and their order throughout the process. Instead, the knowledge worker has the control over the tasks to be performed and their order that will achieve the goals in the process. Case management [3, 25] is an approach for managing KiPs, and Case Management Model and Notation (CMMN) [6] is the industry standard process modeling notation for Case Management. CMMN is a well suited notation for modeling the flexible and goal-oriented nature of KiPs [7, 19]. Moreover, being the industry standard, there are already available tools for modeling and execution of CMMN models. Therefore, in this paper, we chose to focus on KiP models using CMMN.

For a KiP model using CMMN, most of the time, there are multiple tasks that are enabled, and the knowledge worker decides which enabled task to do next. If the context is dynamic, it is difficult for the knowledge worker to prioritize the enabled tasks since different contexts require different tasks to achieve the goals, and the set of required tasks change with the dynamic context within a single process execution. In such a case, it is challenging for the knowledge worker to prioritize the enabled tasks while considering the effect of dynamic context.

This paper focuses on supporting knowledge workers performing KiPs under dynamic contexts in efficiently addressing the KiP goals. Here, we focus on KiPs which have inherently dynamic contexts that changes based on the interpretations and decisions made by the knowledge worker during process execuriton. We provide a heuristic method that supports knowledge workers in prioritizing their tasks such that they efficiently collect the information required to assess the achievement of goals under dynamic contexts. Our method provides a list of prioritized tasks to the knowledge workers, based on the amount of information, provided by the task, required to assess the achievement of process goals. Our method aims to guide the knowledge worker in prioritizing their tasks, such that the information required to assess the achievement of the goals is gathered more efficiently (with lesser tasks) under dynamic contexts.

There are several approaches that propose support for KiPs [5,11,12,15, 17,21,23,27–30]. These approaches focus on guiding KiPs with some machine learning/artificial intelligence(AI) techniques based on historical information [11, 15,21,30], modeling and planning of KiPs using AI (or automated planning) techniques and Markov Decision Process (MDP) [12,23,27–29], and optimization of declarative processes [5,17]. KiPs are hardly repeatable [7], therefore useful historical information does not always exist. Different from existing approaches [5,11,12,15,17,21,27–30], we focus on guiding knowledge workers on such cases where no historical data is present.

Considering the approaches in [5,17], the focus of our method is different. We guide knowledge workers to address the goals in a dynamic context where the context affects how the goals are achieved. In [5,17], the effect of context on the way that the goals are achieved is not considered. Also, we focus on information gathering aspect of tasks when prioritizing them, which is also not the focus of the existing approaches in [5,17]. Lastly, to the best of our knowledge, the notion of dynamic context and its integration for guiding knowledge workers in executing flexible KiPs, has not been investigated in the existing work [5,11,12, 15,17,18,23,27–30].

The remainder of this paper is organized as follows. Section 2 presents the motivation for our problem and introduces a running example. Section 3 presents the step by step description of our task prioritization method. In Sect. 4, we demonstrate our method on a real-life example and provide the results of our evaluation using simulation. Section 5 discusses the related work. Lastly, Sect. 6 concludes this paper and briefly discusses next steps.

2 Running Example

In this section we motivate the use of our method on a running example, the differential diagnosis in the abdominal pain treatment process [2,13].

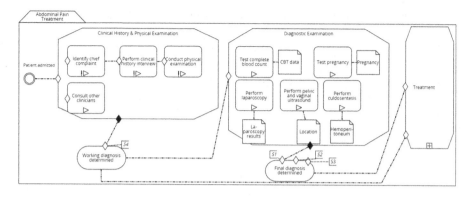

Fig. 1. CMMN model of the running example, abdominal pain treatment process

The diagnosis process is the process of information gathering and clinical reasoning with the goal of determining the patients' health problem. The process starts with a patient with abdominal pain seeking for a treatment. Then, based on the information provided by the patient and physical examination, the clinician determines a working diagnosis, i.e., a potential diagnosis explaining the patient's symptoms. The working diagnosis may be a single diagnosis or a list of potential diagnoses. Usually, clinicians come up with a list of potential diagnoses and refine this list as more information is gathered, through tests, throughout the diagnosis process. This process is called a differential diagnosis process [2,13].

If the diagnosis cannot be determined based on the information provided by the patient and physical tests alone, the next step is diagnostic testing. A set of diagnostic tests are done to gather information about the potential causes of the patient's problem. Each potential diagnosis requires the results of a set of tests to be confirmed. The clinician decides which tests to do and in which order. Diagnostic tests are costly and sometimes can be risky for the patients. Therefore, unnecessary tests should be avoided. In other words, the goal is to come up with a reasonable final diagnosis in an effective and efficient manner.

In Fig. 1, this process is modeled using CMMN. On this figure, the folder shape represents a case plan or, in other words, a process model. A stage (rectangle with cut edges) groups a set of related tasks and represent a phase or an episode in a case. A task (box shape) represents an atomic unit of work. A milestone (rounded rectangles) represent achievable targets in a process. They are usually used to follow the progress in the case execution. Event listeners (circles) listen for external events that can occur during case execution and trigger tasks, stages or milestones in the process accordingly. Lastly, the diamond-like shapes attached to the tasks, stages or milestones are called sentries. Sentries are boolean expressions that involve a combination of event and/or data conditions. Sentries specify when a task, stage or milestone becomes enabled (empty diamond) or complete (black diamond).

Table 1. Milestones, sentries and contexts, abdominal pain treatment process

Sentry-1 (S1)	Pregnancy is collected & Hemoperitoneum is collected & Location is collected	Context-1: Ectopic pregnancy
Sentry-2 (S2)	Location is collected & CBT is collected	Context-2: Appendicitis
Sentry-3 (S3)	Laparoscopy is collected & Hemoperitoneum is collected & CBT is collected	Context-3: Pelvic inflammatory disease
Sentry-4 (S4)	Clinic. histor. stage is completed	Context-1, Context-2, Context-3

From the process modeling view, diagnostic testing of differential diagnoses corresponds to having alternative sets of tasks and data required to achieve an objective under different dynamic contexts. Here, the context is determined by the diagnosis since the tests that should be performed to achieve Final diagnosis determined goal depend on the specific diagnosis being investigated by the clinician.

There is usually a list of diagnoses considered throughout the process and the final diagnosis is determined by the interpretations made by the clinician based on the test results obtained through executing the differential diagnosis process. Therefore multiple contexts (diagnoses) are investigated and context is subject to changes until the final diagnose is made. This makes the context is dynamic, dependent on the interpretations made by the clinician i.e., knowledge worker. Consequently, the dynamism of the context is not uncontrolled or unexpected but a part of the business logic.

In the process model in Fig. 1, using Case Management Model and Notation (CMMN) [6], contextual goals are modeled as different sentry conditions on the milestone Final diagnosis determined. The combination of a sentry and a milestone represent alternative ways to achieve objectives under different contexts. For instance, sentry-1 represent how the Final diagnosis is determined milestone is achieved in the context of Ectopic Pregnancy, and sentry-2 represent how this goal is achieved if the context is Appendicitis (See Table 1). In such a case, our method can be used to guide the clinician in prioritizing the diagnostic tests to be done and to finalize the diagnosis more efficiently, i.e., with less number of tests. For example, the clinician can use the recommendations given by our approach to prioritize the test that can rule out some potential diagnoses or to prioritize the tests that give more information for multiple potential diagnoses.

3   Guiding Knowledge Workers with Task Prioritization Method

In this section, we provide the step by step description of our method in Fig. 2, using the running example introduced in Sect. 2.

Our method takes a CMMN model as input (See Fig. 1 and Table 1) and, through some intermediate steps and outputs, provides a list of prioritized tasks

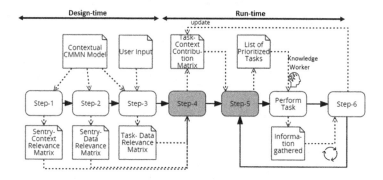

Fig. 2. Method steps

Table 2. Sentry-context relevance matrix, $R(S, C)$, abdominal pain treatment process

Sentry/Context	C1: Ectopic pregnancy	C2: Appendicitis	C3: Pelvic inf. disease
S1	1	0	0
S2	0	1	0
S3	0	0	1
S4	0	0	1

to guide the knowledge worker in choosing among the enabled tasks. Steps-1&2&3 are pre-processing steps performed by the process analyst to structure the inputs of our method during design-time. Steps-4&5 are the main steps of our method, automated in a tool, which provides the prioritized list of enabled tasks at the instant when the prioritization support is needed by the knowledge worker. This tool takes the outputs of Steps-1&2&3 as input, performs the calculations in Steps-4&5 and outputs a list of prioritized tasks. After Step-5, a knowledge worker performs a task and inputs the information gathered (the task that is performed) to the tool. Lastly, in Step-6 the tool makes the calculations to account for the changes in the output of Step-4 after a task is executed. This is followed by Step-5 again, i.e., the cycle in Fig. 2 is repeated every time a knowledge worker performs a task. The tool automating Steps-4&5&6 is a python code in which the calculations in these steps are done automatically. In the following paragraphs, we discuss each step in details.

Input: Our method takes a contextual CMMN model as input. This CMMN model has information on different dynamic contexts and their associated sentry expressions, as in Table 1. Milestones represent achievable targets in a CMMN model. Therefore, there is a natural correspondence between functional process goals and milestones. The input CMMN model has functional goals modeled as milestones. Each sentry on a milestone represents alternative ways to achieve the milestone. Therefore, different sentries on the same milestone are associated to different dynamic contexts that are possible in a single execution of a process.

Table 3. Sentry-data relevance matrix, $R(S, D)$, abdominal pain treatment process

Sentry/Data	Pregnancy	Hemoperitoneum	Location	CBT data	Laparoscopy data	Stage clinic. hist. completed
S1	1	1	1	0	0	0
S2	0	0	1	0	0	0
S3	0	1	0	1	1	0
S4	0	0	0	0	0	1

Table 4. Task-data relevance matrix, $R(T, D)$, abdominal pain treatment process

Task/Data	Pregnancy	Hemoperitoneum	Location	CBT data	Laparoscopy data	Stage clinic. hist. completed
Test comp.	0	0	0	1	0	0
Perf. lap.	0	0	0	0	1	0
Test preg.	1	0	0	0	0	0
Perf. pel.	0	0	1	0	0	0
Perf. culdo.	0	1	0	0	0	0
Stage clinic. hist.	0	0	0	0	0	1

Table 1 shows the sentry conditions and their related dynamic contexts. Note that, we are currently developing a method that supports analysts in deriving this contextual CMMN model.

Step-1: Looking at the Table 1, create a table of alternative dynamic contexts and related sentries on the available milestones ($R(S, C)$, Table 2).

Step-2: Create a table of data items in the if- and on-part expressions of the sentries listed in Step-1 ($R(S, D)$, Table 3).

Note that we treat if-part and on-part of sentries similarly. The if-part of a sentry checks if a condition regarding data holds. The on-part checks the occurrence of an event. Both parts are required to be able to check if the sentry is true or not. Therefore, if we have a task/event in the on-part of a sentry (e.g., S4), then we associate it to a virtual data item representing the completion of this task (e.g., Stage Clinic. Hist. Completed) and add to the tables.

Step-3: Create a table showing the relation between data items and tasks gathering these data items ($R(T, D)$, Table 4). For the tasks that are not directly associated to a data item of the process model, input from the process analyst is required. The process analyst checks the table of task-data relevance table derived automatically from the process model and overwrites the relevance relations, if necessary. For tasks which are not linked to a data item in the process model, the analyst states if a task contributes to the acquisition of a data item in the process model. If multiple tasks are required for a single data item, the contribution of each task for getting the data item is then 1/number of tasks. In our running example, each task is related to only one data item, so the contribution is either 0 or 1 in Table 4.

Table 5. Task-context contribution matrix, $ContTC(T, C)$, abdominal pain treatment process

Context/Task	Test comp.	Perf. lap	Test preg.	Perf. pel.	Perf. culdo.
C1:Ectopic pregnancy	0	0	0.33	0.33	0.33
C2:Appendicitis	0.5	0	0	0.5	0
C3:Pelvic inf. disease	0.33	0.33	0	0.33	0.33
$ContTOT(T_z)$	0.83	0.33	0.3	1.16	0.66

Step-4: Next, leave out the tasks/stages/sentries of milestones that are not enabled at the instant when task prioritization support is needed. For our running example, we assume that the stage Clinical History & Physical Examination is complete, so we eliminated the row for S4 from Tables 2 and 3, and Stage Clinic. Hist. from Table 4. Note that, we also eliminated the data item Stage Clinic. Hist. Completed from the tables, since it is not relevant for other tasks or sentries.

Then, using the reduced Table 2 and reduced Table 3 determine the contribution of each data item for the achievement of milestones of each context, as follows.

For each context $C_k \in K$, where K is the finite set of contexts, total goals/sentries per context, $TG(C_k)$:

$$TG(C_k) = \sum_{S_i \in S} R(S_i, C_k), \text{ where } S \text{ is the finite set of sentries in the CMMN model.}$$

For each sentry $S_i \in S$, total data items required per sentry, $TT(S_i)$:

$$TT(S_i) = \sum_{D_j \in D} R(S_i, D_j), \text{ where } D \text{ is the finite set of data-items.}$$

For each context $C_k \in K$, contribution of each data item $D_j \in D$ to the achievement of milestones per context, $ContDC(D_j, C_k)$;

$$ContDC(D_j, C_k) = \sum_{S_i \in S} \left(\frac{R(S_i, D_j)R(S_i, C_k)}{TG(C_k)TT(S_i)} \right)$$

Then, using $ContDC(D_j, C_k)$ and $R(T_z, D_j)$, determine the contribution of tasks to contexts, $ContTC(T_z, C_k)$, as follows (Table 5).

For each $C_k \in K$, contribution of each task $T_z \in T$ where T is the finite set of enabled tasks, $ContTC(T_z, C_k)$;

$$ContTC(T_z, C_k) = \sum_{D_j \in D} (ContDC(D_j, C_k)R(T_z, D_j))$$

Step-5: Prioritize tasks based on their overall contribution to different contexts. Overall contribution is calculated as below. Note that, depending on the strategy followed by the user the tasks can also be prioritized in Step-4, based on their contribution to a specific context (Table 5).

For each task $T_z \in T$, overall contribution of a tasks to different contexts, $ContTOT(T_z)$;

$$ContTOT(T_z) = \sum_{C_k \in K} ContTC(T_z, C_k)$$

After this step, a task is chosen and performed. When a task is performed, a certain percentage of the data required to assess the achievement of the milestones will be gathered.

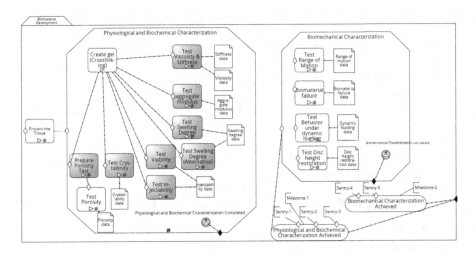

Fig. 3. CMMN model of the biomaterial development process

Step-6: Update Table 5 by replacing contribution values with contribution to the remaining information percentage of each context. For example, if task Test complete blood count is performed by the knowledge worker, then the contribution of remaining tasks of Context-2 and Context-3 are updated by dividing the current contribution values by 0.5 and 0.66, respectively. If a new task is enabled, then this is also introduced to Table 5.

Then, the cycle shown in Fig. 2 is repeated whenever a task is chosen and performed. If, a new milestone becomes available after performing a task, all steps should be performed again starting from Step-1.

4   Evaluation

In this section, we demonstrate the use of our method on an example. The example is about the medicinal product development process taking part in the Horizon2020 iPSpine project[1].

---

[1] https://ipspine.eu/.

4.1 Case Study

Advanced Therapy Medicinal Products (ATMPs) are medicinal products based on advanced biomedical technologies [1]. ATMP development processes are shaped by knowledge-intensive actions and decisions of the expert scientists to develop a safe and effective product.

Being a medicinal product for human use, ATMPs have to comply with a set of regulatory requirements regarding their safety and efficacy [9]. Scientists demonstrate the tests performed and data collected during the scientific development process as a proof of safety and efficacy of the ATMP.

Table 6. Milestones, sentries and contexts, biomaterial development process

Milestone-1, Sentry-1	Viscosity is collected & Stiffness is collected & Porosity is collected	Contex-1
Milestone-1, Sentry-2	Injectability is collected & Swelling is collected & Crystallinity is collected & Viscosity is collected	Context-2
Milestone-1, Sentry-3	Injectability is collected & Stiffness is collected & Swelling is collected & Aggregate modulus is collected & Viscosity is collected	Contex-3
Milestone-2, Sentry-4	Injectability is collected & Range of Motion is collected & Biomaterial Failure is collected & Disc Height Restoration is collected	Contex-1, Contex-3
Milestone-2, Sentry-5	Injectability is collected & Swelling is collected & Biomaterial Failure is collected & Disc Height Restoration & Dynamic Loading is collected	Context-2

Table 7. Step-4: task context contribution matrix, biomaterial development process

Context/ Data	Test viscosity & stiffness	Test aggregate modulus	Test swelling degree	Test swelling degree (alternative)	Test injectability	Test viability	Test crystallinity	Preparation test porosity
C1	0.333333	0.0	0.000000	0.000000	0.0625	0.0625	0.000000	0.083333
C2	0.166667	0.0	0.266667	0.266667	0.0500	0.0500	0.166667	0.000000
C3	0.200000	0.1	0.100000	0.100000	0.1125	0.1125	0.000000	0.000000

Depending on the regulatory context of development, compliance to different regulations needs to be ensured. For instance, different experiments are done to demonstrate the physiological and biochemical properties of the ATMP to check its compliance with related regulations under different regulatory contexts. There are alternative regulatory contexts for an ATMP being developed, e.g., classifying the biomaterial in the ATMP as starting material or as a medical device. The scientists investigate all possible regulatory contexts throughout the scientific development to find out the appropriate option for their product by considering the results of the tests they perform. Although the scientists starts the investigation with an initial assumption on the regulatory context that will be chosen, this can change depending on the results. Therefore the context change is an inherent part of the ATMP development processes and the context dynamically changes based on the interpretations and decisions made by the scientist during process execution.

Figure 3 shows the case plan for a biomaterial development process, which is a part of ATMP development studies. Here, when the Create gel task is completed, there are multiple tasks enabled and the scientist can choose the next one to be performed. There are alternative ways to achieve the milestones Physiological and Biochemical Characterization Achieved and Biomechanical Characterization Achieved depending on the dynamic regulatory context, represented by different sentries on these milestones. It is important for the scientists to make informed decisions about which tasks to perform and how to prioritize them, to reach these milestones in a faster and more efficient manner.

Table 6 shows the milestones, sentries and related contexts for the process model in Fig. 3. Context-1, 2 and 3 are mutually exclusive dynamic contexts. Using the information in Table 6 and the process model in Fig. 3 as input, we calculate the contribution of each task to different contexts (See Table 7) and provide a prioritization ranking for the available tasks (See Table 8).

Table 8. Step-5: list of prioritized tasks, biomaterial development process

Priority	Task	Overall contribution
1	Test viscosity & stiffness	0.700000
2	Test swelling degree	0.366667
2	Test swelling degree (alternative)	0.366667
3	Test injectability	0.225000
3	Test viability	0.225000
4	Test crystallinity	0.166667
5	Test aggregate modulus	0.100000
6	Preparation test porosity	0.083333

4.2   Evaluation Results

To evaluate if following the recommendations provided by our method improves the process, we used discrete event simulation. We have simulated two different models in ARENA (Rockwell Automation). Model-1 simulates the scenario where the scientist chooses among the enabled tasks randomly. This model represents the current way of working of the scientists. The process model already covers the dependencies between tasks and information, inline with the requirements of the domain, in this case ATMP development. So, when a task is enabled

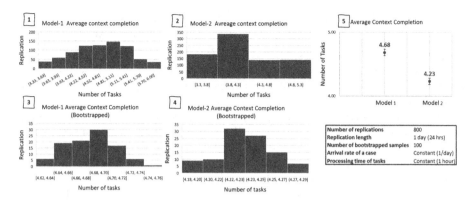

Fig. 4. Simulation results

in the process model, it means that there is no scientific reason included in the process model hindering its execution. This means that the scientist can choose among the enabled tasks randomly. In the second model, Model-2, the scientists follows the prioritization recommendations for choosing among the enabled tasks.

In both models, we measure the total number of tasks performed until the tasks required to assess the milestones of the chosen context, which is defined at a random point throughout the process, are complete. The graph in Fig. 4 shows the output of our simulation study.

In Fig. 4, graphs number-1&2 show the distribution of the replication averages. Note that, to relax any assumptions on the distribution of the output data, we used bootstrapping. In Fig. 4, graphs number-3&4 show the distribution of the bootstrapped sample averages. Then, according to the Central Limit Theorem, we can assume that our data follows a normal distribution. Graph number-5 in Fig. 4 shows the average context completion in two models and their 95% confidence intervals. The confidence intervals do not overlap, therefore we conclude that following our method improves the process.

To further analyze the validity of our results, we calculated the Welch confidence interval [14] of the difference between average number of total tasks in the Model-1 and Model-2. The 95% confidence interval for the difference is [0.445,0.457]. Since this confidence interval excludes zero, we once more conclude that the difference between the averages in Model-1 and Model-2 is significant.

Next, we plan to extend our evaluation to assess the quality of the prioritization recommendations on biomaterial development process with scientists from the iPSpine project.

5 Related Work and Discussion

The notion of context is not new for BPM [8,10,16,18,20,22,24]. However, the focus of those works is either identification and modeling of context in a business process [8,10,16,20,24] or context-aware planning or adaptation of traditional, structured business processes [18,22]. To the best of our knowledge, a contextual goal-based guidance approach for flexible KiPs has not been proposed before. Although the relevance of context for goals [4] and goals for modeling contextual processes [10,16,20] are investigated before, the notion of dynamic context is not covered within these works.

Our aim is to support knowledge workers in working more efficiently by providing guidance in planning their tasks. Within BPM, there has been some work done in guiding flexible, knowledge-intensive processes. In [11,21], the authors provide approaches that give next step recommendations to optimize the execution of cases based on process mining on an event log. In[30], authors use case based reasoning to provide recommendations in case of an exception, based on previously executed similar cases. With their approach, similar past cases are retrieved and the information on how a previous exception is handled is reused to guide the current process. This way they provide guidance in a flexible process and contribute to the efficiency of the process by enabling reuse of the existing information.

There is some work that use Markov Decision Processes (MDPs) to model planning problems in the processes. In [28], the authors use an automated planning approach to produce a sequence of actions to achieve some goal over time in a knowledge-intensive process. They use MDPs to model the planning problem. Goals are formulated as a set of attributes with expected values, activities have probabilistic post conditions, representing their effect on attribute values in the related goals, as well as expected cost and duration. Using this information, their approach provide an optimized execution plan from the current state in the process to the target state in terms of desired goal status. In [12] authors combine MDP and reinforcement learning models to give next step recommendations in flexible, knowledge-intensive processes. Event logs are used as an input to the reinforcement learning model. From there, optimal policies that lead to desired outcomes are derived and provided as next step recommendations to the user. In [23], authors map a data-centric process model into a planning problem and use AI planning techniques to give next step recommendation.

Our method differs from these approaches [11,12,21,23,28,30] since it does not require any historical data such as probabilistic data about outcome of tasks or event-log data. Knowledge-intensive processes are hardly repeatable [7]. Therefore, useful historical data do not always exist for knowledge-intensive processes. Since our method only requires a CMMN model, it is still applicable for such cases.

Another research stream that is relevant for our work is on optimization of declarative processes. In [5], the authors propose a constraint-based approach to generate an optimized execution plan and give next step recommendations to users during execution. As an input for their approach, they extend the declarative process model with additional information, such as resource requirements and durations for each activity. In [17], authors takes a different view on optimizing declarative process models and focus on maximizing flexibility in execution.

Considering the approaches that focus on optimization of declarative processes such as [5,17], our method has a different focus. First, we focus on the notion of dynamic context that results in alternative execution paths during run-time to achieve process goals. Our method supports knowledge worker in managing these alternatives in an efficient way. In the existing papers, alternative execution paths result from the declarative nature of the process model, regardless of the context, any execution path that optimizes the process performance goals is considered as optimal and recommended. In that sense, the effect of dynamic context is not the focus in these papers. Second, we deal with information gathering required to achieve the process goals. We use the relation between tasks and information they provide for the achievement of goals when prioritizing the tasks. This information aspect is not the covered in the existing papers [5,17].

In [15], the authors propose techniques for managing flexible KiPs and providing automated adaptation support for such processes in case of an exception. Their focus is to make use of artificial intelligence techniques for automated adaptation of processes so that such adaptations can be made without intervention of the expert. By doing so, they aim to reduce the error-prone and costly job of doing ad-hoc changes done by experts and hence supporting them. In this sense, their focus is different from ours. Therefore, we conclude that it is not a highly relevant paper for us.

Two works are especially relevant for our work [27,29]. In [27], MDPs are used to optimize the execution of Product Data Models (PDM). A product data model specifies information and operations required to gather other information in a process. This model allows alternative execution paths to gather the information required. Each operation in the PDM has an associated cost, duration and failure and success probability. Then, at any state of the process, based on the optimization objective such as minimizing completion time or costs, a next best step recommendation that, optimizes the objective globally, is provided. In [29], the authors translate a declarative artifact-centric process model into a MDP. Using the MDP, authors provide decision support on planning of the tasks in the process to support efficient information gathering throughout the process.

Our method is similar to [27,29] in the sense that they both focus on information gathering in a process. However, our method uses a case model in CMMN, whereas the approach in [26,27] is built upon a PDM. In [29], a Guard-Stage-Milestone schema is translated into MDP, which requires specification of additional inform such as state transition probabilities, which are calculated using the historical information on the process. Similarly, in [27] additional information, such as probability of success or failure, on tasks is required. In general, the approaches that rely on MPD [12,27–29] needs additional input information that does not exist or is very difficult and expensive to get for some processes [28]. KiPs are usually unique processes and they are hardly totally repeatable. In such a case, gathering the information required by the MDP is not always feasible.

We provide a simple heuristic method that is applicable when such information is not available.

All in all, our method differs from the existing work with respect to three aspects. First, we introduce the notion of contextual goals, and we provide recommendations considering the achievement of goals under different contexts. Second, we introduce the notion of dynamic context for business processes, as the context of a KiP that is inherently dynamic and change based on the interpretations and decisions made by the knowledge worker during process execution. Third, our method does not depend on historical data, which does not always exist for KiPs.

6   Conclusion

In this paper, we have introduced a method for guiding knowledge workers under dynamic contexts. Our method provides a prioritization ranking for the available tasks in the process, to help knowledge workers collect the information they need to evaluate the fulfillment of goals with less number of tasks in dynamic contexts.

Our method is easily adjustable for more complex scenarios. For instance, the prioritization can be made considering the user's preferences in choosing a specific context by introducing different weights to contexts. Similarly, properties such as criticality or risks associated to tasks can be considered for prioritization by introducing weights to tasks. Considering the differential diagnosis example in Sect. 2, for instance, if a test should be less prioritized since it is risky for the patient, although it reveals important information for the determination of the actual diagnosis, the effect of risks associated to a test will also be reflected on the list of prioritized tasks provided by our method.

The method we present is a heuristic method, therefore it does not guarantee optimal solutions. Yet, results show that it provides improvement in the process when the recommendations from our method are followed. For KiPs, gathering detailed input information for more sophisticated methods might be challenging [28]. With limited input available on the KiP, our method provides improvement.

A limitation in our current method is that it does not cover the assessment of the degree of achievement of a milestone but rather focuses on gathering the information required for this assessment and the assessment is done by the knowledge worker. As a next step, we plan to extend our method such that it also considers the degree of achievement of milestones in different contexts and take this into account when giving recommendations on task prioritization.

Another limitation is the lack of a user interface (UI) for the final users who will use this method, i.e., knowledge workers. Although the complex calculations in our method is currently automated in a tool, development of a UI for knowledge workers to use our method is future work. Additionally, a drawback of our method is the manual work performed by the process analyst in Steps-1&2&3, which can be time and effort intensive for more complex scenarios. However, this is a one-time design-time effort and therefore, does not hinder the generalizability and scalability of our method for more complex scenarios. Lastly, the UI would also improve the generalizability and scalability of our method for more complex scenarios by enabling an easy and understandable interaction with both process analysts and the knowledge workers.

Acknowledgements. The work presented in this paper is part of iPSpine project that has received funding from the European Union's Horizon 2020 research and innovation programme under grant agreement No. 825925.

References

1. Advanced Therapy Medicinal Products: Overview. www.ema.europa.eu/en/human-regulatory/overview/advanced-therapy-medicinal-products-overview. Accessed 05 Oct 2021
2. National Academies of Sciences, Engineering, and Medicine: Improving Diagnosis in Health Care. The National Academies Press (2015)
3. van der Aalst, W.M.P., Weske, M., Grünbauer, D.: Case handling: a new paradigm for business process support. Data Knowl. Eng. **53**, 129–162 (2005)
4. Ali, R., Dalpiaz, F., Giorgini, P.: A goal-based framework for contextual requirements modeling and analysis. Requirements Eng. **15**, 439–458 (2010)
5. Barba, I., Weber, B., Valle, C.D., Ramirez, A.J.: User recommendations for the optimized execution of business processes. Data Knowl. Eng. **86**, 61–84 (2013)
6. BizAgi, et al.: Case management model and notation (CMMN), v1.1. OMG Document Number formal/16-12-01, Object Management Group, December 2016
7. Di Ciccio, C., Marrella, A., Russo, A.: Knowledge-intensive processes: characteristics, requirements and analysis of contemporary approaches. J. Data Semant. **4**(1), 29–57 (2014). https://doi.org/10.1007/s13740-014-0038-4
8. de la Vara, J.L., Ali, R., Dalpiaz, F., Sánchez, J., Giorgini, P.: COMPRO: a methodological approach for business process contextualisation. In: Meersman, R., Dillon, T., Herrero, P. (eds.) OTM 2010. LNCS, vol. 6426, pp. 132–149. Springer, Heidelberg (2010). https://doi.org/10.1007/978-3-642-16934-2_12
9. Elsallab, M., Bravery, C., Kurtz, A., Abouel Enein, M.: Mitigating deficiencies in evidence during regulatory assessments of advanced therapies: a comparative study with other biologicals. Mol. Therapy Methods Clin. Dev. **18** (2020)
10. Heravizadeh, M., Edmond, D.: Making workflows context-aware: a way to support knowledge-intensive tasks. In: Conceptual Modelling (APCCM), vol. 79, pp. 79–88 (2008)
11. Huber, S., Fietta, M., Hof, S.: Next step recommendation and prediction based on process mining in adaptive case management. In: Proceedings of S-BPM, pp. 3:1–3:9 (2015)
12. Khan, M.A., Ghose, A., Dam, K.H.: Decision support for knowledge intensive processes using RL based recommendations. In: Proceedings of BPM Forum, pp. 246–262 (2021)
13. Knechtel, M.A.: Formulating a Differential Diagnosis for the Advanced Practice Provider. Springer, Heidelberg (2017). https://doi.org/10.1891/9780826152237
14. Law, A.M.: Simulation Modeling & Analysis. McGraw-Hill, New York (2015)
15. Marrella, A., Mecella, M., Sardiña, S.: SmartPM: an adaptive process management system through situation calculus, indigolog, and classical planning. In: Proceedings of Principles of Knowledge Representation and Reasoning (2014)

16. Mattos, T.D.C., Santoro, F.M., Revoredo, K., Nunes, V.T.: A formal representation for context-aware business processes. Comput. Ind. **65**(8), 1193–1214 (2014)
17. Mertens, S., Gailly, F., Poels, G.: Generating business process recommendations with a population-based meta-heuristic. In: Proceedings of BPM Workshops, pp. 516–528 (2014)
18. Nunes, V.T., Santoro, F.M., Werner, C.M.L., Ralha, C.G.: Real-time process adaptation: a context-aware replanning approach. IEEE Trans. Syst. Man Cybern. Syst. **48**, 99–118 (2018)
19. Pillaerds, J., Eshuis, R.: Assessing suitability of adaptive case management. In: Proceedings of ECIS, p. 37 (2017)
20. Rosemann, M., Recker, J., Flender, C.: Contextualisation of business processes. Int. J. Bus. Process. Integr. Manag. **3**(1), 47–60 (2008)
21. Schonenberg, H., Weber, B., van Dongen, B., van der Aalst, W.: Supporting flexible processes through recommendations based on history. In: Dumas, M., Reichert, M., Shan, M.-C. (eds.) BPM 2008. LNCS, vol. 5240, pp. 51–66. Springer, Heidelberg (2008). https://doi.org/10.1007/978-3-540-85758-7_7
22. Serral, E., Smedt, J.D., Snoeck, M., Vanthienen, J.: Context-adaptive petri nets: supporting adaptation for the execution context. Expert Syst. Appl. **42**, 9307–9317 (2015)
23. Sid, I., Reichert, M., Ghomari, A.R.: Enabling flexible task compositions, orders and granularities for knowledge-intensive business processes. Enterp. Inf. Syst. **13**, 376–423 (2019)
24. Song, R., Vanthienen, J., Cui, W., Wang, Y., Huang, L.: Towards a comprehensive understanding of the context concepts in context-aware business processes. In: Proceedings of S-BPM, pp. 5:1–5:10 (2019)
25. Swenson, K.: Mastering the Unpredictable: How Adaptive Case Management will Revolutionize the Way that Knowledge Workers Get Things Done. Meghan Kiffer, FL (2010)
26. Vanderfeesten, I.T.P., Reijers, H.A., van der Aalst, W.M.P.: Product based workflow support: dynamic workflow execution. In: Proceedings of CAiSE, pp. 571–574 (2008)
27. Vanderfeesten, I.T.P., Reijers, H.A., van der Aalst, W.M.P.: Product-based workflow support. Inf. Syst. **36**, 517–535 (2011)
28. Venero, S.K., Schmerl, B.R., Montecchi, L., dos Reis, J., Rubira, C.M.F.: Automated planning for supporting knowledge-intensive processes. In: Proceedings of CAiSE, pp. 101–116 (2020)
29. Voorberg, S., Eshuis, R., van Jaarsveld, W., van Houtum, G.: Decision support for declarative artifact-centric process models. In: Proceedings of BPM Forum, pp. 36–52 (2019)
30. Weber, B., Wild, W., Breu, R.: CBRFlow: enabling adaptive workflow management through conversational case-based reasoning. In: Proceedings of Advances in Case-Based Reasoning, pp. 434–448 (2014)

Natural Language Processing Techniques in IS Engineering

Context Knowledge-Aware Recognition of Composite Intents in Task-Oriented Human-Bot Conversations

Sara Bouguelia[1]([✉])[iD], Hayet Brabra[1][iD], Boualem Benatallah[2][iD],
Marcos Baez[1][iD], Shayan Zamanirad[2][iD], and Hamamache Kheddouci[1][iD]

[1] LIRIS - University of Claude Bernard Lyon 1, Villeurbanne, France
{sara.bouguelia,hayet.brabra,marcos.baez,
hamamache.kheddouci}@univ-lyon1.fr
[2] University of New South Wales (UNSW), Sydney, Australia
{boualem,shayanz}@cse.unsw.edu.au

Abstract. Task-oriented dialogue systems employ third-party APIs to serve end-users via natural language interactions. while existing advances in Natural Language Processing (NLP) and Machine Learning (ML) techniques have produced promising and useful results to recognize user intents, the synthesis of API calls to support a broad range of potentially complex user intents is still largely a manual and costly process. In this paper, we propose a new approach to recognize and realize complex user intents. Our approach relies on a new rule-based technique that leverages both (i) natural language features extracted using existing NLP and ML techniques and (ii) contextual knowledge to capture the different classes of complex intents. We devise a context knowledge service to capture the requisite contextual knowledge.

Keywords: Task-oriented conversational bots · Complex intent recognition · Context knowledge · Slot value inference

1 Introduction

Task-oriented dialogue systems (or simply bots) use natural language conversations to enable interactions between humans and software-enabled services [3]. In these, fulfilling a user request consists of: (1) understanding the *user utterance* expressed in natural language (e.g., "What is the weather in Paris?"), (2) recognizing the *user intent* (e.g., `GetWeather`), (3) extracting relevant *slot-value* pairs (e.g., (`location, Paris`)), (4) invoking the corresponding API (e.g., `OpenWeatherMap` to get weather condition), and (5) returning a natural language response to the user (e.g., "We have light rain in Paris").

Ideally, the bot should detect intents and infer slot values with the least possible interactions with the user (i.e., the bot asks the user for a missing value only when it cannot infer it from other sources). A key challenge to achieve this objective is devising robust intent recognition and slot inference despite the

© Springer Nature Switzerland AG 2022
X. Franch et al. (Eds.): CAiSE 2022, LNCS 13295, pp. 237–252, 2022.
https://doi.org/10.1007/978-3-031-07472-1_14

potentially ambiguous and complex utterances. An utterance may not always follow a simple conversation pattern, where the bot recognizes a *basic intent* and infers all required slot values from the utterance, as in the previous example.

Natural user conversations can be rich, potentially ambiguous, and express *complex user intents* [6,21]. An intent is complex when its realization requires the bot to break it down into a list of atomic actions and infer potentially missing values from different sources, not directly from the utterance. Given the utterance "Can you book a table for 2 people at Mirazur restaurant for the next public holiday?", the bot should be able to infer the information such as number of people and restaurant from this utterance; however, it also needs to search when will the next holiday be. Failing to support such complex intents can lead to repetitive and less natural interactions affecting the user experience [11].

Existing NLP and ML techniques have produced useful results to recognize basic intents [19]. ML based techniques rely on the availability of massive amounts of annotated data. Using these techniques to recognize complex intents requires laborious, costly and hard to acquire training datasets. In addition, each time a new complex intent is identified, extending or producing a new dataset is needed as well. Therefore, more advanced and flexible techniques that cater for complex intent recognition are needed.

In our previous work, we identified and characterized a set of composite dialog patterns that naturally emerge when conversing with services [2]. In this paper, we focus on the *recognition* of complex intents in human-bot conversations. We take the view that complex intent recognition could be significantly improved by considering composite dialog patterns in addition to basic intent features. We propose an approach that relies on (i) existing NLP and ML techniques to extract natural language features (e.g., basic intents, dialog acts) and (ii) a rule-based approach that leverages these features together with contextual knowledge, enabled by composite dialog patterns and other metadata, to define complex intent recognition rules. These rules enable a higher-level of abstraction that offers flexibility for an *extensible* library of composite dialog patterns. When a new complex intent class is identified, a new rule template is added to recognize intents of this class from utterances. This approach requires to capture fairly complex context knowledge in addition to basic intents in order recognize complex intents. Thus, there is a need for advanced context representation and exploitation techniques that go beyond conversation history to include information inference that leverage metadata such as intent and API schemas (e.g., intents, slots, API methods) and relationships between their elements. Our contributions in this work are summarized as:

- We propose a rule-based approach that combines (i) natural language features (ii) composite dialog patterns and contextual knowledge to capture different classes of complex intents in a generic way.
- We propose major extensions to the preliminary context knowledge service (CKS) presented in [2]. These extensions consist of an improved context knowledge model and a set of new services providing the contextual knowledge that is needed for the rules to recognize complex intents.

– Empirical evidence showing the effectiveness and user experience of the CKS and complex intent recognition. The user study showed that endowing bots with the complex intent recognition allow more natural interactions, as perceived by users and confirmed by performance metrics.

This paper is organized as follows: Sect. 2 describes a scenario and the general architecture; Sect. 3 details the CKS; Sect. 4 shows the rules to recognize and realize complex intents; Sect. 5 presents the experimentation; Sect. 6 presents the related work; Sect. 7 presents the conclusion and future work.

2   Scenario and Architecture

Before delving into the main contributions, we first introduce a scenario illustrating the proposition value of the CKS, and the supporting architecture.

2.1   Scenario

Consider a user who wants to plan some activities by conversing with a bot, as shown in Fig. 1. The user interacts with the bot using complex intents where there may exist missing values. Existing state-tracking[1] (ST) techniques support these interactions only in some cases and tend to be chatty and prompt users for the missing values. Slot values can be inferred by leveraging different sources:

Infer Slot Value from Conversation History. The composite pattern called *slot-value-flow* allows resolving a missing value of a slot by extracting it from conversation history. Existing ST techniques provide a limited support to this pattern. For example, in utterance #2, they can deduce that the missing value of the slot `cinema-area` is the same as the value of the slot `restaurant-area` and reuse it. However, in utterance #3, they use a *coreference* model to replace the expressions "the cinema" and "the restaurant" with the mentions "UGC cinema" and "LaGoulette restaurant", respectively, which are wrong values because they should be addresses. This will lead the bot to ask the user to provide the precise addresses values. A bot improved with CKS can infer these values by detecting that the `departure` is more likely related to the `cinema-address` than the `cinema-name` and thus reusing the address value.

Infer Slot Value by Calling Another API Method. The composite pattern called *nested-method* allows resolving a missing value of a slot by triggering another method. For example, in utterance #4, the user wants to send a message. Instead of giving the recipient's phone number (i.e., `tel`), the user gives an expression that refers to the recipient's name (i.e., "my friend" to refer to "Hayet"). While existing ST techniques can deduce that the expression "my friend" refers to "Hayet", they cannot infer the value of the slot `tel`. A bot improved with CKS can detect that there is an API method having an output

---

[1] State-tracking consists of determining user intent and its required slot values.

Fig. 1. Example of user-bot conversation where there are some complex intents.

similar to the missing slot and therefore invokes this API method to infer the missing value.

Identify the Dependent Method to Get a Value of an id. The composite pattern called *API-calls ordering* allows mapping an intent to a sequence of API calls to satisfy order constraints. For example, in utterance #5, the user wants to start a playlist, but the value of the slot playlist_id is missing. In existing ST techniques, unless the bot developer implements an intermediate method that combines the two API methods Spotify-Search and Spotify-Player, the bot will ask the user for the value of the slot playlist_id. A bot improved with CKS will automatically map the user intent (i.e., StartPlaylist) to a sequence of API calls to get the value of the id.

Infer Slot Value from an External Data Service. The composite pattern called *entity-enrichment* allows resolving a missing value of a slot from an external data service. The user is not always precise; she might refer to an entity mention that is common knowledge to inform a slot value. For example, in utterance #6, the user provides "Eiffel Tower" as a taxi destination instead of the precise address. Since they leverage only the conversation history, existing ST techniques will fail to infer the value of the destination slot. A bot improved with CKS, however, can enrich the "Eiffel Tower" entity with additional information such as its address, which is the target destination value.

2.2   Architecture

To empower bots in handling the previous scenario, the bot needs services that initiate, monitor, and control conversations. Figure 2 shows the workflow between these services. When a bot receives a new utterance, (1) the Co-Ref service takes this utterance and the previous messages as input and resolves the potential referenced mentions. We use Neuralcoref[2], as a coreference resolution model. Then, (2) the utterance is sent to the Natural Language Understanding (NLU) service to extract intent and slot values. We use DialogFlow[3] NLU model. The Dialogue Manager (DM) aims to coordinate the information flow in the conversation. In our approach, the DM uses a Conversational State Machine (CSM) model to represent bot behaviors [22] and relies on a Complex Intent Recognition (CIR) technique to identify complex intents (details in Sect. 4). (3) Once the DM gets the intent and slot values, it creates a composite state, in the CSM, if the CIR recognizes a complex intent. Otherwise it creates an ordinary state. (4) The CKS keeps track of conversation knowledge, infers missing slot values, and provides a set of new services supporting the recognition of complex intents (details in Sect. 3). Once the DM collects all required information for the current state, (5) it calls the related API method and (6) sends the results to the Natural Language Generator (NLG). (7) NLG uses then predefined templates to generate human-like responses to the user.

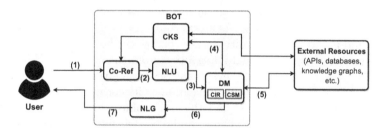

Fig. 2. General architecture supporting our approach.

3   Extended Context Knowledge Service

3.1   Context Knowledge Model

The context knowledge model consists of: (1) the metadata of bot schema, user profile and external services and (2) the data stored as conversation progresses.

Metadata is denoted as a context knowledge graph that includes mainly: (i) the definition of intents, slots, API methods, API parameters, and entity types, and

---

[2] NeuralCoref: https://spacy.io/universe/project/neuralcoref.
[3] DialogFlow: https://dialogflow.com/.

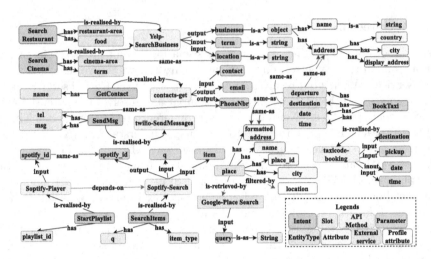

Fig. 3. Context knowledge graph related to the conversation of Fig. 1. For clarity purpose we do not represent all nodes and edges.

(ii) relationships between these elements (e.g., `SearchCinema` intent is realized by the method `Yelp-SearchBusiness`, `departure` slot is same-as `address` parameter, etc.). Figure 3 illustrates an example of this graph related to the conversation scenario. The context knowledge graph includes also the metadata of external data services (e.g., Google KG, wikidata) and user profiles. The key intuition behind including external data services is to endow the bot with the capability of enriching entities with additional information from these services. However, an external data service may return several entities for a given mention. Thus, having a mechanism that links the entity mention to its corresponding entity in the data service is necessary. This is where the user profile comes into play. User profile attributes like location, preferences can be used as filters to select the appropriate entity. Thus, we introduce the following node types: `External service`, `Profile attribute` and relationship types: `is-retrieved-by`, `filtered-by`. `External service` refers to a data service used for an entity enrichment. Often, a data service has an input parameter that takes a text query, which in our case will be filled by the entity mention (e.g., "Eiffel Tower"). `is-retrieved-by` is defined between an entity type and an external service, (e.g., the entity type `place` can be retrieved from `Google-PlaceSearch` service). `filtered-by` is defined between an entity type and a profile attribute, meaning that entities of that entity type can be filtered by the given attribute (e.g., `place` entities can be filtered by `location`). The generation of `filtered-by` edges is based on computing the cosine similarity [18] between the vector embedding[4] of each pair of entity type attributes and profile attributes. Assume that a user profile is defined by this set of attributes (`gender`, `location`, `dietary`) and the entity type `place` has the attribute `city` among others, a `filter-by` edge will be added

---

[4] Vector embeddings are obtained using the off-the-shelf spaCy NLP model.

between `place` and only `location` since it is similar to `city`. We assume that the external data services and their input parameters, the related `is-retrieved-by` relationships and the user profile attributes[5] are specified by the bot developer.

Data includes relevant information that should be memorized during user-bot conversations for later reuse. Two memory structures are used to store this data: Local Context Memory (LCM) and External Context Memory (ECM). The LCM keeps track of all the traces related to each intent fulfillment. This includes the utterance, the intent, the method call, alongside with its timestamp, its inputs, and its outputs. The ECM, on the other hand, keeps track of all entities mentions in user utterances. It also provides all information that external data services extract to enrich these entities mentions. We structure ECM in terms of entities; each is associated with its mention, entity type, and its retrieved attribute values. Examples of data related to the scenario are documented in online appendix[6].

3.2   CK Services

The CKS features four services, two of which are devoted to supporting the inference of slot values from the conversation history and external data services, whereas the two others aim at providing the contextual knowledge that is needed for the rules to recognize complex intents.

History Search: This service allows inferring slot values from the conversation history. It is enabled by the endpoint "`CKS/history? ms & u`" which takes as inputs the missing slot `ms`, and the utterance `u` and returns the value of the slot `ms` when possible. First, the service extracts the relevant entity-mention pairs from the utterance. An entity-mention is relevant if the extracted entity has an attribute same-as the missing slot. Consider utterance #3,, the entity-mention (`restaurant, LaGoulette`) is relevant because the entity `restaurant` has an attribute `address` same-as the missing slot `taxi-destination`. Second, the service rewrites the utterance by replacing each mention with the corresponding attribute's value. For example, the utterance "book a taxi from UCG cinema to LaGoulette restaurant" will be "book a taxi from [UCG-address] to [LaGoulette-address]". The rewriting is important to know if the value of `taxi-destination` is the restaurant or the cinema address. The service then extracts the missing value from the new utterance. If there is no relevant entity-mention in the utterance, the service returns the most recent value of the parameters same-as the missing slot. For example, in utterance #2, there is no entity-mention, so the service returns the value of the restaurant's area.

Entity Enrichment: This service allows enriching entity attributes from external data services. It is enabled by the endpoint "`CKS/invoke_external_service? s & em & a`". Consider utterance #6, the service takes as inputs: the external data service `s`: `Google-PlaceSearch`, the entity-mention `em`: (`place, Eiffel`

---

[5] Updating user profiles from conversations is out of the paper scope.

[6] Examples of data: https://tinyurl.com/scenario-data.

Tower), and the attribute a: address and it returns the value of a. To obtain the attribute value from the appropriate entity, three steps are followed. First, the service invokes the external data service related to the given entity-mention em, which returns a set of entities. Then, it filters the returned entities by discarding any entity, whose similarity with the entity-mention em is less than a predefined threshold and it does not contain the target attribute value. The similarity is computed on the basis of the cosine distance between the embedding vectors of the entity-mention em and the name of the entity returned by the external service. After this step, if only one entity is returned, the service retrieves the target attribute value from it. Otherwise, in order to identify the right entity, the service proceeds a second filtering step based on the filter attributes related to the mention entity type in the metadata. This filter step is expected to return one entity that matches the most of filters while giving a high priority to the location filter.

Nested Method Identification: This service allows identifying an API method that needs to be invoked to obtain the missing value. It is enabled by the endpoint "CKS/nested_method? ms & set_em". Consider utterance #4. The service takes as inputs the missing slot ms: tel, and the set of detected entity-mentions set_em: {(person, Hayet)}. It then gets from the metadata the methods that have an output parameter same-as the slot. For example, the service gets the set of methods {contacts-get, businessDetails-get} where the missing slot tel is the same-as one of the outputs of contacts-get (i.e., phoneNbr) and also the same-as one of the outputs of businessDetails-get (i.e., phone). The service relies on the detected entity-mentions to select the relevant method from the set of methods. For example, in contrast to the method businessDetails-get, the method contacts-get has an input parameter contact same-as to one of the detected entity person. Thus, the service selects contacts-get as the nested method and returns it along with its input values {(contact, Hayet)} and one of its outputs phoneNbr that is same-as the slot tel.

Dependent Method Identification: This service allows identifying a dependent method to get a value of an id. It is enabled by the endpoint "CKS/dependent _method? i" where i is the given intent. This endpoint first gets the method m1 that realize the intent i. Then, it gets the dependent method m2 where m1 depends on m2. For example, in utterance #5, the endpoint takes the intent StartPlaylist as input and returns: the dependent method Spotify-Search, its input parameters {q, item}, and its id output parameter spotify_id.

4 Complex Intent Recognition

We propose a new rule-based approach to support Complex Intent Recognition (CIR). Our approach offers flexibility for an extensible library of dialog patterns, i.e., when a new class of a complex intent is identified, we can add its new rule to recognize the intents of this class from user utterances. We express a rule using a combination of natural language features and contextual knowledge. In what follows, we first define functions that we use to specify the rules, then we specify the rule of each pattern introduced in Sect. 2.1.

4.1 Functions

Functions are the primitives that we use to define the rules. We consider function input and output types to be standard data types found in common programming languages such as `string` and `boolean`; as well complex data types such as `Tuple` or `Set`. Thus, we can leverage the standard operators designed for these data types. We distinguish two types of functions: dialog act functions to capture natural language features and context metadata functions to capture contextual knowledge. These functions are offered by the NLU and the CKS, respectively.

Table 1. Examples of boolean functions to express triggers

Functions	Inputs	Description
IS_NEW_INTENT()	u: string	Returns true if the identified intent in the utterance u is a new intent.
HAS_MISSING_SLOT()	u: string s: string	Returns true if the value of the given slot s is not recognized in the utterance u.
HAS_SAMEAS_PARA()	s: string	Returns true if there is at least one parameter that is the same-as the slot s.
EXIST_NESTED()	s: string	Returns true if there is at least one output parameter that is the same-as the slot s.
IS_DEPENDENT()	i: string	Returns true if the method that realize i depends on another method.
HAS_SAMEAS_ATT()	set_em: set s: string	Returns true if at least one entity in set_em has an attribute that is the same-as the slot s.

Dialog Act functions identify hidden actions in user or bot messages. Whether the user is providing information, or asking a question, or the bot is providing suggestions, are all hidden acts in user or bot messages. We focus on two dialog act functions: `INTENT_OF()`, which identifies the intent i expressed in a given utterance u, and `SLOT_VALUE()`, which returns the value of a given slot s recognized in the utterance u or `NULL` if no value of s is recognized in u.

Context Metadata functions allow to access and query the metadata graph defined in Sect. 3.1 to get the contextual knowledge. For example: `GET_SAMEAS_ PARA()` is a metadata function that returns a set of parameters that are the same-as a given slot s; `DEPENDS_ON()` returns a method name m_b given a method name m_a where m_a depends on m_b or it returns `NULL` if there is no dependent method.

4.2 Complex Intent Recognition Rules

A rule consists of *trigger* and *action* clauses. The trigger clause specifies the conditions that need to be verified to recognize complex intents. Then, the sequence

```
Rule ("slot-value-flow")
when
IS_NEW_INTENT(i).equals(true)    AND
HAS_MISSING_SLOT(u, ms).equals(true)    AND
HAS_SAMEAS_PARA(ms).equals(true)
then
mv := "CKS/history? ms & u"
set_sv_i := set_sv_i ∪ {(ms, mv)}
INVOKE(i, set_sv_i)
```

```
Rule ("nested-method")
when
IS_NEW_INTENT(i).equals(true)    AND
HAS_MISSING_SLOT(u, ms).equals(true)    AND
EXIST_NESTED(ms).equals(true)
then
(m_nes, set_iv_nes, o_nes) := "CKS/nested_method? ms & set_em"
mv := GET_OUTPUT_VALUE(m_nes, set_iv_nes, o_nes)
set_sv_i := set_sv_i ∪ {(ms, mv)}
INVOKE(i, set_sv_i)
```

```
Rule ("entity-enrichment")
when
IS_NEW_INTENT(i).equals(true)    AND
HAS_MISSING_SLOT(u, ms).equals(true)    AND
HAS_SAMEAS_ ATT(set_em, ms).equals(true)
then
(s, em, a) := GET_REQUIREMENTS(set_em, ms)
mv := "CKS/invoke_external_service? s & em & a"
set_sv_i := set_sv_i ∪ {(ms, mv)}
INVOKE(i, set_sv_i)
```

```
Rule ("API-calls-ordering")
when
IS_NEW_INTENT(i).equals(true)    AND
IS_DEPENDENT(i).equals(true)
then
(m_dep, set_i_dep, id_dep) := "CKS/dependent _method? i"
set_iv_dep := GET_VALUES_ASKUSER(m_dep, set_i_dep)
idv := GET_OUTPUT_VALUE(m_dep, set_iv_dep, id_dep)
set_sv_i := set_sv_i ∪ {(id, idv)}
INVOKE(i, set_sv_i)
```

Fig. 4. Rules of composite dialog patterns

of operations specified in the action clause are executed to fulfill the related complex intent. The following statement specify a rule:

Rule "name of the rule" **when trigger then action**

Triggers are expressed as boolean conditions over functions, including dialog act and metadata functions. Table 1 provides examples of boolean functions that are used to define triggers. Conditions may be combined using conjunction operator (AND). The action is a sequence of operations. For instance, an operation can be an assignment of a value to a given variable, or an invocation of a CKS service. Figure 4 shows the definition of rules for each composite pattern:

Slot-Value-Flow Rule. The first condition checks if the identified intent i is a new intent. The second condition checks if the value of the slot ms is missing. These two conditions are the same for nested-method and entity-enrichment rules. The third condition checks if there is at least one already fulfilled parameter that is the same-as the slot ms. If the conditions are satisfied, the bot: (1) invokes the history search CKS service to get the missing value, (2) adds this value to the set of slot-value pairs, and (3) invokes the method that realize the intent i.

Nested-Method Rule. The third condition checks if there is at least one output parameter that is the same-as the slot ms. If the conditions are satisfied, the bot: (1) invokes the nested method CKS service to identify: the nested method m_{nes}, its input values set_iv$_{nes}$, and its output parameter o_{nes}. Then, the bot (2) invokes the method m_{nes} to get the value of o_{nes}, (3) uses this value as a value for the slot ms, and (4) invokes the method that realize the intent i.

API-Calls-Ordering Rule. The first condition is similar to the first condition of the other rules. The second condition checks if the method that realize the intent i depends on another method. If the conditions are satisfied, the bot: (1) invokes the CKS service to identify: the dependent method

m_{dep}, its inputs set_i_{dep}, and the id parameter id_{dep}. Then, the bot **(2)** calls GET_VALUES_ASKUSER() to get the input values of the method m_{dep} by extracting them from the utterance, the history, or by asking the user. After getting the input values, **(3)** invokes m_{dep} to get the value of id_{dep}, **(4)** uses this value as a value for the parameter id, and **(5)** invokes the method that realize the intent i.

Entity-Enrichment Rule. Given a set of entities mentions set_em, extracted from u, the third condition checks if there is at least one attribute of an entity-mention that is the same-as the slot ms. If the conditions are satisfied, the bot: **(1)** calls the metadata function GET_REQUIREMENTS() to get the following information: the related service s, the entity-mention em, and the attribute a. Note that this function chooses one entity-mention from set_em based on the one that has an attribute same-as the slot ms, **(2)** invokes the entity enrichment CKS service to get the value of the attribute, **(3)** uses this value as a value for the slot ms, and **(4)** invokes the method that realize the intent i.

5 Experiments

The first objective of the study was to explore the *effectiveness* and limitations of (i) the proposed CKS (i.e., its capability of inferring slots' values correctly and reducing unnecessary interactions) and (ii) the CIR (i.e., its capability of recognizing correctly the composite dialog patterns mentioned previously). The second objective was to evaluate the user experience (i.e., *naturalness, repetitiveness, understanding*) in interacting with a bot improved with CIR and CKS.

5.1 Methods

Experimental Design. Participants were recruited via email from the extended network of contacts of the authors. The call for volunteers resulted in a total of 20 participants. We prepared an evaluation scenario that required participants to interact with a set of API methods through a bot to plan an evening activity in Paris. Participants were asked to complete four different tasks in this scenario (T1: checking the weather and searching for restaurants, T2: booking a restaurant table, T3: booking a taxi, and T4: sending a confirmation message to the travel partner). The tasks were designed to leverage the type of support provided by the CKS, if the composite dialog patterns were to be effectively recognized (T1: inferring slot value from conversation history, T2: identifying dependent method, T3: using an external data source, and T4: identifying nested method). We followed a within-subjects design,[7] tasking participants to interact with two bots representing the following experimental conditions:

- *DM-Baseline.* The baseline implements a standard conversational management, without composite dialog patterns and CKS support.

---

[7] Study materials and in-depth results available at https://tinyurl.com/study-materials.

– *DM-CKS*. This bot is implemented with the CIR and CKS support.

The two bots relied on the same NLU implementation (in DialogFlow), bot interface, and differed only in the composite patterns and CKS support.

Procedure. The study was conducted online. Participants received a link to an online form that included an informed consent, all the instructions, links to the bots and feedback required. In the study, participants were introduced to the evaluation scenario and tasks, and were asked to perform those tasks with the two bots. The order in which the bots were presented to users was counterbalanced. For each bot, participants were asked to provide open-ended feedback on the pros and cons of their experience. The last part of the study then asked participants about their preferred bot, the reason why, and a quantitative feedback on their user experience. We adopted the user experience questions from prior work [9], to get feedback on the perceived *naturalness* (i.e., ability to fulfill user tasks in human-like conversations), *repetitiveness* (i.e., ability to avoid redundant questions) and *understanding* (i.e., ability to interpret user requests).

Data Analysis. We performed an analysis of conversation logs so as to assess the effectiveness of the CKS and the CIR. These are calculated in relation to optimal conversation scenarios[8] that we designed based on participants conversations. The CKS effectiveness is calculated by considering the following metrics: number of (M1) conversation turns, (M2) prompts asking for missing slot values, and (M3) missing slot values correctly inferred. The effectiveness of the CIR (only available in DM-CKS) is calculated by considering the number of (M4) complex intents correctly detected. These metrics are calculated per user conversation, aggregated (mean) and then used to compute the relative performance against the optimal scenario. We also performed a qualitative analysis of open-ended responses and conversation logs to contextualise the results from the metrics and identify limitations.

5.2   Results

Effectiveness of CKS and CIR. Table 2 shows the relative performance by task of both bots DM-Baseline and DM-CKS in relation to the optimal reference scenario. For the four tasks, we can see that DM-CKS bot experienced a boost in performance for M1 and M2 metrics (mean across tasks 94.66% and 88.4% respectively), approaching the efficiency in terms of number of turns and prompts of the reference ideal scenario. This level of performance is possible due to the accuracy of the slot value inference (M3) performed by the CKS services supporting each task – a mean relative performance across tasks of 96%. In contrast, not having the support of the CKS services lead the DM-Baseline bot to perform poorly in comparison, with the best performance being at around 37.18% for the metrics considered. These results provide evidence for the benefits and effectiveness of the CKS support. Table 2 also shows the relative performance of

---

[8] Scenarios assuming ideal accuracy of slot-value inference and intent recognition.

recognizing complex intent (M4) by the bot DM-CKS in relation to the reference scenario. By analyzing the conversations, we noticed that the recognition error of the composite dialog patterns is mostly caused by the detection error of the correct intent by the NLU during the conversation. For example, if the NLU detects the intent SearchRestaurant instead of BookTaxi, in the utterance "I want to go to this restaurant", this will lead to an error in detecting the slot-value-flow pattern that takes the restaurant address as the destination address. However, for the four tasks, we can see that DM-CKS bot is close to the reference scenario with a mean relative performance across tasks of 94.86%.

User Experience. All but one participant (19/20 participants) expressed a preference towards the DM-CKS bot as opposed to the baseline. The one exception was due to NLU limitations in recognizing user expressions that led to the enactment of the wrong services. The feedback to the specific user experience questions, as well as the open-ended feedback, highlighted the reasons behind the preference. Participants agreed with DM-CKS interactions describing *naturalness* (14/20), less *repetitiveness* (16/20) and *understanding* (15/20), whereas the baseline was poorly rated on these fronts (1/20). Interestingly, these qualities were linked to the CKS support, such as the ability to infer missing slot values from conversation history (e.g., "saying that the drop-off address was the restaurant I have just booked was enough", P1), or from external services (e.g., "[it] found the address when I said Eiffel Tower", P6). The ability to handle complex intents also emerged as a defining feature (e.g., "[DM-CKS] is capable of undertaking complex tasks and retaining previous information", P16). In contrast, participants reported having to copy & paste previous values or google some information during their interactions with the baseline bot.

Table 2. Bot performance for each task according to relevant metrics. Values in bold denote best performance. Percentages denote the relative performance with respect to the reference (optimal) scenario.

Task (service)	DM-Baseline			DM-CKS			
	M1 (TURNS)	M2 (PROMPTS)	M3 (SLOTS)	M1 (TURNS)	M2 (PROMPTS)	M3 (SLOTS)	M4 (PATTERN)
T1 (history)	59.70%	21.18%	49.24%	**98.04%**	90%	**96.97%**	**95%**
T2 (dependent)	61.18%	42.11%	17.86%	**92.86%**	**95.24%**	**95.24%**	**94.44%**
T3 (external)	46.97%	32.39%	3.17%	**91.18%**	**88.37%**	**95.24%**	**95%**
T4 (nested)	52.97%	20%	39.41%	**96.55%**	80%	**96.55%**	**95%**
Mean	55.21%	28.92%	27.42%	**94.66%**	**88.4%**	**96%**	**94.86%**

Limitations. The conversation analysis revealed some limitations in supporting the natural language interaction described by the users:

Enumerating Entities when the Number of Entities Is Expected. In the context of T2, when asked "For how many people do you want to book a table?", some participants would respond with "For me and my friend". The bot could not infer the number of seats from the participant's utterance because it expected to extract a number. This would be an acceptable answer in a natural conversation, and represent as a new type of inference that needs to be considered.

Introducing Typos when Providing Slot Values. When booking a taxi in the context of T3, some participants spelled "Eiffel tower" incorrectly (e.g., "Book a Taxi from the Eifeltower"), which led to the failure of the CKS service for inferring values from a external data source. Handling mistakes when performing inferences is a situation that needs to be addressed.

6   Related Work

Our work is related to the ST process that aims to infer the dialog state in terms of the user intent and its slot-value pairs during conversations [15]. Depending on the leveraged knowledge sources, existing ST approaches can be organized into history-based, schema-based, and Linguistic patterns (LPs) based.

History-based approaches rely on the whole or window-size of the dialogue history to predict the dialog state. Deep learning models including HRNN [8], LSTM [7] and BERT [23] are utilised to encode the dialog history. Other works [4,17] leverage only on the previous dialog states to predict the current state instead of taking the whole history. More advanced approaches [10,14,20] focused first on the learning of slot dependencies from the history and then incorporated them into the ST model, allowing it to infer slot values from similar slots. Most of the ST approaches either focused on recognizing only basic intents or ignored their recognition at all. Similar to some of these, we build upon advances in ML techniques to enable the recognition of basic intents but contribute a new rule-based approach to recognize complex intents.

Schemas-based approaches leverage schemas capturing the structural representation of conversation data to predict the dialog state. Works like [5,13,19] use a slot-level schema graph that captures dependencies between slots. The aim is to allow the ST model to infer slot values from similar slots. Other efforts like [12] leverage the backend database schema in ST model to allow slot inference from the database entities. These methods, however, work with bots integrated only with databases, where the inferred slot-value pairs are used to frame the query. Since our context knowledge model integrates API/Service schema, where each intent is associated with its corresponding API method, our approach can handle flows supported by software-enabled services. The work [1] represents the dialogue state as a dataflow graph and the complex user intent as a dataflow program. For each user utterance, a trained model allows predicting the corresponding dataflow program. This approach relies on datasets where each utterance must be annotated with the corresponding dataflow program; however, it is not intuitive task to annotate utterances with programs. The closest work to ours is [15] which introduced a unified schema defining a service or API as a combination of intents and slots. A BERT-based ST model then takes this schema as input to enable the recognition of intents and inferring their slot-value pairs. The captured knowledge (i.e., the unified schema), however, can only help in the recognition of basic intents. In our work, we devise the CKS mainly to capture the contextual knowledge that is required to recognize complex intents. In addition to the conversation history and intent/slot schemas, this knowledge includes API/Service schemas and enriched entities. Our CIR technique exploits both this knowledge and basic intent features to recognize the complex intents.

LPs-based approaches leverages linguistic patterns that are drawn mainly from human conversation to handle some complex intents and inferring their slots [6,16]. For example, IRIS [6] draws on two existing LPs *dependent questions* (i.e., one question depends on the answer to some subsequent request), and *anaphora* (i.e., expressions that depend on previous expressions) to allow composition and sequencing of intents. These approaches, however, are not enough to capture complex intents that naturally emerge when conversing with services. For instance, while this utterance "Send the message 'I will be at UGC cinema at 3 pm' to Hayet" refers to a complex intent requiring a composition of two API methods, it cannot be recognized by IRIS. The reason is that IRIS can recognize composition based only on linguistic features (e.g., A composition is recognized when a user answers with a new intent to the bot request for a missing slot). In contrast to the LPs-based approaches, we focus on using composite dialog patterns that cater to the inherent features in interactions between humans, bots, and services in addition to the linguistic ones. These patterns are used to enable the contextual knowledge required by the CIR to recognize complex intents.

7 Conclusions and Future Work

We proposed reusable and extensible rule-based technique that uses a sophisticated context service to recognize and realize complex intents. We believe that our approach charts novel abstractions that unlock the seamless and scalable integration of natural language-based conversations with software-enabled services. We devised a novel complex intent recognition that allows the incremental acquisition of rule templates to identify composite intents from basic dialog acts and context features. The contextual knowledge required at run-time to recognise complex intents and infer slot values from user-bot conversations is extracted from conversation history, enriched entities, intents and API schemas and represented in graph structure. Future work includes identifying new composite patterns (e.g., supporting conversations with business process models) and developing privacy-aware task-oriented bots by reasoning about privacy-preserving conversations.

References

1. Andreas, J., et al.: Task-oriented dialogue as dataflow synthesis. Trans. Assoc. Comput. Linguist. **8**, 556–571 (2020)
2. Bouguelia, S., et al.: Reusable abstractions and patterns for recognising compositional conversational flows. In: Proceedings CAiSE (2021)

3. Brabra, H., et al.: Dialogue management in conversational systems: a review of approaches, challenges, and opportunities. IEEE TCDS (2021)

4. Chao, G.L., Lane, I.: BERT-DST: scalable end-to-end dialogue state tracking with bidirectional encoder representations from transformer, pp. 1468–1472, September 2019

5. Chen, L., et al.: Schema-guided multi-domain dialogue state tracking with graph attention neural networks. In: Proceedings of the AAAI Conference on Artificial Intelligence (2020)

6. Fast, E., et al.: Iris: a conversational agent for complex tasks. In: Proceedings of the 2018 CHI Conference on Human Factors in Computing Systems (2018)

7. Gao, S., Sethi, A., Agarwal, S., Chung, T., Hakkani-Tür, D.Z.: Dialog state tracking: a neural reading comprehension approach. In: SIGdial (2019)

8. Goel, R., Paul, S., Hakkani-Tür, D.: HyST: a hybrid approach for flexible and accurate dialogue state tracking. In: Interspeech (2019)

9. Holmes, S., et al.: Usability testing of a healthcare chatbot: can we use conventional methods to assess conversational user interfaces? In: Proceedings of the ECCE (2019)

10. Hu, J., et al.: SAS: dialogue state tracking via slot attention and slot information sharing. In: ACL. Association for Computational Linguistics (2020)

11. Jain, M., Kumar, P., Kota, R., Patel, S.N.: Evaluating and informing the design of chatbots. In: Proceedings of the 2018 Designing Interactive Systems Conference (2018)

12. Liao, L., Long, L.H., Ma, Y., Lei, W., Chua, T.S.: Dialogue state tracking with incremental reasoning. TACL **9**, 557–569 (2021)

13. Lin, W., Tseng, B., Byrne, B.: Knowledge-aware graph-enhanced GPT-2 for dialogue state tracking. CoRR (2021)

14. Ouyang, Y., et al.: Dialogue state tracking with explicit slot connection modeling. In: ACL (2020)

15. Rastogi, A., et al.: Towards scalable multi-domain conversational agents: The schema-guided dialogue dataset. ArXiv abs/1909.05855 (2020)

16. Rastogi, P., Gupta, A., Chen, T., Lambert, M.: Scaling multi-domain dialogue state tracking via query reformulation. In: NAACL, pp. 97–105 (2019)

17. Ren, L., Ni, J., McAuley, J.: Scalable and accurate dialogue state tracking via hierarchical sequence generation. In: EMNLP (2019)

18. Sitikhu, P., et al.: A comparison of semantic similarity methods for maximum human interpretability. In: Proceedings of the AITB (2019)

19. Wu, P., et al.: GCDST: a graph-based and copy-augmented multi-domain dialogue state tracking. In: Findings of the ACL: EMNLP 2020 (2020)

20. Ye, F., et al.: Slot self-attentive dialogue state tracking. In: WWW. ACL (2021)

21. Zamanirad, S.: Superimposition of natural language conversations over software enabled services (2019)

22. Zamanirad, S., et al.: Hierarchical state machine based conversation model and services. In: Proceedings of the CAiSE (2020)

23. Zhang, J., et al.: Find or classify ? Dual strategy for slot-value predictions on multi-domain dialog state tracking. In: STARSEM (2020)

Crowdsourcing Syntactically Diverse Paraphrases with Diversity-Aware Prompts and Workflows

Jorge Ramírez[1](✉)(iD), Marcos Baez[1](iD), Auday Berro[1](iD),
Boualem Benatallah[2](iD), and Fabio Casati[3](iD)

[1] LIRIS – University of Claude Bernard Lyon 1, Villeurbanne, France
{jorge-daniel.ramirez-medina,auday.berro}@univ-lyon1.fr
[2] University of New South Wales, Kensington, Australia
[3] ServiceNow, Santa Clara, USA

Abstract. Task-oriented bots (or simply bots) enable humans to perform tasks in natural language. For example, to book a restaurant or check the weather. Crowdsourcing has become a prominent approach to build datasets for training and evaluating task-oriented bots, where the crowd grows an initial seed of utterances through *paraphrasing*, i.e., reformulating a given seed into semantically equivalent sentences. In this context, the resulting *diversity* is a relevant dimension of high-quality datasets, as diverse paraphrases capture the many ways users may express an intent. Current techniques, however, are either based on the assumption that crowd-powered paraphrases are naturally diverse or focus only on *lexical* diversity. In this paper, we address an overlooked aspect of diversity and introduce an approach for guiding the crowdsourcing process towards paraphrases that are *syntactically* diverse. We introduce a workflow and novel prompts that are informed by syntax patterns to elicit paraphrases avoiding or incorporating desired syntax. Our empirical analysis indicates that our approach yields higher syntactic diversity, syntactic novelty and more uniform pattern distribution than state-of-the-art baselines, albeit incurring on higher task effort.

Keywords: Crowdsourcing · Paraphrasing · Diversity · Task-oriented bots

1 Introduction

Task-oriented chatbots (or simply bots) allow users to interact with software-enabled services in natural language, for example, to perform tasks such as booking a restaurant or checking the weather. Such interactions require bots to process utterances (i.e., user input) like *"find restaurants in Milan"* to identify the user's intent (e.g., *"find restaurant"*) and the entities (i.e., slots) associated with the intent (e.g., *location = "Milan"*). The success of intent recognition

© Springer Nature Switzerland AG 2022
X. Franch et al. (Eds.): CAiSE 2022, LNCS 13295, pp. 253–269, 2022.
https://doi.org/10.1007/978-3-031-07472-1_15

models depends entirely on the quality (and size) of the dataset of user utterances used for training and evaluating these models. A prominent approach to build datasets to support the training and evaluation of intent recognition models involves expanding an initial set of seed utterances (for the intents) by means of *paraphrasing*. Paraphrasing is a task that aims to reformulate a given utterance into its many possible variations to generate semantically equivalent sentences [18].

An important dimension to measure quality in paraphrasing is *diversity*, i.e., the breath and variety of paraphrases in the resulting corpus, which dictates the ability to capture the many ways users may express an intent. In this context, paraphrasing techniques generally rely on approaches that aim at introducing *lexical* and *syntactic* variations [22]. Lexical variations refer to changes that affect individual words, such as substituting words by their synonyms (e.g., *"search restaurants in Milan"*). Syntactic variations, instead, refer to changes in sentence or phrasal structure, such as transforming the grammatical structure of a sentence (e.g., *"Where can we eat in Milan?"*). This richness of human language (and its potential ambiguity [24]) emphasizes the importance of paraphrasing for building diverse datasets. Missing to train models on such variations of language may result in bots failing to recognize intents and slots, thus performing tasks diverging from a user's actual intention and degrading their experience [27].

Having more control over the type of variations introduced can steer the paraphrase generation process towards more diverse and useful paraphrases for training and testing models for downstream tasks [3,6]. For any real-world usage, it is critical to test the generalization capabilities of models. Adversarial examples, crafted by introducing syntactic variations (besides lexical changes) to seeds, can help "break" models and identify the boundaries of their capabilities [9]. Robustness may be increased by training models on augmented data, resulting from applying transformations (like paraphrasing) to training datasets. Thus having more control over the paraphrasing process can help increase the overall diversity of the training datasets to counteract adversarial examples [9].

However, while the development of specific techniques to guide the paraphrase generation process towards syntactic variations is the focus of ongoing work in automatic paraphrasing [3], they are currently greatly under-explored in the crowdsourcing literature. Among the few contributions towards diversity in crowdsourcing, a prominent data collection framework involves turning crowd-based paraphrasing into an iterative and multi-stage pipeline, chaining together multiple paraphrasing rounds. A different approach aims at increasing diversity by focusing on the task design itself [13,27]. While valuable, these state of the art approaches assume workers would naturally produce diverse paraphrases or focus primarily on lexical variations (see Sect. 2).

In this paper, we present a multi-stage paraphrasing pipeline designed to guide the crowdsourcing process towards producing paraphrases that are syntactically diverse and balanced. Unlike prior work, the pipeline supports a *workflow* that can extract syntax patterns from crowdsourced paraphrases, and identify target patterns that should guide the generation task. We adopt the definition of syntax pattern, as the top two levels of a constituency parse tree [9], and select target patterns based on a pattern selection strategy (e.g., frequent or infrequent patterns). The paraphrase generation task then includes novel *prompts* that can elicit paraphrases conforming to the target syntax patterns (patterns by example), or avoiding frequent patterns (taboo patterns). With this approach, we are exploring strategies to elicit more diverse paraphrases by steering the crowd away from over-represented syntax patterns, or guide workers towards less frequent patterns that should have more representation.

Contribution. The contributions of the work are in (i) an approach to guide the crowdsourcing process towards syntactically diverse paraphrases, (ii) workflows and prompts that can elicit paraphrases informed by syntax patterns, (iii) empirical evaluation of state-of-the art approaches, and the proposed strategies, for the generation of syntactically diverse paraphrases, and (iv) we contribute crowdsourced datasets to further study syntactic diversity.

2   Related Work

Crowdsourcing is a widely used approach to paraphrase generation [23]. It is a popular strategy as it can help scale the paraphrases generation efforts while reducing the costs, compared to hiring experts [14]. Two important aspects when it comes to diversity in this context are the *workflow* and *task design*.

In a crowdsourced process, an initial seed utterance, usually provided by an expert or generated using generative models or grammars [21], is presented as a starting point, and workers are asked to paraphrase the seed to new variations. A standard approach to introduce diversity in this context is to see the crowdsourcing task as a brainstorming session [1], where different perspectives are sought after. Here the assumption is that relying on crowd workers from different countries, backgrounds and demographics, will introduce diversity in the paraphrase generation process [1].

An improvement over the standard process involves turning crowd-based paraphrasing into an iterative and multi-stage workflow. This approach chains together multiple rounds of paraphrasing. The seed utterances for a round come from a previous round by using different seed selection strategies [10,12,17]. An approach to this is to use random sampling [10], which replaces a seed by randomly selecting one of its paraphrases from the previous round. An alternative is to replace the seed using semantic outliers [12], where the idea is to look for unique yet valid paraphrases to show to workers. This strategy uses sentence embeddings to represent each paraphrase to then scores these based on their distance to the mean vector. The paraphrases further away from the mean vector are defined as outliers. Another strategy is to just choose all the paraphrases from the previous round as seeds, looking for a multiplier effect, an approach known as Chinese whispers [17]. The focus of these strategies is to ultimately reduce the priming effect of seed utterances and examples [23] that would influence workers towards similar sentences.

Task design is another important aspect that affects the diversity of crowd-based paraphrasing [10,17]. Jian et al. [10] explored relevant task design dimensions including number and type of examples in the prompts, number of paraphrases requested and workflows, assessing their impact on general diversity. The study found that the number of paraphrases requested did not significantly affect the diversity of the outcome, but that workflows and prompts do have a significant contribution. Prompts providing only lexical examples lead to higher semantic relevance but lower diversity than showing a mix of syntactic and lexical examples. They also observed that a workflow based on Chinese whispers [17] can increase the diversity but at the cost of a lower semantic relevance. Overall, although the study did not focus on syntactic diversity, it provides further support for exploring prompts and workflows to improve diversity.

Early work on prompts focused on exploring general priming effects of different types of prompts. Wang et al. [23] explored paraphrasing prompts such as *sentence-based*, based on presenting seed sentences, *scenario-based*, that adopts a story-telling approach instead of directly showing a seed, and *list-based*, where only the goal is presented along with the required slot values. This study found that the list method is the one introducing less priming, with the other two priming workers with their choice of words and language. Most recent work has explored prompts to guide workers towards lexical diversity. Some words in the seed may be swapped with images (e.g., replacing the entity flight with the image of an airplane) [20]. However, this may be hard to apply beyond entities (e.g., finding images for verbs). *Taboo words* have been used instead to constraint the crowd from using frequently-used words [13], and *word recommendations* to help workers in choosing words to incorporate [27] Although these works focus on lexical diversity, they inspired our approach to steer workers towards or away from syntactic patterns to drive the process towards syntactic diversity.

In contrast to the crowdsourcing literature, the controlled generation of syntactic paraphrases has been the focus of research in *automatic* paraphrasing (e.g., [4,8,9]). Works on automatic paraphrasing models have proposed different architectures to disentangle semantic and syntactic properties, and allow for an additional input denoting the target syntax. Relevant to our discussion is the representation of syntactic templates guiding the generation. As syntactic specification, these approaches have leveraged explicit representations, such as constituency parse tree [8,9] or learn more abstract syntax representations from the data [4]. In the latter, the input to the model are exemplars (i.e., sentences providing example expressions to mimic). We stress, however, that despite automatic approaches being a promising and emerging direction (with its own quality issues to address [2,18,25]), crowdsourcing is still a very important technique that can greatly benefit from the research on diversity. Crowdsourcing is actively used for collecting training data, generating adversarial examples for intent recognition models, and even to support the training and evaluation of automatic paraphrasing techniques.

The above tells us that using workflows and prompts for syntactic diversity is an unexplored area in crowdsourced paraphrasing. This also means that it is unclear to what extent current state-of-the-art approaches are able to deliver on syntactic diversity. In this paper, we draw inspiration from automatic paraphrasing based on syntactic patterns, as well as lessons learned from crowdsourced paraphrasing. We explore whether crowdsourcing workflows and prompts can guide the paraphrase acquisition process towards syntactic diversity.

3   Crowdsourcing Syntactically Diverse Paraphrases

In this section, we present our approach to guide the paraphrase generation process towards syntactically diverse paraphrases. In what follows we describe the syntax-aware workflows and prompts that are at the core of our approach.

3.1   Paraphrase Generation Workflow

Figure 1 depicts our approach that *abstracts* and *extends* state of the art paraphrasing workflows [11,12,17] into an iterative and multi-stage pipeline targeting syntactic diversity. We can define the typical data collection process as broken into multiple rounds of three main steps: *paraphrase generation, paraphrase validation*, and *seed selection*.

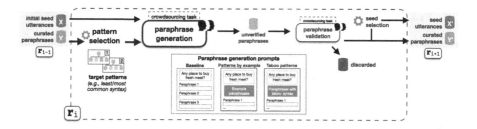

Fig. 1. Our approach consolidates and extends state-of-the-art paraphrasing workflows into an iterative and multi-stage pipeline aiming for syntactic diversity.

A data collection round r, for a typical workflow, takes as input a dataset of seeds utterances X and a curated collection of paraphrases Y (initially, Y can be empty) and proceeds by querying the crowd for paraphrases via predefined prompts. The prompts in the paraphrase generation step ask workers to provide a set m paraphrases for an utterance $x \in X$. These prompts generally rely on instructions and examples explaining the concept of paraphrasing, expecting workers to provide valid paraphrases according to the instructions. The resulting collection of unverified paraphrases $\bar{Y}$ is fed to the paraphrase validation step, where another crowd helps to assess the quality of candidate paraphrases, typically assessing semantic relevance[1]. The valid paraphrases are then appended to the collection of curated paraphrases Y. Finally, the seed selection step updates (or fully replaces) the seeds in X by sampling from the correct paraphrases to create the set of seeds for the next round. In this abstraction, we can model state-of-the-art workflows as instances implementing different seed selection strategies (e.g., random sampling [10], or identifying outliers [12]).

---

[1] Refer to [26,28] for other relevant quality aspects in crowdsourced paraphrases.

To steer the process towards syntactic diversity, we introduce the notion of syntax patterns into the workflow as well as pipeline components that can extract and identify target patterns from an input paraphrase corpus to guide the generation task. In this extended workflow, an input paraphrase corpus Y is provided along with the initial seed utterances X. The input paraphrase corpus provides a curated list of paraphrases from where syntactic exemplars will be derived. Note that this curated list can be the output from a previous round (Y_{r_i-1}) or provided by experts. The *pattern selection* component then extracts the syntactic *patterns* for each paraphrase in the input paraphrase corpus, capturing the different syntactic variations present in the corpus. To direct the crowd away from (or towards) specific syntax, the pattern selection step proceeds by narrowing down this list to a set of *target patterns*, according to a selection strategy. These target patterns and the associated paraphrases in the corpus are handed over to the paraphrase generation step, where novel *prompts* take advantage of this additional input to query the crowd for paraphrases—ensuring workers conform with (or avoid) specific syntax. In the following subsections, we expand on these components and the notion of patterns in more detail.

3.2 Pattern Representation and Selection

To capture and control syntax, we follow [9] and define a pattern as the top two levels of a constituency parse tree, as shown in Fig. 3a. For example, the extracted syntax pattern for *"search for a restaurant"* in bracket notation would be (S (VP)). This pattern denotes a simple declarative clause, with a verb and dependants. Instead, the syntax pattern for *"where to eat?"* would be (SBARQ(WHADVP)(S)) which can be interpreted as a direct question introduced by a wh-word or a wh-phrase.[2] The pattern is thus a relaxed version of the full syntax tree, since the nodes at the top two levels are mostly clause/phrase level nodes. This takes syntax comparisons at a higher level of abstraction, which was deemed appropriate for guiding syntactic variations in prior work [8,9].

Based on this definition of pattern, the *pattern selection* component aims at identifying target patterns that would inform the generation process. The component starts by first extracting the underlying syntax pattern for each paraphrase in Y. To do so, we obtain the linearized parse tree for the paraphrase using the Stanza NLP toolkit [19] and the Stanford CoreNLP package [16]. The pattern (the top two levels) is extracted from the full syntax tree based on the algorithm and code shared in [9]. As a result of this step, we have K unique syntax patterns, where each p_k is associated with one or more paraphrases in the input corpus Y of curated paraphrases.

To support the selection of the pattern, the component then builds a pattern frequency table. This is calculated by looking at each unique syntax pattern p_k, and counting the number of paraphrases in the corpus it is associated with. The pattern selection component then selects a subset of n patterns as the target patterns, by applying a pattern *selection strategy*. In the context of this work

---

[2] Reference for bracket labels at https://gist.github.com/nlothian/9240750.

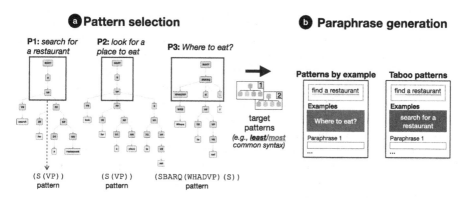

Fig. 2. A pattern is defined as the top two levels of a constituency parse tree. Patterns identified with pattern selection strategy inform paraphrase generation prompts.

these strategies are based on pattern frequency table a) *least-frequent patterns* (bottom-n) or *most-frequent patterns* (top-n). Either choice (top-n or bottom-n) informs the paraphrase generation step differently, producing different prompts.

It is relevant to mention that for practical reasons, this component expects well-formed and grammatically correct paraphrases as part of the input corpus Y. The tools we employ for extracting the parse tree and deriving the patterns [16,19] may interpret errors in the paraphrases (e.g., typos, misused verb forms) as part of new patterns. As relevant literature suggests, crowdsourced paraphrases are subject to such errors [26].

3.3 Paraphrase Generation Prompts

In a crowdsourced paraphrasing process, the paraphrase generation is modeled as a crowdsourcing task, generally deployed on a crowdsourcing platform. The typical task provides instructions explaining the concept of paraphrasing, and prompting crowd workers to provide x paraphrases for a given seed (refer to Fig. 1 for an illustrative example of this baseline task). Except for the work on lexical diversity (see Sect. 2), current paraphrasing prompts rely on the assumption that engaging workers of diverse demographic and background will naturally lead to diversity. In this work, we propose two novel prompts that aim at eliciting workers paraphrases that conform or differ from a target pattern (informed by the *pattern selection* strategy). We posit that by designing syntax-aware prompts we can more effectively guide the crowd towards syntactic variations.

Patterns by Example. The *patterns by example* prompt (Fig. 3b) aims to guide crowd workers towards providing paraphrases featuring desired target patterns. While these patterns could also be provided by experts, in this work we explore the use of least-frequent patterns inferred from the corpus Y. In feeding the prompt with target patterns identified with the least-frequent pattern selection strategy (bottom-n patterns), the idea is to elicit paraphrases conforming with patterns that are currently unrepresented in the input corpus. The design of the prompt, as seen in the figure, incorporates elements of the baseline task, but includes additional instructions, syntactic examples, and validators. The *instructions* request workers to provide (m = 3) paraphrases inspired by the sentence structures illustrated in concrete example sentences. These *syntactic examples* are k example paraphrases (in our experiments $k = 2$),[3] randomly sampled from the list of paraphrases in Y, featuring the target syntax patters (one example per target pattern). The *validators* are a list of checks we built into the task to ensure workers do not provide paraphrases with the same pattern as the input seed x, but did not enforce strict compliance with the target patterns. Thus, we relied on the priming effect of the examples but still allowed for novel syntax (i.e., a patterns not found in any example).

Taboo Patterns. The taboo patterns prompt is inspired by existing work on lexical diversity [13], and it aims to steer the crowd away from over-represented syntax patterns. The prompt is thus informed by the target patterns obtained with the most-frequent pattern selection strategy (top-n patterns). As with the previous prompt, the design of taboo pattern prompt extends the baseline with additional instructions, example taboo syntax and validators. The *instructions* in this case instructs workers to provide (m = 3) paraphrases featuring structures different from those given in syntactic examples. These *taboo pattern examples*, are k example paraphrases (in our experiments $k = 2$), selected for each taboo pattern by randomly sampling one paraphrase featuring the given pattern. The *validators* then ensure that workers do not provide paraphrases with the same pattern as the input seed x and any of the taboo patterns.

To avoid certain well known issues in crowdsourced paraphrasing [26], we incorporated additional checks among the task validators: (i) checking for duplicates, by comparing the workers' contribution to the input seed and examples, after preprocessing (lemmatizing and lowercasing), (ii) avoiding gibberish, as in [15], (iii) ensuring the paraphrases feature the parameters (or slots) in the input seed. If a worker's contribution failed to pass these checks, and the prompt-specific checks, the worker was informed of the issue and reminded of the instructions.

4   Experiment Design

The experiment is set to explore whether our approach can effectively steer the crowd towards syntactic variations. We focus on the impact of the syntactic control introduced on relevant dimensions such a syntactic diversity and pattern distribution as well as important crowdsourcing metrics such as task effort. We compare our approach to state-of-the art workflows and assess their ability to generate syntactic variations. In what follows we summarize the design of the

---

[3] We set $k = 2$ as prompts from prior art typically include two examples [17].

experiment, and provide additional details on datasets, annotations, and data analysis as supplementary materials.[4]

Datasets. We considered seed utterances representing a broad set of intents and domains, drawn from three relevant datasets. We selected 20 seeds from ParaQuality [26], a dataset that contains seed utterances (and their paraphrases) for intents from domains including Scopus, Spotify, Open Weather, Gmail, AWS, among other services. All seven intents from the SNIPS dataset [5] were also considered, randomly sampling three utterances per intent to be used as seeds. Finally, we used utterances from the ATIS dataset [7], where intents corresponds to interactions with a flight-booking bot. We considered the top-5 intents from the training set[5] and sampled 10 utterances (2 per intent) as seeds for our experiment. The resulting dataset contains 51 seed utterances for a total of 24 intents. We provide the list of input seeds as part of our supplementary material.

Experimental Conditions. For the experimental conditions, we chose as baselines the three multi-stage approaches to diversity from the literature (see Sect. 2). We considered these as meaningful baselines as they had the potential to introduce syntactic variations, whereas the approaches focused on lexical diversity were not considered, due to their focus on word-level changes (e.g., replacing words by synonyms) rather than syntax. We compared these baselines to our two strategies based on taboo and example patterns.

All baseline conditions follow the reference state-of-the-art workflow (see Sect. 3.1) with two rounds ($r = 2$). They rely on the same baseline prompt that simply queries for three paraphrases for a given input seed, but implement different seed selection strategies. The ❶ *baseline* condition comprises a workflow that uses the baseline prompt for paraphrase generation and random sampling [10] for seed selection, which substitutes the each seed from the previous round (r_{i-1}) with one correct paraphrase. The ❷ *baseline-cw* condition represents a similar workflow but the seed selection step chooses 8 valid paraphrases per input seed (instead of one), mimicking the Chinese whispers approach [17]. Similarly, the ❸ *baseline-outliers* condition constitute a workflow that for seed selection, it selects one semantic outlier (but correct) paraphrase per input seed, resembling [12].

The two other experimental conditions constitute our approach. Both shared the same extended workflow, and as the baseline conditions were conducted in two rounds. The ❹ *patterns by example* condition sets a workflow where the pattern selection step chooses the bottom-k patterns as targets, and these are used to set up the pattern by example prompt for paraphrase generation. The ❺ *taboo patterns* condition, instead, sets the top-k patterns as targets, and these are used to set up the taboo patterns prompt to elicit paraphrases from workers. We set $k = 2$ for both prompts (i.e., workers are shown two example paraphrases). In these workflows, the seed selection step does not update the input seeds in X

---

[4] Online supplementary material available at https://tinyurl.com/caise-2022-diversity.

[5] We used the dataset available at https://www.kaggle.com/siddhadev/atis-dataset-from-ms-cntk. The top-5 intents are those with the highest number of training items.

(i.e., subsequent rounds use the same seeds). We should note that the specific task designs were refined through internal and external pilots.

Procedure. We conducted two full rounds of the pipeline shown in Fig. 1. The first round (r_1) helped to bootstrap a dataset of curated paraphrases for the 51 seeds of the experiment. This round was shared by all the experimental conditions, using the baseline prompt for paraphrase generation. The bootstrap round collected 1224 paraphrases in total (24 per seed). The paraphrase validation was performed manually by the researchers as explained in the next subsection.

The second and main round (r_2) of the experiment ran all the experimental conditions in parallel, using as input the output dataset from the bootstrap round. In this context, we applied the seed selection, pattern selection and prompts configured based on the specific experimental condition.

Table 1. Relevance criteria used in manual paraphrase validation [28]. Paraphrases correspond to the intent BookTaxi and seed *"Request a taxi from the airport to home"*

Criteria	Examples mistake
Semantic similarity to seed	*Where do I need to go to pick a taxi from airport to home?* (asking for location)
No extra parameter/slots should be added	*I need a taxi from the airport to home for tomorrow*
Generalizations and specializations beyond the scope of the intent are not allowed	*How can I get home from the airport?* (generalization)
Only spelling mistakes such as missing/duplicated articles and typos are tolerated	*Now get a taxi to make me from the airport to my home*
Slot values should not be swapped	I need a taxi from home to the airport
The paraphrase should contain the action	~~*Request*~~ *A taxi from the airport to home*
Turning the original intent into a "composite intent" is not allowed	*Search a taxi from the airport to home and __book__ it for me*
Example valid paraphrase:	*Please book a taxi from the airport to home*

We ran the experiment on Toloka and recruited workers who had passed an English test (set by the platform) and were ranked top-40%. In all conditions, except for *baseline-cw*, each seed was assigned to 8 workers, and each worker wrote 3 paraphrases for a seed (yielding 24 paraphrases per input seed). Since *baseline-cw* relies on 8 seeds per intent, instead of one, we assigned one seed (yielding a total of 24 paraphrases as in the other conditions). Workers were paid 0.15 USD per solved prompt. This reward stems from multiple pilots aimed to estimate task completion time and target a minimum hourly wage.

Paraphrase Validation. A manual validation of the two rounds was performed based on as set of criteria informed by previous work on crowdsourced paraphrasing mistakes [28], which we summarize in Table 1. Two researchers first annotated a small sample of paraphrases to calibrate the criteria, to then tag a 20% of randomly selected seeds, from which a random 20% of paraphrases were selected. The resulting inter-coder agreement was 95%. After this, the researchers split the rest of the dataset and independently performed the annotation. The researchers were condition-blinded, meaning that all paraphrases from all conditions were mixed together with the associated condition hidden, to avoid any condition induced bias. As part of this process, the researchers also labeled borderline cases, and potentially valid paraphrases with minor typos or grammar mistakes. Borderline cases were discussed between the researchers resolved by consensus. The minor typos and mistakes were fixed in a clean version to minimize the chances of generating incorrect parse trees [19].

Data Analysis. In understanding the effectiveness of our approach, we focus first on its ability to inform syntactic variations, i.e., the ability of the proposed prompts to steer workers away or towards the target prompts. For this, we use a measure of *syntactic similarity* proposed in [4] to compare target patterns with produced paraphrases. This metric applies the tree edit distance algorithm (TED) between two (full) syntax parse trees, after removing word tokens. Here, a low value suggests a high syntactic similarity, i.e., less number of edits in the syntax tree of one sentence to transform into the other.

We then focus on the impact of prompts on the quality of the resulting paraphrases as measured by metrics of semantic relevance, general and syntactic diversity, and the resulting pattern distribution. We should note that quality in crowdsourced paraphrasing is a much more involved concept (see [28]), and that here we focus specifically on how the elicited variations influence diversity and syntactic properties, while also assessing that resulting paraphrases are still semantically related and valid. For *semantic relevance* we rely on the manual paraphrase evaluation criteria previously described, and a complementary metric, BertScore [29], which is an automatic text similarity metric[6] based on contextual embeddings. For general *diversity*, we adopted DIV [11], computes diversity at corpus level by calculating n-grams changes between all pairs of utterances sharing the same intent. To measure *syntactic diversity* we relied on the syntactic similarity metric and applied to all pairs of utterances sharing the same intent to compute the mean syntactic distance. We also characterized the resulting *pattern distribution*, and observed to what extent the number of paraphrases per pattern were balanced. In particular, the mean distance of the paraphrase count per pattern in a seed to a uniform distribution.

---

[6] We stress that BertScore was not designed specifically for assessing paraphrases, so it does not capture the full range of criteria of the more specific manual evaluation.

Finally, we also assessed task completion time and task abandonment as a proxies for the percieved and actual effort incurred on workers.

5   Results

We collected a total of 7344 paraphrases from 877 workers, obtained from the bootstrap round (1224 paraphrases) and the main experiment (6120 paraphrases). We made the full crowdsourced dataset available[7], and summarize the distribution by condition in Table 2. While we have an overall high participation and representation of workers across conditions, some conditions attracted more participants (we discuss some reasons in Sect. 5.3).

5.1   Impact on the Relevance of Crowdsourced Paraphrases

The results of the relevance by condition can be seen in Table 2 for the manual and automatic assessment. While improving relevance was not the focus of this work, we analyzed relevance to understand whether the experimental conditions impacted negatively on this quality dimension.

Human Judgement. Even though the baseline conditions rely on the same baseline prompt, the seed selection strategy had an effect on the relevance of resulting paraphrases. We can see that BASE-OUT featured the lowest number of relevant paraphrases among the baselines (56.29%), which we attribute to having a semantic outlier as input seed. Albeit still relevant, the outlier might be pushing workers to contribute paraphrases that get semantically further from

Table 2. Summary of metrics and dataset distribution for the experimental conditions

Dataset	BASE	BASE-OUT	BASE-CW	PAT-TABOO	PAT-EXAMP
N	1224	1224	1224	1224	1224
Workers	203	209	166	164	135
Relevance	BASE	BASE-OUT	BASE-CW	PAT-TABOO	PAT-EXAMP
%Manual	**67.24**	56.29	63.56	53.10	65.60
BertScore	0.516	0.489	0.522	0.501	**0.528**
Diversity	BASE	BASE-OUT	BASE-CW	PAT-TABOO	PAT-EXAMP
S-Novel	3	2	3	**5**	**5**
S-TED$_{main}$	12.06	11.99	7.82	**15.58**	15.35
S-TED$_{workflow}$	12.36	12.95	11.27	**14.02**	13.82
DIV$_{main}$	0.677	0.672	0.494	0.729	**0.730**
DIV$_{workflow}$	0.691	0.706	0.666	**0.710**	0.703

---

[7] The datasets can be found at https://github.com/jorgeramirez/syntactic-diversity.

the original seed (i.e., seed in the bootstrap round). In the literature, BASE-CW has also shown to produce less relevant paraphrases from the initial seed at each iteration [10], but in our experiments having based the seed selection on valid paraphrases reduced this effect (63.56%). We can see having BASE rely on random sampling for seed selection strategy resulted in a higher percentage of relevant paraphrases (67.24%) We see PAT-EXAMP coming second (65.6%) to the performance of the baseline (BASE), hinting that the specific steering strategy did not affect negatively on the relevance. However, PAT-TABOO came last (53.1%), suggesting that workers experienced difficulties contributing with paraphrases that avoided the taboo patterns. We expand on this aspect in Sect. 5.3.

Automatic Assessment. By applying BertScore to the paraphrases we can see similar performances across conditions, but again with the conditions with the semantic outliers (BASE-OUT) and taboo patterns (PAT-TABOO) ranked last. We note that while BertScore has shown to correlate well with human judgement [29], the manual assessment relied on more specific criteria (see Table 1).

5.2   Guiding the Crowd Towards Syntactic Variations

We analyze the effectiveness of the proposed pipeline to steer the process towards syntactic variations by assessing: the syntactic control introduced by the prompts, the impact on diversity, and the overall pattern distribution. This analysis is performed over the subset of relevant paraphrases (manual evaluation).

Syntactic Control. We started by assessing the level of syntactic control introduced by the proposed prompts. In the case of *taboo patterns*, the validators incorporated as part of the prompt design were effective in avoiding paraphrases featuring the given patterns. We observed no paraphrases matching the patterns presented as taboo. As for *patterns by example*, we also look at the conformity of paraphrases with the syntactic examples introduced by the prompt. Recall that patterns by example does not enforce conformity with the target patterns but use them to prime workers. Indeed, we see only a 19% of paraphrases in this condition matching the exact pattern of the examples shown to the workers. Taking the baseline prompt as a reference, the priming effect in this case results in 15% of paraphrases featuring the same pattern as the seed seen by the workers.

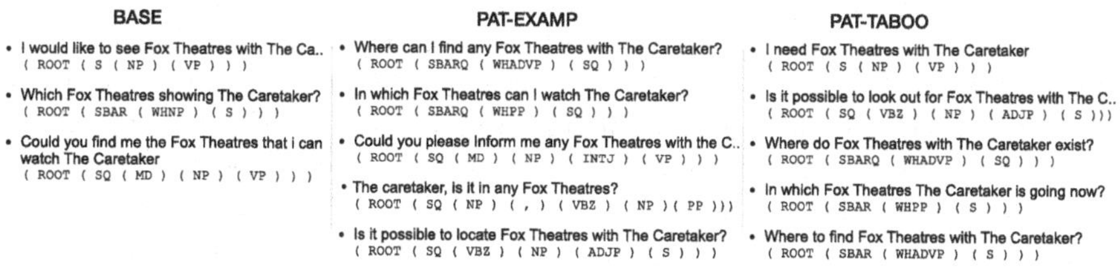

Fig. 3. Novel patterns and representative paraphrases for the seed *"find Fox Theatres with The Caretaker"*, illustrating results generated by BASE and the proposed prompts.

The syntactic similarity metric (Sect. 4) shows the mean edit distance to be 14.70 for PAT-TABOO, which is a higher distance than the 11.92 for PAT-EXAMP. This indicates the ability of these prompts to guide the syntactic variations.

Syntactic Novelty. We then looked at the mean number of *unique syntax patterns* underlying the paraphrases contributed in each condition (main round only). Among the baselines, those where same seed is presented to all workers resulted in the lower mean number of unique patterns (BASE = 5 and BASE-OUT = 5). Chinese whispers did better (BASE-CW = 6) and we attribute this to workers being primed with different seeds. The syntax-aware conditions were more effective, with patterns by example taking the first spot (PAT-EXAMP = 8) followed by taboo patterns (BASE-CW = 7). This suggests that examples priming workers towards less represented syntax might steer workers towards more unique syntax variations.

Taking the entire workflow perspective, we then looked at the *novel syntax patterns* introduced by the conditions with respect to the bootstrap round. That is, we calculated for each condition how many unique patterns were not present in the bootstrap round. As shown in Table 2 (S-Novel row), both syntax-aware approaches were more effective than the baselines in eliciting novel syntactic variations. The Friedman test shows the differences between the conditions are statistically significant ($X_F^2(5) = 90.06269$, $p < .0001$). According to pairwise comparisons using the Wilcoxon signed-rank test (with Bonferroni correction), the number of novel patterns for PAT-TABOO and PAT-EXAMP is significantly higher than the baseline conditions ($p < .001$).

Diversity. We now look at the syntactic and general diversity metrics. Considering the paraphrases for the main round only (S-TED$_{main}$), we observe the syntactic-aware conditions featuring higher *syntactic diversity* than the baseline counterparts. Taboo patterns performed only slightly better (15.58) than patterns by example (15.35). Looking at the entire workflow (S-TED$_{workflow}$), the general trend still favors the syntactic-aware conditions. These results ultimately highlight the benefits of introducing the notion of patterns into the workflow, as seen by the syntactic diversity reached by the conditions rendering our approach.

We also assessed diversity with DIV. Focusing on the paraphrases for the main round (DIV$_{main}$), we see the syntax-aware conditions resulted in a higher mean DIV score than the baselines, with both conditions featuring virtually the same scores (DIV = 0.730). Among the baselines, BASE and BASE-OUT featured very similar scores (DIV = 0.678 and DIV = 0.672, respectively), leaving BASE-CW with a way lower performance than the rest of the conditions (DIV = 0.494). This means that when considering general diversity (lexical and syntactic) the proposed prompts still result in higher performance. Taking the workflow perspective to assess the contribution of the conditions to the bootstrap round, we see the scores balancing out (DIV$_{workflow}$). This indicates that the focus on syntactic variations might produce less lexically diverse paraphrases.

Pattern Distribution. Our analysis of the pattern distribution showed that the syntactic-aware conditions lead to a distribution that is closer than the baselines to an equal representation of syntax patterns. PAT-TABOO displayed the overall lowest mean distance (1.94). In prompting users to avoid the top two common patterns, taboo patterns elicited paraphrases distributed among other patterns. Pattern by example, instead, contributed to some extent those specific syntax patterns shown to the workers (19% conformity as discussed part of syntactic control). In general, in providing no syntactic guidance, the baselines contributed more to a long tail-type distribution, with fewer patterns dominating the dataset.

5.3 Impact on Task Effort

Overall, the syntactic-aware prompts demanded a higher level of effort from workers. The median task completion time was 287 s for BASE, 251 s for BASE-OUT, 244 s for BASE-CW, 321 s for PAT-TABOO, and 326 s for PAT-EXAMP. A Kruskal-Wallis test indicates the differences are significant ($H(4) = 42.56$, $p < .001$), with the Dunn's test of multiple comparisons (with Benjamini-Hochberg adjustment) showing PAT-TABOO and PAT-EXAMP were significantly slower than the baselines.

A high task abandonment was observed in the different experimental conditions—ranging from 45% to 67%. While this is common in crowdsourcing tasks, the task abandonment topped at 47% for the different baselines but was higher for patterns by example (57%) and taboo patterns (67%). Both PAT-EXAMP and PAT-TABOO introduced additional requirements to the task, making the it more challenging. Especially for PAT-TABOO, paraphrases needed to feature a pattern different than a seed and examples, and judging by the resulting relevance, this led to comparatively fewer valid paraphrases.

6 Discussion and Conclusion

Our results provided insights into the effectiveness of the syntactic-aware approach, and shed light into the extent to which the assumptions of diversity of the baseline approaches apply. We summarize our main findings below.

The Syntactic Control is Effective in Eliciting Unique and Novel Syntax Patterns. The proposed prompts were effective in guiding workers towards (or away from) specific syntax, as indicated by the conformity and syntax similarity metrics. This control ultimately yields a higher number of unique syntax patterns, showing the potential of running our approach in a unique round (e.g., with input from experts). When taking a workflow perspective, our approach elicited more novel syntax (almost double) when compared to the literature.

Effective in Eliciting Syntactically Diverse Paraphrases. Our results confirm the added benefits of steering individual workers towards (or away) specific syntax patterns, in eliciting paraphrases featuring more diverse syntax structures (S-TED); these results applied when considering one or two rounds.

Reduced Long-Tail Effect with Syntactic Guidance. We have seen that our syntactic-aware approach is able to elicit more uniform pattern distributions, while the baselines with no guidance lead to paraphrases accumulated around certain patterns. In particular, we observed taboo patterns to contribute more to this uniformity than patterns by example.

Higher Perceived and Actual Task Effort in Syntax-Aware Prompts. The proposed prompts were generally more challenging for workers as indicated by the higher task completion time and abandonment, especially for taboo patterns. Asking workers to avoid popular structures incur in effort that can lead to higher abandonment as well as more non-relevant results.

The above results tell us that improvements in syntactic diversity will come at the price of an increased task effort (23%–25% more effort and, therefore, budget). This makes our proposal a suitable approach when looking to effectively inject novel and more diverse syntactic structures, but not necessarily as a general approach. However, having specialized mechanisms, as the ones proposed in the paper, can provide workflow designers with more control over the type of variations introduced depending on the goal (e.g., generating adversarial examples, training a model). Indeed, combining techniques in paraphrasing workflows and ensembles is an emerging strategy in paraphrase acquisition [2].

Limitations. Despite the systematic approach we followed to the experimentation, we should note some existing limitations. The differences in perceived task difficulty affected participant distribution between conditions, but in eliciting high number of paraphrases per conditions we ensured a high and representative minimum. The experiments were run on the crowdsourcing platform Toloka, which has a majority of crowd workers from east European countries. We mitigated this limitation by engaging workers with proven English level.

Conclusion. This paper empirically showed how a pipeline that incorporates a workflow and prompts informed by syntax patterns could guide the crowdsourcing process towards producing syntactic variations. Comparing to state-of-the-art baselines, our approach results in higher syntactic diversity and more uniform pattern distribution in the generated dataset, albeit with demanding more effort from the crowd. Our ongoing and future work investigates workflows that rely on combinations of techniques and prompts, including automatic approaches.

References

1. Bapat, R., Kucherbaev, P., Bozzon, A.: Effective crowdsourced generation of training data for chatbots natural language understanding. In: Mikkonen, T., Klamma, R., Hernández, J. (eds.) ICWE 2018. LNCS, vol. 10845, pp. 114–128. Springer, Cham (2018). https://doi.org/10.1007/978-3-319-91662-0_8
2. Berro, A., Baez, M., Benatallah, B., Benabdeslem, K., Fard, M.-A.Y.Z.: Automated paraphrase generation with over-generation and pruning services. In: Hacid, H., Kao, O., Mecella, M., Moha, N., Paik, H. (eds.) ICSOC 2021. LNCS, vol. 13121, pp. 400–414. Springer, Cham (2021). https://doi.org/10.1007/978-3-030-91431-8_25
3. Berro, A., et al.: An extensible and reusable pipeline for automated utterance paraphrases. In: Proceedings of the VLDB Endowment (2021)
4. Chen, M., et al.: Controllable paraphrase generation with a syntactic exemplar. In: ACL (2019)

5. Coucke, A., et al.: Snips voice platform: an embedded spoken language understanding system for private-by-design voice interfaces. CoRR abs/1805.10190 (2018)
6. Goyal, T., Durrett, G.: Neural syntactic preordering for controlled paraphrase generation. In: ACL (2020)
7. Hemphill, C.T., et al.: The ATIS spoken language systems pilot corpus. In: Workshop Held at Hidden Valley, Pennsylvania, USA (1990)
8. Huang, K.H., Chang, K.W.: Generating syntactically controlled paraphrases without using annotated parallel pairs. arXiv preprint arXiv:2101.10579 (2021)
9. Iyyer, M., et al.: Adversarial example generation with syntactically controlled paraphrase networks. In: NAACL (2018)
10. Jiang, Y., Kummerfeld, J.K., Lasecki, W.S.: Understanding task design trade-offs in crowdsourced paraphrase collection. In: ACL (2017)
11. Kang, Y., et al.: Data collection for dialogue system: a startup perspective. In: Proceedings of the HLT, vol. 3, pp. 33–40 (2018)
12. Larson, S., et al.: Outlier detection for improved data quality and diversity in dialog systems. In: NAACL-HLT (2019)
13. Larson, S., et al.: Iterative feature mining for constraint-based data collection to increase data diversity and model robustness. In: EMNLP (2020)
14. Lee, W., et al.: Effective quality assurance for data labels through crowdsourcing and domain expert collaboration. In: EDBT (2018)
15. Liu, P., Liu, T.: Optimizing the design and cost for crowdsourced conversational utterances. In: KDD-DCCL (2019)
16. Manning, C.D., et al.: The Stanford CoreNLP natural language processing toolkit. In: ACL (2014)
17. Negri, M., et al.: Chinese whispers: cooperative paraphrase acquisition. In: LREC (2012)
18. Park, S., et al.: Paraphrase diversification using counterfactual debiasing. In: AAAI (2019)
19. Qi, P., et al.: Stanza: a Python natural language processing toolkit for many human languages. In: ACL (2020)
20. Ravichander, A., et al.: How would you say it? Eliciting lexically diverse dialogue for supervised semantic parsing. In: SIGDIAL (2017)
21. Su, Y., et al.: Building natural language interfaces to web APIs. In: CIKM (2017)
22. Thompson, B., Post, M.: Paraphrase generation as zero-shot multilingual translation. arXiv:2008.04935 (2020)
23. Wang, W.Y., et al.: Crowdsourcing the acquisition of natural language corpora: methods and observations. In: (SLT) (2012)
24. Wasow, T., Perfors, A., Beaver, D.: The puzzle of ambiguity. Morphology and the web of grammar: essays in memory of Steven G. Lapointe, pp. 265–282 (2005)
25. Xu, Q., et al.: D-page: Diverse paraphrase generation. arXiv:1808.04364 (2018)
26. Yaghoub-Zadeh-Fard, M., et al.: A study of incorrect paraphrases in crowdsourced user utterances. In: NAACL-HLT (2019)
27. Yaghoub-Zadeh-Fard, M., et al.: Dynamic word recommendation to obtain diverse crowdsourced paraphrases of user utterances. In: IUI (2020)
28. Yaghoub-Zadeh-Fard, M., et al.: User utterance acquisition for training task-oriented bots: a review of challenges, techniques and opportunities. IC (2020)
29. Zhang, T., et al.: BERTScore: evaluating text generation with BERT. arXiv:1904.09675 (2019)

A Subject-aware Attention Hierarchical Tagger for Joint Entity and Relation Extraction

Yawei Zhao[✉][ID] and Xiang Li[ID]

School of Engineering Sciences, University of Chinese Academy of Sciences,
Beijing, China
zhaoyw@ucas.edu.cn, lixiang194@mails.ucas.edu.cn

Abstract. Joint entity and relation extraction aims to detect entities and relations from unstructured text by a single model. This task becomes challenging due to the problem of overlapping relational triples and the lack of internal interaction of triples. In this paper, we propose a **S**ubject-aware **A**ttention **H**ierarchical **T**agger (SAHT) to overcome these challenges. Firstly, this model identifies all subjects through a subject tagger. Secondly, the subject-aware attention mechanism that incorporates the subject features is designed to construct the specific sentence representation for each subject. Finally, the object multi-relation tagger is utilized to extract objects and relations by this representation, and this process is regarded as a multi-label task. Based on this hierarchical extraction, SAHT can make full use of the internal characteristics of subjects to closely contact with the corresponding objects and relations. Experiments on two public datasets demonstrate that our SAHT achieves significant improvement in extracting overlapping relational triples compared with previous joint extraction models.

Keywords: Entity recognition · Relation extraction · Overlapping relational triples · Attention mechanism

1 Introduction

Extracting entities and relations from unstructured text is a key technology for automatic knowledge graph construction, which has received increasing attention in recent years. The extraction task of entities and relations aims to extract triples containing entity pairs and their semantic relations, represented as (*subject, relation, object*).

Now this extraction task is divided into two main strategies: the pipeline method and the joint method. The pipeline method decomposes the task into two steps, that is, first extract entities and then determine the relations between them [5,12]. However, due to the complete separation of two steps, this method ignores the correlation between entities and relations, and also leads to the error

© Springer Nature Switzerland AG 2022
X. Franch et al. (Eds.): CAiSE 2022, LNCS 13295, pp. 270–284, 2022.
https://doi.org/10.1007/978-3-031-07472-1_16

Normal	The [United States] president [Donald Trump] met with [Jack Ma], the founder of [Alibaba]. ⬇ ⎰ (Donald Trump, President_of, United States) ⎱ (Jack Ma, Company_Founder, Alibaba)
SEO	[Steve Jobs], the founder of [Apple], was born in [San Francisco]. ⬇ ⎰ (**Steve Jobs**, Place_of_Birth, San Francisco) ⎱ (**Steve Jobs**, Company_Founder, Apple)
EPO	[Beijing], the capital of [China], is one of the most populous cities in the world. ⬇ ⎰ (**China**, Capital, **Beijing**) ⎱ (**China**, Contains, **Beijing**)

Fig. 1. Examples of the Normal, SingleEntityOverlap (SEO) and EntityPairOverlap (EPO) classes. Overlapping entities are marked in bold.

propagation problem. The joint method is able to effectively integrate the information between entities and relations [14,16]. With the development of deep learning, some researchers [13,18] try to construct entity extractor and relation classifier through neural networks, and then jointly optimize the two subtasks. Despite their success, these models still predict entities and relations separately, thus not fully exploiting the connection between the two subtasks. Unlike previous works, Zheng et al. [26] fuse the two subtasks into a sequence labeling task that assigns each token one and only one entity-relation tag. But this tagging principle allows each token to only participate in one triple, which eventually causes incomplete extraction.

In fact, the reason for this incomplete extraction is not only that a sentence usually includes multiple triples, but also that there are different degrees of overlap between multiple triples. Zeng et al. [23] first consider the cases of overlapping relational triples and divide sentences into three classes according to the overlap degree, namely Normal, SingleEntityOverlap (SEO) and Entity-PairOverlap (EPO). As shown in Fig. 1, a sentence belongs to the Normal class when all of its triples have no overlapping entities. A sentence belongs to the SEO class when some of its triples share a single entity, such as *Steve Jobs*. A sentence belongs to the EPO class when some of its triples have overlapping entity pair, such as *China* and *Beijing*. It is very common to appear these classes in texts, whereas most existing models only focus on the Normal class. To handle the other two classes, models based on the sequence-to-sequence (Seq2seq) framework have been widely concerned. Such models directly generate triples by a Seq2seq framework with copy mechanism [21–23]. But the triples generated by this method are very limited. Therefore, Dai et al. [6] design several tagging sequences according to the position of each query word to simultaneously label entities and relations. Nevertheless, this tagging process does not implement the internal dependencies of subjects, objects and relations. As the improvement, a strategy of decomposing triples and sequentially performing sequence labeling for multiple turns is adopted. However, these models [4,20] either do not fully address all cases of overlapping relational triples, or they just apply the results of the previous part directly to the subsequent extraction work, ignoring internal interactions of triples.

In summary, although above models have achieved some results, the joint extraction of entity and relation remains challenging, mainly in: (1) How to solve all cases of overlapping relation triples and improve the quality of extracted triples; (2) How to enhance the internal interaction of triples. It is well known that decomposing a complex task into easier parts is an efficient solution [4, 24]. We believe that the problem of overlapping relational triples cannot be completely solved by a single process, so triples are extracted hierarchically. In addition, the role of subject in a triple cannot be ignored because its related semantics can guide the extraction of subsequent object and relation. Accordingly, we incorporate a subject-aware attention mechanism into a hierarchical architecture to realize the internal interaction of triples.

Specifically, we propose a subject-aware attention hierarchical tagger (SAHT) for joint entity and relation extraction. It extracts entities and relations hierarchically, which is divided into subject tagger, subject-aware attention mechanism, and object multi-relation tagger. Firstly, the subject tagger labels the entity type at the start and end positions of each subject. Secondly, according to each subject extracted, the subject-aware attention mechanism constructs its specific sentence representation by fusing the type and semantic information of the subject. Finally, through the specific sentence representation, the object multi-relation tagger labels the relation type at the start and end positions of each corresponding object, and this tagging process is regarded as a multi-label task. In summary, the main contribution of this paper are as follows:

- We propose a joint entity and relation extraction model named SAHT. Due to its hierarchical extraction strategy and the integrated multi-label strategy, SAHT is more suitable for the extraction of overlapping relational triples.
- We apply the subject-aware attention mechanism to construct different sentence representations under different subject features. This attention mechanism provides fine-grained information related to the subject for the object and relation extraction, which realizes the internal interaction of triples.
- We evaluate SAHT on two public datasets: NYT and WebNLG. Experiments show that SAHT obtains more competitive evaluation results than previous joint extraction models.

2   Related Work

Several methods have been extensively studied to extract both entities and relations. Traditional works employ a pipelined manner to address this task, which recognizes entities first and then extracts their relations [5, 12]. However, this pipelined method misses the interaction between entity recognition and relation classification, which causes error propagation. To alleviate this problem, several joint models have been proposed. Traditional joint models rely on feature engineering and require relevant tools for feature extraction [14, 16]. Consequently, most of the current joint models are based on neural network architectures, which are roughly divided into Table, Seq2seq and Tagging methods.

Table method [10,14] enumerates all token pairs for each sentence to construct a table. This method maps the joint extraction problem to a table-filling problem in that entity and relation labels are assigned to table cells. To reduce the sparsity caused by enumerating all token pairs, researchers [13,18] first predict all entities, and then perform table-filling operations for all entity pairs. In addition, they usually utilize a parameter sharing strategy to jointly optimize the two subtasks. Recently, Fu et al. [7] also divide the task into two parts and improve their dependencies by relation-weighted graph convolutional network (GCN). However, these models still suffer from redundant predictions because there are fewer entity pairs with relations.

Seq2seq method extracts all triples sequentially. Zeng et al. [23] introduce a Seq2seq framework with copy mechanism to extract overlapping relational triples, but this model cannot predict multi-token entities and order of triples. In response to these problems, a multi-task learning strategy [21] and a reinforcement learning method [22] are respectively applied to such framework. Even so, triples generated by these models based on the Seq2seq framework are limited.

Tagging method provides effective tagging schemes for entity and relation extraction. Zheng et al. [26] propose a general tagging strategy that assigns an entity-relation label to each token in a sentence. Nevertheless, this strategy neglects the problem of overlapping relational triples. Bekoulis et al. [2,3] first recognize all entities, and then regard the step of relation extraction as a multi-head selection problem to extract overlapping triples. Dai et al. [6] design n tagging sequences for a sentence of length n, but this way is too complex and ignores the connection between subjects, objects and relations. In particular, Yu et al. [4] also carry out a multi-round labeling strategy, which labels objects and relations after labeling subjects. But they believe that each relation is mutually exclusive, which leads to poor performance in the situation with EPO class. Wei et al. [20] adopt the same strategy, but ignore the rich semantic information provided by subjects to objects and relations.

In this paper, we explore an efficient tagging scheme to jointly extract triples in sentences while addressing all the problems in above models. On the one hand, our hierarchical architecture can extract all overlapping relational triples. On the other hand, we incorporate entity features and attention mechanism into this hierarchical architecture to better utilize the interaction information of triples. Attention mechanism [1] is originally derived from machine translation task, and now has been successfully applied to other natural language processing (NLP) tasks [19,25].

3   Methodology

In this section, we first introduce our tagging scheme, which converts the extraction of entities and relations into several sequence labeling problems. Then we explain in detail the subject-aware attention hierarchical tagger based on this tagging scheme.

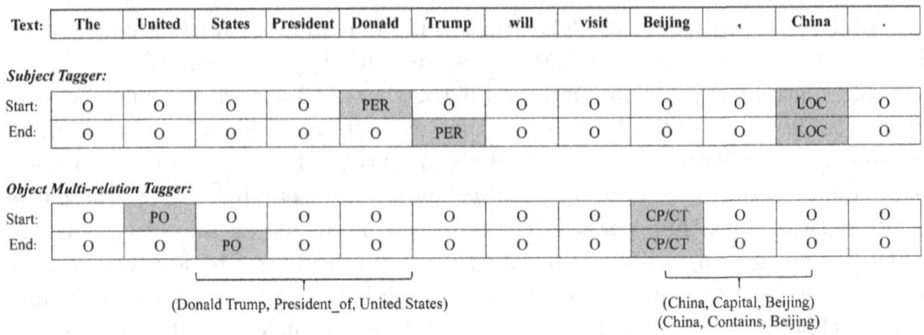

Text:	The	United	States	President	Donald	Trump	will	visit	Beijing	,	China	.
Subject Tagger:												
Start:	O	O	O	O	PER	O	O	O	O	O	LOC	O
End:	O	O	O	O	O	PER	O	O	O	O	LOC	O
Object Multi-relation Tagger:												
Start:	O	PO	O	O	O	O	O	O	CP/CT	O	O	O
End:	O	O	PO	O	O	O	O	O	CP/CT	O	O	O

(Donald Trump, President_of, United States)   (China, Capital, Beijing)
(China, Contains, Beijing)

Fig. 2. An example of our tagging scheme. PER is short for entity type PERSON, and LOC is short for LOCATION. PO is short for relation type *President_of*, CP is short for *Capital*, and CT is short for *Contains*.

3.1   Tagging Scheme

In our tagging scheme, we use subject tagger and object multi-relation tagger to perform sequence labeling tasks. An entity may include multiple tokens, so we respectively predict positions of the entity, including the start and the end. Subject tagger labels its type at positions of each subject. As for each subject extracted, object multi-relation tagger labels the semantic relations between them at positions of each object. Because the corresponding objects and relations are extracted for each subject, the SEO class can be tackled (as shown in Fig. 1). For the EPO class, the solution adopted is to predict multiple relations at positions of each object, transforming it into a multi-label problem.

Figure 2 illustrates our tagging scheme. According to the text in the example, subjects include *Donald Trump* and *China*. Therefore, the subject tagger labels their types PERSON and LOCATION at the start and end positions of these two subjects, and only cares about those words that belong to the subjects. For each subject, the object multi-relation tagger only focuses on those words that belong to the corresponding objects. Like the subject *Donald Trump*, the object multi-relation tagger extracts the object *United States*, and labels the relation *President_of* between them in the corresponding positions. Similarly, the subject *China* corresponds to the object *Beijing*. Because of the two relations between them, the start and end positions of *Beijing* are labeled as *Capital* and *Contains*. Besides, other unrelated words are labeled as *O* (Outside). Finally, we extract three triples as explained in Fig. 2, including (*Donald Trump, President_of, United States*), (*China, Capital, Beijing*) and (*China, Contains, Beijing*).

3.2   Subject-aware Attention Hierarchical Tagger

Based on our tagging scheme, Fig. 3 gives an overview of SAHT. First, we encode the input text by a shared BiLSTM encoder to provide support for the subject

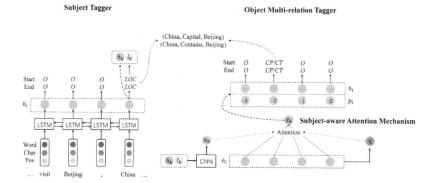

Fig. 3. The architecture of SAHT. The left part is subject tagger, and the right are subject-aware attention mechanism and object multi-relation tagger. By this hierarchical extraction, SAHT returns the triples (*China, Capital, Beijing*) and (*China, Contains, Beijing*).

tagger. For each subject extracted by the subject tagger, we design a subject-aware attention mechanism to obtain the specific sentence representation under subject features. Next given this specific sentence representation, we extract objects and relations through the object multi-relation tagger that combines the subject and context information. Finally, we implement this joint training method of hierarchical extraction.

Shared Encoder. Given a sentence that contains n words $S = \{x_1, x_2, ..., x_n\}$, we denote $\mathbf{x}_i$ as the representation of the i-th word. Formally, the $\mathbf{x}_i$ is calculated by concatenating the pre-trained word embeddings $\mathbf{w}_i^w$, the part-of-speech (POS) embeddings $\mathbf{w}_i^p$ and the character-based word features $\mathbf{w}_i^c$. The pre-trained word embeddings are obtained by Glove [15], and the character-based word features are extracted by a convolution neural network (CNN). Then we utilize BiLSTM to capture the dependencies of the words through the final word representation sequence $\{\mathbf{x}_1, \mathbf{x}_2, ..., \mathbf{x}_n\}$:

$$\mathbf{x}_i = [\mathbf{w}_i^w; \mathbf{w}_i^p; \mathbf{w}_i^c] \tag{1}$$

$$\mathbf{h}_i = [\overrightarrow{LSTM}(\mathbf{x}_i); \overleftarrow{LSTM}(\mathbf{x}_i)] \tag{2}$$

We concatenate the forward and backward LSTM hidden states as the contextual sentence representation $\{\mathbf{h}_1, \mathbf{h}_2, ..., \mathbf{h}_n\}$.

Subject Tagger. Subject tagger aims to identify all the subjects in the input sentence. As discussed in the tagging scheme, the positions of entities are divided into start and end. As shown in the left part of Fig. 3, the subject tagger takes the contextual sentence representation generated by the shared encoder as input, and adopts two linear layers to predict their type at the positions of subjects.

For each token, the detailed operations of the subject tagger are as follows:

$$P(y_i^{sub\_s}) = Softmax(\mathbf{W}_{sub}^s \mathbf{h}_i + \mathbf{b}_{sub}^s) \tag{3}$$

$$P(y_i^{sub\_e}) = Softmax(\mathbf{W}_{sub}^e \mathbf{h}_i + \mathbf{b}_{sub}^e) \tag{4}$$

where $\mathbf{W}_{sub}^s$, $\mathbf{b}_{sub}^s$, $\mathbf{W}_{sub}^e$ and $\mathbf{b}_{sub}^e$ are the trainable parameters, and softmax is selected as the activation function. Finally, $P(y_i^{sub\_s})$ and $P(y_i^{sub\_e})$ represent the probability of tagging the entity type when the i-th token is predicted as the start and end positions of a subject.

We optimize the following loss function L_{sub_t} for the subject tagger, where $\hat{y}_i^{sub\_s}$ and $\hat{y}_i^{sub\_e}$ are the true start and end tags of the i-th token, and n is the length of the input sentence:

$$L_{sub\_t} = \frac{1}{n} \sum_{i=1}^{n} -(logP(y_i^{sub\_s} = \hat{y}_i^{sub\_s}) + logP(y_i^{sub\_e} = \hat{y}_i^{sub\_e})) \tag{5}$$

Subject-aware Attention Mechanism. In a triple, the extraction of object and relation is based on the subject and context information. The potentially different characteristics of each subject lead to different objects and relations. According to the shared encoder and subject tagger, we can get subject features including its semantics and type. To this end, we utilize a CNN (a convolution layer with a max-pooling layer) to extract the subject features:

$$\mathbf{u}_k = CNN([\mathbf{h}_k; \mathbf{l}_k]) \tag{6}$$

where $\mathbf{h}_k$ represents the hidden state of the k-th subject extracted, and $\mathbf{l}_k$ represents its type embedding. Note that the subject may contain several tokens, so $\mathbf{h}_k$ and $\mathbf{l}_k$ contain all the representations between the start and end positions of the subject.

The words in the sentence play different roles under the different subjects, resulting in different contextual information. Based on this assumption, we propose a subject-aware attention mechanism as illustrated in the lower right part of Fig. 3, which calculates the relevant weight for each word in sentence by the subject features. The attention score α_{ik} is obtained as follows:

$$\mathbf{q} = avg\{\mathbf{h}_1, \mathbf{h}_2, ..., \mathbf{h}_n\} \tag{7}$$

$$\mathbf{a}_{ik} = \mathbf{v}^T tanh(\mathbf{W}_k \mathbf{u}_k + \mathbf{W}_q \mathbf{q} + \mathbf{W}_h \mathbf{h}_i) \tag{8}$$

$$\alpha_{ik} = \frac{exp(\mathbf{a}_{ik})}{\sum_{j=1}^{n} exp(\mathbf{a}_{jk})} \tag{9}$$

where $\mathbf{v}$, $\mathbf{W}_k$, $\mathbf{W}_q$ and $\mathbf{W}_h$ are the trainable parameters. Here $\mathbf{q}$ indicates the representation of the global sentence information. In this way, the attention score measures the importance of each word under the subject features, and integrates the entire sentence information. Finally, the sentence representation $\mathbf{z}_k$ under the subject features $\mathbf{u}_k$ is calculated as follows:

$$\mathbf{z}_k = \sum_{i=1}^{n} \alpha_{ik} \mathbf{h}_i \tag{10}$$

Object Multi-relation Tagger. The object multi-relation tagger aims to identify all the objects and the relations. Similar to the subject tagger, the object multi-relation tagger also uses two linear layers to predict the relation type at the start and end positions of objects. The difference is that its input fully incorporates the information of the corresponding subject. As detailed in the upper right part of Fig. 3, we not only add the sentence representation $\mathbf{z}_k$ that fused subject features, but also inspired by Zhang et al. [25] to add the distance representation $\mathbf{p}_i$ between each token and subject. Specifically, the final input representation $\bar{\mathbf{h}}_i$ is denoted as follows:

$$\bar{\mathbf{h}}_i = [\mathbf{h}_i; \mathbf{z}_k; \mathbf{p}_i] \tag{11}$$

The other difference is that the object multi-relation tagger needs to implement a multi-label strategy at the positions of the object, because there are multiple relations between entity pair. Therefore, here two binary classifiers are adopted to determine whether the current token is the start and end positions of the object for each relation type. The detailed operations of the object multi-relation tagger are as follows:

$$P(y_i^{obj\text{-}s}) = Sigmoid(\mathbf{W}_{obj}^s \bar{\mathbf{h}}_i + \mathbf{b}_{obj}^s) \tag{12}$$

$$P(y_i^{obj\text{-}e}) = Sigmoid(\mathbf{W}_{obj}^e \bar{\mathbf{h}}_i + \mathbf{b}_{obj}^e) \tag{13}$$

where $\mathbf{W}_{obj}^s$, $\mathbf{b}_{obj}^s$, $\mathbf{W}_{obj}^e$ and $\mathbf{b}_{obj}^e$ are the trainable parameters, and sigmoid is selected as the activation function. Finally, $P(y_i^{obj\text{-}s})$ and $P(y_i^{obj\text{-}e})$ represent the probability that the i-th token is predicted to be the start and end positions of an object under a certain relation.

We optimize the following loss function L_{obj_t} for the object multi-relation tagger, where $\hat{y}_i^{obj\text{-}s}$ and $\hat{y}_i^{obj\text{-}e}$ are the true start and end tags of the i-th token, and n is the length of the input sentence:

$$L_{obj\_t} = \frac{1}{n} \sum_{j \in (obj\_s, obj\_e)} \sum_{i=1}^{n} -(\hat{y}_i^j log P(y_i^j) + (1 - \hat{y}_i^j) log(1 - P(y_i^j))) \tag{14}$$

Training. According to Eq. 5 and Eq. 14, we get two losses: L_{sub_t} and L_{obj_t}. Therefore, we add them together as the final loss to achieve joint training. Note that during training, we randomly select a gold subject for each input sentence to extract objects and relations. However, all predicted subjects are considered during the test.

4   Experiments

4.1   Datasets

We use two public datasets to evaluate our model: NYT and WebNLG. NYT dataset is constructed by distant supervision method [17], which contains 24

Table 1. The number of sentences for Normal, SEO and EPO classes. Note that a sentence can belong to both SEO class and EPO class.

Class	NYT		WebNLG	
	Train	Test	Train	Test
Normal	37013	3266	1596	246
SEO	14735	1297	3406	457
EPO	9782	978	227	26
ALL	56195	5000	5019	703

relation types. WebNLG dataset is built for natural language generation tasks [8], which contains 246 relation types. The sentences in NYT and WebNLG datasets contain rich overlapping relational triples, hence both datasets are suitable for evaluating our model performance. The number of sentences for Normal, SEO and EPO classes are illustrated in Table 1. To compare with previous models, we split datasets according to the data preprocessing method provided by Zeng et al.[1]. For the NYT dataset, they selected 5000 sentences as the test set in the filtered dataset. For the WebNLG dataset, they used the original development set containing 703 sentences as the test set.

4.2   Implementation Details

We set the dimension of word embedding to 300, POS embedding to 20, and character embedding to 50. The distance embedding between the subject and each word is set to 20 dimensions. The window size of CNN for character-based word feature vector is set to 3, the maximum length of words is set to 15, and the number of filters is 50. Both the hidden state of BiLSTM encoder and the attention are set to 200 dimensions. Moreover, the window size of CNN for subject feature extraction is set to 2, and the number of filters is 200. Parameter optimization is performed using Adam [11] with learning rate 0.001 and batch size 64. To prevent overfitting, dropout with a rate of 0.4 is applied to the word embedding and the hidden state.

4.3   Baselines and Evaluation Metrics

We choose the following models as baselines for comparison: (1) NovelTagging [26] adopts a unified entity-relation tagging strategy to jointly decode entities and relations; (2) CopyRE [23] handles the extraction task through a Seq2seq model and designs multiple decoders; (3) MultiHead [3] first performs the entity recognition task, and then considers relation extraction as a multi-head selection problem; (4) GraphRel [7] introduces the relation-weighted GCN to realize

---

[1] The filtered dataset can be downloaded at: https://github.com/xiangrongzeng/copy_re..

Table 2. Main results of the compared models on NYT and WebNLG datasets.

Model	NYT			WebNLG		
	Precision	Recall	F1	Precision	Recall	F1
NovelTagging	0.328	0.306	0.317	0.525	0.193	0.283
CopyRE	0.610	0.566	0.587	0.377	0.364	0.371
MultiHead	0.607	0.586	0.596	0.575	0.541	0.557
GraphRel	0.639	0.60	0.619	0.447	0.411	0.429
CopyMTL	0.757	0.687	0.720	0.580	0.549	0.564
OrderRL	0.779	0.672	0.721	0.633	0.599	0.616
ETL-Span	0.855	0.717	0.780	0.843	0.820	0.831
SAHT	0.834	**0.806**	**0.819**	**0.858**	0.819	**0.839**

the interaction of entities and relations; (5) CopyMTL [21] applies a multi-task learning framework on the basis of CopyRE to solve the problem of entity extraction with multiple tokens; (6) OrderRL [22] integrates the reinforcement learning method in the Seq2seq model to deal with the extraction order of triples; (7) ETL-Span [4] first identifies all subjects, and then extracts the corresponding objects and relations.

We use standard Precision, Recall and F1 score as evaluation metrics. A triple is considered correct if and only if its entity pair and relation type are all correct, where the entity is considered correct when its start and end offsets are correct.

4.4   Experimental Results and Analyses

Main Results. Table 2 shows the experimental results on NYT and WebNLG datasets. For ETL-Span that also uses the BiLSTM encoder and decomposes the extraction task, SAHT improves 3.9% and 0.8% in F1 score respectively on NYT and WebNLG dataset. Compared with other models, the advantages of SAHT are more prominent. Such performance gains are attributed to the following reasons: (1) Subject-aware attention mechanism provides a selection process for the object and relation extraction, aiming to select contexts related to the subject; (2) Object multi-relation tagger introduces a multi-label strategy, making it possible to extract more relation types.

In addition, we find that SAHT improves more on the NYT dataset than the WebNLG dataset. Because ETL-Span can only tag a relation type at positions of the object, which leads to a failure in the EPO class. However, our SAHT is able to tag multiple relations. According to statistics, the proportion of EPO instances in the NYT test set is 19.6%, while the proportion of EPO instances in the WebNLG test set is only 3.7%. Therefore, the performance of SAHT is similar to that of ETL-Span for the WebNLG data set. Moreover, we notice that SAHT is better than models based on Seq2seq, such as CopyRE, CopyMTL and

Table 3. Ablation study of SAHT on NYT dataset.

Model	Precision	Recall	F1
SAHT	**0.834**	**0.806**	**0.819**
– Subject type	0.832	0.788	0.810
– CNN for subject features	0.824	0.798	0.811
– Subject-aware attention	0.826	0.794	0.809

OrderRL. Because the hierarchical extraction strategy adopted is more conducive to entity and relation extraction than the generation method.

Ablation Study. We conduct ablation experiments on the NYT dataset to verify the effectiveness of subject type, CNN for subject features and subject-aware attention. We delete one component at a time to observe the changes in experimental results, which are summarized in Table 3. (1) We utilize the subject tagger to label 0/1 instead of the entity type when extracting subjects, and remove l_k in Eq. 6. The experimental results show that the entity type is helpful for the extraction task; (2) We add and average the subject information to replace the CNN module. The experimental results show that the CNN module is beneficial to capture local features of the subject; (3) We ignore the operation of subject-aware attention, that is, replace u_k in Eq. 6 with z_k in Eq. 11. We believe that the shallow information of subject is learned when directly using its feature representation, so the evaluation metrics all drop. In contrast, subject-aware attention can automatically capture the subject-related part in the sentence, which ensures the quality of subsequent extraction of objects and relations.

Results on Different Triple Types. To illustrate the extraction ability of our model for overlapping relational triples, we conduct further experiments on the NYT dataset. The sentences in the test set are divided into three overlapping

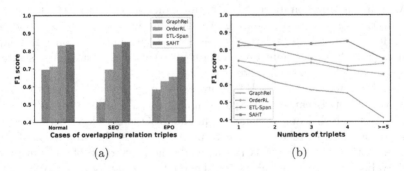

Fig. 4. Results on different sentence types for NYT dataset. (a) F1 score by different cases of overlapping relational triples. (b) F1 score by different numbers of triplets.

Table 4. Case study of SAHT on NYT dataset.

Texts	True triples	Predicted triples
Since the toppling of [Saddam Hussein], American officials tried unsuccessfully to disband [Iraq]'s myriad private armies, from Kurdish pesh merga in the mountainous north to the black-clad Mahdi Army patrolling poor Shiite enclaves in [Baghdad] and [Basra]	(Saddam Hussein, Nationality, Iraq) (Saddam Hussein, Place_of_Birth, Iraq) (Saddam Hussein, Place_of_Death, Iraq) (Iraq, Capital, Baghdad) (Iraq, Contains, Baghdad) (Iraq, Contains, Basra)	(Saddam Hussein, Nationality, Iraq) (Saddam Hussein, Place_of_Birth, Iraq) (Saddam Hussein, Place_of_Death, Iraq) (Iraq, Capital, Baghdad) (Iraq, Contains, Baghdad), (Iraq Contains, Basra)
[John D'Amico], a member of the Hockey Hall of Fame who worked as a National Hockey League linesman for 23 years, died Sunday in [Toronto].	(John D'Amico, Place_Lived, Toronto)	(John D'Amico, Place_Lived, Toronto) (John D'Amico, Place_of_Death, Toronto)

classes, like Normal, SEO and EPO. We select several latest models as baselines for comparison. As demonstrated in Fig. 4(a), SAHT outperforms all other models, especially for the EPO class. The success factor of our model in the EPO class is that the multi-label strategy adopted can predict multiple relations of the entity pair. For other classes, our unique subject-aware attention mechanism makes full use of subject information to realize the internal interaction of triples, and improve the results by a hierarchical strategy.

Furthermore, we also verify the capability of our model to extract different numbers of triples in a sentence. There are five categories of sentences in the NYT test set, indicating that the number of triples is 1, 2, 3, 4, and >=5. As shown in Fig. 4(b), SAHT make significant progress compared with other models. Although the F1 score of SAHT decreases when the number of triples >=5, it still shows more stable performance overall. These two experiments fully indicate that SAHT is more suitable for handling complex joint extraction situations.

Case Study. We select two texts from the NYT test set for case study, as shown in Table 4. In the first case, the predicted results of our model are still the same as the ground truth for such complex sentence. This sentence contains six triples, of which multiple triples belong not only to the SEO class, but also to the EPO class. For example, the entity *Iraq* appears in all triples and implements multiple relations with multiple different entities. This case further illustrates the strong extraction performance of our model for complex texts.

In the second case, our model predicts two triples of which only one is true. Nevertheless, the entity pair *John D'Amico* and *Toronto* should have another relation *Place_of_Death* from the semantics of this sentence. In practical applications, most of the existing datasets are incompletely labeled due to expensive labor costs. We find that SAHT can be used as a triple tagging tool in incompletely labeled datasets. This is a significant advantage of SAHT in that it is able to extract more possible triples in texts.

However, SAHT is limited if there are no more possibilities in the original sentence. For some NLP platforms, such as AllenNLP [9], they deal with too many tasks but not enough focus. For the joint entity and relation extraction task, they are better at simple and delicate sentences, while our model is more suitable to sentences with overlapping relational triples.

5   Conclusion

In this paper, we propose a subject-aware attention hierarchical tagger named SAHT for the joint entity and relation extraction task. It adopts hierarchical and multi-label strategies to decompose the extraction of overlapping relational triples into several sequence labeling tasks, and applies the subject-aware attention mechanism to realize the internal interaction of triples. Experimental results on NYT and WebNLG datasets show that SAHT gains great improvement. Further experiments and analysis demonstrate the advantages of SAHT in dealing with cases of overlapping and multiple triples. Notably, SAHT plays an important role in incompletely labeled datasets by tagging more possible triples. In the future, our work will focus on how to further improve performance and consider integrating our model into a general extractor to achieve more NLP tasks.

Acknowledgment. This work was supported in part by the National Key Research and Development Program of China under Grants 2020YFC1807104.

References

1. Bahdanau, D., Cho, K., Bengio, Y.: Neural machine translation by jointly learning to align and translate. In: 3rd International Conference on Learning Representations (2015)
2. Bekoulis, G., Deleu, J., Demeester, T., Develder, C.: Adversarial training for multi-context joint entity and relation extraction. In: Proceedings of the 2018 Conference on Empirical Methods in Natural Language Processing, pp. 2830–2836 (2018)
3. Bekoulis, G., Deleu, J., Demeester, T., Develder, C.: Joint entity recognition and relation extraction as a multi-head selection problem. Expert Syst. Appl. **114**, 34–45 (2018)
4. Bowen, Y., Zhang, Z., Su, J., Wang, Y., Liu, T., Wang, B., Li, S.: Joint extraction of entities and relations based on a novel decomposition strategy. In: Proceedings of the European Conference on Artificial Intelligence (2020)
5. Chan, Y.S., Roth, D.: Exploiting syntactico-semantic structures for relation extraction. In: Proceedings of the 49th Annual Meeting of the Association for Computational Linguistics: Human Language Technologies, pp. 551–560 (2011)
6. Dai, D., Xiao, X., Lyu, Y., Dou, S., She, Q., Wang, H.: Joint extraction of entities and overlapping relations using position-attentive sequence labeling. In: Proceedings of the AAAI Conference on Artificial Intelligence, pp. 6300–6308 (2019)
7. Fu, T.J., Li, P.H., Ma, W.Y.: Graphrel: modeling text as relational graphs for joint entity and relation extraction. In: Proceedings of the 57th Annual Meeting of the Association for Computational Linguistics, pp. 1409–1418 (2019)
8. Gardent, C., Shimorina, A., Narayan, S., Perez-Beltrachini, L.: Creating training corpora for NLG micro-planning. In: 55th annual meeting of the Association for Computational Linguistics (ACL) (2017)

9. Gardner, M., et al.: AllenNLP: a deep semantic natural language processing platform. In: Proceedings of Workshop for NLP Open Source Software (NLP-OSS), pp. 1–6, July 2018

10. Gupta, P., Schütze, H., Andrassy, B.: Table filling multi-task recurrent neural network for joint entity and relation extraction. In: Proceedings of COLING 2016, the 26th International Conference on Computational Linguistics: Technical Papers, pp. 2537–2547, December 2016

11. Kingma, D.P., Ba, J.: Adam: A method for stochastic optimization. In: 3rd International Conference on Learning Representations (2015)

12. Mintz, M., Bills, S., Snow, R., Jurafsky, D.: Distant supervision for relation extraction without labeled data. In: Proceedings of the Joint Conference of the 47th Annual Meeting of the ACL and the 4th IJCNLP of the AFNLP, pp. 1003–1011 (2009)

13. Miwa, M., Bansal, M.: End-to-end relation extraction using LSTMs on sequences and tree structures. In: Proceedings of the 54th Annual Meeting of the Association for Computational Linguistics (Volume 1: Long Papers), pp. 1105–1116 (2016)

14. Miwa, M., Sasaki, Y.: Modeling joint entity and relation extraction with table representation. In: Proceedings of the 2014 Conference on Empirical Methods in Natural Language Processing (EMNLP), pp. 1858–1869 (2014)

15. Pennington, J., Socher, R., Manning, C.D.: Glove: global vectors for word representation. In: Proceedings of the 2014 Conference on Empirical Methods in Natural Language Processing (EMNLP), pp. 1532–1543 (2014)

16. Ren, X., et al.: Cotype: joint extraction of typed entities and relations with knowledge bases. In: Proceedings of the 26th International Conference on World Wide Web, pp. 1015–1024 (2017)

17. Riedel, S., Yao, L., McCallum, A.: Modeling relations and their mentions without labeled text. In: Joint European Conference on Machine Learning and Knowledge Discovery in Databases, pp. 148–163 (2010)

18. Sun, C., et al.: Extracting entities and relations with joint minimum risk training. In: Proceedings of the 2018 Conference on Empirical Methods in Natural Language Processing, pp. 2256–2265, October–November 2018

19. Vaswani, A., et al.: Attention is all you need. In: Advances in Neural Information Processing Systems, vol. 30 (2017)

20. Wei, Z., Su, J., Wang, Y., Tian, Y., Chang, Y.: A novel cascade binary tagging framework for relational triple extraction. In: Proceedings of the 58th Annual Meeting of the Association for Computational Linguistics, pp. 1476–1488 (2020)

21. Zeng, D., Zhang, H., Liu, Q.: Copymtl: copy mechanism for joint extraction of entities and relations with multi-task learning. In: Proceedings of the AAAI Conference on Artificial Intelligence, pp. 9507–9514 (2020)

22. Zeng, X., He, S., Zeng, D., Liu, K., Liu, S., Zhao, J.: Learning the extraction order of multiple relational facts in a sentence with reinforcement learning. In: Proceedings of the 2019 Conference on EMNLP and the 9th IJCNLP, pp. 367–377 (2019)

23. Zeng, X., Zeng, D., He, S., Liu, K., Zhao, J.: Extracting relational facts by an end-to-end neural model with copy mechanism. In: Proceedings of the 56th Annual Meeting of the Association for Computational Linguistics, pp. 506–514 (2018)

24. Zhang, X., Goldwasser, D.: Sentiment tagging with partial labels using modular architectures. In: Proceedings of the 57th Annual Meeting of the Association for Computational Linguistics, pp. 579–590, July 2019

25. Zhang, Y., Zhong, V., Chen, D., Angeli, G., Manning, C.D.: Position-aware attention and supervised data improve slot filling. In: Proceedings of the 2017 Conference on Empirical Methods in Natural Language Processing, pp. 35–45 (2017)
26. Zheng, S., Wang, F., Bao, H., Hao, Y., Zhou, P., Xu, B.: Joint extraction of entities and relations based on a novel tagging scheme. In: Proceedings of the 55th Annual Meeting of the Association for Computational Linguistics, pp. 1227–1236 (2017)

Process Monitoring and Simulation

Estimating Activity Start Timestamps in the Presence of Waiting Times via Process Simulation

Claudia Fracca[1,2], Massimiliano de Leoni[1(✉)], Fabio Asnicar[2], and Alessandro Turco[2]

[1] University of Padua, Padua, Italy
deleoni@math.unipd.it
[2] ESTECO SpA, Trieste, Italy
{fracca,asnicar,turco}@esteco.com

Abstract. Process Mining aims to analyze and improve processes to enable organizations to provide better services or products. The starting point of Process Mining is an event log that is extracted from the organization's information systems that support the process' executions. Several techniques require event logs to record the timestamp when process' activities have started and been completed. Unfortunately, information systems do not always record the timestamps when process activities start, preventing the application of these techniques. This paper reports on a technique based on process simulation that aims to estimate the start event timestamps when missing. In a nutshell, the idea is to build an accurate process model from the initial event log without start timestamps, to simulate it with alternative activity-duration profiles, and to select the model with the profile that generates the runs that are the closest to the initial log. This activity-duration profile is used to add the missing, start timestamps to the initial log. Experiments were conducted with two event logs with start timestamps, and aimed at their rediscovery: the results show our estimation of the start event timestamps is more accurate than the state of the art.

Keywords: Start timestamps · Time perspective · Waiting time · Log repair · Process simulation

1 Introduction

Process mining is a research discipline that sits between machine learning and data mining on the one hand and process modeling and analysis on the other hand. The idea behind it is to discover, monitor, and improve real processes to provide better services or products by extracting knowledge from event logs readily available in today's organization's information systems [1]. As briefly elaborated in Sect. 2, several process mining techniques need event logs that store both start and complete life-cycle transitions of activities. These techniques, e.g., [8, 13], specifically rely on knowing the timestamps when process' activities were started. Unfortunately, most information systems that support the process executions only record the completion of the different process' phases

© Springer Nature Switzerland AG 2022
X. Franch et al. (Eds.): CAiSE 2022, LNCS 13295, pp. 287–303, 2022.
https://doi.org/10.1007/978-3-031-07472-1_17

and activities. As a consequence, event logs often only store the events when activities are completed, thus missing events when activities started.

Existing techniques naïvely estimate the timestamps related to the start of activities under the assumptions that activity instances start as soon as possible, namely when the activities that come before are completed and a suitable resource is available (e.g.,[14]). This corresponds to assuming no waiting times, and it is often unrealistic in practice [4, 8]: *(i)* resources work on multiple processes and continuously switch from one to the other while event logs refer to one process, *(ii)* take breaks during the working days (e.g., when tired), *(iii)* carry on additional duties that lead no trail in the event logs (e.g., when answering the phone).

This paper proposes a new technique to estimate the timestamps of the start events, namely of the events related to the start of activities. The starting point is an event log $\mathcal{L}$ of a given process $\mathcal{P}$, and a simulation model $\mathcal{M}$ of $\mathcal{P}$. This simulation model consists of a model of a process $\mathcal{P}$ (e.g., a BPMN model)[1] extended with additional information for the simulation aspects (case inter-arrival time, activity durations, routing probabilities, resource allocation, and utilization, etc.). The simulation model can be constructed by combining different process mining techniques (see the case studies discussed in Sect. 5). In a nutshell, the idea is that event log $\mathcal{L}$ is augmented with the missing start events using n different activity duration profiles, thus obtaining a set of event logs $\mathcal{L}_1, \ldots, \mathcal{L}_n$. Using each log $\mathcal{L}_i$, it is possible to compute the activity duration probabilities to be included in $\mathcal{M}$, lead to n simulation model $\mathcal{M}_1, \ldots, \mathcal{M}_n$. Each simulation model $\mathcal{M}_i$ is used to generate a simulated event log $\mathcal{L}_i^{sim}$. The technique returns the event log $\mathcal{L}_i$ with start events such that the corresponding simulation model $\mathcal{M}_i$ generated an event log $\mathcal{L}_i^{sim}$ that is the closest to $\mathcal{L}$ with the respect that certain properties, such as the probability distribution of trace duration.

The technique has been evaluated in two case studies using two event logs about the process for credential recognition of students in a university and a purchase to pay process (cf. Sect. 5). These event logs contain both start and completion events. For the evaluation, we removed the start events and aimed to rediscover through our technique. The evaluation outcome shows that the our technique was able to rediscover start-event timestamps that were more accurate than what could be achieved by existing techniques that naïvely assume no waiting time.

2   Related Work

Several techniques rely on the availability of the start activity timestamps, namely the timestamps of the start events. In business process simulation complete and precise event logs, including information about completion and start of activities, is highly valuable and necessary as the starting point for many simulation parameters discovery algorithms, such as techniques for multi-perspective information extraction. For example, Martin et al. [13] present a discover technique for the resource availability calendars and in [8] a technique to detect the presence of multitasking. These techniques start from event log assuming both start and complete life-cycle transitions of activities. A complete event log is necessary as input also for certain techniques for automated discovery

---

[1] https://www.bpmn.org/.

of business process models, such as in [10], to better distinguish between true concurrency and interleaving. The construction of a business simulation model that accurately model resources also requires the presence of the timestamps of start and completion events [5, 18]. In particular, Carmargo et al. [5] confirm the difficulty to find real-life event logs with both start and completion timestamps, thus limiting the applicability of their simulation model construction. The same applies to techniques to discover the resource availability calendars [13] or the detection of multitasking [8].

The problem of estimating the start activity timestamps is somehow related to queue mining, namely assessing the queue lengths and waiting times of process activities [2, 19]. However, queue mining uses stochastic approaches to provide probability distributions, confidence intervals, etc., without focusing on computing punctual values for each start event. Rogge-Solti and Weske use stochastic Petri nets to determine the probability distribution of the duration of process instances, but their goal is not to estimate the start-event timestamps [17]. Techniques to repair, clean, and restore event data before analysis have been suggested in other works: classical trace alignment algorithms are used to restore missing events but without restoring their timestamps [6]. In [7], Denisov et al. propose an alternative technique to restoring missing timestamps, under the strong assumption, which does not generally hold, that the model is acyclic and contains no parallelism constructions (e.g., AND splits). Pegoraro et al. have proposed a repertoire of process mining techniques over missing event data, but they have aimed at process discovery and conformance checking [15, 16], without focusing on repairing event logs andto adding the missing start events and their respective timestamps.

3 Preliminaries

An event log and a simulation model are the starting points of our framework to estimate the starting timestamps for computing the activity durations. Since we do not need to make any assumption of the modeling language and the simulation parameters, we remain very abstract in this respect. A **simulation model** is a tuple $\mathcal{M} = (\mathcal{N}, \mathcal{S})$ composed by a business process model $\mathcal{N}$ (e.g., a BPMN model), and a set $\mathcal{S}$ of the parameters to define the simulation specifications for the different process perspectives (time, resources, decisions, etc.). Examples of parameters are the case inter-arrival time, activity durations, routing probabilities, resource allocation, and utilization. Events and logs are defined as follows.

Definition 1 (Events). *Let $\mathcal{A}$ be a set of activity labels. Let $\mathcal{T}$ be the universe of timestamps. Let $\mathcal{R}$ be a set of resources. Let $\mathcal{I} = \{$start, complete$\}$ be the life-cycle information. An event $e \in \mathcal{A} \times \mathcal{T} \times \mathcal{R} \times \mathcal{I}$ is a tuple consisting of an activity label, a timestamp of occurrence, a resource performing the activity, and the life-cycle information.*

In the remainder, given an event $e = (a, t, r, i)$, $act(e) = a$ returns the activity label, $time(e) = t$ returns the timestamp, $res(e) = r$ returns the resource, and $life(e) = i$ is the information whether e refers to the starting or completion of an activity.

In practice, several event logs are composed of events where the life-cycle information

Table 1. A fragment of an event log of a train ticket compensation request procedure.

Case ID	Activity	Timestamp	Resource	Life-cycle
123	Check Ticket	16-07-21 00:21	Paul	Complete
124	Register Request	16-07-21 00:27	Ann	Start
124	Register Request	16-07-21 00:32	Ann	Complete
124	Check Ticket	16-07-21 00:40	Paul	Start
124	Check Ticket	16-07-21 00:49	Paul	Complete
123	Decide	16-07-21 00:50	Ann	Start
123	Decide	16-07-21 01:10	Ann	Complete
124	Decide	16-07-21 01:20	Ann	Start

is not present. In this case, we assume that those events refer to the completion. The log might include events not related to starting or completing activities; we ignore those events. Additional details attached to the events are also ignored. Sometimes events carry a payload consisting of attributes taking on values; we also ignore these attributes.

Definition 2 (Traces and Event Logs). *Let $\mathcal{E}_A$ the universe of the events defined over a set A of (labels of) activities. A trace $\sigma = \langle e_1, \ldots, e_m \rangle \in \mathcal{E}_A^*$ is a sequence of events, with the constraint that, for all $0 < i < j \leq m$, $time(e_i) \leq time(e_j)$. An event log $\mathcal{L}$ is a set of traces, namely $\mathcal{L} \subset \mathcal{E}_A^*$.*

In the remainder, we use the shortcut $e \in \mathcal{L}$ to indicate that there is a trace $\sigma \in \mathcal{L}$ such that $e \in \sigma$. Also, the subscript A is omitted when it is clear from the context.

Example 1. Consider the fragment of an event log presented in Table 1. This event log contains information about the handling of a request for compensation of train tickets. The arrival of a ticket compensation request initiates a process instance. After the request is received, the ticket is checked, and a decision is made. The compensation request is either rejected or paid. Each case, identified by CASE ID, is composed of a list of events that has an activity label, a timestamp of occurrence, a resource performing the activity, and life-cycle information, i.e., starting or completion of activities. As mentioned before, we assume that the timestamps of the events are ordered within the case.

Definition 3 (Trace Duration). *Let $\sigma = \langle e_1, \ldots, e_m \rangle$ a trace in an event log $\mathcal{L}$. Let denote with $TD(\sigma)$ the trace duration related to the trace σ. A trace duration $TD(\sigma) = time(e_m) - time(e_1)$ is the difference between the timestamps of the last and the first event in the trace σ.*

Given an event log $\mathcal{L}$, we aim to compute the **probability distribution of trace durations of $\mathcal{L}$** as a function $\mathcal{D} : \mathbb{R}_0^+ \to [0, 1]$ that best fits the multiset of trace durations

$\uplus_{\sigma \in \mathcal{L}} TD(\sigma)$.[2] Note that the domain of function $\mathcal{D}$ coincides with the possible trace durations, namely any non-negative real value.

The discussion of our technique requires the introduction of the concept of the duration of an activity instance, namely the difference between the timestamp of the completion event and that of the start event:

Definition 4 (Activity Instance Duration). *Let $\sigma = \langle e_1, \ldots, e_i, \ldots, e_m \rangle$ be a trace in $\mathcal{L}$. Let $e_i \in \sigma$ be an event such that $life(e_i) = $ complete. Let e_j be the latest, previous event in σ referring to the starting of the same activity as e_i, namely $j < i$, $act(e_j) = act(e_i)$, $life(e_j) = $ start, and there is no start event for the same activity between the j-th and the i-th event, namely $\forall k \in]j, i[$. $act(e_k) \neq act(e_j) \lor life(e_k) \neq $ start. The duration of the activity instance related to the completion event e_i is $AD(e_i) = time(e_i) - time(e_j)$.*

Similarly, the concept of waiting time of an activity instance is necessary hereafter, intended as the difference between the timestamp of start event e and that of the latest event that precedes e in the trace:

Definition 5 (Activity Instance Waiting Time). *Let $\sigma = \langle e_1, \ldots, e_i, \ldots, e_m \rangle$ be a trace in $\mathcal{L}$. Let $e_i \in \sigma$ be an event such that $life(e_i) = $ start. Let e_j be the latest, previous event in σ referring to the completion of an activity, namely $j < i$, $life(e_j) = $ complete, and there is no completion event between j and i, namely $\forall k \in]j, i[$. $life(e_k) \neq $ complete. The waiting time of the activity instance related to the start event e_i is $WD(e_i) = time(e_i) - time(e_j)$.*

Example 2. Considering the example before. Let take case 124 and the event related to the activity *Check Ticket*. In this case, the start timestamp is 16-07-21 00:40, and the completion timestamp is 16-07-21 00:49, and the previously completed timestamp is 16-07-21 00:32. Therefore, in this case, the activity instance duration is equal to 9 min, and the activity instance waiting time is equal to 8 min.

Let $\mathcal{L}$ be an event log defined over a set $\mathcal{A}$ of activities. For each activity $a \in \mathcal{A}$, it is possible to compute the **activity-duration probability distribution** as the probability distribution functions $d_{p,a} : \mathbb{R}_0^+ \longrightarrow [0, 1]$ that best fits the multisets $\uplus_{e \in \mathcal{L}|act(e)=a} AD(e)$ of duration of instances of activity a in $\mathcal{L}$. Similarly, the **waiting time probability distribution** of a is the distribution $d_{w,a} : \mathbb{R}_0^+ \longrightarrow [0, 1]$ that best fits the multisets $\uplus_{e \in \mathcal{L}|act(e)=a} WD(e)$ of waiting times for instances of activity a ins $\mathcal{L}$.

In the remainder, we denote with $dist\_p : \mathcal{A} \to S$, the function that for each activity a returns $d_{p,a}$ the activity-duration probability distribution in the universe S of probability distribution functions $f : \mathbb{R}_0^+ \longrightarrow [0, 1]$. And with $dist\_w : \mathcal{A} \to S$ the function that returns for an activity a the waiting time probability distribution $d_{w,a}$.

The following definition presents the concept of a previous event in a trace by control-flow, which, given an event $e \in \sigma$ related to completion, represents the previous event in σ that also refers to a completion.

Definition 6 (Previous Event in a Trace by Control-Flow). *Let $\sigma = \langle e_1, \ldots, e_m \rangle$ a trace in an event log $\mathcal{L}$. For each $e_i \in \sigma$ s.t. $life(e_i) = $ complete and $\exists j < i :$*

---

[2] Symbol $\uplus$ indicates the union of elements to form a multiset.

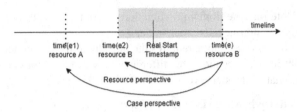

Fig. 1. Schema representing the concepts of previous event in a trace by control-flow and previous event performed by a resource. For the event e, $time(e)$ is the timestamp related to the event e, and $res(e) = resourceB$ the resource performing the activity $act(e)$. Looking at the trace perspective, e_1 is the previous event in a trace by control-flow $prev\_t_{\mathcal{L}}(e)$, and e_2 the previous event performed by a resource $prev\_r_{\mathcal{L}}(e)$ with $res(e_2) = res(e) = resourceB$. The green box represents the timeline range in which the event e could be started. (Color figure online)

$life(e_j) = \texttt{complete}$, *the previous event* $prev\_t_{\mathcal{L}}(e_i)$ *in a trace by control-flow related to the event* e_i, *is defined as follows:*

$$prev\_t_{\mathcal{L}}(e_i) = e_k \ s.t. \ life(e_k) = \texttt{complete} \ and \ \forall k < l < i \ life(e_l) \neq \texttt{complete}.$$

If the event log contains resource information, we can thus define the previous event $prev\_r_{\mathcal{L}}(e)$ as the completion event with the closest timestamp smaller than $time(e)$, among those referring to activities performed by the same resource $res(e)$:

Definition 7 (Previous Event Performed by a Resource). *Let e an event in the event log $\mathcal{L}$. Let now assume that $life(e) = \texttt{complete}$ and $\exists e_j \in \mathcal{L} : life(e_j) = \texttt{complete}$, $res(e_j) = res(e)$ and $time(e_j) < time(e)$. The previous event performed by the resource $res(e)$, is defined as follows:*

$$prev\_r_{\mathcal{L}}(e) = e_k \ s.t. \ life(e_k) = \texttt{complete}, \ res(e_k) = res(e) \ and$$
$$\nexists \ \hat{e} \in \mathcal{L} \mid res(\hat{e}) = res(e),$$
$$life(\hat{e}) = \texttt{complete}, \ and$$
$$time(prev\_r_{\mathcal{L}}(e)) \leq time(\hat{e}) \leq time(e).$$

In Fig. 1 a schema representing these two concepts. Note that, given an event $e \in \mathcal{L}$, $prev\_t_{\mathcal{L}}(e)$ and $prev\_r_{\mathcal{L}}(e)$ may not always be defined, e.g. when the current activity instance is the first one executed by a resource, or when the activity instance is the first one in a trace, or for the first activity instance recorded in the event log.

Example 3. Considering the example before. Let consider the case 123 and the event related to the activity *Decide* with life-cycle information equal to $\texttt{complete}$. In this case the event e is the tuple *(Decide*, 16-07-21 01:10, Ann, $\texttt{complete}$). For this event the related $prev\_t_{\mathcal{L}}(e)$ is the tuple *(Check Ticket*, 16-07-21 00:21, Paul, $\texttt{complete}$) and it is the previous event completed in the same trace 123. Therefore $time(prev\_t_{\mathcal{L}}(e))$ is equal to 16-07-21 00:21. And the related $prev\_r_{\mathcal{L}}(e)$ is *(Register Request*, 16-07-21 00:32, Ann, $\texttt{complete}$) and it is the previous completion event performed by the same resource Ann. Therefore $time(prev\_r_{\mathcal{L}}(e))$ is equal to 16-07-21 00:32.

Fig. 2. BPMN model related to the event log in Table 1.

The estimation of the timestamp related to the starting of activity requires defining the minimum timestamp when the activity could have started, considering the different process constraints, e.g., on resource and control flow. Given an event log $\mathcal{L}$, denoted the set of completion events in $\mathcal{L}$ with $E_{\mathcal{L}} = \{e \in \mathcal{L} : life(e) = \texttt{complete}\}$, this computation is abstracted as a *minimum-timestamp oracle* $mintime_{\mathcal{L}} : E_{\mathcal{L}} \to \mathcal{T}$ where $\mathcal{T}$ is the universe of timestamps. For each event in $e \in E_{\mathcal{L}}$, $mintime_{\mathcal{L}}(e)$ is the earliest timestamp when the activity instance related to e could have started.

The abstraction as a minimum-timestamp oracle is motivated by the fact this can be defined in multiple ways, also depending on the information available in the $\mathcal{L}$. As an example, if we have both defined for an event e the events $prev\_t_{\mathcal{L}}(e)$ and $prev\_r_{\mathcal{L}}(e)$, the related $mintime\_res\_time_{\mathcal{L}}(e) = max(time(prev\_t_{\mathcal{L}}(e)), time(prev\_r_{\mathcal{L}}(e)))$. Another example, if it is possible to compute $prev\_t_{\mathcal{L}}(e)$ but we do not have information about the resource perspective, then $mintime\_time_{\mathcal{L}}(e) = time(prev\_t_{\mathcal{L}}(e))$. In the remainder, when evident from the context, we omit the subscript $\mathcal{L}$.

Example 4. Considering the example before. Let consider the case 123 and the event related to the activity *Decide*, therefore $e = (Decide, 16\text{-}07\text{-}21\ 01{:}10, Ann, \texttt{complete})$. In this case the $mintime\_res\_time_{\mathcal{L}}(e)$ is equal to 16-07-21 00:32, i.e. the maximum between the $time(prev\_t_{\mathcal{L}}(e))$ and $time(prev\_r_{\mathcal{L}}(e))$.

4   Technique

In the remainder, event logs are assumed to contain no events related to the starting of activities. This is to keep the explanation simple: however, the extension is simple to tackle the hybrid case where a fraction of the start events are present.

Given an event log $\mathcal{L}$ without start events defined over a set $\mathcal{A}$ of activities, the technique aims to build a new event log $\mathcal{L}'$ that include the start events. In particular, for each trace $\sigma \in \mathcal{L}$, $\mathcal{L}'$ includes a trace σ' that contains every event of σ. For each event $e \in \sigma$, σ' additionally includes a matching start event e': $act(e') = act(e)$, $res(e') = res(e)$ and $life(e') = \texttt{start}$. The timestamp $time(e')$ needs to be estimated. To do so, we formulate the problem as finding a value for a parameter $\alpha(e) \in [0, 1]$ related to the event e such that:

$$time(e') = \alpha(e) \cdot mintime(e) + (1 - \alpha(e)) \cdot time(e) \qquad (1)$$

where $mintime(e)$ is some instance of the minimum-timestamp oracle (cf. Sect. 3). Note that, if $\alpha(e) = 0$, $time(e') = time(e)$, namely the duration of the activity instance to which e refers is zero. Conversely, if $\alpha(e) = 1$, $time(e') = mintime(e)$, namely the activity instance to which e refers starts at the earliest possible moment.

In practice, to keep the problem tractable, we assume to find the same $\alpha(e)$ for all events e related to the same activity a, namely:

$$time(e') = \alpha(a) \cdot mintime(e) + (1 - \alpha(a)) \cdot time(e) \tag{2}$$

where $act(e') = a$. The assumption is that waiting times for different instances of the same activity a are similar, i.e., these instances are executed by the same type of resources, which exhibit similar behavior. The remainder of this section details how our technique computes function $\alpha : \mathcal{A} \rightarrow [0,1]$, namely each value $\alpha(a)$ for every activity a.

Along with event log $\mathcal{L}$, we need an initial simulation model $\mathcal{M}_0 = (\mathcal{N}, \mathcal{S}_0)$ without a specification about activity durations.

Example 5. The event log in Table 1 could be potentially associated to a simulation model $\mathcal{M}_0 = (\mathcal{N}, \mathcal{S}_0)$ where $\mathcal{N}$ is the process model in Fig. 2, and the simulation parameters $\mathcal{S}_0$ contain: (i) the case inter-arrival time parameterized as an exponential distribution with mean 20 min, (ii) the routing probabilities for the XOR gateway: 65% for the Pay Compensation branch and 35% for the other, and (iii) a resources allocation where Ann performs the activities *Register Request* and *Decide*, while Paul does the others.

Given n functions $\alpha_1 : \mathcal{A} \rightarrow [0,1], \ldots, \alpha_n : \mathcal{A} \rightarrow [0,1]$, we extend the original event log $\mathcal{L}$ with the starting events computed using Eq. 2. Using $\alpha_j : \mathcal{A} \rightarrow [0,1]$, we obtain an event log $\mathcal{L}_j^{sc}$, which can be used to compute the probability distribution function $\mathcal{D}_j^{sc}$ of trace duration, along with the waiting time probability distribution $dist\_w_j^{sc}(a)$ for each activity $a \in \mathcal{A}$ (see Sect. 3).

The probability distributions $dist\_p_j^{sc}(a)$ for all $a \in \mathcal{A}$ can be added to the initial simulation model $\mathcal{M}_0 = (\mathcal{N}, \mathcal{S}_0)$, yielding a simulation model $(\mathcal{N}, \mathcal{S}_j)$. The simulation model $(\mathcal{N}, \mathcal{S}_j)$ can be run so as to obtain an event log $\mathcal{L}_j^{sim}$. Log $\mathcal{L}_j^{sim}$ can be used to compute the probability distribution function $\mathcal{D}_j^{sim}$ of trace duration, and the waiting time probability distribution function $dist\_w_j^{sim}(a)$ for each activity $a \in \mathcal{A}$.

Event logs $\mathcal{L}_j^{sc}$ and $\mathcal{L}_j^{sim}$ can now be compared considering the distance of the respective trace-duration distributions:

Definition 8 (Trace Duration Distance). *Let $\mathcal{L}_1$, $\mathcal{L}_2$ be two event logs. Let $\mathcal{D}_1 : \mathbb{R}_0^+ \rightarrow [0,1]$ and $\mathcal{D}_2 : \mathbb{R}_0^+ \rightarrow [0,1]$ be the probability distribution functions of the trace durations of $\mathcal{L}_1$ and $\mathcal{L}_2$ respectively. The trace duration distance is the integral difference between the probability distribution functions:* $\varepsilon_{(\mathcal{L}_1, \mathcal{L}_2)} = \int_0^{+\infty} |\mathcal{D}_1(x) - \mathcal{D}_2(x)| dx$.

Logs $\mathcal{L}_j^{sc}$ and $\mathcal{L}_j^{sim}$ can also be compared with respect to the distance of the waiting-time distributions:

Definition 9 (Waiting Time Distance). *Let $\mathcal{L}_1$, $\mathcal{L}_2$ be two event logs defined over the same set $\mathcal{A}$ of activities. For each activity $a \in A$, let $d_{w,a}^1 : \mathbb{R}_0^+ \rightarrow [0,1]$ and $d_{w,a}^2 : \mathbb{R}_0^+ \rightarrow [0,1]$ be the probability distribution functions of the waiting times for activity instance of a in $\mathcal{L}_1$ and $\mathcal{L}_2$, respectively. The waiting time distance for a is*

```
input  : Event log: L.
input  : Simulation model: M₀ = (N, S₀).
input  : Mintime function: mintime : E_L → T.
input  : Granularity parameter: δ.
α_best ← set_start_alpha(L, M₀, δ) ;
ε_best ← compute_distance(α_best, L, M₀, mintime) ;
for a ∈ activities(N) do
    Q_tried ← [α_best(a)] ;
    Q_next ← [prev_succ(α_best, δ), next_succ(α_best, δ)] ;
    while Q_next ≠ [] do
        α ← α_best ;
        α(a) ← pick_and_remove(Q_next) ;
        if α(a) ∉ Q_tried then
            Q_tried ← Q_tried ∪ [α(a)] ;
            ε ← compute_error(α, L, M₀, mintime) ;
            if ε ≤ ε_best then
                α_best ← α, ;
                ε_best ← ε;
                Q_next ← [prev_succ(α_best, δ), next_succ(α_best, δ)] ;
            end
        end
    end
end
return α_best

Function compute_distance(α, L, M₀, mintime) : ℝ₀⁺
    L^sc ← add_start_event(L, mintime, α) ;
    dist_p ← find_processing_time(L^sc) ;
    M ← set_duration_distribution(M₀, dist_p) ;
    L^sim ← simulate(M) ;
    logs_distance ← Δ(L^sc, L^sim) ;
    return logs_distance
end
```

Algorithm 1: Local search-based algorithm to estimate activity start timestamps via simulation.

the integral difference between the probability distribution functions of waiting times:
$\phi_{(\mathcal{L}_1, \mathcal{L}_2)}(a) = \int_0^{+\infty} |d^1_{w,a}(x) - d^2_{w,a}(x)| dx$.

As mentioned, for each alpha function $\alpha_k \in \{\alpha_1, \ldots, \alpha_n\}$, we obtain a real event log $\mathcal{L}^{sc}_k$ augmented with start events, and a simulated event log $\mathcal{L}^{sim}_k$. We opt for the α_k that minimizes the distance $\Delta(\mathcal{L}^{sc}_k, \mathcal{L}^{sim}_k)$ between $\mathcal{L}^{sc}_k$ and $\mathcal{L}^{sim}_k$, which consider the distances between the respective trace-duration and waiting-time distributions:

Definition 10 (Logs Distance). *Let $\mathcal{L}^{sc}$ be the original event log augmented with start events. Let $\mathcal{L}^{sim}$ be the event log obtained via simulation. Let $\varepsilon_{(\mathcal{L}^{sc}, \mathcal{L}^{sim})}$ be the trace duration distance for the two logs $\mathcal{L}^{sc}$ and $\mathcal{L}^{sim}$. Let $\phi_{(\mathcal{L}^{sc}, \mathcal{L}^{sim})}(a)$ be the waiting time distance for any activity $a \in \mathcal{A}$. The distance between $\mathcal{L}^{sc}$ and $\mathcal{L}^{sim}$ is computed as follows:*

$$\Delta(\mathcal{L}^{sc}, \mathcal{L}^{sim}) = \varepsilon_{(\mathcal{L}^{sc}, \mathcal{L}^{sim})} + \sum_{a \in \mathcal{A}} \phi_{(\mathcal{L}^{sc}, \mathcal{L}^{sim})}(a) \tag{3}$$

So far, the set of configurations were given. However, these configurations need to be computed on the fly to find a (sub)optimal minimum error. To this aim, we will use a local search based algorithm for this minimization problem. The pseudo-code in Algorithm 1. The proposed method takes as input an event log $\mathcal{L}$, an initial simulation model

$\mathcal{M}_0 = (\mathcal{N}, \mathcal{S}_0)$, a $mintime_{\mathcal{L}}$ function, and a granularity parameter $\delta \in (0, 1)$. Using the δ parameter we can define the succession $alpha\_succ(\delta) = \{x_t | x_t = x_{t-1} + \delta, x_0 = 0, x_t \leq 1\}$, in such way we can obtain a different configuration obtained via function $\alpha(a) = x_t$ for each activity $a \in \mathcal{A}$. For example, using the parameter $\delta = 0.1$, the succession is $alpha\_succ(\delta) = \{0, 0.1, 0.2, \ldots, 1\}$.

The first step of the Algorithm 1 is to initialize the function α with random values. Starting from the initial function α, we select one activity $a \in \mathcal{A}$ and try to optimize $\alpha(a)$ using local search. In particular, for each activity and the corresponding value $\alpha(a) = x_t \in alpha\_succ(\delta)$, for the next values of $\alpha(a)$ in $\mathcal{Q}_{next}$, we add the previous value $x_{t-1} \in alpha\_succ(\delta)$ and the consecutive value $x_{t+1} \in alpha\_succ(\delta)$. We store the value with the smallest logs distance and we keep going in the next updates in the direction with decreasing logs distance until no improvements are permitted, see Algorithm 1. To compute the logs distance given a configuration of the function α, we can create the new event log $\mathcal{L}^{sc}$ as discussed above, here abstracted as a function $add\_start\_event()$. The next step is, given the completed event log $\mathcal{L}^{sc}$, compute the function $dist\_p(a)$ that for each $a \in \mathcal{A}$. Then we incorporate the activity-duration probability distribution function $dist\_p()$ in the structure of the simulation model $\mathcal{M}_0$, obtaining the updated simulation model $\mathcal{M} = (\mathcal{N}, \mathcal{S})$. Given as input the simulation model $\mathcal{M} = (\mathcal{N}, \mathcal{S})$ the next step is to call the $simulate(\mathcal{M})$ function that calls a simulator and returns the simulated event log $\mathcal{L}^{sim}$ related to the simulation model $\mathcal{M}$. The last step is to calculate the logs distance $\Delta(\mathcal{L}^{sc}, \mathcal{L}^{sim})$, according to Eq. 3. If the logs distance decreases then we update the function α_{best} and the logs distance ϵ_{best}, and we continue until no further improvement are observed.

5   Implementation and Experiments

This section assess the quality of the estimation of the timestamp of start activities for two case studies. In our experiments, we used the inductive miner algorithm [10] for the discovery of the process model because it guarantees the soundness of the discovered models. The resulting Petri-net models are later translated into BPMN models [11]. Then, using process mining and statistical techniques, we complement the BPMN model with the other simulation parameters, namely:

The resource perspective. We extract the pool of resources from the log events, and we group them in roles, finally linking BPMN-model tasks to roles. In particular, we leverage on the role-discovery algorithm by Burattin et al. [3].

Working calendar. We discover the working calendar hours for each role by analyzing the day of the week and the hour of the day in which each role most frequently completed tasks.

The inter-arrival time. We calculate the time difference between subsequent traces, also consider the working calendar. Then, we compute the inter-arrival time distribution that best fits, namely which minimizes the error.

Branching probabilities. For each XOR split in the BPMN model, we compute the probability to continue via each available branch.

These parameters focus on different process perspectives (resource, time and control-flow, respectively) and allow configuring a sufficiently-precise simulation model, with

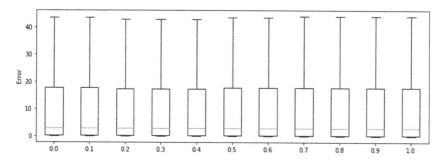

Fig. 3. The estimation error when varying the noise parameter of the inductive miner algorithm for the process for student credential recognition. The estimation error is measured in days, and is the absolute number of the between the estimated and the real timestamps.

evident benefits on the accuracy of the estimation of the start events and their respective timestamps. The BPMN-model branching probabilities are derived via from the corresponding probabilities on the Petri net discovered through the Inductive leveraging, by using the Multi-perspective Process Explorer [12]. The other simulation parameters are obtained through a combination of the results of the process-mining library PM4Py[3] with other Python libraries for machine learning, data science and statistics.

To put together all the simulation parameters with the BPMN model into a single data structure the implementation is through a Python library BPSimpy [9]. It can be downloaded from the Github repository.[4] We used the Lanner simulator (L-sim)[5] using the generated simulation model as input, to perform the simulation. All the experiments were run on an Intel Core i7-8550U CPU @ 1.80 GHz with 16 GB RAM with duration of ca. 3.5 h per analysis.

5.1 Case Study of the Process for Student Credential Recognition

This section reports a case study of a real business process for credential recognition of students in a Colombian University that contains both starting and completion events.[6] It contains 954 traces, 18 activities, 6870 events and involves 561 resources. In the remainder, we translate the activity labels into English for clarity. The start events were removed, aiming to assess the accuracy of their rediscovery via our simulation-based techniques. Once we discovered the BPMN process model and the simulation parameters, we have the initial simulation model $\mathcal{M}_0$. Using the $mintime_{\mathcal{L}}$ oracle based on control-flow and resources (cf. Sect. 3) and the granularity parameter $\delta = 0.1$, we apply Algorithm 1 to find the best α function.

---

[3] https://pm4py.fit.fraunhofer.de/documentation.

[4] https://github.com/claudiafracca/BPSimpyLibrary.

[5] https://www.lanner.com/en-us/technology/l-sim-bpmn-simulation-engine.html.

[6] https://github.com/AutomatedProcessImprovement/Simod/blob/master/inputs/ConsultaDataMining201618.xes.

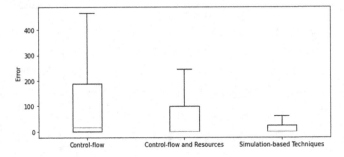

Fig. 4. Comparison of the estimation error of the start timestamp for the student credential-recognition process when using our simulation-based technique and the naïve techniques The first and second boxplots respectively report on the naïve techniques that use the control-flow information only, and both the control-flow and resource information. The third refers to our technique. Errors are reported in days.

Sensitivity with Respect to the Model. The first question of the evaluation is how much the quality of the model influences our technique, in terms of precision and fitness [1]. As mentioned we employed inductive miner to mine model, which allows the discovery of models with different sensitivity levels as function of a noise parameter that takes values between 0 and 1: value 0 indicates that no part of behaviour is considered as noise and the model allows for the whole behavior observed in the event log, whereas larger and larger values indicate that less and less event-log behavior is incorporated into the model. Since lower values produce models with a larger set of admissible behavior, in general lower values produce models with higher fitness but less precise. Figure 3 shows the estimation error when applying our technique and using the different models that are obtained varying the noise parameter of the inductive-miner algorithm and extended with the simulation parameters mentioned above. The estimation error is measured in days and is the absolute number of the between the estimated and the real timestamps. We can notice that the error does not change with the noise parameter and, hence, with the model precision and fitness. This can be explained: the possible lack of precision is balanced by the branching probabilities for the XOR splits. If the model is not precise, the probabilities for certain infrequent branches might become so low that it is in fact equivalent to not having them.

Comparison with Naïve Techniques. The second evaluation question refers to a comparison between our and some naïve techniques. The naïve techniques assume no waiting time and that the new activities start as soon as possible. In a first case, the new activity starts when the previous completes; a second case also considers the availability of resources and assumes that the new activity starts when the previous completes and when the resource that performs the new activity is available. Figure 4 uses boxplots to show the distribution of the estimation error between the two naïve techniques and our technique. The error for our technique is built on the model that scores the best when varying the noise parameter (cf. Fig. 3). Our technique clearly outperforms the naïve technique that is based on only control-flow information: The mean and media values

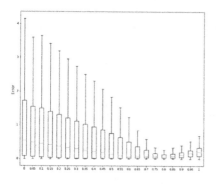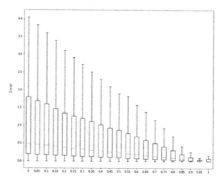

Fig. 5. Comparison by estimation error in days for the activities *Course revision (Revisar curso)* and *Validate the application (Validar solicitud)* between different parameter values α in $alpha\_succ(\delta) = \{0, 0.1, 0.2, \dots, 1\}$ for the process for student credential recognition.

of the estimation error are certainly smaller, and the error's standard deviation reduced to ca. 10% of the case of the naïve technique based on control-flow information. Compared with the naïve technique that also employs resource information, our technique is characterized by a similar error's mean value, but the error's standard deviation is reduced to ca. 20% of the naïve-technique case that also uses the resource information.

Accuracy with Respect to the α Configuration. The next question of the evaluation is how the estimation error varies for a specific activity a with respect to $\alpha(a)$. Figure 5 reports for the activities *Course revision (Revisar curso)* and *Validate the application (Validar solicitud)* a comparisons between error boxplots one for each values of function α in $alpha\_succ(\delta) = \{0, 0.1, 0.2, \dots, 1\}$. This figure shows a typical distribution of the error function when varying α: the error has a convex trend, with the minimum for some value between zero and one. In this case, the minimum corresponds to the $\alpha(a) = 0.8$ and $\alpha(a) = 0.95$, illustrating that activities tend to be started soon after it is possible, but not immediately (cf. Eq. 2).

Table 2. Average and standard deviation of process-instance duration of simulated process executions when activity duration is estimated via the naïve approach (first two table rows) and ours (third row). The last row refers to actual average and standard deviation of process-instance durations, observed in the event log.

	Average	Standard Deviation
Estimating using control-flow only	138 d 09 h 11 m 28 s	180 d 19 h 25 m 53 s
Estimating using control-flow and resources	58 d 08 h 10 m 32 s	107 d 09 h 34 m 31 s
Estimating using our simulation-based technique	10 d 19 h 01 m 56 s	18 d 20 h 35 m 21 s
Actual process-instance durations in the event log	14 d 10 h 18 m 11 s	27 d 03 h 40 m 51 s

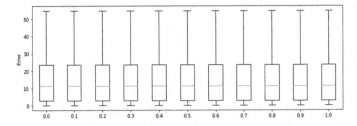

Fig. 6. The estimation error when varying the noise threshold of the inductive miner algorithm for the purchase process case study.

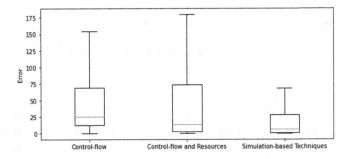

Fig. 7. Comparison of the estimation error of the start timestamp for the purchase process case study, when using our simulation-based technique and some naïve techniques that assume no waiting time.

Effects on Process-Instance Duration in Simulation. In sum, our technique allows a better estimation of the duration of the activity instances observed in the event log. We previously mentioned that this provides large benefits to the application of several Process-Mining techniques, including for more accurate simulation models. Assuming no waiting times, naïve techniques would lead to estimating distributions of activity-instance durations that are larger than the reality. If activity-instance durations are simulated to be larger than reality, simulations would highlight a unreal overestimation of the utilization of the resources that perform such activities, as well as they would report on overly long duration of process instances. To empirically verify this, we first used the durations estimated via our techniques and via the naïve techniques to learn the probability distributions of the durations of the instances of different process' activities, which were later added to the simulation model. So-constructed simulation models were run for so many instances as those recorded in the event log. We measured the average and standard deviations of process-instance durations. Table 2 summarizes the findings: the comparison highlights that our technique allows analysts to build simulation models that simulate realistic process-instance durations. Indeed, the average of 10 days and ca. 19 h and the standard deviation of 18 days and ca. 21 h is close to the actual durations (see last table row). Conversely, the two naïve techniques estimated activity-instance durations that produced distributions for the simulation model that generate process-instance runs whose durations are of an order of magnitude larger than reality.

5.2 Purchase Process Case Study

This section reports the experiment results based on an event log that record executions of a purchase-to-pay process of 21 activities and 27 resources.[7] This event log is composed by 9119 events, both start and complete, divided in 608 traces. Analogously to the previous case study, we removed the start events, aiming to assess the accuracy of their rediscovery via our simulation-based techniques. As the case study before, the simulation model was created via Inductive Miner, extended with the simulation parameters that are mentioned at the beginning of this section and discovered as there indicated. The same sensitivity analysis of the model wrt. different noise-parameter values was carried out (see Fig. 6): analogously to the previous case study, the accuracy of the estimations was not influenced by the quality of the model to well balance fitness and precision. So did we compare our techniques with the same naïve techniques that use control-flow and, possibly, resource information. The results are shown in Fig. 7, which confirm the findings of the first case study: our technique reduces both the average and the standard deviation of the estimation error.

6 Conclusion

Process mining techniques allows process analysts to discover, monitor, and extract information from an event log related to different perspectives of a business process. However, most of the techniques required event logs that stored both start and complete life-cycle transitions to extract the different multi perspectives aspects. Unfortunately, event logs often record the completion only. This paper focuses on the approximating of the start events. Naïve techniques assume activity instances to start as soon as possible, thus assuming no waiting times. In reality, resources can work on different processes, take breaks, and perform other duties that are not recorded in the logs. In these cases, the actual durations are over-estimated, yielding simulations that report an untrue over-utilization of resources and/or process-instance durations that are far longer than the reality. This paper reports on an technique to estimate the start event, assuming waiting times to be possible. The idea is to estimate the start event by simulating different activity-duration configurations and comparing the simulation results to find the configuration for which the process-instance durations follow a probability distribution that is close to that of the original event log. The idea hint is that the duration of simulated traces are closer to those of the original event log if the activity durations are better estimated. The validation has been conducted on processes whose event logs record both starting and completion timestamps for each activity instance. The starting timestamps were removed and estimated: the results show that our technique computes better duration estimation with respect to techniques that assume no waiting time.

As future work, we aim to optimize our technique. Each configuration (i.e. vector) of α parameters needs to be simulated, and currently we simulate as many traces as those of the original event log in an attempt to fade any simulation warm-up effects. In fact, it might actually be statistically sufficient to simulate fewer traces, so as to speed up the simulation steps, while still fading the warm-up effects.

---

[7] https://fluxicon.com/academic/material/.

We acknowledge that there might be some threats to the validity of our technique, on which we aim to work in the future. First and foremost, the accuracy of the estimations of the start timestamps might depend on the accuracy of the simulation model. Secondly, our technique still assumes resources to work on at most one activity instance at the same time, which might not always be true: we aim to extend support for resources that carry on multiple activity instances at the same time [8].

References

1. van der Aalst, W.M.P.: Process Mining: Data Science in Action. Springer, Cham (2016). https://doi.org/10.1007/978-3-662-49851-4
2. Berkenstadt, G., Gal, A., Senderovich, A., Shraga, R., Weidlich, M.: Queueing inference for process performance analysis with missing life-cycle data. In: Proceedings of 2nd International Conference on Process Mining (ICPM 2020), pp. 57–64. IEEE (2020)
3. Burattin, A., Sperduti, A., Veluscek, M.: Business models enhancement through discovery of roles. In: Proceedings of the 2013 IEEE Symposium on Computational Intelligence and Data Mining (CIDM), pp. 103–110 (2013)
4. Camargo, M., Dumas, M., González Rojas, O.: Learning accurate business process simulation models from event logs via automated process discovery and deep learning. arXiv abs/2103.11944 (2021)
5. Camargo, M., Dumas, M., González-Rojas, O.: Automated discovery of business process simulation models from event logs. Decis. Support Syst. **134**, 113284 (2020)
6. Carmona, J., van Dongen, B.F., Solti, A., Weidlich, M.: Conformance Checking - Relating Processes and Models, 1st edn. Springer, Cham (2018). https://doi.org/10.1007/978-3-319-99414-7
7. Denisov, V., Fahland, D., van der Aalst, W.M.P.: Repairing event logs with missing events to support performance analysis of systems with shared resources. In: Janicki, R., Sidorova, N., Chatain, T. (eds.) PETRI NETS 2020. LNCS, vol. 12152, pp. 239–259. Springer, Cham (2020). https://doi.org/10.1007/978-3-030-51831-8_12
8. Estrada-Torres, B., Camargo, M., Dumas, M., García-Bañuelos, L., Mahdy, I., Yerokhin, M.: Discovering business process simulation models in the presence of multitasking and availability constraints. Data Knowl. Eng. **134**, 101897 (2021)
9. Fracca, C., Bianconi, A., Meneghello, F., de Leoni, M., Asnicar, F., Turco, A.: BPSimpy: a python library for WfMC-standard process-simulation specifications. In: Proceedings of the Demo Session at the 19th International Conference on Business Process Management (2021)
10. Leemans, S.J.J., Fahland, D., van der Aalst, W.M.P.: Discovering block-structured process models from incomplete event logs. In: Ciardo, G., Kindler, E. (eds.) PETRI NETS 2014. LNCS, vol. 8489, pp. 91–110. Springer, Cham (2014). https://doi.org/10.1007/978-3-319-07734-5_6
11. de Leoni, M., van der Aalst, W.M.P.: The feature prediction package in ProM: correlating business process characteristics. In: Proceedings of the Demo Session at the 14th International Conference on Business Process Management (BPM 2014). CEUR, vol. 1295 (2014)
12. Mannhardt, F., de Leoni, M., Reijers, H.A.: The multi-perspective process explorer. In: Proceedings of the Demo Session at the 13th International Conference on Business Process Management, vol. 1418, pp. 130–134. CEUR-WS.org (2015)
13. Martin, N., Depaire, B., Caris, A., Schepers, D.: Retrieving the resource availability calendars of a process from an event log. Inf. Syst. **88**, 101463 (2020)
14. Nakatumba, J.: Resource-aware business process management: analysis and support. Ph.D. thesis, Technische Universiteit Eindhoven (2013)

15. Pegoraro, M., van der Aalst, W.M.P.: Mining uncertain event data in process mining. In: Proceedings of the 2nd International Conference on Process Mining (ICPM 2019), pp. 89–96. IEEE (2019)
16. Pegoraro, M., Uysal, M.S., van der Aalst, W.M.P.: Discovering process models from uncertain event data. In: Di Francescomarino, C., Dijkman, R., Zdun, U. (eds.) BPM 2019. LNBIP, vol. 362, pp. 238–249. Springer, Cham (2019). https://doi.org/10.1007/978-3-030-37453-2_20
17. Rogge-Solti, A., Weske, M.: Prediction of business process durations using non-Markovian stochastic Petri nets. Inf. Syst. **54**, 1–14 (2015)
18. Rozinat, A., Mans, R., Song, M., van der Aalst, W.: Discovering simulation models. Inf. Syst. **34**(3), 305–327 (2009)
19. Senderovich, A., Leemans, S.J.J., Harel, S., Gal, A., Mandelbaum, A., van der Aalst, W.M.P.: Discovering queues from event logs with varying levels of information. In: Reichert, M., Reijers, H.A. (eds.) BPM 2015. LNBIP, vol. 256, pp. 154–166. Springer, Cham (2016). https://doi.org/10.1007/978-3-319-42887-1_13

Updating Prediction Models for Predictive Process Monitoring

Alfonso E. Márquez-Chamorro[1,2](✉)[ID], Isabel A. Nepomuceno-Chamorro[1][ID], Manuel Resinas[1,2][ID], and Antonio Ruiz-Cortés[1,2][ID]

[1] I3US Institute, Universidad de Sevilla, Seville, Spain
{amarquez6,inepomuceno,resinas,aruiz}@us.es
[2] SCORE Lab, Universidad de Sevilla, Seville, Spain

Abstract. Predictive monitoring is a key activity in some Process-Aware Information Systems (PAIS) such as information systems for operational management support. Unforeseen circumstances like COVID can introduce changes in human behaviour, processes, or computing resources, which lead the owner of the process or information system to consider whether the quality of the predictions made by the system (e.g., mean time to solution) is still good enough, and if not, which amount of data and how often the system should be trained to maintain the quality of the predictions. To answer these questions, we propose, compare, and evaluate different strategies for selecting the amount of information required to update the predictive model in a context of offline learning. We performed an empirical evaluation using three real-world datasets that span between 2 and 13 years to validate the different strategies which show a significant enhancement in the prediction accuracy with respect to a non-update strategy.

Keywords: Predictive process monitoring · Process mining · Process-aware information systems · Prediction models · Model updating

1 Introduction

Predictive process monitoring (PPM) provides proactive and corrective actions to improve the process performance and mitigate potential risks in real time. PPM retrieves information from Process-Aware Information Systems (PAIS) stored in event logs to make predictions of evaluation metrics, also known as process performance indicators (PPIs) [1]. A path extensively followed in the literature for predictive monitoring is adapting existing machine learning techniques [2] such as decision trees, clustering methods or neural networks to obtain predictive models with higher accuracy. When these approaches are used, the

Work funded by grants RTI2018-101204-B-C21 and RTI2018-101204-B-C22 funded by MCIN/ AEI/ 10.13039/501100011033/ and ERDF A way of making Europe; grant P18-FR-2895 and US-1381595 funded by Junta de Andalucía/ERDF, UE.

X. Franch et al. (Eds.): CAiSE 2022, LNCS 13295, pp. 304–318, 2022.
https://doi.org/10.1007/978-3-031-07472-1_18

typical procedure for predictive monitoring comprises two steps. First, a training stage in which the predictive models are trained using data collected in the event logs. Second, once the model is built, it is deployed and it is used to predict PPIs for current and/or future process executions.

In the absence of significant changes, *ceteris paribus* (all else being equal), this approach works fine, but processes are subject to continuous changes. For instance, the response to COVID may introduce new ways of performing activities, users can behave in a different way, or human or computing resources can change over time. These changes may negatively affect the performance of the predictive model since the data used to train them does not reflect reality any more. Therefore, the only way to keep this performance over a desired threshold is by adapting the model to the changes.

In the machine learning community, there are two main adaptation approaches for that, namely, online and offline learning. In online learning, the predictive model is being updated continuously from the data it receives. Conversely, in offline learning, the predictive model is rebuilt again from the ground. In this paper, we decide to focus on offline learning mainly for two reasons. Firstly, the pace of change and the pace of new events in the processes we are interested in, gives enough time to completely rebuild new models. Secondly, its use allows one to reuse a huge amount of machine learning techniques that are available for offline learning, which is much more comprehensive than that of online learning. Furthermore, these techniques do not need to make compromises to keep a reasonable learning time.

In this context, the goal of this paper is to provide details on how to face two of the questions that arise in the update of predictive models: "Which data should be considered in the new model that is being built?" and "How the selection of data does impact on the performance of the predictive models?".

By answering these questions, we contribute to the state of the art on PPM by proposing six different strategies for updating predictive models (baseline, cumulative, non- cumulative, ensemble, sampling, and concept drift) and comparing their performance. Our experimentation was validated using three real-life event logs that span between 2 and 13 years. We have also performed a comparison of different well-known classifiers used in related literature.

The reminder of this paper is organized as follows. Section 2 summarises basic concepts in predictive monitoring. Section 3 presents the strategies for updating predictive models. The experiment and the discussion of the obtained results are presented in Sect. 4. Section 5 summarises the related work. Finally, Sect. 6 concludes the work and presents possible future directions.

2   Predictive Process Monitoring

In the following, we introduce some basic concepts of predictive process monitoring. As defined in [3], an *event log* (L) is composed of a set of *traces* (T). Each trace (T_i) reflects an execution of a process instance. Formally, we can express a trace as an ordered list of *events* $T_i = [E_{i_1}, \ldots, E_{i_m}]$ where E_{i_1} represents the first event and E_{i_m} the final event of trace T_i. Similarly, a log can be expressed as the set of traces for the instances that have finished in an interval of time $L = [T_1, \ldots, T_n]$ where T_1 is the first and T_n is the last executed trace in the time interval. Finally, an event represents the execution of an activity of the process. Each event contains a set of *attributes* (a), which represents information related to such event, *e.g.* timestamp, the resource that executes the activity, or the value of some data used throughout the instance, $E_j = [a_{j_1}, \ldots, a_{j_o}]$ where o determines the total number of attributes of the event.

A process *indicator* (I) is a quantifiable metric focused on measuring the progress toward a goal or strategic objective. Indicators can be classified into two types: single-instance indicators or aggregated indicators. The former is computed for each trace in the log using the values of the attributes of the events that compose this trace. Therefore, it can be defined as a function of a trace T_i, *i.e.* $I(T_i)$. This function can return a binary value, *e.g* a determined condition fulfilled by the trace, or a real value, *e.g* the duration of an activity. Instead, an aggregated indicator is computed for a set traces by aggregating a single-instance indicator using some aggregation function, *e.g.* sum or average. An example of this type of indicator could be the percentage of incidents solved in a certain period of time.

A predictive model for an indicator I is a function $P_I([E_{i_k}, \ldots, E_{i_l}])$, with $k \leq l$, that computes a prediction for I from the partial trace $[E_{i_k}, \ldots, E_{i_l}]$, where E_{i_l} is the last event that have occurred in trace T_i at a given moment. If $k = 1$, then all events that have occurred in the process instance at hand are considered. Instead, if $k = l$, then only the last event of the process instance is considered.

In order to train a predictive model $\hat{I}$ for a key performance indicator (KPI) I, an encoded fixed-size representation $\mathcal{C}$ of all the cases C, where $C \subseteq \mathcal{C}$, included in the training set is required. This encoding, generally represented as a feature matrix (X), should store enough information of the process, and will be used as input for the machine learning technique employed to build the model together with the value of the KPI I for each case in C, which represents the target variable (y). The feature matrix X is obtained after applying a sequence encoding function $\mathcal{F}$, which receives a set of cases C and returns a matrix X. Each row of the matrix represents an event E, i.e. the execution of an activity of the process, of a case $c \in C$ and each column represents the different (encoded) attributes a of the event. Various sequence encoding techniques have been proposed in the literature for this task such as last state encoding [4], aggregation encoding [5], or index-based encoding [6]. The other decision is if only one classifier is trained for the whole dataset or, on the contrary, if cases are grouped into several buckets and a different classifier is trained for each one. Several case bucketing techniques have been proposed in the literature [7]: Zero bucketing [5], prefix length bucketing [6], or cluster bucketing [8]. After these two decisions are made, a predictive model is built using some machine learning algorithm using the pair (X, y) as the input.

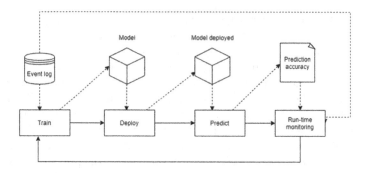

Fig. 1. Updating models system in a predictive monitoring process.

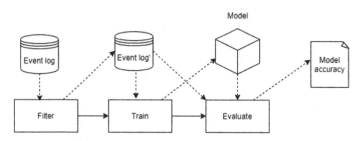

Fig. 2. Training stage.

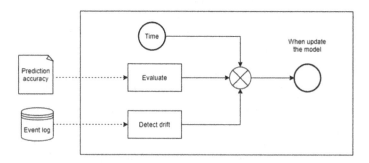

Fig. 3. Run-time monitoring stage.

An indicator I can represent different issues, such as a certain outcome, the next activity of the process or remaining cycle time of a given process case. In this work we have focused on the outcome-based prediction. Therefore, we are predicting an outcome value per case instead of a value per each event.

3   Updating Predictive Models

Once the predictive models are generated following the mechanisms described in the previous section are deployed into production, they start making predictions that can be used to timely react to operational issues. However, after a while, the way the process was performed might have changes; resources participating in the process may come and go; even the structure of the process may suffer changes. All these changes are ignored by the predictive model that was deployed some time ago, so these changes may negatively affect the performance of the predictive model. Therefore, it is necessary to provide mechanisms to update the predictive model. Figure 1 shows a system for the updating of predictive models described below. It consists of a training stage depicted in Fig. 2 (which involves the filtering of the event log, the generation of the predictive model and the evaluation of this model), the deployment of this model, the prediction using this model, and finally, a mechanism for the update of the deprecated models, named Run-time monitoring process as shown in Fig. 3. This mechanism can evaluate the model in terms of the performance of the predictions and decide when the predictive model should be updated according to three possible parameters: the time elapsed from the last deployed model, the accuracy of predictions and the possible occurrence of a concept drift [9].

As mentioned in the introduction, there are two approaches for updating predictive models, namely online and offline learning. In this paper, we focus on offline learning because it allows one to use the huge amount of machine learning techniques for offline learning, which is much more comprehensive than that of online learning and, furthermore, these techniques do not need to make compromises in order to keep a reasonable learning time. To the best of our knowledge, any other work related to offline strategies for updating predictive models appears in the literature, so that comparison with other papers is not possible. In the context of offline learning, two basic questions need to be answered to update the predictive model:

1. When should the predictive model be updated?
2. Which data should be considered in the new model that is being built?

For the first question, several strategies can be considered (Run-time monitoring stage in Fig. 3). The most straightforward is a periodical update of the model [10]. A reasonable deadline for the change of the model can be fixed, e.g. six-monthly periodicity, and then, a new generation of the model will be carried out. A different strategy might involve monitoring the accuracy of our predictions. When it begins to decrease over an uninterrupted period of time, it may be recommended to change the predictive model. A threshold of error can be set, and if the prediction exceeds this threshold, the prediction model will be updated. Finally, a third strategy could involve using the detection of drifts in processes [11] to trigger updates in the predictive model [10]. Several strategies could be also combined to design a more robust system.

Our focus in this paper is, however, on the second question. This question is relevant because of two reasons that involve the quality and cost of predictive models. Concerning the former, if the reason for updating the predictive model is because the process has changed, it is reasonable to think that learning past behaviours of the process may not be beneficial for the performance of the predictive model, so it might make sense not to include the whole data set, but only the most recent behaviour. As for the latter, the computational cost of building a predictive model increases with the size of the input data set. Therefore, a goal should be to achieve the best predictive performance by using the smallest possible input data set. In [10], authors propose two possible solutions to the second question: retraining and incremental update of a predictive model, however, all predictive algorithms cannot learn incrementally (e.g. random forests). Therefore, we have collected a set of strategies for choosing the data set used for building a new predictive model regardless of the predictive algorithm used.

A strategy for choosing the data set used for building a new predictive model can be seen as a function S that receives a training and test set pair (X, y) and returns another training and test set pair (X', y'), such that $X' \subseteq X$ and $y' \subseteq y$. Next we detail several possible data selection strategies. We use the notation $X_{[i,j]}$ to select the subset of X that is between i and j, where i and j could be either an instant in time such as the 7th of March of 2019, or an instance number since the first one received. Furthermore, if they take the value 0, it refers to the first event in the data set and if they take the value c, it refers to the last event received in the data set. Therefore, $X_{[0,c]} = X$.

In the following, we present the different strategies for the selection of data. Figure 5 shows a graphical representation of the different strategies described in this section. Figure 4 depicts an event log that will be used to explain the different strategies in Fig. 5. This event log is split into several intervals from t_1 to t_n. Each interval represents all the process instances executed during a certain period of time, e.g. six months.

1. **Baseline strategy (S_B):** In this strategy the model is not updated throughout the life of process:

$$S_B(X, y) = (X_{[0,c]}, y_{[0,c]})$$

   Figure 5a shows a graphical representation of the baseline strategy. With this strategy, a first interval is selected as the training set, and it is not updated throughout the life of the process. We use the rest of the intervals as test sets.

2. **Cumulative strategy (S_C):** This strategy involves including all the cases that are available for training since the beginning:

$$S_C(X, y) = (X_{[0,c]}, y_{[0,c]})$$

   Cumulative strategy is represented in Fig. 5b. This strategy involves adding all instances of a process as training set. We split the event log into training and test sets, and we incrementally add each interval from t_1 to t_n in the training set and use the rest for the test set.

3. **Non-cumulative strategy (S_N):** This strategy involves choosing only the most recent cases for training. It includes a parameter tn that determines how many recent cases should be included in the training:

$$S_N(X, y) = (X_{[c-tn,c]}, y_{[c-tn,c]})$$

The advantage of this strategy in comparison to the cumulative strategy is that it is more efficient computationally and it might solve problems derived from using cases that do not follow the current behaviour of the process. The drawback is that having less training instances might hurt the performance of the predictive model.

For the non-cumulative strategy (Fig. 5c), we select an unique interval in the training phase. In this manner, we only include the most recent cases for training.

4. **Ensemble strategy** $(\mathcal{S}_E)$: This strategy is similar to the non-cumulative strategy because it only includes the most recent ts cases in training a new model. The difference is that, unlike the non-cumulative strategy, this strategy do not throw away older models, but keep them and combine them using some ensemble technique [12]. For instance, one can use a weighted voting technique in which the prediction of each model is considered a vote and combined using different weights for each model to make the final prediction. These weights can be updated each time a new model is added to the ensemble so that older models have a lower weight. To this end, weights can be modeled using an exponential decay function like $e^{-\lambda t}$. Furthermore, besides these weights, if the last model had very bad performance, we might be interested in removing it from the ensemble so that it does not hurt the overall performance. To this end, we set a threshold parameter so that if the quality metric of choice, e.g. f-score, of the previous model did not meet the threshold in the last interval, it is removed from the ensemble.

The advantage of this strategy is that it has almost the same computational cost as the non-cumulative strategy, but it helps to avoid discarding all of the old cases. However, the combination of the different models might not be as powerful as a model built using the cumulative strategy that includes all previous cases.

In this strategy, depicted in Fig. 5d, we choose the same training and test sets and keep older models to combine them using some ensemble technique to achieve better predictions.

5. **Sampling strategy** $(\mathcal{S}_S)$: This strategy involves a weighted sampling of all the cases that are available for training since the beginning. It includes a parameter ts that determines the number of samples that must be obtained from the data:

$$\mathcal{S}_S(X, y) = (sampling(X_{[0,c]}, ts), sampling(y_{[0,c]}, ts))$$

Where sampling is a function that takes ts samples from X or y, respectively. Sampling can also be weighted so that it is more likely to obtain more recent samples than older samples. A similar approach as the one used in the ensemble strategy can be used here to define these weights. The advantage of this approach in comparison to the cumulative strategy is that it limits the computational cost of the new model. Furthermore, unlike the ensemble strategy it relies on the machine learning algorithm instead of in the voting mechanism to combine both information from old and recent cases.

Fig. 4. Representation of a split event log.

Figure 5e shows the Sampling strategy. We build the training set in a incremental way using a weighted strategy where recent samples are more likely to be selected than older samples.

6. **Drift strategy (S_D):** This strategy is similar to the non-cumulative one. It includes the most recent cases for training and, when a concept drift is detected, we include as training set, all the cases after a certain time has passed since the drift has occurred.

   Figure 5f shows the drift strategy. When the concept drift is detected, training set is built only with those cases executed after the drift detection.

4 Experimental Evaluation

As we stated in Sect. 1, the goal of this paper is to define the different strategies for the selection of data (described in Sect. 3) and compare the predictive performance of the different strategies proposed. Based on this goal, we define a research question for our experimentation: What is the impact of the different updating strategies on the accuracy of predictions?

The rest of the section is organized as follows: the experiment setup is detailed in Sect. 4.1. The different datasets used in the experimentation are described in Sect. 4.2. Finally, a discussion of the obtained results is provided in Sect. 4.3.

4.1 Experiment Setup

As predictive algorithm we have used random forest [13] as seen in previous works in the literature [14]. This technique combines predictor trees such that each tree depends on the values of a random vector tested independently and with the same distribution for each of them. In [14], authors highlight extreme gradient boosting (XGBoost) and random forest as two of the best techniques in predictive monitoring. Thus, we have selected random forest because the quality of results with respect to XGBoost is similar and it consumes less computational time.

We have selected a typical aggregation encoding described in [14] as one of the most used in the literature to encode the process cases and also one of the best performers [14]. Thus, all events since the beginning of the case are considered. An aggregation function is applied to the values taken by a specific attribute throughout the case lifetime. In our case, this function is the number of times that each specific attribute appears in the case (frequency encoding). We have not divided the cases in the event log into different buckets. This technique is named Zero bucketing as defined in [14]. We have also incorporated the order of the events as a new attribute in all the logs, as well as the elapsed time between

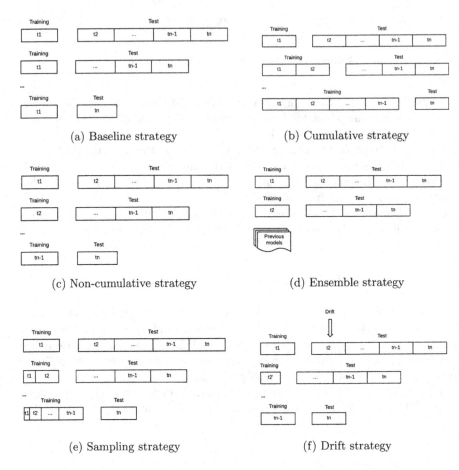

Fig. 5. Graphical representation of different proposed strategies for choosing the data set used for building a new predictive model.

the event and the beginning of the case and the time between the previous event and the current one. The details and the code of the experimentation are available online[1].

4.2   Event Logs

Three different real-life event logs were considered in our experiments: IT Department of an Andalusian organisation (ITA), BPI 2015 (BPI15) [15] and Traffic fines (TRAFFIC) [16]. These logs were chosen because they span several years: 2, 5 and 12, respectively, so they are useful to evaluate the effect of possible changes on the process over time.

---

[1] https://github.com/isa-group/predictive-monitoring-evolution.

ITA was extracted from the IT Department of an organisation in Andalusia. This dataset represents the incident management log of the IT Department in two years. In this scenario, a service level agreement (SLA) is established considering certain key performance indicators (KPIs). This SLA determines the penalties derived from the under-fulfilment of a threshold for each of the KPIs. Thus, predictive monitoring is necessary to warn the possibility of violation of the SLA. For the experiment, we used as target for the prediction if the incident is going to be put in a waiting state by the employee.

BPI15 is provided by five Dutch municipalities. The data contains all building permit applications over a period of approximately five years. There are many different activities present, denoted by both codes (attribute concept:name) and labels. The cases in the log contain information on the main application as well as objection procedures in various stages. Furthermore, information is available about the resource that carried out the task and on the cost of the application. This log covers the period October 2010 - March 2015. This log consists of five different datasets, one for municipality, where Log 1 includes 1,199 cases, Log 2 832 cases, Log 3 1,409 cases, Log 4 1,053 cases and Log 5 1,156 cases. All the logs contain between 40,000 and 60,000 events. The LTL rule used in the labelling function is described as $\varphi = G(\text{"send confirmation receipt"}) \rightarrow F(\text{"retrieve missing data"})$.

TRAFFIC represent a road traffic fine management process from Italian police. The log contains information about notifications sent about the fines and information about repayments. The targeted label to be predicted is based on whether the fine is repaid in full or is sent for credit collection. The resulting event log contains 129,615 cases, which were recorded between January 2000 and June 2012. Most of the cases consist of four events only.

4.3 Results

To perform the experimentation, we encode each dataset and split X into a set of intervals $X_{[I_1]}, ..., X_{[I_n]}$. We also compute the target value y and split it into a set of possibly different intervals $y_{[I_1]}, ..., y_{[I_m]}$. Like before, the size of intervals depends on the size of the dataset. With this setup, we train a predictive

Table 1. Average results of F-score for the different updating strategies.

	Strategy					
Dataset	Baseline	Non-Cum.	Cumulat.	Ensemble	Sampling	Drift
ITA	0.206883	**0.265163**	0.216884	0.250157	0.218832	NA
BPI city 1	0.858889	0.907668	0.900652	**0.921329**	0.908680	0.895364
BPI city 2	0.804032	0.849116	**0.907067**	0.881576	0.849492	0.790812
BPI city 3	0.710348	0.790268	0.815853	**0.840622**	0.756128	0.725569
BPI city 4	0.883692	**0.925582**	0.905460	0.925150	0.890478	0.832110
BPI city 5	0.896918	0.915899	0.913034	**0.921801**	0.915416	0.904564
TRAFFIC	0.652358	0.694372	0.703657	**0.714230**	0.705357	NA

model for each interval $X_{[I_i]}$ and evaluate it against all test intervals $y[I_k]$ such that I_k is after I_i. We have used F-score as accuracy measure [17] as seen in other works of the literature [14]. The F-score is the harmonic average of the precision and recall. F-score reaches its best value at 1. We have also detected the concept drifts for the different datasets using the algortihm included in the process mining framework PM4PY described in [18]. Specifically, we have found one concept drift for BPI city 1, two for BPI city 2, one for BPI city 3 and BPI city 4 and two for BPI city 5. We have not detected any drift for TRAFFIC and ITA datasets. These concept drifts have been used for the Drift strategy.

Table 1 summarises the results of the executions for the three datasets. The table is built assuming that the new model generated for each training interval is the one that is used to predict the values until a new model is created. In other words, we do not throw away models that are not performing better than a previous one. Furthermore, to ensure a fair comparison between approaches, we define training and test intervals using the number of instances instead of time. This avoids those cases in time intervals with fewer cases weight more than cases in others.

The values that we used for the intervals depend again on the dataset. For ITA, the training size was 39,000 cases, the interval between new models was 52,000 cases and the test interval was 13,000 cases. For all BPI datasets, the train size was 300 instances, and both the interval between new models and the test interval were 150 cases. Finally, for the TRAFFIC dataset, the train size was 8,641 cases, and the interval between new models and the test interval were 4,320 cases. In addition, for the Ensemble and Sampling strategies we assign weights to each interval using a decaying parameter of $e^{-x/3}$ and we set a threshold for the Ensemble of 0.5 except for ITA for which we set a threshold of 0.25.

From the table, we can conclude that there are no big differences between strategies in terms of F-Score. Nonetheless, as it was expected, the worst results are obtained with the Baseline strategy for all datasets (5–6% points on average less than the other strategies). On the other hand, the Ensemble strategy seems to perform better than the others in most datasets (4 out of 7), the second one is the Non-cumulative strategy (2 out of 7), and the third one is the Cumulative strategy (1 out of 7). The Sampling strategy is the one that seems to perform a bit worse. However, for the datasets in which we use large training

Table 2. Average results of F-score for the executions of different classifiers using BPI15 dataset.

Dataset	RF	BOOST	BN
BPI city 1	0.895364	0.7646200	0.533489
BPI city 2	0.790812	0.8395537	0.468736
BPI city 3	0.725569	0.7122018	0.440710
BPI city 4	0.832110	0.8472612	0.493650
BPI city 5	0.915416	0.9155702	0.450492
Average	**0.831854**	0.8158410	0.477415

sets like ITA and TRAFFIC, its performance is almost the same as the Cumulative strategy even when it uses much less instances as in input and hence, its computational cost is much more reduced. We can also conclude that Drift strategy does not perform as well as could be expected. This may be due to the fact that a low representative number of instances has been collected as training set after the concept drift has happened. On average, the three winner strategies (Non-cumulative, Cumulative and Ensemble) overcome the Baseline strategy in 4.71, 5 and 6.5% points. Considering the computational cost, it is quite evident that Cumulative strategy consumes more resources than the other two. Ensemble strategy has almost the same computational cost as the Non-cumulative strategy, however the use of older models, which are discarded in the Non-cumulative strategy, provides extra information that help to increase the accuracy prediction in almost 2 points more.

An extra experiment was performed to justify the use of random forest as machine learning algorithm in our experimentation. To this aim, we have compared the results obtained by random forest (RF) with those obtained by other three well-known classifiers also used in related literature [14]: Gradient Boosting (BOOST), and Bayesian Network (BN). For this experimentation we have used BPI15 dataset and drift strategy. We have used the Scikit-learn implementation of all the cited algorithms and we set the parameters of the algorithms by default. Regarding the F-score results in Table 2, we can appreciate a slight improvement of the results using random forest with respect to boosting algorithm. BN presents worse accuracy than RF and BOOST.

In summary, the main conclusion that can be drawn is that using all of the available data to rebuild the models is not a good choice because there is no win in performance and the computational cost is much higher. Furthermore, a significant improvement of accuracy prediction can be obtained using updated models versus non-updated models (Baseline strategy). This percentage can be increased from 5 to 15 points at best (Ensemble strategy). The Ensemble strategy provides good results and it reuses all models created previously, so it is more efficient computationally.

5   Related Work

Model updating has received increasing interest in the data mining community using diverse terminology such as, e.g., concept drift, incremental learning, stream data mining, or dynamic data mining [19]. However, a few works considers the updating of prediction models in the context of predictive process monitoring. Some of them [20,21] describe the notion of concept drift which is a term applied in machine learning and data mining refers to situations when the relation between the input data and the target variable, which the model is trying to predict, changes over time in unforeseen ways [20]. In [21] authors introduce a paradigm to handle concept drift in predictive process monitoring and also present a systematic experimental study to define different incremental learning strategies and encodings of process traces suited for the predictive monitoring of continuously evolving processes. Apart from that, a framework and specific techniques to detect when a process changes and to localize the parts of the process that have changed, are proposed in [20].

In [22], a remaining time prediction method along with a concept drift adaptation method is presented. As a predictor, they used an annotated transition system with probabilities obtained from Fuzzy Support Vector Machines based on process instance data. The predicted remaining time is obtained by summing up the durations of future activities estimated using Support Vector Machines. The concept drift adaptation method is based on a multimodel which is trained over different intervals of previous data, and assigns weights to the predictions of each model based on the difference in time between the model and the test data, factoring in an exponential decay and a periodic function.

Authors in [9] analyze which data should be selected for the retraining of the machine learning model after the detection of a concept drift. Therefore, they use different data selection strategies and consider the effects of the different retraining options in a real-life use case in process mining.

CONDA-PM is presented in [23], a four-phased framework that may guide process mining practitioners in assessing the maturity level of a concept drift analysis method. It covers a complete lifecycle of a concept drift analysis method with four phases. This method describes the phases and requirements of a concept drift analysis.

In [10], authors present a switching algorithm which combines the advantages of retraining and incremental updates. They test several drift detectors regarding performance on a real-world data set with incremental drift. They also provide a comparison among drift handling strategies and static models, showing that static models wear out over time and their performance decreases. Furthermore, a comparison among different drift handling strategies is provided.

Authors develop an incremental predictive process monitoring technique (Incremental Clustering-based and Incremental Index-based) applied to logs containing concept drifts in [24]. The updating of models is carried out at runtime; once a new case ends, it is added as a training example to generate a new model, through two algorithms (Hoeffding tree (HT) and Adaptive Hoeffding tree (AT)) and compare them with a standard classification algorithm (random forests). They also examine the impact of incremental learning techniques on real event logs with respect to traditional offline learning in terms of prediction accuracy and conclude that the incremental techniques allow for getting predictions are as accurate as the ones obtained with the periodic rediscovery of the predictive models.

The main highlights of our work are summarized in the following. Our proposal follows an offline strategy for prediction (some of the cited papers follow an online strategy and conclude that the results do not improve [24]), and propose six different strategies to decide how much data should be included in the model rebuild are presented and experimentations with three real-life datasets are performed to validate them. Although some works in the literature propose several strategies to retrain or update a predictive model, they are only focused on the occurrence of concept drifts [9,10]. Strategies defined in this work are not necessarily applied after the occurrence of a concept drift, they can be applied since the beginning of the running process instance. Furthermore, they are not limited by the ability to accurately detect concept drifts in the event log.

6   Conclusions

The goal of this paper is to propose and compare several strategies to choose the amount of data that should be used while rebuilding a predictive monitoring model in an offline learning setting. Based on this goal, we performed an empirical evaluation using three real-world datasets that span between 2 and 13 years and obtained the following conclusions.

We analysed the performance of the six data selection strategies described in Sect. 3 (Baseline, Cumulative, Non-cumulative, Ensemble, Sampling and Drift). To this aim, we summarised the results (F-score) of the executions for each of the datasets and we concluded that the Ensemble strategy provides better results and it reuses all models created previously, so it is more efficient computationally. A prediction improvement of up to 15% is achieved with this strategy.

Further research will include the development of techniques that help to decide when the predictive model should be updated. To this end, we plan to include some of the ideas included in the introduction to detect changes in the process. The generalizability of our results are subject to certain limitations. Despite these first promising results, our findings are based on three data sets only. In future work, we want to broaden the field of application by analyzing additional real-word data sets. Furthermore, only one predictive technique has been used to evaluate the strategies. Novel deep learning approaches can be considered for further works.

References

1. del Río-Ortega, A., Resinas, M., Durán, A., Bernárdez, B., Ruiz-Cortés, A., Toro, M.: Visual PPINOT: a graphical notation for process performance indicators. Bus. Inf. Syst. Eng. **61**, 137–161 (2019)
2. Márquez-Chamorro, A., Resinas, M., Ruiz-Cortés, A.: Predictive monitoring of business processes: a survey. IEEE Trans. Serv. Comput. **11**(6), 962–977 (2017)
3. Márquez-Chamorro, A.E., Revoredo, K., Resinas, M., Del-Río-Ortega, A., Santoro, F.M., Ruiz-Cortés, A.: Context-aware process performance indicator prediction. IEEE Access **8**, 222050–222063 (2020)
4. Polato, M., Sperduti, A., Burattin, A., Leoni, M.: Time and activity sequence prediction of business process instances. Computing **100**(9), 1005–1031 (2018). https://doi.org/10.1007/s00607-018-0593-x
5. de Leoni, M., van der Aalst, W.M., Dees, M.: A general process mining framework for correlating, predicting and clustering dynamic behavior based on event logs. Inform. Syst. **56**, 235–257 (2016)
6. Verenich, I., Nguyen, H., La Rosa, M., Dumas, M.: White-box prediction of process performance indicators via flow analysis. In: ICSSP 2017, pp. 85–94 (2017)

7. Teinemaa, I., Dumas, M., La Rosa, M., Maggi, F.: Outcome-oriented predictive process monitoring: Review and benchmark. CoRR abs/1707.06766 (2017)
8. Folino, F., Guarascio, M., Pontieri, L.: Discovering context-aware models for predicting business process performances. In: Meersman, R., et al. (eds.) OTM 2012. LNCS, vol. 7565, pp. 287–304. Springer, Heidelberg (2012). https://doi.org/10.1007/978-3-642-33606-5_18
9. Baier, L., Reimold, J., Kühl, N.: Handling concept drift for predictions in business process mining. In: CBI 2020, vol. 1, pp. 76–83 (2020)
10. Baier, L., Kellner, V., Kühl, N., Satzger, G.: Switching scheme: a novel approach for handling incremental concept drift in real-world data sets. In: HICSS-54 (2021)
11. Maaradji, A., Dumas, M., La Rosa, M., Ostovar, A.: Detecting sudden and gradual drifts in business processes from execution traces. IEEE Trans. Knowl. Data Eng. **29**(10), 2140–2154 (2017)
12. Rokach, L.: Ensemble-based classifiers. Artif. Intell. Rev. **33**(1–2), 1–39 (2010)
13. Breiman, L.: Random forests. Mach. Learn. **45**(1), 5–32 (2001)
14. Verenich, I., Dumas, M., La Rosa, M., Maggi, F., Teinemaa, I.: Survey and cross-benchmark comparison of remaining time prediction methods in business process monitoring. arXiv:1805.02896 (2018)
15. Van Dongen, B.: Bpi challenge 2015. tu delft. dataset. 10.4121/uuid:31a308ef-c844-48da-948c-305d167a0ec1 (2015)
16. De Leoni, M., Mannhardt, F.: Road traffic fine management process. Eindhoven university of technology. Dataset. https://doi.org/10.4121/uuid:270fd440-1057-4fb9-89a9-b699b47990f5 (2015)
17. Powers, D.: Evaluation: From precision, recall and F-Factor to ROC, informedness, markedness & correlation. Mach. Learn. Technol. **2** (2008)
18. Bose, R., Aalst, W., Žliobaitė, I., Pechenizkiy, M.: Handling concept drift in process mining. In: CAISE 2011, pp. 391–405 (2011)
19. Guajardo, J., Weber, R., Miranda, J.: A model updating strategy for predicting time series with seasonal patterns. Appl. Soft Comput. **10**(1), 276–283 (2010)
20. Bose, R., Aalst, W., Žliobaitė, I., Pechenizkiy, M.: Dealing with concept drifts in process mining. IEEE Trans. Neural Netw. Learn. Syst. **25**(1), 154–171 (2014)
21. Maisenbacher, M., Weidlich, M.: Handling concept drift in predictive process monitoring. In: SCC 2017, pp. 1–8 (2017)
22. Firouzian, I., Zahedi, M., Hassanpour, H.: Investigation of the effect of concept drift on data-aware remaining time prediction of business processes. Int. J. Nonlinear Anal. Appl. **10**(2), 153–166 (2019)
23. Elkhawaga, G., Abuelkheir, M., Barakat, S., Riad, A., Reichert, M.: CONDA-PM-a systematic review and framework for concept drift analysis in process mining. Algorithms **13**(7), 161 (2020)
24. Francescomarino, C.D., Ghidini, C., Maggi, F.M., Rizzi, W., Persia, C.D.: Incremental predictive process monitoring: how to deal with the variability of real environments. arXiv:1804.03967v1, p. 1 (2018)

Multi-model Monitoring Framework for Hybrid Process Specifications

Anti Alman[1]([✉])[iD], Fabrizio Maria Maggi[2][iD], Marco Montali[2][iD], Fabio Patrizi[3][iD], and Andrey Rivkin[2][iD]

[1] University of Tartu, Tartu, Estonia
anti.alman@ut.ee
[2] Free University of Bozen-Bolzano, Bolzano, Italy
{maggi,montali,andrey}@inf.unibz.it
[3] Sapienza University of Rome, Rome, Italy
patrizi@diag.uniroma1.it

Abstract. So far, business process monitoring approaches have mainly focused on monitoring executions with respect to a single process model. This setting aptly captures monolithic scenarios from domains in which all possible behaviors can be folded into a single model. However, this strategy cannot be applied to domains where multiple interacting (procedural) sub-processes work under additional (declarative) constraints. For example, in healthcare, co-morbid patients may be subject to multiple clinical pathways at once, in the presence of additional, general constraints capturing basic medical knowledge. To support monitoring of thus emerging hybrid specifications, we propose a Multi-Model Monitoring Framework. On the one hand, the framework allows for a hybrid representation of a process, using both procedural and declarative models. This admits more flexible process model design as domain experts can focus on specific procedures and domain constraints without needing to merge them into one single specification. On the other hand, the framework includes an automata-based monitoring technique to simultaneously account for multiple models within one execution while resolving conflicts caused by the interplay of such models. We describe the overall framework, report on a prototypical implementation of the monitoring technique, and demonstrate its feasibility with a healthcare scenario.

Keywords: Business process monitoring · Data Petri net · Declare · Automaton · Hybrid process

1 Introduction

A key functionality of any process-aware information system is *monitoring* [12]. Monitoring concerns the ability to detect, and therefore handle, deviations appearing in ongoing process instances and, in most cases, requires the expected behavior of the process to be specified in advance. Such specifications are commonly created in the form of procedural or declarative process models, depending on the scenario at hand. In general, procedural models are more suitable for

© Springer Nature Switzerland AG 2022
X. Franch et al. (Eds.): CAiSE 2022, LNCS 13295, pp. 319–335, 2022.
https://doi.org/10.1007/978-3-031-07472-1_19

relatively structured processes (e.g., an automated manufacturing line), while declarative models are more suitable for flexible and knowledge-intensive processes (e.g., the management of a natural disaster).

The majority of existing monitoring approaches rely on the assumption that the full knowledge-base (control-flow, decision rules, temporal aspects, etc.) required for monitoring each possible process instance can be embedded into a single process specification. While this is a reasonable assumption for processes with homogeneous behavior (i.e., either structured or knowledge-intensive), there are domains in which processes are characterized by a combination of several (independently defined) procedural sub-processes working under additional (declarative) domain constraints. A prime example of this can be found in the medical domain, where patients with co-morbidities may be subject to multiple clinical pathways at once (consisting of various medical actions) that can be enriched with additional, context-dependent constraints. Monitoring such multimodel scenarios becomes a challenging task as it requires not only to account for checking a process instance against multiple heterogeneous models, but also to provide mechanisms for handling the interplay of those models. For example, prescribing a certain treatment without taking into consideration patient's preexisting conditions may result in adverse effects causing a worsening of the patient's state. Ideally, these conflicts should be detected at early stages of the process execution and reported to health providers so as to avoid undesired treatment outcomes.

To address these problems, we present a Multi-Model Monitoring Framework for hybrid process specifications (M3 Framework). In this work, our focus lies on the lifecycle and conceptual features of the framework, while all related formal and algorithmic details are delegated to a technical report [1]. The framework consists of multiple phases, starting from knowledge elicitation prior to process execution, and ending with the successful completion of a scenario specific monitoring task. We outline the main steps of these phases and present a prototypical implementation of the corresponding multi-model monitoring approach. This approach can seamlessly handle the interplay of process specifications, detect inevitable violations in advance, and provide recommendations on the next course of action based on a violation cost model (either avoiding violations or, if that is not possible, minimizing the total cost of violations). The key benefits of the M3 Framework are (1) support for monitoring process executions with respect to multiple process specifications simultaneously, thus circumventing the need to embed the full knowledge-base required for the execution of every possible process instance into a single process specification, and (2) support for both procedural and declarative process specifications, thus circumventing the need to force declarative knowledge into procedural specifications and vice versa.

The rest of this paper is structured as follows. Section 2 provides an example scenario for the M3 Framework. Section 3 describes the process components used in this paper. Section 4 and Sect. 5 outline the main phases of the M3 Framework and the proposed monitoring approach respectively. Section 6 reports on initial monitoring experiments. Section 7 provides an overview of related work and Sect. 8 concludes the paper by outlining directions for future research.

2   Example Scenario

To motivate the need for our Multi-Model Monitoring Framework for hybrid process specifications, we use the healthcare scenario from [22] that shows interactions between seemingly disjoint clinical guidelines (CGs) and basic medical knowledge (BMK). In what follows, we provide a description of the scenario and abbreviations of activities used in the next sections.

The first CG that we consider defines a "default" process for patients with hip fractures. It begins with an initial assessment (AP) of the patient's condition, which is then followed by a decision on performing a surgery (SD). If the patient has a high fever, cough, or there are reasons to reconsider any immediate surgical intervention, then it may be decided to postpone the surgery (PS) and repeat the assessment after the blocking issues have been resolved. Otherwise, the patient is taken into a room where pre-surgery anesthesia (preSA) is delivered, and then into an operating room where the surgery is performed (S). After the surgery, the patient is prescribed with post-surgery analgesia (postSA) for pain relief as well as physiotherapy for mobilizing the hip (M). Both activities can be repeated until the patient feels better and can end the treatment (HFend).

The second CG provides a process for diagnosing and treating a potential chest infection. First, a patient with a suspected chest infection is prescribed a chest X-ray (CXray). By analyzing the X-ray images, the health provider decides whether there are serious signs of a chest infection that have to be urgently treated (TCI) or the suspicions were not corroborated (noCI). In the former case, the patient is immediately prescribed with an amoxicillin therapy (AT).

Usually, in medical practice, surgical interventions are avoided or postponed whenever the patient suffers from other conditions that can cause additional complications. For example, the general anesthesia required for performing a surgery cannot be performed together with an amoxicillin therapy. This is a common BMK rule that should be considered with any combination of CGs and the best way of doing so is to represent it as a global, declarative constraint, requiring that a decision to perform a surgery cannot coexist with an amoxicillin therapy, thus connecting two seemingly disconnected CGs. Similarly, a constraint can be used to specify that, if a patient has high body temperature or cough, then an X-ray check must be performed. Constraints can also be used to further specify the behavior of already existing CGs. For example, to prescribe that mobilization therapy should be delayed in case of leg pain after the hip surgery reported during a regular post-operational assessment (postOA).

Based on the first constraint, if the patient is diagnosed with a chest infection, but it is also decided to perform a hip surgery, then there is a conflict between that constraint and the two CGs. In this outlier, but possible situation there would be three alternatives: violate the first CG (by skipping the surgery and further treatment), violate the second CG (by not prescribing amoxicillin therapy), or violate the constraint (and prioritize the CGs).

Informing medical experts about the presence of a conflict is crucial to help them in assessing the current situation, weigh the implications of one choice over the others, and finally make an informed decision. These decisions can be further supported by assigning a violation cost to each CG and BMK specification. In this case, we can assume that highest violation costs should be given to the constraint, as any surgical complications should be avoided, and to the second CG specification, since there are no alternatives to the antibiotic therapy.

The formal models used for representing CGs and BMK specifications and how to address the above conflicts are discussed in the following sections.

3 Process Components

In this section, we define representations of declarative and procedural data-aware process specifications by relying on data Petri nets (DPNs) [11,16] and a variant of multi-perspective DECLARE (MP-DECLARE) [5] respectively. Note that DPNs and MP-DECLARE can be both translated into an equivalent finite-state automaton by using data abstraction and automata construction techniques [9]. This will be leveraged in Sect. 5 to monitor hybrid specifications.

Events and Traces. An *event signature* is a tuple $\langle n, A \rangle$, where: n is the *activity name* and $A = \{a_1, \ldots, a_\ell\}$ is the set of event *attribute (names)*. We assume a finite set $\mathcal{E}$ of event signatures, each having a distinct name. By $\mathcal{N}_{\mathcal{E}}$, we denote the set of all event names from $\mathcal{E}$ and by $\mathcal{A}_{\mathcal{E}}$ the set of all attribute names occurring in $\mathcal{E}$.

An *event* of event signature $\langle n, A \rangle$ is a pair $e = \langle n, \nu \rangle$, s.t. $n \in \mathcal{N}_{\mathcal{E}}$, and $\nu : A \mapsto \mathbb{R}$ is a total function assigning actual values for the attributes of the corresponding signature. For simplicity, we assume attributes ranging over reals equipped with comparison predicates (simpler types such as strings with equality and booleans can be seamlessly encoded). As usual, we call a finite sequence $\sigma = e_1 \cdots e_\ell$ of events a *trace*, where each e_i is an event of some signature in $\mathcal{E}$.

Data Petri Nets. As a language for procedural specifications, we opt for data Petri nets (DPNs) [11,16]. DPNs extend traditional place-transition nets with the possibility to manipulate scalar case variables, which are used as basic building blocks to constrain the evolution of the process through data-aware read-write constraints (called *guards*) assigned to transitions.

A *data Petri net* D over a set $\mathcal{E}$ of event signatures is a tuple $\langle P, T, F, l, V, r, w \rangle$, where: (i) (P, T, F) is the Petri net graph; (ii) $l : T \to \mathcal{N}_{\mathcal{E}} \cup \{\tau\}$ is a *labeling* function (here τ denotes a *silent* transition); (iii) $V \subseteq \mathcal{A}_{\mathcal{E}}$ is the set of net's *variables*; (iv) $r : T \to \mathcal{G}_{\mathcal{E}}$ (resp., $w : T \to \mathcal{G}_{\mathcal{E}}$) is a *read* (resp., *write*) *guard-assignment* function, mapping every transition $t \in T$ into a read (resp., write) guard – a boolean formula whose components are atomic expressions of the form $a \odot c$, where $\odot$ is a type-specific comparison predicate.

Example 1. Figure 1 shows two DPNs encoding the two CG fragments discussed in Sect. 2. Notice that the net in Fig. 1(a) models also a case in which the patient has a high fever and cough, but one of the doctors still recommends to risk performing the surgery (e.g., due to severe blood loss caused by the trauma). In this case, the model offers a choice: proceed with the surgery or postpone it (and possibly treat the blood loss together with fever and cough).

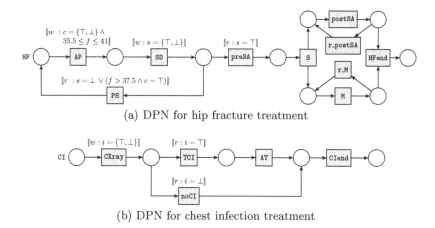

(a) DPN for hip fracture treatment

(b) DPN for chest infection treatment

Fig. 1. DPN representations for two clinical guideline fragments. We use prefixes r: and w: to distinguish read and write guards respectively. Models use the following CG parameters: coughs (c), fever (f), surgery decision (s), infection (i). Trivial, true-valued guards are omitted for brevity.

The execution semantics of DPNs extends that of place-transition nets with the ability to check and manipulate the net's variables via transition guards. In particular, a transition is *enabled* only if its read and write guards are satisfied under a given "firing mode" – a function that assigns values only to variables of the guards – and all the input places of the transition contain sufficiently many tokens to consume. Here, to check the read guard, the firing mode function picks values currently available in the net's state, while for the write guard it assigns to its variables any real values that would satisfy the guard (this accounts for "constrained" user input). When a transition is enabled, it may *fire* by consuming the necessary amount of tokens from its input places and producing the necessary amount of tokens in its output places, and by updating all the values assigned to variables in the write guard using the firing mode function. Values assigned to all other variables remain untouched.

In this paper, we deal only with DPNs that are 1-*bounded* and well-formed over their respective set of event signatures. The well-formedness means that a silent transition cannot update net variables and the write guard of each $t \in T$ uses variables matching attributes of event signature $\langle n, A \rangle$, for which $\ell(t) = n$. Such requirements appear naturally in the context of monitoring: we can always assume that variables are only manipulated by a fired visible transition, triggered by the corresponding event. At the same time, an event does not bring more data than is foreseen by the system design, and its payload is used to update the net variables (proviso that the corresponding write guard is satisfied).

Multi-perspective Declare with Local Conditions. To represent declarative process components, we opt for a multi-perspective extension of the well-known DECLARE language [5]. A DECLARE model describes *constraints* that must be satisfied throughout the system (or process) execution. Constraints, in turn, are based on *templates*. Templates are patterns that define parameterized classes of properties, and constraints are their concrete instantiations. The syntax of such constraints is defined using the following grammar:

$$\Phi := \top \mid \varphi \mid \mathbf{X}\,\Phi \mid \mathbf{F}\,\Phi \mid \mathbf{G}\,\Phi \mid \Phi_1 \mathbf{U}\,\Phi_2 \mid \neg\Phi \mid \Phi_1 \wedge \Phi_2$$

Here, φ is a boolean combination of attribute-to-constant comparisons and event variables ranging over $\mathcal{N}_\mathcal{E}$. Notice that the language of such boolean combinations without event variables closely resemble the guard language of DPNs, thus providing a good basis for combining declarative constraints with procedural models expressed with DPNs. As in standard LTL_f, $\mathbf{X}$ denotes the *strong next* operator (which requires the existence of a next state where the inner formula holds), while $\mathbf{U}$ stands for *strong until* (which requires the right-hand formula to eventually hold, forcing the left-hand formula to hold in all intermediate states).

We refer to the above constraints as LMP-DECLARE, i.e., MP-DECLARE constraints with local conditions. Their syntactic and semantic definition corresponds to LTL_f formulae [17] with attribute-to-constant comparisons and event variables as atomic formulae, interpreted over traces of the form given above.

Example 2. Here, we show how BMK constraints discussed in Sect. 2 can be formalized in LMP-DECLARE. The first constraint prohibits a positive surgery decision when the patient is undergoing amoxicillin therapy (NOT COEXISTENCE(AT, SD$\{s = \top\}$)):

$$\big(\mathbf{F}(\text{AT}) \rightarrow \neg\mathbf{F}(\text{SD} \wedge s = \top)\big) \wedge \big(\mathbf{F}(\text{SD} \wedge s = \top) \rightarrow \neg\mathbf{F}(\text{AT})\big)$$

The second constraint stipulates that if a patient has high body temperature (i.e., greater than 37.5°) or cough, then an x-ray check for detecting a chest infection has to be performed (RESPONSE(AP$\{f > 37.5 \vee c = \top\}$, CXray)):

$$\mathbf{G}\big(\text{AP} \wedge (f > 37.5 \vee c = \top) \rightarrow \mathbf{F}(\text{CXray})\big)$$

The third constraint prescribes that, whenever a patient suffers from pain in lower limbs (here modeled with variable llp) that is reported during a post-operational assessment, any mobilization therapy has to be delayed (NOT SUCCESSION(postOA$\{llp = \top\}$, M)):

$$\mathbf{G}\big((\text{postOA} \wedge llp = \top) \rightarrow \neg\mathbf{F}(\text{M})\big)$$

4   Multi-model Monitoring Framework for Hybrid Process Specifications

To address scenarios like the one described in Sect. 2, we introduce the Multi-Model Monitoring Framework (M3 Framework) for eliciting, managing, and monitoring hybrid process specifications. More specifically, the framework can be used in scenarios with multiple procedural and declarative specifications, where the former can be executed concurrently and the latter work as global constraints

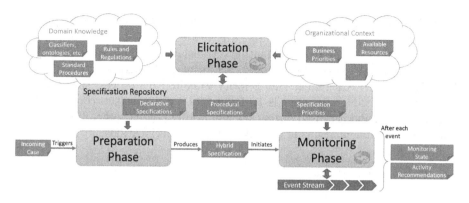

Fig. 2. Conceptual overview of the M3 Framework.

that implicitly induce additional dependencies between procedural specifications. In the following, we describe in more detail the three phases interconnected by a specification repository (Fig. 2), which is constantly updated during the model elicitation phase, and then used for monitoring individual cases in the case-specific preparation and monitoring phases.

4.1 Elicitation Phase

The elicitation phase of the M3 Framework is envisioned as a continuous case-agnostic phase, during which domain knowledge (standard procedures, classifiers, etc.) and organizational context (business priorities, available resources, etc.) are transformed into concrete process specifications, which are then stored in a dedicated specification repository. Both declarative and procedural specifications are supported, and multiple specifications of either paradigm can be used to represent a single global process, thus supporting not only hybrid process specifications, but also, for example, component-based and aspect-oriented modeling approaches [10]. Full agreement between the individual process specifications is not assumed, instead each specification is associated with a priority value that is used during monitoring to provide guidance to the user in resolving any potential conflicts. The elicitation phase consists of four main steps:

Extraction — Analysis of changes in the domain knowledge and organizational contexts to determine if new process specifications need to be created or existing ones need to be updated or removed. Relevant knowledge is extracted from standard procedures, regulations, etc., and the corresponding process specifications are identified.

Harmonization — Comparison of the extracted knowledge to common classifiers, ontologies, etc., to ensure that the same vocabulary is used across all process specifications. For example, specifications in the medical domain should adhere to the classifiers published by the World Health Organization.[1]

---

[1] Classifiers available at: https://www.who.int/standards/classifications.

Modeling — Transformation of the extracted knowledge into concrete process specifications via process modeling. Any modeling language (declarative or procedural) can be used, assuming that a translation into an equivalent finite-state automaton is possible (see Sect. 5.2 for more details).

Prioritization — Assignment of a priority value to each process specification. The priority value corresponds to the cost of violating the corresponding specification, and it is used during the monitoring phase (Sect. 4.3) to provide activity recommendations in case of conflicting specifications.

4.2 Preparation Phase

The preparation phase of the M3 Framework is envisioned as a case-specific non-recurrent phase in which an incoming case is assessed, relevant process specifications are selected, and a corresponding hybrid specification is automatically created as an input for the following monitoring phase. This hybrid specification will encompass the combined behavior of all selected specifications, the corresponding specification priorities (Sect. 4.1, Prioritization step), and, if required, also additional case-specific modifications. The selected process specifications can be smaller fragments of a single business process, but also fragments or full specifications of multiple, separately defined (but concurrently executed) business processes. The preparation phase consists of three main steps:

Case Assessment — Selection of relevant process specifications from the specification repository based on the features of the incoming case. In some domains, this step can be partially automatized. For example, in healthcare, potential conflicts between drugs used in different process specifications could be detected automatically using already existing knowledge bases.[2]

Fine-tuning — Optional modification of the selected specifications, including the specification priorities, and addition of custom specifications in order to tailor the monitor behavior to the specific needs of the incoming case. In healthcare, for example, this would include constraining the use of specific drugs or procedures because of some underlying conditions, co-morbidities, or preferences of the patient.

Automated Assimilation — Automated creation of a hybrid specification, which combines the outcome of case assessment and fine-tuning steps into a single case-specific hybrid specification, which also serves as the monitoring automaton. This step is further discussed in Sect. 5.2.

4.3 Monitoring Phase

The monitoring phase of the M3 Framework is envisioned as an ongoing case-specific phase, covering the entire duration of the case being monitored. During this phase, the state of the monitor and the set of next recommended actions

---

[2] For example: https://reference.medscape.com/drug-interactionchecker.

(with payloads) are updated after the occurrence of each event, therefore providing guidance towards the successful completion of the case. The monitoring phase consists of three main steps:

Automated Event Processing — Update of the monitor state, including both the global state and the states of individual process specifications, and update of the set of next recommended activities, including the corresponding data payloads. This step is further discussed in Sect. 5.3.

Case Reassessment — Optional modification of the current hybrid process specification to handle emerging case characteristics that were unforeseen during the preparation phase. For example, case reassessment would be necessary in the medical domain if a previously unknown underlying condition is discovered during the ongoing treatment case. Additionally, this step is useful for handling any imperfections that may be detected in the original process specifications during the ongoing monitoring case. Case reassessment is currently unsupported in the preliminary implementation of the monitor.

Next Event Execution — Execution of the next event based on the current monitoring state and activity recommendations. While we see recommendations as an important input for guiding the process execution to a successful completion, the execution of other (not recommended) events is also possible.

5   Automata-Based Monitoring

There are two central challenges in the proposed M3 Framework. First, the assimilation of input process specifications into a single hybrid specification (required for Sect. 4.2). Second, the interpretation of incoming events against this hybrid specification (required for Sect. 4.3). From an algorithmic perspective, these challenges can be addressed by encoding each DPN and LMP-DECLARE specification into a corresponding guarded finite-state automaton (GFA) that fully captures the execution semantics of the specification. This is possible, even in the presence of data, thanks to the specific shape of data guards (Sect. 3), which allows the usual automata constructions to be augmented with data abstraction and consequent propositionalization techniques [3]. In the following, we give a conceptual overview of the necessary steps, while formal and algorithmic details are delegated to the technical report [1].

5.1   Monitoring Semantics

A prerequisite of any monitoring approach, especially in a novel hybrid setting such as the one induced by the M3 Framework, is to set the corresponding monitoring semantics. At the level of individual process specifications, the standard execution semantics of data Petri nets or LMP-DECLARE constraints are followed. However, the execution semantics of a hybrid specification, produced in the Preparation phase (Sect. 4.2), is specific to the M3 Framework and therefore warrants further discussion. The following rules apply:

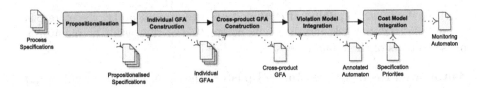

Fig. 3. Main steps and intermediate artefacts for creating the monitoring automaton.

- Each DPN ignores events that are not included in that DPN. This is a natural consequence of modularity which requires not to assume that a single DPN explicitly describes the full control flow (and therefore all potential activities) of the global process. Note that this rule does not apply to LMP-DECLARE, since declarative constraints are interpreted globally. In particular, that would break the execution semantics of templates imposing a directly-follows relation between activities (e.g., CHAIN RESPONSE(x,y)).
- A DPN is considered to be permanently violated if an event included in that DPN occurs while no corresponding transition can be successfully fired in its current state.
- A DPN is considered to be temporarily violated until the final marking of that DPN is reached or a permanent violation occurs. Furthermore, a DPN is considered permanently satisfied if its final marking is reached. This captures the intuition that a DPN specifies some procedural sequence of events to be carried out once during the full process control flow.
- The occurrence of each event is processed against all process specifications simultaneously (except the specifications ignoring that event). This captures the intuition of concurrent execution: if multiple specifications require the same event to occur, then its single occurrence should satisfy all of them.
- The variables of each DPN are local to that DPN. This keeps the semantic meaning of each DPN intact in the assimilated hybrid process specification.
- An LMP-DECLARE specification is considered permanently satisfied iff all individual constraints within that specification are permanently satisfied. This captures the intuition that an LMP-DECLARE specification represents declarative knowledge applicable throughout the full process control flow.
- An LMP-DECLARE specification is considered permanently violated iff at least one individual constraint within that specification is permanently violated. This captures the intuition that the constraints in a single LMP-DECLARE specification form a single logical entirety.

5.2   Monitoring Automaton

The proposed monitoring approach relies on a GFA, which is further annotated with violation and cost models, thus forming the hybrid process specification of the M3 Framework (Fig. 3). A GFA is a standard finite-state automaton, with the only difference that the transitions of the automaton are decorated with data conditions, imposing additional restraints on when a specific transition is allowed. This representation allows for capturing the semantic meaning of each individual process specification (including the data perspective), while also fully accounting for the execution semantics outlined in Sect. 5.1. Additionally, the annotated monitoring automaton enables early conflict detection and next activity recommendations as outlined in Sect. 5.3.

The creation of the monitor automaton occurs at the end of the preparation phase of the M3 Framework (Sect. 4.2, Automated Assimilation) and consists of the following main steps:

Propositionalization — Translation of the original process specifications into propositionalized specifications based on interval abstraction. Activities and attribute-constant combinations (including intervals between the constants) used in the process specifications are extracted and enumerated to form propositions. The activity names and conditions are then replaced in the original process specifications with equivalent sets of propositions to form propositionalized specifications similarly to the approach presented in [3].

Individual GFA Construction — Creation of an equivalent GFA for each propositionalized process specification. LTL_f-based automata construction techniques are used for LMP-DECLARE and a reachability-based algorithm is used for DPNs. In case of DPNs, additional self loops are added to all states of the GFA for handling events that the DPN should ignore, and an additional trap state is added for handling permanent violations.

Cross-product GFA Construction — Combining the individual GFAs into a cross-product GFA. A standard automata cross-product algorithm can be used, given that the guards of the transitions are encoded as simple propositional strings.

Violation Model Integration — Annotation of the cross-product GFA states with a corresponding global monitoring status and a corresponding monitoring status of each individual process specification. In the current implementation, this is performed by concurrent traversal of the cross-product GFA and individual GFAs, however this can be further improved in the future.

Cost Model Integration — Fixpoint computation procedure based on the priorities of the input process specifications and the violation model from the previous step. The procedure begins by annotating each GFA state with the total cost of temporary and permanent violations incurred in that state. Here, the cost is equivalent to the priority of the specification, thus making the highest priority specifications also the most costly to violate. A copy of these annotations is made and then updated iteratively, based on the corresponding values of the successor states, so that the lowest value is used after each iteration. As a result, each state of the cross-product GFA is annotated with the total cost of stopping the process execution in the given state and the lowest possible total cost of violations achievable from the given state.

5.3   Event Processing

Event processing in the proposed monitoring approach is somewhat analogous to other existing automata based monitoring approaches [14]. The main differ-

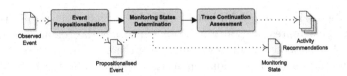

Fig. 4. Main steps and intermediate artifacts for processing a single event.

ences are that each incoming event must be translated into a propositionalized form accepted by the monitoring automaton, and two additional post-processing steps are performed after updating the state of the monitoring automaton, one for determining the monitor state, and one for determining the next activity recommendations. An overview of the event processing steps is provided on Fig. 4.

Processing of each observed event occurs at the beginning of the monitoring phase of the M3 Framework (Sect. 4.3, Automated Event Processing) and consists of the following main steps:

Event Propositionalization — Translation of the observed event into the equivalent propositionalized event. The propositionalized event is required to correspond to one of the propositions used in the monitoring automaton (Sect. 5.2, Propositionalization step) and can therefore be used directly to transition the monitor automaton into its corresponding next state.

Monitor State Determination — Determination of the monitor state based on the propositionalized event. The monitoring state can be looked up directly based on the corresponding GFA annotations and consists of a global monitoring state and the monitoring state of each individual process specification (Sect. 5.2, Violation Model Integration).

Trace Continuation Assessment — Determination of the next activity recommendations based on cost model annotations of the GFA. Each immediate successor state of the current monitor automaton state is evaluated to determine the set of states that can lead to a minimum total cost of violations. The propositional labels of the transitions leading to the best successor states are translated into equivalent events (including the data perspective) and returned as the set of activity recommendations.

6   Preliminary Experiments

A prototypical implementation of the monitoring approach presented in Sect. 5 was developed to perform preliminary experiments. In this section, we give an overview of these experiments by providing an example of the monitoring results and discussing scalability with respect to the number of input process specifications. For reproducibility purposes, the implemented tool, all models, and all event logs used in the experiments are available at https://git.io/JM0iA.

Monitoring Results. To demonstrate the monitoring results, we rely on the example scenario introduced in Sect. 2. We have modeled both the hip fracture

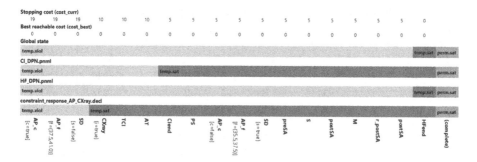

Fig. 5. Example of monitoring results (excluding activity recommendations) for a case where the patient is required to do a surgery and, at the same time, has a chest infection.

and the chest infection DPNs, as well as the constraint requiring an X-ray check if a patient has high body temperature or cough. The DPNs are assigned a violation cost of 5, while the constraint is assigned a violation cost of 9. This gives us a total of three process specifications, which, along with their violation costs, are automatically combined into a single hybrid process specification for monitoring.

A screenshot of the monitoring results, for a case where suspicion of a chest infection causes the surgery to be postponed, is provided in Fig. 5. There are a few key observations that we can make based on these monitoring results. First, the stopping cost drops after certain events, indicating that some process specifications have been completely and correctly carried out. Second, the best reachable cost is always zero, indicating that there is always at least one possible sequence of future events (including payloads) that would satisfy all process specifications. The last process specification (the declarative part of the hybrid specification) is temporarily violated after the first event because cough is detected, thus requiring a chest X-ray to be performed. While these are the main observations based on the given scenario, a more in-depth description, including an overview of the activity recommendations, is available at https://youtu.be/ f9gy74Ikl8s.

Scalability. Multiple copies of the chest infection treatment DPN from Sect. 2 were used to asses the scalability of the monitoring approach. All activities in each copy were renamed to be distinct and a constraint such as Chain Response(noCIcopy01, CXraycopy02) was used to connect each new DPN copy to the previous one, therefore allowing to scale up the experiments in a predictable manner that would also include interplay of the process specifications. The same event log, consisting of four traces of three to four events, was used for all tests.

Based on the test results (Table 1), it is clear that, for the offline task of building the monitoring automaton, the scalability of the current implementation is reasonable when the number of input process specifications is not very large. While the memory usage and the size of the monitoring automaton are relatively

Table 1. Results of the syntetic scalability experiments.

Specifications		Monitoring Automaton		Event Processing(ms)			Implementation
DPN	LMP-Declare	Time(ms)	States	Min.	Max.	Mean	Memory(mb)
1	0	25	7	5	40	11	226
2	1	53	83	5	40	15	232
3	2	167	1010	4	45	15	269
4	3	1997	12092	5	47	15	829
5	4	18774	143272	4	49	16	8886

small for 3 DPN models with 2 LMP-DECLARE constraints, both requirements quickly ramp up with higher number of input specifications. Meanwhile, the performance of event processing is minimally affected by the number of input specifications and remained near instantaneous in all tests.

The potential scalability issues of the current implementation are mainly caused by two factors. First, we focused on demonstrating that multiple declarative and procedural process specifications can be combined for monitoring, thus advancing the state-of-the-art by overcoming the assumption that the process behavior should be embedded into a single process model. Given this focus, we opted for a naïve implementation that could be used as a baseline for future optimizations. Second, the approach itself has some inherent complexity issues due to propositionalization, which leads to a state explosion in the constructed automaton. We believe that these potential scalability issues can be mitigated; however, this requires further research.

7   Related Work

Monitoring Petri Net Models. There are various works that rely on different classes of Petri nets for capturing inappropriate system behaviors. One of the first works studies a monitoring approach that detects errors by controlling the number of tokens inside P-invariants [19]. Another work [18] proposes a workflow management system that encompasses workflow monitoring and delay prediction modules based on resource-aware Petri nets. While there are other Petri-net based monitoring approaches, all of them share the common assumption that the full process specification is given as a single Petri net, which can be insufficient in domains with highly flexible and knowledge-intensive processes.

Monitoring Declarative Specifications. Here, we restrict ourselves to approaches related to DECLARE (for comparisons with other approaches please refer to [12]). While existing DECLARE approaches in general assume that a single specification is used, splitting it into multiple specifications (e.g., one specification per constraint) would be semantically equivalent. This is well exemplified in [14], where the truth value of each constraint is monitored individually and possible global conflicts are handled by the conjunction of all the constraints being monitored. The DECLARE language has also been extended to account for multiple perspectives by considering activity payloads and corresponding monitoring approaches have been developed (see, e.g.,[6,13]). However, none of these works studied monitoring of LMP-DECLARE constraints in hybrid specifications.

Conformance Checking. The interplay of multiple process specifications (both procedural and declarative) has however been addressed to some extent from the perspective of conformance checking. A recent work [8] studies the conformance checking task for mixed-paradigm process models that integrate Petri nets and DECLARE constraints. However, this setting does not consider any activity payloads and, as customary to conformance checking, the authors focus on alignment of complete traces and not on monitoring ongoing incomplete process executions. There are two other research lines that consider multiple process and constraint specifications, both related to the medical domain. The first one focuses on interactions between CGs and BMK from the view-point of the conformance checking problem [4]. The second one studies the same interactions, but from the perspective of explainability [22] (i.e., how can the actions taken during the treatment of a specific patient be automatically explained given the presence of multiple CGs and BMK). While these approaches consider the interplay of procedural and declarative models, their respective tasks of interest are performed on historical data and do not consider streams of events.

Hybrid Models. In addition to the aforementioned approaches, research in relation to hybrid business process representations (HBPRs) is currently ongoing. The term hybrid refers, in this case, to combining declarative and procedural modeling paradigms into a unified modeling approach which would allow expressing both strict and flexible aspects of a single process in the same model. A conceptual framework and a common terminology for these types of models has been proposed recently [2] and a number of open research challenges related to HBPRs have been identified [21]. Some process mining approaches for HBPRs [7,15,20] have also been developed. However, to the best of our knowledge, there are currently no monitoring approaches suitable for hybrid settings.

8   Conclusion

In this paper, we have presented M3, a framework for monitoring hybrid process specifications in domains where multiple interacting (procedural) sub-processes work under additional (declarative) constraints. We developed a prototypical implementation of the monitoring approach as a proof-of-concept and performed initial scalability experiments showing that, even without optimizations, the tool scales reasonably well when using a limited number of specifications.

The avenues for future work can be divided into three categories. First, the scalability of the approach should be improved, both by code optimizations and by exploring heuristics for reducing the monitoring automaton size. Second, the functionality should be extended to support the time perspective, recovery strategies, and runtime modifications of the hybrid specification. These would respectively allow the process analysts to monitor time critical aspects of a process (e.g., a mandatory checkup after a surgery within a certain time period), continue monitoring after a permanent violation (thus enabling the detection of multiple violations of a single constraint), and handle unforeseen circumstances (e.g., a COVID-19 infection during an ongoing treatment or adaptations of a clinical guideline). Finally, while we have presented a general framework for utilizing our monitoring approach, there are additional socio-technical aspects that should be explored, e.g., how to integrate the framework into an organizational context, and what skills would be necessary to support its different phases.

Acknowledgements. The work of A. Alman was supported by the European Social Fund via "ICT programme" measure and by the Estonian Research Council grant PRG1226. F.M. Maggi was supported by the UNIBZ project CAT.

References

1. Alman, A., Maggi, F.M., Montali, M., Patrizi, F., Rivkin, A.: Monitoring hybrid process specifications with conflict management: The automata-theoretic approach. Technical report, arXiv.org (2021)
2. Andaloussi, A.A., Burattin, A., Slaats, T., Kindler, E., Weber, B.: On the declarative paradigm in hybrid business process representations: a conceptual framework and a systematic literature study. Inf. Syst. **91**, 101505 (2020)
3. Bergami, G., Maggi, F.M., Marrella, A., Montali, M.: Aligning data-aware declarative process models and event logs. In: BPM, pp. 235–251 (2021)
4. Bottrighi, A., Chesani, F., Mello, P., Montali, M., Montani, S., Terenziani, P.: Conformance checking of executed clinical guidelines in presence of basic medical knowledge. In: BPM Workshops, pp. 200–211 (2011)
5. Burattin, A., Maggi, F.M., Sperduti, A.: Conformance checking based on multiperspective declarative process models. Expert Syst. Appl. **65**, 194–211 (2016)
6. De Masellis, R., Maggi, F.M., Montali, M.: Monitoring data-aware business constraints with finite state automata. In: ICSSP, pp. 134–143. ACM (2014)
7. De Smedt, J., De Weerdt, J., Vanthienen, J.: Fusion miner: process discovery for mixed-paradigm models. Decis. Support Syst. **77**, 123–136 (2015)
8. van Dongen, B.F., De Smedt, J., Di Ciccio, C., Mendling, J.: Conformance checking of mixed-paradigm process models. Inf. Syst. **102**, 101685 (2021)
9. Hopcroft, J.E., Motwani, R., Ullman, J.D.: Introduction to automata theory, languages, and computation, 3rd Edition. Addison-Wesley (2007)
10. Jalali, A., Maggi, F.M., Reijers, H.A.: A hybrid approach for aspect-oriented business process modeling. J. Softw. Evol. Process. **30**(8), e1931 (2018)
11. de Leoni, M., Felli, P., Montali, M.: A holistic approach for soundness verification of decision-aware process models. In: Trujillo, J.C., et al. (eds.) ER 2018. LNCS, vol. 11157, pp. 219–235. Springer, Cham (2018). https://doi.org/10.1007/978-3-030-00847-5_17
12. Ly, L.T., Maggi, F.M., Montali, M., Rinderle-Ma, S., van der Aalst, W.M.P.: Compliance monitoring in business processes: functionalities, application, and toolsupport. Inf. Syst. **54**, 209–234 (2015)
13. Maggi, F.M., Montali, M., Bhat, U.: Compliance monitoring of multi-perspective declarative process models. In: EDOC, pp. 151–160. IEEE (2019)
14. Maggi, F.M., Montali, M., Westergaard, M., van der Aalst, W.M.P.: Monitoring business constraints with linear temporal logic: an approach based on colored

automata. In: Rinderle-Ma, S., Toumani, F., Wolf, K. (eds.) BPM 2011. LNCS, vol. 6896, pp. 132–147. Springer, Heidelberg (2011). https://doi.org/10.1007/978-3-642-23059-2_13

15. Maggi, F.M., Slaats, T., Reijers, H.A.: The automated discovery of hybrid processes. In: Sadiq, S., Soffer, P., Völzer, H. (eds.) BPM 2014. LNCS, vol. 8659, pp. 392–399. Springer, Cham (2014). https://doi.org/10.1007/978-3-319-10172-9_27

16. Mannhardt, F., de Leoni, M., Reijers, H.A., van der Aalst, W.M.P.: Balanced multiperspective checking of process conformance. Computing **98**(4), 407–437 (2015). https://doi.org/10.1007/s00607-015-0441-1

17. Montali, M., Pesic, M., van der Aalst, W.M.P., Chesani, F., Mello, P., Storari, S.: Declarative specification and verification of service choreographiess. ACM Trans. Web **4**(1), 3:1–3:62 (2010)

18. Pla, A., Gay, P., Meléndez, J., López, B.: Petri net-based process monitoring: a workflow management system for process modelling and monitoring. J. Intell. Manuf. **25**(3), 539–554 (2012). https://doi.org/10.1007/s10845-012-0704-z

19. Prock, J.: A new technique for fault detection using petri nets. Automatica **27**(2), 239–245 (1991)

20. Sadiq, S.W., Orlowska, M.E., Sadiq, W.: Specification and validation of process constraints for flexible workflows. Inf. Syst. **30**(5), 349–378 (2005)

21. Slaats, T.: Declarative and hybrid process discovery: recent advances and open challenges. J. Data Semant. **9**(1), 3–20 (2020)

22. Spiotta, M., Terenziani, P., Theseider Dupré, D.: Temporal conformance analysis and explanation of clinical guidelines execution: an answer set programming approach. IEEE Trans. Knowl. Data Eng. **29**(11), 2567–2580 (2017)

Graph and Network Models

Mining Valuable Collaborations from Event Data Using the Recency-Frequency-Monetary Principle

Leen Jooken[✉][iD], Mieke Jans[iD], and Benoît Depaire[iD]

Hasselt University, Martelarenlaan 42, 3500 Hasselt, Belgium
leen.jooken@uhasselt.be

Abstract. Collaborative work leads to better organizational performance. However, a team leader's view on collaboration does not always match reality. Due to the increased adoption of (online) collaboration systems in the wake of the COVID pandemic, more digital traces on collaboration are available for a wide variety of use cases. These traces allow for the discovery of accurate and objective insights into a team's inner workings. Existing social network discovery algorithms however, are often not tailored to discover collaborations. These techniques often have a different view on collaboration by mostly focusing on handover of work, resource profile similarity, or establishing relationships between resources when they work on the same case or activities without any restrictions. Furthermore, only the frequency of appearance of patterns is typically used as a measure of interestingness, which limits the kind of insights one can discover. Therefore we propose an algorithm to discover collaborations from event data using a more realistic approach than basing collaboration on the sequence of resources that carry out activities for the same case. Furthermore, a new research path is explored by adopting the Recency-Frequency-Monetary (RFM) concept, which is used in the marketing research field to assess customer value, in this context to value both the resource and the collaboration on these three dimensions. Our approach and the benefits of adopting RFM to gain insights are empirically demonstrated on a use case of collaboratively developing a curriculum.

Keywords: Collaboration network · Mining resource behavior · RFM · Social network analysis

1 Introduction

Collaborative work leads to better organizational performance in terms of efficiency and quality when the teams are well implemented, managed and supported [11,25]. This requires that team leaders have accurate insights into the

Supported by the Special Research Fund (BOF19OWB10) of Hasselt University.

X. Franch et al. (Eds.): CAiSE 2022, LNCS 13295, pp. 339–354, 2022.
https://doi.org/10.1007/978-3-031-07472-1_20

collaboration characteristics, in order to improve team effectiveness through team-oriented interventions [11]. However, a team leader's view on how collaboration is taking place does not always match reality [18,23]. Research has shown that people have difficulties in accurately perceiving the informal structure of groups and that there is a negative relationship between the hierarchy level and the accuracy of perception [7,10,18].

Due to the increasing digitization however, more digital traces on collaboration have become available as teamwork is increasingly supported by communication and coordination tools [9]. The global COVID pandemic has further sped up the adoption of these information systems that support online collaboration out of necessity to keep businesses running. This shift provides a great opportunity as the data in these systems provide a more objective and complete view on the work that actually took place in reality.

In this study we aim to extract the resources (the actors in the team) and the collaboration relationships between these resources (based on the objects they worked on) from this type of data. This work is related to existing work in the field of Organisational Network Analysis (ONA) [9,28], the organisational perspective in Process Mining [1], and Developer Social Networks (DSN) [12], but these are all subject to some limitations when applied to this collaboration context. The main shortcomings are that the data from collaboration systems is not suitable to use with these existing techniques, and that the existing techniques have a view on collaboration that differs from the view adopted in this paper. This will be further elaborated on in Sect. 2. Furthermore, for all these research areas there is often no clarity or agreement on what constitutes a valuable resource or a valuable relationship. Therefore we will expand on related work by also assessing the value of a resource and a relationship in the collaborative context, based on the Recency-Frequency-Monetary (RFM) model [6] presented in marketing literature. This model is a widely used tool designed to measure customer value, which, given an event of interest, measures how recent the event occurred (R), how frequently it occurred (F) and the monetary aspect of the event (M) [22]. Since the concept of an event can be interpreted broadly, the RFM model can be adapted to many different contexts [22]. This is usually done by modifying one or more RFM segmentation variables, such as redefining, adding or excluding variables [15]. This concept has already been successfully applied in other data mining applications to find interesting patterns, not solely based on their frequency of appearance (see Sect. 2).

Therefore the contribution of this paper is twofold: (1) we provide an algorithm that, using realistic constraints, can uncover how collaboration takes place in reality. The input data can come from any information system that captures digital traces of collaboration, as long as the resources, the objects of collaboration, and the timestamps of when a resource worked on an object can be extracted from it. The output is the set of resources and the set of collaboration relationships between these resources, which could be represented as a network. Furthermore (2) we substantiate the value of resources and their relationships by adopting and redefining the RFM model to gain valuable insights.

The remainder of this paper is structured as follows. In Sect. 2 the relevant related work on ONA, Process Mining, DSN and RFM-enriched networks is discussed. Section 3 elaborates on the algorithm's design and implementation, and formalization of the RFM concepts in the context of collaboration. A demonstration on a use case is given in Sect. 4. Finally, this paper is concluded in Sect. 5.

2   Related Work

2.1   Organizational Network Analysis

Organizational Network Analysis (ONA) is a type of Social Network Analysis (SNA) that tries to uncover and provide insights into relationships between people in an organisation [9,28]. There exists a broad array of research within this domain, as it covers all sorts of different networks. Research on collaborative networks has covered actors in movies [17], co-authors on research papers [17], software developers on a project [4,12,17], problem-solving collaborations [9] and more. A downside of the ONA approach is that it requires the input data to explicitly state the collaboration relationships (usually collected through surveys [9]), which is not necessarily the case for the data in these collaboration systems. Often only information on who worked on what and when this happened, is recorded in this data. Therefore firstly, a method is needed that can discover collaboration relationships from this type of data. The two other domains on the other hand, can handle this type of input data, but have shortcomings in other areas. As for the value of resources and their relationships, ONA provides metrics such as degree, closeness and betweenness centrality, and modularity [28]. One could for example derive the core members and boundary spanners, but these insights are limited to the network structure, not the actual importance of a resource or a relationship for collaboration.

2.2   Process Mining

The goal of the field of Process Mining is to turn data on events in a process, collected by process-aware information systems, into insights and actions [1]. The lion's share of research in this field is focused on control-flow discovery [16, 26], which aims to discover a model that best represents the process in terms of activities and their dependencies [1]. There has been some attention, albeit limited, to the organizational perspective of Process Mining, where the focus lies on the resources that carry out the activities in the process [1]. The view on collaboration that is put forward in this literature is strongly intertwined with the process context and therefore differs from the view on collaboration adopted in this paper. In this paper, a collaboration relationship between resources is assumed when they work on the same objects in close proximity in time. In the Process Mining field a relationship between resources is not established on object level, but either on the level of working on the same case (i.e. the specific process instance) or activities [2,3,23,24,26]. Therefore analyses mostly focus on handover of work networks [2,3,26] or resource profile similarity [3]. As for the value of relationships in these networks, if this value exists at all, it is based on its frequency of appearance [2,3]. The resources itself are almost never given an importance value, with the exception of the work of Pika et al. [23] where resource utilization and productivity is analysed.

2.3 Developer Social Networks

Lastly there is a large body of work dedicated to Developer Social Networks (DSN), which focuses on constructing social networks that represent the collaborative effort of writing software code [12]. Often however, the most commonly used definition of collaboration is very lax, stating that two developers are connected when they worked on the same code file, without taking into account any constraints [4,5,29]. In reality however, collaboration is often more nuanced than this. Therefore some efforts have been made to refine this definition (some of them we will also adopt in this work): by using a time window in which collaboration must take place [19]; taking a granularity measurement into account so that collaboration on one object differs from that on a dozen objects [19]; incorporating an object importance value [13]; or adopting similarity measures to establish relationships between two resources [13]. Another well known problem is that developers can choose how often they log their work: if they log it in 1 big chunk or several small chunks. Therefore the number of times a developer worked on a code file is in itself not an objective metric and cannot be used in calculations or comparisons without some kind of modification. This will also be taken into account in our work by grouping the work of a resource into work sessions.

As for the value of resources and relationships: the resources in DSN literature only very seldomly get assigned a weight value, whereas the collaboration relationships get assigned a weight value in some studies [4,13,19,27], but the methods vary and there is no universal agreement. The value of a relationship is sometimes given as part of the survey data [27], or calculated using a similarity or distance metric [13]. However we criticize that similarity between developers does not necessarily entail collaboration.

2.4 Recency-Frequency-Monetary Model

The RFM model [6] is a widely used tool designed to measure customer value, and therefore mostly used for customer segmentation and to predict customer churn, retention, loyalty and profitability [8]. The RFM model has been combined with data mining techniques, such as sequential pattern mining [8], bayesian networks [20] and deep neural networks [14] for prediction and pattern mining tasks. To the best of our knowledge there are no studies that incorporate the RFM dimensions in a social network discovery algorithm. There are however several studies that enrich pre-mined network representations with RFM information [14,20–22,30]. The work of Mitrović et al. [20–22] lies closest to the work presented in this paper. It focuses on enriching telecom call graphs with RFM information in order to include both interaction and structural features as explanatory variables for churn prediction. Their work covers two approaches: an RFM-embedded and an RFM-augmented graph. In the first approach the relationship between two customers is given a weight based on the distance between the RFM vectors of both customers. This differs from the approach in this paper as we calculate the RFM values for the edge directly and do not combine these into a summarized score, hence losing information. In their second approach Mitrović et al. augment the network by adding the RFM information as nodes to the network itself, hence changing its topology. Here no RFM value is calculated for the relations between the customers. The approach in this paper refrains from changing the topology of the network and provides RFM values for the relationships as well.

To the best of our knowledge, no studies adopting the RFM model for a network representation in the context of collaboration between resources have been carried out yet.

3   Algorithm Design

This section elaborates on the input data requirements and the different steps taken to discover collaboration relationships between resources and to value both the relationships and the resources on the three RFM dimensions.

First of all, it is important to note that the assumption is made that a resource can log their work as frequently as desired, as based on and justified in Sect. 2.3. This means that a resource can choose to register their work often in small chunks or less often in big chunks, and therefore the amount of times work is registered does not necessarily entail how often a resource has worked or collaborated. To tackle this we introduce the concepts of a work session and a collaboration session, which group work that is registered in close proximity in time together. The high-level algorithm design is then as follows. First the collaboration relationships between resources are mined from the data, making use of the concept of a collaboration session. Next, the value of such a relationship on the RFM dimensions is calculated. To also calculate these values for a resource, the preparatory step in which the resource's work is divided into work sessions is carried out first. The RFM model is redefined for this collaboration context as follows. The recency value is based on how recent a resource worked or how recent a collaboration took place. The frequency value indicates how frequent a resource worked or collaborated, and the monetary value indicates the importance of a resource or collaboration based on the importance value of the objects that were worked on. These different steps will all be elaborated on in the next subsections.

3.1   Input Requirements

The algorithm's input data can come from any information system that captures collaboration relationships, as long as it is possible to extract a set of events in which a resource worked on an object at a specific moment of time. The accepted input data structure is therefore an event log, a concept adopted from the Process Mining field [1]. A typical Process Mining event log is constructed as a list of events, in which each event must specify a case ID (i.e. a specific instance of a process) and an event ID. Furthermore information on how to (partially) order events in time must be present. Additional attributes such as an activity label, the exact timestamp and the resource that carries out the activity are optional, but appear in most event logs in practise. The input requirement for our algorithm differs in the way that the case ID is not required, but the exact timestamp, the resource and the object of the activity are. This is formalized in Definition 1.

Definition 1. *An event is defined as a tuple (event ID, resource A, object O, timestamp T) and represents a specific point in time T when resource A worked on object O.*

3.2   Mining the Collaboration Relationships

The existence of a collaboration relationship between two resources depends on whether these resources engaged in a collaboration session, as stated in Definition 2 and 3. Note that all objects that both resource A and B worked on are considered when determining if a collaboration relationship between these two resources exists. To determine the set of collaboration sessions between resource A and B on an object O (Algorithm 1), two user-specified parameters are required:

- A minimal time value t_{min} in minutes, indicating that if the time between two consecutive events exceeds this threshold, these events certainly belong to separate collaboration sessions
- The maximum length of a collaboration session t_{max} in minutes

The set of collaboration sessions between two resources is further also used in Sect. 3.3 to calculate the RFM values for a collaboration relationship.

Definition 2. *There exists a collaboration relationship between two resources A and B if and only if there exists ≥ 1 collaboration session between these two resources.*

Definition 3. *A collaboration session between resources A and B is a time window with size $\leq t_{max}$ that contains ≥ 1 event in which A worked on an object O, and ≥ 1 event in which B worked on that same object O. The time between 2 consecutive events in this window is always $\leq t_{min}$. The set of collaboration sessions between resources A and B on an object O is calculated as stated in Algorithm 1.*

Algorithm 1: Get collaboration sessions for resource pair (A,B) on object O

> Input   : The set of events in which resource A worked on object O $\cup$ the set of events in which resource B worked on object O, t_{min}, t_{max}
> Output : Set of collaboration sessions for resource pair (A,B) on object O

```
 1  timestamps ← order timestamps of all the events chronologically;
 2  t_current ← timestamps [0];
 3  e_current ← corresponding event of t_current;
 4  session [e_current];
 5  for i ← 1 to len(timestamps) do
 6      t_next ← timestamps [i];
 7      e_next ← corresponding event of t_next;
 8      if t_next − t_current > t_min then
 9          ProcessCollabSession(session, t_max) ;              /* See Algorithm 2 */
10          session ← [ ]
11      end
12      append e_next to session;
13      t_current ← t_next;
14      e_current ← e_next;
15  end
16  ProcessCollabSession(session, t_max) ;                      /* See Algorithm 2 */
```

Algorithm 2: ProcessCollabSession($session, t_{max}$)

> Input   : A set of events with as resource A OR B and as object O, t_{max}
> Output : Set of collaboration sessions for resource A and B on object O

```
 1  timestamps ← order timestamps within this session chronologically;
 2  t_first ← timestamps [0];
 3  t_last ← timestamps [-1];
 4  if t_last − t_first > t_max then
        /* Session needs to be split up in parts                                */
 5      window1, window2 ← find the largest gap between 2 consecutive timestamps in this
        window and split here the window into 2 parts;
        /* if there are multiple options choose the one that lies closest to the midpoint of the current
           window under consideration                                          */
        /* process these 2 new session windows by recursively calling this function again   */
 6      ProcessCollabSession(window1, t_max);
 7      ProcessCollabSession(window2, t_max);
 8  else
        /* This session is not too long, check if collaboration took place      */
 9      if session contains ≥ 1 event which has A as the resource AND ≥ 1 event which has
        B as the resource then
10          collaborationsessions ← save this window with the including events as one
            collaboration session to a global container;
11      end
12  end
```

3.3   RFM Values for a Relationship

To calculate the values of the three RFM dimensions for a collaboration relationship between resources A and B, their set of collaboration sessions is required. This set is obtained by taking the union of the sets of collaboration sessions on every object they collaboratively worked on, as discussed in Sect. 3.2.

Recency

Definition 4. *The recency value of a collaboration relationship between resource A and B is an indication of how recent their collaboration sessions fall on the timeline of the log that is under consideration, calculated as indicated in Algorithm 3.*

To calculate the recency value, the timeline of the event log that is examined is divided into time windows of a predefined width (user-specified parameter *'windowsize'*). These windows are numbered starting from the least recent one (number 1) to the most recent one (number n, with n the total number of windows). Next, each window gets assigned a weight equal to their window number over the total number of windows. This results in the least recent one having a weight of $1/n$, to the most recent one having a weight of 1. The collaboration sessions of a resource pair then get assigned to their corresponding windows, based on the median timestamp of a session's included events. The recency value of this collaboration relationship is then the relative number of items (number/total number of collaboration sessions) in a window times the window weight, and this summed over all the windows. This is formalized in Algorithm 3.

Algorithm 3: Recency(resource A, resource B)

Input   : Set of all collaboration sessions between resource A and B, windowsize as the size of the bins, t_{first} the first timestamp of the entire project event log, t_{last} the last timestamp of the entire project event log

Output : Recency value for the collaboration relationship between resource A and B

/* Divide the timeline into bins   */
1 bins ← divide the timeline between t_{first} and t_{last} into bins of width windowsize starting from t_{last} and working towards t_{first};

/* Give each bin a working weight   */
2 **for** i ← 1 **to** $len(bins)$ **do**
3 | binweights [i] ← $i/$ len(bins);
4 **end**

/* Get for each collaboration session the median time value for the included events; these become the data points to bin   */
5 datapoints ← [ ];
6 **for** i ← 1 **to** $len(collaborationsessions)$ **do**
7 | timestamps ← list of timestamps of all the events in collaborationsessions[i];
8 | datapoints [i] ← median(timestamps);
9 **end**
10 add each data point from datapoints into the appropriate bin from bins;

/* Calculate the relative frequency of data points in each bin   */
11 **for** i ← 1 **to** $len(bins)$ **do**
12 | bincount ← # datapoints in bins [i];
13 | relativeBinCount [i] ← bincount / len(datapoints);
14 **end**

/* Calculate final recency value   */
15 recency ← 0;
16 **for** i ← 1 **to** $len(relativeBinCount)$ **do**
17 | recency + ← relativeBinCount [i] · binweights [i];
18 **end**
19 **return** *recency*

Frequency

Definition 5. *The frequency value of a collaboration relationship between resource A and B is defined as the total number of collaboration sessions that exist between A and B, taking into account all the objects they worked on, as calculated using Algorithm 1 in Sect. 3.2.*

$$F(A, B) = \sum_O \# \; collaboration \; sessions(A, B, O) \tag{1}$$

Monetary. The monetary value of a collaboration relationship represents the importance of the work package, i.e. the collection of objects, both resources collaboratively worked on. In order to calculate this value a notion of *"the importance value of an object"* is necessary. These object importance values are highly project-dependent and therefore it is difficult to provide a default method of calculation that makes sense in all cases. Therefore these values can best be included in the event log as attributes, or calculated based on a user-defined function.

The method that was chosen for the demonstration in Sect. 4 is adopted from the software development context. An object (or file in that context) is considered important for collaboration if it continues to *"grow over time"*. Files that get altered regularly are good candidates for collaboration since multiple people having knowledge of them secures their further evolution. Based on these assumptions, Formula 2 is used to calculate the object importance. To ensure that objects that have been around for a long time are not favored over relatively new ones, we work with a ratio that takes the life span of the object into account. (Note that in this case information on the creation and deletion of an object must be available.) This also results in a larger importance value for objects created towards the end of the event log, however they are considered important as they are most relevant at this very moment in the project stage.

$$I(O) = \frac{\# \; months \; in \; which \; O \; got \; worked \; on}{\# \; months \; O \; existed} \tag{2}$$

Definition 6. *The monetary value of a collaboration relationship between resource A and B is defined as the number of collaboration sessions on an object O times the importance value of that object, and this summed over all the objects the pair of resources (A,B) collaborated on.*

$$M(A, B) = \sum_O \# \; collaboration \; sessions(A, B, O) \cdot Importance(O) \tag{3}$$

The number of collaborations on an object is included in the equation to distinguish between a pair that worked once on an important object and often on less important objects, compared to a pair that constantly worked on an important object and seldom on less important ones. If we would not take the number of collaborations into account, both pairs would have the same monetary value, while the latter should actually have a bigger monetary value.

3.4   Constructing the Work Sessions

As highlighted in the beginning of Sect. 3, in order to calculate the RFM values for a resource, the resource's work package must first be divided into work sessions. Such a work session consists of several events in which the resource worked on any object, that are grouped together when they occur in close proximity in time.

Definition 7. *A work session of resource A is a time window with size $\leq t_{max}$ that contains ≥ 1 event, with all these events having A as the resource, and the time between 2 consecutive events in this window is always $\leq t_{min}$.*

   The set of work sessions of a resource A is calculated almost identical to Algorithm 1, with two differences. First, the set of events as input just consists of all the events that have A as the resource (regardless of the object that was worked on). Note that this means that the work sessions are not calculated per object, as was the case for the collaboration sessions. Secondly, the check if collaboration took place becomes redundant, which means that the session always gets saved as a work session.

3.5   RFM Values for a Resource

The work sessions that were calculated for a resource in the previous section will serve as the starting point for the calculation of the resource's RFM values, similar to the approach for the relationships.

Recency

Definition 8. *The recency value of a resource A is an indication of how recent their work sessions fall on the timeline of the log that is under consideration. This value is calculated in the same way as the recency value for a collaboration relationship, as indicated in Algorithm 3, with the difference that instead of the collaboration sessions between two resources, the set of all work sessions of resource A is used as input.*

Frequency

Definition 9. *The frequency value of a resource A is defined as the total number of work sessions identified for resource A, as explained in Sect. 3.4.*

$$F(A) = \# \ work \ sessions(A) \qquad (4)$$

Monetary. The monetary value of a resource represents the importance of their work package. There are different metrics that can be used to calculate this value, depending on the end user's goal. The method presented here is analogous to the reasoning followed to calculate the monetary value of a relationship in Sect. 3.3. Possible alternative methods include: using the betweenness centrality when the interest lies in cross-functional team members; or using the eigenvector centrality to emphase resources that are very central in the team.

Definition 10. *The monetary value of a resource A is defined as the number of work sessions that include ≥ 1 event that has O as object, times the importance value of that object, and this summed over all the objects resource A worked on.*

$$M(A) = \sum_{O} \# \ work \ sessions(A) \ that \ include \ O \cdot Importance(O) \quad (5)$$

4   Demonstration

The tool is implemented in Python and available on Github[1]. In this section a demonstration of the tool and possible interesting insights will be provided. As a use case the "Machine Learning for Beginners curriculum"[2] project is used, which is an initiative of the Azure Cloud advocates at Microsoft. This team of authors, illustrators and Microsoft Student Ambassadors has come together to create a freely available 26-lesson curriculum on machine learning. Furthermore it is open to the public to contribute translations, fix bugs, or suggest and provide new lessons. The incremental traces of collaboratively developing the lessons and translations are available for study. The data was extracted from GitHub, which is a version control system mainly used for software development projects. However, it also harbors collaboration information on other topics such as this use case of developing a curriculum. Do note that the tool's strength lies in its applicability to data from any information system that captures digital traces of collaboration, beyond only GitHub.

An event log consisting of events that describe the timestamp when a resource worked on a file (i.e. the object of collaboration) was extracted based on the log of Git commits. The resulting event log analyzed in this demo includes the work between January 31 2021 and November 13 2021. The parameter settings for the demonstration were set to t_{min} and t_{max} respectively equal to 2 weeks and to 7 days for the discovery of the collaboration sessions; and 24 h and 4 h for the identification of the work sessions. The window size for the recency calculation for both a resource and a collaboration relationship was set to 24 h. All the resources' names are anonymized in the discussion to maintain their privacy.

The collaboration network that was discovered using our tool is shown in Fig. 1. The color codes were added manually based on the available project information. To analyze the RFM values for both the resources and relations, the recency, frequency, and monetary ranges are divided into five segments, similar to how RFM has been traditionally used for market segmentation in the marketing field [8]. The resulting segments for each dimension and the number of elements that fall within each segment are shown in Table 1. This table will be used to highlight a selected number of insights, by discussing groups that are formed using a set intersection of segments from each dimension. For example, resource group $1 - x - 4/5$ refers to the all the resources that have a recency

---

[1] https://github.com/LeenJooken/RFMCollaborationMiner.
[2] https://github.com/microsoft/ML-For-Beginners.

value in segment 1 ([0.00, 0.25[), any possible frequency value, and a monetary value in segment 4 or 5 (≥20), as described below.

$$Resource\ group\ 1 - x - 4/5\ =\ \forall\ resources \in segment\ R1\ \cap$$
$$(\ \forall\ resources \in segment\ M4\ \cup\ \forall\ resources \in segment\ M5\ )$$
$$(6)$$

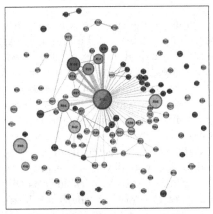

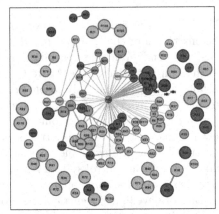

| (a) Monetary values as weights | (b) Recency values as weights |

Fig. 1. The mined collaboration network with as node and edge weights respectively the monetary value (a) and the recency value (b). Therefore in (a) bigger nodes and thicker edges represent higher monetary values, in (b) they represent higher recency values. The color codes: author (blue), illustrator (green), MS student (yellow), bug fixer (red), translator (purple), bot (black). (Color figure online)

First of all, the core resources of the network, that are mostly authors and illustrators, are characterized by the highest monetary values (segments 3 to 5) (Fig. 1 (a)), mostly also high frequency values (segments 4 and 5), but very low

Table 1. Segmentation of the RFM dimensions. The number of elements (resources or collaboration relationships) that fall within each segment for each dimension is indicated between brackets. (Sums to total number of elements by column.)

#	Resource			Collaboration relationship		
	R	F	M	R	F	M
1	[0.00, 0.25[(3)	[0, 2 [(60)	[0, 3 [(69)	[0.00, 0.25[(2)	[0 - 3 [(80)	[0 - 0.6 [(23)
2	[0.25, 0.60[(40)	[2, 5 [(30)	[3, 10[(28)	[0.25, 0.50[(15)	[3 - 5 [(10)	[0.6 - 2 [(64)
3	[0.60, 0.75[(24)	[5, 10[(10)	[10, 20[(7)	[0.50, 0.65[(51)	[5 - 10[(6)	[2 - 5 [(9)
4	[0.75, 0.90[(17)	[10, 25[(9)	[20, 50[(6)	[0.65, 0.80[(19)	[10 - 20[(6)	[5 - 10[(5)
5	[0.90, 1.00] (27)	≥25 (2)	≥50 (1)	[0.80, 1.00] (16)	≥20 (1)	≥10 (2)

recency values (segment 2) (Fig. 1 (b)), (resulting in group 2 − 4/5 − 3/4/5). This means that they worked often and that their work package is important, but that this work took place in the beginning of the project. This is also reflected in their internal collaboration relationships that are not recent, but have a large monetary value (group 2 − x − 4/5). Figure 1 (b) shows then that the resources with recency values in the highest segment (group 5 − x − x) are all translators or bug fixers. This makes sense as the lessons first had to be created before they were made available for translations and fixes. The 4th recency segment (group 4 − x − x) contains one author that added a lesson at a later stage in the project (Fig. 1 (b) resource R11). Next, it is easy to notice that resource R52 stands out above all in terms of monetary and frequency value (group x − 5 − 5) and turns out to act as the lead for this project. This resource is also involved in the most collaboration relationships, namely 48 (with the second highest being 6 for reference). If we further look at resources with a high monetary value (group x − x − 4/5) (Fig. 1 (a)), we notice that resources R69 and R86 barely engage in collaborations (0 and 1 respectively), which makes them crucial resources for further knowledge retention of this project. Lastly, if we take a look at group 1-1-1, it shows that this group consists of three bot resources (microsoft open source, microsoft-github-operations[bot] and azure static web apps) that were all only used by the lead resource R52 to initiate the project. These are depicted as black nodes in Fig. 1.

5   Conclusions, Limitations, and Future Work

Insights into a team's collaborative characteristics are essential to improve organizational performance. Nowadays, accelerated by the rise of COVID, more and more digital traces on all sorts of collaboration are available as collaborative work is increasingly supported by information systems. In this study we explored the potential of this data to provide realistic and valuable insights into collaborative work. Existing methods from the domains of Organizational Network Analysis, Process Mining and Developer Social Networks are subject to certain shortcomings when applied to this collaboration context. Therefore in this study we presented an algorithm designed to mine collaboration relationships between resources from event data extracted from these systems, which captures the exact timestamp of when a resource worked on which object. Furthermore, we expanded on existing literature by exploring a new research path on how to value a resource and a relationship, by adopting and redefining the RFM model from marketing research. This model allows to gain insights beyond how frequently collaboration took place, by also providing a recency and monetary dimension. The algorithm was demonstrated on a use case of collaboratively and incrementally developing a curriculum on machine learning. The demonstration showed that insights into the general structure of the collaboration network could be provided, as well as insights into how resources and relationships are positioned on the different RFM dimensions.

    There are however some limitations that should be addressed. The work presented in this paper starts from the premise that a project is available for analysis that clearly indicates the objects on which collaboration took place. This will not always be the case when data is extracted from information systems, and often data cleaning and preprocessing might be required. Further, the method that was chosen to calculate the importance value of an object for the demonstration in Sect. 4 values objects based on their importance for collaboration and not necessarily their business value. This solution could be appropriate for several use cases. However, note that if applied to a traditional software development project, the method should be fine-tuned, as the current one could point to objects that required frequent bug fixes and not necessarily those objects that are the most valuable in terms of feature criticality.

To conclude, there are several possible extensions to this work that could be addressed in the future. First of all, a validation study on a use case with expert feedback is planned for the future. Next, it may be difficult for an end-user to provide (the optimal) parameter values. Possible future directions may be working with fuzzy constraints instead of hard boundaries when calculating the work and collaboration sessions; or providing a method that calculates an optimal default parameter setting. Furthermore, different methods to determine the importance value of an object might be explored. Lastly, the methods of calculating a work or collaboration session could be handled in an alternative way by positioning them as optimization problems to find the most optimal grouping of events in sessions. Examining the effects of repositioning these methods could be interesting further research.

References

1. van der Aalst, W.: Process mining: Data science in action (2016). ISBN 978-3-662-49851-4
2. van der Aalst, W.M.P., Reijers, H.A., Song, M.: Discovering social networks from event logs. Comput. Supp. Cooper. Work (CSCW) **14**(6), 549–593 (2005)
3. van der Aalst, W.M.P., Song, M.: Mining social networks: uncovering interaction patterns in business processes. In: Desel, J., Pernici, B., Weske, M. (eds.) BPM 2004. LNCS, vol. 3080, pp. 244–260. Springer, Heidelberg (2004). https://doi.org/10.1007/978-3-540-25970-1_16
4. Aljemabi, M.A., Wang, Z.: Empirical study on the similarity and difference between vcs-dsn and bts-dsn. In: Proceedings of the 2017 International Conference on Management Engineering, Software Engineering and Service Sciences. ICMSS 2017, New York, NY, USA, pp. 30–37. Association for Computing Machinery (2017)
5. Bird, C., Pattison, D., D'Souza, R., Filkov, V., Devanbu, P.: Latent social structure in open source projects. In: Proceedings of the 16th ACM SIGSOFT International Symposium on Foundations of Software Engineering. SIGSOFT 2008/FSE-16, pp. 24–35. Association for Computing Machinery (2008)
6. Bult, J.R., Wansbeek, T.: Optimal selection for direct mail. Mark. Sci. **14**(4), 378–394 (1995)
7. Casciaro, T.: Seeing things clearly: social structure, personality, and accuracy in social network perception. Soc. Networks **20**(4), 331–351 (1998)
8. Chen, Y.L., Kuo, M.H., Wu, S.Y., Tang, K.: Discovering recency, frequency, and monetary (RFM) sequential patterns from customers' purchasing data. Electron. Commer. Res. Appl. **8**(5), 241–251 (2009)

9. Cross, R., Ehrlich, K., Dawson, R., Helferich, J.: Managing collaboration: improving team effectiveness through a network perspective. Calif. Manage. Rev. **50**(4), 74–98 (2008)
10. Cullen, K.L., Palus, C.J., Appaneal, C.: Developing Network Perspective: Understanding the Basics of Social Networks and their Role in Leadership [White paper]. Technical report, Center for Creative Leadership (2014). https://doi.org/10.35613/ccl.2014.1019
11. Guzzo, R.A., Dickson, M.W.: Teams in organizations: recent research on performance and effectiveness. Annu. Rev. Psychol. **47**(1), 307–338 (1996)
12. Herbold, S., Amirfallah, A., Trautsch, F., Grabowski, J.: A systematic mapping study of developer social network research. J. Syst. Softw. **171**, 110802 (2021)
13. Jermakovics, A., Sillitti, A., Succi, G.: Mining and visualizing developer networks from version control systems. In: Proceedings of the 4th International Workshop on Cooperative and Human Aspects of Software Engineering. CHASE 2011, New York, NY, USA, pp. 24–31, Association for Computing Machinery (2011)
14. Lai, C.Y., Li, Y.M., Lin, L.F.: A social referral appraising mechanism for the e-marketplace. Inf. Manage. **54**(3), 269–280 (2017)
15. Li, J., Cao, S.: The study on high-value user identification of localized information platform. J. Phys: Conf. Ser. **1883**(1), 012109 (2021)
16. Ly, L.T., Rinderle, S., Dadam, P., Reichert, M.: Mining staff assignment rules from event-based data. In: Bussler, C.J., Haller, A. (eds.) BPM 2005. LNCS, vol. 3812, pp. 177–190. Springer, Heidelberg (2006). https://doi.org/10.1007/11678564_16
17. Madey, G., Freeh, V., Tynan, R.: The open source software development phenomenon: an analysis based on social network theory. In: AMCIS 2002 Proceedings, pp. 1806–1813. Association for Information Systems (2002)
18. Mehra, A., Smith, B.R., Dixon, A.L., Robertson, B.: Distributed leadership in teams: The network of leadership perceptions and team performance. Leadersh. Q. **17**(3), 232–245 (2006)
19. Meneely, A., Williams, L.: Socio-technical developer networks: should we trust our measurements? In: Proceedings of the 33rd International Conference on Software Engineering. ICSE 2011, pp. 281–290. Association for Computing Machinery (2011)
20. Mitrovic, S., Baesens, B., Lemahieu, W., De Weerdt, J.: tcc2vec: RFM-informed representation learning on call graphs for churn prediction. Inf. Sci. **557**, 1–16 (2019)
21. Mitrovic, S., De Weerdt, J.: Dyn2Vec: Exploiting dynamic behaviour using difference networks-based node embeddings for classification. In: Proceedings of the International Conference on Data Science. pp. 194–200. CSREA Press (2019)
22. Mitrovic, S., Singh, G., Baesens, B., Lemahieu, W., De Weerdt, J.: Scalable RFM-enriched representation learning for churn prediction, vol. 2018-January, pp. 79–88. IEEE (2017)
23. Pika, A., Leyer, M., Wynn, M.T., Fidge, C.J., Hofstede, A.H.M.T., Aalst, W.M.P.V.D.: Mining resource profiles from event logs. ACM Trans. Manag. Inf. Syst. **8**(1), 1:1–1:30
24. Pika, A., Wynn, M.T., Fidge, C.J., ter Hofstede, A.H.M., Leyer, M., van der Aalst, W.M.P.: An extensible framework for analysing resource behaviour using event logs. In: Jarke, M., et al. (eds.) CAiSE 2014. LNCS, vol. 8484, pp. 564–579. Springer, Cham (2014). https://doi.org/10.1007/978-3-319-07881-6_38
25. Recardo, R., Wade, D., Mention, C.: Teams: Who Needs Them and Why? Teams: Who Needs Them and Why?, Gulf Publishing Company (1996)
26. Song, M., van der Aalst, W.M.P.: Towards comprehensive support for organizational mining. Decis. Support Syst. **46**(1), 300–317 (2008)

27. Tymchuk, Y., Mocci, A., Lanza, M.: Collaboration in open-source projects: Myth or reality? In: 11th Working Conference on Mining Software Repositories, MSR 2014 - Proceedings (2014)

28. Wasserman, S., Faust, K., et al.: Social Network Analysis: Methods and Applications. Cambridge University Press, Cambridge (1994).ISBN 0-521-38707-8

29. Wolf, T., Schroter, A., Damian, D., Nguyen, T.: Predicting build failures using social network analysis on developer communication. In: 2009 IEEE 31st International Conference on Software Engineering, pp. 1–11 (2009)

30. Xue, Y., Chen, J., Zhou, Y.: Research on user discovery based on loyalty in SNS. In: Proceedings of the 2017 International Seminar on Social Science and Humanities Research (SSHR 2017), pp. 399–406. Atlantis Press, December 2017

Querying Temporal Property Graphs

Landy Andriamampianina[1,2]($\boxtimes$) (iD), Franck Ravat[1] (iD), Jiefu Song[1,2] (iD),
and Nathalie Vallès-Parlangeau[1] (iD)

[1] IRIT-CNRS (UMR 5505) - Université Toulouse 1 Capitole (UT1),
2 Rue du Doyen Gabriel Marty, 31042 Toulouse Cedex 09, France
{landy.andriamampianina,franck.ravat,jiefu.song,
nathalie.valles-parlangeau}@irit.fr
[2] Activus Group, 1 Chemin du Pigeonnier de la Cépière, 31100 Toulouse, France
{landy.andriamampianina,jiefu.song}@activus-group.fr

Abstract. Nowadays, in many real-world problems, objects are characterized by properties and interactions that evolve over time. Several temporal property graph models associated with query languages are proposed in the literature to manage the temporal and interconnectivity features of such problems. However, they are not widely used due to the lack of a conceptual view. To overcome this drawback, we propose user-oriented operators to analyze temporal evolution of property graphs. We also define translation rules between our operators and existing property graph query languages to implement them directly. To illustrate the feasibility of our solution, we present two case studies based on a Neo4j and an OrientDB implementations of our operators and show some real-world querying examples.

Keywords: Operators · Temporal evolution · Implementation ·
Neo4j · OrientDB

1 Introduction

Many activities involve people (or objects) that interact in many ways over time [26]. For instance, an infectious disease spreads over time through the contacts among a population. Developing applications to manage these activities requires taking into account both the interconnectivity and the temporal features of the latter. In the context of the Information System, the interconnectivity can be managed by a property graph, which connects entities together through relationships and describes them with attributes [4]. The temporality, however, is not studied in this field. In other words, changes in interconnected data over time (adding, removing and updating entities, relationships as well as their attributes) are neither represented nor exploitable in existing property graph based systems. Our research question is therefore how to model and query interconnected data, taking into account their different types of changes over time.

Temporal management of data has been studied in other domains, such as relational databases [14] and Semantic Web [13]. In light of this work, the graph

© Springer Nature Switzerland AG 2022
X. Franch et al. (Eds.): CAiSE 2022, LNCS 13295, pp. 355–370, 2022.
https://doi.org/10.1007/978-3-031-07472-1_21

community has been working on classic graph modelling [7] and graph-oriented databases [3] that have failed to manage data temporality up to now [18,23]. Some works propose different extensions of classic graph data models to integrate time dimension [27]. In parallel, some works have developed their own management systems for temporal graph data [10,11,15,20]. The overall observation is thus that there is no unified framework for both modelling and querying temporal interconnected data [6,24]. Existing solutions focus mainly on specific implementations and lack of a conceptual view to meet the needs of designers and developers [3,6,24].

The contribution of our work is to provide a conceptual solution (independent of any implementation aspects) for designers and developers to model and query temporal interconnected data. To do so, we propose operators for querying temporal graph data, which are based on a model proposed in our previous work [2]. The remainder of the paper is organized as follows. First, we review the literature on the management of temporal graph data (Sect. 2). Second, we define our conceptual model (Sect. 3.1) and operators (Sect. 3.2). Third, we present translation rules of our solution into technical environments in Sect. 3.3. Fourth, we evaluate the feasibility of our operators, presented in Sect. 4. Finally, we conclude the paper.

2   Related Work

Temporal evolution of interconnected data shows how entities, relationships and their attributes may evolve in time. This evolution can be categorized into two categories: topological evolution (addition and removal of entities and relationships) and attributes evolution (addition, removal and update of attributes of entities and relationships) [27]. To address the management of such data, we study their modelling and querying in the literature.

Property-graph and RDF data models are commonly used in the context of graph data management [3]. The property graph model allows for representing entities and relationships, using nodes linked by edges, and their attributes, using properties contained in nodes and edges [4]. The RDF model allows for representing the semantic links between data, using nodes linked by edges, but does not allow the nesting of data such as properties contained in nodes and edges [17]. Several graph query languages rely on the previous models such as SPARQL (W3C)[1] for the RDF data model, Cypher (Neo4j)[2], G-Core (LDBC) [5] and PQGL (Oracle) [25] (and so on) for the property graph model. However, they only provide basic graph operations for interconnected data [6,24]. To query temporal aspects of interconnected data, it requires an underlying data model that traces evolution. Although the property graph model incorporates some aspects of data we are interested in, it does not take into account the different types of changes that may occur on interconnected data.

---

[1] https://www.w3.org/TR/rdf-sparql-query/.

[2] https://neo4j.com/developer/cypher/querying/.

To support temporal evolution, some works propose to extend current graph query languages, based on temporal property graph models, to support basic graph operations and add expressions for time dimension querying [10,11,15]. However, graph query languages are database-dependent but not user-oriented. Implementation details behind graph query languages need to be understood to formulate queries. Therefore, the use of these extended graph query languages can be difficult for designers and developers [9]. Moreover, graph query languages may evolve over time (the addition or removal of functionalities) so they are not very consistent as a basis of a new query language [9]. The work of [20] proposes a graph query language independent of current graph query languages. However, it has the same limited composability as for graph query languages. Composability[3] allows complex queries to be built up from smaller (or simpler ones). This facilitates the understanding of complex queries and the reuse of existing operations [5].

Other works propose an algebra of composable operators for querying temporal property graphs models, in the same idea as the relational algebra [19,22]. They extend existing graph operations [3,6,24], such as the *basic graph pattern matching*[4], to incorporate temporal operators functionally similar to Allen operators [1]. They also introduce novel operators such as the *snapshot* operator, which extracts subgraphs (nodes and edges) that existed at a user-defined time range. They allow operators to be combined for advanced analysis, such as comparing two graphs obtained by the snapshot operator to observe changes between the two. However, the algebra in [19] relies on the sequence of property graph snapshots, a graph-specific adaptation of the temporal data modelling strategy in the relational databases [12]. This approach fails to trace changes at the level of the graph component (node and edge). Therefore, it does not allow direct querying of temporal graph data at the graph component level [16]. Both [19] and [22]'s operators manipulate data-oriented concepts from their underlying models, such as nodes and edges, instead of user-oriented concepts, such as entities and relationships. Moreover, there is no technical environment that implements them directly.

To sum up, existing works fail to either provide a user-oriented solution or support all temporal analysis operations. To do so, we propose a solution to query temporal graph data according to the following user-oriented criteria (i, ii and iii) and analysis criteria (iv and v): (i) to rely on a user-oriented conceptual model, (ii) to be composable to facilitate the formulation of temporal queries and their combination, (iii) to be directly implementable, (iv) to support basic and temporal graph operations, and (v) to support direct querying at all levels of the graph (a component, a set of components and the whole graph). To satisfy the previous criteria, we introduce in the following section our conceptual model and operators for representing and querying temporal interconnected data.

---

[3] Graphs are input and output of queries [5].

[4] Basic graph pattern matching consists in retrieving subgraphs that match a user-defined pattern (or graph structure).

3   Proposition

3.1   Model

We define a conceptual model of temporal property graphs, on which rely our operators. All the details of this model are available in [2].

Our model provides concepts to represent objects, relationships between objects and their evolution in terms of (i) topology i.e., their addition and removal over time as well as (ii) attributes (or properties) i.e., the addition and removal of new attributes and the change in attribute values. To handle such evolution, the model manages time through the concept of *valid time interval*, which represents when something has occurred or changed in the real world. We denote it $T = [t_s, t_f[$ which indicates a time interval starting from the time instant t_s and extending to but excluding the time instant t_f.

To describe an object, we propose the concept of *temporal entity*. A *temporal entity* e_i has an identifier *id* and a label l that describes its semantic. At each change of an entity, in terms of topology and attributes, a new state of the entity is created instead of overwriting the old state version to keep track of changes. Therefore, a temporal entity is composed of a non-empty set of states S^{e_i}. Each state $s_j \in S^{e_i}$ describes the characteristics of the entity through a set of attributes A^{s_j}, the related set of attribute values V^{s_j} and a valid time interval T^{s_j} indicating the time during which A^{s_j} and V^{s_j} do not change. The function Σ_e returns for a temporal entity all of its states:

$$\Sigma_e : e_i \rightarrow \{s_1, ..., s_m\}$$

A relationship between two objects does not have an independent existence. Its existence depends on the objects it links. To describe such relationship, we propose the concept of *temporal relationship*. A *temporal relationship* r_i is defined according to the same concepts and functions as a temporal entity. Its particularity is to describe the link between two entity states (s_k, s_j). The function ρ returns, for two entity states s_k and s_j and a relationship label l, a temporal relationship r_i if it exists:

$$\rho : s_k \times s_j \times l \rightarrow r_i$$

Following these definitions, a *Temporal Property Graph* is defined by $TG = \langle E, R \rangle$ where $E = \{e_1, ..., e_g\}$ is a finite set of temporal entities and $R = \{r_1, ..., r_h\}$ is a finite set of temporal relationships. Subsets of entities (or relationships) in the graph can share the same semantic. The function δ returns for a label l, the set of entities E_k (or relationships R_k) having the label l:

$$\delta_e : l \rightarrow E_k \text{ where } E_k \subset E$$
$$\delta_r : l \rightarrow R_k \text{ where } R_k \subset R$$

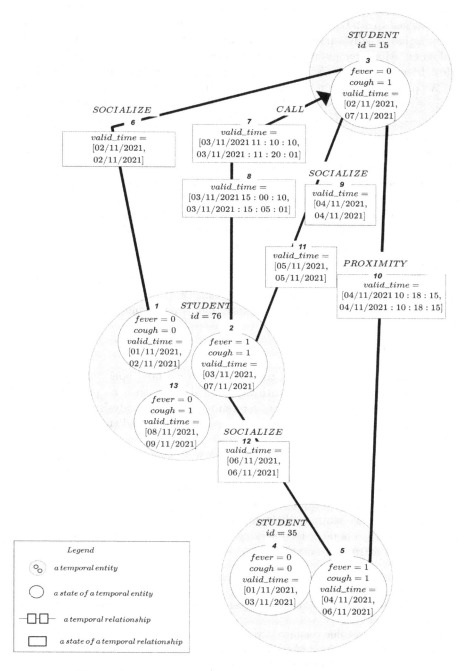

Fig. 1. Graphical notation of our temporal property graph.

Example 1. In this example, we propose a real-world use case of our temporal property graph model to present its graphical notation. A social experiment[5] was designed to study the contagion of flu symptoms of students from MIT. The study includes daily surveys about the flu symptoms of students: cough, fever and so on. Moreover, it includes information about interpersonal relationships (close friends, socialize[6], etc.) and physical information (proximity[7], call, etc.).

We present in Fig. 1 a short example of the temporal property graph representation of such dataset. Students are modelled as labelled temporal entities and illustrated by nodes in grey. All descriptive information, such as flu symptoms of students, are modelled through attributes. Students evolve in terms of their attribute values. Indeed, they have different states (illustrated by the white nodes) because their flu symptoms can change over time[8]. For instance, the student identified 35 has two states numbered 4 and 5 because he got fever and cough at state 5 that he did not have at state 4. The interpersonal relationships and physical information between students evolve only according to their topology (addition and removal over time). Each of them is modelled as a temporal relationship between two states of students and illustrated by a black edge. Each temporal relationship is labelled with its semantic (socialize, proximity or call etc.). It can have several states (illustrated by white rectangles) as they occur several times. For instance, the student 76 calls two times the student 15 that is why the relationship $CALL$ has two states numbered 7 and 8.

3.2   Operators

In this section, our objective is to propose user-oriented operators. Instead of proposing a set of operations with a technical view (such as projection), we propose two emblematic operators for temporal graph analysis: (i) extraction of a subgraph satisfying selection and temporal criteria and (ii) extraction of a subgraph satisfying pattern criteria.

Our proposed operators rely on the previous model of temporal property graph (Sect. 3.1). They return a temporal subgraph TG_{output} whose entities and relationships are subsets of an input temporal property graph TG_{input}.

In the context of temporal interconnected data, users may reason over time dimension to express their analyses [26]. To do so, we propose the $matching_{predicate}$ operator for querying temporal property graphs according to conditions on attributes and time.

---

[5] Available on the Reality Commons website http://realitycommons.media.mit.edu/socialevolution.html.

[6] Participate at least one common activity.

[7] Bluetooth signal sent from whose mobile phone and received by whose mobile phone and time, indicating the sender's mobile phone was within 10 m of the receiver's mobile phone at the time of the record.

[8] The value of a symptom attribute equals 0 if the student does not have the symptom and 1 if the student has the symptom.

Table 1. Predicate matching operator.

Operator:	$matching_{predicate}(TG_{input}, \pi)$
Input:	an input graph TG_{input};
	a set of user-defined predicates π
Output:	a subgraph TG_{output}
Actions:	1. Extract all the labels in π
	2. $TG_{output} \leftarrow \langle \emptyset, \emptyset \rangle$
	3. For each $l \in \pi$
	4. Extract the set of entities or relationships labelled l
	from TG_{input} using $\delta_e(l)$ or $\delta_r(l)$
	5. For each $e_h \in \delta_e(l)$ or $r_h \in \delta_r(l)$
	6. Get the states of e_h or r_h using $\Sigma_e(e_h)$ or $\Sigma_r(r_h)$
	7. For each $s_i \in \Sigma_e(e_h)$ or $s_i \in \Sigma_r(r_h)$ linking (s_j, s_k)
	8. If s_i satisfies all conditions in π
	9. $TG_{output} \leftarrow TG_{output} \cup \langle \{s_i\}, \emptyset \rangle$
	10. or $TG_{output} \leftarrow TG_{output} \cup \langle \{s_j, s_k\}, \{s_i\} \rangle$
	11. End If
	12. End For
	13. End For
	14. End For
	15. Return TG_{output}.

Definition 1. *The $matching_{predicate}$ operator is used to extract the subgraph TG_{output} from an input graph TG_{input} according to a user-defined set of predicates on each element of entity and relationship sets of the input graph. Within a predicate, the user has access to an entity or relationship label l, attributes, valid time intervals and can express a logical condition. The algorithm of the execution of time matching operator is presented in Table 1.*

$$matching_{predicate} : TG_{input} \times \pi \rightarrow TG_{output}$$

where $\pi = \{p_1 \beta p_2...p_{n-1} \beta p_n\}$ is a set of user-defined predicates combined with connective operators β such as AND or OR (etc.).

Each predicate p_i equals $l.a\theta w$ or $l.T\theta w$ where l is an entity or relationship label, a is an attribute, T is a valid time interval, w is a user defined value and θ is a comparison operator.

In the case of an attribute predicate $p_i = l.a\theta w$, θ could be, for instance $=$, $<$ or $>$ (etc.) to express that the attribute a satisfies a given value or range. In the case of a time predicate $p_i = l.T\theta w$, θ is a temporal operator such as an Allen operator presented in Table 2.

Contrary to the filter operation for static property graphs [3,6,24], the proposed $matching_{predicate}$ operator allows filtering graph data not only according

Table 2. Allen operators. $T = [t_s, t_f[$ is a valid time interval. $T_u = [x, y[$ is a user-defined time interval where variables x and y are time instants.

Operators	Description	Relations between time instants
$T < T_u$	T precedes T_u	$t_f < x$
$T_u > T$	T_u is preceded by T	$x > t_f$
$T m T_u$	T meets T_u	$t_f = x$
$T \circ T_u$	T overlaps T_u	$max(t_s, x) < min(t_f, y)$
$T s T_u$	T starts T_u	$t_s = x$
$T d T_u$	T during T_u	$(t_s > x)$ AND $(t_f < y)$
$T f T_u$	T finishes T_u	$t_f = y$
$T = T_u$	T equals T_u	$(t_s = x)$ AND $(t_f = y)$

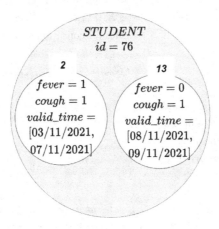

Fig. 2. Result of Example 2.

to predicates on attributes but also on valid time intervals. As we can see in Table 1, the $matching_{predicate}$ operator extracts only entities and relationships that satisfy the set of predicates at the level of states.

Example 2. Following Example 1, we want to know how did evolve the symptoms of the student 76 since 03/11/2021. To do so, we apply $TG_1 = matching_{predicate}(TG,$ $\{(STUDENT.T \circ [03/11/2021, +\infty[) \ AND \ (STUDENT.id = 76)\})$ to the temporal graph TG in Fig. 1. We use the temporal operator "overlaps" denoted $\circ$ in Table 2 to express the time predicate. The previous operation extracts the states of the student identified 76 with a valid time interval overlapping $[03/11/2021, +\infty[$. We obtain the subgraph TG_1 illustrated in Fig. 2. We observe that student 76 has two states, meaning that he experienced a change in its flu symptoms.

A fundamental operation of graph analytics is to explore subgraphs that match a user-defined graph pattern. To do so, we propose the following operator.

Table 3. Graph pattern matching operator.

Operator:	$matching_{pattern}(TG_{input}, (l_{E_i}, l_{R_j}, l_{E_k}))$
Input:	two entity labels l_{E_i} and l_{E_k};
	a relationship label l_{R_j}
Output:	a subgraph TG_{output}
Actions:	1. $TG_{output} \leftarrow \langle \emptyset, \emptyset \rangle$
	2. Extract the set of entities labelled l_{E_i} and l_{E_k}
	from TG_{input} using $\delta_e(l_{E_i})$ and $\delta_e(l_{E_k})$
	3. For each $e_h \in \delta_e(l_{E_i})$
	4. Get the states of e_h using $\Sigma_e(e_h)$
	5. For each $e_f \in \delta_e(l_{E_k})$
	6. Get the states of e_f using $\Sigma_e(e_f)$
	7. For each $s_i \in \Sigma_e(e_h)$
	8. While there exists an entity state $s_j \in \Sigma_e(e_f)$
	such that $\rho(s_i, s_j, l_{R_j}) \neq \emptyset$
	9. $TG_{output} \leftarrow TG_{output} \cup \langle \{s_i, s_j\}, \{\rho(s_i, s_j, l_{R_j})\} \rangle$
	10. End while
	11. End For
	12. End For
	13. End For
	14. Return TG_{output}

Definition 2. *A matching$_{pattern}$ operator returns for an input graph TG_{input}, an output subgraph TG_{output} matching a user-defined graph pattern defined by a starting entity label l_{E_i}, an ending entity label l_{E_k}, and a relationship label l_{R_j} to be traversed between the two entity labels. The algorithm of the execution of graph pattern matching operator is presented in Table 3.*

$$matching_{pattern} : TG_{input} \times (l_{E_i} \times l_{R_j} \times l_{E_k}) \rightarrow TG_{output}$$

Contrary to the graph pattern matching operation for static property graphs [3,6,24], the proposed $matching_{pattern}$ operator allows extracting subgraph structures with time dependent information. Indeed, it extracts subgraphs having the same pattern as the user-defined graph pattern at the level of states (Table 3). It excludes from the result set the states of entities and relationships that are not labelled with the labels specified in the user-defined graph pattern and that do not verify the existence of relationship states between each pair of entity states.

Example 3. Following Example 1, we want to know if students that had fever socialized since 03/11/2021 with students that did not have fever. To do so, we apply to the temporal graph TG in Fig. 1 TG_2 =

$matching_{predicate}(TG, \{(STUDENT_1.fever = 0)\ AND\ (STUDENT_2.fever = 1)\ AND\ (SOCIALIZE.T \circ [03/11/2021, +\infty[)\})$ to select entities and relationships satisfying our attribute and time conditions. Then, we apply $TG_3 = matching_{pattern}(TG_2, (STUDENT_1, SOCIALIZE, STUDENT_2))$ on TG_2 to obtain the relationships between the selected entities. We obtain the subgraph TG_3 in Fig. 3. We observe that the relationship has two states (numbered 9 and 11) meaning that the relationship has changed. Here, as there is no attribute in the relationship, we only have information about its evolution in terms of topology, i.e. the time of its occurrence (when it is added and removed).

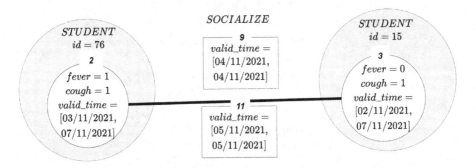

Fig. 3. Result of Example 3.

3.3 Mapping from Temporal Graph Operators to a Property Graph Operators

In this section, our objective is to define translation rules of our operators into existing property graph operations to enable a direct implementation in property-graph based systems.

As a preliminary step, we have to map our conceptual temporal property graph TG into a logical property graph PG [4]. A property graph PG is composed of nodes and edges. Each edge is associated to a pair of nodes. Each node (or edge) can be associated with a set of labels and can contain properties. Each property is a key-value pair. For each state s of an entity e in TG, a node is created in PG with a label corresponding to the label of e and a set of properties corresponding to the identifier of e, the attributes of s, the start and end instants of the valid time interval of s. An entity in the property graph corresponds therefore to a set of nodes having the same identifier. For each state s of a relationship r in TG, an edge is created in PG by connecting the two nodes corresponding to two states that r links, with a label corresponding to the label of r and a set of properties corresponding to the attributes of s, the start and end instants of the valid time interval of s. A relationship in the property graph corresponds therefore to a set of edges linking the same pair of nodes. As a

Table 4. Translation rules of our conceptual model into the logical model of property graph, the property graph in Neo4j and the property graph in OrientDB. **startvalidtime and endvalidtime.* ***with different valid time intervals.*

Temporal property graph	Property graph	Neo4j	OrientDB
A state of a temporal entity s_j	A node	A node	A vertex
A state of a temporal relationship s_b	An edge	An edge	An edge
A valid time interval of an entity state T^{s_j}	Two properties*	Two properties	Two properties
A valid time interval of a relationship state T^{s_b}	Two properties*	Two properties	Two properties
A temporal entity e_i	A set of nodes**	A set of nodes	A set of vertices
A temporal relationship r_i	A set of edges**	A set of edges	A set of edges
A label of a temporal entity l	A label	A label	A vertex class
A label of a temporal relationship l	A label	A type	An edge class
An attribute of a temporal entity $a_q^{e_i}$	A property	A property	A property
An attribute of a temporal relationship $a_d^{r_i}$	A property	A property	A property

Table 5. Graph operations to query property graphs. *Bgpm = Basic graph pattern matching.*

Operator	Description	Notation
Bgpm	Extracts subgraphs from a property graph G according to pattern P	$\tau(G, P)$
Projection	Returns a subset of the output variables O of the result of a bgpm	$\mu(G, O)$
Filter	Extracts subgraphs from G satisfying user-defined conditions C	$\sigma(G, C)$

result, we obtain the translation rules in Table 4 of our temporal property graph into the property graph to implement the model in any graph oriented NoSQL database compatible with the property graph.

In Table 6, we define translation rules of our proposed operators in existing property graph languages. The algorithms of our proposed operators (Tables 1 and 3) define the scope of the sequence of basic operations in existing property graph query languages (Table 5). A $matching_{predicate}(TG_{input}, \pi)$ operation is translatable into property graph query languages through the execution of the filter operation $\sigma(TG_{input}, \pi)$ to extract the subgraphs G_1 from the temporal property graph TG_{input} satisfying user-defined predicates π. Then, the projection operation $\mu(G_1, G_1)$ returns the graph resulting from the previous operation. A $matching_{pattern}(TG_{input}, (l_{E_i}, L_{R_j}, l_{E_k}))$ operation is translatable into property graph query languages through the execution of the basic pattern matching operation $\tau(TG_{input}, (l_{E_i}, L_{R_j}, l_{E_k}))$ to extract subgraphs G_1 with the pattern $(l_{E_i}, L_{R_j}, l_{E_k})$. Then, it uses the μ operator as in the chain of operations of $matching_{predicate}$ to get the result set.

In some environments, existing property graph query languages include sufficient functionalities to translate easily our proposed operators. In other environments, our proposed operators could not be easily implementable via the property graph query language. Due to the rich functionalities of the query languages of Neo4j and OrientDB graph databases, the mapping of our operators is simple.

Table 6. Translation of our temporal graph operators into property graph query languages. $l.p_x$ and $l.p_y$ are user-defined predicates in π. TG = *Temporal Property Graph*, PG = *Property Graph*, QL = *Query Language*.

TG operators	$matching_{predicate}$ (TG_{input}, π)	$matching_{pattern}$ $(TG_{input}, (l_{E_i}, l_{R_j}, l_{E_k}))$
PG operators	1. $G_1 = \sigma(TG_{input}, \pi)$ 2. $G_2 = \mu(G_1, G_1)$	$G_1 = \tau(TG_{input}, (l_{E_i}, l_{R_j}, l_{E_k}))$ $G_2 = \mu(G_1, G_1)$
Neo4j QL	$MATCH\,(a:l)$ $WHERE\,l.p_x\,AND\,l.p_y$ $RETURN\,a$	$MATCH\,(a:l_{E_i}) - (b:l_{R_j})$ $-(c:l_{E_k})$ $RETURN\,a, b, c$
OrientBD QL	$MATCH\{class:l, as:a,$ $where:p_x\,AND\,p_y\}$ $RETURN\,*$	$MATCH\{class:l_{E_i}\}.outE(l_{R_j})$ $.inV(l_{E_k})$ $RETURN\,*$

4   Experimental Evaluation

We run an experiment with the objective of evaluating the feasibility of our solution (our model and operators) through their implementation in technical environments.

4.1   Protocol

To validate the feasibility of our solution, we implement two datasets in two different graph database systems.

We used Neo4j and OrientDB graph database systems. More precisely, we used the following hardware configuration for the experiment: PowerEdge R630, 16 CPUs x Intel(R) Xeon(R) CPU E5-2630 v3 @ 2.40 GHz, 63.91 GB. Two virtual machines are installed on this hardware. Each virtual machine has 6 GB in terms of RAM and 100 GB in terms of disk size. On each of the two virtual machines, we installed respectively a graph database compatible with the property graph model: (i) Neo4j (version 4.1.3) and (ii) OrientDB (version 3.0.4). To avoid any bias in the disk management, we did not use any customized optimization techniques, but relied on default tuning of Neo4j and OrientDB.

To avoid any bias in datasets, we need to include both real and benchmark datasets. The first one we used is the Social experiment dataset presented in Example 1. The second one is a dataset generated from a reference benchmark available online, namely TPC-DS benchmark[9]. We transformed both datasets into the temporal property graph. Then, we stored the Social experiment dataset in Neo4j and the TPC-DS dataset in OrientDB by applying the mapping rules in Table 4. As a result, we obtained two implementations having different volumes (from 0.3 GB to 17 GB), different temporal evolutions (many nodes in one dataset

---

[9] http://www.tpc.org/tpc_documents_current_versions/pdf/tpc-ds_v2.13.0.pdf.

Table 7. Characteristics of datasets. *Y= Yes, N= No, AV = Attribute Value, AS = Attribute Set, T = Topology.*

Implementation	Social experiment	TPC-DS
Number of nodes	33 934	2 348 965
Number of edges	2 168 270	41 898 261
Size in GB	0.3	17
Evolution types of entities	AV,T	AV,AS,T
Evolution types of relationships	T	AV,AS,T

and many edges in another) and different domains (social networks and a retail company). Details of both implementations are presented in Table 7 and available on the website https://gitlab.com/2573869/queryingtemporalpropertygraphs.

Finally, we need temporal analyses adapted for each dataset. The objective is to express them into our operators and then translate them into the graph query languages of the graph database systems we used.

4.2   A Neo4j-Based Implementation

We query the Social Experiment dataset in Neo4j to make temporal analyses based on our operators. The first query concerns the analysis of the evolution of an entity during a period. The second query concerns the analysis of the evolution of several entities at a time point. In the following, we express the previous analyses using our operators and translating them into Cypher, the Neo4j's query language.

Query 1: *How did evolve the symptoms of student 76 during the period from 19/01/2009 to 23/01/2009?* This query corresponds to the following operation in our solution:

- $TG_1 = matching_{predicate}(TG_{input}, \{(STUDENT.id = 76)\,AND$
  $(STUDENT.Td[19/01/2009, 23/01/2009])\}$

The above query is translated (Table 6) into Cypher as:

```
MATCH (s:Student)
WHERE s.id="76"
AND date(s.startvalidtime) > date("2009-01-19")
AND date(s.endvalidtime) < date("2009-01-23")
RETURN s
```

Query 2: *Are there students that had fever and socialized at the day 05/03/2009 with other students that did not have fever?* This query corresponds to the following sequence of operations in our solution:

- $TG_1 = matching_{predicate}(TG_{input}, \{(STUDENT_1.fever = 1)$
  $AND\,(STUDENT_2.fever = 0)$
  $AND\,(SOCIALIZE.T \circ [05/03/2009, 06/03/2009[)\})$
- $TG_2 = matching_{pattern}(TG_1, (STUDENT_1, SOCIALIZE, STUDENT_2))$

The above query is translated (Table 6) into Cypher as:

```
MATCH p=(s1:Student)-[r:Socialize]-(s2:Student)
WHERE  s1.fever="1"
AND s2.fever ="0"
AND date(r.startvalidtime) < date("2009-03-06")
AND date(r.endvalidtime) >= date("2009-03-05")
RETURN p
```

4.3   An OrientDB-Based Implementation

We query the TPC-DS dataset in OrientDB to conduct a temporal analysis based on our operators. The query concerns the analysis of the evolution of a set of entities during a period. In the following, we express the previous query using our operators and translating them into OrientDB query language.

Query 3: *Find the stores that proposed a promotion at the month 03/1996?* This query corresponds to the following sequence of operations in our solution:

- $TG_1 = matching_{predicate}(TG_{input}, \{(Promotion.T \circ ([03/1996, 04/1996[)\})$
- $TG_2 = matching_{pattern}(TG_1, (Store, SS\_Promotion, Promotion))$

The above query is translated (Table 6) into OrientDB query language as:

```
MATCH {class: Store, as: s}.outE("SS_Promotion").inV("Promotion")
{as: p, where: (start_valid_time.asDate().format("yyyy-MM")
< date("1996-04", "yyyy-MM").format("yyyy-MM")
AND end_valid_time.asDate().format("yyyy-MM")
>= date("1996-03", "yyyy-MM").format("yyyy-MM"))}
RETURN *
```

5   Conclusion and Future Work

In this paper, we proposed two conceptual operators to help designers and developers to query temporal property graphs. They combine several advantages compared to current graph query languages and operators. First, they support classic and temporal graph operations. Second, they allow for a direct querying at different levels of the graph and at different time granularity. Third, they manipulate user-oriented concepts instead of database-oriented concepts to facilitate the formulation of queries. Finally, they are directly implementable into existing property graph database systems. To validate their feasibility, we examined use cases based on real and benchmark datasets. We showed how our operators can be used to express real-world analysis cases, and how they can be easily translated into queries in Neo4j and OrientDB using our translation rules.

In our future work, we will have several research directions. First, regarding our proposition, we will make a theoretical study to prove the completeness of our operators and add new operators if necessary. Second, regarding the evaluation of our solution, we are currently working on the performance evaluation of our operators. This evaluation will include several experiments based on several alternative implementations of graph database management systems and graph query languages, and based on different datasets and query types. Then, we will evaluate the query performance via experiments. To do so, we will study different optimization techniques, and propose several scale factors to test scalability. The objective is to propose guidelines for the implementation choice according to the analytical needs. Finally, we identified a possible extension of our solution in other domains, such as the Semantic Web domain [8,21]. We will verify its implementation in new environments and make a performance comparison with classic graph database systems such as the ones used in our paper.

References

1. Allen, J.F.: Maintaining knowledge about temporal intervals. Commun. ACM **26**(11), 832–843 (1983). https://doi.org/10.1145/182.358434
2. Andriamampianina, L., Ravat, F., Song, J., Vallès-Parlangeau, N.: Towards an efficient approach to manage graph data evolution: conceptual modelling and experimental assessments. In: Cherfi, S., Perini, A., Nurcan, S. (eds.) RCIS 2021. LNBIP, vol. 415, pp. 471–488. Springer, Cham (2021). https://doi.org/10.1007/978-3-030-75018-3_31
3. Angles, R.: A comparison of current graph database models. In: 2012 IEEE 28th International Conference on Data Engineering Workshops, pp. 171–177. IEEE, Arlington (2012). https://doi.org/10.1109/ICDEW.2012.31
4. Angles, R.: The property graph database model. In: AMW (2018)
5. Angles, R., et al.: G-CORE: a core for future graph query languages. In: Proceedings of the 2018 International Conference on Management of Data, pp. 1421–1432. ACM, Houston (2018). https://doi.org/10.1145/3183713.3190654
6. Angles, R., Arenas, M., Barceló, P., Hogan, A., Reutter, J., Vrgoč, D.: Foundations of modern query languages for graph databases. ACM Comput. Surv. **50**(5), 68:1–68:40 (2017). https://doi.org/10.1145/3104031
7. Angles, R., Gutierrez, C.: Survey of graph database models. ACM Comput. Surv. **40**(1), 1–39 (2008). https://doi.org/10.1145/1322432.1322433
8. Batsakis, S., Petrakis, E.G., Tachmazidis, I., Antoniou, G.: Temporal representation and reasoning in owl 2. Semant. Web **8**(6), 981–1000 (2017)
9. Bloesch, A., Halpin, T.: ConQuer: A Conceptual Query Language, January 1996
10. Byun, J., Woo, S., Kim, D.: ChronoGraph: enabling temporal graph traversals for efficient information diffusion analysis over time. IEEE Trans. Knowl. Data Eng. **32**(3), 424–437 (2020). https://doi.org/10.1109/TKDE.2019.2891565
11. Debrouvier, A., Parodi, E., Perazzo, M., Soliani, V., Vaisman, A.: A model and query language for temporal graph databases. VLDB J. **30**(5), 825–858 (2021). https://doi.org/10.1007/s00778-021-00675-4
12. Dey, D., Barron, T.M., Storey, V.C.: A complete temporal relational algebra. VLDB J. **5**, 5–167 (1996)

13. Gutierrez, C., Hurtado, C., Vaisman, A.: Introducing time into RDF. IEEE Trans. Knowl. Data Eng. **19**(2), 207–218 (2007). https://doi.org/10.1109/TKDE.2007.34

14. Johnston, T., Weis, R.: A brief history of temporal data management. In: Managing Time in Relational Databases, pp. 11–25. Elsevier, Amsterdam (2010). https://doi.org/10.1016/B978-0-12-375041-9.00001-7

15. Khurana, U., Deshpande, A.: Storing and analyzing historical graph data at scale. In: EDBT (2016)

16. Kosmatopoulos, A., Gounaris, A., Tsichlas, K.: Hinode: implementing a vertex-centric modelling approach to maintaining historical graph data. Computing **101**(12), 1885–1908 (2019). https://doi.org/10.1007/s00607-019-00715-6

17. Lassila, O., Swick, R.R.: Resource description framework (RDF) model and syntax specification (1998)

18. Lazarevic, L.: Keeping track of graph changes using temporal versioning (2019)

19. Moffitt, V.Z., Stoyanovich, J.: Temporal graph algebra. In: Proceedings of The 16th International Symposium on Database Programming Languages. DBPL 2017, pp. 1–12. Association for Computing Machinery, Munich, Germany (2017). https://doi.org/10.1145/3122831.3122838

20. Ramesh, S., Baranawal, A., Simmhan, Y.: A distributed path query engine for temporal property graphs. In: 2020 20th IEEE/ACM International Symposium on Cluster, Cloud and Internet Computing (CCGRID), pp. 499–508. IEEE, Melbourne (2020). https://doi.org/10.1109/CCGrid49817.2020.00-43

21. Ravat, F., Song, J., Teste, O., Trojahn, C.: Efficient querying of multidimensional RDF data with aggregates: comparing NoSQL, RDF and relational data stores. Int. J. Inf. Manag. **54**, 102089 (2020)

22. Rost, C., et al.: Distributed temporal graph analytics with GRADOOP. VLDB J. (2021). https://doi.org/10.1007/s00778-021-00667-4

23. Semertzidis, K., Pitoura, E.: Time traveling in graphs using a graph database. In: EDBT/ICDT Workshops (2016)

24. Sharma, C., Sinha, R., Johnson, K.: Practical and comprehensive formalisms for modeling contemporary graph query languages. Inf. Syst. 101816 (2021)

25. Van Rest, O., Hong, S., Kim, J., Meng, X., Chafi, H.: PGQL: a property graph query language. In: Proceedings of the Fourth International Workshop on Graph Data Management Experiences and Systems - GRADES 2016, pp. 1–6. ACM Press, Redwood Shores (2016). https://doi.org/10.1145/2960414.2960421

26. Wang, Y., Yuan, Y., Ma, Y., Wang, G.: Time-dependent graphs: definitions, applications, and algorithms. Data Sci. Eng. **4**(4), 352–366 (2019)

27. Zaki, A., Attia, M., Hegazy, D., Amin, S.: Comprehensive survey on dynamic graph models. Int. J. Adv. Comput. Sci. Appl. **7**(2), 573–582 (2016). https://doi.org/10.14569/IJACSA.2016.070273

A Supervised Learning Community Detection Method Based on Attachment Graph Model

Yawei Zhao[1]([⊠]), Huafeng Yan[1,2], and Xueying Zhao[3]

[1] School of Engineering Sciences, University of Chinese Academy of Sciences, Beijing, China
zhaoyw@ucas.edu.cn
[2] Goertek Inc., Weifang, China
[3] Beijing Pan Stock Technology Co., Ltd., Beijing, China
https://www.goertek.com

Abstract. Community detection is an important method for network organizations exploration. This method has been widely employed in application systems and proves beneficial. As a complex network, the domain knowledge graph often has a small number of known community structures, and the use of these community structure information can effectively improve the effect of community detection. Based on this community structure and the self-similar characteristics of complex networks, this paper proposes a supervised learning community detection method, the core of which is the Attachment Graph Model (AGM). This model effectively utilizes the known community structure information, calculates the attachment strength between nodes based on supervised learning algorithms, determines the attachment relationship of the nodes to form an attachment matrix, thereby able to perform community testing to the entire domain knowledge graph. The community detection method (AGM) proposed in this paper is compared with the previous community detection methods in the real enterprise investment relationship network. The results show that AGM demonstrates a higher community detection accuracy.

Keywords: Attachment graph · Community detection · Domain knowledge graph · Complex network · Supervised learning

1 Introduction

The rapid development of information technology contributes to the efficiency and convenience of human life. But this development also render the relationship between individuals or groups more complicated than before. The network formed by mapping these relationships has also become intricate, so the mining of complex networks and the analysis of complex network structures have become particularly important. In recent years, in complex networks research,

ⓒ Springer Nature Switzerland AG 2022
X. Franch et al. (Eds.): CAiSE 2022, LNCS 13295, pp. 371–386, 2022.
https://doi.org/10.1007/978-3-031-07472-1_22

many scholars found that most of the real networks share the characteristics of community structure [5,7,10]. The network diagram in Fig. 1 shows four interconnected community structures, and each node in the dashed box belongs to the same community. The mining of community structure in such networks is termed the community detection [18].

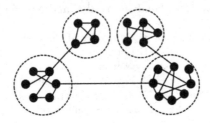

Fig. 1. An example network with community structure

The traditional community detection algorithm is based on the network topology, and their premise is that the network is a full graph. However, in production applications, the graph is often a subgraph, the nodes at the border of the graph will be detected into the wrong community because of the incomplete relationship, and the network in production is often mixed with a lot of business information, which can directly affect the result of community detection. Therefore, the community detection algorithm based entirely on topology is difficult to play a role in practical application. Taking financial business as an instance, an investment institution A chooses to support and help a certain company group to gradually develop in order to maximize its investment return. In this process, the investment institution will invest in many companies under the company group, and the result is shown in Fig. 2. It demonstrates the investment relationship between the investment institution A and its subsidiary companies B, C, D, E, F, and G. Obviously, the relationship between investment institution A and the company group is extremely close, financially. But A neither participates the economic production activities nor belong to the company group. With a community detection model such as label propagation or random walk, the investment institution A would be considered as part of the company group, which is not in line with the real outcome. Meanwhile, not all actions conducted by the company group share the same goal. It is normal for a subsidiary company to behave 'out-of-line' for cash in certain business opportunities. Figure 3 visualizes the network. As illustrated in the diagram, several companies (A, B, C, D, E) are closely connected and F is the opportunity that E took. In the network, F is only connected to E. If we apply the traditional algorithm to detect the community, the network topology will classify the node F into the community where E and other nodes belong to. But in fact, F is an independent individual and does not belong to the company group. The reason for this inaccurate community detection is the current community detection models are based on topology with the assumption of no prior knowledge of any community structure information. However, under some situations, there are few prior knowledge of some communities' information, the community detection algorithms which is based on the network topology is not applicable under these scenarios. As for financial domain knowledge graph, the ideal model outcome provide network structures which can reflect an accurate and reasonable network of real financial production activities. In the process of community detection with limited prior knowledge on community structures, it is necessary that we not only use the relevant data of the network topology, but also consider the known information of communities, which can be traced from the attributes of the nodes in the network. Therefore, it requires a new community detection method to better perform community detection.

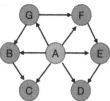

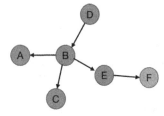

Fig. 2. Investment institutions and group

Fig. 3. Individual and group

In order to solve the above problems, this paper proposes a community detection model based on the self-similarity [1] of complex networks, the Attachment Graph Model (AGM). The basic idea is to use the characteristics of similarity between local and global regions in the network, by learning the relationship between nodes in the known community, the law of attachment between nodes can be summarized, and to be used on predicting the probability of the attachment for each edge. With the probability of attachment between two neighboring nodes, the model can decide whether there is an attachment relationship between these two nodes according to the threshold parameter. If the attachment relationship does not exist, the model deletes the edge between the two adjacent nodes in the network and keeps the edge if the attachment relationship exists. In the end, an attachment graph is completed with several connected sub-graphs and every sub-graph forms a community structure.

2 Related Work

Community detection is used in many fields, such as medical diagnosis [5], biological network analysis [10], web community mining [7], etc. So far, a variety of community detection algorithms have been brought forth. First GN algorithm [6] was proposed by Girvan and Newman Its principle idea is to obtain the result of community detection by continuously deleting the edges in the complex network. But this algorithm needs to predict the number of communities to determine the algorithm termination condition, and thus the time complexity is high. FN algorithm [8] came into being. This algorithm is proposed to quantify the evaluation index for network segmentation – modularity, which solves the problem of slow running speed of GN algorithm due to high time complexity. Then Raghavan and Albert put forward that the label propagation method (LPA) [9] is a community detection algorithm based on graph semi-supervised learning. This method predicts the unlabeled node data through a number of known labelled data. Although it is advantageous in its low complexity, the result of each iteration is unstable, and the accuracy is not high. After that Blondel V. D, Guillaume J. L, Lambiotte R, et al. proposed the method BGLL [25], which is a hierarchical clustering algorithm for community expansion based on local information and has been successfully applied to large-scale weighted networks.

In recent years, some new methods of community detection have been gradually put forward. Jin D, Yu Z, et al. proposed a comprehensive review of the existing community detection methods and introduce a new taxonomy that divides the existing methods into two categories, namely probabilistic graphical model and deep learning [12]. Torghabeh et al. conducts carries out community detection in graphs by constructing Markov random walks [14] on the graphs. The mixing properties of the random walk are then used to identify communities. Xin Y, Yang J, Xie Z proposed a semantic overlapping community detection algorithm based on random walk [11]. This algorithm proposed a semantic modularity model which measured the result of semantic community detection, conducted the detection by random walk strategy, and verified the feasibility through experiments. Lü, Linyuan, Chen D, et al. [21] concluded that ClusterRank is superior to PageRank and LearderRank in terms of algorithm complexity and its final result. The WalkSCAN algorithm proposed by Alexandre Hollocou et al. [19] is an extended model based on the PageRank algorithm. This algorithm uses some low-dimensional embedding of the graph based on random walks starting from the seed nodes to detect community.

With the development of neural networks and deep learning, node embedding is used to assist community detection [17, 20], A Modularized Nonnegative Matrix Factorization (M-NMF) model [16] to incorporate the community structure into network embedding was proposed by scholars such as Xiao W et al. Fan S, Wang X, et al. [22] propose a novel task-guided One2Multi graph autoencoder clustering framework. The One2Multi graph autoencoder is able to learn node embeddings by employing one informative graph view and content data to reconstruct multiple graph views to iteratively improve the clustering results. The technique of deep learning was recently adopted to handle the high dimensional network data and learn low-dimensional representation of network structures. Examples include methods based on the auto-encoder [23, 26] and the generative adversarial approach [27, 28].

As more and more algorithms are proposed, the authenticity of detection results is gradually being paid attention by more scholars. However, because these algorithms are based on network topology information for community detection, the result of sub-graph recognition is often far from the actual situation. The AGM model studied in this paper is different from other models in that AGM is a community detection algorithm based on supervised learning, which depends on the topology of the network and the attachment information between nodes, and AGM has a higher community detection accuracy of subgraphs, which is more suitable for community detection in real scenes.

3 Definition

In the related research of complex networks, graph is represented as $G = (V, E)$, where the set $V = \{v_1, v_2, \cdots, v_n\}$ represents the set of all nodes, $E = \{e_1, e_2, \cdots, e_n\}$ denotes the set of all associated edges and the incidence functions. If the edge in graph G can be represented as either (u, v) or (v, u) in V, the graph is an undirected graph and a directed graph otherwise. Figure 4 (a) is shown as an undirected graph G. If each edge in E has a certain weight in the undirected graph, the graph is a weighted graph, and an unweighted graph otherwise. The community detection task, performed in this paper, is conducted on the foundation of an undirected graph. The concepts of adjacent relationship, attachment strength, attachment relationship, attachment strength matrix, attachment matrix and attachment graph are proposed on the basis of an undirected graph. We will introduce the model in detail below. We summarize all of our notations in Table 1.

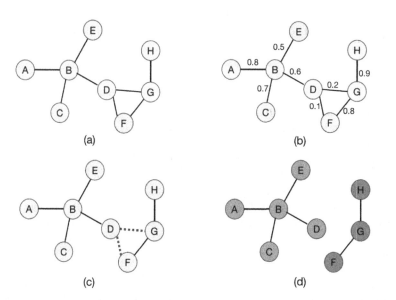

Fig. 4. The construction process of the attachment graph. (a): Original network structure G. (b): Network with attachment strength as weight. (c): Network after deleting weak attached edges. (d): The final attachment graph.

Definition 1. *Adjacent relationship.* In graph theory, any edge is represented as a line connecting its two end points. The edge with two vertices u and v as endpoints is generally denoted as (u, v). Any two nodes, u and v for example, connected by an edge are considered to be adjacent, and denoted as $\exists e_{(u,v)}$. If two nodes are not connected by an edge, it is defined as non-adjacent relationship and denoted as $\neg \exists e_{(u,v)}$. As shown in Fig. 4(a), there are adjacent relationships between nodes in (A, B), (B, C), (B, D), (B, E). Meanwhile, there is no adjacent relationship between nodes such as A and C, E and D, E and H.

Table 1. Notations used in this paper.

Notation	Description
$G(V, E)$	Graph G, nodes V and edges E
u, v	Nodes in Graph G
$C_I \in C$	Community collection
$w_f(u, v)$	Attachment strength between node u and node v
$fr(u, v)$	Attachment relationship between node u and node v
$F_w(G)$	Attachment strength matrix
$F(G)$	Attachment matrix
γ	Attachment strength threshold
G_f	Attachment graph of graph G
ϕ	Activation function
$\vec{\delta_u}, \vec{\delta_v}$	Attribute collection of u, v
$\vec{\alpha}$	The weight of the relationship between u and v
$\vec{\beta}, \vec{\gamma}$	The weight of u, v

Definition 2. *Attachment strength.* The attachment strength of two adjacent nodes u and v is expressed as $w_{fr}(u, v)$ $u, v \in G$, means the probability of node u following node v into the same community. For example, the value of the investment proportion in the enterprise investment network can be used as the value of the attachment strength of two enterprises. If there is a lack of investment proportion in the enterprise relationship network, a classifier can be learned through the known attachment relationship to predict whether there is a attachment relationship at the edge of the unknown investment proportion as the attachment strength between enterprises. The functional relationship is represented as:

$$w_{fr}(u, v) = \phi(\vec{\alpha} \cdot w_{u,v}, \vec{\beta} \cdot \vec{\delta_u}, \vec{\gamma} \cdot \vec{\delta_v}) \tag{1}$$

$\vec{\delta_u}$ means the attributes of the node u, if the node has n attributes, its vector expression is $[\delta_{u1}, \delta_{u2}, \cdots, \delta_{un}]$, the notation goes same for node v. $w_{u,v}$ means the weight of the relationship between its two nodes. where $\vec{\alpha}, \vec{\beta}, \vec{\gamma}$

are weighted hyperparameter vectors and are used to control the importance of different factors, ϕ is the activation function, here it is sigmoid.

Definition 3. *Attachment relationship.* If there are n different communities, $\{C_1, C_2, \cdots, C_n\}$ in the graph G, for any two different communities $\{C_i, C_j \ (i,j = 1, 2, \cdots, n)\}$, there are two different nodes u, v $(u \neq v)$. For these two communities C_i, C_j, there is an edge set E, where the elements in the set are denoted as $E = (u, v)_{u, v \in C_i \cup C_j}$. It is a set of all edges, the adjacent relationships of the nodes in these two communities shared. Given this set E, the adjacent relationship can be divided into two subsets, the attachment relationship and the non-attachment relationship. The attachment relationship is the relationship between two adjacent nodes that both nodes belong to the same community and the non-attachment relationship is the relationship of two adjacent nodes that comes from two different communities. The non-adjacent relationship is not included in the paper because this research focus on the adjacent relationship. There is no ground for classifying a non-adjacent relationship as attachment or non-attachment relationship, since there are two factors on classifying the adjacent relationship, the existence of the adjacent relationship and the facilitation of the community. The symbol of the attachment relationship is $fr(u, v)$, and the result is a binary value. To be more clear, if there is an attachment relationship, the value of $fr(u, v)$ is 1, and 0 otherwise.

$$E = E_1 + E_2 \Rightarrow \begin{cases} E_1 = (u, v)_{u, v \in C_i (i=1,2,3,\cdots)} & \Rightarrow fr(u, v) = 1 \\ E_2 = (u, v)_{u \in C_i \wedge v \in C_j (i \neq j \wedge i, j=1,2,\cdots)} \Rightarrow fr(u, v) = 0 \end{cases} \quad (2)$$

For all edges in edge set E in graph G, it can be divided into an edge set E_1 and E_2, the former includes the node pairs with attachment relationship and the latter includes the node pairs with non-attachment relationship. Consistent with the definition of the attachment relationship, the elements in set E_1 refer to the nodes which have an adjacent relationship and belong to the same community, which is represented as $fr(u, v) = 1$. The elements of the E_2 set refer the nodes which have an adjacent relationship but belong to different communities, which is represented as $fr(u, v) = 0$. As shown in Fig. 4(d), $fr(A, B)$ is an attachment relationship with $fr(A, B) = 1$, and $fr(D, G)$ is a non-attachment relationship with $fr(D, G) = 0$.

At the same time, attachment relationship and attachment strength also have the following relationship:

$$fr(u, v) \begin{cases} 0 \ w_{fr}(u, v) < \gamma \\ 1 \ w_{fr}(u, v) \geq \gamma \end{cases} \quad (3)$$

The γ is the attachment strength threshold, which can be reasonably tuned according to the actual situation to reach the optimal result. When $w_{fr}(u, v) \geq \gamma$, nodes u and v have an attachment relationship. On the contrary, there is no attachment relationship exist between nodes u and v.

Definition 4. *Attachment strength matrix and Attachment matrix.* The attachment strength matrix $F\_w(G)$ is used to describe the attachment strength between all adjacent nodes in graph G. If the relationship between the two nodes is non-adjacent, fill the corresponding position with the symbol "–". Take the network structure in Fig. 4(b) as an example, the value on the edge is the attachment strength value between two nodes, and the corresponding attached strength matrix can be created as follows:

$$
F\_w(G) = \begin{pmatrix}
- & 0.8 & - & - & - & - & - & - \\
0.8 & - & 0.7 & 0.6 & 0.5 & - & - & - \\
- & 0.7 & - & - & - & - & - & - \\
- & 0.6 & - & - & - & - & - & - \\
- & 0.5 & - & - & - & 0.1 & 0.2 & - \\
- & - & - & - & 0.1 & - & 0.8 & - \\
- & - & - & - & 0.2 & 0.8 & - & 0.9 \\
- & - & - & - & - & - & 0.9 & -
\end{pmatrix}
$$

The attachment matrix $F(G)$ means that if there is an attachment relationship between two adjacent nodes, then the value in the corresponding attachment matrix is 1, otherwise it is 0. If the two nodes are non-adjacent, fill the corresponding position with the symbol "–" same as the attachment strength matrix. Take the network structure in Fig. 4(b) as an example, the value on the edge is the attachment strength value between two nodes, and the corresponding the attachment matrix can be created as follows:

$$
F(G) = \begin{pmatrix}
- & 1 & - & - & - & - & - & - \\
1 & - & 1 & 1 & 1 & - & - & - \\
- & 1 & - & - & - & - & - & - \\
- & 1 & - & - & - & - & - & - \\
- & 1 & - & - & - & 0 & 0 & - \\
- & - & - & - & 0 & - & 1 & - \\
- & - & - & - & 0 & 1 & - & 1 \\
- & - & - & - & - & - & 1 & -
\end{pmatrix}
$$

Definition 5. *Attachment graph.* The undirected graph generated by attachment matrix mapping is called the attachment graph and denoted as G_f. In essence, the attachment graph is a graph formed by deleting edges of non-attachment relationship on the basis of the original graph G. As shown in Fig. 4(c), it illustrates the process of deleting the edges that do not have attachment relationship and retaining edges that have attachment relationship. Therefore, the attachment graph is a graph formed by the aggregation of multiple connected sub-graphs, and each connected sub-graph is a community structure. As shown in Fig. 4(d), two communities were detected, the C_1: A, B, C, D, E, and the C_2: F, G, H.

4   Algorithm

AGM (Attachment Graph Model) is a community detection model based on attachment graph. The AGM algorithm is as follows:

Algorithm. 1 AGM

---

input: Graph $G = (V, E)$, prior knowledge X, parameter γ
output: Community Results Collection C
1: $F\_w(G) \leftarrow Pre\ strength(G, X)$ //Build the attachment strength matrix
2: $F(G) \leftarrow Attachment\ matrix(F\_w(G), \gamma)$ //Build the attachment matrix
3: $G_f \leftarrow Attachment\ graph(F(G))$ //Build the attachment graph
4: $C \leftarrow Community\ detection(G_f)$ // Community detection
return: G_f

---

process 1 Pre strength.

input: Graph $G = (V, E)$, prior knowledge X
output: Attachment strength matrix $F\_w(G)$
1: **initialize:** $F\_w(G) = (fr(u, v) = 0), u \in V, v \in V$
2: model $\leftarrow train(X)$ //train () is a supervised training model
3: **for** $e \in E$ **do:** $fr(u, v) \leftarrow pre(model, e)$.
4: **end for**
return: $F\_w(G)$

---

process 2 Attachment matrix.

input: Attachment strength matrix $F\_w(G)$, parameter γ
output: Attachment matrix: F(G)
1: **initialize:** $F(G) = (fr(u, v) = 0), u \in V, v \in V$
2: **for** $w_{fr}(u, v) \in F\_w(G)$ **do:**
3:    **if** $w_{fr}(u, v) \geq \gamma$ **do:** $fr(u, v) \leftarrow w_{fr}(u, v)$
4:    **else:** $fr(u, v) \leftarrow 0$
5: **end for**
return: $F(G)$

---

process 3 Attachment graph.

input: Attachment matrix $F(G) = (fr(u, v))$
output: Attachment graph: G_f
1: **initialize:** $V_f = \{\}, E_f = \{\}$
2: **for** $fr(u, v) \in Fw(G)$ **do:**
3:    **if** $fr(u, v) \neq 0$ **do:** $V_f = V_f + \{u, v\}; E_f = E_f + \{(u, v)\}$
4: **end for**
5: $G_f \leftarrow (V_f, E_f)$
return: G_f

---

process 4 Community detection.

input: Attachment graph: G_f
output: Community Results Collection: C
1: **initialize:** $V \leftarrow V_f = (v_1, v_2, \cdots, v_n), C = \{\}$
2: **for** sub-graph $\in G_f$ **do**
3:    **for** V in sub-graph **do:** $C_i \leftarrow C_i + \{V\}$
4:    **end for**
5:    $C \leftarrow C + C_i$
6: **end for**
return: C

---

1. Calculate the attachment strength between all nodes with adjacent relationships in the network to form an attachment strength matrix.
2. Based on he known attachment relationship in the graph, build a classification model to classify the adjacent relationships of the whole graph into attachment relationship and non-attachment relationship.
3. Keep the edges that represent attachment relationship and delete the edges that represent non-attachment relationship, and form the attachment graph.
4. Search for connected subgraphs in the graph based on the attachment graph to form a community result.

5   Experiments

In this experiment, we compare the performance of our algorithm with the performances of other five algorithms: the GN [6] algorithm, the Fast Newman (FN) [8] algorithm, the LPA [9] algorithm, the WalkSCAN [19] algorithm and the M-NMF [16] algorithm. In order to compare the accuracy of clustering algorithms in a fairly manner, we adopt two widely used precision measures: the Adjusted Rand Index (ARI) [15] and the Normalized Mutual Information (NMI) [20].

5.1   Data

The experiment data in this article are the corporate investment relationship network of the China Market Supervision Bureau. The data includes three parts: node data, relation data and group data. The node data is an enterprise entity, which contains basic information on the corporate dimensions such as number, name, scale, nature, operating status, and region; the relation data is the investment relationsh ip between enterprises; the group data is a community structure formed by a collection of companies. We divided the experimental dataset into Dataset1 and Dataset2. Dataset1 is used to train an attachment relationship prediction model to predict the attachment strength between nodes in Dataset2, Dataset2 is used to compare AGM model with other community partition models. Because the attachment strength prediction model is built by learning the relationship between nodes in the known community, therefore, four known communities of different sizes were used to train four AGM models in Dataset1, finally, the four models are called AMG - (K-1), AMG - (K-2), AMG - (K-3) and AMG - (K-4). To observe the performance of AGM on the community detection of different magnitude data, we test the model with 7 different scales of test sample sets from Dataset2. The descriptive information of the experimental data are displayed with Table 2. N, R and C respectively represent the number of nodes, relationships and communities in the datasets.

Table 2. Experimental data.

	Dataset1				Dataset2						
	K-1	K-2	K-3	K-4	D-1	D-2	D-3	D-4	D-5	D-6	D-7
N	194	953	2825	5619	232	576	2438	5543	20354	54356	235086
R	315	1796	4387	9023	418	752	3732	8486	38256	73264	320454
C	5	26	56	102	10	20	50	100	500	1000	5000

5.2 Experiment Procedures

The experimental steps are as follows:

1. Construct an attachment strength prediction model based on historical data for supervised learning. The experiment starts by randomly selecting a node set containing three nodes (A, B and C) from the Dataset1, on the condition that two of the three nodes (B, C) are the neighbor nodes to the center node A and these two nodes belong to different communities. If the center node and the neighbor node, B for example, belong to the same community, the center node and the neighbor node have an attachment relationship and this relationship is marked as "1". If the center node and the neighbor node come from different communities, there is no attachment relationship between these two nodes and their relationship is marked "0". For each node, we collected the basic information, such as the registered capital, size, nature of the business, industry type, location information and the registration date, as part of the nodes' features. Along with the investment relationship between two enterprises, we construct the complete set of features for each node. Table 3 is a sample of some features for one edge.

Table 3. Features of one edge.

Attribute field	Meaning	Example
ID1/ID2	Id of company	****034
Capital1/Capital2	Registered capital of company	2000
Size1/Size2	Size of company	Large/medium/small
Nature1/Nature2	Nature of company	A/B/C/D
Industry1/Industry2	Industry of company	J,S,T...
Area1/Area2	Area of company	0,1,2...
Date1/Date2	Opening date of company	2001, 2004...
Weight	Investment relation between companies	0.54
label	Label of attachment relationship	"1" or "0"

In the experiment, we use the open source automatic machine learning tool FLAML [17] to train an attachment strength predictor, among them, the parameter "estimator-list" selects "lgbm" [24], "xgboost" [3], "rf" [13], "gbdt" [2], "extra-tree" [4], and the training time parameter "time-budget" is set 7200 s. We applied the predictor to predict the possibility of an attachment relationship between two nodes and evaluate the performance by several indicators such as *Accuracy, Precision, Recall, F1* [3]. Then we choose the best model with the highest *F1* score as the attachment strength prediction model.

2. Determine the attachment relationship by the choice of the parameter γ and form a corresponding attachment graph. After predicting the attachment strength with the attachment strength prediction model, it comes to decide the value of the parameter γ for determining whether the edge in the network is an attachment relationship. First, let's take a closer look at the parameter γ. In order to explore the influence of different parameters γ on the attachment graph model AGM, we construct different attachment graphs based on the Dataset1-(c) by selecting different values for γ between 0 and 1, and compare the attachment graph with the real community results with ARI and NMI indicators. With the experiment of different γ values applied, and the parameter with the best community detection performance determined.

3. Comparison of the community detection results generated by the AGM and other algorithms. In the experiment, GN algorithm, FN algorithm, LPA algorithm, WalkSCAN algorithm and M-NMF algorithm are used to compare with four AGM models on seven different scale of test sets to verify the reliability of AGM model in solving real network community detection. The results were evaluated using ARI and NMI indicators.

5.3   Result

1. The result of the attachment strength prediction. We used FLAML for experimental analysis of Dataset1, after 7200 s of optimization, the AMG-(K-1) selects the gbdt model, the others all choose the xgboost model as the final prediction model to predict the attachment strength of the edges of the network in Dataset2.

2. Parameter γ analysis. The ARI and the NMI scores for the experiment on testing the appropriate values of the γ are shown in Fig. 5. The horizontal axis represents different values of the parameter γ, and the vertical axis represents the values of ARI and NMI corresponding to different values of γ on community detection accuracy.

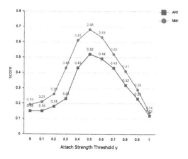

Fig. 5. Parameter γ of AGM. The influence of parameter γ on the result of community detection

As we observe from the graph of the community detection result of different value of the parameter γ, when the parameter γ is set too low or too high, the corresponding attachment graph is constructed inappropriately and produce low quality of community detection result. When the parameter γ is set at 0.5, we are able to obtain high quality community detection result with ARI = 0.52 and the NMI = 0.68. In this case, the community situation predicted with the model is close enough to the actual community situation.

3. Results of community detection. According to the experiment plan for constructing the AGM algorithm, we first predict the attachment strength with the pre-trained FLAML model on the Dataset2. Then we construct the attach-

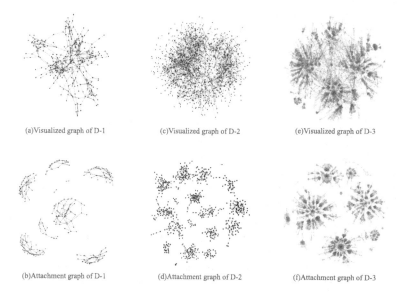

(a)Visualized graph of D-1   (c)Visualized graph of D-2   (e)Visualized graph of D-3

(b)Attachment graph of D-1   (d)Attachment graph of D-2   (f)Attachment graph of D-3

Fig. 6. Visualized graph and attachment graph of dataset

Table 4. Community detection results.

	Method	D-1	D-2	D-3	D-4	D-5	D-6	D-7
ARI	GN	0.32	0.38	0.42	0.37	0.21	0.17	0.23
	FN	0.30	0.25	0.37	0.28	0.23	0.23	0.29
	LPA	0.45	0.45	0.38	0.34	0.31	0.18	0.34
	WalkSCAN	0.37	0.36	0.57	0.47	0.28	0.32	0.28
	M-NMF	**0.53**	0.53	0.62	0.42	0.37	0.37	0.43
	AGM-(K-1)	0.42	0.55	0.63	0.52	0.39	0.48	0.42
	AGM-(K-2)	0.42	0.59	0.67	0.54	0.43	0.52	0.46
	AGM-(K-3)	0.48	**0.65**	**0.73**	0.57	**0.46**	0.62	0.51
	AGM-(K-4)	0.46	0.63	0.71	**0.58**	0.45	**0.65**	**0.53**
NMI	GN	0.48	0.56	0.35	0.41	0.48	0.31	0.38
	FN	0.52	0.57	0.41	0.34	0.39	0.38	0.57
	LPA	0.43	0.47	0.48	0.49	0.46	0.42	0.48
	WalkSCAN	0.37	0.62	0.53	0.58	0.72	0.65	0.62
	M-NMF	0.53	0.48	0.59	0.61	0.63	0.60	0.71
	AGM-(K-1)	0.53	0.68	0.63	0.69	0.63	0.72	0.74
	AGM-(K-2)	0.57	0.72	0.66	0.74	0.76	0.74	0.76
	AGM-(K-3)	**0.62**	**0.76**	0.75	**0.81**	**0.85**	0.76	**0.84**
	AGM-(K-4)	0.61	0.75	**0.77**	0.79	0.82	**0.78**	0.79

ment graph with the parameter γ set to 0.5. It means in the AGM algorithm the edge with attachment strength value higher than γ is kept and the edge with the attachment strength value lower than γ is deleted when we construct the attachment graph. We visualize the attachment graph and the original metadata graph with the Gephi. As show in Fig. 6, we take D-1, D-2, D-3 data as example to illustrate the model's performance on community detection, the graph of (a), (c), (e) are the visualized graph of D-1, D-2, D-3 data and (b), (d), (f) are the attachment graph with AGM-(K-3) algorithm. The community structure is far clearer and more organized in the attachment graph than the visualize graph.

As shown in the Table 4, the AGM model has obviously better performance on 6 out of 7 data sets, D-2 to D-7, on ARI perspective and outperforms all other models with NMI measure. Experiments show that the AGM model can effectively find the existence of community structure in the network. At the same time, the experiment compares the running time of each model on different data sets. As shown in Fig. 7, the efficiency of each model in the network formed by small data sets is not obvious. With the increase of nodes and relationships in the data set, the advantages of AGM model will be enlarged. The execution efficiency of AGM model in large network is higher than that of other competition models, which makes AGM model more applicable in real large networks.

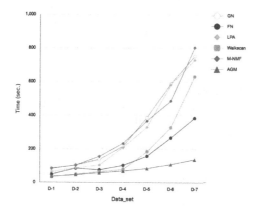

Fig. 7. Comparison of model running time

6   Conclusion

This article proposes an Attachment graph model (AGM) to solve the problem of community detection in financial scenarios. This model integrates the basic concept of the attachment graph and the method of constructing the attachment graph with the practical guidance on community detection. The process of constructing the attachment graph has been described in detail with comprehensive experiments. Validation with the real-world community knowledge known, we found that the community detection results obtained by the AGM model are very accurate and effective. It can effectively solve the problems of traditional community detection algorithms, namely their overlying on the network topology but cannot effectively applied in practice with satisfactory accuracy. At the same time, the attachment graph model demonstrates excellent scalability. As long as a certain potential attachment relationship can be found between nodes in the network, the attachment graph can be constructed for the entire network by using the AGM algorithm and provide a reasonable community detection result. It can be used on detecting communities in practical scenarios.

Acknowledgement. This work was supported in part by the National Key Research and Development Program of China under Grants 2020YFC1807104.

References

1. Karsai, M., Kivelä, M., Pan, R.K., et al.: Small but slow world: how network topology and burstiness slow down spreading. Phys. Rev. E Stat. Nonlinear Soft Matter Phys. **83**(2), 025102 (2011)
2. Friedman, J.H.: Greedy function approximation: a gradient boosting machine. Ann. Stat. **29**(5), 1189–1232 (2001)
3. Chen, T., Guestrin, C.: XGBoost: a scalable tree boosting system. arXiv e-prints (2016)

4. Geurts, P., Ernst, D., Wehenkel, L.: Extremely randomized trees. Mach. Learn. (2006). https://doi.org/10.1007/s10994-006-6226-1
5. Ni, J., Fei, H., Fan, W., Zhang, X.: Cross-network clustering and cluster ranking for medical diagnosis. In: ICDE (2017)
6. Girvan, M., Newman, M.E.J.: Community structure in social and biological networks. Proc. Natl. Acad. Sci. **99**, 7821 (2002)
7. Santo, F.: Community detection in graphs. Phys. Rep. **486**(3–5), 75–174 (2010)
8. Newman, M.E.J.: Fast algorithm for detecting community structure in networks. Phys. Rev. E Stat. Nonlin. Soft Matter Phys. **69**(6 Pt 2), 066133 (2003)
9. Raghavan, U.N., Albert, R., Kumara, S.: Near linear time algorithm to detect community structures in large-scale networks. Phys. Rev. E **76**(3), 36–106 (2007)
10. Sozio, M., Gionis, A.: The community-search problem and how to plan a successful cocktail party. In: KDD (2010)
11. Xin, Yu., Yang, J., Xie, Z.: A semantic overlapping community detecting algorithm in social networks based on random walk. J. Comput. Res. Dev. **52**(2), 499–511 (2015)
12. Jin, D., Yu, Z., et al.: A survey of community detection approaches: From statistical modeling to deep representation, arXiv:2101.01669 (2021) [Online]
13. Saffari, A., Leistner, C., Santner, J., et al.: On-line random forests. In: IEEE International Conference on Computer Vision Workshops. IEEE (2009)
14. Torghabeh, R.P., Santhanam, N.P.: Modeling community detection using slow mixing random walks. In: 2015 IEEE International Conference on Big Data (Big Data). IEEE (2015)
15. Steinley, D.: Properties of the Hubert-Arabie adjusted rand index. Psychol. Methods **9**(3), 386–396 (2004)
16. Wang, X., Cui, P., Wang, J., Pei, J., Zhu, W., Yang, S.: Community preserving network embedding. In: AAAI, pp. 203–209 (2017)
17. Wang, C., Wu, Q., Weimer, M., et al.: FLAML: a fast and lightweight AutoML library (2019)
18. Fortunato, S.: Community detection in graphs. Phys. Rep. **486**(3), 75–174 (2009)
19. Hollocou, A., Bonald, T., Lelarge, M.: Improving PageRank for local community detection. arXiv preprint arXiv: 1610.08722 (2016)
20. Tian, F., Gao, B., Cui, Q., Chen, E., Liu, T.-Y.: Learning deep representations for graph clustering. In: AAAI, pp. 1293–1299 (2014)
21. Lü, L., Chen, D., Ren, X.L., et al.: Vital nodes identification in complex networks. Phys. Rep. **650**, 1–63 (2016)
22. Fan, S., Wang, X., Shi, C., et al.: One2Multi graph autoencoder for multi-view graph clustering. In: WWW 2020: The Web Conference 2020 (2020)
23. Wang, C., Pan, S., Long, G., Zhu, X., Jiang, J.: MGAE: marginalized graph autoencoder for graph clustering. In: Proceedings of CIKM, pp. 889–898 (2017)
24. Ke, G., Meng, Q., Finley, T., et al.: LightGBM: a highly efficient gradient boosting decision tree. Curran Associates, Inc. (2017)
25. Blondel, V.D., Guillaume, J.L., et al.: Fast unfolding of communities in large network. J. Stat. Mech. Theory Exp. **2008**(10), 10008 (2008)
26. Sun, B., Shen, H., Gao, J., Ouyang, W., Cheng, X.: A non- negative symmetric encoder-decoder approach for community detection. In: Proceedings of CIKM, pp. 597–606 (2017)
27. Jia, Y., Zhang, Q., Zhang, W., Wang, X.: CommunityGAN: community detection with generative adversarial nets. In: Proceedings of WWW, pp. 784–794 (2019)
28. Zhang, Y., et al.: SEAL: learning heuristics for community detection with generative adversarial networks. In: Proceedings of SIGKDD, pp. 1103–1113 (2020)

Model Analysis and Comprehension

Soundness of Data-Aware Processes
with Arithmetic Conditions

Paolo Felli[ID], Marco Montali[ID], and Sarah Winkler[(✉)][ID]

Free University of Bozen-Bolzano, Bolzano, Italy
{pfelli,montali,winkler}@inf.unibz.it

Abstract. Data-aware processes represent and integrate structural and behavioural constraints in a single model, and are thus increasingly investigated in business process management and information systems engineering. In this spectrum, Data Petri nets (DPNs) have gained increasing popularity thanks to their ability to balance simplicity with expressiveness. The interplay of data and control-flow makes checking the correctness of such models, specifically the well-known property of soundness, crucial and challenging. A major shortcoming of previous approaches for checking soundness of DPNs is that they consider data conditions without arithmetic, an essential feature when dealing with real-world, concrete applications. In this paper, we attack this open problem by providing a foundational and operational framework for assessing soundness of DPNs enriched with arithmetic data conditions. The framework comes with a proof-of-concept implementation that, instead of relying on ad-hoc techniques, employs off-the-shelf established SMT technologies. The implementation is validated on a collection of examples from the literature, and on synthetic variants constructed from such examples.

Keywords: Soundness · Data Petri nets · Arithmetic conditions · SMT

1 Introduction

Integrating structural and behavioral aspects to holistically capture how information systems dynamically operate over data through actions and processes is a central problem in business process management (BPM) [20] and information systems engineering [23]. This is witnessed by the mutual cross-fertilization of the two areas on this topic, with models and approaches originating from BPM and its underlying formal foundations being then applied to information and enterprise systems [11,18,21], and vice-versa [3,24].

The interplay of data and control-flow makes checking the correctness of such models crucial and challenging. From the formal point of view, the problem is undecidable even for severely restricted models and correctness properties, both

This work is partially supported by the UNIBZ projects DaCoMan, QUEST, SMART-APP, VERBA, and WineId.

X. Franch et al. (Eds.): CAiSE 2022, LNCS 13295, pp. 389–406, 2022.
https://doi.org/10.1007/978-3-031-07472-1_23

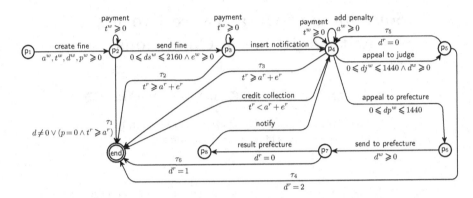

Fig. 1. Data-aware process for road fines [17].

in the case of simple data variables [13] and richer relational structures [5,7]. From the modeling perspective, the difficulty in combining these two dimensions is exacerbated by the fact that, more and more, models are obtained through a two-step approach: a first, automated discovery step produces a baseline model from event data, followed by a refinement and modification step driven by human ingenuity. The following example illustrates the challenge.

Example 1. A management process for road fines from an information system of the Italian police was presented as in [17] using a Data Petri nets (DPN). DPNs have gained increasing popularity thanks to their ability to balance simplicity with expressiveness. They focus on the evolution of a single (case) object evolved by the process (or a fixed number of inter-related objects), combining a Petri net-based control-flow with case variables and data conditions, capturing decisions and constrained updates. The process maintains seven case data variables: a (amount), t (total amount), d (a dismissal code), p (points deducted), e (expenses), and three time intervals ds, dp, dj. The process starts by creating a fine for a traffic offense in the system (create fine). A notification is sent to the offender within 90 d, i.e., 2160 h, by action send fine) and this is entered in the system (insert notification). If the offender pays an amount t that exceeds the fine a plus expenses e, the process terminates via τ_1, τ_2, or τ_3. For the less happy paths, there is a credit collection action if the paid sum was not enough; and the offender may file a protest, via appeal to judge, appeal to prefecture, and subsequent actions. The appeals again need to respect a certain time frame.

For simplicity, in Fig. 1 we present the model as a transition system instead of a Petri net. It was generated from real-life logs through multi-perspective process mining techniques, then enriched manually with more sophisticated arithmetic constraints extracted from domain knowledge [17]. *What is not obvious is that the process gets stuck in state p_7 if send to prefecture writes value $d > 1$.*

Examples like this call for a virtuous circle where process mining, human modelling, and *automated* verification techniques for correctness checking empower each other. A well-established formal notion of correctness for dynamic systems is that of *soundness* [1], defined over the well-known Petri net class of workflow nets. Intuitively, this property requires (i) that there are no activities in the process that cannot be executed in any of the possible executions; (ii) that from every reachable configuration the process can always be concluded by reaching a *final* configuration and (iii) that final configurations are always reached in a 'clean way', without leaving any thread of the process still hanging. After the seminal work in [1], which solely focuses on the evolution of single process instances in pure control-flow terms, several follow-up approaches were brought forward to define and study soundness for richer control-flow structures [2], several isolated cases [12], and presence of resources [22], showing decidability of the problem without entering into the engineering of verification tools.

When considering data-aware processes, the standard formulation of soundness is insufficient, as it does not consider how data affects the execution. This makes prior works not readily applicable to solve the problem. Refined notions of soundness have in fact been put forward to take data into account. Specifically, in [13] the property of *data-aware* soundness was obtained by lifting the standard soundness property of workflow nets to DPNs [13,16] (see the example above), by resorting to a translation to colored Petri nets. However, data conditions attached to activities were restricted to variable-to-constant comparisons. The approach was later extended to DPNs with a guard language that supports direct comparison of case data [8]. In parallel, [4] introduced notions of *decision-aware* soundness, where the focus is on data consumed and produced by (DMN) decision tables attached to the process. It was later shown in [15] how DPNs could be used to capture BPMN processes enriched with DMN S-FEEL decision tables, and how the different decision-aware soundness notions [4] could be recast as data-aware soundness [13].

While data-aware soundness is a crucial notion that captures also the problem in Example 1, a common shortcoming present in the literature is the limited expressivity of data conditions attached to activities and decision rules: *they cannot handle expressions with arithmetic computations*. For instance, one can check that the current credit card balance b is equal or larger than the price p of the purchased item (i.e., that $b \geqslant p$), but not that it is greater than the price plus some threshold amount t that could be obtained through a human task (i.e., that $b \geqslant p + t$). Clearly, this makes the existing technique not applicable to a very large number of real world applications (for instance, Example 1), revealing a research gap in the field that motivates the need of novel results in this spectrum.

Contributions and Methodology. Having identified this open research problem, we aim at contributing to the advancement of the body of knowledge in information systems engineering by answering three research questions:

1. Is soundness checking decidable for DPNs equipped with arithmetic?
2. Is there an operational way to conduct the check?
3. Is this operational way effective from the computational point of view?

We answer these through theoretical and algorithmic research, and through the creation of a concrete IT proof-of-concept artifact for soundness checking.

Specifically, we focus on DPNs supporting unlimited addition of variables but only constant multiplication, that is, *linear arithmetic*, which captures many real-world use cases. We address the first two research questions at once by lifting the approach in [8] to our richer setting, introducing a soundness checking procedure consisting of three algorithmic steps: (1) we transform the DPN into a labelled transition system called *data-aware dynamic system* (DDS) [14]; (2) we construct a *constraint graph*, which acts as a symbolic representation of the reachable state space via a finite set of formulas; (3) a set of satisfiability checks is performed using the formulas in the graph, and we prove that the DPN is unsound if and only if one of these checks succeeds. The constraint graph built for a DDS with arithmetic may in general be infinite. However, it is finite and computable, so that our check becomes a decision procedure, when the given process guarantees that reachable configurations are suitably limited (e.g. in that only a bounded part of the computation history is relevant, or the constraint language is sufficiently restricted). This requirement holds for well-identified classes of processes, formally captured by a *finite history set* [9]. For instance, it applies to all DPNs used in our evaluation, including Example 1.

Towards answering the third research question, we provide a proof-of-concept implementation of our framework in the tool ada. Being research in this setting at an early stage, we cannot rely on well-established empirical or experimental methods to validate this IT artifact. To mitigate this problem, we proceed as follows. First and foremost, instead of relying on ad-hoc techniques, our tool employs off-the-shelf SMT solvers as a backend. This guarantees that the main computation burden, namely the satisfiability checks in the third algorithmic step, is handled by third-party, industrially-validated software. Secondly, since there is no benchmark for DPNs, we set up a preliminary, performance evaluation in two steps: *(i)* we collect, and check soundness of, all DPN examples/case studies present in the literature to model real-world data-aware processes in information systems of various types; *(ii)* we construct synthetic variants of some of these examples, in order to test how the performance of ada changes by increasing actions, variables and conditions present in the model.

The paper is structured as follows. In Sect. 2, we fix our DPN model and define data-aware soundness, illustrating its high-level verification procedure in Sect. 3. The following sections detail the required steps: in Sect. 4 we relate data-aware soundness of a DPN to that of a corresponding transition system. We explain the constraint graph in Sect. 5, and show in Sect. 6 how it can be used to check data-aware soundness. Our implementation and experiments are the topic of Sect. 7. In Sect. 8 we conclude and comment on future work.

Proofs of the technical results are available in an extended report [10].

2   Background

In this section we summarize some background on constraints, DPNs and data-aware dynamic systems, as well as data-aware soundness.

Constraints. We start by fixing a set of data types for the variables manipulated by a process: let $\Sigma = \{\texttt{bool}, \texttt{int}, \texttt{rat}\}$ with associated domains of booleans $\mathcal{D}(\texttt{bool}) = \mathbb{B}$, integers $\mathcal{D}(\texttt{int}) = \mathbb{Z}$, and rationals $\mathcal{D}(\texttt{rat}) = \mathbb{Q}$. We assume a fixed set of *process variables* V, so there is a function $type \colon V \mapsto \Sigma$ assigning a type to each variable. For instance, in Example 1 the set of process variables is $V = \{a, d, dj, dp, ds, p, t\}$ all of type $\texttt{int}$ (i.e., $type(a) = \texttt{int}$, etc.). For a type $\sigma \in \Sigma$, V_σ denotes the subset of variables of type σ. To manipulate variables, we consider expressions c with the following grammar:

$$c := x_{\texttt{bool}} \mid b \mid n_1 \; op \; n_2 \mid r_1 \; op \; r_2 \mid c_1 \wedge c_2$$

$$op := \neq \mid = \mid \geqslant \mid > \qquad n := x_{\texttt{int}} \mid k \mid k_1 \cdot n_1 + k_2 \cdot n_2 \qquad r = x_{\texttt{rat}} \mid q \mid q_1 \cdot r_1 + q_2 \cdot r_2$$

where: $x_{\texttt{bool}} \in V_{\texttt{bool}}, x_{\texttt{int}} \in V_{\texttt{int}}$, and $x_{\texttt{rat}} \in V_{\texttt{rat}}$ respectively denote a boolean, integer, and rational variable, while $b \in \mathbb{B}$, $k \in \mathbb{Z}$, and $q \in \mathbb{Q}$ respectively denote a boolean, integer, and rational constant. We consider booleans, integers, and rationals as three prototypical examples of three datatypes, respectively relying on a finite, infinite discrete, and infinite dense domain. Similar datatypes, such as strings equipped with equality and real numbers, can be seamlessly handled.

These expressions will be used to capture conditions on the values of variables that are read and written during the execution of process activities. For this reason, we call them *constraints*. The set of constraints over V is denoted $\mathcal{C}(V)$.

For our process variables V, we consider two disjoint sets of *annotated* variables $V^r = \{v^r \mid v \in V\}$ and $V^w = \{v^w \mid v \in V\}$ which are read and written by process activities, respectively, as explained below, and we assume $type(v^r) = type(v^w) = type(v)$ for every $v \in V$. For instance, the constraint $t^r \geqslant a^r + e^r$ in Example 1 dictates that the current value of variable t is greater or equal than the sum of the values of a and r; whereas $0 \leqslant dj^w \wedge dj^w \leqslant 1440$ requires that the new value given to dj (i.e., assigned to dj as a result of the execution of the activity to which this constraint is attached) is between 0 and 1440. On the other hand, $a^w > a^r$ would mean that the new value of a is larger than its current value. More generally, given a constraint c as above, we refer to the annotated variables in V^r and V^w that appear in c as the *read* and *written variables*, respectively.

An *assignment* α is a total function $\alpha \colon V \mapsto D$ mapping each variable in V to a value in its domain. We say that α *satisfies* a constraint c over V, written $\alpha \models c$, if the evaluation of c under α is true. For instance, the assignment α such that $\alpha(t) = 10$, $\alpha(a) = 7$, and $\alpha(v) = 0$ for $v \in V$ otherwise, satisfies $t^r \geqslant a^r + e^r$.

Our constraint language is that of linear arithmetic over integers and rationals, which is decidable, and for which a range of mature SMT (satisfiability modulo theories) solvers is available. Moreover, linear arithmetic is known to enjoy *quantifier elimination* [19]: if φ is a formula with atoms in $\mathcal{C}(V \cup \{x\})$, there is some φ' with free variables V that is logically equivalent to $\exists x.\varphi$, i.e., $\varphi' \equiv \exists x.\varphi$. We assume that qe is a quantifier elimination procedure that returns such a formula, as implemented in off-the-shelf SMT solvers.

We adopt the following standard definition of Data Petri Nets (DPNs) [16,17].

Definition 1 (DPN). *A DPN is a tuple* $\mathcal{N} = \langle P, T, F, \ell, \mathcal{A}, V, guard \rangle$, *where (1)* $\langle P, T, F, \ell \rangle$ *is a Petri net with non-empty, disjoint sets of places P and transitions T, a flow relation* $F : (P \times T) \cup (T \times P) \mapsto \mathbb{N}$ *and a labelling function* $\ell : T \mapsto \mathcal{A}$, *where* $\mathcal{A}$ *is a finite set of activity labels; (2) V is a set of process variables (all with a type); and (3) guard:* $T \mapsto \mathcal{C}(V^r \cup V^w)$ *is a guard mapping.*

Example 2. Consider a simple auction process modeled by the DPN in Fig. 2. The initial and final markings are $M_I = \{\mathsf{p_0}\}$ and $M_F = \{\mathsf{p_3}\}$. It maintains the set of variables $V = \{o, t\}$, where o (domain $\mathbb{Q}$) holds the last offer issued by a bidder, and t (domain $\mathbb{Z}$) is a timer. The initial assignment is $\alpha_I(o) = \alpha_I(t) = 0$. We briefly explain the working of the process: the action init initializes the timer t to a positive value (e.g., of days) and the offer o to 0; as long as the timer has not expired, it can be decreased (action timer), or bids can be issued, increasing the current offer (bid); the item can be sold if the timer expired and the offer is positive (hammer). We denote this DPN, consisting of all actions drawn in black in Fig. 2, by $\mathcal{N}$. For illustration purposes, we will also consider two variants of this DPN: $\mathcal{N}_{\mathsf{reset}}$ extends $\mathcal{N}$ by a reset action that restarts the process if the offer in the final state is 0 (drawn in red), and $\mathcal{N}_{\mathsf{thresh}}$ adds to $\mathcal{N}$ the transition thresh which leads to the final state if the offer exceeds a threshold (drawn in blue).

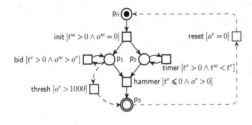

Fig. 2. DPN for simple auction model. (Color figure online)

The variables that are read and written by a transition t are denoted $read(t) = \{v \mid v^r$ occurs in $guard(t)\}$, $write(t) = \{v \mid v^w$ occurs in $guard(t)\}$, respectively. For instance, for t the activity labelled bid in Fig. 2, $write(t) = \{o\}$ and $read(t) = \{o, w\}$.

We call a *state variable assignment*, denoted α, an assignment with domain V. In contrast, a *transition variable assignment*, denoted β, is a (partial) function that assigns values of correct type to the annotated variables $V^r \cup V^w$, used to specify how variables change during activity executions (cf. Definition 2).

For a DPN $\mathcal{N}$ with underlying Petri net (P, T, F, ℓ), a *marking* $M : P \mapsto \mathbb{N}$ assigns every place a number of tokens. A *state* of $\mathcal{N}$ is a pair (M, α) of a marking and a state variable assignment, which thus accounts for both the control flow progress and the current values of variables in V. For instance, $(\{\mathsf{p_0}\}, \left[\begin{smallmatrix} t=0 \\ o=0 \end{smallmatrix}\right])$ is a state for the net of Example 2. We next define when transitions may fire in a DPN.

Definition 2 (Transition firing). *A transition* $t \in T$ *is enabled in a state* (M, α) *if a transition variable assignment* β *exists such that:*

(i) $\beta(v^r) = \alpha(v)$ *for every* $v \in read(t)$, *i.e.,* β *assigns read variables as by* α,
(ii) $\beta \models guard(t)$, *i.e.,* β *satisfies the guard; and*
(iii) $M(p) \geqslant F(p, t)$ *for every* p *so that* $F(p, t) \geqslant 0$.

An enabled transition may fire, producing a new state (M', α'), *s.t.* $M'(p) = M(p) - F(p,t) + F(t,p)$ *for every* $p \in P$, *and* $\alpha'(v) = \beta(v^w)$ *for every* $v \in write(t)$, *and* $\alpha'(v) = \alpha(v)$ *for every* $v \notin write(t)$. *A pair* (t, β) *as above is called (valid) transition firing, and we denote its firing by* $(M, \alpha) \xrightarrow{(t,\beta)} (M', \alpha')$.

Given $\mathcal{N}$, we fix one state (M_I, α_0) as *initial*, where M_I is the initial marking of the underlying Petri net (P, T, F, ℓ) and α_0 is a state variable assignment that specifies the initial value of all variables in V. Similarly, we denote the final marking as M_F, and call *final* any state of the form (M_F, α_F) for some α_F. For instance, the net in Example 2 admits a transition firing $(\{p_0\}, \begin{bmatrix} t=0 \\ o=0 \end{bmatrix}) \xrightarrow{\text{init}} (\{p_1, p_2\}, \begin{bmatrix} t=1 \\ o=0 \end{bmatrix})$ from its initial state, while $(\{p_3\}, \begin{bmatrix} t=0 \\ o=5 \end{bmatrix})$ is one final state.

We say that (M', α') is *reachable* in a DPN iff there exists a sequence of transition firings $(M_I, \alpha_0) \xrightarrow{(t_1, \beta_1)} \ldots \xrightarrow{(t_n, \beta_n)} (M', \alpha')$, denoted also as $(M_I, \alpha_0) \rightarrow^* (M', \alpha')$. Such a sequence is a (valid) *process run* if the resulting state (M', α') is final. For instance, a possible sequence of transition firings in Example 2 (in which the timer t is initialized to 1 day, then decremented) is:

$$(\{p_0\}, \begin{bmatrix} t=0 \\ o=0 \end{bmatrix}) \xrightarrow{\text{init}} (\{p_1, p_2\}, \begin{bmatrix} t=1 \\ o=0 \end{bmatrix}) \xrightarrow{\text{timer}} (\{p_1, p_2\}, \begin{bmatrix} t=0 \\ o=0 \end{bmatrix}) \tag{1}$$

For simplicity of presentation, in the remainder of this paper, we restrict to *bounded* DPNs, that is, DPNs where the number of tokens in reachable markings is bounded by some $m \in \mathbb{N}$. Indeed, detecting unboundedness (which in turn witnesses unsoundness) can be done as in [8], where it is shown that the standard unboundedness detection techniques based on coverability graphs also apply to the data-aware setting. For instance, the DPNs $\mathcal{N}$, $\mathcal{N}_{\text{reset}}$, and $\mathcal{N}_{\text{thresh}}$ in Example 2 are 1-bounded. Next, we define the crucial property of data-aware soundness.

Definition 3 (Data-aware soundness). *A DPN is* data-aware sound *iff:*

(P1) *if* $(M_I, \alpha_0) \rightarrow^* (M, \alpha)$ *there is some* α' *such that* $(M, \alpha) \rightarrow^* (M_F, \alpha')$ *for all* M, α, *i.e., any sequence can be continued to a process run;*
(P2) *if* $(M_I, \alpha_0) \rightarrow^* (M, \alpha)$ *and* $M \geqslant M_F$ *then* $M = M_F$ *for all* M, α, *i.e., termination is clean; and*
(P3) *for all* $t \in T$ *there is a sequence* $(M_I, \alpha_0) \rightarrow^* (M, \alpha) \xrightarrow{(t,\beta)} (M', \alpha')$ *for some* M, M', α, α', *and* β, *i.e., there are no dead transitions.*

For instance, the DPN $\mathcal{N}$ from Example 2 violates (P1) because after the sequence (1) above no further transition is applicable, but the reached state is not final. $\mathcal{N}_{\text{reset}}$ also violates (P3) because the transition reset is dead: if a token reaches the place p_3, o will never have value 0. On the other hand, $\mathcal{N}_{\text{thresh}}$ violates also (P2) as the following steps lead to marking $\{p_2, p_3\} > \{p_3\} = M_F$:

$$(\{p_0\}, \begin{bmatrix} t=0 \\ o=0 \end{bmatrix}) \xrightarrow{\text{init}} (\{p_1, p_2\}, \begin{bmatrix} t=1 \\ o=0 \end{bmatrix}) \xrightarrow{\text{bid}} (\{p_1, p_2\}, \begin{bmatrix} t=1 \\ o=1000 \end{bmatrix}) \xrightarrow{\text{thresh}} (\{p_2, p_3\}, \begin{bmatrix} t=1 \\ o=1000 \end{bmatrix})$$

3 Soundness Checking: The High-Level Perspective

Algorithm 1 gives a bird's-eye view of our soundness checking procedure. The initial step is to transform the given DPN $\mathcal{N}$ into a special kind of transition system (called DDS) $\mathcal{B}$, by unfolding the interleaving semantics. The respective procedure DPNtoDDS is detailed in Sect. 4. Next, in line 3, the procedure COMPUTECG constructs the constraint graph of $\mathcal{B}$ as a symbolic representation of all reachable states, as explained in Sect. 5. In lines 4, 6, and 8 the routines BADTERMINATION, DEADTRANSITION, and BLOCKEDSTATE then use the constraint graph $CG_{\mathcal{B}}$ to check whether $\mathcal{N}$ violates the properties (P2), (P3), and (P1) of Definition 3, respectively (see Sect. 6). If one of these properties does not hold, the procedure returns *false* immediately, otherwise data-aware soundness is confirmed by returning *true* in line 10. The reason why we check (P1) last is that the other two checks are significantly cheaper.

Algorithm 1. Procedure to check data-aware soundness of a DPN

1: **procedure** CHECKSOUND($\mathcal{N}$)
2:     $\mathcal{B} \leftarrow$ DPNtoDDS($\mathcal{N}$)
3:     $CG_{\mathcal{B}} \leftarrow$ COMPUTECG($\mathcal{B}$)
4:     **if** BADTERMINATION($CG_{\mathcal{B}}, \mathcal{N}$) **then return** *false*   ▷ see Alg. 1
5:     **if** DEADTRANSITION($CG_{\mathcal{B}}, \mathcal{N}$) **then return** *false*   ▷ see Alg. 2
6:     **if** BLOCKEDSTATE($CG_{\mathcal{B}}, \mathcal{N}$) **then return** *false*   ▷ see Alg. 2
7:     **return** *true*

---

4 From DPNs to Transition Systems

This section details the first step in our soundness checking procedure: to unfold the interleaving semantics of the given DPN into a labelled transition system called *data-aware dynamic system* (DDS) [14]. We start by defining DDSs.

Definition 4. *A DDS* $\mathcal{B} = \langle B, b_I, \mathcal{A}, \Delta, B_F, V, \alpha_I, guard \rangle$ *is a labelled transition system such that (i) B is a finite set of states, with $b_I \in B$ the initial one; (ii) $\mathcal{A}$ is a set of actions; (iii) $\Delta \subseteq B \times \mathcal{A} \times B$ is a transition relation; (iv) $B_F \subseteq B$ are final states; (v) V is the set of process variables; (vi) α_I is the initial assignment; (vii) guard: $\mathcal{A} \mapsto \mathcal{C}(V^r \cup V^w)$ fixes executability constraints on actions.*

Figure 3 shows three example DDSs (that are in fact obtained from transforming the DPNs in Example 2, as defined below). The action guards are the same as in Fig. 2, but have been omitted for readability. We denote a transition from state b to b' by executing an action $a \in \mathcal{A}$ as $b \xrightarrow{a} b'$. For instance, the DDS $\mathcal{B}$ in Fig. 3 admits a transition $\mathsf{p_0} \xrightarrow{\text{init}} \mathsf{p_{12}}$. A *configuration* of $\mathcal{B}$ is a pair (b, α) where $b \in B$ and α is an assignment. For instance, $(\mathsf{p_0}, \left[\begin{smallmatrix} t=0 \\ o=0 \end{smallmatrix}\right])$ is the initial configuration of $\mathcal{B}$ in Fig. 3. An *action firing* is a pair (a, β) of an action $a \in \mathcal{A}$ and a transition variable assignment β, i.e., a function $\beta \colon V^r \cup V^w \mapsto D$. As defined next, an action firing (a, β) transforms a configuration (b, α) into a new configuration (b', α') by changing state as defined by action a, and updating the assignment α to α', in agreement with the action guard. In the new assignment α', variables that are not written keep their previous value as per α, whereas written variables are updated according to β. Let $write(a) = \{x \mid x^w \in V^w \text{ occurs in } guard(a)\}$.

Definition 5. *A DDS* $\mathcal{B} = \langle B, b_I, \mathcal{A}, \Delta, B_F, V, \alpha_I, guard \rangle$ *admits a step from configuration* (b, α) *to* (b', α') *via action firing* (a, β), *denoted* $(b, \alpha) \xrightarrow{a, \beta} (b', \alpha')$, *if* $b \xrightarrow{a} b'$ *and (i)* $\beta(v^r) = \alpha(v)$ *for all* $v \in V$; *(ii) the new state variable assignment* α' *satisfies* $\alpha'(v) = \alpha(v)$ *if* $v \in V \setminus write(a)$, *and* $\alpha'(v) = \beta(v^w)$ *otherwise;* *(iii)* $\beta \models guard(a)$, *i.e., the guard is satisfied by* β.

Thus, the variable update works exactly as for the case of DPNs. For instance, $\mathcal{B}$ in Fig. 3 admits a step $(\mathsf{p}_0, \left[\begin{smallmatrix} t=0 \\ o=0 \end{smallmatrix}\right]) \xrightarrow{init, \beta} (\mathsf{p}_{12}, \left[\begin{smallmatrix} t=1 \\ o=0 \end{smallmatrix}\right])$ where $\beta(t^r) = \beta(o^r) = \beta(o^w) = 0$ and $\beta(o^w) = 1$. Given a DDS $\mathcal{B}$, a *derivation* ρ of length n from a configuration (b, α) is a sequence of steps:

$$\rho \colon (b, \alpha) = (b_0, \alpha_0) \xrightarrow{a_1, \beta_1} (b_1, \alpha_1) \xrightarrow{a_2, \beta_2} \ldots \xrightarrow{a_n, \beta_n} (b_n, \alpha_n)$$

We also associate with ρ the *symbolic derivation* σ that *abstracts* ρ, i.e., the sequence $\sigma \colon b_0 \xrightarrow{a_1} b_1 \xrightarrow{a_2} \ldots \xrightarrow{a_n} b_n$ where only the state and action sequences are recorded, but no concrete assignments are given. For some $m < n$, $\sigma|_m$ is the prefix of σ that has m steps. We call a *run* of $\mathcal{B}$ a derivation starting from (b_I, α_I), and a *symbolic run* a symbolic derivation starting from b_I. For instance,

$$\rho \colon (\mathsf{p}_0, \left[\begin{smallmatrix} t=0 \\ o=0 \end{smallmatrix}\right]) \xrightarrow{init} (\mathsf{p}_{12}, \left[\begin{smallmatrix} t=1 \\ o=0 \end{smallmatrix}\right]) \xrightarrow{timer} (\mathsf{p}_{12}, \left[\begin{smallmatrix} t=0 \\ o=0 \end{smallmatrix}\right]) \tag{2}$$

is a derivation of the DDS $\mathcal{B}$ from Fig. 3, and also a run because it starts in the initial state p_0; ρ is abstracted by the symbolic run $\mathsf{p}_0 \xrightarrow{init} \mathsf{p}_{12} \xrightarrow{timer} \mathsf{p}_{12}$. One may notice the similarity with the sequence of transition firings (1) in Sect. 2.

Transformation. It is straightforward to define the procedure DPNTODDS($\mathcal{N}$) used in Algorithm 1 to transform a given, bounded DPN $\mathcal{N}$ into a DDS. To this end, we consider in the rest of this section a k-bounded DPN $\mathcal{N} = \langle P, T, F, \ell, \mathcal{A}, V, guard \rangle$ with initial variable assignment α_I, initial marking M_I, and final marking M_F. We define DPNTODDS($\mathcal{N}$) as the DDS $\mathcal{B} = \langle B, M_I, \mathcal{A}, \Delta, \{M_F\}, V, \alpha_I, guard \rangle$ where B is the set of all k-bounded markings of $\mathcal{N}$; and $(M, a, M') \in \Delta$ iff there is some $t \in T$ such that $\ell(t) = a$, $M(p) \geqslant F(p, t)$ for every p so that $F(p, t) \geqslant 0$ and $M'(p) = M(p) - F(p, t) + F(t, p)$ for every $p \in P$. Indeed, Fig. 3 shows the DDSs obtained for the DPNs $\mathcal{N}$, $\mathcal{N}_{\mathsf{reset}}$, and $\mathcal{N}_{\mathsf{thresh}}$ from Example 2.

After having defined the transformation from DPNs to DDSs, it remains to relate data-aware soundness of a DPN with properties of its DDS representation. To that end, we define some notions that turn out to be useful: A DDS $\mathcal{B} = \langle B, b_I, \mathcal{A}, \Delta, B_F, V, \alpha_I, guard \rangle$ has a *blocked state* if there is a run $\rho \colon (b_I, \alpha_I) \to^* (b, \alpha)$ to some configuration (b, α) such that there is no derivation $(b, \alpha) \to^* (b_f, \alpha')$ with $b_f \in B_F$. Moreover, let a state $b \subset B$ be *reachable* if there is a run $(b_I, \alpha_I) \rightarrow^* (b, \alpha)$ for some α; and a transition $(b, a, b') \in \Delta$ be *reachable* if there is a run $(b_I, \alpha_I) \rightarrow^* (b, \alpha) \xrightarrow{a,\beta} (b', \alpha')$ for some α, α', and β. It is then not hard to observe the following relationship between the properties (P1), (P2), and (P3) in Definition 3 and properties of the DDS representation:

Lemma 1. *If $\mathcal{N}$ is a DPN and $\mathcal{B} = \mathrm{DPNToDDS}(\mathcal{N})$ has control states B,*

- *$\mathcal{N}$ satisfies (P1) iff $\mathcal{B}$ has no blocked states,*
- *$\mathcal{N}$ satisfies (P2) iff all $M \in B$ with $M \geqslant M_F$ are unreachable, and*
- *$\mathcal{N}$ satisfies (P3) iff for all transitions $t \in T$ of $\mathcal{N}$ there are some $M, M' \in B$ such that $(M, \ell(t), M') \in \Delta$ is reachable.*

This relationship allows us to check data-aware soundness on the level of DDSs. For instance, **reset** is not reachable in $\mathcal{B}_{\mathsf{reset}}$ as p_3 is only reached via **hammer**, i.e., if $o > 0$, so $\mathcal{N}_{\mathsf{reset}}$ does not satisfy (P3). Also, $\mathcal{B}_{\mathsf{thresh}}$ admits the run (3) below to state p_{23}, corresponding to marking $\{p_2, p_3\}$ in $\mathcal{N}_{\mathsf{thresh}}$, violating (P2). Finally, $\mathcal{B}$, $\mathcal{B}_{\mathsf{thresh}}$ and $\mathcal{B}_{\mathsf{reset}}$ have the blocked state $(\{p_1, p_2\}, \begin{bmatrix} t=0 \\ o=0 \end{bmatrix})$, reachable via run (2).

$$\rho: (p_0, \begin{bmatrix} t=0 \\ o=0 \end{bmatrix}) \xrightarrow{\text{init}} (p_{12}, \begin{bmatrix} t=1 \\ o=0 \end{bmatrix}) \xrightarrow{\text{bid}} (p_{12}, \begin{bmatrix} t=1 \\ o=1001 \end{bmatrix}) \xrightarrow{\text{thresh}} (p_{23}, \begin{bmatrix} t=1 \\ o=1001 \end{bmatrix}) \qquad (3)$$

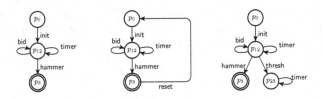

Fig. 3. DDSs $\mathcal{B}$, $\mathcal{B}_{\mathsf{reset}}$, and $\mathcal{B}_{\mathsf{thresh}}$ for DPNs $\mathcal{N}$, $\mathcal{N}_{\mathsf{reset}}$, and $\mathcal{N}_{\mathsf{thresh}}$.

5   Constraint Graph

While numerical data and arithmetic are required to faithfully model processes in many real-life information systems, they render the state space infinite. For instance, the DDS $\mathcal{B}$ in Fig. 3 has infinitely many configurations such as $(p_{12}, \begin{bmatrix} t=1 \\ o=5 \end{bmatrix})$, $(p_{12}, \begin{bmatrix} t=2 \\ o=3 \end{bmatrix})$, and $(p_{12}, \begin{bmatrix} t=0 \\ o=3 \end{bmatrix})$. However, not all state variable assignments differ with respect to possible next actions: action **hammer** requires $o > 0$ and $t \leqslant 0$, while **bid** and **timer** need $t > 0$; but it is irrelevant whether, say, $o > 4$. Therefore, $(p_{12}, \begin{bmatrix} t=1 \\ o=5 \end{bmatrix})$ and $(p_{12}, \begin{bmatrix} t=2 \\ o=3 \end{bmatrix})$ are indeed *equivalent* with respect to possible next steps, but the configurations $(p_{12}, \begin{bmatrix} t=2 \\ o=3 \end{bmatrix})$ and $(p_{12}, \begin{bmatrix} t=0 \\ o=3 \end{bmatrix})$ are not. Now, the key idea of the constraint graph is to symbolically represent equivalent configurations using a tuple (b, φ) of a control state b and a formula φ over variables V. For instance, for $\mathcal{B}$ we will distinguish $(p_{12}, (o = 0) \wedge (t > 0))$ (both **bid** and **timer** apply) from $(p_{12}, (o = 0))$ (we have no information about t, so only **bid** applies).

To formalize this idea, let $\mathcal{B} = \langle B, b_I, \mathcal{A}, \Delta, B_F, V, \alpha_I, \mathit{guard} \rangle$ be a given DDS. We start with some auxiliary notions: The *transition formula* Δ_a of action a is given by $\Delta_a(\overline{V}^r, \overline{V}^w) = \mathit{guard}(a) \wedge \bigwedge_{v \notin \mathit{write}(a)} v^w = v^r$. It simply expresses conditions on variables *before and after* executing the action: $\mathit{guard}(a)$ must hold, and the values of all variables that are not written are copied. E.g., for action bid in Fig. 3, we have $\mathit{write}(\mathsf{bid}) = \{o\}$, and $\Delta_{\mathsf{bid}} = (t^r > 0) \wedge (o^w > o^r) \wedge (t^w = t^r)$. Next, we use the transition formula to define an *update* operation, representing how a current state, captured by a formula φ, changes when executing action a.

Definition 6. *For a formula φ and action a, let $\mathit{update}(\varphi, a) = qe(\exists \overline{U}. \varphi[\overline{U}/\overline{V}] \wedge \Delta_a[\overline{U}/\overline{V}^r, \overline{V}/\overline{V}^w])$, where U is a set of variables that has the same cardinality as V and is disjoint from all variables in φ.*

Here, $\varphi[\overline{U}/\overline{V}]$ is the result of replacing variables $\overline{V}$ in φ by $\overline{U}$, and similar for Δ_a. For instance, if $\overline{V} = (o, t)$ we can take the renamed variables $\overline{U} = (o', t')$; for $\varphi = (t > 0) \wedge (o = 0)$ we then get $\mathit{update}(\varphi, \mathsf{bid}) = qe(\exists o' t'. (t' > 0) \wedge (o' = 0) \wedge (o > o') \wedge (t = t'))$, which is simplified by quantifier elimination to $(t > 0) \wedge (o > 0)$. The use of a quantifier in Definition 6 might look like a complication, but it allows us to remember the previous state φ, even if variables are overwritten by action a; afterwards, quantifier elimination can produce a logically equivalent formula without $\exists$. Next, given assignment α, let C_α be the formula $C_\alpha \doteq \bigwedge_{v \in V} v = \alpha(v)$.

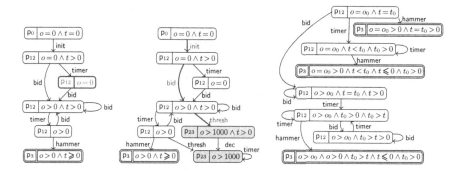

Fig. 4. Constraint graphs $\mathrm{CG}_{\mathcal{B}}$, $\mathrm{CG}_{\mathcal{B}_{\mathsf{thresh}}}$, and $\mathrm{CG}_{\mathcal{B}}(\mathsf{p}_{12})$.

Definition 7. *A constraint graph $\mathrm{CG}_{\mathcal{B}}(b_0, \alpha)$ for $\mathcal{B}$, a state $b_0 \in B$, and assignment α is a triple $\langle S, s_0, \gamma \rangle$ where the set of nodes S consists of tuples (b, φ) for $b \in B$ and a formula φ, and $\gamma \subseteq S \times \mathcal{A} \times S$, inductively defined as follows:*

(i) $s_0 = (b_0, C_\alpha) \in S$ is the initial node; and
(ii) if $(b, \varphi) \in S$ and $b \xrightarrow{a} b'$ such that $\mathit{update}(\varphi, a)$ is satisfiable, there is some $(b', \varphi') \in S$ with $\varphi' \equiv \mathit{update}(\varphi, a)$, and $(b, \varphi) \xrightarrow{a} (b', \varphi')$ is in γ.

Algorithm 2. Checking soundness properties for $\mathrm{CG}_{\mathcal{B}} = \langle S, s_0, \gamma \rangle$ and DPN $\mathcal{N}$

---

procedure BADTERMINATION($\mathrm{CG}_{\mathcal{B}}, \mathcal{N}$)
    return $\exists (b, \varphi) \in S$ such that b corresponds to marking M in $\mathcal{N}$ and $M \geqslant M_F$

procedure DEADTRANSITION($\mathrm{CG}_{\mathcal{B}}, \mathcal{N}$)
    return $\exists$ transition t of $\mathcal{N}$ such that $\nexists (s, \ell(t), s') \in \gamma$ for some s, s'

procedure BLOCKEDSTATE($\mathrm{CG}_{\mathcal{B}}, \mathcal{N}$)
    return $\exists (b, \varphi) \in S$ such that $b \neq b_F$ and $blocked(b, \varphi)$ satisfiable

---

Intuitively, the constraint graph describes symbolically the states reachable in $\mathcal{B}$. Specifically, we write $\mathrm{CG}_{\mathcal{B}}$ for the graph $\mathrm{CG}_{\mathcal{B}}(b_I, \alpha_I)$ starting at the initial state and the initial assignment. This is also the graph returned by the procedure COMPUTECG($\mathcal{B}$) used in Algorithm 1. For instance, the first two graphs in Fig. 4 show $\mathrm{CG}_{\mathcal{B}}$ and $\mathrm{CG}_{\mathcal{B}_{\text{thresh}}}$, respectively. Nodes that have the control state p_3 that is final in $\mathcal{B}$ are drawn with double border; the coloring will be explained later.

For technical reasons, our procedure often requires to consider constraint graphs that are built from an arbitrary state b and that, instead of assigning variables V to specific values, only impose that they have the same value of fresh placeholder variables V_0. We denote this by $\mathrm{CG}_{\mathcal{B}}(b)$. E.g., the rightmost graph in Fig. 4 shows $\mathrm{CG}_{\mathcal{B}}(\mathsf{p}_{12})$, representing the states reachable in $\mathcal{B}$ from p_{12} where $V = \langle o, t \rangle$ is initially assigned the placeholder variables $V_0 = \langle o_0, t_0 \rangle$.

We next establish properties that connect constraint graphs to derivations of the DDS $\mathcal{B}$. For a *path* $\pi \colon (b_0, \varphi_0) \xrightarrow{a_1} (b_1, \varphi_1) \xrightarrow{a_2} \ldots \xrightarrow{a_n} (b_n, \varphi_n)$ in a constraint graph, we denote by $\sigma(\pi)$ the symbolic derivation $b_0 \xrightarrow{a_1} b_1 \xrightarrow{a_2} \ldots \xrightarrow{a_n} b_n$ that has the same control state and action sequences. We now show that every combination of a path in a constraint graph and a satisfying assignment for the formula in its final node corresponds to a run in the DDS, and vice versa. To that end, we need a fixed variable renaming $\hat{\alpha} \colon V \mapsto V_0$.

Lemma 2. *(1)* $\mathrm{CG}_{\mathcal{B}}$ *has a path* $\pi \colon (b_I, C_{\alpha_I}) \to^* (b, \varphi)$ *where* φ *is satisfiable by* α, *iff* $\mathcal{B}$ *has a run* $(b_I, \alpha_I) \to^* (b, \alpha)$ *whose abstraction is* $\sigma(\pi)$.
(2) $\mathrm{CG}_{\mathcal{B}}(b)$ *has a path* $\pi \colon (b, C_{\hat{\alpha}}) \to^* (b', \varphi)$ *s.t.* φ *is satisfiable by* α, *iff* $\mathcal{B}$ *has derivation* $(b, \alpha_0) \to^* (b', \alpha_n)$ *abstracted by* $\sigma(\pi)$ *with* $\alpha_0 = \alpha|_{V_0}$ *and* $\alpha_n = \alpha|_V$.

To illustrate this result, e.g. the run (3) corresponds to the path in $\mathrm{CG}_{\mathcal{B}_{\text{thresh}}}$ shown in red (see Fig. 3). On the other hand, the lemma reveals that $\mathcal{B}$ has runs with the same action sequence for *all* assignments that satisfy $(o > 1000) \wedge (t > 0)$.

As stated above, the construction of the constraint graph according to Definition 7 need not terminate. However, it does in many practical examples, which is related to the following property identified in [9]: A DDS $\mathcal{B}$ has a *finite history set* if the set of formulas φ obtained during the construction of the constraint graph (called *history constraints* in [9]) is finite up to equivalence. Thus, if $\mathcal{B}$ has a finite history set, and the procedure COMPUTECG($\mathcal{B}$) checks eagerly for equivalent nodes while executing Definition 7, the construction must produce a finite graph. Crucially, this holds for a clearly identifiable class of systems used in the literature: it was shown that if either the constraint language in $\mathcal{B}$ is restricted to variable-to-variable and variable-to-constant comparisons, or if the control flow is such that the current state depends only on finitely many actions in the past, the DDS $\mathcal{B}$ has indeed a finite history set [9, Thms 5.2 and 5.9]. All examples of DPNs collected from the literature (see Sect. 7) fall in one of these categories.

6 Data-aware Soundness

In this section we harness the constraint graph to check data-aware soundness. To that end, we assume a DDS $\mathcal{B} = \langle B, b_I, \mathcal{A}, \Delta, \{b_F\}, V, \alpha_I, guard \rangle$ obtained by translating a DPN $\mathcal{N}$, such that $b_I = M_I$ and $b_F = M_F$ correspond to the initial and final markings of $\mathcal{N}$; and we assume that $CG_\mathcal{B}$ is the constraint graph of $\mathcal{B}$. The three requirements of Definition 3 are then checked by the procedures in Algorithm 2:

- BADTERMINATION returns *true* if in the node set S of the constraint graph $CG_\mathcal{B}$ there is a node (b, φ) such that b corresponds to a marking M of the DPN $\mathcal{N}$ with $M \geqslant M_F$. For instance, it returns *true* for $CG_{\mathcal{B}_{thresh}}$ in Fig. 4 since the red nodes correspond to marking $\{p_2, p_3\}$; while it would return *false* for $CG_\mathcal{B}$.
- DEADTRANSITION returns *true* if there is a transition in the DPN $\mathcal{N}$ whose label does not occur in $CG_\mathcal{B}$. For instance, the constraint graph for the DDS $\mathcal{B}_{reset}$ in Fig. 3 coincides with the graph $CG_\mathcal{B}$ in Fig. 4, which does not contain reset. Thus, DEADTRANSITION($CG_\mathcal{B}, \mathcal{N}_{reset}$) returns *true*.
- For BLOCKEDSTATE, we use the formulas $blocked(b, \varphi)$ defined next. For $b \in B$ and constraint graph $CG_\mathcal{B}(b) = \langle S', \gamma', s_0' \rangle$, let $final(b) = \{\varphi \mid (b_F, \varphi) \in S'\}$ be all formulas in $CG_\mathcal{B}(b)$ that occur together with final states. Then,

Definition 8. *For* $CG_\mathcal{B} = (S, \gamma, s_0)$ *and* $(b, \varphi) \in S$, *let*

$$blocked(b, \varphi) = \varphi[\overline{V}/\overline{V}_0] \wedge \neg \left(\exists \overline{V}. \bigvee_{\psi \in final(b)} \psi \right).$$

Now, BLOCKEDSTATE returns *true* if there is some node $(b, \varphi) \in S$ in $CG_\mathcal{B}$ such that $blocked(b, \varphi)$ is satisfiable. This formula expresses that the process reaches control state b that prohibits to reach a final state: Indeed, $\Psi := \exists \overline{V}. \bigvee_{\psi \in final(b)} \psi$ states conditions to reach a final state from b and variables assigned to $\overline{V}_0$ (where $\exists \overline{V}$ reflects that we do not care about the final values of the data variables). Thus, $\neg \Psi$ states that *no* final state can be reached, and we take the conjunction with φ (with variables renamed appropriately) to combine this with the assumptions of the current constraint graph node (b, φ). For instance, we can check whether $\mathcal{B}$ in Fig. 3 admits a deadlock at a run the is captured by the node $(p_{12}, o = 0)$ (drawn in red) of $CG_\mathcal{B}$ in Fig. 4, as follows: There are three final nodes in $CG_\mathcal{B}(p_{12})$ in Fig. 4 labelled $\varphi_1 \doteq (o = o_0 \wedge o_0 > 0 \wedge t = t_0 \wedge t_0 > 0)$, $\varphi_2 \doteq (o = o_0 \wedge o_0 > 0 \wedge t_0 > t \wedge t \leqslant 0 \wedge t_0 > 0)$, and $\varphi_3 \doteq (o > o_0 \wedge o > 0 \wedge t_0 > t \wedge t \leqslant 0 \wedge t_0 > 0)$, so $final(p_{12}) = \{\varphi_1, \varphi_2, \varphi_3\}$. We hence get

$$blocked(\mathsf{p}_{12}, o = 0) = (o_0 = 0) \wedge \neg\, (\exists o\, t.\, (\varphi_1 \vee \varphi_2 \vee \varphi_3))$$

which is simplified using quantifier elimination to $(o_0 = 0) \wedge (t_0 \leqslant 0)$, and e.g. satisfiable by $\alpha(o_0) = \alpha(t_0) = 0$. Thus BLOCKEDSTATE$(CG_\mathcal{B}, \mathcal{N})$ returns *true*, reflecting the blocked sequence (1) shown at the end of Sect. 2.

Note that all checks in Algorithm 2 are effective if $CG_\mathcal{B}$ and all $CG_\mathcal{B}(b)$ are finite. Finally, we relate the procedures in Algorithm 2 to properties of $\mathcal{B}$, which together with Lemma 1 shows that data-aware soundness of DPNs is effectively checked.

Theorem 1. *Let* $CG_\mathcal{B}$ *be a constraint graph for a DDS* $\mathcal{B}$.

(1) BLOCKEDSTATE$(CG_\mathcal{B}, \mathcal{B})$ *returns true iff* $\mathcal{B}$ *has a blocked state.*

(2) DEADTRANSITION$(CG_\mathcal{B}, \mathcal{B})$ *returns true iff* $\mathcal{N}$ *has a transition t of* $\mathcal{N}$ *such that* $(b, \ell(t), b') \in \Delta$ *is unreachable for all* $b, b' \in B$, *and*

(3) BADTERMINATION$(CG_\mathcal{B}, \mathcal{B})$ *returns true iff some* $b \in B$ *corresponding to M with* $M \geqslant M_F$ *is reachable.*

7 Implementation and Experiments

We implemented our approach in the tool `ada` (arithmetic DDS analyzer) in Python; source code, benchmarks, and a web interface are available.[1] The tool takes a (bounded) DPN in `.pnml` format as input, and checks data-aware soundness following Algorithm 1 and Algorithm 2. As output, it produces graphical representations of the DDS $\mathcal{B}$ and the constraint graph $CG_\mathcal{B}$, and if data-aware

Table 1. Experiments with `ada` on DPNs from the literature.

Process			Sound	Time	Checks	$|V|$	$|\mathcal{B}|$	$|CG_\mathcal{B}|$
(1)	Road fines (normative)	[17, Fig. 7]	No P1	3.1 s	3909	8	9/19	29/44
(2)	Road fines (mined)	[16, Fig. 12.7]	No P1	3.1 s	3811	8	9/19	59/104
(3)	Road fines (mined)	[13, Fig. 13]	Yes	2 m 16 s	114,005	5	9/19	234/376
(4)	Hospital billing	[16, Fig. 15.3]	Yes	3 m 1 s	229,467	4	17/40	360/703
(5)	Sepsis (normative)	[16, Fig. 13.3]	Yes	19 s	831	3	301/1630	793/4099
(6)	Sepsis (mined)	[16, Fig. 13.6]	Yes	1 m 43 s	8085	4	301/1630	1117/5339
(7)	Digital whiteboard: register	[16, Fig. 14.3]	Yes	0.1 s	16	2	7/6	7/6
(8)	Digital whiteboard: transfer	[16, Fig. 14.3]	No P1	0.1 s	19	3	7/6	7/6
(9)	Digital whiteboard: discharge	[16, Fig. 14.3]	Yes	0.1 s	30	4	6/6	7/6
(10)	Credit approval	[6, Fig. 3]	Yes	1.2 s	434	5	6/10	26/27
(11)	Package handling	[8, Fig. 5]	No P3	1.3 s	242	5	16/28	68/67
(12)	Auction	[9, Ex. 1.1]	No P1	5.8 s	1007	5	5/7	13/15

---

[1] https://soundness.adatool.dev.

soundness is violated, a witness is constructed. CVC5 (cvc5.github.io) and Z3 (z3prover.github.io), which support all datatypes mentioned in Sect. 2.

As DPNs are a relatively recent framework, an extensive set of benchmarks is still missing. To mitigate this, we have collected all available DPN examples/use cases from the literature, and used ada to check soundness. The results are shown in Table 1, which indicates data-aware soundness (and the violated property of Definition 3), the verification time, number of SMT checks, number of variables in the DDS $\mathcal{B}$, and the sizes of $\mathcal{B}$ and $CG_{\mathcal{B}}$ as number of nodes/transitions. All tests were run on an Intel Core i7 (4×2.60 GHz, 19 GB RAM), using CVC5 as backend.

Benchmarks (1)–(3) model the handling of traffic offenses in an information system of the Italian police; in a normative model and two versions where decision rules were mined automatically. The former two have the same unsoundness issue (see Example 1), related to missing guards on written variables. (4) models the billing process in a hospital, it was mined from a real-life log with 100k traces, discovering guards by overlapping decision mining. (5) and (6) reflect the triage process for sepsis patients, based on a log obtained from a hospital's ERP system for 1,050 patients. (5) is a normative model; for (6), guards were discovered by decision mining. (7)–(9) are activity patterns for patient logistics designed based on domain knowledge and logs of a hospital information system. (10) is a faithful though hand-made process of granting loans to clients of a bank. (11) is a manually designed order-to-delivery process, obtained as a DPN translation of a DBPMN model (a data- and decision-aware model that builds on BPMN and DMN S-FEEL). (12) is a manually designed model for an English auction.

We stress that the benchmarks (1), (5), (7), (10), and (12) are out of reach of the earlier approaches [8,13], as their constraint language cannot express addition and multiplication. Moreover, while example (3) took 1.9h with the technique of [13], soundness can be detected by ada in less than 3 min.

An extensive DPN benchmark set with a wide range of problem sizes is not yet available. To provide some indications on the scalability of our method, we therefore modified some of the above benchmarks, adding (a) up to 100 sequential control states, and (b) up to 10 data variables $z_1, \ldots, z_k$ for every type, in the latter case obfuscating constraints of the form $e \odot e'$ to $e = z_1 \wedge z_1 = z_2 \wedge \cdots \wedge z_k \odot e'$. The results are depicted in Fig. 5, where the x-axis reports the number of added states/variables, and the y-axis the computation time.

The chart in (a) suggests that the addition of sequential tasks in the control-flow increases the computation time only linearly. For (b), we also observe a linear behaviour for many systems; but for benchmarks with a more complex constraint structure such as the credit approval example, performance can be considerably harmed. However, note that the benchmarks generated in (b) exhibit far larger constraints than the real-world systems, and can hence be considered extreme cases. Finally, it it interesting to observe that similar trends are obtained for (b) when using operators other than equality in building the expanded constraints.

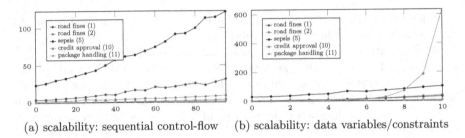

(a) scalability: sequential control-flow   (b) scalability: data variables/constraints

Fig. 5. Scalability of **ada** considering control-flow (a) and data variables (b).

8   Conclusion

The presence of numerical data in data-aware process models, either designed by hand or discovered from logs, render it highly intricate (undecidable in general) to manually check correctness properties such as soundness. We presented the first automatic technique that can verify data-aware soundness for DPNs with linear arithmetic, along with a prototype implementation. Our experiments show that the approach is effective and efficient, and can detect soundness bugs.

In future work, we aim at realizing a tighter integration between manual and automated approaches for data-aware process discovery and correctness analysis. Specifically, we plan to study the integration of this technique with automated approaches for process discovery to either guarantee by design the soundness of the discovered processes, or to provide specific indications on how to repair them. We also intend to deepen our understanding of the scalability of the approach starting from the preliminary evaluation presented here, with the goal of isolating the main sources of computational complexity, and of incorporating specific methods to handle them. Finally, we hope that having a solid foundational framework paired with a proof-of-concept IT artefact will trigger empirical research focussed on on-field validation of soundness for data-aware processes.

References

1. van der Aalst, W.: The application of Petri Nets to workflow management. J. uits Syst. Comput. **8**(1), 21–66 (1998)
2. van der Aalst, W.M.P., van Hee, K.M., ter Hofstede, A.H.M., Sidorova, N., Verbeek, H.M.W., Voorhoeve, M., Wynn, M.T.: Soundness of workflow nets: classification, decidability, and analysis. Formal Aspects Comput. **23**(3), 333–363 (2011)
3. Artale, A., Calvanese, D., Montali, M., van der Aalst, W.M.P.: Enriching data models with behavioral constraints. In: Ontology Makes Sense. FAIA, vol. 316, pp. 257–277. IOS Press (2019)
4. Batoulis, K., Haarmann, S., Weske, M.: Various notions of soundness for decision-aware business processes. In: Mayr, H.C., Guizzardi, G., Ma, H., Pastor, O. (eds.) ER 2017. LNCS, vol. 10650, pp. 403–418. Springer, Cham (2017). https://doi.org/10.1007/978-3-319-69904-2_31

5. Calvanese, D., de Giacomo, G., Montali, M.: Foundations of data-aware process analysis: a database theory perspective. In: Proceedings of 32nd PODS, pp. 1–12 (2013)
6. de Leoni, M., Mannhardt, F.: Decision discovery in business processes. In: Encyclopedia of Big Data Technologies, pp. 1–12. Springer (2018)
7. Deutsch, A., Hull, R., Li, Y., Vianu, V.: Automatic verification of database-centric systems. ACM SIGLOG News **5**(2), 37–56 (2018)
8. Felli, P., de Leoni, M., Montali, M.: Soundness verification of data-aware process models with variable-to-variable conditions. Fund. Inf. **182**(1), 1–29 (2021)
9. Felli, P., Montali, M., Winkler, S.: Linear-time verification of data-aware dynamic systems with arithmetic. In: Proceedings of 36th AAAI (2022)
10. Felli, P., Montali, M., Winkler, S.: Soundness of data-aware processes with arithmetic conditions (ext. version). CoRR (2022). https://arxiv.org/abs/2203.14809
11. Fettke, P., Reisig, W.: Modelling service-oriented systems and cloud services with HERAKLIT. In: Zirpins, C., Paraskakis, I., Andrikopoulos, V., Kratzke, N., Pahl, C., El Ioini, N., Andreou, A.S., Feuerlicht, G., Lamersdorf, W., Ortiz, G., Van den Heuvel, W.-J., Soldani, J., Villari, M., Casale, G., Plebani, P. (eds.) ESOCC 2020. CCIS, vol. 1360, pp. 77–89. Springer, Cham (2021). https://doi.org/10.1007/978-3-030-71906-7_7
12. van Hee, K., Sidorova, N., Voorhoeve, M.: Generalised soundness of workflow nets is decidable. In: Cortadella, J., Reisig, W. (eds.) ICATPN 2004. LNCS, vol. 3099, pp. 197–215. Springer, Heidelberg (2004). https://doi.org/10.1007/978-3-540-27793-4_12
13. de Leoni, M., Felli, P., Montali, M.: A holistic approach for soundness verification of decision-aware process models. In: Trujillo, J.C., Davis, K.C., Du, X., Li, Z., Ling, T.W., Li, G., Lee, M.L. (eds.) ER 2018. LNCS, vol. 11157, pp. 219–235. Springer, Cham (2018). https://doi.org/10.1007/978-3-030-00847-5_17
14. de Leoni, M., Felli, P., Montali, M.: Strategy synthesis for data-aware dynamic systems with multiple actors. In: Proceedings of 17th KR, pp. 315–325 (2020)
15. de Leoni, M., Felli, P., Montali, M.: Integrating BPMN and DMN: modeling and analysis. J. Data Semant. **10**(1), 165–188 (2021)
16. Mannhardt, F.: Multi-perspective Process Mining. Ph.D. thesis, Technical University of Eindhoven (2018)
17. Mannhardt, F., de Leoni, M., Reijers, H.A., van der Aalst, W.M.P.: Balanced multi-perspective checking of process conformance. Computing **98**(4), 407–437 (2015). https://doi.org/10.1007/s00607-015-0441-1
18. Polyvyanyy, A., van der Werf, J.M.E.M., Overbeek, S., Brouwers, R.: Information systems modeling: language, verification, and tool Support. In: Giorgini, P., Weber, B. (eds.) CAiSE 2019. LNCS, vol. 11483, pp. 194–212. Springer, Cham (2019). https://doi.org/10.1007/978-3-030-21290-2_13
19. Presburger, M.: Über die Vollständigkeit eines gewissen Systems der Arithmetik ganzer Zahlen, in welchem die Addition als einzige Operation hervortritt. In: Comptes Rendus du I congres de Mathem. des Pays Slaves, pp. 92–101 (1929)
20. Reichert, M.: Process and data: two sides of the same coin? In: Meersman, R., Panetto, H., Dillon, T., Rinderle-Ma, S., Dadam, P., Zhou, X., Pearson, S., Ferscha, A., Bergamaschi, S., Cruz, I.F. (eds.) OTM 2012. LNCS, vol. 7565, pp. 2–19. Springer, Heidelberg (2012). https://doi.org/10.1007/978-3-642-33606-5_2
21. Ritter, D., Rinderle-Ma, S., Montali, M., Rivkin, A.: Formal foundations for responsible application integration. Inf. Syst. **101**, 101439 (2021)
22. Sidorova, N., Stahl, C.: Soundness for resource-constrained workflow nets is decidable. IEEE Trans. Syst. Man Cybern. Syst. **43**(3), 724 729 (2013)

23. Snoeck, M.: Enterprise Information Systems Engineering - The MERODE App-roach. The Enterprise Engineering Series. Springer (2014)
24. Snoeck, M., De Smedt, J., De Weerdt, J.: Supporting data-aware processes with MERODE. In: Augusto, A., Gill, A., Nurcan, S., Reinhartz-Berger, I., Schmidt, R., Zdravkovic, J. (eds.) BPMDS/EMMSAD -2021. LNBIP, vol. 421, pp. 131–146. Springer, Cham (2021). https://doi.org/10.1007/978-3-030-79186-5_9

Narration as a Technique to Improve Process Model Comprehension: Tell Me What I Cannot See

Banu Aysolmaz[1]([⊠]) [iD], Farida Nur Cayhani[2], and Hajo A. Reijers[1,3] [iD]

[1] Eindhoven University of Technology, Eindhoven, The Netherlands
{b.e.aysolmaz,h.a.reijers}@tue.nl
[2] Vrije Universiteit Amsterdam, Amsterdam, The Netherlands
[3] Utrecht University, Utrecht, The Netherlands
h.a.reijers@uu.nl

Abstract. Conceptual models play a vital role in the engineering of information systems. A variety of stakeholders rely on their use, but they often find it challenging to make sense of such models. This is particularly known to be the case for process models, which capture complex temporal behavior. In practice, professionals often extend process models with textual descriptions to make them easier to understand, but it is not known whether this creates an even higher cognitive burden. In this study, we adopt the dual coding theory and the cognitive theory of multimedia learning, which suggest that people experience a better learning process when materials are presented via two different sensory channels (i.e., auditory and visual). We used this theory to set up and conduct an experiment with 42 participants that involve models of two real-life processes. We also implemented an online environment, which presents additional information on process model elements through the auditory channel in the form of narration. Our findings support that the use of narration may have a positive impact on process model comprehension, although it seems to depend on the kind of model elements that are explained. We discuss the implications of these findings and suggest further directions for research into process model comprehension.

Keywords: Conceptual modeling · Business process models · Process model comprehension · Narration · Cognitive theory of multimedia learning · Experiment

1 Introduction

Conceptual models are essential artifacts for the development of information systems (ISs) [1]. Conceptual models that are developed during systems analysis are then used for various purposes, particularly to establish a common understanding of the system and facilitate communication among diverse stakeholders [2]. Therefore, it is important that users or stakeholders in an organization can understand these conceptual models. However, it is hard for conceptual model users to learn and understand the content by

© Springer Nature Switzerland AG 2022
X. Franch et al. (Eds.): CAiSE 2022, LNCS 13295, pp. 407–422, 2022.
https://doi.org/10.1007/978-3-031-07472-1_24

looking at the models [3]. A business process model, or a *process model* for short, is a type of conceptual model frequently used in IS development [1], which bears similar challenges of understandability to its diverse users [4, 5].

To make process models more understandable, they are frequently extended with textual descriptions [6]. Whether this is an effective practice can be questioned. The task of comprehending inherently complex process models already generates a considerable cognitive load [7]. Reading process models *together* with textual descriptions may exert an even higher cognitive load since users need to process graphical and textual information simultaneously [8]. This matter motivates this paper.

Prior studies on computer-based learning have reported the use of narration, specifically together with animation, as a way of alleviating the cognitive load in the mental process of understanding and learning a material [9–12]. *Narration* in a computer-based environment is a multimedia technique used to deliver information in a verbal mode that is processed by the user's auditory sensors, different than the visual sensory channel [13]. The potential comprehension enhancements through narration are based on the dual coding theory (DCT) [14] and the principles of the cognitive theory of multimedia learning (CTML) [15]. These theories state that presenting learning materials via two different sensory channels, i.e., auditory and visual, helps the user distribute the cognitive load among the two channels, leaving more room to build connections between graphical and textual concepts [13]. Process models, which involve complex graphical information that requires users infer hidden behavior among process elements and additional textual information [16], constitute a relevant learning material for using narration for improving comprehension [17].

In this study, by building on the principles established by the DCT and CTML, we develop a process model environment that implements narration. The purpose of the environment is to display process models, potentially extended with textual process descriptions, to users who want to make sense of such models. It is important to note that, in the context of process models, narration is subject to temporal constraints, since an aspect of a process generally needs to be verbalized in an ordered way ("First, activity A takes places, which is followed up by either activity B or C..."). Thus, it made sense to support the environment with narrations by the use of animation, which is in line with guidelines to coordinate the presentation of verbal and visual explanations that are related (e.g. [13]). To this end, we implemented the process model animation technique from [18].

We report in this study on an online experiment that was conducted to evaluate the process model environment in an organizational setting using two real-life processes. We examined the effect of narration on process model comprehension through a process model comprehension test. In practice, process descriptions are typically used to deliver two types of content: (1) descriptions of the relations of an element with other process model elements, in particular in terms of process flow, shortly *flow descriptions*, and (2) detailed information about elements that are not readily available within the process model, shortly *element descriptions*. Narration can impact the cognitive processing of the two descriptions differently, since graphical elements related to those descriptions are different. Thus, we designed the experimental material to distinguish between the flow and element descriptions. We further evaluated user perceptions about the narration environment through a survey based on the IS adoption literature [19]. The results, as obtained through the involvement of 42 participants, show that process model comprehension was higher in the group using the narration environment; the difference is significant for the test score related to element descriptions. Better perceptions of the narration environment, particularly in terms of ease of use and satisfaction, support the use of narration as an effective technique for comprehension of process models. Our study contributes to the wider IS research by introducing narration as a new multimedia technique for conceptual model use. In what follows, we will discuss potential explanations of the impact of narration, its use in combination with animation, and future directions for conceptual modeling research.

The remainder of this paper is structured as follows. In the next section, we present the theoretical background and develop our hypotheses. In Sect. 3, we describe the experimental research design. Section 4 presents the results, including the test of hypotheses. In Sect. 5, we discuss our results along with its implications and limitations. Finally, we conclude and provide future research directions in Sect. 6.

2   Background and Hypotheses

In this section, we summarize background theory on process model comprehension and use of narration for improving comprehension; and develop our hypotheses.

2.1   Process Models and Comprehension

A process model graphically captures the execution of activities performed as part of a process, the resources associated with the activities, and information regarding the activities as process model elements [20]. The comprehension of process models is cognitively demanding since they are inherently complex. Challenges relate to the hidden dependencies among activities through gateway elements, to the hard mental operations required to understand the relations among elements, and to the difficulty of grasping parts of the model to infer overall process knowledge [21, 22].

The cognitive load theory (CLT) [23] helps to explain the described phenomena by pointing out that working memory has a limited capacity to process any given information. When the presented material is complex and requires a deep understanding, the cognitive load exerted increases, diminishing the learning capacity. To lower the cognitive load while reading process models, various visualization approaches, called secondary notation, have been proposed [7].

It is a typical practice that conceptual models are complemented with textual descriptions [24, 25]. Textual descriptions that accompany business process models mainly serve two purposes. The first purpose relates to improving the understandability of the process model, since some stakeholders may have difficulties in comprehending – they may simply prefer to have textual explanations of the model at their disposal as well [26]. For this purpose, a process element such as an activity is described to explain its position within the process flow, e.g., after which activity and under what conditions it is executed, the responsible roles, its relations with other activities such as inputs or outputs [16]. We name this type shortly *flow description*, which is information that could also have been obtained from the model.

The second purpose is to provide detailed information of a process element that is not readily or completely available on the process model, either because the graphical notation does not allow for it or because the model would otherwise get very complicated [25, 27]. As examples, rare execution conditions and exceptions for an activity are specified; also, if an activity involves data entry, specific data fields are listed. We refer to this type as *element descriptions*. The typical ways of presenting both the *flow* and *element descriptions* are on an accompanying document or on the user interface that appears when the relevant element is chosen [28–30].

When there is additional textual information, cognitive load is increased since the user needs to process both the graphical information of the model and the related text to understand the process. This is called the *split-attention effect* since the user's attention is split between two simultaneous inputs on the visual sensory channel [8]. Previous conceptual model comprehension literature has dealt with this comprehension challenge in different ways. For example, the level of comprehension has been compared when users receive the graphical and textual format together or alone [24] or when they receive them in different orders [16]. Narration, however, can provide a solution by allowing the synchronized delivery of the graphical and textual information in parallel.

2.2 Narration for Learning and Comprehension

DCT explains how human cognitive system processes verbal (auditory) and non-verbal (visual) representations simultaneously to build integrated knowledge [31]. Building on DCT, CTML explains the sources of cognitive overload on the two sensory channels, visual and auditory, such as the split-attention effect [32]. It further provides multimedia principles to harvest the potential of using these two channels in parallel to improve learning [8]. More specifically, the *modality principle* suggests that presenting the textual information as narration rather than as on-screen text provides an off-loading effect for the cognitive load in the visual channel [8]. Moreover, the *temporal contiguity principle* suggests that the presentation of corresponding visual and auditory material should be synchronized rather than offered successively [13]. To provide such a synchronized presentation, narration needs to be used together with a dynamic visualization technique, in particular animation. The *multimedia principle* of CTML explains that deep learning can be achieved through the synchronized use of animation and narration [13].

The effect of using narration with animation on improving comprehension and learning has been established in computer-based learning studies [9–12, 33]. The related theories support that using narration for presenting process model and related textual information can improve process model comprehension. In this way, while the graphical process model is conveyed through the visual channel, textual information is transmitted through the auditory channel, overcoming the split-attention effect and using the modality principle.

2.3 Hypotheses

Based on the theoretical background provided so far, we develop the following hypothesis on the effect of using a verbal explanation (narration) rather than on-screen text to deliver textual information about a process model:

H1: The use of narration for process models will have a positive impact on the comprehension of process model information.

As discussed before, we distinguish two types of textual process descriptions that can be provided through the auditory channel, or narration: *flow descriptions* and *element descriptions*. The use of narration has shown to enhance learning for both procedural knowledge with an order in time [11], i.e., process model information in our study, and factual knowledge of a specific topic [34], i.e., additional process information. However, narration can impact their comprehension differently. For flow descriptions, the information relates not only to the process model element being described but also other graphical elements. Moreover, the user can reach this information also through the visual channel by investigating the model. For element descriptions, by contrast, the information is on one process model element and not readily available on the model. Narration is likely to impact these two descriptions differently. To study this impact, we propose two subhypotheses that complement H1:

H1a: The use of narration for process models will have a positive impact on the comprehension of flow descriptions of process models.

H1b: The use of narration for process models will have a positive impact on the comprehension of element descriptions of process models.

For the adoption and achievement of a new model or system, the positive experience of its users is important [19, 35]. In our case, this translates to the environment we built, and it seems fair to only expect an enduring positive effect of the multimedia techniques it employs if stakeholders are inclined to continuously use them. Literature on IS adoption, which complements the technology acceptance research, has found three important indicators for the adoption of IS artifacts [19]. The first, perceived usefulness (PU), is about the beliefs of the user about the utility and performance of the artifact [36]. The second, perceived ease of use (PEOU), reflects the perceptions on the effort required to use the artifact [19]. Lastly, the level of satisfaction (SAT) captures if the user is content with the artifact because it helps to fulfill the expectations [37]. These measures have been validated also in the context of multimedia learning [38]. With the presence of narration that may alleviate the cognitive load of comprehending a process model, we expect that users have perceptions of the environment in terms of PU, PEOU, and SAT that are better for the narration than the non-narration environment, as stated by the following hypothesis:

H2: The use of narration for process models will have a positive impact on the user perceptions about the process model environment.

Next, we proceed with explaining our experimental research design and the narration environment we used in our experiment to test the hypotheses.

3 Research Design

We conducted an experiment to test the hypotheses described in Sect. 2.3. We used the guidelines from the software engineering domain to design, execute, and analyze the experiment [39]. Aligned with our hypotheses, we identified the independent variable of our study as the use of a process model environment that delivers the verbal explanations of process models. The first set of dependent variables relate to the level of process model comprehension as measured by the total process model comprehension test score, the test score for flow description related questions, and the test score for element description related questions. The second set of dependent variables relate to the user perceptions of the narration environment, which are PU, PEOU, and SAT. We also used control variables such as process modeling knowledge and familiarity with the presented processes. In what follows, we will discuss the experimental design in more detail and also shed light on how the participants were involved in the experiment.

3.1 Experimental Design

The experiment we set up used one factor with two treatments: narration and non-narration. The participants were randomly divided into two groups and were exposed to one of the treatments that used the same process models.

Our first treatment, narration, offers a verbal narration to explain relevant information regarding the elements on the process models. To signal the narrated element, the narration is accompanied by process model animation. The use of narration has proven to improve learning only when used with animations [12, 33]. Accordingly, we implement our narration environment based on an animation solution that has shown to be relevant for process models [18].

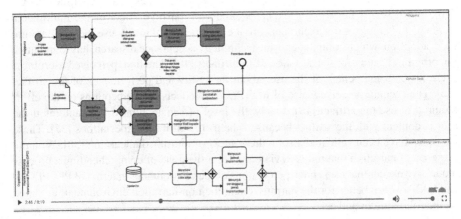

Fig. 1. A screenshot of the environment for the narration treatment.

A screenshot of the environment for the narration treatment is depicted in Fig. 1. Treatment materials are available for both processes as video files (Colocation: https://bit.ly/3iwbFWi, Change management: https://bit.ly/3mo36ho). Each video shows the flow of the process from the start until the end event. At the beginning of the process, all nodes are displayed in white/plain mode. When explaining a particular element (i.e., an activity, gateway, or event), the element turns into yellow. At this time, a narration describes the information related to the corresponding element. After the narration has finished, the color of the node changes into green, and the flow of the process continues to the next element. During this treatment, possible flow alternatives originating from a split gateway are explored. For example, when explaining an outgoing XOR gateway, the animation highlights all outgoing paths. Then, each process flow following these options are alternately described before it continues with the next step. The dynamic visualizations can be paused, restarted, or shown for a certain part only.

The second treatment is designed in the form of a static model. Within the environment we designed, the participant can investigate the process model as a static artifact as the standard way of comprehending process models. Figure 2 shows a screenshot of the environment for the non-narration treatment. When the participant selects one of the process model elements, related textual information is shown as an on-screen text next to the element, following the *spatial contiguity* principle to lower the cognitive load of processing two separate information [8]. The content of this information is the same as the one in the narration representation. The participants can move the absolute position of the model to get a better overview of the process.

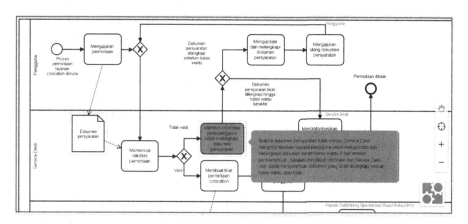

Fig. 2. A screenshot of the environment for the non-narration treatment.

The narration and non-narration environments are based on several other design decisions. In the narration group, the textual information was delivered only through the verbal channel without an additional on-screen text, based on the redundancy principle [13]. Next, we chose not to apply an interactive animation where the participants have control over the animation but rather implemented a continuous mode. This option could potentially increase the cognitive load due to the effort to actively explore the process flow [18] while processing the textual information from the auditory channel. Furthermore, as the duration of the treatment for each participant would vary, it would be difficult to set a standard minimum time to make the narration and non-narration treatments comparable. As for the non-narration treatment, we chose not to use animation since the animation would impose a pace that may not match the participant's reading speed. To make sure that participants exerted a tangible comprehension effort, and to make this effort comparable within treatments, a minimum time limit was implemented to examine the process models; the duration of the corresponding continuous animation was set on the non-narration environment. Participants of both groups could use the environment longer, but only move to the next step, which involved questions, after the minimum time limit.

3.2 Participants and Procedure

This study was conducted in a real business environment. We chose the participants from an organizational unit in the Ministry of Finance of the Republic of Indonesia. The management recognized that sometimes the employees experience difficulty in understanding their processes, which may lead to problems during their execution. Therefore, the management supported the employees to participate in this experiment. The employees were also motivated since this would help them gain a better understanding of the process models. We sent invitation emails to the targeted employees in the organization to recruit participants.

We selected two processes that are commonly executed in the involved organization and where most employees of the unit act as participants; colocation and change management processes. The *colocation process* describes the procedures for requesting a colocation service from a customer to the organization starting when a request is submitted until it is completed or rejected. The *change management process* depicts how a change on IT services, such as a configuration item, service, or service component, is requested and applied in the organization. We modeled the processes using BPMN, an industrial standard for process modeling [40]. For all process model elements, namely activities, split gateways, and events, we developed textual descriptions. The textual descriptions included flow descriptions for all elements and element descriptions for the relevant elements. Process models and other materials were developed in the Indonesian language and narrations were created using the TextAloud text to speech software. We provide English translations of the materials online (https://bit.ly/3nVOgAS). The structural properties of the two processes are shown in Table 1. They depict diverse structural properties with average to high complexity levels [41].

Table 1. Structural properties of the two process models used in the experiment.

Process	Tasks	Split gateways	Join gateways	Total nodes	Arcs	Roles
P1-colocation process	25	6	5	36	43	5
P2-change management process	31	9	9	49	60	8

The participants were given a link to access the experiment page based on the assigned treatment type. The experiment began with a welcoming page in which a brief explanation about the purpose and general summary of the study were presented. Next, a page explaining the BPMN notation was shown. After that, the participants moved to the personal questionnaire to collect data on their background that might influence their comprehension on process models [18]. Here, we used four questions from literature about self-reported process modeling expertise and two questions on the level of domain knowledge regarding the presented processes. These measures were then used as control variables.

Next, the first process model, the colocation process, was shown in the relevant environment based on the assigned treatment. Following the completion of the allocated time, the participants could move to the next page, where a process model comprehension test in the form of ten multiple-choice questions about the given process model were raised. Most of the questions were related to flow descriptions, which could be answered based on the process model. The rest of the questions required the consideration of element descriptions. While answering the questions, a static process model could be accessed as a reference through a particular button in the questionnaire page. The process model was then displayed in the separate window. This feature was offered in both treatment groups. After the participants answered all questions, they were navigated to the second process, change management, in which the same procedure was applied as in the first model.

The last part of the experiment was a questionnaire to measure the user perceptions regarding the implemented environment. This part consisted of five questions on PU, five questions on PEOU, and four questions on SAT [36]. The level of agreement of the participants was measured using five-point Likert scale (1 = strongly disagree, and 5 = strongly agree). The experiment ended with a closing page.

4 Results

Overall, 51 employees responded to our invitation and agreed to participate in the experiment. These employees were from diverse divisions. Nine participants could not finish and dropped out from the experiment; hence, the experiment was completed by 42 participants: 23 participants in the narration group and 19 participants in the non-narration group.

To check if the control variables differed across the groups, we used Chi-square and Fisher's exact (for binary variable) tests. Regarding process modeling-related variables, we could establish that there is no difference among the groups with respect to the intensity of encountering process models (Chi2(1, $N = 42$) = 4.83, .19; M = 2.90/4, SD = .96), knowledge level on process modeling (Chi2(1, $N = 42$) = 7.89, .53; M = 2.80/5, SD = .82), or training on process modeling (p = .17, Fisher's exact test; M = 0.3, SD = .46). The reported domain knowledge regarding the colocation (Chi2(1, $N = 42$) = 3.37, .50; M = 3.38/5, SD = .1.04) and change management (Chi2(1, $N = 42$) = 2.92, .57; M = 3.69/5, SD = 1.09) processes also did not differ significantly.

For the reliability assessment, we checked the internal consistency of our measure comprising the comprehension test score. We calculated Cronbach's α by adding the scores of individual questions as items. Our Cronbach's α value of 0.73 suggests that the reliability was sufficiently adequate. Therefore, we proceeded with the test of our hypotheses on the available data summarized in Table 2.

4.1 Tests of Hypothesis 1: Process Model Comprehension

We measure the first dependent variable, the level of process model comprehension, with the score of the process model comprehension test achieved by the participant. We calculate the overall test score of the two processes (ScoreTot), the test score for questions related to the flow descriptions (ScoreFlDesc), and the test score for questions involving element descriptions (ScoreElDesc). Figure 3 presents the plots for the mean values with error bars related to these variables. As can be seen, mean ScoreTot for the narration group is higher than those in the non-narration group. The same trend holds for the ScoreFlDesc and ScoreElDesc scores.

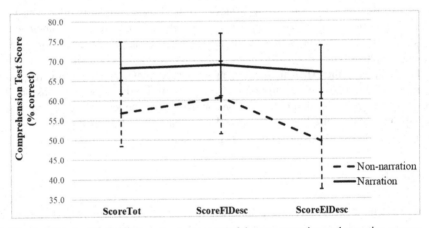

Fig. 3. Plots for the comprehension test scores of the non-narration and narration groups.

To test if the differences in the comprehension test scores are significant among groups, we used Mann-Whitney U test as an alternative of the t-test. We did so since the scores did not follow a normal distribution. We checked split histograms to confirm the data follow a similar shape for the two groups. The results confirmed that the participants in the narration group had statistically significantly higher comprehension on process model based on ScoreTot ($68.3 \pm 15.3\%$ total correct answers) compared to those who are in the non-narration group ($56.8 \pm 17.4\%$), $U(42) = -2.173$, $p = 0.030$, *confirming H1*. The difference in the scores related to flow descriptions (ScoreFlDesc) was higher in the narration ($69.0 \pm 18.3\%$) compared to the non-narration group ($60.7 \pm 19\%$), but the difference was not significant ($U(42) = -1.491$, $p = 0.136$). For the test scores of the element description questions (ScoreElDesc), narration group ($67.0 \pm 15.8\%$) outperformed the non-narration ($49.6 \pm 25.3\%$) with a significant difference ($U(42) =$

-2.235, p $= 0.025$). Interestingly, it seems that the effect can be attributed to the better comprehension of process model aspects that relate to element descriptions (*confirmation of H1b*); the effect is not as strong for the understanding of flow elements (*rejection of H1a*).

4.2 Tests of Hypothesis 2: User Experiences

Figure 4 presents the plots for the mean values with error bars for the variables related to H2, the differences in the perceptions of users about the process model environment. For all three variables, PU, PEOU, and SAT, narration group has higher scores of perception than non-narration. To test if there is significant difference among groups, we used Mann-Whitney U test since the scores did not follow a normal distribution. For PU, there is no statistically significant difference between the two groups, U(42) $= -1.474$, p $= 0.141$. In contrast, the mean comparison across the treatment types for both PEOU (U(42) $= -2.172$, p $= 0.030$) and SAT (U(42) $= -2.297$, p $= 0.022$) resulted in significant differences, which points to an interpretation that the representation of process model using narration was rated higher than those which used non-narration.

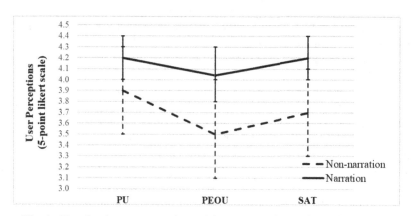

Fig. 4. Plots for the user perceptions of the non-narration and narration groups.

Table 2. Results of hypotheses tests.

	Variable	Total		Narration		Non-narration		p	Result
		M	SD	M	SD	M	SD		
H1	ScoreTot	63.1	17.1	68.3	15.3	56.8	17.4	.030	Confirmed
H1a	ScoreFlDesc	65.2	18.9	69.0	18.3	60.7	19.0	.136	Rejected
H1b	ScoreElDesc	59.1	22.2	67.0	15.8	49.6	25.3	.025	Confirmed
H2	PU	4.07	0.67	4.2	0.50	3.90	0.81	.141	Partly confirmed
	PEOU	3.82	0.73	4.04	0.53	3.55	0.86	.030	
	SAT	3.97	0.73	3.69	0.83	4.20	0.54	.022	

5 Discussion

Our results show that narration can positively influence process model comprehension. Thus, this study contributes to the IS literature by introducing narration as a legitimate multimedia technique for the comprehension of process models. We confirm that the use of visual and auditory channels simultaneously makes sense to deliver process-related information, preventing the so-called split attention effect for multiple inputs. In IS development, it is a common practice to combine multiple information sources in the form of models and text [42]. Narration can provide a solution to the problem of presenting multiple conceptual model information in an integrated way while managing the cognitive load [16, 24].

Our exploration into the impact of narration on two types of process model descriptions reveals interesting differences. We find the effect particularly strong for element descriptions, which refers to detailed information not readily available in the model. When examining the comprehension levels for process model descriptions related to flow descriptions, the impact of narration is still positive yet not significant. Therefore, it seems that the overall positive effect of narration should mainly be attributed to a better comprehension of element descriptions.

Multiple explanations for the differences in the comprehension of diverse descriptions can be considered. One explanation concerns the visual elements related to each description and the availability of information on the model. For flow descriptions, users can infer similar knowledge themselves by investigating the process model closely. Although this requires the investigation of multiple graphical elements, i.e., activities, gateways, and events, expert users specifically are found to be highly proficient at this [7]. Considering that our participants reported high levels of process modeling and domain knowledge (as provided in Sect. 4), the narration of flow descriptions may have been redundant for them, thereby not considerably improving the comprehension of the narration group.

An important property of our process model environment is that it integrates narration with animation. To synchronize the temporal input of the narrations through the auditory channel with the visual input, narration needs to be complemented with animation in some way. The need for the coordination of auditory and visual inputs are dictated by the temporal contiguity and multimedia principles of the CTML [8]. Without the use of animation on a process model, the user cannot make out what the verbalized process model element are, rendering the description useless. Although we used animation as a prerequisite to implement narration, our findings cannot be completely untangled from the effects of animation. Process model animation has been found to improve process model comprehension, particularly for flow-related aspects [18]. The interesting thing, though, is that our present study particularly shows a positive impact through the narration of element descriptions – not the flow aspects of a process. We see this as an indication that narration improves process model comprehension in its own right. Nevertheless, it is relevant to further investigate the impact of narration when animation is used in different ways. For example, interactive animation can be used for both narration and non-narration groups, enabling users to choose the narrations to listen to.

We also find out that user perceptions about the environment used to view the process models have been improved. Despite a higher total perceived usefulness (PU) in the narration group, it did not significantly differ. Overall, the participants considered each representation type useful (4.07 over 5). The perceptions of participants in two treatment groups towards ease of use (PEOU) and satisfaction about the environment (SAT) were significantly different. Process models were perceived to be easier to use by the narration group than in the non-narration group. In general, the process model environment when used with narration was considered to be clear to understand, interesting to use, and to improve the motivation to learn business processes. This finding highlights the practical value of a process model environment with narration features. Organizations can benefit from such an environment in a sustained way due to high user adoption. We invite interested vendors of process modeling solutions to draw inspiration from the animation features already available in the online process model environment (http://www.ays olmaz.com/ProcessModelAnimation/prime.html) and the narration ideas presented in the current paper. Furthermore, thanks to the improvements in text-to-speech algorithms, it is possible to automate the generation of narrations and integration of them to the process models, which would otherwise require a high level of effort for organizations with a high number of process models in their repositories. The environment can also adjust the speed of narration automatically based on a measurement of a user's reading speed.

Some limitations to our study are the following. Although we performed our experiment in an organization using real-life processes, our results are limited to one organization. To increase the generalizability of our findings, the study should be repeated in multiple organizations, using different processes. The sample sizes in our experiment can be said to be of moderate size. However, as in similar studies that require focused time and effort of the participants [18], we opted for high quality input rather than high participation numbers. Our statistical analysis supports the robustness of the findings. Our experimental design decisions may have also introduced limitations. Alternative experiment designs could be considered, such as a paired comparison design in which each participant uses both treatments [39]. Furthermore, since the two process models used in the experiment differ in complexity, a factorial design with an additional factor of complexity could be used (e.g., as in [43]). However, as the complexity of the experiment design increases, additional threats emerge about the validity of the experiment such as interaction effects [39]. User interface may also have an impact on the results, such as the text box overlaying part of the process model when a description is shown on the non-narration environment, which is necessary to prevent the split-attention effect. Lastly, although our participants were selected from diverse units, they showed rather high process modeling and domain knowledge levels. Since user characteristics can be a factor on the impact of narration, it seems wise to involve users a with a more diverse background, cf. [7].

6   Conclusion

In this study, we set out to introduce narration as a new multimedia technique to improve the comprehension of conceptual models, particularly process models. We build on the dual coding theory and principles of the cognitive theory of multimedia learning to design a process model environment that implements narration. We report on an experiment that we conducted in an organization with two real-life processes, involving 42 participants. Our findings confirm that narration can aid in understanding process models and related descriptions by using verbal and auditory sensory channels simultaneously. We distinguish the impact of narration on different types of descriptions. Our results show a significant impact of narration on the comprehension of descriptions that provide detailed information of a specific process model element but not so much on information that describe flow relations of an element with other elements. This finding is important for understanding cognitive effects of narration for different material, which can be important to extend the use of narration and accompanying animation solutions to other conceptual models. Our findings on the increased user perceptions of the environment when narration is used indicate that narration can be used as an effective tool to improve conceptual model comprehension in organizations.

We see three main directions for future research. First, the exploration of the use of narration for other conceptual models can bring opportunities to benefit from the findings more extensively for IS development. Next, to develop most relevant solutions, the criteria of using narrations, for what kind of information and how, need to be further investigated. Specifically, the ways of combining animation and narration and reaping their benefits, individually and synergistically, is a valid research direction. This would also provide practical value to organizations for making better use of their conceptual models. Furthermore, other aspects that may have a role on the impact of multimedia techniques to support model comprehension, such as user characteristics, should be investigated and considered for the design of a process model environment.

References

1. Davies, I., Green, P., Rosemann, M., Indulska, M., Gallo, S.: How do practitioners use conceptual modeling in practice? Data Knowl. Eng. **58**, 358–380 (2006)
2. Bera, P., Burton-Jones, A., Wand, Y.: Research note–how semantics and pragmatics interact in understanding conceptual models. Info. Sys. Res. **25**, 401–419 (2014)
3. Parsons, J.: An experimental study of the effects of representing property precedence on the comprehension of conceptual schemas. J. Assoc. Inf. Syst. **12**, 1 (2011)
4. Reijers, H.A., Mendling, J.: A study into the factors that influence the understandability of business process models. IEEE Trans. Syst. Man, Cybern. - Part A Syst. Humans. **41**, 449–462 (2011)
5. Leyer, M., Brown, R., Aysolmaz, B., Vanderfeesten, I., Turetken, O.: 3D virtual world BPM training systems: process gateway experimental results. In: Advanced Information Systems Engineering, pp. 415–429. Springer (2019). https://doi.org/10.1007/978-3-030-21290-2_26
6. van der Aa, H., Leopold, H., Mannhardt, F., Reijers, H.A.: On the Fragmentation of Process Information: Challenges, Solutions, and Outlook. In: EMMSAD 2015, pp. 3–18. Springer (2015). https://doi.org/10.1007/978-3-319-19237-6_1
7. Figl, K.: Comprehension of procedural visual business process models. Bus. Inf. Syst. Eng. **59**(1), 41–67 (2016). https://doi.org/10.1007/s12599-016-0460-2
8. Mayer, R.E., Moreno, R.: Nine ways to reduce cognitive load in multimedia learning. Educ. Psychol. **38**, 43–52 (2003)
9. Mayer, R.E., Anderson, R.B.: Animations need narrations: an experimental test of a dual-coding hypothesis J. . Educ. Psychol. **83**, 484–490 (1991)

10. Morett, L.M., Clegg, B.A., Blalock, L.D., Mong, H.M.: Applying multimedia learning theory to map learning and driving navigation. Transp. Res. Part F Traffic Psychol. Behav. **12**, 40–49 (2009)
11. Gemino, A.: Empirical comparisons of animation and narration in requirements validation. Requir. Eng. **9**, 153–168 (2003)
12. Hwang, I., Tam, M., Lam, S.L., La,: Review of use of animation as a supplementary learning material of physiology content in four academic years. Electron. J. e-Learning. **10**, 377–386 (2012)
13. Mayer, R.E., Moreno, R.: Animation as an aid to multimedia learning. Educ. Psychol. Rev. **14**, 87–99 (2002)
14. Paivio, A.: Mental Representations: A Dual Coding Approach. Oxford University Press, Oxford (1990)
15. Mayer, R.E.: Multimedia Learning, 2nd edn. Cambridge University Press, Cambridge, UK (2009)
16. Ottensooser, A., Fekete, A., Reijers, H.A., Mendling, J., Menictas, C.: Making sense of business process descriptions: an experimental comparison of graphical and textual notations. J. Syst. Softw. **85**, 596–606 (2012)
17. Aysolmaz, B., Reijers, H.A.: Towards an integrated framework for invigorating process models: a research agenda. In: Lecture Notes in Business Information Processing, pp. 552–558. Springer (2015). https://doi.org/10.1007/978-3-319-42887-1_44
18. Aysolmaz, B., Reijers, H.A.: Animation as a dynamic visualization technique for improving process model comprehension. Inf. Manag. **58**, 103478 (2021)
19. Recker, J.: Continued use of process modeling grammars: the impact of individual difference factors. Eur. J. Inf. Syst. **19**, 76–92 (2010)
20. Aysolmaz, B., Reijers, H.A.: Use cases for understanding business process models. In: Advanced Information Systems Engineering, pp. 428–442. Springer (2017). https://doi.org/10.1007/978-3-319-59536-8_27
21. Petrusel, R., Mendling, J., Reijers, H.A.: How visual cognition influences process model comprehension. Decis. Support Syst. **96**, 1–16 (2017)
22. Green, T.: Cognitive dimensions of notations. In: Proceedings of the Fifth Conference of the British Computer Society Human Computer Interaction Specialist Group - People and Computers V, pp. 443–460 (1989)
23. Sweller, J., Ayres, P., Kalyuga, S.: Cognitive Load Theory. Springer, London (2011)
24. Gemino, A., Parker, D.: Use case diagrams in support of use case modelling: deriving understanding from the picture. J. Database Manag. **20**, 1–24 (2009)
25. Leopold, H., van der Aa, H., Leopold, H., van de Weerd, I., Reijers, H.A.: Causes and consequences of fragmented process information: insights from a case study. In: Organizational Transformation & Information Systems (SIGORSA), p. 10, Boston (2017)
26. Aysolmaz, B., Leopold, H., Reijers, H.A., Demirörs, O.: A semi-automated approach for generating natural language requirements documents based on business process models. Inf. Softw. Technol. **93**, 14–29 (2018)
27. Aysolmaz, B., Iren, D., Reijers, H.A.: Detecting role inconsistencies in process models. In: 27th European Conference on Information Systems (ECIS). AISEL, Stockholm & Uppsala (2019)
28. Aysolmaz, B., Demirörs, O.: Modeling business processes to generate artifacts for software development: a methodology. In: Modelling in Software Engineering (MISE). 2014 ICSE Workshop on, pp. 7–12. Hydarabad, India (2014)
29. Figl, K., Recker, J.: Process innovation as creative problem-solving: an experimental study of textual descriptions and diagrams. Inf. Manag. **53**, 75–78 (2016)

30. Aysolmaz, B., Demirörs, O.: Unified process modeling with UPROM tool. In: Information Systems Engineering in Complex Environments, pp. 250–266. Springer (2015). https://doi.org/10.1007/978-3-319-19270-3_16
31. Clark, J.M., Paivio, A.: Dual coding theory and education. Educ. Psychol. Rev. **3**, 149–210 (1991)
32. Mayer, R.E., Moreno, R.: A split-attention effect in multimedia learning: evidence for dual processing systems in working memory. J. Educ. Psychol. **90**, 312–320 (1998)
33. She, H.-C., Chen, Y.-Z.: The impact of multimedia effect on science learning: evidence from eye movements. Comput. Educ. **53**, 1297–1307 (2009)
34. Hug, T.: Micro learning and narration: exploring possibilities of utilization of narrations and storytelling for the designing of "micro units" and didactical micro-learning arrangements. MiT4 Work Stories, Proc. fourth Media Transit. Conf. May 6–8, MIT, p. 4048 (2005)
35. Leyer, M., Aysolmaz, B., Brown, R., Türkay, S., Reijers, H.A.: Process training for industrial organisations using 3D environments: an empirical analysis. Comput. Ind. **124**, 103346 (2021)
36. Venkatesh, V., Morris, M.G., Davis, G.B., Davis, F.D.: User acceptance of information technology: toward a unified view. MIS Q. **27**, 425–478 (2003)
37. Jasperson, J., Carter, P.E., Zmud, R.W.: A comprehensive conceptualization of post-adoptive behaviors associated with information technology enabled work systems. MIS Q, pp. 525–557 (2005)
38. Tamilmani, K., Rana, N.P., Wamba, S.F., Dwivedi, R.: The extended unified theory of acceptance and use of technology (UTAUT2): a systematic literature review and theory evaluation. Int. J. Inf. Manage. **57**, 102269 (2021)
39. Wohlin, C., Runeson, P., Bost, M., Ohlsson, M.C., Regnell, B., Wessl6n, A.: Experimentation in software engineering An Introduction. Kluwer Academic Publishers, Norwell, MA, USA (2000)
40. Chinosi, M., Trombetta, A.: BPMN: An introduction to the standard. Comput. Stand. Interfaces. **34**, 124–134 (2012)
41. Recker, J.: Empirical investigation of the usefulness of Gateway constructs in process models. Eur. J. Inf. Syst. **22**, 673–689 (2013)
42. Sabegh, M.A.J., Recker, J.: Combined use of conceptual models in practice: An exploratory study. J. Database Manag. **28**, 56–88 (2017)
43. Gopalakrishnan, S., Krogstie, J., Sindre, G.: Adapting UML activity diagrams for mobile work process modelling: experimental comparison of two notation alternatives. In: IFIP Working Conference on The Practice of Enterprise Modeling, pp. 145–161. Springer (2010). https://doi.org/10.1007/978-3-642-16782-9_11

Analyzing Enterprise Architecture Models by Means of the Meta Attack Language

Adina Aldea[1] and Simon Hacks[2(✉)]

[1] University of Twente, Enschede, The Netherlands
a.i.aldea@utwente.nl
[2] University of Southern Denmark, Odense, Denmark
shacks@mmmi.sdu.dk

Abstract. The digital transformation exposes organizations to new threats endangering their business. A way to uncover these threats is threat modeling and attack simulations. However, modeling an entire organization by hand is time consuming and error prone. Therefore, we propose to reuse Enterprise Architecture (EA) models. In this work, we propose a mapping from ArchiMate, a common EA modeling language, to coreLang, a threat modeling language, and use the resulting models to perform attack simulations to foresee possible attack paths. Then, we play back the results of the attack simulations to the EA model and complete the round-trip. To demonstrate our approach, we developed a prototype performing the transformation from ArchiMate to coreLang and applied our approach to the well-known ArchiSurance example.

Keywords: ArchiMate · Attack simulations · Automated analysis · EA security

1 Introduction

Digital transformation has been a topic of interest for many organizations in the past decade, as it changes customer relationships, internal processes and value creation [1]. On the one hand, it offers new possibilities for business model innovation and the ability to disrupt markets to gain lasting competitive advantage [2]. On the other hand, it exposes organizations and customers to new threats. Common types of cyber-attacks include email bombing, information and data theft, Distributed Denial of Service (DDoS) attacks, Trojan viruses, and hacking the data or the system that accesses it [3]. The COVID-19 pandemic has accelerated the process of digital transformation as many organizations needed to support a remote workforce and to provide their products and services online [4]. In 2020 58% of customer interactions were digital compared to 36% in 2019 [5].

While some organizations benefit from the effects of the digital transformation [5], others struggle more than before [4]. Social engineering attacks are especially dangerous in this period of time due to more people working and studying

© Springer Nature Switzerland AG 2022
X. Franch et al. (Eds.): CAiSE 2022, LNCS 13295, pp. 423–439, 2022.
https://doi.org/10.1007/978-3-031-07472-1_25

remote and using videoconferencing software. The US Federal Trade Commission estimated that 12 million dollars were lost from COVID-19 related scams between January and April 2020, with similar reports from other countries [6].

Thus, the importance of cyber security is becoming more apparent. While research in the area of cyber security is progressing, there are not many studies that focus on the security aspects of Enterprise Architecture (EA). EA can be used by organizations to manage their digital transformation by designing, planning, and implementing organizational change from the point of view of their business, application, technology, and physical architecture [7]. One popular language for EA modeling is the ArchiMate specification [7]. We have chosen to use the ArchiMate language for our research due to its popularity [8], it is used by many organizations. However, while the EA models created with ArchiMate can help organizations with visualizing their IT landscape, they do not natively support any kind of security analysis.

Current research addressing this gap has several limitations, such as a manual security analysis [9], the information from the security analysis being used without using the models as input [10], or the use of other languages than ArchiMate as a source for the security analysis [11]. In this research, we aim to address these limitations and contribute to the state-of-the-art by proposing a way to automate the transformation and analysis of ArchiMate models from a security perspective. First, we propose a mapping between the concepts of the ArchiMate language and coreLang. Second, we perform an analysis of the possible security vulnerabilities with the help of the securiCAD attack simulations. Third, we enrich the ArchiMate models with the results of the analysis in a way that illustrates the most likely attacks on the EA of an organization.

Based on these limitations and our previous research [12], we assume the case of an organization that has a large EA model repository (often in the notation of ArchiMate [7,8]) at hand and desires to perform a security analysis to reduce the risk of unwanted compromise of the organization. Usually, one would scan the systems and perform an automated vulnerability analysis. However, this is just partly possible, as EA models usually lack detailed information that is necessary to identify concrete vulnerabilities (such as concrete versions). Due to the size of the repository, it is not feasible, to enrich the EA model itself with this additional security relevant information as proposed by other authors [9,13], because it would be too much effort and enterprise architects classically lack the needed security knowledge. From these observations, we deduct following requirements:

1. *Should contribute towards automation of the cyber security analysis of ArchiMate models.* With the help of model transformation rules, we map the ArchiMate metamodel to the coreLang metamodel, to facilitate the automated transfer of models. Once this step is completed, we can perform the automated cyber security analysis with the help of the securiCAD attack simulations. Thus, the EA models can be reused for security analysis and every time the EA model is updated, the security analysis can be updated as well.

2. *Should reuse existing ArchiMate models.* Effort for security analysis can be substantially reduced by reusing information that is already available in an organization. One possible source for the underlying structure of an organization can be EA models [9], that are often maintained in ArchiMate [7,8]. Thus, we rely on this notation for our approach, while aiming for a generalization for other notations in future. However, most EA practitioners model their architecture at a high level of abstraction. This could pose certain challenges when trying to perform security simulations due to the difference in the levels of abstraction, which we address with the next requirement.

3. *Should not add additional security elements to existing ArchiMate models.* Considering the fact that EA models do not natively support cyber security analysis, it stands to reason that the information that is needed to perform these analyses is also not included in the models (separation of concerns). Thus, we consider that our approach to transfer the models into an environment that is designed with the purpose of performing these analyzes and adding the relevant information is suitable for achieving our goals. Moreover, we close the gap between the high abstraction of EA models and the needed detail level for security simulations by using different configurations of the elements to reflect uncertainty about missing information such as concrete versions of applications [12].

4. *Should show a simple overview of the cyber security analysis results in the original ArchiMate models.* Considering the complexity of data resulting from the attack simulations which can span through 1000s s of scenarios, it stands to reason that not all of the results are useful to transfer back to the ArchiMate models. Especially, managers are usually interested in abstracted information [14]. Thus, the existing elements of the EA model will be enriched with properties reflecting an abstraction of a few scenarios (based on likelihood and impact).

For this research, we adhere to the guidelines of the Design Science Research by Peffers et al. [15], which is also reflected in the structure of this paper. Section 2 presents the background on the ArchiMate and MAL languages and discusses the related work. In Sect. 3 we propose the mapping between the ArchiMate and the coreLang, while in Sect. 4 we demonstrate how this can be used with the help of a case study. Sections 5 and 6 focus on the discussion and conclusions.

2   Background

2.1   ArchiMate

ArchiMate is a language maintained by the Open Group that can be used to model EAs and their transformations in relation to the motivation behind them [16]. The language is structured according to a two-dimensional framework which contains six layers and four aspects.

At the intersection of the six layers and the three aspects (except for Motivation), certain views are defined. These views determine, which concepts and relations can be used to visualize a certain part of the architecture that is relevant to this part of the framework. Thus, for each of the views a metamodel is defined.

For each of these layers and aspects, certain concepts are defined. The Business layer contains concepts relating to the services offered to customers and the processes and actors that support it, while the Application layer includes concepts relating to the software applications and data used to support the business layer, the Technology layer focuses on the infrastructure of the organization with servers where data can be stored and networks that connect the devices, and the Physical layer helps describe how certain physical products can be produced.

The concepts in the Motivation aspect can be used by organizations to model the reasons for the changes in the architecture, while the Strategy layer can help define how these changes can be done at a higher abstraction level than the other four aforementioned layers. The Implementation and Migration layer, on the other hand, helps organizations with planning how these architectural transformations can be performed in order to achieve the best outcomes.

2.2 MAL

MAL is a meta-meta language, which combines probabilistic attack and defense graphs with object-oriented modeling. It is used to create Domain-Specific Languages (DSLs) that provide a meta language, which can be used to create models for attack simulations. Such a DSL defines the required information for the models and specifies the generic attack logic about the domain studied. For a detailed overview of MAL, we refer to the original paper [17].

To create a MAL-based language, one needs to identify all relevant assets and their associations. Each asset is comprised by multiple attack steps, which lead to "−>" 0 to n attack steps. Each attack step is either of the type OR "|" or AND "&". If one parent attack step of an OR attack step is compromised, an attacker can elaborate on this OR attack step. If all parent attack steps of an AND attack step are compromised, an attacker can elaborate on this AND attack step. Additionally, one can define the expected effort an attacker needs to spend on an attack step also called time-to-compromise (TTC). Further, an asset can contain defenses "#". Combining all possible attack paths lead to the attack/defense graph used for the attack simulation.

MAL provides the frame to create a DSL for threat modeling and attack simulations from scratch. At the same time, we recognized that many DSLs created with MAL share common concepts. Thus, we proposed coreLang [18] as means to reduce unnecessary redundant work. coreLang provides a basic set of assets that serve as starting point to model more advanced MAL DSLs or act as a basic language to model simple environments [11]. Figure 1 illustrates the overall structure of coreLang with respect to the concepts used in this work and presented next. For more details, we refer to the original publication [18].

The central concept that we use in this work is Application, which is characterized by its executability i.e., being software. Moreover, an Application is

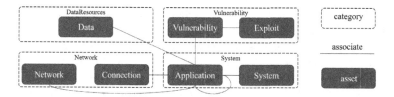

Fig. 1. Excerpt of `coreLang` containing used concepts (adapted from [18]).

able to execute another `Application` such as an operation system executing a program. For the execution itself, some hardware is needed that performs the actual calculations. This functionality is modeled as `System`.

Between two `Application` not just an execution relationship is possible, but they can also communicate with each other e.g., via interfaces. Such a communication is realized by a `Connection`, which is always intended and can take place within the same or different networks. On the other hand, `Application` can be contacted unintended e.g., by performing port scans. To reflect this, an `Application` can be exposed to a `Network`. If an attacker has access to such a `Network`, they can connect to all exposed `Application`.

Usually, an attacker is interested in the `Data` that is processed by the `Application`. Generally, `Data` can have two states. Firstly, it can be stored by an `Application`. Then, an attacker would be able to read, write, or delete the `Data`. Secondly, `Data` can be in transition between two `Application`. Then, the attacker can affect the `Data`, e.g., by a man-in-the-middle (MITM) attack.

While introducing coreLang, we mentioned its basic structure, which causes the abstract nature of the concepts. Thus, these assets cannot contain concrete attack steps and related TTC. Instead, just attack concepts, such as MITM on `Connection`, are contained. To enable the end-user to use coreLang nonetheless, the concepts of `Vulnerability` and `Exploit` have been introduced. They allow the end-user to relate a `Vulnerability` to an `Application`, which allows the attacker to compromise the `Application` via an `Exploit`. Moreover, they mirror the Common Vulnerability Scoring System (CVSS)[1] allowing to compute TTC.

3 Mapping

Before, we presented the basic concepts of ArchiMate, MAL, and coreLang. In our mapping, we rely on ArchiMate, as it is a wide-spread standard for EA modeling [7,8]. We opted for MAL, as it provides a framework for automated attack simulations, while being flexible towards different domains [17,19]. Finally, we opted for coreLang as it represents basic concepts in IT systems [18] and it has already been successfully used in similar contexts [12,20]. Next, we motivate our mapping from ArchiMate to coreLang. However, ArchiMate contains a broad

---

[1] https://www.first.org/cvss/specification document.

range of different element types and, therefore, we reason which categories of element types we consider for being mapped.

First, we check which layers of ArchiMate are eligible to be mapped to core-Lang. The *Strategy* layer models strategic directions and decisions of organizations [16]. As coreLang contains solely technical assets, there are no equivalents and, thus, we neglect this layer. A similar argumentation can be applied to the *Business* layer, as it technological-independently models the organization [16].

The *Application* layer describes the structure, behavior, and interactions of the organization's applications [16]. This relates to the executable assets [18] and, thus, we consider this layer for our mapping. The *Technology* layer models the technical infrastructure of organizations [16], which is classically referred to executables that are not exposed to the end-user. From a security perspective, these executables behave as on the Application layer. Moreover, the Technology layer includes also the *Physical* layer, which is used to model the physical world, i.e., hardware [16]. coreLang also foresees the modeling of hardware components [18], which lets us consider this layer.

The *Implementation & Migration* layer encodes the evolution of the EA [16]. However, MAL DSLs take a static view on the architecture [17], which makes this layer not of interest for our mapping. Finally, the *Motivation* layer depicts the motivation for the EA's evolution [16], which also has no equivalent in coreLang.

As we have determined the layers to be considered, we can shrink further down the number of element types that we need to evaluate for the mapping, as there are basically three different aspects in ArchiMate.

Active Structure element types are performing actions in the EA, i.e., applications serving the business. Consequently, these element types are of interest for security analysis. Such Active Structures perform *Behavior*, which are the dynamic aspects of organizations [16]. Behavior unites the activities of several Active Structures and are a logical grouping. Consequently, we do not consider those elements for our mapping. *Passive Structure* element types represent data objects [16]. Attackers are interested in the data of organizations and, therefore, they constitute the ultimate goal in our attack simulations.

Next, we take a close look at the remaining ArchiMate element types to be mapped to coreLang (cf. Table 1). Obviously, we map *Application Component* to Application and *Data Object* to Data. As *Application Collaboration* represents multiple Active Structure elements [16], it is a logical construct and we do not map it. Similarly, *Application Interface* is a point of contact related to a certain *Application Component* and is not related to an own execution.

Equally, we can argue for *Technology Collaboration* and *Technology Interface*. In contrast, *Node* and *Device* are characterized by hosting executables [16] and are in line with the conceptualization of System. Such executables in the Technology Layer are *System Software*, which execute *Application Component* [16] and are mapped to Application. The communication between several *Node* is modeled by *Path*. This communication can also take place along several networks [16], which leads to a mapping to Connection. If the *Node* share the same network, this connection is codified by a *Communication Network* [16], which is in line with Network. Finally, *Artifact* is "a piece of data" [16], which matches Data.

Table 1. Mapping from ArchiMate to `coreLang`

Layer	Element type	Application	Data	System	Network	Connection	PhysicalZone
Application	Application component	✖					
	Application collaboration						
	Application interface						
	Data object		✖				
Technology	Node			✖			
	Device			✖			
	System software	✖					
	Technology collaboration						
	Technology interface						
	Path					✖	
	Communication network				✖		
	Artifact		✖				
Physical	Equipment			✖			
	Facility						✖
	Distribution network						
	Material						

Equipment are physical machines that process materials [16]. These machines are controlled by software, which they host. Consequently, we map *Equipment* to `System`. A *Facility* is a grouping of *Equipment* deployed at one physical location [16]. The best representation for this is `PhysicalZone`. A *Distribution Network* transports *Material* or energy [16]. As coreLang is not equipped with assets representing physical concepts, there is no representation neither for both.

4   Demonstration

To realize the automated attack simulations for EA models, we follow a five-stepped process. (1) The EA model is translated to its graph representation. (2) The graph is modified to match coreLang specificities. (3) The graph is transformed into its representation, which can be interpreted by securiCAD. (4) Additional vulnerability information is added to the securiCAD model. (5) The simulation results are imported and visualized in the original EA model. Hitherto, the steps (1) to (3) are fully automatized, while (4) and (5) need still some manual work.

4.1   Illustrative Example

We choose to demonstrate the application of our proposed mapping and simulation with the help of the ArchiSurance case study, which is used in several previous papers [7,21]. We expand upon the previous details available in this case and enrich it with information that is necessary for our demonstration. Below, we provide a short description of the case.

ArchiSurance is an insurance merged from three independent insurance organizations, because they could not maintain their competitive advantage without significant investments in IT. By merging, they are able to reduce costs, invest in new technology, maintain customer satisfaction, and explore opportunities in emerging markets. After the merger, ArchiSurance went through several transformations of their landscape in order to unify in the customer facing processes, reduce redundancies, and merge customer data from the different data centers.

Due to these transformations, the organization is concerned that their landscape might be facing new threats. The need for insight into possible security vulnerabilities is emphasized due to a recent increase in cyber-attacks, especially in the insurance industry. Several insurances were subjected to ransomware attacks which resulted in a loss of trust from customers and potential lawsuits.

4.2   Processing

To perform the attack simulations for ArchiSurance, we followed a five-stepped process implemented in our prototype[2]. First, the XML of the ArchiMate model is translated to its graph-representation. Therefore, each element becomes a node and each relationship an edge. Moreover, we preserve the name, id, and ArchiMate element/relationship type as attributes to the node/edge.

Second, we modify the graph to match assumptions made in coreLang. On the one hand, we add additional nodes for certain relationships as the respective relationships are not foreseen in coreLang. This is the case for *Application Component serving* another *Application Component*. In coreLang, `Application` are just linked directly to each other if one is executing the other. A communication as indicated by *"serving"* is realized via a `Connection`. Therefore, we introduce a `Connection` for such relationships and link it to the related `Application`.

Additionally, it is not presumed that *Device* or *Node* (mapped to `System`) are directly exposed to a *Communication Network* (mapped to `Network`). Instead, the operation system (i.e., *System Software*) running on the *Device* or *Node* is communicating via the *Communication Network*. Consequently, we add for each of those communications a *System Software* and related edges.

The last modification is related to the access of ArchiMate elements to *Data Object/Artifact*, which is from the former to the latter. In contrast, coreLang defines that `Data` is accessed by `Application`. To overcome this, we simply inverse the direction of the respective edges in the graph-representation.

Third, the graph is translated into a securiCAD format [19], the tool we use for attack simulations. This translation is guided by the mapping presented in

---

[2] https://github.com/simonhacks/EA-Resilience.

Fig. 2. securiCAD model with external attacker and possible vulnerabilities and exploits

Sect. 3 and if an ArchiMate element type is not in this mapping, the node and related edges will be ignored. Moreover, it takes a MAL DSL as input (e.g., coreLang [18]) to ensure that the produced result conforms to the DSL.

Fourth, we enrich the securiCAD model (cf. Fig. 2) with security relevant information on the attack surface, possible vulnerabilities, and exploits as core-Lang does not provide such information by itself [18]:

- We assume that ArchiSurance uses WordPress to host their *Web portal* and WooCommerce as plugin to sell their insurances to the customers. The used WooCommerce version allows unauthenticated users to upload files even with executable content so that the installation can be overtaken[3].
- As the *Call center application* of ArchiSurance, they use the bitrix24 software. The used version allows for a server-side request forgery (SSRF)[4], which can be exploited to get deeper into ArchiSurance's network.
- *Customer Data Access* is provided by an application, which runs on an oracle cloud instance. Due to CVE-2021-2320[5], an attacker can take over the storage gateway and influence other applications hosted on that infrastructure.

---

[3] https://nvd.nist.gov/vuln/detail/CVE-2021-24212.
[4] https://nvd.nist.gov/vuln/detail/CVE-2020-13484.
[5] https://nvd.nist.gov/vuln/detail/CVE-2021-2320.

- *Home and Away Policy Administration* is an own implementation and, hence, it is not possible to gather vulnerabilities from a central repository. Therefore, we use the `UnknownVulnerability` and `UnknownExploit` with a low probability to be present to express that there might be a security issue in this application.
- *Financial Application* is hosted in an SAP environment and implemented in NetWeaver. A security scan could discover a weakness[6] that allows an attacker to inject commands that endanger the integrity of the system.
- Due to security restrictions, the *Admin Server* is not directly connected to the internet. To provide updates to the machine, it offers a USB interface that uses USB Pratirodh to allow just encrypted devices. However, an attacker can change usernames and passwords to take over the respective `System`[7].

Finally, the attack simulations can be performed, and the results be exported. The export contains information on which attack steps have been compromised by the attacker in which time and with which likelihood. To include this information into the original EA model, we determine for each asset one attack step for which the asset can be seen as fully compromised, i.e., it is annotated with consequences for confidentiality, integrity, or availability. Then, the TTC of that attack step is considered to be reported in the EA model.

4.3   Analysis

While mapping the ArchiMate elements to the coreLang is straightforward, the same cannot be said about incorporating the results of the simulation back into the ArchiMate model. This is mostly due to the complexity of the simulation results which provide a multidimensional perspective on each element that is analyzed. Thus, for each element, several attack steps can be possible, with varying degrees of probability determined based on 1000 simulations.

For example, in Fig. 3 we see that the ArchiSurance organization uses a Policy Data Management application to support their Handle Claims business process. Based on the results of the simulation, this element of the architecture can be exposed to 24 different attack steps, of which 11 attack steps have a probability of success that is higher than 0. Thus, to map this information back to the ArchiMate model, we need to be able to relate all the different attack steps and their probability values to the Policy Data Management application component. However, this mapping is not possible to do automatically, as the language does not currently support this type of data mapping.

Following [22], we propose to use the language extension mechanism and introduce the concept of Metric as a specialization of Driver. With the help of the Metric concept, we can relate the different attack steps and their probability values to each element of the architecture. For this purpose, we create two metrics, namely External Attack (attack steps) and Probability External Attack

[6] https://nvd.nist.gov/vuln/detail/CVE-2021-33663.
[7] https://nvd.nist.gov/vuln/detail/CVE-2017-6911.

(probability). The first metric can store all of the possible attack steps while the second metric can store the numeric values associated with the probabilities.

To make the results of the analysis visible in the ArchiMate model, we use a color and label overlay. The color is used to show the probability while the label shows the attack step. The reason for this is that the most important information, in this case, the probability of an attack succeeding, should be the most visible. Since it is not possible to visualize in one view all the different attack steps and their probabilities, we have chosen to show in Fig. 3 only the most severe attacks that have a probability of success higher than 0. The other attack steps and their probabilities can be visualized in a similar manner.

5 Discussion

Our work contains several points that need discussion. First, one can criticize our decision on the used languages. To our best knowledge, there is no alternative to MAL that would allow automated attack simulation, while already providing an increasing ecosystem of threat modeling languages for different domains [11].

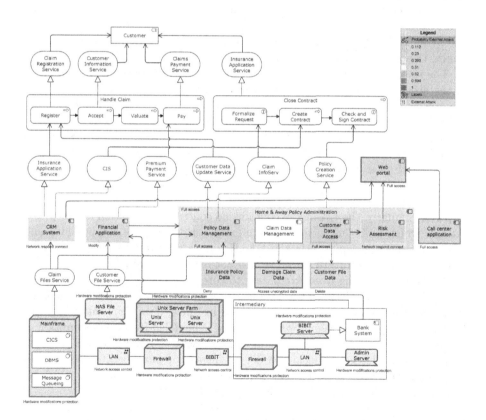

Fig. 3. ArchiSurance security analysis

Adapting our approach to other (not MAL) threat modeling languages, might be challenging as the model transformation would be to be implemented from scratch, while the rest of our approach could remain same.

coreLang is abstract and does not provide security relevant information by itself [18]. However, it is the MAL DSL at hand, which is closest to our needs [11] and has already been used in similar contexts [12,20]. Moreover, other languages are tailored to more concrete domains [23–25] making it challenging to find a mapping to a general-purpose language such as ArchiMate. Considering generalization, there is a growing ecosystem of languages that build on coreLang [11]. Consequently, our approach can be adapted to these languages by further refining the mapping. For languages that are not build on coreLang, a completely new mapping has to be sketched, while the rest of our approach would remain.

ArchiMate is a wide-spread notation for EA models in organizations and research [7,8]. Therefore, our approach is applicable to a broad range of existing EA models. However, recent efforts have been taken, to understand EA models as Knowledge Graphs [26,27]. Considering Knowledge Graph representation of EA models as input to our approach, would allow us to include all EA model notations, which have a graph representation, and thus mean a large step towards generalization from this end. However, this would also include the need to a generalized mapping from EA model notations towards our desired MAL DSL. Unfortunately, such a general representation for EA models does not exist. Hence, this step towards generalization remains for future work.

The second point of improvement is also related to the decision for coreLang, as the absence of vulnerability information forces us to add this by hand. On the one hand, we added just exemplary vulnerabilities to the model to avoid overcrowding the visualization. In a real-world context, one would include all discovered vulnerabilities. For the demonstration purposes, adding a subset of possible vulnerabilities is sufficient as we can perform the related attack simulations and those would just increase in complexity. On the other hand, one could employ automated vulnerability scans to gather the respective vulnerabilities. However, this would demand an infrastructure to scan, which is not at our disposal. Similarly, the EA model contains no concrete information on the applications, which forces us to make assumptions on what exact applications and which versions are deployed in the EA. Having a real-world example at hand, which is planned for future work, we will not experience this issue.

Third, the mapping from ArchiMate to coreLang can be differently realized. The most influential decision was to neglect transitive relations between mapped elements related to the behavior aspect. For instance, if an *Application Component* is executed by a *System Software* but it is modeled by the consumption of a *Technology Service*, this information will be lost. Unfortunately, it is not that simple to solve this issue, because a deeper inspection is needed to determine if a transitive relation should be still contained in the security analysis, which we plan to address in a future iteration of our research.

Fourth, another issue is related to the fact that coreLang does not allow System to communicate directly over Network with each other. Therefore, we introduced additional Application symbolizing the operation system, which take care for the communication. As we tried to keep it simple, we introduced for each connection of a System to a Network such an Application. If a System has several connections to Network, it results in multiple Application added to the model. In the next iteration, we aim for a more realistic solving of this issue, as one System solely can have one operation system.

Fifth, the EA model contains elements named "Firewall", which are translated to System, as we just consider the element type and do not perform a deeper inspection of the elements. However, such a deep inspection is pointless in our case as the firewall is an exception in coreLang and the rest of the assets is on an abstract level. In case that there will be a MAL DSL available, which is more specific than coreLang, then relying the mapping not just on the element types but also on further information available (e.g., element names) might be suitable.

Sixth, the transformation of the simulation results back to the ArchiMate model had to be done manually. Since the ArchiMate language does not support the complexity of the information resulting from the simulation, certain simplifications had to be made. For example, we could not visualize all the attack steps that would affect certain elements of the architecture but had to choose one attack step at a time. To do this, we chose the types of attack steps that had a probability higher than 0 and have the highest impact on the architectural element. Similarly, we did not consider all the values, but rather focus only on the probability value that was calculated. However, this simplified information can still provide enterprise architects with a good overview of which types of attack steps can have the most impact and their probability of success.

Furthermore, the purpose of ArchiMate is to support the high-abstraction modeling of EA elements. Thus, enriching ArchiMate models with the type of data required for a detailed security analysis as presented in this paper (e.g., version or instance number) would not be aligned with the purpose of the language and falls into the realm of IT service management. While previous work has proposed the extension of the ArchiMate language to include Security related concepts [28], this approach is not sufficient to support the simulation-based analysis that we propose in our paper. In future work, the feasibility of using a language extension mechanism to support our proposed approach could be investigated.

Lastly, while we have demonstrated how our approach can be used to conduct a detailed security analysis of ArchiMate models, additional qualitative analysis to validate the results is needed. Thus, we plan interviews with EA and Security experts to validate the usefulness and usability of our approach. Additionally, to better understand the business impact of these potential security threats, the analysis should be extended to encompass the link between the technical and business elements, similar to Ebbers et al. [29].

6   Related Work

There are different efforts to enrich ArchiMate with security information. Grandry et al. [13] mapped the concepts of an information system security risk management to ArchiMate. The main limitation of this work in relation to our goals and requirements is that the cyber security analysis is done manually and based only on a conceptual representation. This relies on the ability of the person analyzing the architecture to analyze all of the relevant architectural risks, as opposed to a simulation-based analysis which is able to run through 1000 s of scenarios.

Band et al. [28] extended this work and demonstrated the connection between ArchiMate and other risk and security concepts. Their conclusion was that most of the common risk and security concepts can be realized in ArchiMate. Aldea et al. [30] identified relevant metrics to assess the overall resilience of a given EA model as a means for future research. These works are characterized by incorporating security or risk relevant information directly into ArchiMate. In contrast, for our approach it is not needed to make changes to the models itself as the security information is codified in MAL. Moreover, we perform simulations to see the architecture's influence on the security.

Manzur et al. [31] took a step further and enhanced ArchiMate to xArchiMate, which can be used to perform simulations, experimentations, and analyze EAs by an extension to the ArchiMate meta-model. A similar work was done by Grov et al. [32] focusing more on risk aspects and developing a tool to visualize the effects in EA. This is similar to our approach, while we leave the ArchiMate meta-model untouched and transform the model instead to an instance of a MAL DSL.

Generally, EA models are a popular input for security assessments. Mathew et al. [9] elaborated on the reuse of EA related information in a security context. Therefore, they identified similarities between the management parts of TOGAF and BSI Grundschutz and proposed a mapping from ArchiMate to the German BSI Grundschutz' meta-model. Similarly, Xiong et al. [33] use EA repositories to predict effects of failing components on the entire architecture. Ebbers et al. [29] use EA models to aggregate vulnerabilities from assets to a level of relevance for the management. Lastly, Pavleska et al. [34] took EA models in a health context and transferred them by hand to securiCAD to perform security analysis. Similarly, Jiang et al. [35] did with models from the power domain. All works are like ours as EA related information is reused for security analysis. However, these were performed by hand, while we aim to automate it.

There are also works reusing security models for EA. Holm et al. [10] proposed a mapping of the NeXpose Scanner to ArchiMate. Later, they use these models as foundation for attack simulations in securiCAD [36]. König et al. [37] mapped the Substation Configuration Language (SCL) to ArchiMate to better ease the stakeholders' understanding of the Substation Automation (SA) system and its architecture. Comparing these works to ours, we recognize that the previous work focuses on models representing reality and including them in EA models, while we perform analysis on these models and solely play back the results.

Finally, there are works focusing on the reuse of existing models for attack simulations in MAL. Firstly, Hacks et al. [38] propose a method to automatically create a MAL DSL based on an EA model. Secondly, Hacks et al. [12] developed a mapping from the Business Process Modeling Notation (BPMN) to coreLang [18], automatically transform these models to a graph representation, and perform attack simulations in securiCAD. We extend the first work by providing a tool that also translates ArchiMate models into instances of MAL DSLs and the second work by enabling such transformation for ArchiMate models.

7 Conclusion

In this work, we have presented an automated transformation from EA models to threat models that are then used to perform attack simulations. Therefore, we proposed a mapping from ArchiMate to coreLang. With the help of this mapping, existing ArchiMate models which do not contain any cyber security information can still be analyzed. This is in line with the first three requirements mentioned in the 1 section of the paper.

Finally, we incorporate the simulation results back to the EA model to visualize the generated insights for the EA practitioners. With the help of this approach, the original ArchiMate models maintain their value as the single source of truth regarding the EA and are enriched with the most relevant cyber security analysis results to help EA practitioners in their decision-making process. To demonstrate our approach, we developed a first prototype and used the well-known ArchiMate example of ArchiSurance. This is in line with the fourth requirement mentioned in Sect. 1.

Still, future work remains. As such, we plan to implement our approach in different organizations to analyze real-world EAs and further investigate the link between technical and business assets. Additionally, we will investigate further a suitable way to cope with the simulation results in the EA model. Moreover, we are looking forward to a MAL DSL that is tailored for office IT environments to avoid the need for adding vulnerabilities by hand.

References

1. Zaoui, F., Souissi, N.: Roadmap for digital transformation: a literature review. Proc. Comput. Sci. **175**, 621–628 (2020)
2. Verhoef, P.C., et al.: Digital transformation: a multidisciplinary reflection and research agenda. J. Bus. Res. **122**, 889–901 (2021)
3. Chowdhury, A.: Recent cyber security attacks and their mitigation approaches – an overview. In: Batten, L., Li, G. (eds.) ATIS 2016. CCIS, vol. 651, pp. 54–65. Springer, Singapore (2016). https://doi.org/10.1007/978-981-10-2741-3_5
4. Lallie, H.S., et al.: Cyber security in the age of COVID-19: a timeline and analysis of cyber-crime and cyber-attacks during the pandemic. Comp. Sec. **105**, 102248 (2021)
5. LaBerge, L., O'Toole, C., Schneider, J., Smaje, K.: How COVID-19 has pushed companies over the technology tipping point - and transformed business forever (2020)
6. Hakak, S., Khan, W.Z., Imran, M., Choo, K.K.R., Shoaib, M.: Have you been a victim of COVID-19-related cyber incidents? Survey, taxonomy, and mitigation strategies. IEEE Access **8**, 124134–124144 (2020)

7. Aldea, A., Iacob, M.E., van Hillegersberg, J., Quartel, D., Franken, H.: Modelling value with ArchiMate. In: Persson, A., Stirna, J. (eds.) CAiSE 2015. LNBIP, vol. 215, pp. 375–388. Springer, Cham (2015). https://doi.org/10.1007/978-3-319-19243-7_35

8. Barbosa, A., Santana, A., Hacks, S., Stein, N.V.: A taxonomy for enterprise architecture analysis research. In: ICEIS, vol. 2, SciTePress, pp. 493–504 (2019)

9. Mathew, D., Hacks, S., Lichter, H.: Developing a semantic mapping between TOGAF and BSI-IT-Grundschutz. MKWI 5, 1971–1982 (2018)

10. Holm, H., Buschle, M., Lagerström, R., Ekstedt, M.: Automatic data collection for enterprise architecture models. Softw. Syst. Model. 13(2), 825–841 (2012). https://doi.org/10.1007/s10270-012-0252-1

11. Hacks, S., Katsikeas, S.: Towards an ecosystem of domain specific languages for threat modeling. In: La Rosa, M., Sadiq, S., Teniente, E. (eds.) CAiSE 2021. LNCS, vol. 12751, pp. 3–18. Springer, Cham (2021). https://doi.org/10.1007/978-3-030-79382-1_1

12. Hacks, S., Lagerström, R., Ritter, D.: Towards automated attack simulations of BPMN-based processes. In: EDOC, pp. 182–191 (2021)

13. Grandry, E., Feltus, C., Dubois, E.: Conceptual integration of enterprise architecture management and security risk management. In: EDOCW, pp. 114–123, September 2013

14. Hacks, S., Brosius, M., Aier, S.: A case study of stakeholder concerns on EAM. In: EDOCW, pp. 50–56. IEEE (2017)

15. Peffers, K., Tuunanen, T., Rothenberger, M.A., Chatterjee, S.: A design science research methodology for information systems research. JIMS 24(3), 45–77 (2007)

16. The Open Group: ArchiMate 3.1 Specification (2019)

17. Johnson, P., Lagerström, R., Ekstedt, M.: A meta language for threat modeling and attack simulations. In: ARES, p. 38. ACM (2018)

18. Katsikeas, S., et al.: An attack simulation language for the IT domain. In: Eades III, H., Gadyatskaya, O. (eds.) GraMSec 2020. LNCS, vol. 12419, pp. 67–86. Springer, Cham (2020). https://doi.org/10.1007/978-3-030-62230-5_4

19. Ekstedt, M., Johnson, P., Lagerström, R., Gorton, D., Nydrén, J., Shahzad, K.: securiCAD by foreseeti: a CAD tool for enterprise cyber security management. In: EDOCW, pp. 152–155. IEEE (2015)

20. Hacks, S., Butun, I., Lagerström, R., Buhaiu, A., Georgiadou, A., Michalitsi Psarrou, A.: Integrating security behavior into attack simulations. In: ARES, pp. 1–13 (2021)

21. Aldea, A., Iacob, M.E., Quartel, D., Franken, H.: Strategic planning and enterprise achitecture. In: ES 2013, pp. 1–8. IEEE (2013)

22. Aldea, A., Iacob, M.E., Daneva, M., Masyhur, L.H.: Multi-criteria and model-based analysis for project selection: an integration of capability-based planning, project portfolio management and enterprise architecture. In: EDOCW, pp. 128–135 (2019)

23. Hacks, S., Katsikeas, S., Ling, E., Lagerström, R., Ekstedt, M.: powerLang: a probabilistic attack simulation language for the power domain. Energy Inf. 3(1), 1–17 (2020). https://doi.org/10.1186/s42162-020-00134-4

24. Ling, E.R., Ekstedt, M.: Generating threat models and attack graphs based on the IEC 61850 system configuration description language. In: SAT-CPS, pp. 98–103. ACM (2021)

25. Katsikeas, S., Johnson, P., Hacks, S., Lagerström, R.: Probabilistic modeling and simulation of vehicular cyber attacks: an application of the meta attack language. In: Proceedings of the 5th ICISSP (2019)

26. Smajevic, M., Bork, D.: From conceptual models to knowledge graphs: a generic model transformation platform. In: ER. Springer. LNCS (2021)
27. Smajevic, M., Hacks, S., Bork, D.: Using knowledge graphs to detect enterprise architecture smells. In: PoEM, Springer International Publishing, pp. 48–63 (2021)
28. Band, I., Engelsman, W., Feltus, C., Paredes, S.G., Diligens, D.: Modeling enterprise risk management and security with the archimate ®. Language, The Open Group (2015)
29. Ebbers, F., Hacks, S., Thakurta, R.: The business impact of IIOT vulnerabilities. In: PACIS 2021 Proceedings, vol. 225 (2021)
30. Aldea, A., Vaicekauskaitė, E., Daneva, M., Piest, J.P.S.: Assessing resilience in enterprise architecture: a systematic review. In: EDOC, pp. 1–10 (2020)
31. Manzur, L., Ulloa, J.M., Sánchez, M., Villalobos, J.: XArchiMate: enterprise architecture simulation, experimentation and analysis. Simulation **91**(3), 276–301 (2015)
32. Grov, G., Mancini, F., Mestl, E.M.S.: Challenges for risk and security modelling in enterprise architecture. In: Gordijn, J., Guédria, W., Proper, H.A. (eds.) PoEM 2019. LNBIP, vol. 369, pp. 215–225. Springer, Cham (2019). https://doi.org/10.1007/978-3-030-35151-9_14
33. Xiong, W., Carlsson, P., Lagerström, R.: Re-using enterprise architecture repositories for agile threat modeling. In: EDOCW, pp. 118–127 (2019)
34. Pavleska, T., Aranha, H., Masi, M., Grandry, E., Sellitto, G.P.: Cybersecurity evaluation of enterprise architectures: the E-SENS case. In: PoEM, pp. 226–241 (2019)
35. Jiang, Y., Jeusfeld, M., Atif, Y., Ding, J., Brax, C., Nero, E.: A language and repository for cyber security of smart grids. In: EDOC, pp. 164–170 (2018)
36. Holm, H., Shahzad, K., Buschle, M., Ekstedt, M.: P^{2}CySeMoL: predictive, probabilistic cyber security modeling language. TDSC **12**(6), 626–639 (2015)
37. König, J., Zhu, K., Nordström, L., Ekstedt, M., Lagerstrom, R.: Mapping the substation configuration language of IEC 61850 to ArchiMate. In: EDOCW, pp. 60–68 (2010)
38. Hacks, S., Hacks, A., Katsikeas, S., Klaer, B., Lagerström, R.: Creating meta attack language instances using ArchiMate: applied to electric power and energy system cases. In: EDOC, pp. 88–97 (2019)

Recommender Systems

Enhancing Semantics-Driven Recommender Systems with Visual Features

Mounir M. Bendouch[1], Flavius Frasincar[1] (ID), and Tarmo Robal[2(✉)] (ID)

[1] Erasmus University Rotterdam, Burgemeester Oudlaan 50,
3062 Rotterdam, PA, The Netherlands
mbendouch@hotmail.com, frasincar@ese.eur.nl
[2] Tallinn University of Technology, Ehitajate tee 5, 19086 Tallinn, Estonia
tarmo.robal@ttu.ee

Abstract. Content-based semantics-driven recommender systems are often used in the small-scale news recommendation domain, founded on the TF-IDF measure but also taking into account domain semantics through semantic lexicons or ontologies. This work explores the application of content-based semantics-driven recommender systems to large-scale recommendations on the example of movie domain. We propose methods to extract semantic features from various item descriptions, including images. In particular, we use computer vision to extract semantic features from images and use these for recommendation together with various features extracted from textual information. The semantics-driven approach is scaled up with pre-computation of the cosine similarities and gradient learning of the model. The results of the study on a large-scale MovieLens dataset of user ratings demonstrate that semantics-driven recommenders can be extended to more complex domains and outperform TF-IDF on ROC, PR, F_1, and Kappa metrics.

Keywords: Semantics-driven recommendation · Ontology · Computer vision · Visual semantic features · Large-scale recommendation

1 Introduction

With the emergence of the Web vast amounts of information have become available with an accelerating increase [44], scaling up to 44 trillion gigabytes in 2020 [38]. This abundance of information has enabled users to explore immerse variety of content (e.g., articles, movies, music), but also introduced the problem of information overload making finding the right information difficult and time consuming. A solution for the latter problem is seen in recommender systems (RS) [28,29], which provide mechanisms to filter and deliver content relevant to the user in the form of recommendations based on information available about the user and domain [30]. Different approaches to RS [28] exist: *collaborative filtering*, where recommendations are based on similarities between preferences

© Springer Nature Switzerland AG 2022
X. Franch et al. (Eds.): CAiSE 2022, LNCS 13295, pp. 443–459, 2022.
https://doi.org/10.1007/978-3-031-07472-1_26

of one user and preferences of others, *content-based filtering*, which recommends items according to their content, and a combination of the two latter known as *hybrid RS* [5].

Here, we focus on content-based RS [26] operating on similarities between content items based on various extractable features, The features available depend on the item type and dataset. Although text (e.g., descriptions) is the common form of information to extract features to measure similarity, other types of information (e.g., music songs include the artist, genre, and the lyrics, movies include the actors, plot, posters) can also serve as a source of features.

A widely used technique to estimate similarity between texts is Term Frequency - Inverse Document Frequency (TF-IDF) [20], where a feature vector based on the frequency counts of terms in the text is constructed and multiplied by the inverse frequency of these terms occurrence in all text sources. The resulting vectors can then be directly compared using measures such as cosine similarity [16]. Several recommenders such as CF-IDF(+), SF-IDF(+) have taken the TF-IDF concept further to provide recommendations of news articles [4,6,11,16], using concepts from domain ontologies or synsets from semantic lexicons for features instead of terms. These methods have further been extended to (Bing)-(C)SF-IDF recommenders [7,19,25] by including semantically related synsets or concepts, or absorbing named-entity similarities using Bing page counts.

Relying on the promising results of the latter semantics-driven RS for news articles, and encouraged by the successful scaling and porting of these methods to large scale recommendations [3], we are now eager to explore the value of semantic information extracted from items more complex than text – digital images – derived by the idea that *a picture may be worth more than a thousand words*! In this paper, we extend the extraction of semantic features from text to digital images (movie posters), and explore whether and to what extent it can contribute to recommendations. In particular, we seek to answer:

RQ1: *How to extract and apply semantic features from images for recommendation?*

RQ2: *How do semantic features from images contribute to recommendation?*

In this paper we continue and extend our previous work on semantics-driven RS [3], resulting in the following contributions:

- A method for extracting of semantic features from digital images using computer vision for the task, and the adjustment of the scaled similarity model [3] for features extracted from images.
- A proposal of novel method for large-scale semantics-driven recommendations based on concepts and synsets extracted from text, and synsets extracted from digital images.
- Demonstration that semantics-driven RS have many unexplored applications and can be utilized effectively with the proposed approach to various domains.

The rest of this paper is organized as follows. Section 2 presents related work, while Sect. 3 discusses data used for the research. Section 4 focuses on the recommendation methodology, and Sect. 5 on its evaluation. Section 6 draws conclusions.

2 Related Work

We start by reviewing the semantics-driven recommenders TF-IDF, CF-IDF, SF-IDF, and their extensions CF-IDF+, SF-IDF+ originally designed for news recommendation. These RS extract features from news article text but can be used to predict similarity between any two texts.

The TF-IDF is of interest as SF/CF-IDF(+) build on its mathematical concept. The TF-IDF [33] recommender consists of two parts, where the TF indicates how often a term occurs in a given document (higher frequencies link to higher relevancy), and the IDF captures the importance and uniqueness of a term in a collection of documents (frequent terms are considered to be common and less important). The resulting feature vector represents terms with scores, which can be compared to user vectors using similarity functions (e.g., the cosine distance). The TF-IDF score is large for terms that occur frequently in single document but not often in all other documents. A certain specified threshold value decides whether an item and the user's interest are considered similar.

The Concept Frequency - Inverse Document Frequency (CF-IDF) [16] is a variant of TF-IDF, where instead of terms concepts of domain ontology are used. The text is processed by a natural language processing (NLP) engine that performs word sense disambiguation (WSD), part-of-speech (POS) tagging, and tokenization to transform the text into a collection of concept candidates. A domain ontology containing concepts and their relationships is checked for each candidate, and if a match is found, a count is added to that concept. The use of concepts represents the domain semantics better as only relevant words of the domain are considered, and results in performance improvement over TF-IDF [16]. CF-IDF+ extends this method further by including directly related concepts in the domain ontology [11]. Each type of relationship (superclass, subclass, or instance) is given a weight to vary the overall importance of the found concepts and their related concepts. The weights are optimized by grid search.

The Synset Frequency - Inverse Document Frequency (SF-IDF) [6] is another variant of TF-IDF, which in addition to all terms looks at synonyms and ambiguous terms using a semantic lexicon (WordNet). Terms having the same meaning will be subsumed in one single concept, and therefore WSD is needed. For terms with multiple meanings, corresponding word senses are counted separately. SF-IDF+ [25] outperforms SF-IDF by including synsets that are directly related over the 27 types of semantic relationships present in WordNet, where each type has a weight optimized by a genetic algorithm.

The TF/CF/SF-IDF(+) content-based RS were originally established for news recommendation, rather small-scale recommendation domain, where they proved their efficiency for the task. The applicability of these methods to large-scale recommendation problem was proven to be successful in [3] on the example of movie domain. To enable large-scale recommendations, new methods to extract semantic features from various item descriptions were established together with a method to efficiently devise a domain ontology for the selected complex dataset in case an external ontology is not available, leveraging the need to manually construct such ontology. Further, the semantics-driven approach was scaled up with pre-computation of the cosine similarities, reduction of dimensionality and gradient learning of the model, allowing to avoid computationally expensive operations [3]. While [3] used semantic information available in the textual form, this work extends it by including also rich semantic information available in graphical form, on the example of the movie domain and posters (digital images) available.

RS for (multi)media are of interest to many researchers due to the large diverse information available. Various approaches have been exercised to provide recommendations: a graphical model and signature-tree-based scheme over social media streams [46], knowledge graphs [18], context-aware social media recommendations [45], ontologies [1,34], Bidirectional Encoder Representations from Transformers (BERT) [13] for conversational RS [27] with experiments on movies, books and music recommendation, Word2Vec algorithm to recommend movies [42] based on metadata (e.g., directors, actors), textual image metadata for recommending socially relevant images [21]. A comprehensive overview of RS for multimedia content is given in [12].

Convolutional neural networks (CNNs) dominate the field of computer vision in terms of performance on a variety of tasks, such as optical character recognition (OCR) [8,9], facial recognition [23,24], face detection [15], or to learn image shapes for recommending apparel goods [32]. On some object classification tasks [36] it can even rival human performance [31]. Guo et al. [17] used CNNs to extract features of semantic image objects, splitting image into a number of image objects, extracting the features, and then summarising the results for an image. Tuinhof et al. [37] used CNNs for image classification on fashion product images to recommend products by texture and category type features. They showed that RS purely relying on visual features are reasonable and could also be helpful in case of lacking user historical data. Yu et al. [43] on the other hand focused on goods RS based on image content represented by weighted feature model using only computationally inexpensive low-level image features such as color, texture, and shape to cut down on computation time. We use computer vision to extract visual-semantic information from movie posters.

3   Recommendation Data

As in [3], we continue to use the MovieLens 20M[1] dataset providing us 20,000,000 user ratings on a scale of 1–5 for 27,278 movies over a ten-year period from 138,493 users who had rated at least 20 movies, and acquire from the MovieLens[2] the title, year of release, genre labels, and IMDB[3] identification numbers for each

---

[1] https://grouplens.org/datasets/movielens/20m/.
[2] https://movielens.org/.
[3] The Internet Movie Database, https://www.imdb.com/.

Table 1. Movie information, descriptive statistics.

Data type and source	N	Missing %	Mean	Min	Max
Title (MovieLens)	27,278				
Genres (MovieLens)*	27,278		1.99	1	10
Genres (OMDb)*	27,207	0.26	2.21	1	5
Directors (OMDb)*	27,003	1.01	1.11	1	41
Plot (OMDb)**	26,327	3.49	63.49	3	1471
Writers (OMDb)*	25,831	5.30	2.41	1	35
Actors (OMDb)*	26,925	1.29	3.93	1	4
Poster (TMDb)	26,827	1.65			

* Multi-class variable, statistics reported for number of classes.
** Full text, statistics reported for number of words.

movie as the item-level information for feature extraction. We use two other sources over IMDB ids: (i) OMDb[4] to query movie plots, and (ii) TMDb[5] to collect movie posters. We use TMDb as it provides posters freely to anyone with free user account, whereas OMDb makes them available only to patrons, and for this reason we need to use TMDb next to OMDb. TMBd provides a movie poster with sufficient resolution for 98.35% of the movies in the dataset, while OMDb provides plots for 96.51% of the movies in MovieLens. We discard movies for which no plot or poster is available. We notice that the plots are substantially shorter (in average 63 words) than typical news articles, which might reduce the amount of available semantic information. For each movie we obtain genres from MovieLens and OMDb, retaining genres from both sources, as we want to ensure no valuable information is lost due to their variability. We discard any movie that has one or more missing values in any of the variables (e.g., director, actor, poster, etc.), leaving us with the final dataset of 25,138 movies for this research. This affects only 0.83% of user ratings available. Table 1 describes the different movie-level variables we use in this research.

4   Recommendation Methodology

This section covers shortly the extraction of semantic features from the plots, described in detail in [3], followed by the extraction of semantic features form digital images. We then proceed with the recommendation method building on the existing TF/CF/SF-IDF(+) recommenders.

4.1   Feature Extraction from Textual Information

In line with TF-IDF [16], CF-IDF(+) [11,16], and SF-IDF(+) [7] recommender systems, we extract semantic information from terms, concepts, and synsets.

---

[4] The Open Movie Database, https://www.omdbapi.com/.
[5] The Movie Database, https://www.themoviedb.org/.

Variables such as genres and persons are readily available and need not to be extracted from text [3]. We use the relationships between persons (*Actors, Directors, Writers*) to construct a domain ontology, detailed in [3].

We use NLP techniques to extract terms and synsets from the plots. Using NLTK[6] package in Python 2.7, each plot is split into a set of sentences and processed separately. Sentences are split into a list of words (tokens) with tokenization using known properties of words (such as they usually occur in the English dictionary). Using part-of-speech (POS), each word is tagged with the POS (e.g., noun, verb, adjective). Stop words, containing negligible semantic information, are then removed, and the Porter [39] stemming algorithm applied to each word to reduce the words to their roots and extract the terms.

Synsets are extracted using the Adapted Lesk [2] WSD algorithm on each word. WSD addresses the problem of identifying the sense of a word – the meaning in its context. Only senses that have the same POS tag as the word from the text are considered. If no sense is found, all senses with any POS are considered. The synset containing the identified sense of the word is extracted.

4.2 Feature Extraction from Images

The posters are generally made to advertise the movies and tend to show the characters and setting of the movie. For example, the poster for the movie *Toy Story* (Fig. 1) shows toys, a cowboy, and an astronaut, delivering the impression of a family movie targeted to young boys. During the study we notice that compared to the movie plot, the poster contains fewer irrelevant elements.

Each pixel in a digital image is represented by 3 colour values for red, green, and blue (RGB). Thereby, an input image of size w wide and h pixels high, can be represented as a matrix of $3 \times h \times w$ values. The most common lossless digital image compression format Portable Network Graphics (PNG) encodes pixels of an image in a 24-bit RGB palette (8 bits per colour). Computer vision libraries (e.g., OpenCV[7]) convert this to a $3 \times h \times w$ matrix of unsigned 8-bit integer values ranging from 0 to $2^8 - 1 = 255$. As most neural network libraries such as Theano[8] take floating-point numbers as inputs, the matrix is normalized by multiplying with $\frac{1}{255}$ to obtain a matrix of values in the range $[0, 1]$.

To extract semantic features from the movie posters we use techniques from computer vision – algorithms to gain high-level understanding from visual information on digital images. In particular, we use CNNs [14] that are state-of-the-art models to extract a vector of synset probabilities and a Visual-Semantic Embedding (VSE) vector from each movie poster.

In order to extract synset vectors from poster images, we exploit the VGG19 – a 19-layer deep CNN from the Visual Geometry Group of the University of Oxford [35]. VGG19 was the highest-performing submission for the ImageNet Large Scale Visual Recognition Challenge (ILSVRC)[9] in 2014. ILSVRC is a com-

---

[6] http://www.nltk.org/.

[7] http://opencv.org/.

[8] http://deeplearning.net/software/theano/.

[9] http://www.image-net.org/challenges/LSVRC/.

Comic book	0.8770	
Book jacket	0.0336	Window 1
Toyshop	0.0294	
Shoe shop	0.0147	
Jigsaw puzzle	0.0098	Window 2
Bookshop	0.0042	
Puck	0.0031	
Tray	0.0030	
Confectionery	0.0016	Window 3
Tobacco shop	0.0013	

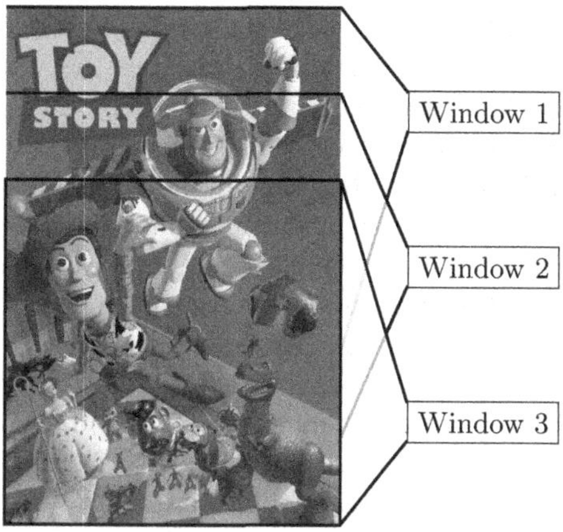

Fig. 1. Crop of three windows of 224×224 px (right), and predicted class (synset) probabilities for each (left), feature values are the maximum probabilities of each synset.

petition where algorithms compete for object detection and image classification, where the challenge for the algorithms is to classify an image in $1,000$ categories that are each represented by a synset. In the tests, for 81.1% of the images the top-5 predictions included the correct class, while human performance on this metric is estimated to be around 88–95% [31]. The trained parameters for this model are publicly available[10]. VGG19's convolutional layers each have a filter size of 3×3 and the input to each of those layers is zero-padded with $p = 1$ such that the outputs are of equal spatial dimensions. Down-sampling occurs only through max-pooling layers. Two fully connected layers are added and connected to a 1,000 dimensional softmax output layer. As substantial semantic content of the posters can be described by the objects that can be recognized from them, we can use VGG19 to extract meaningful synset vectors. The model takes a 224×224 colour image as input, represented as a $224 \times 224 \times 3$ matrix of RGB pixel values, therefore poster images are down-scaled to the width of 224 px keeping the aspect ratio. The height is then still larger than 224 but never larger than 3×224, so we can take 3 vertically overlapping 224×224 windows of the poster as inputs to ensure every part of the image is covered. Figure 1 exemplifies these windows on the poster for the movie *Toy Story* with identified synsets and their probabilities. VGG19 outputs a vector of $1,000$ probabilities, one for each synset. We evaluate the model on each window, after which we take the maximum of the 3 output values for each class (synset). We apply this procedure to the posters to obtain feature vectors of $1,000$ synset values.

The synset values returned by VGG19 are intended to classify an image and do not necessarily describe a poster fully. We therefore also consider another approach called Visual-Semantic Embedding (VSE) [22] that has been used for

---

[10] http://www.robots.ox.ac.uk/~vgg/research/.

the challenge of image captioning [40], where the aim is to generate a natural language caption that best describes the content of an input image (i.e., translating images to text). This is done by mapping the image and the sequence of words of a caption to a common feature space – visual-semantic space – in which semantic distances between an image and a caption can be calculated. From this distance metric the semantic similarity between an image and a caption can be estimated and the nearest-neighbour caption can be returned. Our goal to represent the posters in a semantic space can be considered equivalent to mapping them to a visual-semantic embedding.

The embeddings can be learned with knowledge of pairs of images and their captions. In visual-semantic space, an image and its caption should be close. Let us define this closeness as the cosine similarity between the image's embedding $\vec{m} \in \mathbb{R}^n$ and the embedding of the caption $\vec{c} \in \mathbb{R}^n$. In a properly constructed visual-semantic space, for the image and its caption, $cos(\vec{m}, \vec{c})$ should be relatively high. Reversely, a non-descriptive caption c_r should lead to a relatively low $cos(\vec{m}, \vec{c_r})$. As the image and the caption are mapped to the same visual-semantic space, we can also expect that the more semantically similar $poster_1$ and $poster_2$ are, the higher their $cos(\vec{m_1}, \vec{m_2})$ – which is exactly the aim of our semantics-driven recommender.

Mapping an image to a visual-semantic space is done in [22] by a form of transfer learning [41], where the 4,096 visual features from the second-to-last layer of the pre-trained VGG19 model are transferred to a new model in which they are multiplied by a matrix of trainable weights θ_m, resulting in an embedding vector $\vec{m} \in \mathbb{R}^n$. Transfer learning simplifies the problem from learning the visual-semantic embedding from raw pixels to learning it from high-level visual features trained on the ImageNet Challenge.

Another trainable neural network with weights θ_c transforms the text of the caption in an embedding vector $\vec{c} \in \mathbb{R}^n$. We denote a non-matching caption for image embedding $\vec{m}$ as $\vec{c_r}$ and a non-matching image for caption embedding $\vec{c}$ as $\vec{m_r}$. All weights $\theta = \{\theta_m, \theta_c\}$ are trained simultaneously to minimize the following pairwise ranking loss:

$$\sum_m \sum_r max\{0, \alpha - s(\vec{m}, \vec{c}) + s(\vec{m}, \vec{c_r})\}$$
$$+ \sum_c \sum_r max\{0, \alpha - s(\vec{c}, \vec{m}) + s(\vec{c}, \vec{m_r})\} \tag{1}$$

where $s(\vec{m}, \vec{c}) = \vec{m} \cdot \vec{c}$ is the scoring function. As [22], we first scale the embedding vectors $\vec{m}$ and $\vec{c}$ to unit norm, making s equivalent to cosine similarity $s(\vec{m}, \vec{c}) = cos(\vec{m}, \vec{c})$. For the purpose of extracting semantic features from the movie posters, we are interested in the VSE $\vec{m}$ of the images. The authors of [22] have made an embedding matrix to generate 1,024-dimensional visual-semantic embeddings publicly available[11]. This matrix was trained to optimize Eq. 1 on public image captioning datasets. Our procedure consists of using this

---

[11] https://github.com/ryankiros/visual-semantic-embedding.

pre-trained embedding matrix on the 4,096-dimensional VGG19 visual feature vectors of the movie posters to obtain their visual-semantic embeddings.

The VSE vectors have a more solid theoretical foundation compared to the synset vectors, being derived from a state-of-the-art method whose purpose is to translate images to text. This is a more direct way of achieving our goal of extracting semantic features, and we expect this to improve recommender performance compared to VGG19 synset vectors. The VSE method however has a disadvantage – the features are hidden and have no natural interpretation, making it complicated to link them to an ontology or semantic lexicon.

4.3   Scaling Visual Features

The 1,000 synset values (VGG19) and the 1,024 VSE values extracted from the posters could benefit from scaling as we expect that some features are more relevant to the content of the movies and thus should play a larger role in the cosine distance, therefore scaled higher. We have little information about the relevance of each of the 1,000 synsets, and even less about the 1,024 visual-semantic features. We learn 1,000 scales for the synsets and 1,024 scales for the visual-semantic features simultaneously with optimizing the model through stochastic gradient descent (SGD). We apply the established similarity model scaling [3] also to synsets and visual-semantic features extracted from posters. Denoting the scale as $\vec{c_i}$, if it applies to the i-th feature type t_i, leads $\vec{c_i} \in \mathbb{R}^{1,000} \Leftrightarrow t_i = VGG19$ and $\vec{c_i} \in \mathbb{R}^{1,024} \Leftrightarrow t_i = VSE$. The user-profile vector u_i and the unseen item vector $\vec{v_i}$ are then scaled through $\vec{c_i} \circ \vec{u_i}$ and $\vec{c_i} \circ \vec{v_i}$ respectively, with $\circ$ the element-wise product. These resulting scaled vectors are used in the cosine. We restrict $\vec{c_i} \geqslant 0$ and $\sum \vec{c_i} = 1$ to avoid the over-parametrization caused by $cos(\lambda\vec{u}, \lambda\vec{v}) = cos(\vec{u}, \vec{v}) \ \forall \lambda \neq 0$. Further, we use both the scaled vectors and unscaled original vectors in the model for comparison. Table 2 lists all used feature types.

Table 2. Characterization of used feature types

i	Feature type t_i	Extracted from	Dataset	n_i*	m_i**
1	Directors	Variable	OMDb	12,231	4
2	Actors	Variable	OMDb	45,393	4
3	Writers	Variable	OMDb	27,415	4
4	MovieLens genres	Variable	MovieLens	19	1
5	OMDb genres	Variable	OMDb	27	1
6	Terms	Plot	OMDb	48,083	1
7	Synsets	Plot	OMDb	69,977	19
8	VGG19	Poster	TMDb	1,000	1
9	VSE	Poster	TMDb	1,024	1

* #Features i.e., length of feature vectors. ** #Relations.

To learn scaling for visual feature types, we use the similarity model (Eq. 2) established in [3], where s_i is part similarity (here cosine similarity) and w_i its weight, $\vec{u}_i$ user-profile feature vector, $\vec{v}_i$ unseen item feature vector, $\vec{q}_i$ vector of relation weights, U_i user feature matrix, and V_i feature matrix for unseen item:

$$sim = \sum_{i=1}^{k} w_i s_i = \sum_{i=1}^{k} w_i \cdot cos(\vec{u}_i, \vec{v}_i) = \sum_{i=1}^{k} w_i \frac{\vec{q}_i(U_i V_i^\top)\vec{q}_i^\top}{\sqrt{\vec{q}_i(U_i U_i^\top)\vec{q}_i^\top}\sqrt{\vec{q}_i(V_i V_i^\top)\vec{q}_i^\top}} \quad (2)$$

In the similarity model [3] we insert $\vec{u}_i \leftarrow (\vec{c}_i \circ \vec{u}_i)$ and $\vec{v}_i \leftarrow (\vec{c}_i \circ \vec{v}_i)$, where $\vec{c}_i \in \mathbb{R}^{n_i}$ is the learnable scaling, $\vec{u}_i = U_i$, and $\vec{v}_i = V_i$, because the number of relations $m_i = 1$ for these feature types. We restrict $\sum_{l=1}^{m_i} \vec{q}_{il} = 1$, making $\vec{q}_i = 1$ redundant, and rewrite part-similarity model s_i as given by Eq. 3:

$$sim = \sum_{i=1}^{k} w_i s_i = \sum_{i=1}^{k} w_i \frac{(\vec{c}_i \circ \vec{u}_i)(\vec{c}_i \circ \vec{v}_i)^\top}{\sqrt{(\vec{c}_i \circ \vec{u}_i)(\vec{c}_i \circ \vec{u}_i)^\top}\sqrt{(\vec{c}_i \circ \vec{v}_i)(\vec{c}_i \circ \vec{v}_i)^\top}} \quad (3)$$

The scaling c_i has n_i optimizable parameters and therefore by definition the model is at least n_i-dimensional – this is irreducible. However, when we want to re-use the learned scaling, we can pre-compute $\vec{c}_i \circ \vec{u}_i$ and $\vec{c}_i \circ \vec{v}_i$ because the scaling is known and fixed in that case. Then we can redefine $\vec{u}_i = \vec{c}_i \circ \vec{u}_i$ and $\vec{v}_i = \vec{c}_i \circ \vec{v}_i$ and use our efficient model [3] with pre-computed $U_i U_i^\top$, $U_i V_i^\top$, and $V_i V_i^\top$.

5   Experiments and Results

The similarity model is directly trained on pairs of user-profiles and corresponding unseen items to recommend items for which the predicted similarity is above a certain threshold value, following the procedure established in [3]. The stochastic gradient descent (SGD) is applied on the gradient of the similarity model.

An item is considered to be liked by a user if it is rated with a score ≥ 4.5, otherwise disliked, resulting in an average proportion of 19.12% liked items and 20.9 liked items per user. Further, we shuffle the order of users in our dataset and take the first 1,000 as the test set for evaluation, the following 1,000 as the validation set for the similarity model (including early stopping while training), and the rest 136,493 as the training set to optimize the similarity model.

An observation is a pair of user-profile and unseen item. User-profiles are constructed by sampling $p = 5$ liked items from a user. For each observation the feature matrices $U_i V_i^\top$, $U_i U_i^\top$, and $V_i V_i^\top$ are constructed from the X_i pre-computed data. The $V_i V_i^\top$ are retrieved as blocks of X_i, while $U_i V_i^\top$ and $U_i U_i^\top$ are constructed from sums of p blocks.

For the train and validation sets, the unseen items are defined as all items not in the user-profile. For each user-profile, we sample a liked or a disliked item with equal probability such that we obtain balanced train and validation sets with $E(y) = 0.5$. Each observation is therefore a random user-profile and item, sampled from a random user. We sample 100 batches of 1,024 validation observations and 1,374 training batches of 1,024 observations, for totals of 102,400 and 1,406,976 respectively.

To allow the test set to reflect a realistic recommendation setting, we sample the $p = 5$ user-profile items by shuffling all rated items and then iteratively discarding the first item, adding it to the user-profile if it is liked. We stop as soon as we have obtained $p = 5$ liked items. All discarded liked and disliked items are then considered to be seen. Thus, we simulate the situation when a RS detects that a user has liked $p = 5$ items. We require the unseen items to contain at least one liked and one disliked item to able to measure performance, leaving us with 809 eligible user-profiles from the 1,000 test users. We then construct observations for the user-profile with each unseen item, and save these in a separate batch for each user. The test data is therefore composed of 809 batches of varying sizes, namely the number of unseen items. The comparison between the predicted scores and the actual likes forms the basis of performance measurement. The similarity model is trained with SGD and follows the method (Algorithm 1) described in [3].

We demonstrate the value of semantics-driven recommendations by comparison to the traditional TF-IDF recommender (denoted as T) as a baseline with terms from plots. Our version of SF-IDF+ based on synsets from plots is called S, modified CF-IDF+ holding 5 concept feature types (Directors, Actors, Writers, and genres from MovieLens and OMDb) and operating on the ontology as C, VGG19 as VG, and VSE as VS. When the visual feature scaling of VG or VS is learned (optimized) together with the rest of the parameters, the component is denoted VG_L or VS_L respectively. When the VG scaling is pre-trained in another model and transferred to this model, we denote the component VG_R (each of the 10 restarts uses a pre-trained scaling from a different restart of VG_L) or VG_A (each of the 10 restarts uses the same pre-trained scaling – the average scaling over all 10 restarts of VG_L). Our proposed semantics-driven model is called $C+S+VG_A$, combining the concepts (C) with synsets from plots (S) and posters (VG), where the scaling for the VGG19 synsets is transferred from the average of the 10 optimized VG_L models. Table 3 lists all models used. We test the proposed $C+S+VG_A$ model against the TF-IDF benchmark and against all alternative models.

Table 3. Models and their optimization results, averages over 10 random restarts; n = 102,400 validation and n = 1,406,976 train observations. Scaling transferred from VG_L for $C+S+VG_R$ and $C+S+VG_A$.

Model	k^*	θ^{**}	Logloss***		Training time****		
			Valid.	Train	Epochs	Secs/Epoch	Minutes
T benchmark)	1	2	0.6896	0.6900	10.0	6.4	1.1
C	5	18	0.6815	0.6826	11.9	10.3	2.0
S	1	21	0.6912	0.6914	11.0	14.7	2.7
C+S	6	38	0.6812	0.6822	11.0	22.7	4.2
VG	1	2	0.6924	0.6925	9.4	6.4	1.0
VS	1	2	0.6930	0.6931	8.1	6.3	0.9
VG_L	1	1,002	0.6797	0.6797	26.4	87.3	38.4
VS_L	1	1,026	0.6779	0.6777	39.3	64.4	42.2
C+S+VG	7	39	0.6810	0.6820	11.7	23.3	4.5
$C+S+VG_L$	7	1,039	0.6681	0.6694	35.7	117.0	69.7
$C+S+VG_R$	7	39	0.6708	0.6716	9.4	23.8	3.8
$C+S+VG_A$	7	39	0.6671	0.6680	10.4	23.0	4.0

* Number of feature types (part-similarities) ** Number of parameters.
*** Minimum over all epochs. **** Until early stopping.

We start by describing the results for the computational load of the optimization procedure implemented in Python 2.7 using Keras[12] and Theano[13] libraries, with calculations performed on a regular desktop PC with NVIDIA GTX1060 CPU enabling efficient parallel computations of the gradient updates in batches of 1,024 observations. To optimize $C+S+VG_A$ and $C+S+VG_R$, we first optimize the VG_L model, extract the visual scaling from the 10 restarts, and pre-compute the VGG19 dot-products with this scaling. Table 3 presents the optimization results. We find training within reasonable limits, taking fewer than 70 min for even the heaviest model $C+S+VG_L$. The impact of our scalability method is reflected in a 15x reduction in seconds per epoch of the VG model, which uses pre-computed dot-products, compared to its VG_L counter-part using the traditional approach. Although the VS_L model with visual-semantic embeddings has 1,024 features compared to 1,000 synset features for the VG_L model, it takes about 1.5x as many epochs to converge and results in a slightly better logloss. The sparsity of the VGG19 vectors compared to the VSE vectors could have been a factor in this. For the unscaled visual vectors we see the opposite, as VG needs slightly more epochs and results in a lower loss.

We continue with the comparison between the predicted scores and the actual likes, which forms the basis of performance measurement expressed through area under curve (AUC) for the precision-recall (PR) and receiver operating characteristic (ROC) curve, F_1-measure, and Cohen's kappa [10] coefficient κ. Even though we do not directly optimize for these metrics, a lower logloss results in

---

[12] (https://keras.io).
[13] https://pypi.org/project/Theano/.

higher test performance (Table 4). Table 4 presents the analysis of performance metrics over all models, showing that concepts alone (C) are more informative than both synsets (S) and terms (T), while the combination of C+S [3] outperforms T on all metrics. The inclusion of features captured from poster images further improves (depending on method) the recommendation, as the proposed C+S+VG$_A$ model outperforms C+S, and thereby also the benchmark T.

Comparing the visual feature models we see the unscaled VG outperforms VS, indicating the 1,000 synset feature values we extracted from the posters are more suitable for recommendation than the 1,024-dimensional visual-semantic embeddings. Optimized scaling results in a large performance increase: from an AUC(ROC) of 0.508 to 0.605 for VS$_L$ and from 0.525 to 0.605 for VG$_L$. Under learned scaling VS$_L$ rivals VG$_L$ on some metrics, and closes the gap on AUC(ROC). These results indicate that the visual-semantic embeddings do not improve recommender performance over the synset vectors.

When the mean optimized scales of VG$_L$ are transferred to the C+S+VG$_R$ model, it strongly outperforms its unscaled version C+S+VG and all other recommenders without learned scaling. When we collect the average VG scale over 10 random restarts of VG$_L$ and transfer this to C+S+VG$_A$, we see that it strongly outperforms all other models.

The proposed C+S+VG$_A$ recommender model outperforms the traditional benchmark TF-IDF by a large margin on all metrics. Average AUC(ROC) improves from 0.531 to 0.634, and AUC(PR) from 0.324 to 0.391. We improve $\min_r(F_1)$ from 0.413 to 0.435, and $\max_r(F_1)$ from 0.479 to 0.537. Kappa metrics are improved from 0.038 to 0.137 and from 0.198 to 0.298 for $\min_r(\kappa)$ and $\max_r(\kappa)$ respectively. Given the separately pre-trained visual scaling, we can optimize the model with the scalable approach using pre-computed dot-products

Table 4. Performance on test set, $n = 809$ users, averages over 10 random restarts.

Models	AUC		F_1		κ	
	ROC	PR	$\min_r$	$\max_r$	$\min_r$	$\max_r$
T (TF-IDF, benchmark)	0.535	0.324	0.413	0.479	0.041	0.200
C	0.567	0.358	0.419	0.507	0.081	0.249
S (SF-IDF+)	0.531	0.319	0.411	0.477	0.038	0.198
C+S	0.570	0.361	0.419	0.509	0.083	0.251
VG	0.525	0.308	0.415	0.476	0.036	0.189
VS	0.508	0.299	0.415	0.472	0.018	0.176
VG$_L$	0.605	0.347	0.429	0.519	0.110	0.262
VS$_L$	0.605	0.370	0.422	0.517	0.115	0.268
C+S+VG	0.574	0.362	0.419	0.510	0.087	0.253
C+S+VG$_L$	0.624	0.385	0.431	0.531	0.131	0.289
C+S+VG$_R$	0.624	0.386	0.432	0.532	0.128	0.286
C+S+VG$_A$	0.634	0.391	0.435	0.537	0.137	0.298

just in 4–5 min. It is neither necessary to train the scaling together with the model as a whole, nor to directly optimize on the final performance metrics.

6   Conclusion

In this paper we continued our work on scaling content-based semantics-driven RS to large-scale recommendation task, and extended the approach to include features delivered by computer vision. The paper delivers the second phase of our work earlier work [3]. While previously [3] we showed that semantic information can be extracted not only from articles but also from information of different nature represented as text, established a method for virtual ontology construction, when suitable domain ontology is not readily available, and showed that effective scales can be found through direct optimization of the logloss within minutes on consumer-grade hardware, we now demonstrated that rich semantic information can be extracted from digital images to further improve recommendations. Through a reformulation of how related features are combined, we were able to pre-compute the computationally expensive operations of the cosine similarities and reduced the dimensionality of the similarity model by several orders of magnitude. Overall, we showed that semantics-driven RS can be extended to more complex domains with high-quality recommendations on an extremely large scale.

The proposed semantics-driven recommender $C+S+VG_A$ enhanced with visual features strongly outperformed the baseline TF-IDF, and all other models on ROC, PR, F_1, and κ, even though it was not directly optimized on these metrics but on a cross-entropy loss function that allowed for efficient gradient-based optimization. We showed that semantics-driven RS can be extended to more complex domains with high-quality recommendations on an extremely large scale. The visual synsets extracted from images do not have to be disambiguated but can perhaps be augmented with related synsets from WordNet. The convincing success of learned feature scaling introduces the possibility of models with greater degrees of freedom, especially since the short training time on commodity hardware means that still larger datasets can be utilized.

References

1. Arafeh, M., Ceravolo, P., Mourad, A., Damiani, E., Bellini, E.: Ontology based recommender system using social network data. Future Gener. Comput. Syst. **115**, 769–779 (2021)
2. Banerjee, S., Pedersen, T.: An adapted lesk algorithm for word sense disambiguation using wordnet. In: Gelbukh, A. (ed.) CICLing 2002. LNCS, vol. 2276, pp. 136–145. Springer, Heidelberg (2002). https://doi.org/10.1007/3-540-45715-1_11
3. Bendouch, M.M., Frasincar, F., Robal, T.: Addressing scalability issues in semantics-driven recommender systems. In: IEEE/WIC/ACM International Conference on Web Intelligence (WI-IAT 2021). Association for Computing Machinery, New York (2021). https://doi.org/10.1145/3486622.3493963

4. Brocken, E., Hartveld, A., de Koning, E., van Noort, T., Hogenboom, F., Frasincar, F., Robal, T.: Bing-CF-IDF+: a semantics-driven news recommender system. In: Giorgini, P., Weber, B. (eds.) CAiSE 2019. LNCS, vol. 11483, pp. 32–47. Springer, Cham (2019). https://doi.org/10.1007/978-3-030-21290-2_3
5. Burke, R.: Hybrid recommender systems: survey and experiments. User Model. User-Adapt. Interact. **12**(4), 331–370 (2002)
6. Capelle, M., Frasincar, F., Moerland, M., Hogenboom, F.: Semantics-based news recommendation. In: Proceedings of the 2nd International Conference on Web Intelligence, Mining and Semantics, WIMS 2012. ACM, New York (2012)
7. Capelle, M., Moerland, M., Hogenboom, F., Frasincar, F., Vandic, D.: Bing-SF-IDF+: a hybrid semantics-driven news recommender. In: Proceedings of the 2015 ACM Symposium on Applied Computing, SAC 2015, pp. 732–739. ACM, New York (2015)
8. Cireşan, D.C., Meier, U., Masci, J., Gambardella, L.M., Schmidhuber, J.: Flexible, high performance convolutional neural networks for image classification. In: Proceedings of the Twenty-Second International Joint Conference on Artificial Intelligence, IJCAI 2011, vol. 2, pp. 1237–1242. AAAI Press (2011)
9. Ciregan, D., Meier, U., Schmidhuber, J.: Multi-column deep neural networks for image classification. In: 2012 IEEE Conference on Computer Vision and Pattern Recognition, pp. 3642–3649 (2012)
10. Cohen, J.: A coefficient of agreement for nominal scales. Educ. Psychol. Meas. **20**(1), 37–46 (1960)
11. de Koning, E., Hogenboom, F., Frasincar, F.: News recommendation with CF-IDF+. In: Krogstie, J., Reijers, H.A. (eds.) CAiSE 2018. LNCS, vol. 10816, pp. 170–184. Springer, Cham (2018). https://doi.org/10.1007/978-3-319-91563-0_11
12. Deldjoo, Y., Schedl, M., Cremonesi, P., Pasi, G.: Recommender systems leveraging multimedia content. ACM Comput. Surv. **53**(5), 1–38 (2020)
13. Devlin, J., Chang, M.W., Lee, K., Toutanova, K.: BERT: Pre-training of deep bidirectional transformers for language understanding. In: Proceedings of the 2019 Conference of the North American Chapter of the Association for Computational Linguistics: Human Language Technologies, vol. 1 (Long and Short Papers), pp. 4171–4186. Association for Computational Linguistics, Minneapolis (2019)
14. Egmont-Petersen, M., de Ridder, D., Handels, H.: Image processing with neural networks-a review. Pattern Recogn. **35**(10), 2279–2301 (2002)
15. Farfade, S.S., Saberian, M.J., Li, L.J.: Multi-view face detection using deep convolutional neural networks. In: 5th ACM on International Conference on Multimedia Retrieval, ICMR 2015, pp. 643–650. ACM, New York (2015)
16. Goossen, F., IJntema, W., Frasincar, F., Hogenboom, F., Kaymak, U.: News personalization using the CF-IDF semantic recommender. In: Proceedings of the 1st International Conference on Web Intelligence, Mining and Semantics, WIMS 2011. ACM, New York (2011)
17. Guo, G., Meng, Y., Zhang, Y., Han, C., Li, Y.: Visual semantic image recommendation. IEEE Access **7**, 33424–33433 (2019)
18. Guo, Q., et al.: A survey on knowledge graph-based recommender systems. IEEE Trans. Knowl. Data Eng. (2020)
19. van Huijsduijnen, L.H., et al.: Bing-CSF-IDF+: a semantics-driven recommender system for news. In: Darmont, J., Novikov, B., Wrembel, R. (eds.) ADBIS 2020. CCIS, vol. 1259, pp. 143–153. Springer, Cham (2020). https://doi.org/10.1007/978-3-030-54623-6_13
20. Jones, K.S.: A statistical interpretation of term specificity and its application in retrieval. J. Doc. **28**(1), 11–21 (1972)

21. Karlsen, R., Elahi, N., Andersen, A.: Personalized recommendation of socially relevant images. In: Proceedings of the 8th International Conference on Web Intelligence, Mining and Semantics, WIMS 2018. ACM, New York (2018)

22. Kiros, R., Salakhutdinov, R., Zemel, R.S.: Unifying visual-semantic embeddings with multimodal neural language models. CoRR abs/1411.2539 (2014). http://arxiv.org/abs/1411.2539

23. Lawrence, S., Giles, C.L., Tsoi, A.C., Back, A.D.: Face recognition: a convolutional neural-network approach. IEEE Trans. Neural Netw. 8(1), 98–113 (1997)

24. Matsugu, M., Mori, K., Mitari, Y., Kaneda, Y.: Subject independent facial expression recognition with robust face detection using a convolutional neural network. Neural Netw. 16(5–6), 555–559 (2003)

25. Moerland, M., Hogenboom, F., Capelle, M., Frasincar, F.: Semantics-based News Recommendation with SF-IDF+. In: Proceedings of the 3rd International Conference on Web Intelligence, Mining and Semantics, WIMS 2013. ACM, New York (2013)

26. Pazzani, M.J., Billsus, D.: Content-based recommendation systems. In: Brusilovsky, P., Kobsa, A., Nejdl, W. (eds.) The Adaptive Web. LNCS, vol. 4321, pp. 325–341. Springer, Heidelberg (2007). https://doi.org/10.1007/978-3-540-72079-9_10

27. Penha, G., Hauff, C.: What does BERT know about books, movies and music? probing bert for conversational recommendation. In: 14th ACM Conference on Recommender Systems, RecSys 2020 pp. 388–397. ACM, New York (2020)

28. Rafsanjani, A.H.N., Salim, N., Aghdam, A.R., Fard, K.B.: Recommendation systems: a review. Int. J. Comput. Eng. Res. 3(5), 47–52 (2013)

29. Ricci, F., Rokach, L., Shapira, B.: Recommender Systems Handbook. Springer, Boston (2015). https://doi.org/10.1007/978-0-387-85820-3

30. Robal, T., Haav, H.-M., Kalja, A.: Making web users' domain models explicit by applying ontologies. In: Hainaut, J.L., et al. (eds.) ER 2007. LNCS, vol. 4802, pp. 170–179. Springer, Heidelberg (2007). https://doi.org/10.1007/978-3-540-76292-8_20

31. Russakovsky, O., et al.: Imagenet large scale visual recognition challenge. CoRR abs/1409.0575 (2014). http://arxiv.org/abs/1409.0575

32. Saga, R., Duan, Y.: Apparel goods recommender system based on image shape features extracted by a CNN. In: 2018 IEEE International Conference on Systems, Man, and Cybernetics (SMC), pp. 2365–2369 (2018)

33. Salton, G., Buckley, C.: Term-weighting approaches in automatic text retrieval. Inf. Process. Manag. 24(5), 513–523 (1988)

34. Sheridan, P., Onsjö, M., Becerra, C., Jimenez, S., Dueñas, G.: An ontology-based recommender system with an application to the Star Trek television franchise. Future Internet 11(9), 182 (2019)

35. Simonyan, K., Zisserman, A.: Very deep convolutional networks for large-scale image recognition. CoRR abs/1409.1556 (2014). http://arxiv.org/abs/1409.1556

36. Szegedy, C., et al.: Going Deeper with Convolutions. CoRR abs/1409.4842 (2014). http://arxiv.org/abs/1409.4842

37. Tuinhof, H., Pirker, C., Haltmeier, M.: Image-based fashion product recommendation with deep learning. In: Nicosia, G., Pardalos, P., Giuffrida, G., Umeton, R., Sciacca, V. (eds.) Machine Learning, Optimization, and Data Science, pp. 472–481. Springer, Cham (2019). https://doi.org/10.1007/978-3-030-13709-0_40

38. Turner, V., Gantz, J.F., Reinsel, D., Minton, S.: The Digital Universe of Opportunities: Rich Data and the Increasing Value of the Internet of Things. International Data Corporation, White Paper, IDC_1672 (2014)

39. Van Rijsbergen, C., Robertson, S., Porter, M.: New Models in Probabilistic Information Retrieval. British Library research & development report, Computer Laboratory, University of Cambridge, Cambridge, England (1980)
40. Vinyals, O., Toshev, A., Bengio, S., Erhan, D.: Show and tell: a neural image caption generator. In: The IEEE Conference on Computer Vision and Pattern Recognition (CVPR) (2015)
41. Weiss, K., Khoshgoftaar, T.M., Wang, D.: A survey of transfer learning. J. Big Data 3(1), 9 (2016)
42. Yoon, Y.C., Lee, J.W.: Movie recommendation using metadata based word2vec algorithm. In: 2018 International Conference on Platform Technology and Service (PlatCon), pp. 1–6. IEEE (2018)
43. Yu, L., Han, F., Huang, S., Luo, Y.: A content-based goods image recommendation system. Multimedia Tools Appl. 77(4), 4155–4169 (2017). https://doi.org/10.1007/s11042-017-4542-z
44. Zhang, G.Q., Zhang, G.Q., Yang, Q.F., Cheng, S.Q., Zhou, T.: Evolution of the internet and its cores. New J. Phys. 10(12), 123027 (2008)
45. Zhou, X., Qin, D., Chen, L., Zhang, Y.: Real-time context-aware social media recommendation. VLDB J. 28(2), 197–219 (2018). https://doi.org/10.1007/s00778-018-0524-7
46. Zhou, X., Qin, D., Lu, X., Chen, L., Zhang, Y.: Online social media recommendation over streams. In: 2019 IEEE 35th International Conference on Data Engineering (ICDE), pp. 938–949. IEEE, Piscataway (2019)

Assisting Mentors in Selecting Newcomers' Next Task in Software Product Lines: A Recommender System Approach

Raul Medeiros[(✉)] and Oscar Díaz

University of the Basque Country (UPV/EHU), San Sebastián, Spain
{raul.medeiros,oscar.diaz}@ehu.eus

Abstract. Onboarding (i.e., the process of incorporating new people) is relevant because it introduces employees to their role, the company's culture, and what the company has to offer. Onboarding is then dependent on the company's culture and practices. When it comes to software development, these practices include the methods, the tools or the developers' organigram. Accordingly, there is not a one-size-fits-all onboarding, rather this procedure needs to be tuned for the practice at hand. This work tackles the specifics brought about by Software Product Line Engineering w.r.t. traditional software development, namely: larger code base, larger code variability, and larger and more heterogeneous teams. Specifically, this works advocates for feature-centric onboarding. Features (i.e., functional characteristics that are visible for a user) already play a key role throughout the SPL lifecycle. In this context, we advocate for defining the onboarding process as a journey where milestones are equated with features. Unfortunately, finding the most appropriate feature for a newcomer, if conducted manually by mentors, would be time-consuming, given the sheer number of features. To face this problem, we advocate for Recommender Systems based on the similarity between the feature's codebase and the code previously explored by the newcomer. To this end, we resort to Topic Modeling, and specifically, Latent Dirichlet Allocation. We provide proof-of-concept through *RecomMentor*, a recommender system for *pure-variants* as the variability management system. *RecomMentor* is put to test against ranking metrics of the Information Retrieval literature. The first evaluation suggests that LDA could be an appropriate technique, paving the way towards using Recommender Systems in feature-based onboarding scenarios.

Keywords: Onboarding · Mentoring · Software Product Line Engineering · Recommender Systems · Latent Dirichlet Allocation

1 Introduction

The process of incorporating a new person into a company is known as onboarding, and software teams are not strangers to it. Distinct onboarding models have

© Springer Nature Switzerland AG 2022
X. Franch et al. (Eds.): CAiSE 2022, LNCS 13295, pp. 460–476, 2022.
https://doi.org/10.1007/978-3-031-07472-1_27

been proposed (refer to [32] for an overview). One popular approach is mentoring, i.e., connecting a newcomer ('the mentee') and a more experienced senior colleague ('the mentor'). Mentoring is correlated with higher levels of activity from the side of the newcomer [18]. On the down side, appointing senior developers as mentors can detract useful resources [31]. Hence, a mentor 'is not like a tutor who is there all of the time, but rather the mentor checks up on the newcomer, perhaps once per day, monitoring the newcomer's progress and providing feedback and advice' [15]. As a result, most development teams expect newcomers to explore and understand the source code by themselves [34]. However, even if mentees progress at their own pace, mentors should provide milestones during the onboarding journey, otherwise risking mentees' disappointment and frustration [22]. Research shows that successful onboarding relates to *systematic* onboarding programs (aka institutionalized onboarding). The more complex the receiving organization, the more important it is to be systematic in the onboarding process [12]. Systematic implies to be methodical in the implementation of onboarding. However, there is not a one-size-fits all onboarding process but this very much depends on context [30]. This work tackles onboarding in Software Product Lines (SPL). A *Software Product Line (SPL)* is a set of software-intensive systems sharing a common, managed set of *features* that satisfy the specific needs of a particular market segment or mission and that are developed from a common set of core assets in a prescribed way [14].

Problem Space. By addressing an entire 'market segment' (rather than a single product), no wonder SPLs are complex both organizationally and software wise. SPLs support planned reuse (as opposed to opportunistic reuse) by making code variability intensive [14]. Variability is realized in terms of features. Features are functional abstractions that serve to communicate, reason, and distinguish between individual products [3]. Features are then problem-oriented (close to the terms in which customers express requirements) but also solution-meaningful (used for scoping functional units, describing areas of responsibility or reporting bugs). This sits features in-between customers and developers. We conjecture these very characteristics make features appropriate for the mentee-mentor interaction. Mentees might better grasp features than other more elaborated technicalities. On the other hand, chances are that tasks in the backlog are framed in terms of features, or at least, mentors would be able to promptly link features to code files or functional profiles of the staff. Hence, our first premise is that the features might serve as the middle ground between newcomers and experienced members. The drawback is the sheer number of features, in the range of hundreds [23]. This raises our research question: how would a feature-driven onboarding intervention for SPL organizations might look like?

Solution Space. Our second premise is that 'simple-to-complex' is an appropriate strategy for SPL onboarding. This is not new. This strategy by which newcomers start with simple tasks that gain in difficulty as mentees progress, is common in one-off development environments [22]. The difference stems from the task scope. Whereas in one-off settings, tasks are framed within classes or functions, we advocate for onboarding tasks to be framed within features. On this premise, a task is 'simple' if it is framed within a feature the newcomer is familiarized with. And the other way around, a large degree of complexity is expected if the newcomer is moved outside his 'zone of comfort'. Hence, onboarding becomes a journey to gradually take newcomers out of their comfort zone. However, finding an appropriate set of features that matches the newcomer background, if conducted manually, would be time-consuming, given the sheer number of features involved. This is when Recommender Systems come in.

Recommender Systems (RSs) are an established approach to cope with a large set of resources (e.g., the SPL's features) where users (e.g., mentors) might have difficulties finding interesting items (e.g., features) in a reasonable amount of time (e.g., the onboarding set-time). Broadly, our vision is for an RS to predict whether a particular newcomer would be better 'fitted' to an SPL feature or not based on the newcomer's profile. The challenge rests on profiling both features and newcomers in terms of appropriate facets. Inspired by previous work on similar code detection [4,15,26,35], we resort to code to profile both features and users. Features are fleshed out in terms of *if-def* blocks while newcomers are characterized in terms of their previous code activities. The latter is not unusual. Recruiters are increasingly relying on online activities of developers to find a suitable candidate [24]. Although the newcomer might ignore the SPL domain (e.g., automotive), it might be knowledgeable about the underlying technologies and programming frameworks. These first technical skills can be gradually enriched as the newcomer faces onboarding tasks throughout the onboarding journey, similar to the purchasing story in on-line markets. We contribute to this vision by providing proof-of-concept (Sect. 4) and preliminary proof-of-value (Sect. 5).

2   Onboarding in Software Projects

Software development is contingent on the practices and settings in which the software is created. This section places SPL practices together with other software practices, as far as onboarding is concerned. Specifically, we resort to the Balali et al.'s barriers to characterize mentees' hassles [7]:

- *personal barriers*, e.g., newcomers' reluctance to ask for help,
- *interpersonal barriers*, e.g., communication issues due to different goals, different cultures and different interpersonal skills,
- *process barriers*, e.g., difficulties in having a holistic perspective of the software they are there to contribute to and in finding where to start working; and
- *technical barriers*, e.g., complexity of the systems being developed, lack of prior knowledge of the domain.

Table 1 reviews onboarding interventions w.r.t the barriers being tackled. Specifically, three software practices are examined: Global Software Development (GSD), Agile Software Development (ASD), and Software Product Line Engineering (SPLE). The aim: making the case for onboarding practices to be tuned to SPLE specifics.

Table 1. Onboarding specifics: GSD vs. ASD vs. SPLE. In bold the barrier and intervention approached in this work.

Context	GSD	ASD	SPLE
Interpersonal B.	Cultural differences, Offshore socialization, Geographical dispersion [10] Geographical dispersion [9] Communication issues [28]		Communication between teams with different aims (i.e. AE vs DE)
Process B.	Strategy fragmentation, Difficulty of remote mentoring [10] Strategy fragmentation, Difficulty of remote mentoring [9]	Conveying agile principles, Mindset change [20]	Reuse awareness
Technical B.	–	–	Scope of concerns, **program structure**
Interventions	Remote mentoring, Feedback and review [10] Socialization emphasis [9] Remote mentoring, Feedback and review, Onshore mentoring [28]	Mentoring Ceremonies, Process documentation, Physical task board, Guided task allocation, Feedback and review [20] Daily, Explicit mentoring responsibilities [11]	Feature-centric documentation [5] **Feature-driven semi-automatic mentoring**

Global Software Development (GSD). The Internet allows for software professionals to team up no matter the time and the place. This confers GSD very specific social characteristics. Here, challenges rest on offshore socialization (i.e. difficulties to integrate into the team due to its distributed nature), geographical dispersion and communication issues (i.e. problems to communicate between teams with different time zones or difficulties to conduct remote mentoring), overcoming cultural differences and strategy fragmentation (i.e., maintaining the same onboarding process in the whole organization) [9,10,28]. Remote mentoring, onshore workshops (i.e. gathering together different teams in the same place to work together, for example, through pair programming) or frequent feedback are some strategies taken by GSD companies to mitigate these barriers [9,10,28].

Agile Software Development (ASD). ASD refers to a group of software development methodologies based on iterative development, where requirements and solutions evolve through collaboration between self-organizing cross-functional teams. From an onboarding perspective, main concerns include the change of mindset and the independent way of working (i.e., selecting your own tasks from the backlog, calling your own meetings, or getting used to daily meetings and developing by sprints) [11,20]. To fight this back, ASD teams resort to mentoring ceremonies (i.e., special mentoring meetings where mentors try to teach agile principles to newcomers) or emphasizing agile principles through daily meetings or physical task boards [11,20].

Software Product Line Engineering (SPLE). SPLs excel at reuse, better said, planned reuse. To this end, two main activities intertwine: (1) *Domain*

```
230    // PVSCL:IFCOND(Autocomplete,LINE)
231    // Load datalist with previously used texts
232    const themeOrCode = CommentingForm.getCodeOrThemeForAnnotation(anno
233    CommentingForm.retrievePreviouslyUsedComments(themeOrCode).then((pr
234        const awesomeplete = new Awesomplete(document.querySelector('#com
235            list: previousComments,
236            minChars: 0
237        })
238        // On double click on comment, open the awesomeplete
239        document.querySelector('#comment').addEventListener('dblclick', (
240            awesomeplete.evaluate()
241            awesomeplete.open()
242        })
243    })
244    // PVSCL:ENDCOND
245    // PVSCL:IFCOND(LookupLiterature, LINE)
246    // Add the option to delete a suggestedLiterature from the comment
247    $('.removeReference').on('click', function () {
248        $(this).closest('li').remove()
249    })
```

Fig. 1. Features as crosscuts. SPL codebase is frequently interspersed with feature variants, i.e., *#ifdef* blocks that are annotated with feature names (e.g., *Autocomplete*, *Loou224pLiterature*), i.e., the block directives . At configuration time, depending on the product's feature, blocks are kept if their directives include the product's feature. Otherwise, the blocks are removed.

Engineering (DE), where the scope and variability of the system is defined in terms of features, and reusable assets are developed to conform the SPL platform; and (2) *Application Engineering (AE)*, where products are derived from the SPL platform by selecting the features to be exhibited by the product [3]. This approach to software development accounts for many benefits [3], yet it results in complex structures both technically and organizationally. The impact on onboarding is many-fold:

– *Technical Barriers.* Technically, the impact is double. First, the large SPL *scope*. SPLs do not tackle a product but a class of products. Hence, the size of concerns to be considered are those of a 'domain' rather than those involved in a single 'product'. This variability is reflected in terms of 'features' (see later). SPLs might account for hundreds of features, complicating both mentoring and onboarding. Second barrier comes from *the program structure*. In variability-intensive systems like SPLs, the code should account for reuse. Often, this is achieved by enclosing variants within *#ifdef* and *#endif* marks, and associated with precompilation directives, i.e. features (see Fig. 1). The point is that features tend to be crosscuts, being frequently scattered along distinct methods, and tangled with other features. As a result, code comprehensibility is diminished [27].

- *Interpersonal Barriers.* Different units might interplay during SPL development. DE is dedicated to keeping up the platform, while AE develops products out of the platform, frequently involving adaptations that will eventually feedback the platform itself. This *DE-AE communication* might involve tens of developers with different agendas and aims [6].
- *Process Barriers.* SPLE is all about developing *for* reuse (domain engineers) and developing *by* reuse (application engineers). *Reuse-awareness* is to SPLE what agility is to ASD: a major cultural shift in code development. Reuse-awareness departs from traditional one-off development [1]. The code might run in different settings, integrated by developers other than the original authors. Newcomers need to become aware of the importance of reuse, its drivers and practices.

The bottom line is that SPLE brings its own onboarding challenges. The question arises about how traditional onboarding strategies are adapted to this new setting. We argue that the notion of 'feature' is an appropriate construct for the mentee-mentor interaction. Yet, for a mentor to select one feature out of hundreds is very time-consuming. To assist in this selection, we rely on Recommender System.

3   Adopting Recommender Systems for SPLE Mentoring

Recommender Systems (RSs) comprise three main modules: the content analyzer, the profile learner, and the filtering component [25]. The former abstracts content (e.g., pictures, news) in terms of meaningful facets (e.g., painting style), i.e., the content profile. The profile learner collects data representative of the user, and tries to generalize this data, to build up a profile. Finally, the filtering component exploits the learner profile to suggest similar content based on profile similarity (refer to [19] for a survey on RSs). Next, we adapt this architecture for the SPLE case.

3.1   Content Analyzer

The goal of a recommender system is to generate recommendations to a collection of users for items (e.g., books, movies). Here, this item is the code that implements a feature, i.e., the feature codebase. This code is commonly scattered across different files, and tangled with other features. Features are rarely mapped to a single programming construct (i.e., file, class, method). Rather, a feature codebase tends to be scattered across different constructs, normally as code snippets embedded as *ifdef* blocks in the methods' code. To obtain the codebase, each and every code file of the SPL needs to be parsed. For each *#ifdef-block* whose annotation directive refers to feature f_i, the block code is extracted and stored in *codebase$_i$*. This is our counterpart to books in Amazon or movies in Netflix.

The Content Analyzer is in charge of taking a set of codebase as input, and returning a set of **Feature Profiles**. A feature profile characterizes a codebase in terms of the facets that are considered meaningful for the task at hand. Our task is instructional. Here, studies report that the primary way a developer comprehends a code is by reading identifier names which make up, on average, about 70% of the characters found in a body of code [16]. On these premises, we conjecture that newcomers would feel more confident looking at a code whose identifiers semantically related, to a certain extent, with those explored in previous tasks. Accordingly, we characterize the feature codebase in terms of 'topics'.

Topic Modeling is a natural language processing method to discover the abstract 'topics' (i.e., a collection of relevant words) in a collection of documents. Here, the documents are the features' codebases, and the topics are inferred from the identifiers of variables, classes, methods or comments. A popular approach to Topic Modeling is Latent Dirichlet Allocation (LDA). Here, each topic has the probabilities to generate various words, and a word can be generated from multiple topics with different probabilities. In this way, the Feature Profile is obtained out of a mixture of several topics. Specifically, a Feature Profile is realized as a vector $F = [t_1, t_2, ..., t_{tnum}] = 1, where\ t_i$ shows the likelihood of the feature to belong to the ith topic. Table 2 (a) shows the presentation of feature "Linking" in terms of topics. Part (b) depicts the representation of "Topic0" in terms of code identifiers. Therefore, the Content Analyzer outputs a set of topic-probability distributions.

Table 2. An example of Content Analyzer topic and feature representation

A: Feature profile representation in terms of topics

	topic0	topic1	topic2	topic3	topic4	topic5	topic6	topic7
Linking	3.11E-02	2.41E-06	5.13E-04	1.44E-06	5.21E-07	4.23E-06	7.74-05	0.94

B: An excerpt of topic0 representation in terms of code identifiers

	abwa	access	account	actions	activate	activated	activity	adds
Topic0	0.00E+00	1.45E-02	3.45E-03	2.22E-04	3.12E-02	5.2E-01	6.42E-02	0.02

3.2   Profile Learner

This module collects data representative of the newcomer to construct the **Newcomer Profile**. Usually, the generalization is realized through machine learning techniques, which are able to infer a model of user interests starting from items liked or disliked, e.g., based on previous purchases. We adopt as the counterpart of 'previous purchases', the notion of 'previous programming'. Specifically, two scenarios are possible:

- If the newcomer comes from within the company (crossboarding), then chances are they have already been involved in some SPLE activities. In this case, we take this code as the starting point.
- If the newcomer is external, then the mentor needs to select the feature that might better reflect the background of the newcomer through interview.

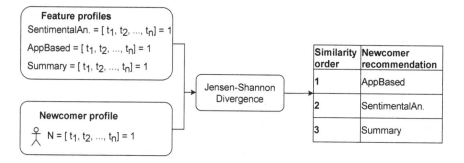

Fig. 2. An example of *RecomMentor*'s filtering component outcome.

Wherever this 'previous coding' is obtained, the Newcomer Profile is also abstracted from this codebase, using Topic Modeling. Therefore, this profile is also realized as a topic-probability distribution.

3.3 Filtering Component

This module exploits the Newcomer Profile to suggest similar Feature Profiles. Both profiles are equally characterized as a topic-probability distribution. It is up to the Filtering component to set the similarity between both profiles. To this end, we resort to the Jensen-Shannon Divergence. This results in a newcomer[feature] vector $N = [f_1, f_2, ..., f_{tnum}]$, where f_i holds the likelihood of Newcomer Profile N being similar to the i th feature. For example, in Fig. 2 similarity values between features *SentimentalAn*, *AppBased* and *Summary*, and the Newcomer Profile are calculated using the Jensen-Shannon divergence. Then, based on these similarity values, features are presented to the mentor ordered by most similar to most dissimilar. Finally, the mentor can select from the ordered list which feature the newcomer should explore next.

4   Proof-of-Concept: *RecomMentor*

RecomMentor is a Recommender Systems for SPLE that uses *pure::variants* as the variability management system [8], and built on top of *LASCAD* for similar application detection based on source code [2]. *RecomMentor* is available at https://github.com/onekin/RecomMentor. *RecomMentor* proceeds along with three stages (see Fig. 3): *Feature-codebase extraction, Topic matrix generation* and, *Similar-feature recommendation*.

Feature-Codebase Extraction. For each *#ifdef-block* whose annotation directive refers to feature f_i, *RecomMentor* extracts this block code and stores it in *codebase_i*. The result is a map $M = (f_1, codebase_1)$, $(f_2, codebase_1), ...(f_n, codebase_n)$.

Topic Matrix Generation. With the help of *LASCAD*, *codebase_i* is now parsed: (1) identifiers are extracted from code and words in comments; (2) terms

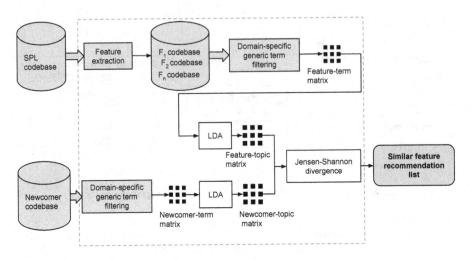

Fig. 3. *RecomMentor* process overview. Steps in blue refer to those tuned specifically for SPLE. (Color figure online)

are refined by removing English and programming language-specific stop words; and (3) overly common and overly rare terms from the corpus are removed. In addition, the fact that features pertain to a single organization might increase the chances of similarity due to naming conventions within the organization. We then perform a finer-grained, SPL-specific removal of non-discriminatory terms. This results in *the feature-term matrix*. This matrix feeds the LDA to obtain *the feature-topic matrix*: each row (i.e., feature) denotes a vector $F = [t_1, t_2, ..., t_{tnum}] = 1$, where the vector depicts the probability distribution of feature F of belonging to topics 1 to $tnum$. The same process is conducted for the newcomer's codebase. The result is a 'newcomer profile'-topic single row matrix where the row is a vector $N = [t_1, t_2, ..., t_{tnum}] = 1$ that presents the probability distribution of Newcomer N of belonging to topics 1 to $tnum$.

Feature Recommendation. Once the Feature Profile and the Newcomer Profiles are worked out, *RecomMentor* resorts to the Jensen-Shannon similarity divergence method to work out a list of features pondered by their similarity with the newcomer's code (see Fig. 2). From this list the mentor can select which feature should the newcomer explore next.

5   Proof-of-Value: *WACline* Evaluation

Recommender systems tend to be evaluated based on IR effectiveness metrics (e.g. recall or precision) [13]. The importance of both precision and recall very much depends on the domain, specifically, the impact of incurring in false positives or false negatives. In our case, recommending a dissimilar feature (i.e., false positives) might disturb newcomers to a larger extent that *not* recommending a feature that is similar (i.e., false negatives). In other words, precision turns out to be a more critical concern than recall.

More to the point, identifying the right features is important, but also how these features are ranked in terms of similarity. For a given Newcomer Profile, and using similarity as the ranking criterion, suppose the expected ideal ranked result set is *(fa, fb, fc, fd)*, where the recommender system outputs *(fb, fa, fc, fd)*. While returning all the expected hits (precision = 100% and recall = 100%), the recommender system failed to return the ideal expected ranking, by reporting a less relevant result *fb* prior to the more relevant one *fa*, hence misguiding the mentor towards selecting a less appropriate feature fb. Therefore, we evaluated *RecomMentor* along three top-weighted metrics [13]:

- *First False Positive:* the position of the first false positive. In our setting this refers to the position of the first feature that is not similar to the Newcomer Profile,
- *Precision at K:* the proportion of recommended items in the top-k results that are true positive. In our setting, we take 'k' as 5 as this tends to be the number of features *WACline* mentors tend to look at,
- *Normalized Discounted Cumulative Gain (NDCG)*: the quality of the ranked results in terms of how well relevant items are highly ranked.

5.1 WACline Dataset

The Target SPL. We put *RecomMentor* at work for the *WACline* SPL. *WACline* is an Open Source SPL for Web Annotation browser extensions[1], is implemented in JavaScript as the programming language, and *pure::variants* as the variability management tool. *WACline* accounts for 25K lines of code and 85 features from which 60 are optional features. This result in $5.77*10^{13}$ different possible configurations. Despite its small-medium size for an SPL, mastering *WACline* involves understanding over a hundred different notions and their inter-dependencies.

The Users. We consider a scenario where newcomers come from within the company. Specifically, we consider they were working on the development of one of the sixty *WACline* optional features. This provides us with sixty Newcomer Profiles.

The Instrument. Usually, recommender systems are evaluated against a ground truth [13]. We asked *WACline's* potential mentors to provide an oracle for evaluating *RecomMentor*. The oracle consists of a *Feature x Feature* matrix (of all the optional features in *WACline*) where cells hold a feature-to-feature similarity value from 0 (totally dissimilar) to 3 (identical) (check Appendix A). They built the oracle performing three steps: (1) develop a personal oracle independently (i.e. put a similarity value for each feature pair in WACline), (2) put the two oracles in common and check for discrepancies, and (3), reach an agreement on discrepancies, and deliver the final oracle. We measure to what extent the results provided by *RecomMentor* for a particular Newcomer Profile match the oracle developed by WacLine's maintainers, i.e., to what extent would *RecomMentor* select features dissimilar from those of a human mentor.

---

[1] *WACline's* source code is available at https://github.com/onekin/WacLine.

5.2   Results

First False Positive. We tested *RecomMentor*'s results against the oracle. In this case, we treated as similar all the feature pairs with a rating bigger than or equal one. Our results show that the value of the first false positive metric range is placed from 1 to 11 (i.e., for the 60 first false positive metric measured against WACline's oracle, the results oscillate from 1 to 11). Figure 4 (left) shows that 75% of the tests placed their First False Positive above the third position, and 50% above the fourth position. We consider these results quite satisfactory especially if we consider that the mentor only has to choose one feature at a time, and that on average only 9 out of 60 features per Newcomer Profile were actually rated with one or more. This means that on average half of the similar features were located in the first results. This measure's main limitation is the high dependence on both the SPL data set and the Newcomer Profile. For example, if the SPL data has only X actual true positives for a given Newcomer Profile, the best achievable result using this measure is $X + 1$. This issue affects the applicability of this measure.

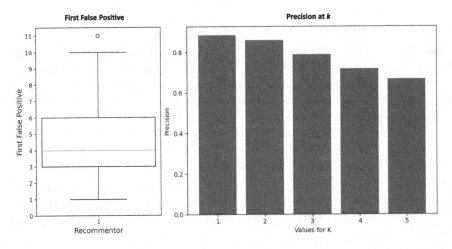

Fig. 4. *First False Positive* (on the left) and *Precision@K* (on the right) metrics for the *WACline* evaluation.

Precision@K. We consider mentors' attention rarely goes up to more than 5 features at a time. Figure 4 (right) depicts the average precision@k for values of the sixty Newcomer Profiles from 1 to 5, being 0.67 the lowest one obtained for $k = 5$.

$$Precision_k = \frac{tp_k}{tp_k + fp_k} \ where \ tp \ and \ fp \ are$$

$$limited \ to \ the \ top \ K \ hits$$ (1)

NDCG. NDCG resorts to an oracle to set the ideal result where features are orderdered based on their relevance (i.e. ordered by similarity). To calculate the

NDCG (Eq. 3), we need to calculate the Ideal DCG (IDCG). IDCG returns the ideal (highest achievable) DCG (Eq. 2) using the given relevance score set (from the oracle). That is, the DCG of the best system is the same as the value of the IDCG. The maximum value for the NDCG function is 1.0 for a result set that exactly matches the one from the oracle, and the minimum value is 0.0 for result sets with no true positive. Finally, using DCG and IDCG, we can now calculate the NDCG:

$$DCG(q, n) = r(q, 1) + \sum_{i=2}^{n} \frac{r(q, i)}{log_2(i))} \tag{2}$$

$$NDCG(q, n) = \frac{DCG(q, n)}{IDCG(q, n)} \tag{3}$$

Table 3. An example of ranked results for a Newcomer Profile.

RecomMentor	SentimentAn.	SuggestedLiterature	Import	TXT	Summary
Newcomer Profile	1	2	0	4	2

Oracle	TXT	SuggestedLiterature	Summary	SentimentAn.	Import
Newcomer Profile	4	2	2	1	0

The function $r(q,i)$ in Eq. 2 returns the relevancy score for the given Newcomer Profile in the position (i) from the ranked results. For example, on the first part of Table 3 (RecomMentor) $r(Newcomer\ Profile,1)$ would be 1, whereas on the oracle part it would be 4. In Table 3 we can see an example of ranked results for a Newcomer Profile. The first part of the table refers to the results given by the recommender system, while the second one refers to those established by the oracle. In this example, if we apply Eqs. 2 and 3 to the ranked results we get that: $IDCG = 7.76$, while $DCG = 5.87$ and $NDCG = 5.87/7.76 = 0.75$. Back to the evaluation, *RecomMentor* was compared with the oracle, achieving an average NDCG of 0.87 for the Newcomer Profiles at hand.

This first evaluation seems to suggest that *First-False-Positive, Precision@k* and *NDCG* could be appropriate measures, paving the way towards using RSs in feature-based onboarding scenarios.

5.3 Threats to Validity

Construct Validity. We take code-term similarity as a proxy for semantic-closeness, and hence, mentors' criteria. So far, however, we have only involved mentors indirectly in the study, so we cannot claim that feature similarity really results in a more gradual and engaging onboarding experience. However, our first aim was to measure to what extent *RecomMentor* matches mentors' opinion. In this aspect, obtained ranked metrics are quite promising. We also used features as surrogates of newcomer profiles, and this can be seen as inappropriate. However, our newcomer profiles are built upon the code of features with which the newcomers are being involved. This means that in a preliminary stage, if the newcomer is external, then the newcomer profile will always consist only of one feature.

Internal Validity. We resort to Topic Modeling and software similarity. Yet, Topic Modeling has been tested in Open Source Software whereas our code is that of feature realizations. We tuned *LASCAD*'s Topic Modeling functionality to consider some SPL specifics, yet differences in size might influence the results.

External Validity. We focus on annotated SPLs where variability is supported through *ifdef* directives. Other approaches to variability handling (e.g., feature-based, component-based or model-based) might require a different treatment. In addition, the evaluation is being conducted for a medium-size SPL. Recommentor's performance can be impacted by a bigger size of the feature pool both in terms of scalability and the quality of the obtained results. Yet, *WACline* uses pure::variants as the variability manager and follows the Chrome recommendation for web extension architecture. On the other hand, we measured to what extent *RecomMentor* matches *WACline*'s mentors' criteria, but this may not be generalizable to other SPL mentors' criteria.

6 Related Work

We introduce related studies on onboarding using the following framework for comparison: (1) setting, i.e., the environment in which the onboarding takes place; (2) intervention, i.e., the type of action to take in response to the onboarding challenges; (3) population, i.e., the stakeholders who are affected by the intervention; and (4) results, i.e., the reported impact.

Setting. Most of the works tackling onboarding consider single-off application development, with differences on the nature of the application context, either Open Source [15,17,26,33,35] or commercial. We are only aware of one work set in an SPL scenario: [5].

Intervention. Different interventions have been proposed to facilitate onboarding: a dedicated web portal for newcomers [33]; chatbots to assist newcomers [17]; gamification for onboarding [21]; using augmented reality in diary tasks [29]; or using concept maps for newcomer guidance [5]. We depart from these interventions in the setting (SPL organizations), the subject of the recommendation (features), and the approach (Recommender Systems). *RecomMentor* takes inspiration from [15,26,35]. Main differences from this work rest on the subject of the recommendation (i.e., features vs. bug, snippets and emails) and the process of obtaining each feature codebase.

Population. The target audiences being addressed exhibit small differences: undifferentiated [15,17,26,29,33,35], generation Y and Z [21] or Application Engineers [5]. Our work can be characterized as 'undifferentiated' as we do not make any main assumption about the newcomer profile.

Results. Not all aforementioned interventions provide an evaluation. Some exceptions include: subjective onboarding improvement [5, 21] and softened social barriers [33]. As for Recommentor, we use IR metrics as the goodness criteria. These metrics were used to assess the difference between Recommentor's answers and those provided by a human expert who acts as the oracle.

7   Conclusions and Future Work

This work presents *RecomMentor*, an RS to assist feature-based onboarding in SPL organizations. We use Topic Modeling for characterizing both the Feature Profile and the Newcomer Profile based on the features' codebase and the newcomer's explored features' code, respectively. Using *WACline* as the dataset, the evaluation seems to suggest that Topic Modeling upon the features' codebase performs quite well on matching mentors criteria (i.e. *WACline*'s oracle). That said, the evaluation is limited, and hence, results should be interpreted with caution. All in all, these findings might provide a basis for informed onboarding that assists mentors in selecting appropriate features for their mentees. Next follows-on include extending the evaluation to other SPLs of bigger size and onboarding experiences. Here, a limitation is the involvement that building an oracle implies for Domain Engineers. Besides, *RecomMentor* builds Feature Profiles based on the features' raw codebase. We also plan to extend Recommentor's recommendation interface and provide it with functionalities that will aid mentors on detecting wrong (false positive) recommended features. More elaborated characterization might be also conducted where extraction is not only focused on variables, classes or methods but also on metrics present in SPLE such as scattering or tangling metrics.

Acknowledgments. This work is supported by the Spanish Ministry of Science and Innovation (RTI2018-099818-B-I00). R. Medeiros enjoys a doctoral grant from the Ministry of Science and Innovation.

A   The Oracle

The *WACline* oracle used in the evaluation consists of a *Feature x Feature* matrix (of all the optional features in WACline) where cells indicate similarity values between the optional features of the SPL, values go from 0 (totally dissimilar) to 3 (identical) (check Table 4 for an example). Two developers were involved in the construction process. The process follows: (1) an oracle is provided by each of the developers, (2) both oracles are disclosed, and (3) an agreement on discrepancies is reached.

Table 4. An excerpt of the WACline oracle. The oracle is available at: https://tinyurl. com/fep4jyhs.

	ACM	Alphabetical	Annotated PDF	Annotati-onList	Assessing	Autocom-plete	Browser Storage	Built In
ACM	X	0	0	0	0	0	0	0
Alphabetical	0	X	0	0	0	0	0	0
AnnotatedPDF	0	0	X	1	0	0	0	0
AnnotationList	0	0	2	X	0	0	0	0
Assessing	0	0	0	0	X	1	0	0
Autocomplete	0	0	0	0	1	X	0	0
BrowserStorage	0	0	0	0	0	0	X	0
BuiltIn	0	0	0	0	0	0	0	X

References

1. Abbas, M., Jongeling, R., Lindskog, C., Enoiu, E.P., Saadatmand, M., Sundmark, D.: Product line adoption in industry: an experience report from the railway domain. In: SPLC (A), pp. 3:1–3:11. ACM (2020). https://doi.org/10.1145/3382025.3414953

2. Altarawy, D., Shahin, H., Mohammed, A., Meng, N.: Lascad: language-agnostic software categorization and similar application detection. J. Syst. Softw. **142**, 21–34 (2018). https://doi.org/10.1016/j.jss.2018.04.018

3. Apel, S., Batory, D.S., Kästner, C., Saake, G.: Feature-Oriented Software Product Lines - Concepts and Implementation. Springer (2013). https://doi.org/10.1007/978-3-642-37521-7

4. Auch, M., Weber, M., Mandl, P., Wolff, C.: Similarity-based analyses on software applications: a systematic literature review. J. Syst. Softw. **168**, 110669 (2020). https://doi.org/10.1016/j.jss.2020.110669

5. Azanza, M., Irastorza, A., Medeiros, R., Díaz, O.: Onboarding in software product lines: Concept maps as welcome guides. In: ICSE (SEET), pp. 122–133. IEEE (2021). https://doi.org/10.1109/ICSE-SEET52601.2021.00022

6. Azanza, M., Montalvillo, L., Díaz, O.: 20 years of industrial experience at SPLC: a systematic mapping study. In: SPLC (A), pp. 172–183. ACM (2021). https://doi.org/10.1145/3461001.3473059

7. Balali, S., Steinmacher, I., Annamalai, U., Sarma, A., Gerosa, M.A.: Newcomers' Barriers. . . Is That All? An Analysis of Mentors' and Newcomers' Barriers in OSS Projects. Computer Supported Cooperative Work (CSCW), 679–714 (2018). https://doi.org/10.1007/s10606-018-9310-8

8. Beuche, D.: Industrial variant management with pure: : variants. In: SPLC (B), pp. 64:1–64:3. ACM (2019). https://doi.org/10.1145/3307630.3342391

9. Britto, R., Cruzes, D.S., Smite, D., Sablis, A.: Onboarding software developers and teams in three globally distributed legacy projects: a multi-case study. J. Softw. Evol. Process. **30**(4) (2018). https://doi.org/10.1002/smr.1921

10. Britto, R., Smite, D., Damm, L., Börstler, J.: Evaluating and strategizing the onboarding of software developers in large-scale globally distributed projects. J. Syst. Softw. **169**, 110699 (2020). https://doi.org/10.1016/j.jss.2020.110699

11. Buchan, J., MacDonell, S.G., Yang, J.: Effective team onboarding in agile software development: techniques and goals. In: ESEM, pp. 1–11. IEEE (2019). https://doi.org/10.1109/ESEM.2019.8870189

12. Cable, D.M., Parsons, C.K.: Socialization tactics and person-organization fit. Pers. Psychol. **54**(1), 1–23 (2001). https://doi.org/10.1111/j.1744-6570.2001.tb00083.x
13. Cañamares, R., Castells, P., Moffat, A.: Offline evaluation options for recommender systems. Inf. Retrieval J. **23**(4), 387–410 (2020). https://doi.org/10.1007/s10791-020-09371-3
14. Clements, P., Northrop, L.: Software Product Lines - Practices and Patterns. Addison-Wesley (2001)
15. Čubranić, D., Murphy, G.C., Singer, J., Booth, K.S.: Hipikat: a project memory for software development. IEEE Trans. Softw. Eng. **31**(6), 446–465 (2005). https://doi.org/10.1109/TSE.2005.71
16. Deissenboeck, F., Pizka, M.: Concise and consistent naming. Softw. Qual. J. **14**(3), 261–282 (2006). https://doi.org/10.1007/s11219-006-9219-1
17. Dominic, J., Houser, J., Steinmacher, I., Ritter, C., Rodeghero, P.: Conversational bot for newcomers onboarding to open source projects. In: ICSE (Workshops), pp. 46–50. ACM (2020). https://doi.org/10.1145/3387940.3391534
18. Fagerholm, F., Guinea, A.S., Münch, J., Borenstein, J.: The role of mentoring and project characteristics for onboarding in open source software projects. In: Proceedings of the 8th ACM/IEEE International Symposium on empirical software engineering and measurement, pp. 1–10 (2014). https://doi.org/10.1145/2652524.2652540
19. Gasparic, M., Janes, A.: What recommendation systems for software engineering recommend: a systematic literature review. J. Syst. Softw. **113**, 101–113 (2016). https://doi.org/10.1016/j.jss.2015.11.036
20. Gregory, P., Strode, D.E., AlQaisi, R., Sharp, H., Barroca, L.: Onboarding: how newcomers integrate into an agile project team. In: Stray, V., Hoda, R., Paasivaara, M., Kruchten, P. (eds.) XP 2020. LNBIP, vol. 383, pp. 20–36. Springer, Cham (2020). https://doi.org/10.1007/978-3-030-49392-9_2
21. Heimburger, L., Buchweitz, L., Gouveia, R., Korn, O.: Gamifying onboarding: how to increase both engagement and integration of new employees. In: Goossens, R.H.M., Murata, A. (eds.) AHFE 2019. AISC, vol. 970, pp. 3–14. Springer, Cham (2020). https://doi.org/10.1007/978-3-030-20145-6_1
22. Ju, A., Sajnani, H., Kelly, S., Herzig, K.: A case study of onboarding in software teams: tasks and strategies. In: ICSE, pp. 613–623. IEEE (2021). https://doi.org/10.1109/ICSE43902.2021.00063
23. Kamali, S.R., Kasaei, S., Lopez-Herrejon, R.E.: Answering the call of the wild?: thoughts on the elusive quest for ecological validity in variability modeling. In: SPLC (B), pp. 81:1–81:8. ACM (2019). https://doi.org/10.1145/3307630.3342400
24. Kuttal, S.K., Chen, X., Wang, Z., Balali, S., Sarma, A.: Visual resume: exploring developers' online contributions for hiring. Inf. Softw. Technol. **138**, 106633 (2021). https://doi.org/10.1016/j.infsof.2021.106633
25. Lops, P., de Gemmis, M., Semeraro, G.: Content-based recommender systems: state of the art and trends. In: Ricci, F., Rokach, L., Shapira, B., Kantor, P.B. (eds.) Recommender Systems Handbook, pp. 73–105. Springer, Boston, MA (2011). https://doi.org/10.1007/978-0-387-85820-3_3
26. Malheiros, Y., Moraes, A., Trindade, C., Meira, S.: A source code recommender system to support newcomers. In: COMPSAC, pp. 19–24. IEEE Computer Society (2012). https://doi.org/10.1109/COMPSAC.2012.11
27. Melo, J., Narcizo, F.B., Hansen, D.W., Brabrand, C., Wasowski, A.: Variability through the eyes of the programmer. In: ICPC, pp. 34–44. IEEE Computer Society (2017). https://doi.org/10.1109/ICPC.2017.34

28. Moe, N.B., Stray, V., Goplen, M.R.: Studying onboarding in distributed software teams: a case study and guidelines. In: EASE, pp. 150–159. ACM (2020). https://doi.org/10.1145/3383219.3383235

29. Ohri, İ, Öge, İ, Orkun, B., Yilmaz, M., Tuzun, E., Clarke, P., O'Connor, R.V.: Adopting augmented reality for the purpose of software development process training and improvement: an exploration. In: Larrucea, X., Santamaria, I., O'Connor, R.V., Messnarz, R. (eds.) EuroSPI 2018. CCIS, vol. 896, pp. 195–206. Springer, Cham (2018). https://doi.org/10.1007/978-3-319-97925-0_16

30. Petersen, K., Wohlin, C.: Context in industrial software engineering research. In: ESEM, pp. 401–404. IEEE Computer Society (2009). https://doi.org/10.1109/ESEM.2009.5316010

31. Pham, R., Kiesling, S., Singer, L., Schneider, K.: Onboarding inexperienced developers: struggles and perceptions regarding automated testing. Software Qual. J. **25**(4), 1239–1268 (2016). https://doi.org/10.1007/s11219-016-9333-7

32. Sharma, G.G., Stol, K.: Exploring onboarding success, organizational fit, and turnover intention of software professionals. J. Syst. Softw. **159** (2020). https://doi.org/10.1016/j.jss.2019.110442

33. Steinmacher, I., Gerosa, M., Conte, T.U., Redmiles, D.F.: Overcoming social barriers when contributing to open source software projects. Computer Supported Cooperative Work (CSCW) (4), 247–290 (2018). https://doi.org/10.1007/s10606-018-9335-z

34. Viviani, G., Murphy, G.C.: Reflections on onboarding practices in mid-sized companies. In: CHASE@ICSE, pp. 83–84. IEEE/ACM (2019). https://doi.org/10.1109/CHASE.2019.00027

35. Wang, J., Sarma, A.: Which bug should I fix: helping new developers onboard a new project. In: CHASE, pp. 76–79. ACM (2011). https://doi.org/10.1145/1984642.1984661

Conceptual Models, Metamodels and Taxonomies

Towards Interoperable Metamodeling Platforms: The Case of Bridging ADOxx and EMF

Dominik Bork[1]([envelope]) [ORCID], Konstantinos Anagnostou[1], and Manuel Wimmer[2] [ORCID]

[1] TU Wien, Business Informatics Group, Vienna, Austria
{dominik.bork,konstantinos.anagnostou}@tuwien.ac.at
[2] Johannes Kepler University Linz, CDL-MINT, Linz, Austria
manuel.wimmer@jku.at

Abstract. Metamodeling platforms are an important cornerstone for building domain-specific modeling languages in an efficient and effective way. Two prominent players in the field are ADOxx and the Eclipse Modeling Framework (EMF) which both provide rich ecosystems on modeling support and related technologies. However, until now, these two worlds live in isolation while there would be several benefits of having a bridge to exchange metamodels and models for different purposes (e.g., reuse of features and plugins that are only available on one platform, access to additional modeler and developer communities). Therefore, in this paper, we propose first steps toward establishing interoperability between ADOxx and EMF. For this, we thoroughly analyze the metamodeling concepts employed by both platforms before proposing a bridge that enables bidirectional exchange of metamodels. We evaluate the bidirectional bridge with several openly available metamodels created with ADOxx and EMF, respectively. Moreover, we quantitatively and qualitatively analyze the bridge by an evaluation that incorporates the instantiation and use of the metamodels on both platforms. We show that the metamodels can be exchanged without information loss and similar modeling experiences with respect to the resulting models can be achieved.

Keywords: Metamodeling · ADOxx · EMF · Language engineering · Tool interoperability

1 Introduction

Modeling languages are ubiquitous in information systems, e.g., consider the different process modeling languages, data modeling languages, or multi-viewpoint enterprise modeling languages to mention just a few prominent examples. Metamodeling platforms are an important cornerstone for building modeling languages in an efficient and effective way [7,8]. Such metamodeling platforms provide dedicated support to specify the modeling concepts and their relationships, i.e., the abstract syntax of the modeling language, as well as dedicated

© Springer Nature Switzerland AG 2022
X. Franch et al. (Eds.): CAiSE 2022, LNCS 13295, pp. 479–497, 2022.
https://doi.org/10.1007/978-3-031-07472-1_28

support to develop the visualization of the models in terms of textual, graphical, or even hybrid languages, i.e., the concrete syntax of the modeling language. In addition, several other technologies, such as transformation engines, simulation frameworks, or code generators are provided based on the common abstraction referred to as the meta-metamodel. Although there are standards for meta-metamodels [8], current metamodeling platforms still use different meta-metamodels based on their particular development history, user base, or targeted use cases for the hosted modeling languages.

Two prominent players in the field are ADOxx [1] and the Eclipse Modeling Framework (EMF) [26] which both provide rich ecosystems on modeling support and related technologies. However, until now, these two worlds live in isolation while there would be several benefits of having a bridge to exchange metamodels and models for different purposes. The main reason for this is that they employ different meta-metamodels. However, thoroughly investigating if these meta-metamodels share similarities is of interest as it would allow to exchange metamodels – and eventually models – between these two worlds by dedicated model transformations [27] and benefit from reuse, particular support offered by a particular platform, and reaching additional users which are operating in the other platform. As such the integration proposed in this paper not only bridges the technological spaces but also the associated modeler and developer communities, it enables the creation of powerful tool-chains that span ADOxx and EMF, and facilitates the mutual strengths while mitigating potential shortcomings.

In this paper, we propose first steps toward establishing interoperability between ADOxx and EMF concerning the abstract syntax of the modeling languages, so to speak the foundation of the languages. For this, we thoroughly analyze the metamodeling concepts employed by both platforms before proposing a bridge that enables bidirectional exchanges of metamodels. We evaluate the bidirectional bridge with several openly available metamodels created with ADOxx and EMF, respectively. Moreover, we quantitatively and qualitatively analyze the bridge by an evaluation that incorporates the instantiation and use of the metamodels on both platforms. Our results show that the metamodels can be exchanged without information loss and also pragmatic issues such as providing the same modeling experiences with respect to the instantiated models can be achieved.

The rest of the paper is structured as follows. The foundations of metamodeling, ADOxx, and EMF are introduced in Sect. 2. Related work on bridging metamodeling platforms is presented in Sect. 3, before Sects. 4 and 5 describe our approach of bridging ADOxx and EMF in detail. Section 6 evaluates our approach based on different characteristics. Finally, we conclude this paper in Sect. 7 and elaborate on future research directions.

2   Foundations

In this section, we provide the foundations for this work: (*i*) the general metamodeling architecture, and (*ii*) the two metamodeling platforms ADOxx and EMF.

2.1   Metamodeling

Metamodeling platforms support the development of modeling tools by providing an abstract meta-metamodel that is adequate even for non-programmers to specify (domain-specific) metamodels – and corresponding modeling tools – by modeling modeling languages, thus metamodeling [16].

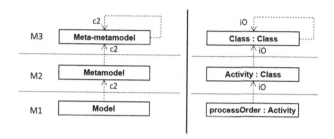

Fig. 1. Metamodeling stack: Macro view (left hand side), Micro view (right hand side)

Figure 1 shows the metamodeling stack on a macro and micro view. Most metamodeling platforms are based on three modeling layers. Let us start with the macro view. M3 – the top layer – is providing the metamodeling language of a platform to define metamodels on M2, i.e., the modeling languages. The models build with these languages are situated on the next lower level M1. The relationships between the different artefacts on the different layers are very important. Between adjacent layers, the upper layer provides the building plan for the lower layer. Thus, we speak about *conforms To* (c2) relationships, i.e., an artefact on layer n is valid with respect to the artefact on layer $n + 1$. Finally, please note that M3 is reflexive in most platforms, i.e., it is defined by itself.

The right hand side of Fig. 1 shows the micro view, i.e., looking inside the artefacts shown in the left hand side of Fig. 1. It shows a basic modeling concept called *Activity* on M2. This concept is modeled as a *class* – a concept provided on M3. Then, the activity concept is instantiated on M1 for defining the activity *processOrder*. Please note that for the micro view, we have *instance-of* (iO) relationships between the elements of different levels.

Furthermore, such platforms provide pre-configured, method agnostic functionality like model management, user management, and user interaction which are attached to abstract and generic meta-metamodel classes thereby considerable contributing to the efficient realization of modeling tools with metamodeling platforms. The language engineer only needs to adapt the platform's meta-metamodel to her domain.

2.2   ADOxx

The ADOxx [1] metamodeling platform matured from industry and is nowadays widely used in academia for the development of modeling tools [7]. ADOxx is focusing on realizing graphical conceptual modeling tools with built-in generic features like graph-based model simulation and support to define model queries that can be easily customized to domain-specific modeling languages (cf. [6]). Moreover, a powerful language to realize static and dynamic graphical concrete syntaxes that go beyond tree structures is provided. ADOxx is open use and provides several extension mechanisms to plug-in or interact with third-party services and tools. In order to realize a new modeling tool with ADOxx, language engineers only need to [4]: (*i*) configure the specific metamodel by referring its concepts to the meta-metamodel concepts of ADOxx, optionally constrained using the platform-specific scripting language AdoScript; (*ii*) provide a visualization for the concepts; (*iii*) combine the concepts into logical chunks, i.e., ADOxx modeltypes; and (*iv*) realize additional model processing functionality such as model transformations or simulations.

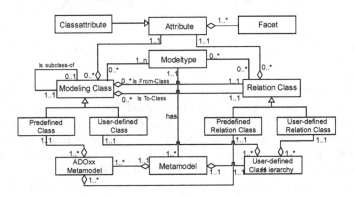

Fig. 2. Excerpt of the ADOxx dynamic meta-metamodel [5]

ADOxx metamodels are composed of *modeltypes* which themselves compose pre-defined and user-defined *modeling classes* and *relation classes* (Fig. 2). Modeling and relation classes may both have attributes. Functionality in ADOxx is inherited from the abstract pre-defined classes of the ADOxx meta-metamodel. The ADOxx metamodel is decomposed into two parts, a static part that features pre-defined abstract classes to represent organizational structures like, departments, actors, and roles, and a dynamic part (visualized in Fig. 3) that features pre-defined abstract classes that enable the realization of graph-based process-like metamodels.

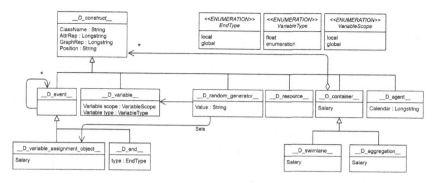

Fig. 3. Excerpt of the ADOxx metamodel

2.3 EMF

The Eclipse Modeling Framework (EMF) provides a meta-metamodel called Ecore[1] which can be considered as the Java-based realization of the Meta-Object Facility (MOF) standard [8]. With Ecore, language developers can define their own modeling languages in terms of metamodels and use different code generators to produce model APIs to load, store, and process models as well as to provide modeling editors. A rich set of extensions and plug-ins are available which build on EMF for different concerns. This is due to the fact that EMF is entirely open source with a large Java developer community.

The Ecore meta-metamodel comes with a plethora of pre-defined meta-classes which originate in MOF but also reflect their refinement for using Java as a code generation target. Relevant for conceptual modeling are particularly the classes visualized in Fig. 4. Ecore-based metamodels are clustered in *EPackages* which compose *EClasses* as complex data types and *EDataTypes* for primitive data types. Every EClass itself is composed of *EStructuralFeatures*. Two special kinds of features are further distinguished: *EReferences* relate two EClass

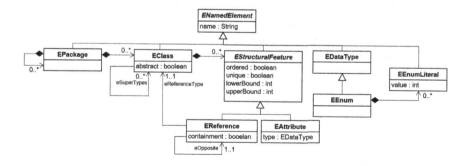

Fig. 4. Excerpt of the Ecore meta-metamodel

---

[1] https://download.eclipse.org/modeling/emf/emf/javadoc/2.9.0/org/eclipse/emf/ecore/package-summary.html.

instances to each other, whereas *EAttributes* define additional intrinsic properties of EClasses. By defining an *eSuperType* relationship between two EClasses, these EClasses are related by means of an inheritance relationship to one another. Please note that in Ecore multiple inheritance is allowed.

An important concept in Ecore is the composition relationship, i.e., an EReference with containment property set to true. By this concept, a corresponding model becomes a primary tree structure which can be exploited in several scenarios. First, it allows deletion propagation, but also other means are provided such as using reflective editors which allow to fold/unfold parts of a model or when building generic transformations which focus on container/containee relationships. Please note that features such as references and attributes can be single valued or multi-valued based on their multiplicities, see the attributes lowerBound and upperBound in the meta-class *EStructuralFeature*.

3   Related Work

Several previous works targeted interoperability concerns for different modeling platform combinations. In the following, we summarize these previous efforts.

Concrete metamodeling platforms have been bridged in the past, especially when it comes to EMF. For instance, the Microsoft DSL Tools have been integrated with EMF in [9]. The bridge is based on model transformations which provides exchange capabilities on the metamodel-level as well as on the model-level. A similar bridge has been presented in [20] and further developed in [18] for achieving model exchange between EMF and ARIS, MetaEdit+, and Visio, respectively. Another work which targeted EMF is presented in [2] for the integration with the Generic Modeling Environment (GME). Bridging metamodeling platforms such as EMF with UML modeling tools has been the subject in [28]. UML profiles are derived to exchange models from EMF to UML and back again with the help of model transformations.

Going beyond concrete metamodeling platforms was first presented and discussed by Bezivin et al. [3]. Their main idea is to introduce technical spaces which provide a dedicated and representative meta-metamodel for a technical space as well as associated meta-modeling architecture and associated tools. This seminal work gave rise to a bunch of work on bridging several concrete technical spaces. When it comes to the modelware technical space, which is the technical space of metamodeling platforms, concrete approaches for providing bridges with Grammarware [29], XMLware [23], JSONware [11], and OntoWare [24] have been presented.

An approach that establish a new meta-layer on top of several existing metamodels in the business process modeling domain is presented by Heidari et al. [15]. The authors generalize and integrate the M2-level concepts of seven business process modeling language by proposing a generic M3-level domain metamodel.

From the perspective of ADOxx, several integrations with third-party tools (e.g., [10]) and concepts for metamodel patterns [21] and method chunks [25] as foundations for integrating heterogeneous metamodels have been proposed. To the best of our knowledge, an integration between ADOxx and other metamodeling platforms has not been discussed or realized in the past.

Synopsis. To the best of our knowledge, there is a lack of approaches which consider the establishment of a bridge between ADOxx and EMF for exchanging metamodels and models between these two popular metamodeling platforms. However, previous interoperability architectures exploiting metamodeling stacks in combination with model transformations is a general solution scheme which is also employed in this paper. Nevertheless, the focus of this work is on the concrete interoperability challenges between the two modeling platforms as is discussed next.

4   Comparative Analysis of ADOxx and EMF Meta-Metamodels

In this paper, we are focusing on the abstract syntax definition exchange between both platforms. Thus, we only consider ADOxx and EMF without additional plug-ins and extensions – we leave these investigations as subject for future work. The comparative analysis in the following thus focuses on a thorough investigation of the meta-metamodels of the two platforms and their underlying metamodeling concepts. As can already be grasped from the introduction of the platform foundations in Sect. 2, ADOxx and EMF share many similarities while they also differ in some details. We now focus our attention to the core of the two platforms, their meta-metamodels and the metamodeling concepts they employ. The thorough analysis that follows is inspired by previous works (cf., e.g., [17]) and the experiences of the authors in realizing modeling tools with ADOxx and EMF.

Table 1 summarizes the findings of our analysis, differentiated along several categories. The table shows, whether and how a particular criteria is supported by the two platforms. In the following, some of the most interesting differences will be highlighted as they establish the major challenges for realizing interoperability – the concepts we developed to address these challenges are discussed in detail in Sect. 5.

Table 1. Comparison of M3 Level features of ADOxx and Ecore meta-metamodels

Criteria	ADOxx	Ecore
Core modeling concepts		
Class	Class	EClass
Relationship	Relation class	EReference
Attribute	Attribute/Class attribute	EAttribute
Classes		
Abstract classes	✓	✓
User-defined root element	✗[1]	✓
Relationships		
Arity	binary[2]	binary
Inverse	✗[3]	✓
Composition	✗[3] (only visual)	✓
Multiplicity	✓	✓
Endpoints	Class	EClass
Unique names	✓ (per Metamodel)	✓ (per Class)
Link to model	✓	✗
Attributes		
Applicable to	Class/Relation class	EClass
multiplicity	single-/multi-valued	single-/multi-valued
Unique	✓	✓
Ordered	✗[3]	✓
Default value	✓	✓
Custom data type	✓[4]	✓
Inheritance		
Single/Multiple	single	multiple
Instantiation	single	single
Class Inheritance	✓	✓
Relationship inheritance	✗	✗
Grouping	ModelTypes	EPackage

[1] every class in ADOxx inherits from a predefined abstract class
[2] n-ary with *Interref*
[3] realization via AdoScript possible
[4] via Record Classes

Composition. In EMF metamodels, composition plays an essential role. Any EMF metamodel needs to have a user-defined root class that contains directly or transitively any other metamodel class. On the ADOxx side, composition is not natively supported. ADOxx features an abstract pre-defined class _D_container_ with additional abstract subclasses (see Fig. 3). These abstract classes feature an automated detection mechanism that recognizes objects that are located geographically *inside* a _D_container_ object. Additional behavior such as cascaded deletion of composite objects is not natively supported.

Single- vs. multiple inheritance. EMF supports multiple inheritance between classes whereas ADOxx supports single inheritance.

Relation Class Uniqueness. Relation classes names in ADOxx are unique whereas for Ecore metamodels, no uniqueness of EReferences names is required as they are contained by the classes, thus having their own name space.

Pre-defined Metamodel. The ADOxx metamodel comprises both, the abstract pre-defined classes and the user-defined classes whereas Ecore metamodels are solely composed of the user-defined classes, i.e., direct instantiations from M3.

5   Metamodel Transformation Approach

For operationalizing the mapping specified in Table 1, we implemented a bi-directional transformation chain. In particular, to achieve bidirectional transformations between ADOxx and EMF metamodels, we realized two unidirectional transformations (see Fig. 5), one transforming an ADOxx metamodel into an equivalent EMF metamodel and one the other way around. Note, that due to specific heterogeneities of the two platforms, roundtrip transformations between ADOxx and EMF will not result in an identical metamodel compared to the initial metamodel the roundtrip started from (see a discussion of selected heterogeneities in the previous section). Our approach therefore aims to achieve equivalence between the source and the target (i.e., transformed) metamodel when being used in the source and target metamodeling platforms, respectively. A detailed discussion on this matter is part of our evaluation in Sect. 6.

5.1   From ADOxx to EMF Metamodels

For transforming ADOxx metamodels into EMF, we first use the XML export functionality provided by ADOxx. The derived XML-based metamodel specification is then parsed and processed in Java using JAXB. Eventually, we use the EMF API to create an equivalent Ecore metamodel and to serialize it into standardized XMI format which enables direct loading into EMF.

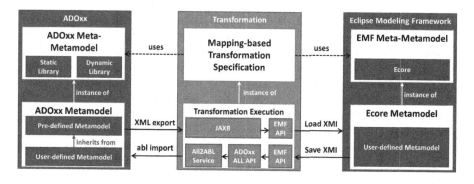

Fig. 5. Technological view on the two unidirectional transformations

Pre-defined metamodel. As mentioned earlier already, ADOxx metamodels are composed of abstract pre-defined classes and user-defined classes. In order to not obscure the EMF metamodel and to enable focus on the user-defined metamodel, we separated the two metamodels into two *EPackages*.

User-defined root class. As any Ecore metamodel needs to have a single, user-defined root class that has no counterpart in ADOxx metamodels, we generate a root class with the name of the ADOxx library the transformation was initiated with.

Enumerations. Enumerations in ADOxx are treated as conventional attributes of modeling and relation classes whereas in Ecore-based metamodels, enumerations are special classes. Consequently, all enumerations in an Ecore-based metamodel also need to have unique names which is not ensured from the ADOxx side, as enumerations attributes only need to have a unique name per class, not per library. We solve this challenge by prefixing the name of a transformed enumerations class in Ecore with the name of the ADOxx class the enumerations attribute originally belongs to.

Java Identifiers. ADOxx allows to use various characters in class and attribute names (e.g., dots and spaces), which are not allowed in Ecore where all names need to follow the naming rules of Java identifiers. We solved this issue by replacing all prohibited characters by either an underscore, or omitting them all together.

5.2   From EMF to ADOxx Metamodels

For transforming EMF metamodels into ADOxx, we first use the standardized XMI serialization. We then use the Java EMF API to process the Ecore-based metamodel and apply the respective transformation rules. To generate the equivalent ADOxx metamodel, we use the *ADOxx ALL API*[2]. Once the generation is concluded, the *ALL2ABL web service*[3] transforms the textual metamodel specification in ALL into an ADOxx application library (.abl) file that can be imported into ADOxx.

Composition. To simulate composition in ADOxx, we generate two AdoScript event handlers for each composition in Ecore. One event handler is executed when a modeler triggered the creation of a new instance of a modeling class (i.e., *AfterCreateModelingNode* event in ADOxx) and one in cases where the modeler has triggered the deletion of a modeling instance (i.e., *BeforeDelete-Instance* event in ADOxx). Aside from the event handlers, the transformation creates a library attribute named *compositeClasses* that stores all class names of composite classes and, for each composite class in Ecore, an attribute *compositumClass* in the ADOxx metamodel. These attributes are used in the event handlers to navigate from composite to compositum and vice versa. Algorithm 1 describes these two event handlers in pseudo code. The first ensures, that each newly created composite needs to be linked to a valid

---

[2] https://www.adoxx.org/live/adoxx-java.
[3] https://www.adoxx.org/live/all2abl-converter-service.

Algorithm 1: AdoScript code for handling composition.

Input: *classid*, *objid*, and *modelid* of the object *o* to be created

1 *ON_EVENT "AfterCreateModelingNode"*
2 compositeClasses ← LibraryMetaData.compositeClasses()
3 **if** *compositeClasses contains classid* **then**
4 | compositumClass ← o.compositumClass()
5 | availableCompositumObjects ← GET_ALL_OBJS_OF_CLASSNAME(modelid, compositumClass)
6 | **if** *availableCompositumObjects.size() > 0* **then**
7 | | selectedCompositumObject ← LISTBOX(availableCompositumObjects).selection()
8 | | ADD_INTERREF(selectedCompositumObject, o)
9 | **else**
10 | | DELETE_OBJ(o)
11 |
12

Input: *classid*, *objid*, and *modelid* of the object *o* to be deleted

13 *ON_EVENT "BeforeDeleteInstance"*
14 compositeClasses ← LibraryMetaData.compositeClasses()
15 compositumClasses ← LibraryMetaData.compositumClasses()
16 **if** *compositumClasses contains classid* **then**
17 | **for** *Composite c : o.composedInstances()* **do**
18 | | DELETE_OBJ(c)
19 | **end**
20 **else if** *compositeClasses contains classid* **then**
21 | compositumClass ← o.compositumClass()
22 | availableCompositumObjects ← GET_ALL_OBJS_OF_CLASSNAME(modelid, compositumClass)
23 | **for** *Compositum com : availableCompositumObjects* **do**
24 | | **if** *com.composedInstances().contains o* **then**
25 | | | REMOVE_INTERREF(com, o)
26 | |
27 | **end**
28

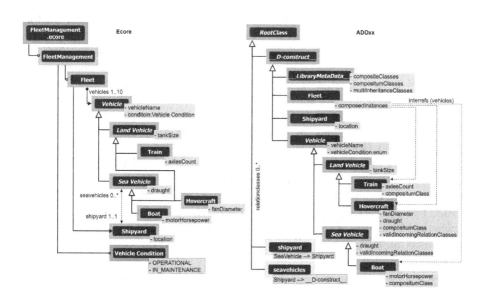

Fig. 6. Illustrative multiple inheritance transformation example: EMF to ADOxx

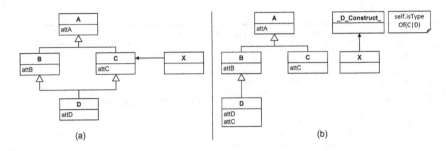

Fig. 7. Multi-inheritance example (a) and the adapted expansion pattern (b)

compositum, whereas the second ensures that the deletion of a compositum is cascaded to all it's composite objects.

Multiple Inheritance. Several approaches have been proposed in the literature to translate multiple inheritance structures into equivalent single inheritance structures (cf. [12,13]). After carefully studying potential solutions, we opted to apply an adapted version of the *expansion pattern* originally proposed by Crespo et al. [12]. Figure 7 visualizes the pattern in detail. Our transformation picks the first superclass to inherit from, the properties of all remaining super classes are then reproduced to ensure that the subclass (class D in Fig. 7) has the same expressiveness as when actually inheriting from multiple classes. Figure 6 summarizes the explained mapping by example. Note that *Vehicle Condition* is an enumeration, *shipyard* and *seavehicles* are relationships.

Additionally, we need to make sure to handle the incoming relationships of the remaining super classes (class C in Fig. 7) as these shall be also valid for the inheriting class D. We decided to solve this by changing the endpoint of the relation class from the specific class (in this case class C) to the abstract super class _D_Construc_ in ADOxx (i.e., now this relation can be incoming to any user-defined class). To restrict the possible endpoints to the valid ones, we further generate an event handler in AdoScript and create a LibraryMetaData *multiInheritanceClasses* attribute in ADOxx that stores the class names of all remaining classes and the inheriting class of multiple inheritance (i.e., the classes C and D in Fig. 7).

Algorithm 2 describes the event handler for realizing multiple inheritance in ADOxx. It is executed when the modeler triggered the creation of a new relation and checks, whether the class name of the *to object* of the newly created relation participates in multiple inheritance. Then, the algorithm checks, whether the relation class is valid to be connected with the *from object* by means of an incoming relation.

Algorithm 2: AdoScript code for handling multiple inheritance.

Input: *classid, relationid, modelid, toObj*, and *fromObj* of the relation r to be created

1 ON_EVENT "*AfterCreateModelingConnector*"
2 multiInheritanceClasses ← LibraryMetaData.multiInheritanceClasses()
3 **if** *multiInheritanceClasses contains classid* **then**
4   validIncomingRelationClasses ← toObj.validIncomingRelationClasses()
5   **if** *!validIncomingRelationClasses contains classid* **then**
6   DELETE_CONNECTOR(r)
7   **end**
8 **end**

Relation class uniqueness. As EReferences only require unique names on class level and not in the entire Ecore metamodel, but Relation Class names in ADOxx are unique in the entire metamodel, we adjusted the transformation in such a way, that the name of the target Relation Class in ADOxx is composed as follows: *<source-classname><EReference-name><target-classname>*.

6 Evaluation

For evaluating our transformation chain, we conducted a set of experiments and applied different means of quantitatively and qualitatively testing the transformation.

6.1 Research Questions and Evaluation Methods

With the evaluation, we aim to respond to the following three major research questions.

RQ1-Metamodel Validity: *Does our transformation produce valid metamodels in the target metamodeling platform?* For testing the validity of the transformed metamodels, we use platform-specific built-in functionality. For validating Ecore metamodels, we first apply the *EMF Validator* and secondly register the metamodel. The ADOxx metamodels are automatically validated once an .abl file is imported.

RQ2-Metamodel Expressivity: *Is the expressivity of the source and target metamodel equivalent?* To test the expressivity equivalence, we imported the transformed metamodels and manually investigated their expressivity on both platforms. We further developed metrics on both platforms that enable the automated evaluation of the metamodel expressivity.

RQ3-Model Processing Equivalence: *Is the behavior of processing a model in the two platforms equivalent?* Here, we instantiated sample models using the source and the target metamodels in their respective platforms. We then applied CRUD operators to see, whether the models adhering to the transformed metamodel in the target platform behave equivalent to the behavior of the model adhering to the source metamodel in the source platform.

6.2   Study Setup

For the study we used 45 ADOxx metamodels, reported in [5], that were transformed into Ecore metamodels. Furthermore, we used 33 randomly selected Ecore metamodels of the ATL zoo[4], to transform them into equivalent ADOxx metamodels. Table 2 provides some descriptive statistics on the metamodels we used in our evaluation experiments. It shows the minimal, median, and maximal number of classes, number of abstract classes, number of classes with multiple inheritance, relationships, attributes, enumerations, and the maximal inheritance depth of the metamodels.

6.3   Results

RQ1-Metamodel Validity. None of the generated metamodels yield errors or warnings when being imported into EMF (see Table 3). The implementation of semantically appropriate procedures for renaming classes and attributes in order to comply to naming conventions, separating various elements into different packages in order to avoid name clashes, have thus been validated. Initial tests pointed us to these issues. Another issue was resolved by ensuring that attributes with the same name are neither defined in the same class nor in one of its super classes.

One remaining issue we observed relates to the data types. In one instance, a certain value of an attribute is too long for the datatype STRING, which is limited to a max length of 3699 symbols in ADOxx. This error occurs in the *AttributeInterRefDomain* facet, which has a non-changeable datatype of STRING. We set this facet for defining all composed instances of a compositum class in order to enable composition on ADOxx side. For one particular library of our experiments, so many composed instances exist, that the generated string is simply too long for this datatype. We already have a workaround in mind but need to test it thoroughly in future experiments.

RQ2-Metamodel Expressivity. We have analyzed the expressivity of a rpresentatice sample of the transformed metamodels by analyzing their structure and their created classes, attributes, and relationships. We found that the mapping of the different elements corresponds to our specification. In some cases, such as in the ADOxx to EMF transformation, we verified that the correct amount of additional Enum-Classes was created and correctly assigned to the appropriate metamodel class. In other cases, we verified that relations are correctly assigned from the source to the target class, as well as their cardinalities are set correctly. Further, in the EMF to ADOxx transformation, we verified that the correct metadata for multiple inheritance and composition is set in the correct classes on ADOxx side.

---

[4] https://www.eclipse.org/atl/atlTransformations/.

RQ3-Model Processing Equivalence. As a final evaluation step, we have created sample models by using the generated metamodels. Here, we could verify that the class creation, attribute value modification, composition features, and multiple inheritance features behave equivalent in both platforms. For the composition part on the ADOxx side, we verified that the transformed event handlers work correctly. For this, we generated compositum and composite elements, then deleted the compositum element, and verified, that all composite instances are deleted as well. For the multiple inheritance transformation on ADOxx side, we checked, that for any class that inherits multiple classes in the Ecore metamodel, the additional attributes from the non-inherited super class are present in the corresponding ADOxx class instance. Additionally, we verified the correct behaviour of our event handler in allowing also incoming relationships from the other multi-inheritance super classes.

Limitations. Our study of course also comes with limitations, some of which will be briefly discussed in the following. First, we need to limit the generalizability of our outcomes. We cannot generalize our results to other metamodels having different structures, sizes, etc. Our experiments incorporated 33 EMF and 45 ADOxx metamodels of different nature (see Table 2 for some statistics), still more experiments need to be conducted to further generalize our findings. Second, our transformations may not be representative or amenable for language engineers who may have other patterns in mind to represent the metamodels in the other platform. We took deliberate decisions, based on the literature and also the experience of the authors working with both platforms, when designing the transformations, esp. for the challenging parts reported on in Sect. 5, still others may prefer to, e.g., follow a different multi-to-single inheritance transformation pattern, etc. Third, some metamodel functionalities provided by ADOxx (e.g., *conversion*) and EMF (e.g., *eOpposite* and *move*) are not considered yet in the transformation as we focus on information loss exchange between the

Table 2. Metrics of the source ADOxx and EMF metamodels used in the experiments

	ADOxx			EMF		
	Min	Med	Max	Min	Med	Max
Classes	5	30	180	1	7	93
Abstract classes	0	2	24	0	1	12
Relations	1	11	81	0	2	59
Compositions	0	2	13	0	2	36
Attributes	2	86	1165	1	6	64
Inheritance depth	1	3	6	0	1	4
Multi inheritance classes	–	–	–	0	0	4
Enumerations	0	17	270	0	0	7

Table 3. Outcomes of the conducted metamodel transformation experiments

Transformation direction	Cases	No errors	Error	Success rate
ADOxx → Ecore	45	45	0	100 %
Ecore → ADOxx	33	32	1	96.97 %

platforms. Future research will investigate how to consider such features in the transformation.

Future Research. In order to mitigate some of the limitations, a detailed analysis at the transformed source and target metamodels will be conducted. Work on this task has started, where we compare different features such as class size, relation size, enumeration size and so forth for each individual source and generated target metamodel. These metrics provide a better understanding of the nature of the different metamodels and were inspired from previous work [5,14, 19,22]. A comparison on the individual metamodel-level will reveal the concrete impacts of a transformation, e.g., how many attributes have been created in the target metamodel from a set of attributes in the source metamodel. General findings about the complexity of the generated metamodels and the performance of the transformation can be found this way.

On the other hand, this procedure can support the validation of the transformation by comparing the different metrics in source and target metamodel to derive conclusions. For instance, since our algorithm transforms Interrefs from an ADOxx source metamodel to relationships in Ecore, we may verify that the total amount of expected relationships in Ecore can be calculated as follows: Given the ADOxx relationships count as $|R_{ado}|$ and the ADOxx Interrefs count $|IR_{ado}|$, the total amount of generated relationships in the target Ecore metamodel $|R_{emf}|$ would need to be $|R_{emf}| = |R_{ado}| + |IR_{ado}|$.

7   Conclusion

In this paper, we have presented a transformation-based framework to exchange metamodels between ADOxx and EMF. We evaluated the resulting bridge by transforming a representative set of metamodels and evaluated the outcomes with respect to validity, expressivity, and modeling equivalence. From a scientific point of view, this work investigated the different concepts provided by ADOxx and EMF. Although, there are several differences, we have also shown that there is a common core which can be used to simulate the missing parts in both worlds. From a practical point of view, this work supports the exchange of metamodels between both platforms which allows for reuse of existing metamodels available only for one platform as well as using a wide variety of tools for the metamodels which are available in both platforms. The bridge is deployed openly and can be used via: http://me.big.tuwien.ac.at/.

The evaluation conforms already a very high level of interoperability enabled by our bridge. The single remaining error is minor and we already have ideas for solving it. Future research will focus on mitigating this remaining issue, drilling down other edge cases that we did not yet encounter, and extending the transformation in two ways. First, we are currently investigating the extent to which the graphical concrete syntax of the metamodel concepts can be transformed between the two platforms. Second, we aim to extend the transformation to be also applicable to models instantiated from the transformed metamodels to allow not only metamodel exchange between the platforms, but model exchange as well.

Acknowledgments. Work partially funded by the Austrian Science Fund (P 30525-N31) and by the Austrian Federal Ministry for Digital and Economic Affairs and the National Foundation for Research, Technology and Development (CDG).

References

1. ADOxx.org: Official homepage of the ADOxx meta-modeling platform (2021). http://adoxx.org, Accessed 27 Mar 2022
2. Bézivin, J., Brunette, C., Chevrel, R., Jouault, F., Kurtev, I.: Bridging the generic modeling environment (GME) and the eclipse modeling framework (EMF). In: Proceedings of the Best Practices for Model Driven Software Development at OOPSLA (2005)
3. Bézivin, J., Devedzic, V., Djuric, D., Favreau, J.M., Gasevic, D., Jouault, F.: An M3-Neutral infrastructure for bridging model engineering and ontology engineering. In: Interoperability of enterprise software and applications, pp. 159–171. Springer, Heidelberg (2006). https://doi.org/10.1007/1-84628-152-0_15
4. Bider, I., Perjons, E., Bork, D.: Towards on-the-fly creation of modeling language jargons. In: Proceedings of the 17th International Conference on ICT in Education, Research and Industrial Applications. CEUR, vol. 3013, pp. 142–157. CEUR-WS.org (2021)
5. Bork, D.: Metamodel-based analysis of domain-specific conceptual modeling methods. In: Buchmann, R.A., Karagiannis, D., Kirikova, M. (eds.) PoEM 2018. LNBIP, vol. 335, pp. 172–187. Springer, Cham (2018). https://doi.org/10.1007/978-3-030-02302-7_11
6. Bork, D., Buchmann, R., Hawryszkiewycz, I., Karagiannis, D., Tantouris, N., Walch, M.: Using conceptual modeling to support innovation challenges in smart cities. In: IEEE 14th International Conference on Smart City, pp. 1317–1324 (2016)
7. Bork, D., Buchmann, R.A., Karagiannis, D., Lee, M., Miron, E.T.: An open platform for modeling method conceptualization: the OMiLAB digital ecosystem. Commun. Assoc. Inf. Syst. **44**, 673–697 (2019)
8. Brambilla, M., Cabot, J., Wimmer, M.: Model-Driven Software Engineering in Practice, 2nd edn. Morgan & Claypool Publishers, San Rafael (2017)
9. Brunelière, H., Cabot, J., Clasen, C., Jouault, F., Bézivin, J.: Towards model driven tool interoperability: bridging eclipse and microsoft modeling tools. In: Kühne, T., Selic, B., Gervais, M.-P., Terrier, F. (eds.) ECMFA 2010. LNCS, vol. 6138, pp. 32–47. Springer, Heidelberg (2010). https://doi.org/10.1007/978-3-642-13595-8_5

10. Buchmann, R.A., Karagiannis, D.: Domain-specific diagrammatic modelling: a source of machine-readable semantics for the Internet of Things. Cluster Comput. **20**(1), 895–908 (2016). https://doi.org/10.1007/s10586-016-0695-1
11. Colantoni, A., Garmendia, A., Berardinelli, L., Wimmer, M., Bräuer, J.: Leveraging model-driven technologies for JSON artefacts: the shipyard case study. In: 24th International Conference on Model Driven Engineering Languages and Systems (MODELS), pp. 250–260. IEEE (2021)
12. Crespo, Y., Marques, J.M., Rodríguez, J.J.: On the translation of multiple inheritance hierarchies into single inheritance hierarchies. In: Proceedings of the Inheritance Workshop at ECOOP, pp. 30–37 (2002)
13. Dao, M., Huchard, M., Rouge, T.L., Pons, A., Villerd, J.: Proposals for multiple to single inheritance transformation. In: MASPEGHI: Managing SPEcialization/Generalization Hierarchies, pp. 21–26. Laboratoire I3S (Rapport de recherche) (2004)
14. Di Rocco, J., Di Ruscio, D., Iovino, L., Pierantonio, A.: Mining metrics for understanding metamodel characteristics. In: Proceedings of the 6th International Workshop on Modeling in Software Engineering (MiSE). ACM (2014)
15. Heidari, F., Loucopoulos, P., Brazier, F.M.T., Barjis, J.: A meta-meta-model for seven business process modeling languages. In: IEEE 15th Conference on Business Informatics (CBI), pp. 216–221. IEEE (2013)
16. Kelly, S., Lyytinen, K., Rossi, M.: MetaEdit+ a fully configurable multi-user and multi-tool CASE and CAME environment. In: Constantopoulos, P., Mylopoulos, J., Vassiliou, Y. (eds.) CAiSE 1996. LNCS, vol. 1080, pp. 1–21. Springer, Heidelberg (1996). https://doi.org/10.1007/3-540-61292-0_1
17. Kern, H.: The interchange of (meta) models between MetaEdit+ and eclipse EMF using M3-level-based bridges. In: Tolvanen, J., Gray, J., Rossi, M., Sprinkle, J. (eds.) 8th Workshop on Domain-Specific Modeling at OOPSLA. ACM (2008)
18. Kern, H.: Model interoperability between meta-modeling environments by using M3-level-based bridges. Ph.D. thesis, Leipzig University, Germany (2016)
19. Kern, H., Hummel, A., Kühne, S.: Towards a comparative analysis of meta-metamodels. In: 11th Workshop on Domain-Specific Modeling at OOPSLA, pp. 7–12. ACM (2011)
20. Kern, H., Kühne, S.: Model interchange between ARIS and eclipse EMF. In: 7th Workshop on Domain-Specific Modeling at OOPSLA, vol. 2007 (2007)
21. Kühn, H., Bayer, F., Junginger, S., Karagiannis, D.: Enterprise model integration. In: Bauknecht, K., Tjoa, A.M., Quirchmayr, G. (eds.) EC-Web 2003. LNCS, vol. 2738, pp. 379–392. Springer, Heidelberg (2003). https://doi.org/10.1007/978-3-540-45229-4_37
22. Langer, P., Mayerhofer, T., Wimmer, M., Kappel, G.: On the usage of UML. In: Fill, H.G., Karagiannis, D., Reimer, U. (eds.) Modellierung 2014, pp. 289–304. GI (2014)
23. Neubauer, P., Bergmayr, A., Mayerhofer, T., Troya, J., Wimmer, M.: XMLText: from XML schema to Xtext. In: Proceedings of the ACM SIGPLAN International Conference on Software Language Engineering (SLE), pp. 71–76. ACM (2015)
24. Parreiras, F.S., Staab, S.: Using ontologies with UML class-based modeling: the TwoUse approach. Data Knowl. Eng. **69**(11), 1194–1207 (2010)
25. Ralyté, J., Backlund, P., Kühn, H., Jeusfeld, M.A.: Method chunks for interoperability. In: Embley, D.W., Olivé, A., Ram, S. (eds.) ER 2006. LNCS, vol. 4215, pp. 339–353. Springer, Heidelberg (2006). https://doi.org/10.1007/11901181_26
26. Steinberg, D., Budinsky, F., Merks, E., Paternostro, M.: EMF: Eclipse Modeling Framework. Addison-Wesley, Boston (2008)

27. Tratt, L.: Model transformations and tool integration. Softw. Syst. Model. **4**(2), 112–122 (2004). https://doi.org/10.1007/s10270-004-0070-1
28. Wimmer, M.: A semi-automatic approach for bridging DSMLs with UML. Int. J. Web Inf. Syst. **5**(3), 372–404 (2009)
29. Wimmer, M., Kramler, G.: Bridging grammarware and modelware. In: Bruel, J.-M. (ed.) MODELS 2005. LNCS, vol. 3844, pp. 159–168. Springer, Heidelberg (2006). https://doi.org/10.1007/11663430_17

Services Engineering and Digitalization

Situation Awareness for Autonomous Vehicles Using Blockchain-Based Service Cooperation

Huong Nguyen$^{(\boxtimes)}$ ⓘ, Tri Nguyen$^{(\boxtimes)}$ ⓘ, Teemu Leppänen ⓘ, Juha Partala ⓘ, and Susanna Pirttikangas ⓘ

ITEE, University of Oulu, Oulu, Finland
{huong.nguyen,tri.nguyen,teemu.leppanen,juha.partala,
susanna.pirttikangas}@oulu.fi

Abstract. Efficient Vehicle-to-Everything enabling cooperation and enhanced decision-making for autonomous vehicles is essential for optimized and safe traffic. Real-time decision-making based on vehicle sensor data, other traffic data, and environmental and contextual data becomes imperative. As a part of such Intelligent Traffic Systems, cooperation between different stakeholders needs to be facilitated rapidly, reliably, and securely. The Internet of Things provides the fabric to connect these stakeholders who share their data, refined information, and provided services with each other. However, these cloud-based systems struggle to meet the real-time requirements for smart traffic due to long distances across networks. Here, edge computing systems bring the data and services into the close proximity of fast-moving vehicles, reducing information delivery latencies and improving privacy as sensitive data is processed locally. To solve the issues of trust and latency in data sharing between these stakeholders, we propose a decentralized framework that enables smart contracts between traffic data producers and consumers based on blockchain. Autonomous vehicles connect to a local edge server, share their data, or use services based on agreements, for which the cooperating edge servers across the system provide a platform. We set up proof-of-concept experiments with Hyperledger Fabric and virtual cars to analyze the system throughput with secure unicast and multicast data transmissions. Our results show that multicast transmissions in such a scenario boost the throughput up to 2.5 times where the data packets of different sizes can be transmitted in less than one second.

Keywords: Vehicle-to-everything · Autonomous vehicles · Situation awareness · Edge computing · Blockchain

1 Introduction

Automatic driving and connected vehicles have specific requirements for high-quality connectivity [24]. Enhancing the autonomous vehicles' performance can

---

H. Nguyen and T. Nguyen—These authors contribute equally.

© Springer Nature Switzerland AG 2022
X. Franch et al. (Eds.): CAiSE 2022, LNCS 13295, pp. 501–516, 2022.
https://doi.org/10.1007/978-3-031-07472-1_29

partly be enabled with a clear situational picture constructed from a large amount of environmental context data generated during a journey. These data, e.g., weather, road condition, and data from traffic situations, needs to be delivered with low latency through secure and reliable connections and computing infrastructure. Autonomous navigation and decision-making rely on different sensory systems whose flawless operation is a key factor. Ensuring the technical robustness, as well as the validity of data are also means towards accountability of systems [10] - developing them are concrete steps on our path towards answering "Who will be responsible in case of an accident?", for example. New efficiency and safety designs can increase the resiliency and security of the whole autonomous vehicle systems of systems.

Notably, the real-time data transmission and Intelligent Transportation System (ITS) service access from autonomous vehicles to the backend Internet-of-Thing (IoT) systems is a significant bottleneck due to mobility and physically long distances across networks [13]. Hence, edge computing as a next-generation IoT platform provides a solution by bringing services, applications, and data into the close proximity of vehicles. In such a decentralized IoT platform, based on local edge servers deployed at a one-hop distance in the (mobile) network infrastructure, data transmission and processing latencies can be significantly reduced and application execution localized. Real-time capabilities for ITS and Vehicle-to-Everything (V2X) systems, in general, are thus improved, for example, related to vehicle sensor data processing and sharing of information between vehicles on the road and access to services by different stakeholders. Moreover, privacy can be enhanced with localized data processing.

As a state-of-the-art technology, blockchain promises the connection among participants in a decentralized environment. To tackle the possible lack of trust among various participants in a decentralized environment, blockchain targets to transparency, immutability, and security and serving as a public distributed database. Trust formation is realised as the confirmed information in blockchain can be witnessed but cannot be modified by anyone [23]. Furthermore, the successful formation of a smart contract system is based on blockchain technology. With the utilization of the blockchain concept for trust generation in a decentralized system, a smart contract platform distributes execution transactions to system participants for autonomous execution. Via blockchain and smart contract, the most recent survey [19] indicates many blockchain's benefits to Internet-of-Vehicles scenarios in ensuring integrity, privacy, fault tolerance, trust, and system connectivity with performance and automation. In regard to the data exchange and management, recent works [12,16,17] gain reliability and security in data exchange among vehicles via the deployment of blockchain by Road Side Units (RSUs) or Local Aggregators (LAs). However, although these approaches proposed potential architectures and reputation schemes for qualified data evaluation, a question about the network infrastructure is still open. Also, these existing works have not evaluated a Proof-of-Concept (PoC) related to blockchain performance. Finally, these studies have not mentioned the interpretation of information exchange in the decision-making improvement of autonomous vehicles.

With the existing questions, the research aims to leverage a permissioned blockchain in the enhancement of vehicles' decision-making ability within the vehicular network, where data storage, exchange, and service access are based on smart contracts as the agreements between service providers' edge servers in the system. The proposal is a trusted platform exchanging information among participants[1] through services deployed on edge servers that consume vehicle's, traffic's, weather's, contextual data to produce information related to situation awareness of the road condition, congestion, incidents, and traffic control. In which, distributed services at the edge platform share their information to build a big picture of the traffic and contextual environment that supports autonomous vehicles in their decision-making as well as enables them to adapt the operations according to the situation awareness in real-time. Furthermore, with the lack of a PoC from previous works, this study proposes a scenario for a blockchain-based information exchange system among virtual vehicles in a specific context, taxi companies' cooperation. We emphasize our contribution to the experiments and simulations that demonstrate the feasibility of our proposed system in the real-world application as a robust and lightweight service delivery for situation awareness among vehicles, with promising low latency in both unicast and multicast transmissions.

The remaining of this paper is organized as: Sect. 2 mentions related works. The proposal and system setup are described at Sect. 3 and Sect. 4, respectively. Section 5 is about the experiments and results. Section 6 concludes the paper through the discussion and future works.

2   Related Work

With the development of ITS, Zhang et al. [28] indicates practical issues for ITS, such as traffic accidents, traffic congestion, and the limitation of land resources. Along with those challenges, a prominent solution considered by [28] is to analyze a large amount of traffic data to form new functions and services in an ITS, for example, the GPS data can support for user behavior prediction. The study therefore envisions the growth of ITS as a data-driven ITS which gathers data as much as possible. Leveraging data for processing in a data-driven ITS, Zhang et al. [28] mentions two major categories, including vision-driven ITS and multisource-driven ITS. In vision-driven ITS, a set of applications includes traffic behavior prediction, traffic object vision related to detection or recognition, and tracking through video sensor. Meanwhile, the multisource-driven ITS consists of sensor data, such as inductive-loop detector, laser radar, and GPS, assist the recognition of environment changes as snow, glare, slippery, and rain. Leveraging traffic information in ITS enables autonomous vehicle systems with efficiency and safety.

---

[1] The terms "participant", "station", "node", and "peer" interchangeably use with the same meaning, while the term "network" and "system" are also interchangeable.

Due to the importance of data in both vision-driven and multisource-driven ITS [28], the evolution of ITS needs a secure, reliable connectivity for data exchange. As the infrastructure for data exchange, an architecture for ITS demands components, including, data generators as vehicles through sensors, edge computing, and data information transmission among stakeholders. To further clarify the gap among the prior literature and how this proposal addresses the problem, hereby, we consider autonomous vehicles in general and the leveraging blockchain in ITS.

Proposed works from the fog and edge layers have been given out to address these latencies [5,8,26]. Among edge, fog, and cloud architectures, the key difference is related to deployment servers and data stores across the platform; as computational power increases in layers towards the cloud, so do the latencies across networks. One of the approaches related to our PoC in solving traffic congestion is [5], which took advantages of YOLOv3 and DeepSORT algorithm to detect the traffic flow based on vehicles surveillance. Recently, Tang et al. [26] have introduced their π-edge system as the first complete and super lightweight edge computing system of an autonomous production vehicle, which was successfully evaluated on Nvidia Jetson to support multiple autonomous driving services while only consuming 11 W of power.

Security is another issue since autonomous vehicles are vulnerable to attacks in many ways. As regards this, [14] mentioned all the possible attack categories and cases that can be happened for driverless vehicles. To be more specified, intrusions may occur to automotive control system, such as ECU [25], driving system components, such as sensors [1,27], and during the vehicle-to-everything communications [4,9]. Besides, outstanding defense approaches in the last decade were also discussed in the paper [11]. According to that, a fused model from CertainLogic and Dempster-Shafer Theory has been introduced by [6] to measure the trust value of each participated vehicle in the system considering On-Board Unit components, GPS data, and safety messages.

Related to this work, [16,17] are attracted from the idea of blockchain-based cryptocurrencies for the construction of coins to encourage the information exchange among vehicles. A blockchain-based incentive announcement network is proposed by [16] utilizing a reputation point for evaluating information and gaining reputation scores from sharing information. Also, study [17] mentions the use of blockchain to build a vehicle sharing system with data coins and energy coins.

Notably, [12] exploited a consortium blockchain for a secure sharing of vehicular data in vehicular edge computing and networks. Edge servers are RSUs that contain and exchange vehicular data in blockchain from vehicles via smart contracts and a reputation scheme for the reliable data source. This work describes the architecture and experiments related to reputation schemes with a dataset but lacks an evaluation of the system's performance. Another point from this study is the utilization of cloud setup and a proof-of-work consensus for a consortium blockchain. Those usages of blockchain in the vehicle system agree that blockchain maintenance is from RSU and LAs or even official public vehicles to verify and validate blockchain operations, such as consensus tasks. By exploiting the cooperation among service transport providers based on blockchain, Nguyen et al. [20] proposed utilization of blockchain to form a Mobility-as-a-Service with trustworthiness.

Despite many studies for autonomous vehicle systems utilizing blockchain in the field, evaluation and PoC for this study are still questions from our perspectives. Also, instead of forming a setup with connectivity among transportation service providers, for example, taxi companies, the existing studies do not detail to clarify infrastructure for the system; these studies utilize the incentive strategies of blockchain to gain attraction and fairness among participants. Recognize this lack of knowledge; this work proposes a blockchain-based situation awareness for autonomous vehicles, constructs a PoC, and evaluates the throughput.

3   Our Proposal: Blockchain-Based Service Cooperation for Autonomous Vehicles

In the context of sharing data with a higher standard of safety, along with the need for cooperation among transport vehicles, we propose a secure, reliable collaborating system that takes advantage of the embedded blockchain technology.

3.1   Blockchain-Based Service Cooperation in a Vehicle System

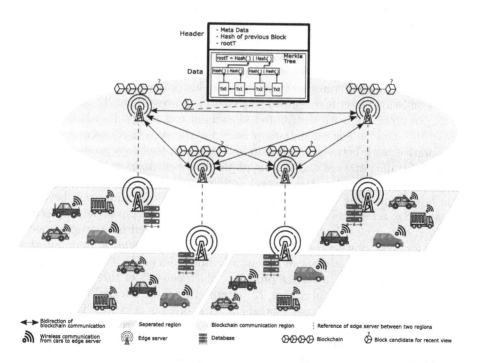

Fig. 1. General system design for the proposal

The proposal is a platform encompassing many types of entities in a transportation scenario to handle the lack of context knowledge from the perspective of autonomous vehicles. As a question for the lack of contextual and situational awareness, autonomous vehicles process an amount of data generated by themselves and require much more environmental and traffic information to produce high-performance decisions. Therefore, forming information exchanges among autonomous vehicles is a crucial deliberation; however, this has an obstruction related to trust in the connection among participants. As a prominent solution for trust construction, a distributed deployment of roadside edge servers maintains a unique blockchain by which the data is distributed and stored at every part of the network.

Basically, blockchain is a chain of data blocks, as the green zone in Fig. 1, where each block contains two main components: header and data. The header is about metadata, including hashing values of the previous block and Merkle tree [18] to guarantee integrity, while the data part is a list of ordered messages as system's data. Moreover, without intermediaries, a blockchain system requires a consensus mechanism to form agreement and validation on blockchain proposals; for example, at the green zone in Fig. 1, four edge servers communicate and validate the block candidate.

Thus, the system provides trust among the participants to access the vehicle data via blockchain's secure, transparent, and immutable sharing mechanism. Moreover, although the system's failure can be from data transmission or even crashed participants, blockchain technology enables the fault tolerance for the system based on a consensus mechanism.

With the distributed data, an edge server at a specific location shares to vehicles within its coverage. Those servers handle computational tasks before emitting recommendations to vehicles in the local environment. As local edge servers facilitate short-range communications, less latency is experienced, and less transmission power is consumed when data is processed locally before transmitting or storing it with distributed blockchain technology. In addition, processing the data on edge maintains privacy for the system. Consequently, the collaborative work between blockchain and edge can lead to a promising, fast, and effective data storage and sharing platform in real-time.

With this perspective, the general architecture proposal encompasses two main layers, including blockchain communication and communication between cars and edge servers as green and yellow zones in Fig. 1, respectively. Referred to Fig. 1, our proposed system provides a blockchain-based infrastructure as a channel for collaborative communication among service providers. In detail, the system separates into an array of regions as yellow sides in Fig. 1. An edge server manages each region as a service provider, which consists of three main tasks: (1) collecting vehicles' information, (2) interpreting from vehicles' information, and (3) maintaining a unique blockchain with other service providers. With the consideration, vehicles at a specific region share captured data related to the contextual environment, for example, road conditions or traffic information, to the edge server of the region via pre-defined smart contracts. Although the contextual environment is vision and multisource data, we primarily focus on vision information through this work. For example, a vehicle can capture images of the surrounding environment and send them to the edge nearby with its identity and GPS as location information. After gathering vehicles' information, the edge server analyses to understand the region's situation and broadcasts the knowledge to other edge servers. Consequently, the information of each yellow region is broadcast to entire edge servers and waits for wrapping and validating into a block as a new confirmed state. Once accepting a new state, edge servers send contextual information and knowledge of the new state to vehicles in their region to enhance the decision-making ability of the vehicles. In other words, the edge servers as a set of service providers maintain a unique blockchain storing vehicles' sensor information and interpreting knowledge of any participants.

An interest for a blockchain-based vehicle system is a wide range of services. These can be deployed with the smart contract concept as a platform that supplies standards and infrastructure through network participation. For example, with a blockchain-based smart contract for insurance, the proposal can provide and construct an insurance system. Once existing accidents, the system automatically collects evidence and sends specs to the insurance company. These shreds of evidence can include the log of the car's speed, the latest image before the incident, the latest car inspection time, or the history of owners.

A blockchain-based system could be a promising solution to the problem of resource distribution. For example, when numerous cars in a zone send their acquired data to the same server, the workload turns heavy, and it becomes bottlenecked while the others are idle. The possible answer for this issue is based on the rank of the received requests, by which the peer forwards tasks with low priority to the neighbors for assistance in offloading. For example, following [7], the definition of high-level data is the knowledge related to emergencies, congestion, drivers' behaviors, vehicles' condition, roads' condition, and neighboring vehicles. Meanwhile, the low-level data is about accurate position, drivers information, and vehicles information.

Whenever data is stored in the blockchain, its correctness needs to be ensured by the validating nodes. Due to such public verifiability requirements, data privacy poses a significant problem for any blockchain application that stores private data. Regarding the storage of vehicular information, one needs to be very careful not to violate the privacy of the drivers and passengers. Therefore, anonymization techniques need to be applied to remove all personally identifiable information. In our system, all information is pseudonymized. Each vehicle is identified by its unique public key and no other identification information is stored. Furthermore, requests from the vehicles to the edge servers need to be encrypted and mutually authenticated in order to prevent eavesdropping and impersonation. For smart contract applications that need to store personal data, zero-knowledge arguments can be used to mitigate privacy issues by showing the correctness of statements without disclosing any other information. There are non-interactive zero-knowledge-based schemes, such as Hawk [15] and Zexe [3], that can be used to protect blockchain-based smart contracts and enable them to encrypt data. For a survey and comparison of such schemes, see for example [22]. Such methods need to be applied together with anonymization techniques to remove any personally identifiable information before data is stored in the system.

Instead of considering the infrastructure providers, the proposal system is a collaborative platform, attracting service providers through their fascination. In collaboration with an array of edge servers, the infrastructure for the system is a question. Thus, the system can cooperate among different organizations, such as transport service providers, to maintain the blockchain. The proposed system is a collaborative channel that permits organizations to provide their infrastructure and define the agreement as supporting services. Also, instead of forming a cluster of vehicles through connecting smart vehicles, the edge server as the central point provides the channel gathering smart vehicles in the locality with robust computation, reliability, and security.

3.2 Proof-of-Concept in Situation Awareness for a Blockchain-Based Taxi Service

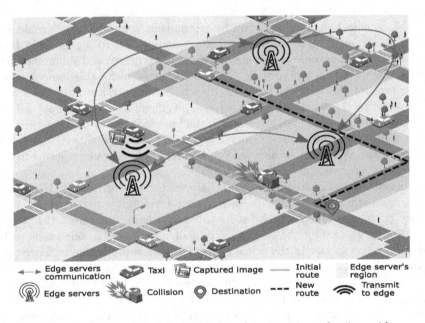

Fig. 2. Proof-of-Concept for blockchain-based taxi service: adaptive guidance

For the PoC, we aim to create a friendly sharing environment for a specific group of targets: the taxi. In particular, our platform encompasses multiple taxi companies as participants to join and share their data. To be more specified, two or more taxis will share their locations and image data to the nearest edge server, which is known as the base station, without concern about which taxi company the server belongs.

According to that, data after being stored in one server will be replicated to others within the network, which belongs to other companies. This broadcasting mechanism enables every car throughout the cooperated network to have the access to all data almost simultaneously and accurately. Cars are also able to be constantly aware of critical factors affecting the transportation process, such as road conditions based on other cars' status. For example, we can know about the current location's situation from the image data, understand the surrounding context, and process the information to detect early congestion or unexpected incidents. Consequently, a pre-defined route to a destination in a car will be automatically changed to another if there is a congestion or any incidents detected. The voice navigation is updated accordingly to guide the drivers to safely switch the route to reach the same target. Shortly, adaptive routing will be an indispensable feature for cars, compatible, easy to integrate with multiple in-car applications. Hence, it becomes beneficial for the drivers to avoid unexpected events and have a smoother road trip towards the ITS.

We present an illustration for the use case of adaptive guidance in Fig. 2. Three edge servers placed in the same-color zones respond to three taxi companies: red, green, and blue. As can be seen, a taxi from the red company has witnessed an accident on its way of travel and later sent the captured image along with the GPS data *(longitude, latitude)* to the base station in its zone *(the green server)*. Meanwhile, another car from the green company, being in the blue zone and trying to reach the destination, will instantly receive an updated message from the blue's server. This car will then change its pre-defined route *(solid turquoise line)* to a new one *(dashed black line)* to avoid accidents and congestion. This process can be done due to the broadcasting from green's server to all the participants, including the blue one, shortly after receiving the captured image from the red car. As a result, all vehicles working within the blue zone will be notified about the collision. Furthermore, the integrated routing application in each car will automatically adjust its route in response to the impact of the occurrence.

4   Blockchain-Based Service Cooperation Setup

The simulation for the blockchain is based on a permissioned blockchain platform called Hyperledger Fabric[2]. As two primary services for Hyperledger Fabric [2], *Peers* are to maintain a unique ledger as blockchain data and smart contract environments. In detail, the peers have two roles, including endorser and committer. The endorser task is to simulate transactions and prevent non-deterministic transactions while committer peers are appending validated transactions. Notice that a peer can act in both roles. With this consideration, the peer from our setup carries both two roles. In contrast, *Orderers* are responsible for arranging endorsed transaction proposals to form a block candidate as the

---

[2] www.hyperledger.org/projects/fabric.

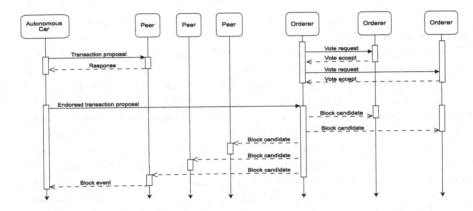

Fig. 3. Diagram for leveraging blockchain into an autonomous car system

consensus operation. Also, as a permissioned blockchain platform, the system leverages a certificate authority to provide certificates to participants as identity; hence, the consensus for the permissioned blockchain is based on traditional aspects, such as Paxos or Raft. Additionally, Fabric proposes a procedure called execute-order-validate that describes a system that first receives requests from clients for handling operators at peers before submitting to orderers to arrange and form a data block. This block is then broadcast to all system's peers for validating at the validation phase before updating the blockchain. As the PoC for the blockchain-based vehicles proposal, a simulation is set up as Fig. 3 with several peers and orderers handling a permissioned blockchain system.

Our system's setup needs to encompass at least three peers and three orderers to simulate a blockchain system that supposes to handle a single failure from a system; meanwhile, the number of autonomous cars can vary. Therefore, if one of the peers or orderers crashes with any issues, the other can alternate the tasks. Regarding the consensus mechanism in our simulation, Raft [21] is deployed on three Orderers to arrange for the chronological order of requests. As a brief description for the setup as Fig. 3, several system's peers, in the beginning, gather information and requests generated by vehicles for executing. After that, these peers return the vehicle's execution results, forming endorsed transaction proposals and sending them to orderers. Finally, the orderers collect those requests and arrange them into a block candidate for the specific consensus round before broadcasting to all system's peers.

With the PoC scenario, a set of smart contracts are deployed as services provided by the system. Following Fig. 4, the system receives requests that update information from the autonomous vehicles. For example, the smart contract's update information includes the sequence of owners, inspection history, GPS, currently connected edge server, and even insurance information. Also, the car captures data related to the surrounding environment for updating the local state to the edge nearby, such as images or information about the congestion, traffics, road conditions, and weather. On the other hand, the request of information

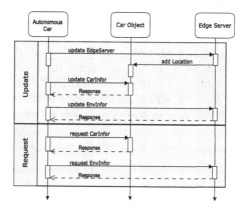

Fig. 4. The sequence diagram of the smart contract in the proposal

consists of two main procedures: revealing the car information and requiring for environmental information. Therefore, the system swiftly reacts to cars' requests; for example, once an accident exists between two vehicles, the accident information can be transmitted to the system that autonomously contacts the insurance of the violating vehicle. Further, if the edge server receives any urgent situations, such as congestions or accidents, the system directly emits notifications to cars nearby.

5 Experiments and Results

The main idea of experiments is to evaluate the throughput of our proposal with a simulation to demonstrate feasibility and practicability. Due to the demand for communications among servers in a decentralized environment, throughput is an important performance indicator. Further, throughput has not been considered in the related work.

5.1 Resource Configuration

The setup for the blockchain network is based on six virtual machines (three for Peers and three for Orderers) as Fig. 3. Those virtual machines are deployed on a physical machine with Intel(R) Core(TM) i7-8700 CPU @ 3.20 GHz, 3.19 GHz, 64-bit OS, x64-based processor, and 32 GB memory through a virtual machine program called Virtual Box Version 5.2.22 r126460 (Qt5.6.2). Meanwhile, the experiments consider three virtual vehicles, for each is set up on a virtual machine with 4 GB memory and 4 cores in processors, as described in Table 1. Virtual machines deploy some Hyperledger Fabric's containers, such as fabric-orderer, fabric-peer, fabric-ca, and fabric-tools, through a docker version 18.09.7. In our particular setting, the edge servers deploy a peer, whereas the virtual vehicles utilize Fabric's tools to interact with peers. The orderer service can be deployed in the same machine with a peer or separated, but we decide the separation. The sizes of multiple microservices are presented in Table 1, especially the fabric-ca' size being 157.9 MB. In particular, peer machines deploy fabric-peer via docker container while fabric-orderer is set up on orderer machines. Moreover, one of the orderer machines maintains a certificate authority for the system via fabric-ca container. Similarly, a peer machine uses fabric-ca to distribute certificates to other peers. Besides, virtual cars utilize fabric-tools to interact with peers and orderers.

Table 1. Detailed resources and containers for system's components

	Resources	Container info	Arch
Orderer	Process: 2, Memory: 2 GB	Fabric-orderer: 2.2.1–38.42 MB	x86_64
Peer	Process: 4, Memory: 6 GB	Fabric-peer: 2.2.1–49.41 MB	x86_64
Virtual car	Process: 4, Memory: 4 GB	Fabric-tools: 2.2.3–513.30 MB	x86_64

5.2 Simulation

As an experiment for throughput of the simulated system, virtual vehicles generate numerous requests to edge servers with results in Table 2. Notice that since we utilize three Peers and three Orderers as the edge servers, the experiments separate into *single* and *multiple* standing for a request sending to one Peer and a request sending to three Peers as unicast and multicast, respectively. Also, the experiment has diverse requests capacity, for example, 16 KiB, 32 KiB, 64 KiB, 100 KiB in each request. By different capacities, each virtual vehicle sends a sequence of 1000 requests to a Peer; hence, with single communication at Table 2, the total requests that the system has to handle are 3000, whereas this figure in multiple communication is 9000. The experiment indicates the number of transactions that the system can process in a second. Especially, *multiple* experiment's results are double as *single*'s, and even gains more 2.5 times than *single* result with the request capacity of 100 KiB.

Another consideration from the throughput is the notification to update the change from the edge server to vehicles. In this case, we deploy an experiment in which the throughput is calculated by the total time from the update request called by a virtual car to another via the confirmation of edge servers. Like the previous setup, this experiment is based on a diversity of capacity, including 16 KiB, 32 KiB, 64 KiB, and 100 KiB for capturing the throughput. In *single*, a virtual car calls 1000 update requests to the system that notifies those changes to another virtual car, whereas, with *multiple*, the system receives multicast transmissions from a virtual car before notifying another. The results in Table 3 indicate the higher capacity leading to the lower amount of transactions that the virtual car can receive in both unicast and multicast. Similar to the aforementioned experiment, the results of *multiple* double the *single*; however, at the requests with 100 KiB, the gap between *single* and *multiple* is smaller than the others.

An interesting observation from two Table 2 and Table 3 indicates the high amount of processed KiB per second with the high capacity carried by transactions. In detail, the increase of capacity that transactions carry is the higher amount of KiB/s; meanwhile, that leads to the lower number of transactions are processed by the system. For example, in *single* part of Table 2, the number of transactions 16 KiB is averagely processed about 1.973 in a second, which regards to a mean of 31.568 KiB/s stored by the system. On the other hand, with transactions higher capacity as 32 KiB, 64 KiB, and 100 KiB, the average amount of data that the system stores is 59.328, 92.928, and 106.126, respectively. At the same time, the number of transactions processed by the system reduces according to the higher capacity carried by transactions; particularly, those are 1.973, 1.854, and 1.061 regarding the transactions' capacities 16 KiB, 32 KiB, 64 KiB, and 100 KiB. This consideration is similar to others, including *single* part of Table 3, *multiple* part of Table 2 and Table 3.

Table 2. The throughput of our proposed system with various capacities of the requests in two types of communication: singe and multiple as unicast and multicast transmission

	Single				Multiple			
Capacity (KiB)	16	32	64	100	16	32	64	100
#transactions/s	1.973	1.854	1.452	1.061	4.637	3.665	2.785	2.559
#KiB/s		31.568	59.328	92.928	106.126	74.192	117.280	178.240	255.907

Table 3. Situation awareness's throughput with various capacities of requests in two types of communication: singe and multiple as unicast and multicast transmission

	Single				Multiple			
Capacity (KiB)	16	32	64	100	16	32	64	100
#transactions/s	1.506	1.328	1.107	0.953	3.271	2.807	2.383	1.538
#KiB/s	24.096	42.496	70.848	95.336	52.336	89.824	152.512	153.851
#s/transaction	0.66	0.75	0.94	1.05	0.31	0.36	0.42	0.65

6   Discussion and Future Works

The paper proposes a blockchain-based vehicle system that supports situation awareness for vehicle decision-making. Interestingly, the system provides a smart contract platform; hence, an array of services for a vehicle system can be deployed in our proposal. By leveraging blockchain technology, the system achieves trust in the collaboration among parties and fault tolerance in a vehicle system. Also, the concept of edge computing is to manage and handle data as close as the data capture, which contributes towards a real-time ITS/V2X system. From this perspective, the proposal is a blockchain-based system encompassing a set of edge servers furnishing real-time decision-making based on situation awareness of vehicles' locality and transparent history.

The experiments evaluate the throughput for the proposal with the unicast and multicast transmission. The results of the experiments indicate the auspicious proposal with the high number of processed transactions per second, especially the multicast transmission obtaining double in comparison with the unicast transmission. Notably, although the number of transactions that the system can handle is less in the transactions' large capacity than transactions having lower capacity, the total amount data in a second (KiB/s) from processed transactions with high capacity is higher. In addition, due to the decentralized environment that broadcasts most information, the numerous participants in both vehicles and edge servers impact the system performance. Especially in the scalability aspect of a decentralized system, like the proposal, a raised question is about ensuring the system's performance with different numbers of participants who synchronize client requests to gain the agreement of validation and confirmation. Therefore, this perspective is a dilemma for decentralized systems. Interestingly, despite the decentralization, blockchain-based service cooperation leverages a permissioned blockchain that inquires participants' permission and separated organizations before becoming a part of the system, which leads to a restriction for exploding the significant number of participants. Further, blockchain-based service cooperation indicates specific services limited to specific organizations can supply.

Since the proposal experiments' components are virtual machines, some gaps connect to realistic deployments. Firstly, virtual cars are stable without movement, especially interchange between two regions. Another gap from the proposal is the limitation of resources from edge servers and virtual cars. Further, although the blockchain setup foundation is on different machines, the setup configuration is a centralized station without detailed consideration of distance connection among edge servers. Therefore, the simulation indicates a reflection of an actual model instead of considering the accurate result for deployment. Besides, a fully autonomous vehicle needs to be liable for any at-fault collisions under existing automobile products liability laws, but its ethical values are still debated.

For a practical application of our system, privacy issues need to be thoroughly investigated. Currently, all vehicles are identified by their pseudonyms and no other identification information is stored. However, it is a significant threat that individuals and their movement patterns could be inferred from the data stored on the blockchain. Therefore, any personally identifiable information and other information that could lead to the identification of individuals needs to be purged from the data before it is stored in the system. Zero-knowledge argument schemes can be applied to encrypt data stored in the smart contracts while simultaneously providing assurances of its correctness. Differential privacy can also be used to prevent the identification of individuals and to anonymize data that cannot be encrypted. However, in this paper, our focus is on the performance of our proposal, and, therefore, such considerations are left for future work.

Acknowledgment. This research is done in a strategic research project *TrustedMaaS* under focus institute Infotech Oulu, University of Oulu, and ECSEL JU FRACTAL (grant 877056). A personal grant by the Nokia foundation for Mr. Tri Nguyen. The researchers operate under Academy of Finland, 6G Flagship (grant 318927).

References

1. Amoozadeh, M., et al.: Security vulnerabilities of connected vehicle streams and their impact on cooperative driving. IEEE Commun. Mag. **53**(6), 126–132 (2015)
2. Androulaki, E., et al.: Hyperledger fabric: a distributed operating system for permissioned blockchains. In: Proceedings of the Thirteenth EuroSys Conference. EuroSys 2018. Association for Computing Machinery, New York (2018)
3. Bowe, S., Chiesa, A., Green, M., Miers, I., Mishra, P., Wu, H.: Zexe: enabling decentralized private computation. In: 2020 IEEE Symposium on Security and Privacy (SP), pp. 947–964 (2020)
4. Checkoway, S., et al.: Comprehensive experimental analyses of automotive attack surfaces. In: 20th USENIX Security Symposium (USENIX Security 2011), San Francisco, CA. USENIX Association, August 2011
5. Chen, C., Liu, B., Wan, S., Qiao, P., Pei, Q.: An edge traffic flow detection scheme based on deep learning in an intelligent transportation system. IEEE Trans. Intell. Transp. Syst. **22**(3), 1840–1852 (2021)
6. Chowdhury, A., Karmakar, G., Kamruzzaman, J., Islam, S.: Trustworthiness of self-driving vehicles for intelligent transportation systems in industry applications. IEEE Trans. Ind. Inform. **17**, 961–970 (2020)
7. Dimitrakopoulos, G., Demestichas, P.: Intelligent transportation systems. IEEE Veh. Technol. Mag. **5**(1), 77–84 (2010)
8. Feroz, B., Mehmood, A., Maryam, H., Zeadally, S., Maple, C., Shah, M.A.: Vehicle-life interaction in fog-enabled smart connected and autonomous vehicles. IEEE Access **9**, 7402–7420 (2021)
9. Foster, I., Prudhomme, A., Koscher, K., Savage, S.: Fast and vulnerable: a story of telematic failures. In: 9th USENIX Workshop on Offensive Technologies (WOOT 2015), Washington, D.C. USENIX Association, August 2015
10. High-Level Expert Group on Artificial Intelligence: Ethics guidelines for trustworthy AI. Technical report, European Commission (2019)
11. Jain, S., et al.: Blockchain and autonomous vehicles: recent advances and future directions. IEEE Access **9**, 130264–130328 (2021)
12. Kang, J., et al.: Blockchain for secure and efficient data sharing in vehicular edge computing and networks. IEEE Internet Things J. **6**(3), 4660–4670 (2019)
13. Khan, M.A., et al.: Robust, resilient and reliable architecture for v2x communications. IEEE Trans. Intell. Transp. Syst. **22**(7), 4414–4430 (2021)
14. Kim, K., Kim, J., Jeong, S., Park, J.H., Kim, H.K.: Cybersecurity for autonomous vehicles: review of attacks and defense. Comput. Secur. **103**, 102150 (2021)
15. Kosba, A., Miller, A., Shi, E., Wen, Z., Papamanthou, C.: Hawk: the blockchain model of cryptography and privacy-preserving smart contracts. In: 2016 IEEE Symposium on Security and Privacy (SP), vol. 00, pp. 839–858, May 2016

16. Li, L., et al.: CreditCoin: a privacy-preserving blockchain-based incentive announcement network for communications of smart vehicles. IEEE Trans. Intell. Transp. Syst. **19**(7), 2204–2220 (2018)

17. Liu, H., Zhang, Y., Yang, T.: Blockchain-enabled security in electric vehicles cloud and edge computing. IEEE Netw. **32**(3), 78–83 (2018)

18. Merkle, R.C.: A digital signature based on a conventional encryption function. In: Pomerance, C. (ed.) CRYPTO 1987. LNCS, vol. 293, pp. 369–378. Springer, Heidelberg (1988). https://doi.org/10.1007/3-540-48184-2_32

19. Mollah, M.B., et al.: Blockchain for the internet of vehicles towards intelligent transportation systems: a survey. IEEE Internet Things J. **8**(6), 4157–4185 (2021)

20. Nguyen, T.H., Partala, J., Pirttikangas, S.: Blockchain-based mobility-as-a-service. In: 2019 28th International Conference on Computer Communication and Networks (ICCCN), pp. 1–6 (2019)

21. Ongaro, D., Ousterhout, J.: In search of an understandable consensus algorithm. In: 2014 USENIX Annual Technical Conference (USENIX ATC 2014), Philadelphia, PA, pp. 305–319. USENIX Association, June 2014

22. Partala, J., Nguyen, T.H., Pirttikangas, S.: Non-interactive zero-knowledge for blockchain: a survey. IEEE Access **8**, 227945–227961 (2020)

23. Queralta, J.P., Westerlund, T.: Blockchain for mobile edge computing: consensus mechanisms and scalability. In: Mukherjee, A., De, D., Ghosh, S.K., Buyya, R. (eds.) Mobile Edge Computing, pp. 333–357. Springer, Cham (2021). https://doi.org/10.1007/978-3-030-69893-5_14

24. Rebbeck, T., Steward, J., Lacour, H.A., Killeen, A., McClure, D., Dunoyer, A.: Final report for 5gaa socio-economic benefits of cellular v2x. Technical report, Analysys Mason Limited (2017)

25. Salfer, M., Schweppe, H., Eckert, C.: Efficient attack forest construction for automotive on-board networks. In: Chow, S.S.M., Camenisch, J., Hui, L.C.K., Yiu, S.M. (eds.) ISC 2014. LNCS, vol. 8783, pp. 442–453. Springer, Cham (2014). https://doi.org/10.1007/978-3-319-13257-0_27

26. Tang, J., Liu, S., Yu, B., Shi, W.: PI-Edge: a low-power edge computing system for real-time autonomous driving services. arXiv preprint arXiv:1901.04978 (2018)

27. Wyglinski, A.M., Huang, X., Padir, T., Lai, L., Eisenbarth, T.R., Venkatasubramanian, K.: Security of autonomous systems employing embedded computing and sensors. IEEE Micro **33**(1), 80–86 (2013)

28. Zhang, J., Wang, F.Y., Wang, K., Lin, W.H., Xu, X., Chen, C.: Data-driven intelligent transportation systems: a survey. IEEE Trans. Intell. Transp. Syst. **12**(4), 1624–1639 (2011)

How Big Service and Internet of Services Drive Business Innovation and Transformation

Haomai Shi⬡, Hanchuan Xu⬡, Xiaofei Xu⬡, and Zhongjie Wang$^{(\boxtimes)}$⬡

School of Software, Harbin Institute of Technology, Harbin 150001, China
shihaomai0109@163.com, {xhc,xiaofei,rainy}@hit.edu.cn

Abstract. The concepts "Big Service" and "Internet of Services (IoS)" arise along with the flourish of Internet-based service paradigm and services computing technologies. Business functionalities belonging to different organizations, regions or domains are encapsulated as *services* and publicized to outside world, and these services are further aggregated by public platforms, then complicated and flexible collaborations among services could be constructed for the fulfillment of personalized customer demands. Big Service and IoS have drastically fostered a new approach for business innovation and transformation of various types of industries. In this paper, we introduce the fundamental concepts and reference architecture of Big Service and IoS, then summarize the corresponding roadmap of business innovation and transformation, and analyze the intrinsic drivers of such roadmap. Referential development and execution environment of Big Service and IoS is presented, along with several candidate technological architecture for companies to adopt in different application scenarios.

Keywords: Big Service · Internet of Services (IoS) · Business innovation · Business transformation · Reference architecture

1 Introduction

With the development of cloud computing, Internet of Things (IoT) and other emerging technologies, people's daily use of the Internet has evolved from initial information sharing to large-scale service consumption. More and more services and resources are provided through the Internet, and the Internet of Services (IoS) [4,16,21] has come into being. Those resources that are available through the Web are registered on specific public platforms, so they can be discovered, tagged, and mixed and matched according to user requirements, and ultimately delivered to users to create value for them [22]. We have entered a service-dominant world, and many innovative service-dominant business models are emerging rapidly and changing industries and societies drastically [8].

To meet the increasingly sophisticated and personalized requirements of users, services from multiple domains and networks are aggregated and interconnected to form a huge complex service network, or called service ecosystem

© Springer Nature Switzerland AG 2022
X. Franch et al. (Eds.): CAiSE 2022, LNCS 13295, pp. 517–532, 2022.
https://doi.org/10.1007/978-3-031-07472-1_30

[5,13,25]. This service ecosystem is named Big Service [32]. In this ecosystem, service providers from different organizations or domains are linked to work together to fulfill large scale and complex user requirements. In this process, new value chains or value networks are constructed to help organizational entities in the service ecosystem capture or develop new market shares and create business value. Compared to the five characteristics of Big Data (Volume, Variety, Velocity, Veracity, Value), the characteristics of Massiveness, Heterogeneity, Complexity, Convergence and Customer focus can effectively respond to the challenges brought by the era of Big Service.

The emergence of IoS and Big Service has led to increased productivity in the service industry, accelerated the servitization of manufacturing, and, most importantly, facilitated industrial convergence. It can be seen that this is a business transformation driven by "user requirements". Traditional business model innovation aims to improve operational efficiency and reduce operating costs by analyzing new requirements put forward by target users, using new information technology tools (such as data mining, artificial intelligence) and other means to discover new knowledge to achieve optimization and improvement of business [1,11]. Under the concept of IoS and Big Service, the new business model innovation unfolds broadly through the following approaches:

(1) Service Publicization. Through service publicization, information about services is available to both end customers and other service providers, promoting the diversification of services on the Internet and gradually form a large service market.
(2) Service Aggregation. The aggregation of services from the same or different fields on the Internet is conducive to exploring new service models.
(3) Service Collaboration. Through the collaboration between services from different fields on the Internet, the existing service value network is reconstructed to form a new value network, which can give rise to a new business model or even a new industry.

The above three business innovation methods are divided into six specific phases, which will be described in detail in Sect. 3. Meanwhile, to accomplish the aggregation and collaboration of services, an operation platform and its development environments are introduced in Sect. 5 for the integration and management of service resources because the interests of multiple service providers. And on this basis, we consider two platform architectures, centralized and distributed, to meet the challenges in different scenarios. For the remainder of this paper, in Sect. 2, we introduce the concepts of IoS and Big Service. The market drivers of the proposed business innovation approaches are described in Sect. 4.

2   Concepts of Big Service and Internet of Services

Internet of Services (IoS) was first proposed by the European Union in 2007 in the 7th Framework Programme (FP7), and together with "Internet by and of

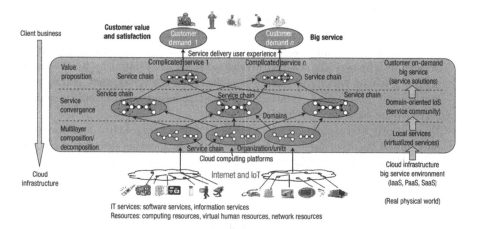

Fig. 1. The reference architecture of Big Service [32].

People" "Internet of Content and Knowledge" and "Internet of Things", constituting the four pillars of the future Internet and networked society [18,22]. IoS is a network space constituted by the collaboration of many service entities in the Internet environment, a complex service networked application form in the Internet. It realizes and provides various business services in the form of integrated services across networks, domains and the cyber-physical world, and it supports service collaboration and transactions among various service participants for realizing various service business functions and achieving the creation and delivery of service values [4].

Big Service refers to the massive complex aggregated services that exist in internet virtual world and real world are formed through cross-network and cross-domain aggregation [32]. It is closely related to the laws of Big Data and various intelligent business services, and is used to solve the problem of Big Data-related business processing and business application in enterprises or society supported by physical information systems, creating service value [23,27]. As shown in Fig. 1, Big Service is a typical hierarchical structure. This structure supports scattered and autonomous Big Service resources to form service ecosystems and networked forms of different granularity through layer-by-layer service aggregation, and ultimately provides each customer with service solutions that meet their individual requirements. The five layers from the bottom to up are: IT infrastructure layer, local services layer, domain-oriented services layer, demand oriented services layer, and the client layer.

The following are specific descriptions of each layer:

(1) IT infrastructure layer. This layer serves as the "interface layer" to connect the "physical world" through the infrastructure, and connects various "services" in the physical world into the Big Service system through terminal devices and local networks to facilitate easy aggregation, virtualization, and standardization of various services and things in the real world.

(2) Local services layer. This layer physically divides the services accessed through the IT infrastructure layer according to organizational or geographical boundaries, forming a "service subnetwork" within each organization or region. The services within the sub-network are related by local service chains, each of which represents a collection of services that collaborate locally and form stable relationships, and together with atomic services, serve as the base services for Big Service.

(3) Domain-oriented services layer. This layer further aggregates and connects all kinds of basic services or service chains in the local services layer according to the industry or domain boundary, forming a wider range of relatively stable service collaboration relationships and realizing the business functions of large-grained services in the field or industry. This is the core resource layer of Big Service.

(4) Demand oriented services layer. This level directly faces the large-scale personalized customer requirements and aggregates services from multiple fields to form complex service solutions across domains, networks and cyber-physical world to maximize customer value.

(5) The client layer. This layer is mainly concerned with the interaction interface between Big Service systems and large scale personalized customers. Various technologies such as intelligent interaction and service requirements engineering are used to properly capture customer requirements and deliver service solutions to customers to achieve optimal customer satisfaction and service value.

Logically, the Big Service ecosystem can be regarded as a "big network" built on top of IoS, but in terms of the realization mechanism, the Big Service is constructed by layer-by-layer iterative aggregation. This layer-by-layer iterative mechanism also provides a layer-by-layer approach for business model innovation and business reconstruction.

3   Big Service and IoS Based Business Innovation and Transformation

3.1   Business Innovation and Transformation

Business model innovation and transformation is an important part of digital innovation and transformation. The earliest business innovation focused on two dimensions of product innovation and process innovation [15]. Later, companies increasingly focus on business model innovation driven by digital technology and complete the integration of digital technology and business processes [34]. On the one hand, manufacturing companies improve survival efficiency based on automated intelligent technologies, and on the other hand, integrate supply chains through big data technologies to meet individual users' personalized needs [14]. Digital transformation is the combined effect of these innovations that change or complement the existing rules of the game within an organization, ecosystem, industry or field [9].

The innovation is an iterative process that broadly consists of three phases: retrieving information about the environment, encouraging new ideas, and learning from mistakes [3]. Driven by demand and technology, companies have explored ways to innovate and transform their business in many ways: (1) Forming a new business model [20] by re-planning and defining the organization's target customers, new customer requirements to be met, value network, core competencies, channels, resource allocation, profit model, etc. (2) Improving service efficiency and reducing service operation costs by applying new information technology (e.g. new technical architecture, distributed computing, cloud computing, mobile computing, embedded software, Internet of Things, blockchain, etc.) to the original business [10,24]. (3) By means of artificial intelligence, data mining, natural language processing, etc., the labor-intensive services are upgraded to knowledge-intensive services [12], and potential knowledge is discovered from the massive service data and used in new services to achieve optimization and improvement for the business.

Gradually, three forms of "innovative products" have emerged in the market. These include the novel digital organizational form, such as ride-hailing platforms, whose emergence has disrupted the business form of the traditional rental industry [9]; the digital institutional building blocks [9], for example, integrating socially recognized payment services in enterprise applications to break the traditional internal innovation [15]; and the infrastructures that go beyond a single organization, for example, blockchain-based distributed platforms that guarantee trusted interactions among multiple participants [14]. Customers formed new value expectations and their satisfaction has been improved, which increases the profits of service providers.

3.2   Roadmap of Big Service/IoS Based Business Innovation and Transformation

The emergence of Big Service and IoS is one of the new driving forces for business innovation and transformation. Based on the Big Service architecture, we summarize the Big Service-based business model innovation and transformation approaches into the following six types, which are shown in Fig. 2. These types are recursive relationships, with the front being the basis for the back.

Phase 1: Servitization of Localized Operations Within the Organization Using the Atomic Service Innovation Model. A variety of typical service innovation models have been developed to address the business characteristics of different service industries. For example, breaking down certain activities from traditional business chains and forming specialized service delivery (service outsourcing [7]), changing certain businesses from a single service provider to a crowd-sourcing service provider using group intelligence [19], transforming certain business activities/products/resources/environments provided offline into Internet-based online service delivery (Everything as a Service [6]), and introducing social, location, sharing, and mobile factors into existing businesses to

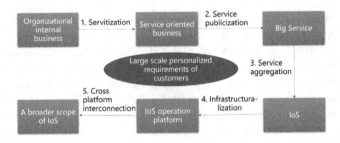

Fig. 2. Business innovation and transformation roadmap based on Big Service.

enhance the resources, capabilities, scope, and precision of service delivery and service use (SoLoMo [33]). These tools are driving more and more aspects of traditional business into the form of services (the so-called "business transformation" or "servitization") [2], which can be in the form of pure software or a combination of online + offline (O2O). This lays the foundation for the formation of Big Service and IoS.

Phase 2: Publicization of Private Mass Services. Publicize services within an enterprise or organization to end customers and other service providers has led to a boom in services in the public market, leading directly to the emergence of "Big Service". Universal Description, Discovery and Integration (UDDI) is a common service description specification for publicizing services to the Internet, and Web Services providers use Web Services Description Language (WSDL) to describe the services they provide, including the protocols and message formats that need to be bound when interacting with other services. Based on the WSDL description, the UDDI registry updates the service catalog and publishes it on the Internet in accordance with the UDDI agreement. In this way, other services can send requests to the registry to obtain the address and service interface information of the Web Services provider to communicate.

Phase 3: The Formation of IoS Under the Massive Service Aggregation. Cooperation between enterprises extends from supply chain based cooperation to service connection based cooperation. Services not originally belonging to the same field are connected together across borders, and the existing service value network is reconstructed to form a new value network, which can give rise to a new business model or even a new industry, leading directly to the emergence of IoS. This service ecosystem is formed through service aggregation, where the types of individuals include atomic services and service symbioses consisting of multiple atomic services that are frequently used together. New business forms are formed through service aggregation within organizations/territories and fields, as well as cross-field service aggregation to gradually cater to user requirements and create value for service providers. This type of innovation is the most dynamic innovation.

Phase 4: The Introduction of IoS Operation Platforms. The massive services publicly released by each enterprise or organization would be difficult and complex to operate and govern entirely on their own. For this reason, a third-party IoS operation platform (i.e., following the BIRIS (Bi-lateral Resource Integration Service Model) [29] innovation model, shown in Sect. 4) is introduced to help enterprises or organizations manage the services provided to the public. In general, such platforms are usually operated by large companies or organizations that dominate in a specific field. In Sect. 5, a detailed description of the operational platform construction methodology for IoS and Big Service scenarios to support the implementation and operation of the BIRIS innovation model is presented.

Phase 5: Cross-operation Platform Service Interconnection Network. Further, considering that a single IoS operation platform is often constrained and limited by geography, business areas and commercial barriers, in order to better meet the increasingly granular requirements of customers, a common trend of innovation and transformation is service interconnection across operation platforms, forming the Internet of Services that aggregates more services, spans a wider range of fields, and has a stronger ability to meet requirement. Blockchain technology provides a guarantee to cope with the trusted delivery of complex distributed platforms, while distributed service solution construction methods, such as distributed service composition, provide technical support for the delivery of cross-operating platform service solutions.

Phase 6: Large-scale Personalization for Individual Customer Requirements. In the traditional service scenarios customer requirement satisfaction is limited by time, space, geography, domain and other aspects, the efficiency of service provision and use is low. It is difficult to find the optimal balance between large-scale generalized service provision (low cost but low customer satisfaction) and highly personalized service provision (high cost but high customer satisfaction). Using the infrastructure created by the Big Service and IoS, the individual requirements of customers can be met in a cost effective manner through customization of the service network.

In contrast to traditional business model innovation and transformation approaches that emphasize "providing holistic solutions to meet overall customer requirements", "using new technologies to improve user experience", and "making business decisions based on data analysis", the approach based on Big Service and IoS emphasizes "servitization", "service interconnection", "solution customization", and "cross-domain innovation", "value-driven", "platform-based" and so on, the customer's requirements can be met to the maximum extent of personalization.

4   Drivers of Service Publicization, Aggregation and Collaboration

The business innovation approaches described in Sect. 3.1 above have all contributed to the development of industry, information and services to some extent. All of these innovative business models revolve around the two drivers of "user requirement" and "digital technology". The business innovation approach based on Big Service and the IoS proposed in Sect. 3.2 is a process of building services through a highly personalized offer built on the specific requirements of different customer segments [15]. Service publicization, aggregation and collaboration are the basis of business innovation and an important part of the layered solution in the Big Service architecture. In fact, the formation of Big Service and IoS is driven by "user requirement", and the purpose is to increase the competitiveness of the services they provide and win more markets.

Given the correlation between user behaviors, the changing requirements of users are mainly reflected in the trend of increasing granularity and personalization, which are often difficult to be met by individual services and often require the integration and collaboration of multiple services, the so-called "one-stop-shop". Big Data and IoS offer the possibility of building "one-stop shop" across multiple domains, networks and the real physical world. Two real-life examples illustrate this trend, for example, one-stop elderly care solution includes monitoring the physical status of the elderly at all times through IoT facilities, providing real-time alerts and assistance in case of accidents, and finding and scheduling services for the elderly that match their preferences, such as home care, insurance, social and travel services. When booking "tourism vacation products" on online service platforms such as Ctrip and Fliggy, each candidate product has already packaged and aggregated air tickets, hotels, classic tickets, car rentals, restaurants and other services, and arranged a reasonable time and route. Users can also personalize them to make them more in line with their personal preferences.

It can be seen that the competition in modern service industry is no longer simply about reducing costs through effective ways and thus gaining competitive advantage, but more about aggregating more services and interconnecting them effectively to form a holistic solution delivered to users for a more advanced experience. We define this service model as BIRIS, which has become one of the mainstream forms of modern service industry at present.

From the perspective of the service provider, the reasons for gaining competitive advantage through service aggregation can be attributed to the following two aspects.

(1) Extension and expansion of the value chain, full-chain solution provision, reducing the cost of user selection and aggregation of services. For example, on the basis of its own Taobao C2C platform, Alibaba B2B platform, Tmall B2C platform, Alipay payment and credit services, Cainiao intelligent logistics services, and Ali cloud computing services, Ali Group has constructed a "manufacturing-marketing-consumption-logistics-payment" e-commerce industry chain, integrating IT, channels, services, marketing, warehousing, logistics

and other aspects of the service, forming a huge ecosystem, providing a one-stop service experience for merchants and customers. Amazon, as an e-commerce giant, started from an online bookstore and gradually expanded its value chain, which has formed three major service lines: a digital product service network built around Kindle, e-books, online publishing, online music and video, intelligent dialogue robots, etc. A physical service network built around B2C services such as paper books, department store goods and fresh food, FBA (Fulfillment by Amazon) warehousing services, supply chain services, transportation services, Amazon Go unmanned stores, etc. The cloud computing service network formed around AWS.

(2) From single-enterprise competition to service ecosystem-based competition, reflecting the "winner-takes-all" principle. After all, the service capacity provided by one enterprise is limited. If multiple enterprises can join together to aggregate each other's services to form a larger granularity of solutions, it will make the overall competitiveness greatly enhanced. Even "giants" such as Ali need to use external forces to build their e-commerce empire, small businesses or start-ups trying to use a single innovative service/product to win the market is becoming increasingly difficult, which reflects the "winner-takes-all" principle. The reason is that service provision in the Internet environment can be expanded from serving small-scale users to serving large-scale users at very low cost, and physical and human resources are no longer key factors affecting competition.

5   Development Environment and Operational Architecture for Big Service

In the six phases of business innovation and transformation based on Big Service and IoS, to accomplish cross-domain and cross-network service solution formation and delivery requires the introduction of a Big Service and IoS operation platform to support the implementation of a series of business innovation and transformation measures (as shown in Phase 4 of Sect. 3.2). In Sect. 5.1, we present the overall architecture of the Big Service and IoS development environment and operational platform, which is equipped to cope with the large granularity of individualized user requirements. In Sect. 5.2, a centralized architecture is introduced to describe the deployment and operation process of the Big Service development environment. At the same time, given the limitations of a single IoS operation platform in terms of geography and coping with commercial barriers, trusted cross-platform service delivery mechanisms are needed to address these challenges (as shown in Phase 5 of Sect. 3.2). In Sects. 5.3 and 5.4, the distributed architecture of Big Service operation platform and the blockchain-based trusted operation guarantee mechanism are described, respectively.

5.1   Overall Architecture

The overall architecture of the Big Service and IoS development environment and operation platform is shown in Fig. 3, which consists of four parts.

(1) Model Driven and Value Aware Big Service Design and Development Environment (SDEnv). It is an integral part of the development environment and provides a set of tools to support the Big Service design and development team to develop and test a collection of operational services, starting from the requirements and value expectations of all parties involved and building the model layer by layer through model-driven and value-aware means.

(2) Bi-Lateral Pattern Development Environment (PDEnv). It is part of the development environment, providing a series of tools to support the requirement pattern and service pattern management in the Big Service development paradigm RE2SEP [31], obtaining historical service requirements from the Big Service solution development environment SSEnv, and carrying out requirement pattern mining accordingly; obtaining historical Big Service solutions and logs formed during the operation of each solution from the Big Service operation platform RPEnv, and carrying out service pattern mining, update and maintain the co-occurrence probability matrices between the two, and manage the service knowledge graph.

(3) Specific Customer Requirement Oriented Big Service Solution Development Environment (SSEnv). It belongs to both development environment and operation platform. Specific users present their personalized requirement in the form of intent tree on the portal, and the environment provides a series of tools to support requirement modeling, requirement recommendation, requirement completion and requirement rewriting based on intent tree and requirement knowledge graph. Based on the Bi-Lateral Pattern information and Incidence Matrices provided by PDEnv, the personalized requirements are precisely matched with the service pattern, and the executable Big Service solution is constructed and released to RPEnv, the Big Service operation platform, and returned to PDEnv for subsequent service pattern update and Incidence Matrices update.

(4) Multiple Architectural Big Service Run-time Platform (RPEnv). The services constructed by SDEnv and the services from external access are integrated into the unified Big Service repository management, and the Big Service solutions from SSEnv are deployed and executed with the support of the distributed cloud service platform, providing infrastructure support for service routing, quality (trustworthiness, security, performance, etc.) assurance, solution dynamic evolution and online modification, and intelligent interaction. Finally, delivery to the user who initially initiated the requirement.

5.2 Centralized Architecture of Big Service Platforms

This subsection introduces the first architecture of the Big Service platform: centralized architecture. As shown in Fig. 4(a), the Big Service platform in this architecture has only one logical operation node (called "Big Service node"). All the functional modules of PDEnv and RPEnv are deployed on this node, and each participant of the Big Service accesses the corresponding functions through the Portal provided by this node to complete the tasks of personalized requirement

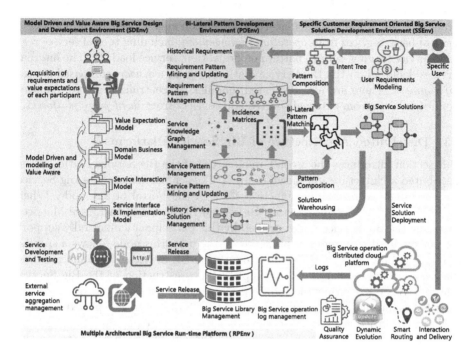

Fig. 3. Development environment and operational architecture of Big Service.

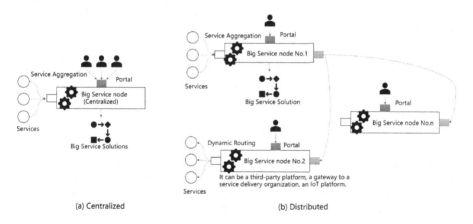

(a) Centralized   (b) Distributed

Fig. 4. Centralized and distributed Big Service platform architecture.

modeling, Bi-Lateral Pattern matching, Big Service solution construction, Big Service solution operation, Big Service delivery and interaction.

The architecture is described in detail as follows: the topmost layer is the *business layer*, and after the Big Service Solution (in the form of BPMN) is constructed according to user requirements, it starts to run with the support of the *execution* engine and carries out scheduling according to the BPMN process structure. The above business layer and execution engine need the support of a series of basic services from *operation management*, including toos of service registry, service logging, service pattern orchestration, service load etc. The internal services deployed on the Big Service platform run in a *Kubernetes-based cluster environment*. There are also dedicated modules for centralized access management of services from external sources and services from *third-party platforms*.

5.3   Distributed Architecture of Big Service Platforms

This section introduces the second architecture of the Big Service Platform: the distributed architecture. As shown in Fig. 4(b), each participant of a Big Service can access the corresponding function through the Portal of any node. When executing each task, if the services, Bi-Lateral Pattern, and Incidence Matrices owned by the Big Service node accessed by this participant cannot fully support the personalized requirements proposed by the user, this node follows a specific protocol to send the request to one or more other Big Service nodes, and multiple Big Service nodes collaborate to complete the construction of the Big Service solution. When executing the solution, the services deployed on this node are regarded as internal services and directly invoked; the services deployed on other nodes are regarded as external services that are connected to this node, and the distributed solution execution is completed through the protocols between the Big Service nodes.

Collaboration among multiple Big Service nodes is achieved through appropriate information exchange as well as resource sharing. Specific functions include:

(1) Big Service node management. Rely on an independent node registry to complete the registration, withdrawal and other management of Big Service nodes, and have the ability to discover Big Service nodes.
(2) Distributed service registration management. Each Big Service node needs to be responsible for service registration in its respective region or organization, and to store relevant information as well as service lifecycle management. It also needs to exchange information with other nodes in the vicinity at regular intervals for service repository synchronization.
(3) Distributed quality of service monitoring. Considering that some business indicators and business logic implementations are closely integrated, the platform uses a combination of logs and fixed protocol interfaces for monitoring. The control center gets the final service quality through the user-defined service quality calculation formula.
(4) Distributed Bi-lateral Pattern matching and Big Service solution construction. Since some of the user requirements and service patterns cannot be realized by deployed services on a single Big Service node, the Big Service node needs to be responsible for pattern identification and management within the region or organization, and also needs to have the ability to maintain the service patterns and requirement patterns across nodes. The information exchange and resource sharing among the nodes ensures the high quality of the final solution.

(5) Distributed service solution execution: The deployment, deletion, and migration of service instances are realized inside the node by integrating container runtime environments (e.g., Kubernetes, Docker Swarm, etc.), and each node implements cross-node service invocation through a fixed interface.

5.4 Blockchain-Based Trustworthy Guarantee for Big Service

Since Big Service operation involves integration of service resources from different fields and organizations. "Trustworthiness" is a performance indicator that must be considered in the Big Service operation platform. The Big Service platform needs to provide users with trustworthy guarantee for the services they access from different providers to avoid fraud in the process of using the services; provide fairness proof for each provider to ensure that the services they provide are treated fairly in the process of constructing the Big Service solution (to ensure that their opportunities to participate in the Big Service solution are only related to their functions and quality); ensure mutual trust between multiple Big Service nodes; guarantee the rationality of evolutionary operations such as the superiority and inferiority of services, and protect the rights and interests of service providers.

Based on the decentralized characteristics of blockchain [17], tamper-evident and information traceable, the trust guarantee system of Big Service is constructed using blockchain to solve the above trust problem. As shown in Fig. 5, in the distributed Big Service platform architecture, on the one hand, the blockchain guarantees the mutual trust of all participants in the construction, operation and maintenance of Big Service solutions, and on the other hand, the blockchain is used as a "connector" to connect multiple Big Service nodes to achieve cross-node data exchange and business.

Supported by the above blockchain architecture, the trusted operating mechanism of the Big service platform includes the following four aspects of detailed design.

(1) Architecture design for a single Big Service node. As the basic unit of the distributed architecture, each Big Service node needs to be connected to a blockchain, and use a combination of on-chain and off-chain storage, information such as service, service pattern, requirement, and Incidence Matrices is reasonably distributed on the blockchain and local nodes. The virtual chain technology is used to achieve fast bookkeeping in the blockchain.

(2) Cross-chain architecture design for cross-node collaboration. Virtual chain technology is used to smoothen the underlying interface inconsistency and protocol inconsistency of different heterogeneous chains, while cross-chain technology of notary group is established, and the function of fast bookkeeping under the chain and synchronization on the chain is accomplished on the basis of virtual chain.

(3) Blockchain architecture design for bilateral pattern matching and solution building. Based on the cross-chain platform in the previous step, multiple distributed matching methods are implemented to realize the generation of

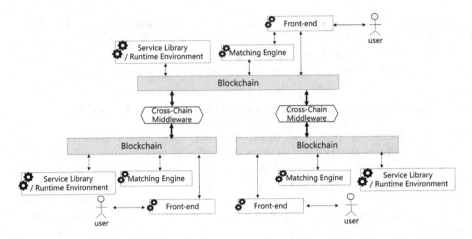

Fig. 5. Blockchain-based distributed big service platform architecture [28].

Big Service solutions from user customized requirements. The Big Service scheme construction adopts two methods of distributed constraint satisfaction and asynchronous backtracking, while combining virtual chain technology for performance optimization.

(4) The Big Service solution as a distributed business process (BPMN form) can be executed in a blockchain-driven manner [30], this step focuses on the generation of smart contracts [26] from Big Service solutions, deployment of smart contracts, and cross-chain execution of Big Service solutions based on smart contracts. The service solution contracts are dispersed across multiple chains in the form of multiple contracts.

6   Conclusions

With more and more services appearing on the Internet and the increasing complexity and personalization of user requirements, IoS and Big Service have emerged. Through the publicization, aggregation and collaboration of services, a transboundary service interconnection network is formed to meet the large-scale personalized requirements of users, and this process promotes the innovation and transformation of business. Considering the resource management needs of multiple participants, we introduce a Big Service platform and its development environments and analyze the centralized architecture, distributed architecture and blockchain-based Big Service architecture to solve challenging issues such as cross-regional and trustworthiness assurance. We do hope this paper would shed light on the research and practice of service-oriented business innovation and transformation in today's service-dominant world.

Acknowledgements. Research in this paper is supported by the National Key Research and Development Program of China (No 2018YFB1402500) and the National Science Foundation of China (61832004, 61832014).

References

1. Akter, S., Michael, K., Uddin, M.R., McCarthy, G., Rahman, M.: Transforming business using digital innovations: the application of AI, blockchain, cloud and data analytics. Ann. Oper. Res. **308**, 7–39 (2022)
2. Baines, T., Bigdeli, A.Z., Sousa, R., Schroeder, A.: Framing the servitization transformation process: a model to understand and facilitate the servitization journey. Int. J. Prod. Econ. **221**, 107463 (2020)
3. Bouwman, H., Nikou, S., de Reuver, M.: Digitalization, business models, and SMEs: how do business model innovation practices improve performance of digitalizing SMEs? Telecommun. Policy **43**(9), 101828 (2019)
4. Cardoso, J., Voigt, K., Winkler, M.: Service engineering for the internet of services. In: Filipe, J., Cordeiro, J. (eds.) ICEIS 2008. LNBIP, vol. 19, pp. 15–27. Springer, Heidelberg (2009). https://doi.org/10.1007/978-3-642-00670-8_2
5. Chandler, J.D., Danatzis, I., Wernicke, C., Akaka, M.A., Reynolds, D.: How does innovation emerge in a service ecosystem? J. Serv. Res. **22**(1), 75–89 (2019)
6. Duan, Y., Fu, G., Zhou, N., Sun, X., Narendra, N.C., Hu, B.: Everything as a service (XaaS) on the cloud: origins, current and future trends. In: 2015 IEEE 8th International Conference on Cloud Computing, pp. 621–628. IEEE (2015)
7. Feng, T., Ren, Z.J., Zhang, F.: Service outsourcing: capacity, quality and correlated costs. Prod. Oper. Manag. **28**(3), 682–699 (2019)
8. Grefen, P.W., Türetken, O.: Design of service-dominant business models for a digital world. In: Dustdar, S., Yu, E., Salinesi, C., Rieu, D., Pant, V. (eds.) CAiSE 2020. LNCS, vol. 12127, pp. 563–565. Springer, Cham (2020). https://doi.org/10.1007/978-3-030-49435-3
9. Hinings, B., Gegenhuber, T., Greenwood, R.: Digital innovation and transformation: an institutional perspective. Inf. Organ. **28**(1), 52–61 (2018)
10. Huang, M.H., Rust, R.T.: Engaged to a robot? The role of AI in service. J. Serv. Res. **24**(1), 30–41 (2021)
11. Keiningham, T., et al.: Customer experience driven business model innovation. J. Bus. Res. **116**, 431–440 (2020)
12. Khatri, N., Baveja, A., Agrawal, N.M., Brown, G.D.: HR and IT capabilities and complementarities in knowledge-intensive services. Int. J. Hum. Resour. Manag. **21**(15), 2889–2909 (2010)
13. Liu, M., Tu, Z., Zhu, Y., Xu, X., Wang, Z., Sheng, Q.Z.: Data correction and evolution analysis of the programmable web service ecosystem. J. Syst. Softw. **182**, 111066 (2021)
14. Liu, Z.: Digital economic technology and innovation. In: Principles of Digital Economics. CE, pp. 13–21. Springer, Singapore (2022). https://doi.org/10.1007/978-981-16-9020-4_2
15. Morabito, V.: Trends and Challenges in Digital Business Innovation. Springer, Cham (2014). https://doi.org/10.1007/978-3-319-04307-4
16. Moreno-Vozmediano, R., Montero, R.S., Llorente, I.M.: Key challenges in cloud computing: enabling the future internet of services. IEEE Internet Comput. **17**(4), 18–25 (2012)

17. Nofer, M., Gomber, P., Hinz, O., Schiereck, D.: Blockchain. Bus. Inf. Syst. Eng. **59**(3), 183–187 (2017)
18. Pan, J., Paul, S., Jain, R.: A survey of the research on future internet architectures. IEEE Commun. Mag. **49**(7), 26–36 (2011)
19. Pedersen, J., et al.: Conceptual foundations of crowdsourcing: a review of is research. In: 2013 46th Hawaii International Conference on System Sciences, pp. 579–588. IEEE (2013)
20. Rachinger, M., Rauter, R., Müller, C., Vorraber, W., Schirgi, E.: Digitalization and its influence on business model innovation. J. Manuf. Technol. Manag. **30**(8), 1143–1160 (2018)
21. Reis, J.Z., Gonçalves, R.F.: The role of internet of services (IoS) on industry 4.0 through the service oriented architecture (SOA). In: Moon, I., Lee, G.M., Park, J., Kiritsis, D., von Cieminski, G. (eds.) APMS 2018. IAICT, vol. 536, pp. 20–26. Springer, Cham (2018). https://doi.org/10.1007/978-3-319-99707-0_3
22. Schroth, C., Janner, T.: Web 2.0 and SOA: converging concepts enabling the internet of services. IT Prof. **9**(3), 36–41 (2007)
23. Sellami, M., Mezni, H., Hacid, M.S.: On the use of big data frameworks for big service composition. J. Netw. Comput. Appl. **166**, 102732 (2020)
24. Sestino, A., Prete, M.I., Piper, L., Guido, G.: Internet of things and big data as enablers for business digitalization strategies. Technovation **98**, 102173 (2020)
25. Sklyar, A., Kowalkowski, C., Tronvoll, B., Sörhammar, D.: Organizing for digital servitization: a service ecosystem perspective. J. Bus. Res. **104**, 450–460 (2019)
26. Szabo, N.: Formalizing and securing relationships on public networks. First Monday **2**(9) (1997). https://firstmonday.org/ojs/index.php/fm/article/download/548/469
27. Taherkordi, A., Eliassen, F., Horn, G.: From IoT big data to IoT big services. In: Proceedings of the Symposium on Applied Computing, pp. 485–491 (2017)
28. Wang, Y., Tu, Z., Bai, Y., Yuan, H., Xu, X., Wang, Z.: A blockchain-based infrastructure for distributed internet of services. In: 2021 IEEE World Congress on Services, pp. 108–114. IEEE (2021)
29. Wang, Z., Xu, X.: Bilateral resource integration service mode for value innovation. Comput. Integr. Manuf. Syst. **15**(11), 2216–2225 (2009)
30. Weber, I., Xu, X., Riveret, R., Governatori, G., Ponomarev, A., Mendling, J.: Untrusted business process monitoring and execution using blockchain. In: La Rosa, M., Loos, P., Pastor, O. (eds.) BPM 2016. LNCS, vol. 9850, pp. 329–347. Springer, Cham (2016). https://doi.org/10.1007/978-3-319-45348-4_19
31. Xu, X., Motta, G., Tu, Z., Xu, H., Wang, Z., Wang, X.: A new paradigm of software service engineering in big data and big service era. Computing **100**(4), 353–368 (2018). https://doi.org/10.1007/s00607-018-0602-0
32. Xu, X., Sheng, Q.Z., Zhang, L.J., Fan, Y., Dustdar, S.: From big data to big service. Computer **48**(7), 80–83 (2015)
33. Yang, H.L., Lin, R.X.: Determinants of the intention to continue use of SoLoMo services: consumption values and the moderating effects of overloads. Comput. Hum. Behav. **73**, 583–595 (2017)
34. Ziyadin, S., Suieubayeva, S., Utegenova, A.: Digital transformation in business. In: Ashmarina, S.I., Vochozka, M., Mantulenko, V.V. (eds.) ISCDTE 2019. LNNS, vol. 84, pp. 408–415. Springer, Cham (2020). https://doi.org/10.1007/978-3-030-27015-5_49

Time-Cost Tradeoffs for Composed Services

Franziska S. Hollauf[ID], Marco Franceschetti[(✉)][ID], and Johann Eder[ID]

Department of Informatics-Systems, Universität Klagenfurt, Klagenfurt, Austria
{franziska.hollauf,marco.franceschetti,johann.eder}@aau.at

Abstract. Time and cost are crucial criteria in Service Level Agreements. Frequently, the time when and how long a service can be provided or used and the cost for utilizing a service are related and hence users are confronted with a trade-off between time and cost. Besides the fundamental direct and indirect proportional relationship between time and cost, composed services might also have more complex non-monotonic relationships. We introduce a novel way of expressing the trade-offs between time and cost in form of TC-Maps as a set of piece-wise linear functions. For calculating the duration, cost and their relation for service compositions, we introduce specific operations used in a bottom-up procedure resulting in an overall TC-Map. The proposed structure allows us to derive the minimum cost of a composed service given a duration limit, or for analyzing possible durations for a provided budget. TC-Maps offer the basis for optimizing the utilization of composed services according to user preferences, resources and objectives.

Keywords: Service Level Agreements · Duration · Cost · Time-cost relation

1 Introduction

Service Level Agreements (SLAs) define what a client can expect from the provider of a service [5]. An SLA includes a definition of the service in terms of scope and quality, in particular, the measures of the qualities. Prominent quality dimensions are temporal properties such as the duration of a service, the date and time a service is provided, etc. [10,11,22]. Service contracts also include the cost of service provision.

Frequently, there are trade-offs between quality and price of a service [28], in particular between the duration and the price of a service offering [9]. Here, we focus on the relationship between time and cost of services, which is important for both service provider and service client [14]. Basically, directly proportional (longer duration - higher cost) and indirectly proportional (shorter duration - lower cost) relations between service duration and cost are considered. Combinations of services with directly and indirectly proportional costs, however, have more complex relationships, as we will discuss in detail below.

© Springer Nature Switzerland AG 2022
X. Franch et al. (Eds.): CAiSE 2022, LNCS 13295, pp. 533–548, 2022.
https://doi.org/10.1007/978-3-031-07472-1_31

Service clients rely on the time-cost relation to adjust the requested qualities to their needs and budgets. In particular, clients should have the possibility to check the cost for a given duration, or which durations are offered for a given budget. Providers compute the time/cost relation for composed services based on the SLAs of all necessary component services to be able to calculate adequate prices for different service levels. It is our ambition to support the representation of time-cost relations, to provide the means for computing time-cost relations for composed services and for business processes and thus contribute to the selection of appropriate quality parameters for clients.

In [14], we introduced a data structure called *time-cost table* for representing the time-cost relations encoding the possible durations of a service and the costs associated to these durations in the form of step functions supporting the frequent pricing model as a set of discrete price levels for different service levels (e.g., different prices for silver, gold, platinum maintenance contracts depending on the maximum reaction time).

While this model was adequate to represent the time-cost trade-offs for a relevant set of service offerings, we observed that the model is not expressive enough in other domains with complex time-cost relations, e.g., with non flat-rate pricing models. Therefore, in this paper, we introduce *TC-Maps* as a representation of the relation between time and cost in the form of piece-wise linear functions. This new representation is strictly more expressive than the previous step functions we used in [14]. The techniques we introduce here are useful for a wider range of application areas than those supported by our prior work. This new data structure, however, requires completely new formal specification and implementation of the necessary operations to compute TC-Maps for combined services.

This research is of course based on the design science paradigm. It addresses a recurring issue in many information systems (Service Level Agreements, service composition, business processes, decision support systems, etc.): to adequately deal with trade-offs between temporal aspects and cost and to develop a generic solution that can be used in the engineering of such systems.

The main contributions of this paper are:

- the definition of TC-Maps for representing time-cost relations for basic and composed services with high expressiveness
- a formal specification of operations on TC-Maps to calculate the time-cost relation of composed services.
- an implementation of these operations to demonstrate the feasibility of the approach.

The remainder of this paper is structured as follows. In Sect. 2, we present a motivating example. In Sect. 3, we introduce the notion of TC-Maps and define basic properties of TC-Maps. In Sect. 4, we propose constructor operators and a procedure for computing TC-Maps for composed services and discuss a prototype implementation of our approach. Section 5 (Related Work) and Sect. 6 (Conclusions) conclude the paper.

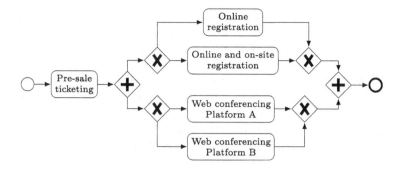

Fig. 1. Example process for a service composition in BPMN.

2   Motivating Example

As a motivating example, let us consider the service composition for the (simplified) process of managing a conference during the COVID-19 pandemic, shown in Fig. 1. The conference is held in hybrid mode, i.e., online with the option of in-presence attendance if allowed by the local restrictions.

The process starts with the use of an online service for ticket pre-sale. Then, the conference takes place. For the duration of the conference, a Web conferencing platform is used to stream the sessions online. We assume that the organizers can choose between two platforms only (A and B in the figure). At the same time, registrations are open. Depending on the local restrictions, over which there is no control from the conference organizers, an in-presence conference with on-site registration may be allowed or not. Therefore, either an online-only ticketing service is used, or a service offering both online and on-site ticketing.

For each of these services, we assume that the cost is known for the different possible durations of service usage. The prices are as follows:

- The pre-sale ticketing service provider offers two flat rates: for a usage duration between 1 and 15 days the cost is 150EUR, between 15 and 30 days the cost is 250EUR.
- The cost for conferencing platform A is as follows: for one day 340EUR; for two days 400EUR; for three days 460EUR; for four days 520EUR; from the fifth day, each additional day (up to 20 days) costs 50EUR.
- The cost for conferencing platform B is as follows: 100EUR per day up to five days; 110EUR per day from the sixth day (up to 20 days).
- The online registration service costs 50EUR per day, up to 10 days; 40EUR per day from the eleventh day on (up to 20 days).
- The online/on-site registration service costs 150EUR for one day; 270EUR for two days; 380EUR for three days; from the fourth day, each additional day (up to 20 days) costs 100EUR.

Now, the conference organizers need to know the relation between the duration of the composed services invocation and the overall cost. Such information is needed for both deciding how to orchestrate the composition and offer the composed service. However, due to the different pricing models and the composition structure involving decisions and observed conditions, it is not trivial to compute such information. Thus, we need to address the following question: *how to determine the time-cost relation for a service composition, given the composition structure and the time-cost relations of its component services in the presence of various pricing models?*

The above example is focused on a cost that has a monetary value, which the service provider strives to minimize. However, here we consider a generalized cost associated to the duration of a service. Examples of such cost generalization are, e.g., energy consumption or CO_2 emissions. For an example, when calculating the time-cost trade-offs between time and cost of driving an electrically powered vehicle a certain distance, the energy cost for the power train is decreasing with the duration (lower speed), while the energy consumption of the AC unit and the headlights are directly proportional to the duration.

In [14], we provided means to represent different time-cost relationships and a bottom-up procedure to calculate the overall time-cost relation for a composed service based on its composition structure and the time-cost relations of its component services. However, our previous work focused on the pricing model of a set of flat rates for services. In mathematical terms, our previous proposed approach can only handle step functions. Here, we aim to extend the approach to other pricing models (in particular "pay-per-use"), like those of all component services except the ticket service of our motivating example. This requires a new representation model for time-cost relationship with a greatly increased expressiveness and new specifications and implementations of the calculation operators on this new data structure. The proposed piece-wise linear relations between time and cost can approximate any other time-cost relations with any necessary precision.

3   TC-Maps for Modeling Time-Cost Relations

This section introduces the composition model for services we use and defines TC-Maps for representing time-cost relations. We make the following assumptions (see also [14]):

1. We aim at computing the time-cost relation for a composition that is given along with the time-cost relations of the component services.
2. The controller of a service can make decisions about service invocations, and in particular choose among different quality characteristics.
3. The controller can choose the service duration.
4. The controller may delay the invocation of a service (which is modelled by wait (or dummy) services without costs).

We do not make any assumptions about the controller's objective function, whether duration is minimized or maximized, etc.: we only assume that for any particular duration the option with the lowest cost is preferred.

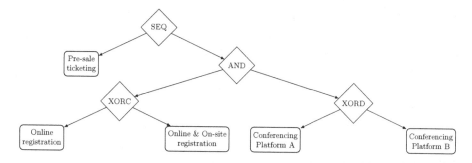

Fig. 2. Composition tree for the composition example in Fig. 1.

3.1 Service Composition Model

Service compositions are represented by a *composition tree*: a binary tree representing the composition of a complex service out of component services with composition constructors. The tree root represents the overall service composition; leaves represent basic services; inner nodes are services composed by applying composition constructors on component services.

Currently, we offer the following constructor types: sequence (SEQ), parallel execution (AND), conditional alternative (XORC), and decisional alternative (XORD). Conditional alternative and decisional alternative differ in how the choice between two alternative sub-services is made: for XORC it depends on the evaluation of an observed condition, while for XORD it depends on the free choice of the composition provider. Hence, at run-time, for XORC only one sub-service is enabled (by the condition evaluation), while for XORD each of the sub-services can be invoked.

Definition 1 (Composition Tree). *Let A be a set of services. A composition tree T is recursively defined as follows:*

- *$a \in A$ is a composition tree*
- *If T_1 and T_2 are composition trees, then*
  $SEQ(T_1, T_2)$, $XORC(T_1, T_2)$ $XORD(T_1, T_2)$, and $AND(T_1, T_2)$
  are composition trees.

Figure 2 shows the composition tree for the example described in Sect. 2 and depicted in Fig. 1.

3.2 TC-Maps

We introduce TC-Maps for expressing time-cost relations as piece-wise linear functions, i.e., as a set of duration intervals with associated costs at the endpoints of the intervals allowing the computation of cost of any duration within an interval by linear interpolation.

Table 1. TC-Map T-I of a service I

d_1	c_1	d_2	c_2
5	30	15	20
15	20	30	5

Table 2. TC-Map T-II of a service II

d_1	c_1	d_2	c_2
10	null	15	null
20	10	30	20
18	15	40	37

Definition 2 (TC-Maps).
A TC-Map is a set of tuples $T = \{\langle d_1, c_1, d_2, c_2 \rangle\}$, where:

- $d_1, d_2 \in \mathbb{R}_0^+$, *with $d_1 < d_2$, represent the two endpoints of a duration interval* $[d_1, d_2)$;
- $c_1, c_2 \in \mathbb{R}_0^+ \cup \{null\}$ *represent the costs associated to the respective interval endpoints.*

Tables 1 and 2 show example TC-Maps. The tuples of the tables are intervals which open on the right side and closes on the left side. So the cost for duration 5 is 30 and the cost for duration 15 is 20. For any duration d with $5 \leq d < 15$ the cost is computed by linear interpolation between the points $(5, 30)$ and $(15, 20)$. A cost of *null* as in Table 2 means that this duration is not available. Including these *null* values is necessary for the definition of functions below.

Various pricing models expressed by partial linear functions can be represented by TC-Maps, in particular also step functions, which are the basis for the time-cost tables in [14]. Partial linear approximation permits the representation of non-linear cost functions with any approximation precision.

With the TC-Map of a service, it is possible to answer questions such as:

1. Which is the minimal cost of the service for a given duration d?
2. Which is the minimal cost, if the duration is between d_1 and d_2 time units, respectively, if it is at most d_2 time units?
3. Which durations are offered within a given budget?
4. Which is the optimal duration, if a duration unit saved is worth 2 cost units?

Answering such questions allows for optimizations with respect to temporal and budgetary constraints, objective functions on durations and costs, and further, allows to properly select services. In this paper, however, we focus on the computation rather than on the exploitation of TC-Maps.

3.3   Properties of TC-Maps

Here, we formalize properties of TC-Maps that will be useful for defining TC-Map operations.

The *gradient* of a tuple of a TC-Map represents the trend of the cost between the interval endpoints.

Definition 3 (Gradient of a Tuple).
Let $t = \langle d_1, c_1, d_2, c_2 \rangle$ be a tuple of a TC-Map. The gradient g_t of t is

$$g_t = \frac{c_2 - c_1}{d_2 - d_1}.$$

For example, the gradient for the first tuple of the TC-Map represented in Table 1 is -1. With the gradient, one can determine the cost associated to any particular duration within the corresponding interval by linear interpolation. Considering again Table 1, one can see that for a duration of 10 the cost is 25.

We call two tuples of a TC-Map T *joinable*, if one of their duration intervals is directly consecutive to the other, and they have the same gradient:

Definition 4 (Joinable Tuples).
Given two tuples $t = \langle d_1, c_1, d_2, c_2 \rangle$, $t' = \langle d'_1, c'_1, d'_2, c'_2 \rangle$ in a TC-Map T, let g_t and $g_{t'}$ be the respective gradients. We call t and t' joinable iff either

$$\begin{cases} d_1 < d'_1 \rightarrow d_2 = d'_1 \wedge c_2 = c'_1 \text{ or} \\ d_1 > d'_1 \rightarrow d'_2 = d_1 \wedge c'_2 = c_1 \end{cases}$$

is true, and $g_t = g_{t'}$.

If two tuples are joinable, they can be joined into a single tuple composed of the non-overlapping endpoints and the corresponding cost values. For instance, the tuples $\langle 5, 1, 10, 4 \rangle$ and $\langle 10, 4, 20, 10 \rangle$ are joinable into the tuple $\langle 5, 1, 20, 10 \rangle$.

We call the right-open interval from the smallest endpoint to the greatest endpoint over all tuples of a TC-Map the *range* of the TC-Map:

Definition 5 (Range of a TC-Map).
Given a TC-Map T, let $d_{min} = min(\{d_1 | \langle d_1, c_1, d_2, c_2 \rangle \in T\})$ and let $d_{max} = max(\{d_2 | \langle d_1, c_1, d_2, c_2 \rangle \in T\})$. The range of T is $r_T = [d_{min}, d_{max})$.

For example, the range of the TC-Map depicted in Table 1 is [5,30); for the TC-Map in Table 2 it is [10,40).

If there are no gaps between the duration intervals, we call the TC-Map *dense*. An example for a dense TC-Map is presented by Table 1, while an example for a non-dense TC-Map is shown in Table 2.

Definition 6 (Dense TC-Map).
Given a TC-Map T, let $r_T = [a, z)$ be the range of T. We call T dense iff $\forall a \leq x < z \, \exists t = \langle d_1, c_1, d_2, c_2 \rangle \in T$ with $d_1 \leq x < d_2$.

A TC-Map T is *functional* if each of the values within the range r_T is included in at most one duration interval, i.e., the intervals from the tuples in T are non-overlapping. For an example, the TC-Map in Table 1 is functional, while the TC-Map in Table 2 has overlapping duration intervals, hence is non-functional.

Definition 7 (Functional TC-Map).
Given a TC-Map T, we call T functional iff
$\forall t = \langle d_1, c_1, d_2, c_2 \rangle \in T \, \nexists t' = \langle d'_1, c'_1, d'_2, c'_2 \rangle \in T \setminus \{t\}$ such that $d'_1 \leq d_1 < d'_2$.

Given the definitions of basic TC-Maps properties, we can now define how to compute TC-Maps for service compositions.

4   Computing TC-Maps

The representation of the time-cost relation of (basic) services in form of TC-Maps calls for procedures to compute TC-Maps for composed services. Here, we give a formal specification of all the necessary operations and functions. We then show how to combine these operators into a procedure to compute the TC-Map for a service composition. Most of the operators have already been introduced in [14], but the different data structure required completely new and more complex specifications. These formal specifications do not lead directly to efficient implementations but are useful for checking the correctness of implementations.

4.1   Basic Operations

We first present basic operations that are essential for defining the TC-Map constructor operations. We start with the addition of cost values and the selection of minimum and maximum cost values from cost sets, also handling *null* cost values representing impossible durations.

Definition 8 (Addition of Cost Values of TC-Maps).
Let c and c' be cost values. The addition $c + c'$ of c and c' is defined as $c + c'$ if both $c, c' \neq null$, and null otherwise.

Definition 9 (Min and Max of a Set of Cost Values).
Let C be a set of cost values. $min(C)$ and $max(C)$ are defined as:

$$min(\emptyset) = null, \; min(C) = min(\{c \in C | c \neq null\}).$$
$$null \in C \vee C = \emptyset \to max(C) = null; \; otherwise \; max(C) = max(\{c \in C\}).$$

For an example of addition: $50 + null = null$, whereas $50 + 30 = 80$. For an example of min and max: $min(\{null, 30, 40, 70\}) = 30$, $max(\{null, 12, 24\}) = null$.

We define the selection of the set of all duration interval endpoints of a TC-Map, called *point set*, as follows:

Definition 10 (Point Set Selection).
Let T be a TC-Map. The point set $\pi(T)$ of T is

$$\pi(T) = \{d | \langle d, c_1, d_2, c_2 \rangle \in T \vee \langle d'_1, c'_1, d, c'_2 \rangle \in T\}.$$

The point set for the TC-Map in Table 2 is $\{10, 15, 18, 20, 30, 40\}$. Given a set of duration endpoints, like a point set, the *interval set construction* creates a dense set of duration intervals for a dense TC-Map:

Definition 11 (Interval Set Construction).
Let D be a set of durations. The interval set $I(D)$ is defined as:

$$I(D) = \{(d, d') | d \in D \setminus \{max(D)\}, d' = min(\{d'' \in D | d'' > d\})\}.$$

Continuing the above example, for $D = \{10, 15, 18, 20, 30, 40\}$, the corresponding interval set is $I(D) = \{(10, 15), (15, 18), (18, 20), (20, 30), (30, 40)\}$.

We define functions to select the minimum, resp. maximum cost associated with a given duration in a TC-Map. σ_0 selects the cost of a duration within a TC-Map tuple by linear interpolation. $\sigma_1(d, T)$ selects the cost of duration d in the TC-Map T, while $\sigma_2(d, T)$ selects the cost "up to d", i.e., the cost of the endpoint of an interval ending in d. This distinction is necessary to care for non continuous functions. Example: $\sigma_1(30, \text{T-II}) = 27$, while $\sigma_2(30, \text{T-II}) = 20$.

Definition 12 (Cost Selection).
Given a functional TC-Map T, let d be a duration in T and let $\langle d_1, c_1, d_2, c_2 \rangle \in T$.
$\sigma_0(d, \langle d_1, c_1, d_2, c_2 \rangle) = c_1 + (c_2 - c_1)/(d_2 - d_1) * (d - d_1)$ *if* $d_1 \leq d < d_2$*, null else.*
$\sigma_1(d, T) = min(\{\sigma_0(d, \langle d_1, c_1, d_2, c_2 \rangle) | \exists \langle d_1, c_1, d_2, c_2 \rangle \in T\})$.
$\sigma_2(d, T) = min(\{c | \exists \langle d_1, c_1, d_2, c_2 \rangle \in T, \ d_1 < d \leq d_2, \ c = c_1 + (c_2 - c_1)/(d_2 - d_1) * (d - d_1)\})$.
$\Sigma_1(d, T) = max(\{\sigma_0(d, \langle d_1, c_1, d_2, c_2 \rangle) | \exists \langle d_1, c_1, d_2, c_2 \rangle \in T\})$.
$\Sigma_2(d, T) = max(\{c | \exists \langle d_1, c_1, d_2, c_2 \rangle \in T, \ d_1 < d \leq d_2, \ c = c_1 + (c_2 - c_1)/(d_2 - d_1) * (d - d_1)\})$.

We now define operations to make a TC-Map functional and of minimal size. The *compression* operation transforms any TC-Map T into a dense functional TC-Map. If duration intervals overlap, the smallest cost is selected. The compression has to partition the range of T in a set of non-overlapping duration intervals representing non-intersecting piece-wise linear functions.

First, we formalize a support operation for retrieving all intersection points of tuples in a TC-Map.

Definition 13 (Intersection Points).
Let T be a TC-Map. The set of intersection points $\Psi(T)$ is defined as $\Psi(T) = \{d | \exists t = \langle d_1, c_1, d_2, c_2 \rangle, t' = \langle d_1', c_1', d_2', c_2' \rangle \in T : d_1 \leq d_1' < d_2, \ max(d_1, d_1') \leq d \leq min(d_2, d_2') : \sigma_0(d, \langle d_1, c_1, d_2, c_2 \rangle) = \sigma_0(d, \langle d_1', c_1', d_2', c_2' \rangle) \wedge g_t \neq g_t' \}$.

Definition 14 (Compression).
Let T be a TC-Map. The compression of T is $\Phi(T) = \{\langle d_1, c_1, d_2, c_2 \rangle | (d_1, d_2) \in I(\pi(T) \cup \Psi(T)), c_1 = \sigma_1(d_1, T)), c_2 = \sigma_2(d_2, T))\}$.

The *normalization* operation minimizes the number of tuples in any functional TC-Map. It combines joinable tuples, and deletes tuples with cost value *null*, since these correspond to durations that are not admissible.

Definition 15 (Normalization).
Let T be a functional TC-Map. The normalization $\Upsilon(T)$ of T is
$\Upsilon(T) = \{\langle d_1, c_1, d_2, c_2 \rangle \mid \langle d_1, c_1, d_2, c_2 \rangle \in T : c_1, c_2 \neq null, \ \forall \langle d_1', c_1', d_2', c_2' \rangle \in T : d_1' < d_1 : \exists \ d_1' \leq d_1'' \leq d_1 : (d_1, c_1) \neq (d_2'', c_2'') \vee (c_2 - c_1)/(d_2 - d_1) \neq (c_2'' - c_1'')/(d_2'' - d_1'')$ *and* $\forall \langle t_1, z_1, t_2, z_2 \rangle \in T : d_2 \leq t_2 : \exists \ d_2 \leq t_2' < t_2 : (d_2, c_2) \neq (t_1', z_1') \vee (c_2 - c_1)/(d_2 - d_1) \neq (z_2' - z_1')/(t_2' - t_1')\}$.

Now we have all the ingredients to define the constructor operations allowing us to compute TC-Maps resulting from the composition of other TC-Maps.

Table 3. Compression and normalization of service

Service							Compression						Normalization			
d1	c1	d2	c2	||	d1	c1	d2	c2	||	d1	c1	d2	c2
7	55	9	55				7	15	9	15				7	15	16	15
7	40	14	40				9	15	14	15							
7	15	9	15				14	15	16	15							
9	15	16	15														

4.2 Constructor Operators

Constructor operators are binary operations for the composition of the TC-Maps of two services, which are connected by one of the service constructors SEQ, AND, XORC, and XORD.

Sequence: Consider two services executed in sequence. For the TC-Map of a sequence, the combination of two table entries is based on the following observations: (1) the minimum duration is $d_1 + d_1'$ when both are at their minimum duration with cost $c_1 + c_1'$, (2) the maximum duration is $d_2 + d_2'$ with cost $c_2 + c_2'$. The increase in cost for an increase in duration is always smaller when the duration of the activity (tuple) with the lower gradient of the tuple is increased (lower marginal cost). Therefore, for the tuple for the sequence, first, the duration of the tuple with the lower gradient is increased, and then the duration of the tuple with the greater gradient. This leads to two tuples as defined below.

Definition 16 (Concat).
*Let A and B be TC-Maps in a sequence, and let $a = \langle d_1, c_1, d_2, c_2 \rangle \in A, b = \langle d_1', c_1', d_2', c_2' \rangle \in B$ be respective TC-Map entries with gradients g_a, resp. g_b.
If $g_a < g_b$ then the concatenation $a||b$ of a and b is:*
$$a||b = \{\langle d_1 + d_1', c_1 + c_1', d_2 + d_1', c_2 + c_1'\rangle, \langle d_2 + d_1', c_2 + c_1', d_2 + d_2', c_2 + c_2'\rangle\},$$
otherwise:
$$a||b = \{\langle d_1 + d_1', c_1 + c_1', d_1 + d_2', c_1 + c_2'\rangle, \langle d_1 + d_2', c_1 + c_2', d_2 + d_2', c_2 + c_2'\rangle\}.$$

For computing the TC-Map for a sequence of services, we compute the pairwise concatenations of all their TC-Map entries and then compress the result.

Definition 17 (SEQ).
Let A and B be functional TC-Maps for two services to be executed in sequence. The TC-Map $SEQ(A, B)$ for the sequence of A and B is

$$SEQ(A, B) = \Phi(\bigcup\{a||b|a \in A, b \in B\}).$$

Extension: To meet some temporal constraint it might be necessary to delay the invocation of a service by introducing a dummy service call after the invocation of a previous service. The EXT function extends the TC-Map of a service with a dummy duration with an associated cost of 0.

Table 4. SEQ, EXT, and AND of Services A and B

Service A				Service B				EXT(B,20)=SEQ(B,{⟨0,0,20,0⟩})				AND(A,B)			
d1	c1	d2	c2	d1	c1	d2	c2	d1	c1	d2	c2	d1	c1	d2	c2
1	340	2	340	1	50	11	550	1	50	11	50	1	390	21	390
2	400	3	400	11	540	20	900	11	50	21	50	21	390	22	439
3	460	4	460					21	50	31	540	22	499	23	548
4	520	5	520					31	540	40	900	23	608	24	657
5	570	20	1320									24	717	25	766
												25	816	31	1410
												31	1410	40	2220

Definition 18 (EXT).
Let A be the functional TC-Map for a service; let d be the maximum duration that may elapse after the completion of the call of the service. The TC-Map for the extension $EXT(A,d)$ of A with d is $EXT(A,d) = SEQ(A, \{\langle 0,0,d,0\rangle\})$.

Parallel Execution: To calculate the TC-Map of a service consisting of the parallel execution of two sub-services, the two TC-Maps A and B of the sub-services have to be partitioned so that the result has no overlapping intervals. Thus, we need to make intervals out of the point set of the union of the interval endpoints of both A and B. The associated cost for the created interval endpoints is the sum of the costs derived from each TC-Map by taking the lower cost for the left interval endpoint and by taking the upper cost for the right interval endpoint. To guarantee that the two parallel executions span the same amount of time, dummy wait tasks may be added with the application of EXT.

Definition 19 (AND).
Let A and B be functional TC-Maps for two services executed in parallel. The TC-Map $AND(A, B)$ for the parallel execution of A and B is

$$AND(A, B) = \Phi(\{\langle d_1, c_1, d_2, c_2\rangle | (d_1, d_2) \in I(\pi(EXT(A,m)) \cup \pi(EXT(B,m)),$$
$$c_1 = \sigma_1(d_1, EXT(A,m)) + \sigma_1(d_1, EXT(B,m)),$$
$$c_2 = \sigma_2(d_2, EXT(A,m)) + \sigma_2(d_2, EXT(B,m)),$$
$$where\ m = max(\{d' | \langle d, c, d', c'\rangle \in A \cup B\})\}).$$

Table 4 visualises in the first two columns the TC-Maps for services A and B, with A representing the conferencing platform A and B representing the online registration of our motivating example. The third column shows the EXT of service B with the duration $d = 20$, which actually performs a SEQ on B and the TC-Map $\{\langle 0,0,20,0\rangle\}$. The selection of $d = 20$ was made because it is the value of m in the $EXT(B,m)$, which is used in the AND operation of A and B. The last column shows the result of the operation $AND(A, B)$.

Conditional and Decisional Alternatives: Since, in the case of XORC, the condition evaluation result cannot be known before it is observed, the worst case

Table 5. XORC and XORD of Services A and B

Service A				Service B				XORC				XORD			
d1	c1	d2	c2	d1	c1	d2	c2	d1	c1	d2	c2	d1	c1	d2	c2
1	340	2	340	1	50	11	550	1	340	2	340	1	50	2	100
2	400	3	400	11	540	20	900	2	400	3	400	2	100	3	150
3	460	4	460					3	460	4	460	3	150	4	200
4	520	5	520					4	520	5	520	4	200	5	250
5	570	20	1320					5	570	11	870	5	250	11	550
								11	870	20	1320	11	540	20	900

has to be assumed and we assign the maximum cost of the two TC-Maps for each duration. For a XORD, the controller decides which sub-service to execute. Here, we assume that for a given duration the controller always selects the sub-service with the lowest cost. Table 5 presents examples for the application of XORC and XORD.

Definition 20 (XORC, XORD).
Let A, B be functional TC-Maps for alternative services to be executed depending on an observed condition. The TC-Maps $XORC(A, B)$, resp. $XORD(A, B)$ resulting from the conditional, resp. decisional alternative are

$$XORC(A, B) = \Phi(\{\langle d_1, c_1, d_2, c_2 \rangle | (d_1, d_2) \in I(\pi(A) \cup \pi(B) \cup \Psi(A \cup B)),$$
$$c_1 = max(\Sigma_1(d_1, A), \Sigma_1(d_1, B)), c_2 = max(\Sigma_2(d_2, A), \Sigma_2(d_2, B))\}.$$
$$XORD(A, B) = \Phi(\{\langle d_1, c_1, d_2, c_2 \rangle | (d_1, d_2) \in I(\pi(A) \cup \pi(B) \cup \Psi(A \cup B)),$$
$$c_1 = min(\sigma_1(d_1, A), \sigma_1(d_1, B)), c_2 = min(\sigma_2(d_2, A), \sigma_2(d_2, B))\}.$$

Having formally defined the constructor operators, we have now the building blocks for a procedure to compute the TC-Map for a service composition.

4.3 Computing the TC-Map for a Service Composition

Following the approach we presented in [14], we combine the basic and constructor operations into a bottom-up procedure for computing the TC-Map for a service composition. Since the procedure works in the same way as the procedure we presented in [14], here we only give an overview of it.

The procedure follows the structure of a service composition: starting from the leaf nodes, which represent basic services, traverses the tree up to the root. We assume that the TC-Maps for each service at the leaf nodes is known as part of the service SLAs. For each internal node, the procedure calculates the corresponding TC-Map by applying the appropriate operation, depending on the node type (SEQ, AND, XORC, XORD), to the children node TC-Maps. The procedure terminates when the TC-Map for the root is calculated.

4.4 Implementation and Evaluation

We implemented all of the presented operations in Java in a Maven project. We used a Windows 10 machine with 16 GB of RAM and with JUnit for tests. We

Table 6. Measured times (in milliseconds) for executing constructor operations on TC-Maps of varying size in the prototype implementation

# Tuples per TC-Map	AND constr.	SEQ constr.	XORC constr.	XORD constr.
10	2.89	3.36	0.21	0.15
20	2.48	54.23	0.26	0.28
30	4.37	210.94	0.5	0.58
40	6.78	811.04	0.68	0.94

defined an XML schema for the input as XML files, and used "Apache POI" to export the resulting TC-Maps as Excel tables. All the TC-Maps resulting from operations shown in tables in this paper have been computed using our implementation.

To evaluate the feasibility of our approach, we ran experiments measuring the execution times for the constructor operations on pairs of TC-Maps of increasing size: 10, 20, 30, and 40 tuples each. For each operation, we ran the implementation 100 times and computed the average execution time for these repeated runs.

The source code for the implementation, the data-sets used for the experiments and the complete results are publicly available in an online repository[1]. In Table 6 we summarize the execution times in milliseconds for the constructor operations SEQ, AND, XORC and XORD.

In a nutshell, our experiments indicated the practical applicability of our proposed approach, even for a non-optimized proof-of-concept implementation, with running times under one second for operations on the largest TC-Maps. We consider these execution times acceptable, since for a composition the number of TC-Map operations is equal to the number of constructors, and the computation is done only once during the design of a composition. Nevertheless, we intend to further optimize the prototype implementation in future work.

5 Related Work

The time and cost aspects of service compositions have been investigated by several prior works - see for instance the overviews in [8,19,20,26]. In particular the temporal aspect is recognized as crucial for designing service compositions, orchestrations and workflows and defining temporal SLAs [5,9,15,16,21,22,27,29]. Examples of prior work towards design and verification of temporal aspects are [2,4,11,17,18,24]. These approaches rely on formalisms such as timed transition systems, interval temporal logic, and temporal constraint networks, and focus on verifying the existence of schedules or absence of conflicting constraints. Besides, they considered the temporal aspect in isolation, not in relation to other aspects, thus missing the interplay and trade-offs between time and cost.

---

[1] The repository is found at https://github.com/ziss05/CAISE2022.

Cost of service invocation in isolation has been considered in several prior works, especially aimed at maximizing Quality of Service of Web service compositions. For instance, in [4], authors propose a heuristic approach for service selection to maximize Quality of Service. The approach proposed in [4] may indeed include cost as one of the non-functional aspects.

Works considering both time and cost are, e.g., [1,3,12,25]. Nevertheless, their considerations of a time-cost relation are not explicit as we do here. The "MoDe4SLA" approach by Bodenstaff et al. [7] considers time and cost as part of a set of impact factors that influence the outcome of a composed service execution. There, a composition tree, similar to the one we use, is representing the dependencies between the component services together with their impact factors and the composed service. In their successive "MoC-SCo" approach [6], time and cost as impact factors are identified to be dependent on each other, but no complex relationships are considered. While Bodenstaff et al. focus on monitoring given SLAs at run time, here we consider the dependencies between time and cost for defining SLAs at design time. On the other hand, in [13], authors address the problem of allocating cloud resources optimizing cost under temporal constraints, relying on linear programming. The cloud broker service STRATOS [23] as well strives for cost minimization in complex relations with other aspects. While these works are towards an explicit representation of the interplay between time and cost, they do not address the composition of complex, and therefore expressive, time-cost relationships.

When it comes to the relation between time and cost, we observe that most prior works generally assumed *the faster a service invocation is, the better*, i.e., the optimal solution is the one that minimizes the service invocation duration. This is not always the case and there is, in general, a more complex relation between time and cost, as we argued in our previous work [14]. There, we showed that the time-cost relation is not always directly proportional, and introduced the notion of indirectly proportional relation. To the best of our knowledge, [14], with time-cost tables, was the first to consider a time-cost relationship in an explicit manner. It was, however, limited by the assumption that the time-cost relation can always be expressed as a step-function. Here, we have shown that this assumption is too strict and we provided new more adequate means to represent the time-cost relation by means of piece-wise linear functions.

6   Conclusions

Adequately modeling the time and cost dimensions is essential for designers of service compositions. The reason for such a need is two-fold: on the one hand, designers need to know which SLAs they can offer; on the other hand, clients need to know which time-cost trade-offs are available to them.

In this paper, we propose TC-Maps for representing the time-cost relations for services in a highly expressive way which can be applied for encoding broad range of time-dependent pricing models. Procedures for computing TC-Maps for composed services are formally specified and implemented in a proof-of-concept prototype that clearly shows the feasibility of the approach.

Our results contribute to the design information systems in which time and cost are not independent orthogonal dimensions. The proposed representation supports also various complex objective functions for the optimization of composed services besides the usual minimum time or minimum cost. As the cost dimension does not need to be a monetary category, the concept of TC-Maps also addresses requirements of many technical application areas dealing with trade-offs between durations and the consumption of some resources.

References

1. Aggarwal, R., Verma, K., Miller, J., Milnor, W.: Constraint driven web service composition in meteor-s. In: IEEE International Conference on Services Computing 2004. (SCC 2004). Proceedings, pp. 23–30. IEEE (2004)
2. Ahmed, W., Wu, Y., Zheng, W.: Response time based optimal web service selection. IEEE Trans. Parallel Distrib. Syst. 26(2), 551–561 (2013)
3. Ardagna, D., Pernici, B.: Global and local QoS constraints guarantee in web service selection. In: IEEE International Conference on Web Services (ICWS 2005). IEEE (2005)
4. Berbner, R., Spahn, M., Repp, N., Heckmann, O., Steinmetz, R.: Heuristics for QoS-aware web service composition. In: 2006 IEEE International Conference on Web Services (ICWS 2006), pp. 72–82. IEEE (2006)
5. Bichier, M., Lin, K.J.: Service-oriented computing. Computer 39(3), 99–101 (2006)
6. Bodenstaff, L., Wieringa, R., Wombacher, A., Reichert, M.: Towards management of complex service compositions - position paper. In: Proceedings of the 2009 World Conference on Services - II. SERVICES-2 2009, pp. 160–167. IEEE Computer Society, USA (2009). https://doi.org/10.1109/SERVICES-2.2009.27
7. Bodenstaff, L., Wombacher, A., Reichert, M., Jaeger, M.C.: Analyzing impact factors on composite services. In: Proceedings of the 2009 IEEE International Conference on Services Computing. SCC 2009, pp. 218–226. IEEE Computer Society, USA (2009). https://doi.org/10.1109/SCC.2009.20
8. Dustdar, S., Schreiner, W.: A survey on web services composition. Int. J. Web Grid Serv. 1(1), 1–30 (2005)
9. Eder, J., Franceschetti, M.: Time and business process management: problems, achievements, challenges (invited talk). In: 27th International Symposium on Temporal Representation and Reasoning (TIME 2020). Schloss Dagstuhl-Leibniz-Zentrum für Informatik (2020)
10. Franceschetti, M., Eder, J.: Checking temporal service level agreements for web service compositions with temporal parameters. In: 2019 IEEE International Conference on Web Services (ICWS), pp. 443–445. IEEE (2019)
11. Franceschetti, M., Eder, J.: Computing admissible temporal slas for web service compositions. In: 2020 IEEE International Conference on Web Services (ICWS), pp. 318–326. IEEE (2020)
12. Guidara, I., Al Jaouhari, I., Guermouche, N.: Dynamic selection for service composition based on temporal and QoS constraints. In: 2016 IEEE International Conference on Services Computing (SCC), pp. 267–274. IEEE (2016)
13. Halima, R.B., Kallel, S., Gaaloul, W., Jmaiel, M.: Optimal cost for time-aware cloud resource allocation in business process. In: 2017 IEEE International Conference on Services Computing (SCC), pp. 314–321. IEEE (2017)

14. Hollauf, F.S., Franceschetti, M., Eder, J.: Towards representing time-cost tradeoffs for service compositions. In: 2021 IEEE International Conference on Services Computing (SCC), pp. 79–88 (2021). https://doi.org/10.1109/SCC53864.2021.00020

15. Ismail, A., Yan, J., Shen, J.: Verification of composite services with temporal consistency checking and temporal satisfaction estimation. In: Vossen, G., Long, D.D.E., Yu, J.X. (eds.) WISE 2009. LNCS, vol. 5802, pp. 343–350. Springer, Heidelberg (2009). https://doi.org/10.1007/978-3-642-04409-0_35

16. Jayathilaka, H., Krintz, C., Wolski, R.: Service-level agreement durability for web service response time. In: 2015 IEEE 7th International Conference on Cloud Computing Technology and Science (CloudCom), pp. 331–338. IEEE (2015)

17. Kallel, S., Charfi, A., Dinkelaker, T., Mezini, M., Jmaiel, M.: Specifying and monitoring temporal properties in web services compositions. In: 2009 Seventh IEEE European Conference on Web Services, pp. 148–157. IEEE (2009)

18. Kazhamiakin, R., Pandya, P., Pistore, M.: Representation, verification, and computation of timed properties in web. In: 2006 IEEE International Conference on Web Services (ICWS 2006), pp. 497–504. IEEE (2006)

19. Lemos, A.L., Daniel, F., Benatallah, B.: Web service composition: a survey of techniques and tools. ACM Comput. Surv. (CSUR) **48**(3), 33 (2016)

20. Milanovic, N., Malek, M.: Current solutions for web service composition. IEEE Internet Comput. **8**, 51–59 (2004)

21. Müller, C., Martín-Díaz, O., Ruiz-Cortés, A., Resinas, M., Fernández, P.: Improving temporal-awareness of WS-agreement. In: Krämer, B.J., Lin, K.-J., Narasimhan, P. (eds.) ICSOC 2007. LNCS, vol. 4749, pp. 193–206. Springer, Heidelberg (2007). https://doi.org/10.1007/978-3-540-74974-5_16

22. Müller, C., Ruiz-Cortés, A., Fernández, P.: Temporal-awareness in SLAs: why should we be concerned? In: Di Nitto, E., Ripeanu, M. (eds.) ICSOC 2007. LNCS, vol. 4907, pp. 165–173. Springer, Heidelberg (2009). https://doi.org/10.1007/978-3-540-93851-4_16

23. Pawluk, P., Simmons, B., Smit, M., Litoiu, M., Mankovski, S.: Introducing stratos: a cloud broker service. In: 2012 IEEE Fifth International Conference on Cloud Computing, pp. 891–898. IEEE (2012)

24. Pichler, H., Wenger, M., Eder, J.: Composing time-aware web service orchestrations. In: van Eck, P., Gordijn, J., Wieringa, R. (eds.) CAiSE 2009. LNCS, vol. 5565, pp. 349–363. Springer, Heidelberg (2009). https://doi.org/10.1007/978-3-642-02144-2_29

25. Pistore, M., Barbon, F., Bertoli, P., Shaparau, D., Traverso, P.: Planning and monitoring web service composition. In: Bussler, C., Fensel, D. (eds.) AIMSA 2004. LNCS (LNAI), vol. 3192, pp. 106–115. Springer, Heidelberg (2004). https://doi.org/10.1007/978-3-540-30106-6_11

26. Rodriguez-Mier, P., Pedrinaci, C., Lama, M., Mucientes, M.: An integrated semantic web service discovery and composition framework. IEEE Trans. Serv. Comput. **9**(4), 537–550 (2016)

27. Wang, D., Ding, H., Yang, Y., Mi, Z., Liu, L., Xiong, Z.: QoS and SLA aware web service composition in cloud environment. KSII Trans. Internet Inf. Syst. (TIIS) **10**(12), 5231–5248 (2016)

28. Zhang, L., Ardagna, D.: SLA based profit optimization in autonomic computing systems. In: Proceedings of the 2nd International Conference on Service Oriented Computing, pp. 173–182 (2004)

29. Zou, G., Lu, Q., Chen, Y., Huang, R., Xu, Y., Xiang, Y.: QoS-aware dynamic composition of web services using numerical temporal planning. IEEE Trans. Serv. Comput. **7**(1), 18–31 (2014)

Tutorials

The Anatomy of Conceptual Models

Heinrich C. Mayr[1]([⊠]) [iD] and Bernhard Thalheim[2] [iD]

[1] Alpen-Adria University of Klagenfurt, Klagenfurt, Austria
heinrich.mayr@aau.at
[2] Christian Albrechts University in Kiel, Kiel, Germany
bernhard.thalheim@email.uni-kiel.de

Keywords: Conceptual modeling · Model characteristics · Model as a program · Model centered architecture · Model-based system realization

1 Introduction

Humans use models as instruments for describing, analyzing and developing. Besides the traditional use of models for (requirements) specification in database and software development, we observe a growing interest in approaches like "Model Driven Software Development" (MDSD), "Model Driven Architecture" (MDA), "Model Centered Architecture" (MCA), or "Model as a Program" (MaaP), partly supported by software environments like metamodeling frameworks, transformers, generators, "programming machines" etc.

Many modeling paradigms have evolved over time, a central one in computer science being that of conceptual modeling. We address here the "anatomy" of conceptual models and show how they can be characterized by a signature. We combine this with a transparent explanation of the nature of conceptual models as the link between the dimension of linguistic terms and the encyclopedic or ontological dimension of notions.

Such a short paper does not provide the space to cover the rich body of knowledge in the field. We therefore limit ourselves to mentioning the works [1–5] as they are the main source for this paper and contain rich reference lists.

2 A Brief Look at the Essential

According to [3] we propose as signature a set of six general characteristics that are common to all models: (1) *Relation to Origins*, (2) *Concern and Usage*, (3) *Purpose and Function*, (4) *Domain and Context*, (5) *Focus*, and (6) *Representation*. For conceptual models we additionally identify the two characteristics (7) *Concept Space* and (8) *Concept Relationship*.

Figure 1 shows the essential terminology including semantic relationships. The lower level describes the epistemological basis according to which cognitive processes produce ideas, which are mental objects. These form the cognitive structure of a person.

© Springer Nature Switzerland AG 2022
X. Franch et al. (Eds.): CAiSE 2022, LNCS 13295, pp. 551–553, 2022.
https://doi.org/10.1007/978-3-031-07472-1

Linguistic perception makes it possible to infer from symbols (words of any language) the ideas represented by them.

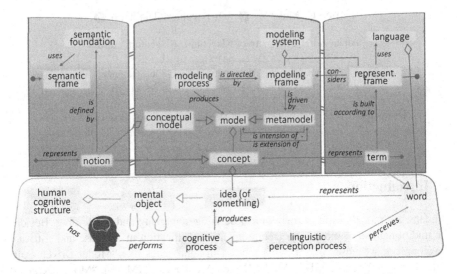

Fig. 1: The "anatomy" of conceptual modeling organized on a triptych

The triptych shows on its tableaus the three dimensions of conceptual modeling: on the right the terms as elements of a language, which are formed and associated according to certain rules ("representation frame"). In the middle the model hierarchies (regulated by a "modeling frame") as collections of concepts and on the left the dimension of notions, semantically founded for example by encyclopedias or ontologies (regulated by a "semantic frame").

Based on such a view of conceptual modeling, we can develop a systematic approach to a theory and practice of model-based system realization.

References

1. Embley, D.W., Thalheim, B.: Handbook of Conceptual Modeling: Theory, Practice, and Research Challenges. Springer, Heidelberg (2011). https://doi.org/10.1007/978-3-642-15865-0
2. Mayr, H.C., Michael, J., Ranasinghe, S., Shekhovtsov, V.A., Steinberger, C.: Model centered architecture. In: Cabot, J., Gómez, C., Pastor, O., Sancho, M., Teniente, E. (eds.) Conceptual Modeling Perspectives, pp. 85–104 (2017). Springer, Cham. https://doi.org/10.1007/978-3-319-67271-7_7
3. Mayr, H.C., Thalheim, B.: The triptych of conceptual modeling. Softw. Syst. Model **20**, 7–24 (2021). https://doi.org/10.1007/s10270-020-00836-z

4. Thalheim, B.: Conceptual model notions – a matter of controversy: conceptual modelling and its lacunas. EMISA J. **13**, 9–27 (2018). https://doi.org/10.18417/emisa.si.hcm.1

5. Thalheim, B.: From Models_For_Programming to Modelling_To_Program and Towards Models_As_A_Program. In: Dahanayake, A., Pastor, O., Thalheim, B. (eds.) M2P 2020. CCIS, vol. 1401, pp. 3–44. Springer, Cham (2021). https://doi.org/10.1007/978-3-030-72696-6_1

Engineering Information Systems in Smart Manufacturing

Francesco Leotta$^{(\boxtimes)}$ ⓘ, Massimo Mecella ⓘ, and Flavia Monti ⓘ

Sapienza Universitá di Roma, Rome, Italy
{leotta,mecella,monti}@diag.uniroma1.it

Abstract. The continuous evolution of digital technologies applied to the more traditional world of industrial automation led to smart manufacturing (also known as Industry 4.0), which envisions production processes subject to continuous monitoring and able to dynamically respond to changes that can affect the product life cycle at any stage (resilient factory). The goal of this tutorial is to instruct the attendees about the employment of information systems engineering at different levels of granularity in smart manufacturing. In particular, this tutorial focuses on the role of technologies, including Artificial Intelligence (AI), on the full supply chain (inter-actor interaction), at the level of single actors and production sites, and at the level of the specific machinery. Involved technologies are different at each level of granularity and their integration is sometimes difficult to imagine, as proposed approaches focus on very limited aspects of complex information systems.

Keywords: Smart manufacturing · Information systems engineering · Artificial intelligence · Digital twins · Software architectures

Industry 4.0 represents the fourth revolution of manufacturing processes and practices. With respect to Industry 3.0, which already introduced interconnection between machines through so called fieldbuses, here the employment of wireless technologies and AI techniques make acquired information not only a tool for diagnostic but also for prognostic, opening to a wide range of applications including predictive and prescriptive maintenance. For these reasons, the term *smart manufacturing* is also used. In addition, information is intended to come from all the actors involved, including machines, humans and organizations. A variety of reference architectures are available to describe assets, functions and product life cycle in Industry 4.0, both proposed by regulatory institutions (e.g., RAMI [3]) and by researchers [2].

The application of Industry 4.0 concepts and approaches is finalized at different goals including agile supply chains [1], Zero Defect Manufacturing (ZDM) [6], resilience, certification of production quality. These goals strongly impact on companies' business, allowing them to provide customers with smart products and optional smart services (e.g., analytics services).

© Springer Nature Switzerland AG 2022
X. Franch et al. (Eds.): CAiSE 2022, LNCS 13295, pp. 554–556, 2022.
https://doi.org/10.1007/978-3-031-07472-1

The term Digital Twin (DT) is often associated to Industry 4.0. A DT is a digital representation of a physical asset and originally it was intended as a means for simulation at design time. Over the years, the concept evolved, also including the possibility of monitoring and executing remote maintenance on products and equipment [2]. To this aim, commercial and open source platforms are available (e.g., Eclipse Ditto, Bosch IoT Things). Modern DTs can implement techniques from computer vision, machine learning and, in general, AI, for monitoring the quality of the production and the health status of a product/machine. The huge amount of information produced by DTs must be managed by information systems, which provide the actual added value to the manufacturing process. Information systems can be specific of single production sites or single actors, or they can span different organizations.

At a specific site, classical information systems include:

- Those usually employed to manage the provisioning, orders, suppliers and production scheduling. The goal here is the optimization of the production.
- Manufacturing Execution Systems (MES), which acquire information about the manufacturing line.
- Industrial Internet of Things (IIoT) systems and Cloud/Fog/Edge.
- Business Processes Management Systems (BPMS) and their employment with IIoT [4]. In particular, BP-Meet-IoT [4] is the research trend focusing on applying BPM and Process Mining where traditional information systems coexist with IoT-based information systems, where acquired data are completely different in terms, for example, of quality, quantity and rate.
- AI systems handling uncertainty and unexpected events, which can be used to cope with events disruptive for the production chain.
- AI systems for data analysis and correlation.

When information systems involve different organizations or sites, different challenges must be addressed. Among them, we have granting production quality and respect of agreements (e.g., through the employment of blockchains). In this tutorial, we attempt to provide a systematic view over the above topics, in order to provide guidelines to practitioners and researchers for studying and developing smart manufacturing in different scenarios.

References

1. Bicocchi, N., Cabri, G., Mandreoli, F., Mecella, M.: Dynamic digital factories for agile supply chains: an architectural approach. J. Ind. Inf. Integr. **15**, 111–121 (2019)
2. Catarci, T., Firmani, D., Leotta, F., Mandreoli, F., Mecella, M., Sapio, F.: A conceptual architecture and model for smart manufacturing relying on service-based digital twins. In: 2019 IEEE International Conference on Web Services (ICWS) (2019)
3. Hankel, M., Rexroth, B.: The Reference Architectural Model Industrie 4.0 (RAMI 4.0). ZVEI **2**(2), 4–9 (2015)
4. Janiesch, C., et al.: The internet-of-things meets business process management: a manifesto. IEEE Syst. Man Cybern. Mag. **6**(4), 34–44 (2020)

5. Leotta, F., Marrella, A., Mecella, M.: IoT for BPMers. challenges, case studies and successful applications. In: Hildebrandt, T., van Dongen, B.F., Röglinger, M., Mendling, J. (eds.) BPM 2019. LNCS, vol. 11675, pp. 16–22. Springer, Cham (2019). https://doi.org/10.1007/978-3-030-26619-6_3

6. Psarommatis, F., May, G., Dreyfus, P.A., Kiritsis, D.: Zero defect manufacturing: state-of-the-art review, shortcomings and future directions in research. Int. J. Prod. Res. **58**(1), 1–17 (2020)

Mining and Simulation for Process-Aware Information Systems

Fernando Brito e Abreu[(⊠)] [iD]

ISTAR-Iscte, University Institute of Lisbon, Lisbon, Portugal
fba@iscte-iul.pt

Abstract. The overall goal of this tutorial is to show how process mining and simulation techniques can be used to optimize resource assignment in process-aware information systems and outline the resulting service level. A meta-process of the proposed approach will serve as a backbone for the presentation, which will go through the following questions:

- How can we use process mining to discover the "as is" process model when we dont have one?
- Which are the parameters required for running a simulation?
- How can we reverse engineer the actual values of those parameters for the "as is" scenario?
- Which are the outputs of a process simulation and how can they be interpreted?
- How can we define a process execution optimization function?
- Which simulation scenarios should we consider in the quest forbreak process optimization?
- How can we express a service level agreement (SLA) based on the optimized simulation scenario?

Keywords: Process mining · Process simulation · Process-aware information systems

1 Process Mining

Process mining is a set of data science techniques that, taking as input event logs from operational process-aware information systems (PAIS), allow to provide insights into what people, machines, and organizations are doing (process discovery), address their performance and compliance problems (conformance checking), and identify process improvement opportunities (process enhancement). Each event in the log should contain a unique identifier for the process instance (aka case id), an identifier of the occurring activity (the actual "event"), and a timestamp.

In this tutorial, we will take as input an event log to (i) discover the underlying process model, (ii) derive the statistical distribution of process instance arrivals, and (iii) identify the statistical distribution of the effort spent in each

© Springer Nature Switzerland AG 2022
X. Franch et al. (Eds.): CAiSE 2022, LNCS 13295, pp. 557–559, 2022.
https://doi.org/10.1007/978-3-031-07472-1

process activity. If information regarding resource costs cannot be obtained from PAIS logs or other internal IS (e.g. HR records in the ERP platform), they can be estimated based on public statistics (e.g. Eurostat statistics on wages per sector and per country), before moving on to the simulation step.

2   Process Simulation

Process simulation is a quantitative analysis method that, by executing many process instances, artificially created according to a given statistical distribution of arrivals and planned effort to be spent in each activity within the process, allows assessing resources adequacy, namely detecting bottlenecks, as well as gathering other performance data such as cost and schedule metrics. Process simulation facilitates impact and risk analysis due to changes in resource assignment, availability (timetables), and cost. Simulation can occur before process deployment or take as input the current ("as is") process scenario and then try to optimize it.

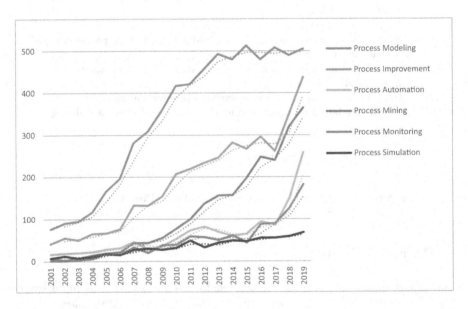

Fig. 1. Google Scholar hits on "Process *" AND "Information Systems Engineering"

Process simulation techniques are widely used in many engineering fields, such as Chemical, Electrical, Nuclear, Mechanical, Civil, Aeronautical, and Automotive. However, while other process perspectives such as process modeling, process improvement, process automation, or process monitoring are also widely used in Information Systems Engineering, process simulation techniques are still relatively novel in the community, as can be concluded by the evolution of published work represented in Fig. 1, where the dotted lines correspond to moving average trends. Data from the last 2 years was excluded on purpose, not to reflect the atypical changes in publication patterns due to the COVID-19 pandemic.

Acknowledgements. This work was partially supported by the Portuguese Foundation for Science and Technology (FCT) project UIDB/04466/2020.

Author Index

Printed in the United States
by Baker & Taylor Publisher Services